DISTRIBUTED NETWORK SYSTEMS

Network Theory and Applications
Volume 15

Managing Editors:

Ding-Zhu Du
University of Minnesota, U.S.A.

Cauligi Raghavendra
University of Southern Califorina, U.S.A.

DISTRIBUTED NETWORK SYSTEMS
From Concepts to Implementations

by

WEIJIA JIA
City University of Hong Kong, P.R. China

WANLEI ZHOU
Deakin University, Australia

Springer

eBook ISBN: 0-387-23840-9
Print ISBN: 1-4899-8341-4
Print ISBN: 978-1-4899-8341-1

©2005 Springer Science + Business Media, Inc.
Softcover re-print of the Hardcover 1st edition 2006

Print ©2005 Springer Science + Business Media, Inc.
Boston

Created in the United States of America

Visit Springer's eBookstore at: http://ebooks.springerlink.com
and the Springer Global Website Online at: http://www.springeronline.com

Contents

Chapter 5 Interprocess Communication using Message Passing 79

Chapter 6 TCP/UDP Communication in Java................... 105

Chapter 8 Group Communications 175

Chapter 9 Reliability and Replication Techniques........... 213

This page intentionally left blank

Preface

Both authors have taught the course of "Distributed Systems" for many years in the respective schools. During the teaching, we feel strongly that "Distributed systems" have evolved from traditional "LAN" based distributed systems towards "Internet based" systems. Although there exist many excellent textbooks on this topic, because of the fast development of distributed systems and network programming/protocols, we have difficulty in finding an appropriate textbook for the course of "distributed systems" with orientation to the requirement of the undergraduate level study for today's distributed technology. Specifically, from up-to-date concepts, algorithms, and models to implementations for both distributed system designs and application programming.

Thus the philosophy behind this book is to integrate the concepts, algorithm designs and implementations of distributed systems based on network programming. After using several materials of other textbooks and research books, we found that many texts treat the distributed systems with separation of concepts, algorithm design and network programming and it is very difficult for students to map the concepts of distributed systems to the algorithm design, prototyping and implementations.

This book intends to enable readers, especially postgraduates and senior undergraduate level, to study up-to-date concepts, algorithms and network programming skills for building modern distributed systems. It enables students not only to master the concepts of distributed network system but also to readily use the material introduced into implementation practices.

The book takes an integrated approach to view the distributed system as a set of programming blocks cooperating on distributed sites. The primary objective of the concept, design and implementation is to meet the requirements or distributed applications based on the networking environment. In this book, networking and distribution design for applications are represented in the form of several dimensions. Therefore, the book describes the distributed systems along a line from general distributed system requirement of applications to system transparency that reflect system structure and algorithm designs and implementation techniques.

The striking features of the book, differs from others, can be illustrated from two basic aspects:

(1) The viewpoint of applications, i.e., what kinds of concepts and programming skill are fitted for the design of distributed systems and applications.

(2) The viewpoint of system designer and implementers, i.e., the system layers and their mapping to the design of distributed algorithms and their implementations.

The book not only provides the basic distributed systems and networks protocols (such as RPC, group communication and Mobile IP), but it also presents the discussion of recent technology development for Internet such as IP for next generation (IPv6 and multicast and anycast communication). As Web/Java

xviii

technology is getting important and popular nowadays, this book illustrates how a distributed system and network protocols can be designed and implemented with distributed system concepts and network programming in today's Internet environment.

The book is composed of 15 chapters. Most chapters contain substantial materials about concepts, algorithm designs and implementation techniques. The outline of the book is given below.

Chapter 1. Overview of Distributed Systems: This chapter outlines the basic concepts of distributed systems and computer networks, such as their purposes, characteristics, advantages, and limitations, as well as their basic architectures, networking and applications.

Chapter 2 introduces the client-server model and its role in the development of distributed network systems. The chapter discusses the cooperation between clients and servers/group servers in distributed network systems, and addresses extensions to the client-server model. Service discovery, which is of crucial importance for achieving transparency in distributed network systems, is also elaborated in this chapter.

Chapter 3. Communication is an important issue in distributed computing systems: This chapter addresses the communication paradigm of distributed network systems, i.e., issues about how to build the communication model for these systems.

Chapter 4. Internetworking. Network software is arranged in a hierarchy of layers: Each layer presents an interface to the layers above it that extends the properties of the underlying communication system. Network functions are achieved through the layered protocols. This chapter discusses the communication protocols in a network, especially, TCP/IP protocols used on the current Internet. The next generation of Internet protocol – IPv6 is also addressed in the chapter.

Chapter 5. Interprocess Communication using Message-Passing: Processes in a distributed network system normally do not share common memory. Therefore, message-passing is one of the effective communication mechanisms between these processes. In this chapter we discuss the most commonly used message-passing based interprocess communication mechanism, i.e., the socket API.

Chapter 6. TCP/UDP Communication in Java: In this chapter we want to address the TCP/UDP programming in Java, since the Java language is currently the most commonly used language to implement a distributed computing system. Java provides the reliable stream-based communication for TCP as well as the unreliable datagram communication for UDP.

Chapter 7. Interprocess Communication using RPC: When using message-passing for interprocess communications, a programmer is aware of the passing of messages between the two processes. However, in a remote procedure call situation, passing of messages is invisible to the programmer. Instead, a language-level concept, the procedure call, is used to mask the actual communication between two processes. In this chapter we discuss two commonly used RPC tools, the DCE/RPC and the SUN/RPC. We have developed a RPC tool, called the Simple RPC tool, which will be described in the chapter. The idea of RPC has been extended to develop interprocess communication mechanisms for object-oriented paradigm, notably the Remote Method Invocation (RMI) in Java. We also introduce this mechanism in the chapter.

Chapter 8. Group Communications is highly desirable for maintaining a consistent state in distributed systems. Many existing protocols are quite expensive and of limited benefit for distributed systems in terms of efficiency. This chapter describes concepts and design techniques of group communication protocol including message ordering, dynamic assessment of membership and fault tolerance. The protocol ensures total ordering of messages and atomicity of delivery in the presence of communication failures and site failures, and guarantees that all operational members belonging to the same group observe a consistent view of ordered events. The dynamic membership and failure recovery algorithms can handle site failures and recovery; group partitions and merges; dynamic members join and leave.

Chapter 9. Reliability and Replication Techniques: A computer system, or a distributed system consists of many hardware/software components that are likely to fail eventually. In many cases, such failures may have disastrous results. With the ever-increasing dependency being placed on distributed systems, the number of users requiring fault tolerance is likely to increase. The design and understanding of fault-tolerant distributed systems is a very difficult task. We have to deal with not only all the complex problems of distributed systems when all the components are well, but also the more complex problems when some of the components fail. This chapter introduces the basic concepts and techniques that relate to fault-tolerant computing.

Chapter 10. Security: There is a pervasive need for measures to guarantee the privacy, integrity and availability of resources in distributed network systems. Designers of secure distributed systems must cope with exposed service interfaces and insecure networks in an environment where attackers are likely to have knowledge of the algorithms used and to deploy computing resources. In this chapter we talk about security issues of distributed network systems, such as integrity mechanisms and encryption techniques, and in particular, the techniques for defense against Distributed Denial-of-Service attacks.

Chapter 11. A Reactive System Architecture for Fault-Tolerant Computing: Most fault-tolerant application programs cannot cope with constant changes in their environments and user requirements because they embed fault-tolerant computing policies and mechanisms together so that if policies or mechanisms are changed the whole programs have to be changed. This chapter presents a reactive system approach to overcoming this limitation. The reactive system concepts are an attractive paradigm for system design, development and maintenance because it separates policies from mechanisms. In the chapter we propose a generic reactive system architecture and use group communication primitives to model it. We then implement it as a generic package, which can be applied in any distributed applications. The system performance shows that it can be used in a distributed environment effectively.

Chapter 12. Web-Based Databases: World Wide Web has changed the way we do business and research. It also brings a lot of challenges, such as infinite contents, resource diversity, and maintenance and update of contents. Web-based database

(WBDB) is one of the answers to these challenges. In this chapter, we classify WBDB architectures into three types: two-tier architecture, three-tier architecture, and hybrid architectures, according to WBDB access methods. Then the existing technologies used in WBDB are introduced as various generations, i.e. the traditional Web (generation 1), fast and more interactive Web (generation 2), Java-based Web (generation 3), and a new generation combining the techniques of XML and mobile agents. Based on the introduction, we provide the challenges and some solutions for current WBDB. Finally we outline a future framework of WBDB.

Chapter 13. Mobile Computing: Mobile computing requires wireless communication, mobility and portability. In the past few years, we have seen an explosion of mobile devices over the world such as notebook, multimedia PDA and mobile phones. The rapidly expanding markets of cellular voice and limited data service have created a great demand for mobile communication and computing. Mobile communications applications include mobile computing and wireless communications. Many of the advances in communications involve the use of Internet Protocol (IP), Asynchronous Transfer Mode (ATM), and ad hoc network protocols. Recently much focus has been directed at advancing communication technology in the area of mobile wireless networks especially on the IP based wireless networks. This chapter focuses on two major issues: Mobile IP and mobile multicast / anycast applications.

Chapter 14. Distributed Network Systems: Case Studies. In the previous chapters we have discussed various aspects of distributed network systems. Distributed network systems are now used everywhere, especially on the Internet. In this chapter we study several well-known distributed network systems, as the examples of our discussion.

Chapter 15. Distributed Network Systems: Current Development. This last chapter outlines the most recent development in distributed network systems. In particular, we present four "hot" topics that have attracted a lot of attention from both academia and industry. These topics include: cluster computing, grid computing, peer-to-peer computing, and pervasive computing. For each topic, we try to outline its current development, its potential applications and benefits, and its challenges. The purpose of this chapter is to broaden the reader's knowledge in distributed network systems.

The book is suitable to any one who needs a informative introduction, basic design and programming strategies of distributed systems and applications. It serves as an idea textbook of one-semester course for senior undergraduates and post-graduates. Chapters 1-6 serve as the basis for the distributed system design and network programming. There are diverse objectives for using the book: (1) For learning of distributed operating system design and implementations: Chapters 7, 8, 9, 10, and 14 can serve the purpose. (2) For readers who are interested in the design and implementations of web-based databases and Internet computing, Chapters 7, 8, 12 and 15 can be used. (3) To learn the concepts of fault-tolerant distributed system design, Chapters 8,9, 11 will serve the purpose. (4) For understanding group, RPC communication protocols and Mobile IP, Chapters 8, 10, 13 will help.

Acknowledgements

We are grateful to many classes students at City University of Hong Kong and Deakin University who have made a lot of feedbacks to our teaching materials as their comments inspire us to write this book. Inspirations also come from Dingzhu Du, Wei Zhao, Qing Li and Andrzej Goscinski.

The following people gave their time to help us to formulate the book, especially, Changgui Chen, who helped to edit the book and contributed partially to Chapter 13. Yang Xiang contributed partially to Chapter 10; Mingjun Lan contributed partially to Chapter 12; and John Casey contributed partially to Section 15.2. Pui-On Au and Yujia Wang helped to format the final version of the book.

We would like to acknowledge some support from research grants we have received, in particular, CityU Strategic grant nos. 7001587/7001446 and UGC grant nos. CityU 1055/01E and CityU 1076/00E, the Austalian Research Council Small Grant no. 0504-32409-0132-3501 and the Deakin University Research Grant 0504-23434-3101. Although the research grants are not directly used to support the writing of the book, some interesting research results presented in the book are taken from our research papers which indeed (partially) supported through these grants. We also would like to express our appreciations to the editors in Kluwer Academic Publishers, especially John Martindale and Angela Quilici, for their excellent professional support.

Finally we are grateful to the family of each of us for their consistent and persistent supports. Weijia would like to present the book to XieMei and Sally. Wanlei would like to present the book to Ling, Lingdi and Andi. Without their support, the book may just become some unpublished discussions.

Weijia

Wanlei

1-May-04

This page intentionally left blank

Biography of Authors

Dr. Weijia Jia is an Associate Professor in Department of Computer Science and Department of Computer Engineering and Information Tech., City University of Hong Kong. He received his BSc and MSc in Computer Science from Center South University (CSU), Changsha, China in 1982 and 1984, respectively. He joined the, CSUT as an Assistant Lecturer in 1984. From 1987 to 1988, as a guest researcher he worked at the Department of Computer Science, University of Ottawa, Canada. From 1988 to 1991, he was a Lecturer in Department of Computer Science, CSU. In 1993, he received his PhD in Computer Science from Faculty Polytechnic of Mons, Belgium and joined German National Research Center for Information Technology (GMD) in St. Augustin as a research fellow. In 1995 he joined the Department of Computer Science, City University of Hong Kong as an assistant professor. His research interest includes computer network and systems with emphasis on parallel/distributed object group system, communication protocols, real-time and Internet communications. He has published extensively in these fields, especially the field of Anycast routing and applications. He is a member of IEEE, IEEE Communication Society and IEEE Computer Society.

Dr. Wanlei Zhou is a Chair Professor and Head of School of Information Technology, Deakin University, Melbourne, Australia. Dr. Zhou received the B.Eng and M.Eng degrees from Harbin Institute of Technology, Harbin, China in 1982 and 1984, respectively, and the PhD degree from The Australian National University, Canberra, Australia, in 1991. Before joining Deakin University, Dr. Zhou has been a Lecturer in Chengdu Institute of Radio Engineering (University of Electronic Science and Technology of China), China, a programmer in Apollo/HP at Massachusetts, U.S.A., a Lecturer in National University of Singapore, Singapore, and a Lecturer in Monash University, Melbourne, Australia. His research interests include distributed computing, computer networks, IT security, performance evaluation, and fault-tolerant computing, and he has published extensively in these research areas. Dr. Zhou is a member of the IEEE and IEEE Computer Society, and the ACM.

This page intentionally left blank

Table of Figures

This page intentionally left blank

CHAPTER 1 OVERVIEW OF DISTRIBUTED NETWORK SYSTEMS

In this Chapter we outline the basic concepts of distributed systems and computer networks, such as their purposes, characteristics, advantages, and limitations, as well as their basic architectures and their applications.

1.1 Distributed Systems

A distributed system is a system consisting of a collection of autonomous machines connected by communication networks and equipped with software systems designed to produce an integrated and consistent computing environment. Distributed systems enable people to cooperate and coordinate their activities more effectively and efficiently. The key purposes of the distributed systems can be represented by: resource sharing, openness, concurrency, scalability, fault-tolerance and transparency [Coulouris et al 1994].

- *Resource sharing.* In a distributed system, the resources - hardware, software and data can be easily shared among users. For example, a printer can be shared among a group of users.

- *Openness.* The openness of distributed systems is achieved by specifying the key software interface of the system and making it available to software developers so that the system can be extended in many ways.

- *Concurrency.* The processing concurrency can be achieved by sending requests to multiple machines connected by networks at the same time.

- *Scalability.* A distributed system running on a collection of a small number of machines can be easily extended to a large number of machines to increase the processing power.

- *Fault-tolerance.* Machines connected by networks can be seen as redundant resources, a software system can be installed on multiple machines so that in the face of hardware faults or software failures, the faults or failures can be detected and tolerated by other machines.

- *Transparency.* Distributed systems can provide many forms of transparency such as:

    1) *Location transparency,* which allows local and remote information to be accessed in a unified way;

2) *Failure transparency,* which enables the masking of failures automatically; and

3) *Replication transparency,* which allows duplicating software/data on multiple machines invisibly.

Computing in the late 1990s has reached the state of Web-based distributed computing. A basis of this form of computing is distributed computing which is carried out on distributed computing systems. These systems comprise the following three fundamental components:

- personal computers and powerful server computers,

- local and fast wide area networks, internet, and

- systems, in particular distributed operating systems, and application software.

In this book we are interested in the last two issues of distributed computing systems: *networks* and *system and application software.*

With the flourishing of the Internet and the current quick development of e-commerce, it is very important in designing distributed systems to consider not only traditional applications but also the requirements of distributed computing based on the Internet.

1.2 Computer Networks

1.2.1 Network History

The following table ([Stallings 1998]) shows a brief networking history.

Table 1.1: Network history

1966	ARPA packet-switching experimentation
1969	First Arpanet nodes operational
1972	Distributed e-mail invented
1973	Non-U.S. computers linked to Arpanet
1975	Arpanet transitioned to Defense Communications Agency
1980	TCP/IP experimentation began
1981	New host added every 20 days
1983	TCP/IP switchover completed
1986	NSFnet backbone created
1990	Arpanet retired
1991	Gopher introduced

1991	WWW invented
1992	Mosaic introduced
1995	Internet backbone privatized
1996	OC-3 (155 Mbps) backbone built

1.2.2 Network Architecture

The early success of the ARPANET (sponsored by the Advanced Research Projects Agency (ARPA) and developed during the late 1960s and early 1970s) and other networks, and the immediate commercial potential of packet switching, satellite, and local network technology made it apparent that computer networking was quickly becoming an important area of innovation and commerce. It was also apparent that to utilize the full potential of such computer networks, international standards would be required to ensure that any system could communicate with any other system anywhere in the world.

In 1978, a new subcommittee (SC16) was created by the International Organization for Standardization (ISO) Technical Committee 97 on Information Processing to develop standards for "open system interconnection (OSI)". The term "open" was chosen to emphasize that by conforming to OSI standards, a system would be open to communication with any other system anywhere in the world obeying the same standards.

The OSI reference model is a seven-layer model for inter-process communication. Its architecture is comprised of application, presentation, session, transport, network, data link and physical layers, and the corresponding protocols, as depicted in Table 1.2. The detailed descriptions of these layers are given in Chapter 4.

Table 1.2: OSI architecture

Application
Presentation
Session
Transport
Network
Data Link
Physical

The early-developed ARPANET adopts another type of network architecture, i.e., four-layer architecture: application, transport, Internet, and network interface, as depicted in Table 1.3. The current Internet based on ARPANET uses this architecture, which is also known as TCP/IP reference model. In this model, the network interface (or access) layer relies on the data link and physical layers of the network, and the application layer corresponds to application and presentation layers of the OSI model, since there is no session layer in the TCP/IP model. The detail of these layers is also given in Chapter 4.

Table 1.3: TCP/IP reference model

Application
Transport
Internet
Network Interface

1.2.3 Network Fault Tolerance

Network reliability refers to the reliability of the overall network to provide communication in the event of failure of a component or components in the network. The term *network fault tolerance* refers to how resilient the network is against the failure of a component.

Why fault tolerance in a networked world? A key indicator of today's global business systems is the reliability and uptime [Grimshaw et al. 1999]. This concern is crucial for e-commerce sites and mission-critical business applications. Expensive and powerful servers and system components that are designed as stand-alone systems can be very reliable, but even an hour of downtime per month can be deadly to online-only businesses.

For example, server clusters are increasingly used in business and academia to combat the problems of reliability since they are relatively inexpensive and easy to build [Buyya 1999] [TBR 1998]. By having multiple network servers working together in a cluster and using redundant components such as more than one power supply and RAID hard drive subsystems, the overall system uptime in theory can approach 100 percent. However, server clusters are only a part of a chain that links business applications together. For example, to access an HTML page of a business web site, a user issues a request that travels from the user's client machine, through a number of routers and firewalls and other network devices to reach the web site. The web site then processes the request and returns the requested HTML page via the same or another chain of routers, firewalls and network devices. The strength of this chain, in terms of reliability and performance, will determine the success or failure of the business, but a chain is only as strong as its weakest link, and the longer the chain, the weaker it is in general. Intuitively, the following two ways can be used to make such a chain stronger: one is the use of redundancy (replication) and concurrency (parallelism) techniques, and the other is to increase the reliability of the weakest link of the chain.

A networked world faces a number of challenges in fault tolerance. In particular, Internet-connected resources have the following characteristics:

- Unreliable communications;

- Unreliable resources (computers, storage, software, etc.);

- Highly heterogeneous environment;

- Potentially very large amount of resources: scalability;

- Potentially highly variable number of resources.

Communication network reliability depends on the sustainability of both hardware and software. It is possible that, depending on failure senario, a variety of network failures can last from a few seconds to days. Traditionally, such failures were primarily from hardware malfunctions that result in downtime (or "outage period") of a network element (a node or a link). Thus, the emphasis was on the element-level network availability and, in turn, the determination of overall network availability. However, other types of major outages have received much attention in recent years. Such incidents include accidental fiber cable cut, natural disasters, and malicious attack (both hardware and software). These major failures need more than what is traditionally addressed through network availability.

These types of failures cannot be addressed by congestion control schemes alone because of their drastic impact on the network. Such failures can, for example, drop a significant number of existing network connections; thus, the network is required to have the ability to detect a fault and isolate it, and then either the network must reconnect the affected connections or the user may try to reconnect it (if the network does not have reconnect capability). At the same time, the network may not have enough capacity and capability to handle such a major simultaneous "reconnect" phase. Likewise, because of a software and/or protocol error, the network may appear very congested to the user. Thus, network reliability nowadays encompasses more than what was traditionally addressed through network availability.

Basic techniques used in dealing with network failures include: retry (retransmission), complemented retry with correction, replication (e.g., dual bus), coding, special protocols (single handshake, double handshake, etc.), timing checks, rerouting, and retransmission with shift (intelligent retry), etc..

1.3 Protocols and QoS

Network software is arranged in a hierarchy of layers. Each layer presents an interface to the layers above it that extends the properties of the underlying communication system. One layer on one machine carries on a conversation with the same layer on another machine. The rules and conventions used in this conversation are collectively known as the *protocol* of this layer. Generally speaking, a protocol is an agreement between the communication parties on how communication is to proceed. The definition of a protocol has two important parts:

- A specification of the sequence of messages that must be exchanged;

- A specification of the format of the data in the messages.

A protocol is implemented by a pair of software modules located in the sending and receiving computers. Each network layer has one or more protocols corresponding to it so that it can provide a service to the layer above it and extend the service provided by the layer below it. Hence these protocols are arranged in a hierarchy of layers as well. For example, in the OSI model, there are seven protocol layers corresponding to each network layer. A complete set of protocol layers is referred to as a *protocol suite* or a *protocol stack,* reflecting the layered structure.

Protocol layering brings substantial benefits in simplifying and generalizing the software interfaces for access to the communication services of networks, but it also carries significant performance costs. The transmission of an application-level message via a protocol stack with N layers typically involves N transfers of control to the relevant layer of software in the protocol suite, at least one of which is an operating system entry, and taking N copies of the data as a part of the encapsulation mechanisms. All of these overheads result in data transfer rates between application processes that are much lower than the available network bandwidth.

Quality of Service (QoS) is a somewhat vague term referring to the technologies that classify network traffic and then ensure that some of that traffic receives special handling. The special handling may include attempts to provide improved error rates, lower network transit time (latency), and decreased latency variation (jitter). It may also include promises of high availability, which is a combination of mean (average) time between failures (MTBF) and mean time to repair (MTTR).

Quality of service facilities in some technologies, such as Asynchronous Transfer Mode (ATM), can be quite detailed, providing users with explicit guarantees of average delay, delay variation and data loss. In ATM terminology, QoS is the performance observed by an end user. The principal QoS parameters are delay, delay variation, and loss. But QoS does not necessarily guarantee particular performance. Performace guarantees can be quite difficult and expensive to provide in packet-switched networks, and most applications and users can be satisfied with less stringent promises, such as prioritization only, without delay guarantees.

QoS also defines the description of how traffic is to be classified. Some QoS implementations provide per-flow classification, in which each individual flow is categorized and handled separately. This can be expensive if there are a lot of flows to be managed concurrently.

1.4 Software for Distributed Computing

1.4.1 Traditional Client-Server Model

The *client-server model* has been a dominant model for distributed computing since the 1980s. The development of this model has been sparked by research and the development of operating systems that could support users working at their personal computers connected by a local area network. The issue was how to access, use and share a resource located on another computer, e.g., a file or printer, in a transparent manner. In the 1980s computers were controlled by monolithic kernel based operating systems, where all services, including file and naming services, were part of that huge piece of software. In order to access a remote service, the whole operating system must be located and accessed within the computer providing the service. This implied a need to distinguish from a kernel based operating system -- that part of software which only provides a desired service -- and embody it into a new software entity. This entity is called a *server*. Thus, each user process, a *client*, can access and use that server, subject to possessing access rights and a compatible interface. Therefore, the idea of the client-server model is to build at least that part of an operating system which is responsible for providing services to users as a set of cooperating server processes.

In the 1990s the client-server model has been used extensively to develop a huge number and variety of applications. The reasons are simple. It is a very clean model that adheres well to the software modularity and usability requirements. This model allows the programmer to develop, test and install applications very quickly. It simplifies maintenance and lowers its costs. It also allows proving correctness of code.

The client-server model has also influenced the building of new operating systems, in particular distributed operating systems [Goscinski and Zhou 1999]. A distributed operating system supports transparency. Thus, when users access their personal computers they have the feeling of being supported by a very powerful computer, which provides a variety of services. This means that all computers and their connection to a communication network are hidden.

However, it is not good enough to use the simple client-server model to describe various components and their activities of a Web-based client-server computing system. The Internet, and in particular Web browsers and further developments in Java programming, have expanded the client-server computing and systems. This is manifested by different forms of cooperation between remote computers and software components.

1.4.2 Web-Based Distributed Computing Models

The Internet and WWW have influenced distributed computing by the global coverage of the network, Web servers distribution and availability, and architecture of executing programs. To meet the requirements of quick development of the Internet, distributed computing may need to shift its environment from LAN to the Internet.

At the execution level, distributed computing/applications may rely on the following parts:

- *Processes:* A typical computer operating system on a computer host can run several processes at once. A process is created by describing a sequence of steps in a programming language, compiling the program into an executable form, and running the executable program in the operating system. While it is running, a process has access to the resources of the computer (CPU time, I/O device and communication ports) through the operating system. A process can be completely devoted to an application, or several applications can use a single process to perform tasks.

- *Threads:* Every process has at least one thread of control. Some OS support the creation of multiple threads of control within a single process. Each thread in a process can run independently from the other threads. The threads may share some memory such as heap or stacks. Usually the threads need synchronization. For example, one thread may monitor input from a socket connection, while another processes users' requests or accesses the database.

- *Distributed Objects:* Distributed Object technologies are best typified by the Object Management Group's Common Object Request Broker Architecture (CORBA) [OMG 1998], and Microsoft's Distributed Component Object Model (DCOM) [Microsoft 1998]. In these approaches, interaction control among components lies solely with the requesting object -- an explicit method call using a predefined interface specification to initiate service access. The service is provided by a remote object through a registry that finds the object, and then mediates the request and its response. Although Distributed Object models offer a powerful paradigm for creating networked applications composed of objects potentially written in different programming languages, hard-coded communication interactions make it difficult to reuse an object in a new application without bringing along all services on which it is dependent, and reworking the system to incorporate new services that were not initially foreseen is a complex task.

- *Agents:* It is difficult to define this overused term, i.e., to differentiate it from a process or an (active) object and how it differs from a program. An agent has been loosely defined as a program that assists users and acts on their behalf. This is called end-user perspective of software agents. In contrast to the software objects of object-oriented programming, from the perspective of end-to-end users, agents are active entities that obligate the following mandatory behavior rules:

  o **R1**: Work to meet designer's specifications;

  o **R2:** Autonomous: has control over its own actions provided this does not violate **R1.**

  o **R3:** Reactive: senses changes in requirements and environment, being able to act according to those changes provided this does not violate **R1.**

An agent may possess any of the following orthogonal properties from the perspective of systems:

  o Communication: able to communicate with other agents.

  o Mobility: can travel from one host to another.

  o Reliability: able to tolerate a fault when one occurs.

o   Security: appear to be trustful to the end user.

Our definitions differ from others in which agents must execute according to design specifications.

According to the client-server model there are two processes, a client, which requests a service from another process, and a server, which is the service provider. The server performs the requested service and sends back a response. This response could be a processing result, a confirmation of completion of the requested operation or even a notice about a failure of an operation. Following this, the current image of Web-based distributed computing can be called the Web-based client-server computing.

1.4.3 Web-based Client-Server Computing

We have categorized the Web-based client-server computing systems into four types: the *proxy computing, code shipping, remote computing* and *agent-based computing* models. The proxy computing (PC) model is typically used in Web-based scientific computing. According to this model a client sends data and programs to a server over the Web and requests the server to perform certain computing. The server receives the request, performs the computing using the programs and data supplied by the client and returns the result back to the client. Typically, the server is a powerful high-performance computer or it has some special system programs (such as special mathematical and engineering libraries) that are necessary for the computation. The client is mainly used for interfacing with users.

The code shipping (CS) model is a popular Web-based client-server computing model. A typical example is the downloading and execution of Java applets on Web browsers, such as Netscape Communicator and Internet Explorer. According to this model, a client makes a request to a server, the server then ships the program (e.g., the Java applets) over the Web to the client and the client executes the program (possibly) using some local data. The server acts as the repository of programs and the client performs the computation and interfaces with users.

The remote computing (RC) model is typically used in Web-based scientific computing and database applications [Sandewall 1996]. According to this model, the client sends data over the Web to the server and the server performs the computing using programs residing in the server. After the completion of the computation, the server sends the result back to the client. Typically the server is a high-performance computing server equipped with the necessary computing programs and/or databases. The client is responsible for interfacing with users. The NetSolve system [Casanova and Dongarra 1997] uses this model.

The agent-based computing (AC) model is a three-tier model. According to this model, the client sends either data or data and programs over the Web to the agent. The agent then processes the data using its own programs or using the received programs. After the completion of the processing, the agent will either send the result back to the client if the result is complete, or send the data/program/midium result to the server for further processing. In the latter case, the server will perform the job and return the result back to the client directly (or via the agent). Nowadays, more and more Web-based applications have shifted to the AC model [Chang and Scott 1996] [Ciancarini *et al* 1996].

1.5 The Agent-Based Computing Models

The basic agent-based computing model has many extensions and variations. However, there are two areas of distinction among these models, which highlight their adaptability and extensibility: one is whether the interactions among components are preconfigured (hard-wired) and the other is where the control for using components or services lies (e.g., requester/client, provider/server, mediator etc.).

Conversational Agent Model

Conversational agent technologies model communication and cooperation among autonomous entities through message exchange based on speech act theory. The best-known foundation technology for developing such systems is the Knowledge Query and Manipulation Language (KQML) [http://www.cs.umbc.edu/kqml/], which is often used in conjunction with the Knowledge Interchange Format (KIF) [http://www.cs.umbc.edu/kqml/]. In these systems, service access control also lies with a client, which requests a service from a service broker or name server, and then initiates peer-to-peer communication with the provider at an address provided by the broker. Although language-enriched interchanges occur, conversational agents suffer from the same restriction as distributed objects in that the interactions among components are hard-coded in the requester, thus making services inflexible and difficult to reuse and extend.

Sun Jini

Sun Microsystems' Jini [Sun 1999] extends the Java runtime environment from a single virtual machine to a network of virtual machines. In Jini, control for resource access lies with the client who requests a service based on type and attributes from a lookup service that holds a collection of service objects (Java object and methods) and attributes posted by providers. Clients filter responses from the lookup service, downloads the service object for the selected service, and invokes remote methods within the provider to obtain the service. Although the capability of downloading the interface between service requester and provider permits a dynamic and extensible assembly of resources, Jini's model still places the burden and responsibility for selecting, acquiring, and managing access with the client.

Blackboard, Publish and Subscribe Approaches

Blackboard approaches such as FliPSiDE [Schwartz 1995] or LINDA [Schoenfeldinger 1995] allow multiple processes to communicate by reading and writing requests and information to a global data store. Requesters post requests on the Blackboard and poll for available results; providers poll to obtain service requests, and use the Blackboard to post results. The Blackboard enables team problem-solving approaches as it can be used for posting problem subcomponents and partial results.

Publish and subscribe approaches such as Talarian [http://www.messageq.com/communications_middleware/talarian_2.html] and Active Web [http://www.pinnaclepublishing.com/AW/AWmag.nsf/home!openform] use a centralized broker as a clearinghouse for requests and information. Clients issue a request to the broker that broadcasts it to available providers; their responses are reflected through the broker to the client. This approach is well-suited to time-critical problems, as its broadcast model facilitates quick responses.

Common to these approaches is their ability to enable dynamic and flexible composition of distributed components because the interaction among components is not predefined at codetime or tightly bound at runtime. But, with this flexibility comes a potential inherent disadvantage because neither approach provides programmatic control for guiding the operation, and at times this control is needed or desired (e.g., to task a provider that best meets known requirements).

OAA's Delegated Computing Model

The Open Agent Architecture (OAA) [http://www.ai.sri.com/~oaa/], a framework for building flexible, dynamic communities of distributed software agents, enables a truly cooperative computing style wherein members of an agent community work together to perform computation, retrieve information, and serve user interaction tasks. OAA's approach to distributed computing shares common characteristics with current distributed computing models, but is distinct in very important ways.

OAA is similar to the above distributed computing models in that it encourages creation of networked applications like Distributed Objects, permits rich and complex interactions like Conversational Agents, and enables building dynamic, flexible, and extensible communities of components like Jini, Blackboard, and Publish and Subscribe.

A key distinguishing feature of OAA is its delegated computing model that enables both human users and software agents to express their requests in terms of what is to be done without requiring specification of who is to do the work or how it should be performed, for example, "When a message for me arrives about security, notify me immediately." A requester delegates control for meeting a goal to the Facilitator -- a specialized server agent within OAA that coordinates the activities of agents for the purpose of achieving higher-level, often complex problem-solving objectives.

The facilitator meets these objectives by making use of knowledge distributed in four locations in OAA:

- The requester, which specifies a goal to the Facilitator and provides advice on how it should be met,

- Providers, who register their capabilities with the Facilitator, know what services they can provide, and understand limits on their ability to do so,

- The Facilitator, which maintains a list of available provider agents and a set of general strategies for meeting goals

- Meta-agents, which contain domain- or goal-specific knowledge and strategies that are used as an aid by the Facilitator.

This knowledge is employed to foster cooperation among a set of OAA agents. The Facilitator matches a request to an agent or agents providing that service, delegates the task to them, coordinates their efforts, and delivers the results to the requester. This style of cooperation among agents can be applied to perform both straightforward and compound, multistep tasks. In addition to delegation, OAA also provides the ability to make direct calls to a specific agent (like distributed objects and conversational agents) and to broadcast requests (like Publish and Subscribe).

OAA's delegation model relieves human and software agents from the responsibility of interfacing, task planning, and execution monitoring. This has several benefits, including

- Reducing complexity for users and agents. Requesters need only specify the work to be done and advise on its execution. Agents then focus on performing their specialized task, not on coordinating execution and results.

- Precipitating a more open and dynamically extensible computing style wherein agents written in many languages and styles can work together. New or different agents can be added or replaced on the fly without requiring reprogramming to take advantage of their capabilities.

- Encouraging reuse across applications and domains because inter-agent interactions are not pre-defined and their interfaces are not hard-coded.

1.6 Summary

The key purposes of distributed systems can be represented by: resource sharing, openness, concurrency, scalability, fault-tolerance and transparency. Distributed computing systems comprise the three fundamental components: computers, networks, and operating systems and application software. Computer networks were first built in the 1960s and there are mainly two reference models for computer networks, one is the OSI model and the other is the ARPANET model. The current Internet is based on ARPANET, which adopts the four-layer network architecture. The layered protocols define the services provided by these network layers. Quality of service is a method for providing enhanced services to network traffic. With the development of networks, especially the Internet, network fault-tolerance is becoming more and more important. A key indicator of today's business systems is the reliability and uptime. Communication network reliability depends on the substainability of both hardware and software.

The client-server model has been a dominent model for distributed computing since the 1980s. It has been used extensively to develop a huge number and variety of applications. However, it is not good enough to describe various components and their activities of a Web-based client-server computing system. The Internet and WWW have influenced distributed computing by the global coverage of the network, Web servers distribution and availability, and architecture of executing programs. The Web-based client-server computing systems are categorized into four types: the *proxy computing* model, the *code shipping* model, the *remote computing* model and the *agent-based computing* model, where the agent-based computing model has many extensions and variations.

Exercises

1.1 What are the purposes of distributed systems? What are the fundamental components of distributed computing systems? 1.1

1.2 When was ARPANET built? When was the Internet invented? 1.2.1

1.3 What is the OSI architecture? What is the Internet architecture? 1.2.2

1.4 Why should we consider fault-tolerance in a networked world? What techniques are used in network fault-tolerance? 1.2.3

1.5 What is the protocol stack? What is the purpose of QoS? 1.3

1.6 Why should we use the client-server model? What types of computing model does the Web-based client-server model have? 1.4.1, 1.4.3

1.7 What components does a Web-based distributed computing application have? 1.4.2

1.8 What variations does the agent-based computing model have? Give examples. 1.5

This page intentionally left blank

CHAPTER 2 MODELLING FOR DISTRIBUTED NETWORK SYSTEMS: THE CLIENT-SERVER MODEL

This chapter is to introduce the client-server model and its role in the development of distributed network systems. The chapter discusses the cooperation between clients and servers/group servers in distributed network systems, and addresses extensions to the client-server model. Service discovery, which is of crucial importance for achieving transparency in distributed network systems, is also elaborated in this chapter.

2.1 Issues Leading to the Client-Server Model

By amalgamating computers and networks into one single computing system and providing appropriate system software, a distributed computing system has created the possibility of sharing information and peripheral resources. Furthermore, these systems improved performance of a computing system and individual users through parallel execution of programs, load balancing and sharing, and replication of programs and data. Distributed computing systems are also characterised by enhanced availability, and increased reliability.

However, the amalgamation process has also generated some serious challenges and problems. The most important, critical challenge was to synthesise a model of distributed computing to be used in the development of both application and system software. Another critical challenge was to develop ways to hide distribution of resources and build relevant services upon them. The development of distributed computing systems is complicated by the lack of a central clock and centrally available data to manage the whole system. Furthermore, amalgamating computers and networks into one single computing system generates a need to deal with the problems of resource protection, communication security and authentication.

The synthesis of a distributed computing model has been influenced by a need to deal with the issues caused by distribution, such as locating data, programs and peripheral resources, accessing remote data, programs and peripheral resources, supporting cooperation and competition between programs executing on different computers, coordinating distributed programs executing on different computers, maintaining the consistency of replicated data and programs, detecting and recovering from failures, protecting data and programs stored and in transit, and authenticating users, etc.

2.2 The Client-Server Model in a Distributed Computing System

A distributed computing system is a set of application and system programs, and data dispersed across a number of independent personal computers connected by a communication network. In order to provide requested services to users the system and relevant application programs must be executed. Because services are provided as a result of executing programs on a number of computers with data stored on one or more locations, the whole computing activity is called *distributed computing*.

2.2.1 Basic Concepts

The problem is how to formalise the development of distributed computing. The above shows that the main issue of distributed computing is programs in execution, which are called *processes*. The second issue is that these processes cooperate or compete in order to provide the requested services. This means that these processes are synchronised.

A natural model of distributed computing is the client-server model, which is able to deal with the problems generated by distribution, could be used to describe computation processes and their behaviour when providing services to users, and allows design of system and application software for distributed computing systems.

According to this model there are two processes, the *client,* which requests a service from another process, and the *server,* which is the service provider. The server performs the requested service and sends back a response. This response could be a processing result, a confirmation of completion of the requested operation or even a notice about a failure of an operation.

From the user's point of view a distributed computing system can provide the following services: printing, electronic mail, file service, authentication, naming, database service and computing service. These services are provided by appropriate servers. Because of the restricted number of servers (implied by a restricted number of resources on which these servers were implemented), clients compete for these servers.

An association between this abstract model and its physical implementation is shown in Figure 2.1. In particular the basic items of the model: the client and server, and request and response are shown. In this case, the client and server processes execute on two different computers. They communicate at the *virtual* (logical) level by exchanging requests and responses. In order to achieve this virtual communication, physical messages are sent between these two processes. This implies that operating systems of computers and a communication system of a distributed computing system are actively involved in the service provision.

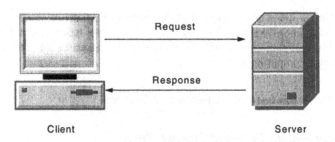

Figure 2.1: The basic client-server model

A more detailed client-server model has three components:

- *Service:* A service is a software entity that runs on one or more machines. It provides an abstraction of a set of well-defined operations in response to applications' requests.

- *Server:* A server is an instance of a particular service running on a single machine.

- *Client:* A client is a software entity that exploits services provided by servers. A client can but does not have to interface directly with a human user.

2.2.2   Features and Problems of the Client-Server Model

The most important features of the client-server model are simplicity, modularity, extensibility and flexibility. Simplicity manifests itself by closely matching the flow of data with the control flow. Modularity is achieved by organising and integrating a group of computer operations into a separate service. Also any set of data with operations on this data can be organised as a separate service. The whole distributed computing system developed based on the client-server model can be easily extended by adding new services in the form of new servers. The servers which do not satisfy user requirements can be easily modified or even removed. Only the interfaces between the clients and servers must be maintained.

There are three major problems of the client-server model:

- The first is due to the fact that the control of individual resources is centralised in a single server. This means that if the computer supporting a server fails, then that element of control fails. Such a solution is not tolerable if a control function of a server is critical to the operation of the system (e.g., a name server, a file server, an authentication server). Thus, the reliability and availability of an operation depending on multiple servers is a product of reliability of all computers and devices, and communication lines.

- The second problem is that each single server is a potential bottleneck. The problem is exacerbated as more computers with potential clients are added to the system.

18

- The third problem arises when multiple implementations of similar functions are used to improve the performance of a client-server based system because of a need to maintain consistency. Furthermore, this increases the total costs of a distributed computing system.

2.3 Cooperation between Clients and Servers

2.3.1 Cooperation Type and Chained Server

A system in which there is only one server and one client would not be able to provide high performance, and reliable and cost effective services to users. As mentioned in the previous section, it is necessary to use one server to provide services to more than one client. The simplest cooperation between clients and servers based on sharing allows for lowering the costs of the whole system and more effective use of resources. An example of a service based on this cooperation is a printing service. Figure 2.2 shows a printer server providing services to n clients, which all are connected by a local area network.

In a distributed computing system there are two different types of cooperation between clients and servers. The first type assumes that a client requests a temporary service. The second one is generated by a client that wants to arrange a number of calls to be directed to a particular serving process. This implies a need for establishing long term bindings between this client and a server.

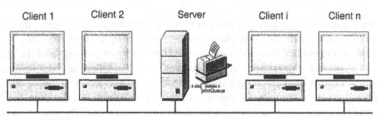

Figure 2.2: Printing service (a service example)

Processes can act as either clients or servers, depending on the context. A file server that receives a request to read a file from a user's client process must check on the access rights of this user. For this purpose the file server sends a request to an authentication server and waits for its response. The response of the file server to the client depends on the response from the authentication server. This implies that the file server acts as a client of the authentication server. Thus, a service provided to the user by a distributed computing system based on the client-server model could require a chain of *cooperating servers.*

2.3.2 Multiple Servers

A distributed computing system has the following functions:

- Improve performance through parallel execution of programs on a cluster (sometimes called network) of workstations,

- Decrease response time of databases through data replication,

- Support synchronous distant meetings,

- Support cooperative workgroups, and

- Increase reliability by service multiplication, etc.

To perform these functions, many servers must contribute to the overall application. This implies a need to invoke multiple services. Furthermore, it would require in some cases simultaneous requests to be sent to a number of servers. Different applications will require different semantics for the cooperation between clients and servers, as illustrated in the following paragraphs.

Cooperation in the systems supporting parallel execution

In a distributed computing system supporting parallel execution, there are some parts of a program which could be executed as individual processes on separate computers. For this purpose a process (parent), which coordinates such parallel processing of individual processes (children), causes them to execute on selected idle computers and waits for computational results. In this case the parent process acts as a client and the child processes as servers, in a one-to-many communication pattern. However, the parent process cannot proceed any further unless all children send back responses.

This example shows that there are two questions which should be answered in order to improve the cooperation between the client and servers: who is responsible for locating idle computers on which servers can run, and who is responsible for setting up those servers on remote computers and coordinating responses.

Cooperation in the systems supporting a distributed database

Similar semantics of cooperation between a client and multiple servers in a distributed computing system occur in supporting a distributed database. To commit a transaction all operations performed on a set of databases must be completed successfully. Thus, a client process which executes a transaction sends operation requests to relevant databases (servers) and waits for the results of the operations. The client process can be involved in other operations, however, responses from all database servers must be received to commit the transaction.

In this case there is no need to set up servers on idle computers — there are servers which already run on dedicated computers. However, there is an issue of who can deal with these database servers, the client process or another entity working on behalf of this client.

Cooperation in the systems supporting a user application

There are different semantics of cooperation between a client and multiple servers in a distributed computing system supporting a user application. This requires identifying a database server which manages relevant data, accesses that database server and carries out some operations on data, and prints that data. There are three servers which must be engaged in supporting the application: a service discovery server, a database server and a printer server. The client process running the application software invokes each server in a sequential order and waits for a response before accessing the next server.

In this case there is again no need to set up servers on idle computers. However, the same issue exists, i.e., who can deal with these database servers, the client process or another entity working on behalf of this client.

Cooperation in the systems supporting mission critical applications

A different form of cooperation between a client and multiple servers is required in reliable distributed computing systems, in particular those which support mission critical applications. In this case a request sent to a group of servers should generate identical responses from all of them. An example of such a system is a redundant computational server on board a space ship, or a fault-tolerant transaction oriented database. In any case only identical operation results are accepted by the client.

These examples show that distributed computing systems have moved from the basic one-to-one client-server model to the one-to-many and chain models in order to improve performance and reliability. Furthermore, the issues identified when discussing the one-to-many communication pattern of the client-server model demonstrate that client and servers cooperation can be strongly influenced and supported by some active entities which are extensions to the client-server model. The following sections address these issues.

2.4   Extensions to the Client-Server Model

The need for extending the client-server model can be specified as an outcome of a study into involvement of other entities in the provision of services, an interface between a client and server, and the behaviour of a client after sending of a request to a server.

2.4.1   Agents and Indirect Client-Server Cooperation

A client and server can cooperate either directly or indirectly. In the former case there is no additional entity that participates in exchanging requests and responses between a client and a server. Indirect cooperation in the client-server model requires two additional entities, called *agents,* to request a service and to be provided with the requested service. Figure 2.3 shows such an extension.

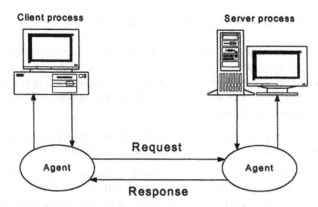

Figure 2.3: Indirect client-server cooperation

The role of these agents can vary from a simple communication module which hides communication network details to an entity which is involved in mediating between clients and servers, resolving heterogeneity issues, and managing resources and cooperating servers. These aspects will be elaborated in other chapters of this book.

As presented in Sections 2.3, a client can invoke desired servers explicitly by sending direct requests to multiple servers. In this case the programmer of a user application must concentrate both on an application and on managing server cooperation and communication. Writing resource management and communication software is expensive, time consuming and error prone. The interface between the client and the server is complicated, differs from one application to another, and the whole service provided is not transparent to the client process (user).

Clients can also request multiple services implicitly. This requires the client to send only one request to a general server. A requested service will be composed by this invoked server cooperating with other servers, based on information provided in the request. After completion of necessary operations by involved servers, the invoked server sends a response back to the client. This coordination operation can be performed by a properly designed agent. Despite the fact that such an agent is quite complicated, the cooperation between the client and the server is based on a single, well-defined interface. Furthermore, transparency is provided to the client which reduces the complexity of the application.

Cooperation between a client and multiple servers can be supported by a simple communication system which employs a direct, one-to-one message protocol. Although this communication model is simple, its performance is poor because each server involved must be invoked by sending a separate message. The overall performance of a communication system supporting message delivery in a client-server based distributed computing system can be dramatically improved if a one-to-many communication pattern is used. In this case a single request is sent by the client process to all servers, specified by a single group name. The use of multicast at the physical/data link layer does improve this system, but it is not essential.

2.4.2 The Three-Tier Client-Server Architecture

Agents and servers acting as clients can generate different architectures of distributed computing systems. The three-tier client-server architecture extends the basic client-server model by adding a middle tier to support the application logic and common services. In this architecture, a distributed application consists of the following three types of components:

- *User interface and presentation processing.* These components are responsible for accepting inputs and presenting the results. They belong to the client tier;

- *Computational function processing.* These components are responsible for providing transparent, reliable, secure, and efficient distributed computing. They are also responsible for performing necessary processing to solve a particular application problem. We say these components belong to the application tier;

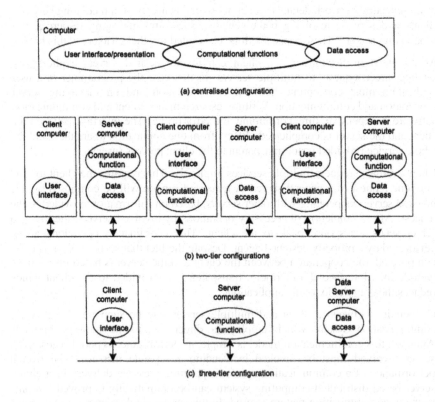

Figure 2.4: Examples of three-tier configurations

- *Data access processing.* These components are responsible for accessing data stored on external storage devices (such as disk drives). They belong to the back-end tier.

These components can be combined and distributed in various ways to create different configurations with varying complexity. Figure 2.4 shows some examples of such configurations ranging from centralised processing to three-tier distribution. In particular, Figure 2.4(a) shows a centralised configuration where all the three types of components are located in a single computer. Figure 2.4(b) shows three two-tier configurations where the three types of components are distributed on two computers. Figure 2.4(c) shows a three-tier configuration where all the three types of components are distributed on different computers.

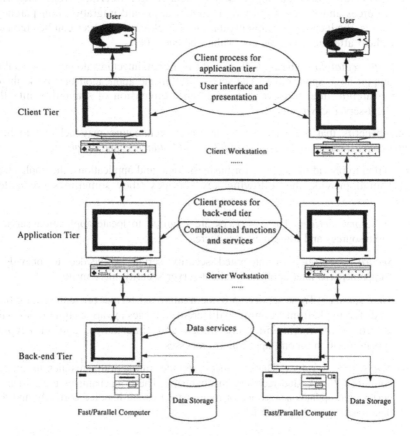

Figure 2.5: An example implementation of the three-tier architecture

Figure 2.5 illustrates an example of implementation of the three-tier architecture. In this example, the upper tier consists of client computers that run user interface processing software. The middle tier contains computers that run computational function processing software. The bottom tier includes back-end data servers. In a three-tier client-server architecture, application clients usually do not interact directly with the data servers, instead, they interact with the middle tier servers to obtain services. The middle tier servers will then either fulfil the requests themselves, sending the result back to the clients, or more commonly, if additional resources are required, servers in the middle tier will act (as clients themselves) on behalf of the application clients to interact with the data servers in the bottom tier or other servers within the middle tier.

Compared with a normal two-tier client-server architecture, the three-tier client-server architecture has the following two important advantages:

- *Better transparency.* The servers within the application tier of the three-tier architecture allow an application to detach user interface from back-end resources and therefore provide better location and migration transparency. That is, the location or implementation of back-end resources can be changed without affecting the programs within the client tier;

- *Better scalability.* The centralised and two-tier architectures do not scale well to support large applications. The servers within the application tier of the three-tier architecture, however, inject another dimension of scalability into the client-server environment.

Other benefits that the three-tier client-server architecture may achieve include better *concurrency, flexibility, reusability, load balancing,* and *reliability.*

In addition to providing services for business logic and applications, the application tier should provide the following key services (they sometimes are called *middleware*):

- *Directory services.* These services are required to locate application services and resources and route messages there.

- *Security services.* An integrated security service is needed to provide a comprehensive inter-application client-server security mechanism.

- *Time services.* These services provide a universal format for representing time on different platforms running in different countries in various time zones. This is critical in maintaining error logs and timestamps, and in keeping synchronisation among application processes.

- *Transaction services.* These services provide transaction semantics to support commit, rollback, and recovery mechanisms. These mechanisms are critical to ensure that updates across one or more databases are handled correctly and that data integrity is not jeopardised.

2.5 Service Discovery

To invoke a desired service a client must know whether there is a server which is able to provide this service and its characteristics if it exists, and its name and location. This is the issue of *service discovery.* In the case of a simple distributed computing system, where there are only a few servers, there is no need to identify an existence of a desired server. Information about all available servers is a priori. This implies that service discovery is restricted to locating the server, which provides the desired service. On the other hand, in a large distributed computing system which is a federation of a set of distributed computing systems, with many service providers who offer and withdraw these services dynamically, there is a need to learn both whether a proper service (e.g., a very fast colour printer of high quality) is available at a given time, and if so its name and location.

It is worth mentioning that a client in a distributed computing system managed by a distributed operating system, which provides *transparency* (one of the most important features of a distributed computing system), should only know a name of either a server or an agent working on behalf of the server. On the other hand, a client in a distributed computing system managed by a set of centralised operating systems and their extensions to access remote resources and services must know both its name and location. The reason is that transparency is not provided.

Service discovery is achieved through the following modes:

- Server computer address is hardwired into client code;

- Broadcast is used to locate servers;

- Name server is used to locate services; and

- Brokers are used to locate servers.

We discuss them in detail next.

2.5.1 Hardwiring Computer Address

This approach requires only a location of the server, in the form of computer address, to be provided. However, it is only applicable in very small and simple systems, where there is only one server process running on the destination computer. Thus, an operating system knows where to deliver an incoming request.

Another version of this approach is based on a much more advanced naming system, where requests are sent to processes rather than to computers. In this case each process is named by a pair *<computer_address, process_name>*. A client is provided with not only a name of a server, but also with the address of a server computer. This solution is not location transparent as the user is aware of the location of the server. The lack of transparency can create a problem when there is a need to move a server to another computer, and a pair *<computer_address, process_name>* has been hardwired in client code.

2.5.2 Broadcast Approach

According to this approach each process has a unique name (e.g., a very long identifier can be used for this purpose). In order to send a request a client knows a name of a destination, in particular of a server. However this is not enough because an operating system of a computer where the server runs must know an address of the server's computer. For this purpose the client's operating system broadcasts a special locate request containing the name of the server, which will be received by all computers on a network. An operating system that finds the server's name in the list of its processes, which means that the named server runs on its computer, sends back a 'here I am' response containing its address (location). The client's operating system receives the response and can store (cache) the server's computer address for future communication. This approach is transparent, however the broadcast overhead is high as all computers on a network are involved in the processing of the locate request.

The cooperation between clients, servers and operating systems supporting them in a distributed computing system using the broadcast approach to locate servers is illustrated in Figure 2.6.

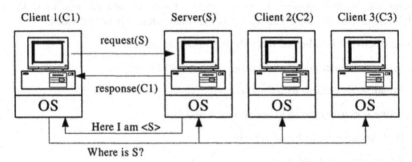

Figure 2.6: Service discovery -- broadcast approach

2.5.3 Name Server Approach

This approach is very similar to the broadcast based approach, however it reduces the broadcast overhead. In order to learn the address of a desired server, an operating system of the client's computer sends a 'where is' request to a special system server, called a *name server,* asking for the address of a computer where the desired server runs. This means that the name and location (computer address) of the name server are known to all operating systems. The name server sends back a response containing an address of the desired server. The client's operating system receives the response and can cache the server's computer address for future communication.

This approach is transparent and much more efficient than the broadcast based approach. However, because the name server is centralised, the overall performance of a distributed computing system could be degraded, as the name server could be a bottleneck. Furthermore, reliability of this approach is low; if a name server computer crashes, a distributed computing system cannot work.

Figure 2.7 illustrates the cooperation between clients, servers and operating systems supporting them in a distributed computing system using the approach of server

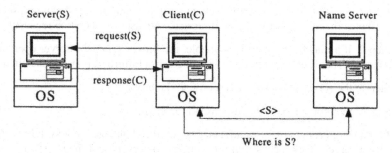

Figure 2.7: Service discovery -- name server and server location lookup

2.5.4 Broker-Based Location Lookup

A client in a distributed computing system supported by any of the above server location approaches must know all servers available in that system and their names (also the server locations (addresses) in systems which do not provide transparency) in order to invoke a desired service. In a large distributed computing system there could be a large number of servers. Moreover, servers of the same type can be characterised by different attributes describing the services they provide (e.g., one laser printer is a colour printer, another is a black and white printer). Furthermore, servers can be offered by some users and revoked dynamically. A user is not able to know names and attributes of all these servers, and their dynamically changing availability. There must be a server which could support users to deal with these problems. This server is called a broker. Thus, a *broker* is a server that

- allows a client to identify available servers which can be characterised by a set of attributes that describe the properties of a desired service;

- mediates cooperation between clients and servers;

- allows service providers to register the services they support by providing their names, locations and features in the form of attributes;

- advertises registered services and makes them available to clients; and

- withdraws services dynamically.

A broker-based approach is very similar to the server location lookup performed via a name server approach. However, there are real conceptual differences between a broker and a name server which frees clients from remembering ASCII names or path names of all servers (and eventually the server locations), and allows clients to identify attributes of servers and learn about their availability. Thus, a broker is a server, which embodies both service management and naming services. There are two basic broker classes, which form two different forms of cooperation between clients and servers:

Forwarding broker

Cooperation between a client and a server mediated by this broker is as follows:

- Step 1: the broker receives from a client a service enquiry in a form of a set of attributes that characterise a desired service, and a server operation request;

- Step 2: if a matching server is available, the broker sends the server operation request to that found server; otherwise, it sends a failure response to the client;

- Step 3: the server sends back a response to the broker;

- Step 4: the broker passes the response to the client.

The forwarding broker possesses advantages and disadvantages of a system with a centralised server. This means that all requests to servers and their responses are going through this broker.

Direct broker

Cooperation between a client and a server mediated by this broker is as follows:

- Step 1: the broker receives from a client a service enquiry in a form of a set of attributes that characterise a desired service;

- Step 2: if a matching server is available, the broker sends back a name and a server computer address to the client; otherwise, it sends a failure response;

- Step 3: the client sends the server operation request to the server;

- Step 4: the server sends back a response to the client.

Despite the fact that the direct broker also possesses advantages and disadvantages of a system with a centralised server, its performance is better than that of the forwarding broker, because only service enquiry messages are sent to this broker.

2.6 Client-Server Interoperability

Reusability of servers is a critical issue for both users and software manufacture due to the high cost of software writing. This issue could be easily resolved in a homogeneous environment because accessing mechanisms of clients may be made compatible with software interfaces, with static compatibility specified by types and dynamic compatibility by protocols.

Cooperation between heterogeneous clients and servers is much more difficult as they are not fully compatible. Thus, the issue is how to make them interoperable. Wegner [Wegner 1996] defines *interoperability* as the ability of two or more software components to cooperate despite differences in language, interface, and execution platform.

There are two aspects of client-server interoperability: a unit of interoperation, and interoperation mechanisms. The basic unit of interoperation is a procedure [Wegner 1996]. However, larger-granularity units of interoperation may be required by software components. Furthermore, preservation of temporal and functional properties may also be required.

There are two major mechanisms for interoperation:

- *Interface standardisation:* the objective of this mechanism is to map client and server interfaces to a common representation. The advantages of this mechanism are: (i) it separates communication models of clients from those of servers, and (ii) it provides scalability, since it only requires $m + n$ mappings, where m and n are the number of clients and servers, respectively. The disadvantage of this mechanism is that it is closed.

- *Interface bridging:* the objective of this mechanism is to provide a two-way mapping between a client and a server. The advantages of this mechanism are: (i) openness, and (ii) flexibility — it can be tailored to the requirements of a given client and server pair. However, this mechanism does not scale as well as the interface standardisation mechanism, as it requires $m * n$ mappings.

2.7   The Relationship

In Section 2.2 we said that in order to allow a client and a server to exchange requests and responses, there is a need to employ a communication network that links computers on which these processes run. We also demonstrated in Section 2.6 that in order to locate a server, the operating systems must be involved. The question is what would be the architecture of a distributed computing system that supports a distributed application developed on the basis of client-server model. Figure 2.8 illustrates the relationship between such a distributed application, the operating system supporting it and communication facility of a distributed computing system.

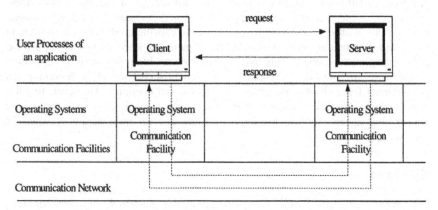

Figure 2.8: A distributed computing system architecture

This figure shows the distributed nature of the operating system, which could be either achieved by:

adding a module to the local centralised operating system of each computer, which allows processes to access remote resources and services; however, in the majority of cases this solution does not fully support transparency, or

30

- employing a distributed operating system, which hides distribution of resources and services; this solution, although futuristic from the current practice point of view, provides location transparency.

It is clear that the extensions to the basic client-server model, described in the previous sections, are achieved through an operating system. Furthermore, network communication services are invoked by an operating system on behalf of cooperating clients and servers.

The overall performance of a distributed computing system developed on the basis of client-server model depends on the performance of a communication facility. Such a facility is comprised of an inter-process communication system of an operating system and network protocols. Communication between clients and servers is discussed in Chapter 5.

Another question is the role of the client-server model in the development of operating systems and communication facilities for distributed computing systems. It will be demonstrated in later chapters that operating systems and network communication systems can also be developed based on the client-server model. This is the current approach to the design of such complicated software following the results of research and practice of software engineering.

2.8 Summary

In this chapter we introduced the client-server model and some concepts related to this model. Partitioning software into clients and servers allows us to place these components independently on computers in a distributed computing system. Furthermore, it allows these clients and servers to execute on different computers in a distributed computing system in order to complete the processing of an application in an integrated manner. This paves the way to high productivity and high performance in distributed computing. The client-server model is becoming the predominant form of software application design and operation. However, to fully benefit from the client-server model, many issues such as client and server cooperation; agents; service discovery; and client-server interoperability, must be investigated.

Exercises

2.1 What challenges does a distributed computing system have when servicing users who share information and peripheral resources? 2.1

2.2 What are the functions of the client-server model? What features does it have? 2.2.1 – 2.2.2

2.3 What is a chain of servers? Give examples. 2.3.1

2.4 Why are multiple servers necessary? 2.3.2

2.5 Describe the indirect client-server cooperation. 2.4.1

2.6 Describe the functions of each tier in the three-tier client-server architecture. 2.4.2

2.7 What methods are used for achieving service discovery? 2.5

2.8 What is client-server interoperability? 2.6

2.9 Describe the relationship between an application, the OS and the communication facility. 2.7

This page intentionally left blank

CHAPTER 3 COMMUNICATION PARADIGMS FOR DISTRIBUTED NETWORK SYSTEMS

Communication is an important issue in distributed computing systems. This chapter addresses the communication paradigm of distributed network systems, i.e., issues about how to build the communication model for these systems.

3.1 Introduction

Distributed computing systems, in particular those managed by a distributed operating system, must be running fast in order to instil in users the feeling of a huge powerful computer sitting on their desks through hiding distribution of resources. Since we have shown in Chapter 2 that the client-server model is commonly used in distributed network systems, this implies that the communication between clients and servers for cooperating by exchanging requests and responses must be fast. Furthermore, the speed of communication between remote client and server processes should not be highly different from the speed between local processes. Distributed systems based on clusters of workstations or PCs do not share physical memory. Thus, requests and responses are sent in the form of messages. The issue is how to build a communication facility within a distributed system to achieve high communication performance.

There is a set of factors which influence the performance of a communication facility. First, the speed of a communication network ranging from slow 10 Mbps to very fast Gbps. Second, the communication protocols that span the connection-oriented protocols such as OSI and TCP, which generate considerable overhead to specialised fast protocols. Third, the communication paradigm, i.e., the communication model supporting cooperation between clients, servers and an operating system support provided to deal with the cooperation. In this chapter we only concentrate on the third factor, i.e., on the communication paradigm.

There are two issues in the communication paradigm. First, as we have shown in Chapter 2, a client can send a request to either a single server or a group of servers. This leads to two patterns of communication: one-to-one and one-to-many (also called *group communication,* see Chapter 9), which are operating system abstractions. Second, these two patterns of inter-process communication could be developed based on two different techniques: Message Passing, adopted for distributed systems in the late 1970s; and Remote Procedure Call (RPC), adopted for distributed systems in mid 1980s. These two techniques are supported by two different sets of primitives provided in an operating system. Furthermore, communication between processes on different computers can be given the same format as communication between processes on a single computer.

The two techniques of interprocess communication are based on different basic concepts. Message passing between remote and local processes is visible to the programmer. The flow of information is unidirectional from the client to the server. However, in advanced message passing, such as structured message passing or rendezvous, information flow is bidirectional, i.e., a return message is provided in response to the initial request. Furthermore, message passing is a completely untyped technique.

The RPC technique is based on the fundamental linguistic concept known as the procedure call. The very general term *remote procedure call* means a type-checked mechanism that permits a language-level call on one computer to be automatically turned into a corresponding language-level call on another computer. Message passing is invisible to the programmer of RPC, which requires a transport protocol to support the transmission of its arguments and results. It is important to note that the term remote procedure call is sometimes used to describe just structured message passing. Remote procedure call primitives provide bidirectional flow of information.

The following topics are discussed in this chapter. First of all, message passing, in particular messages in distributed systems; communication primitives; semantics of these primitives; direct and indirect communication; blocking and non-blocking primitives; buffered and unbuffered exchange of messages; and reliable and unreliable primitives are considered. Second, RPC is discussed. In particular, basic features of this technique; execution of RPC; parameters, results and their marshalling; client-server binding; and reliability issues are presented. Third, group communication is discussed. In particular, basic concepts of this communication pattern; message delivery and response semantics; and message ordering in group communication are presented. The detail implementation of a group communication protocol is discussed in Chapter 9.

3.2 Message Passing Communication

There are two critical issues in message-passing communication: the messages used in the communication and the mechanisms used to send and receive messages. A user is explicitly aware of these two issues during this form of communication. In this section, we discuss the message-passing communication based on these two issues.

3.2.1 What is a Message?

A *message* is a collection of data objects consisting of a fixed size header and a variable or constant length body, which can be managed by a process, and delivered to its destination. A type associated with a message provides structural information on how the message should be identified. A message can be of any size and may contain either data or typed pointers to data outside the contiguous portion of the message. The contents of a message are determined by the sending process. On the other hand, some parts of the header containing system-related information may be supplied by the system.

Messages may be completely unstructured or structured. Unstructured messages have the flexibility that can be interpreted by the communicating pairs. However, the use of unstructured messages that are then interpreted as needed by user processes has problems. That is because some parts of messages (e.g., port names) must be interpreted by the distributed operating system or the communication protocol because they must be translated to be meaningful to another process. Moreover, in heterogeneous networks, only typed information allows the transparent transfer of data items (integers, reals, strings, etc.). Structured messages are also favored for efficiency reasons. Most information transferred between processes is structured in that it represents data items of different types. The use of unstructured messages for such data could be expensive because the encapsulation and decapsulation of structured messages into unstructured linear forms adds a layer of overhead that increases the cost of communication.

In order for any two computers to exchange data value, we need to map data structures and data items to messages. Data structure must be flattened before transmission and rebuilt on arrival. Flattening of structured data into a sequence of basic data is used for the data transmission. Usually a language preprocessor (interface compiler) can be used to generate marshalling/unmarshalling operations automatically. When an IPC primitive is encountered involving data items of the above type, the preprocessor generates code to do the marshalling (for a send) or unmarshalling (for a receive) based on the type description.

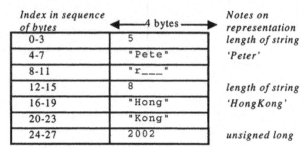

Index in sequence of bytes	◄——4 bytes——►	Notes on representation
0-3	5	length of string
4-7	"Pete"	'Peter'
8-11	"r___"	
12-15	8	length of string
16-19	"Hong"	'HongKong'
20-23	"Kong"	
24-27	2002	unsigned long

The flattened form represents a *Person* struct with value:

{'Peter', ' HongKong', 2002}

Figure 3.1: CORBA CDR message

Example of structured messages:

External data representation (XDR) provided by SUN XDR and Courier for automatic marshalling. Message consists of a sequence of 4-byte objects: (1)

36

Cardinal/integer: 4 bytes; (2) Character: 1 byte; (3) represented as sequences of bytes with the length specified. On receiving a data stream, the data structure must be rebuilt. The diagram in Figure 3.1 is an example of CORBA CDR (Common Data Representation) [OMG 1998].

3.2.2 Message-Passing Mechanisms

Another important issue in the message-passing communication is about the mechanisms used to send and receive messages. These mechanisms involve a set of primitives used for communication.

3.2.2.1 Basic Message-Passing Primitives

There are two issues related to message-passing mechanisms: one is, what is the set of communication primitives, and the other is, what are their semantics? In message-passing communication, a message is sent and received by explicitly executing the *send* and *receive* primitives, respectively. The time diagram of the execution of these two primitives is shown in Figure 3.2. It is obvious that the *receive* primitive must be issued before a message arrives; otherwise the request could be declared as lost and must be retransmitted by the client.

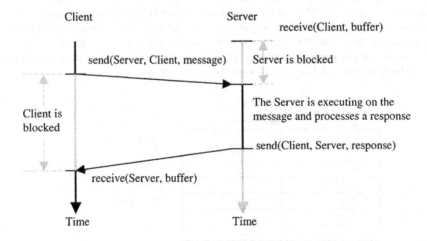

Figure 3.2: Time diagram of the execution of message-passing primitives

Of course, when the server process sends any message to the client process, they have to use these two primitives as well; the server sends a message by executing primitive *send* and the client receives it by executing primitive *receive*.

Several points should be discussed at this stage. All of them are connected with a problem stated as follows: what semantics should these primitives have? The following alternatives are presented:

- Direct or indirect communication ports;

- Blocking versus non-blocking primitives;

- Buffered versus unbuffered primitives;

- Reliable versus unreliable primitives; and

- Structured forms of message passing based primitives.

3.2.2.2 Direct and Indirect Communication Ports

The very basic issue in message-based communication is where messages go. Message communication between processes uses one of two techniques: the sender designates either a fixed destination process or a fixed location for receipt of a message. The former technique is called direct communication and it uses direct names; the latter is called indirect communication and it exploits the concept of a port.

In direct communication, each process that wants to send or receive a message must explicitly name the recipient or sender of the communication. Direct communication is easy to implement and to use. It enables a process to control the times at which it receives messages from each process. The disadvantage of this scheme is the limited modularity of the resulting process definition. Changing the name of the process may necessitate the examination of all other process definitions. All references to the old process must be found, in order to modify them to the new name. This is not desirable from the point of view of separate compilation.

Direct communication does not allow more than one client. That is because, at the very least, issuing the receive primitive would be required for each client. The server process cannot reasonably anticipate the names of all potential clients. Similarly, direct communication does not make it possible to send one request to more than one identical server. This implies the need for a more sophisticated technique. Such a technique is based on ports.

A *port* can be abstractly viewed as a protected kernel object into which messages may be placed by processes and from which messages can be removed, i.e., the messages are sent to and received from ports. Processes may have ownership, and send and receive rights on a port. Each port has a unique identification (name) that distinguishes it. A process may communicate with other processes by a number of different ports.

Logically associated with each port is a queue of finite length. Messages that have been sent to this port, but have not yet been removed from it by a process, reside on this queue. Messages may be added to this queue by any process which can refer to the port via a local name (e.g., capability). A port should be declared. A port declaration serves to define a queuing point for messages, that is, the interface between the client and server. A process that wants to remove a message from a port must have the appropriate receive rights. Usually, only one process may receive

38

access to a port at a time. Messages sent to a port are normally queued in FIFO order. However, an emergency message can be sent to a port and receive special treatment with regard to queuing.

A port can be owned either by a process or by the operating system. If a port is owned by a process, the port is attached to or defined as a part of the process. Ownership of a port can be passed in a message from one process to another. A port can be created by a process which subsequently owns that port. The process also has a receive access to that port. If a single process both owns and has receive access to a port, this process may destroy it. The problem is what can happen to a port when its owner dies. If this process has receive access to that port, the best solution to this problem is automatic destruction of the port. Otherwise, an emergency message is sent to the process which has access rights to it. If the process that is not the owner but has access rights to a port dies, then the emergency message is sent to the owner.

If the operating system owns a port, it provides a mechanism that allows a process to: create a new port (the process is its owner by default); send and receive messages through the port; and destroy a port.

A finite length of the message queues attached to ports is used to prevent a client from queuing more messages to a server than can be absorbed by the system, and as a means for controlling the flow of data between processes of mismatched processing speed. Some implementations can allow the processes owning a port to specify the maximum number of messages which can be queued for that port at any time.

3.2.2.3 Blocking versus Non-blocking Primitives

One of the most important properties of message passing primitives concerns whether their execution could cause delay. We distinguish blocking and non-blocking primitives. We say that a primitive has non-blocking semantics if its execution never delays its invoker; otherwise a primitive is said to be blocking. In the former case, a message must be buffered.

It is necessary to distinguish two different forms of the blocking primitives, in particular send. These forms are generated by different criteria. The first criterion reflects the operating system design, addresses buffer management and message transmission. The blocking and non-blocking send primitives developed following this criterion are illustrated in Figure 3.3. If the blocking send primitive is used, the sending process (client) is blocked, i.e., the instruction following the send primitive is not executed until the message has been completely sent. The blocking receive implies that the process which issued this primitive remains blocked (suspended) until a message arrives, and being put into the buffer specified in the receive primitive. If the non-blocking send primitive is used, the sending process (client) is only blocked for the period of copying a message into the kernel buffer. This means that the instruction following the send primitive can be executed even before the message is sent. This can lead toward parallel execution of a process and message transmission.

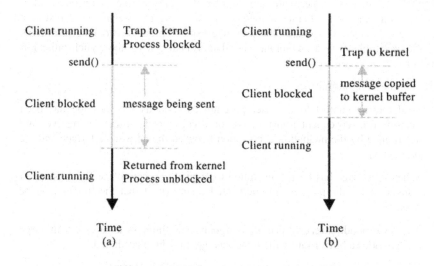

Figure 3.3: Send primitives: (a) blocking; (b) non-blocking

The second criterion reflects the client-server cooperation and the programming language approach to deal with message communication. In this case the client is blocked until the server (receiver) has accepted the request message and the result or acknowledgment has been received by the client. The blocking send primitives developed following this criterion is illustrated in Figure 3.4.

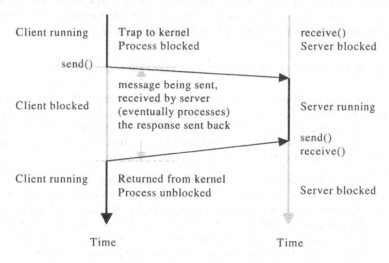

Figure 3.4: Blocked send primitive

There are three forms of receive primitive. The blocking receive is the most common, since the receiving process often has nothing else to do while awaiting receipt of a message. There are also a non-blocking receive primitive, and a primitive for checking whether a message is available to receive. As a result, a process can receive all messages and then select one to process. Blocking primitives provide a simple way to combine the data transfer with the synchronisation function.

With non-blocking primitives:

- Send returns control to the user program as soon as the message has been queued, for subsequent transmission, or a copy made (these alternatives are determined by the method of cooperation between the network interface and the processor);

- When a message has been transmitted (or copied to a safe place for subsequent transmission), the program is interrupted to inform it that the buffer may be reused;

- The corresponding receive primitive signals a willingness to receive a message and provides a buffer into which the massage may be placed; and

- When a message arrives, the program is informed by interrupt.

The advantage of these non-blocking primitives is that they provide maximum flexibility. Moreover, these primitives are useful for real-time applications. The disadvantages of these non-blocking primitives are that they may require buffering to prevent access or change to message contents. These accesses and changes to the message may happen before or during transmission, or while the message is waiting to be received. Buffering may occur on source or destination sites. If a buffer is full, a process must be blocked, which contradicts the original definition of this primitive; make programming tricky and difficult (non-reproducible, timing dependent programs are painful to write and difficult to debug).

3.2.2.4 Buffered versus Unbuffered Message Passing Primitives

In some message-based communication systems, messages are buffered between the time they are sent by a client and received by a server. If a buffer is full when a send is executed, there are two possible solutions: the send may delay until there is a space in the buffer for the message, or the send might return to the client, indicating that, because the buffer is full, the message could not be sent.

The situation of the receiving server is different. The receive primitive informs an operating system about a buffer into which the server wishes to put an arrived message. The problem occurs when the receive primitive is issued after the message arrives. The question is what to do with the message. The first possible approach is to discard the message. The client could time out and re-send, and hopefully the receive primitive will be invoked in the meantime. Otherwise, the client can give up. The second approach to deal with this problem is to buffer the message in the operating system area for a specified period of time. If during this period the appropriate receive primitive is invoked, the message is copied to the invoking server space. If the receive primitive is not invoked and the timeout expires, the message is discarded. Unbuffered and buffered message passing are illustrated in Figure 3.5, where (a) represents unbuffered message passing (messages are discarded before the server issues the receive primitive); and (b) represents buffered message passing (messages are buffered in the OS area for a limited time).

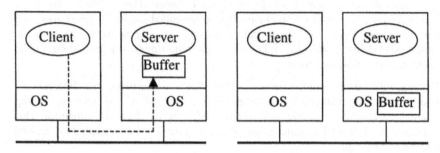

Figure 3.5: Unbuffered and buffered message passing.

Let us consider two extremes: a buffer with unbounded capacity and one with finite bounds. If the buffer has unbounded capacity, then a process is never delayed when executing a send. Systems based on this approach are called systems with asynchronous message passing or systems with no-wait send. The most important feature of asynchronous message passing is that it allows a sender to get arbitrarily far ahead of a receiver. Consequently, when a message is received it contains information about the sender's state that may no longer be valid. If the system has no buffering, execution of send is always delayed until a corresponding receive is executed. Then the message is transferred and both proceed.

When the buffer has finite bounds, we deal with buffered message passing. In this case the client is allowed to get ahead of the server, but not arbitrarily far ahead. In buffered message-passing based systems, the client is allowed to have multiple sends outstanding on the basis of a buffering mechanism (usually in the operating system kernel). In the most often used approach, the user is provided with a system call *create_buffer*, which creates a kernel buffer, of a size specified by the user. This solution implies that the client sends a message to a receiver's port, where it is buffered until requested by the server.

Buffered message-passing systems are characterised by the following features. First, they are more complex than unbuffered message-passing based systems, since they require creation, destruction, and management of the buffers. Second, they generate protection problems, and cause catastrophic event problems, when a process owning a port dies or is killed. In a system with no buffering strategy, processes must be synchronised for a message transfer to take place. This synchronisation is called *rendezvous* see [Gammage and Casey 1985] and [Gammage *et al.* 1987].

42
3.2.2.5 *Unreliable versus Reliable Primitives*

Different catastrophic events, such as a computer crash or a communication system failure may happen to a distributed system. These can cause either a request message being lost in the network, or a response message being lost or delayed in transit, or the responding computer "dying" or becoming unreachable. Moreover, messages can be duplicated, or delivered out of order. The primitives discussed above cannot cope with these problems. These are called *unreliable primitives*. The unreliable send primitive merely puts a message on the network. There is no guarantee of delivery provided and no automatic retransmission is carried out by the operating system when a message is lost.

Dealing with failure problems requires providing *reliable primitives*. In a reliable inter-process communication, the send primitive handles lost messages using internal retransmissions, and acknowledgments on the basis of timeouts. This implies that when send terminates, the process is sure that the message was received and acknowledged.

The question arises of whether reliability should be dealt with at such a high level. Should recovery mechanisms be provided by a network communication facility, in particular either by a transport protocol or lower level protocols? These problems were attacked in [Saltzer *et al.* 1984]. The authors proposed design principles that help guide placement of functions among modules of a distributed system. One of these principles, called end-to-end argument, suggests that "functions placed at a low level of a system may be redundant or of little value when compared with the cost of providing them at that low level". This allows us to suggest that the placement of recovery mechanisms at a process level is sound.

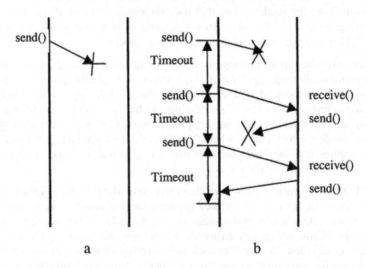

Figure 3.6: Message passing; (a) unreliable; (b) reliable

Reliable and unreliable receives differ in that the former automatically sends an acknowledgment confirming message reception, whereas the latter does not. Two-way communication requires the utilisation of these simple message-passing primitives in a symmetrical way. If the client requested any data, the server sends reply messages (responses) using the send primitive. For this reason the client has to set the receive primitive up to receive any message from the server. Reliable and unreliable primitives are contrasted in Figure 3.6.

Dealing with multiple requests

Two types of semantics are defined, depending on what the server does if it receives multiple copies of a message. It might repeat its processing of the message, even if only one execution was actually desired. Since in this case the reliable primitives do their best to ensure that the request is executed at least once (Figure 3.7(a)). This is called communication with *at-least-once semantics*.

In many cases, of course, repeated execution of a request could destroy the consistency of information, so it is desirable to have primitives which ensure that a request is executed once and only once. This means that a request is idempotent. A primitive with *exactly-once semantics* makes sure that only one execution of the receiver's operation is performed. It is the most desired semantics, but the most difficult to implement.

Exactly-once primitives can be implemented on the basis of a request list maintained by the responding end of the system (Figure 3.7(b)). In this case, each time a request message is received, the server checks whether the *message_id* is on the request list. If yes, this means that this request has been retransmitted and a response message is lost. The previously computed result is sent in a new response message. Otherwise, the *message_id* is placed on the request list, the requested task is performed, a result is associated with a *message_id* entry, and a response message is sent out.

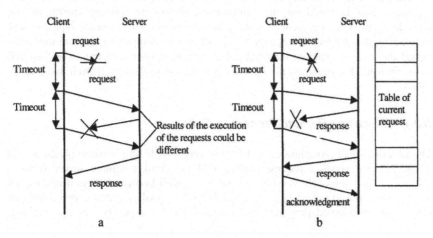

Figure 3.7: Message-passing semantics. (a) at-least-once; (b) exactly-once

3.2.3 Structured Forms of Message-Passing Based Communication

A structured form of communication using message passing is achieved by distinguishing requests and replies, and providing for bidirectional information flow. This means that the client sends a request message and waits for a response. The send primitive combines the previous client's send to the server with a receive to get the server's response. On the other site the receiver (server) acquires a message containing work for them to do and sends the response to the client.

It should be emphasised that different semantics can be linked with these primitives. The result of the send and receive combination in the structured form of the send primitive is one operation performed by the inter-process communication system. This implies that rescheduling overhead is reduced, buffering is simplified (because request data can be left in a client's buffer, and the response data can be stored directly in this buffer), and the transport-level protocol is simplified (because error handling as well as flow control exploit the response to acknowledge a request and authorise a new request) [Cheriton 1988].

When the requesting process is blocked waiting for a reply, it can be blocked indefinitely. This can occur because of a communication failure, a destination computer failure, or simply because the server process does not exist any longer or is too busy to compute a response in a reasonable time. This requires provision of a mechanism to allow the requesting process to withdraw from the commitment to wait for the response.

3.3 Remote Procedure Calls

Message passing between remote and local processes is visible to the programmer. It is a completely untyped technique. Programming message-passing based applications is difficult and error prone. An answer to these problems is the RPC technique that is based on the fundamental linguistic concept known as the procedure call. The very general term remote procedure call means a type-checked mechanism that permits a language-level call on one computer to be automatically turned into a corresponding language-level call on another computer. The first and most complete description of the RPC concept was presented by [Birrell and Nelson 1984].

3.3.1 Executing Remote Procedure Calls

The idea of remote procedure calls (RPC) is very simple and is based on the model where a client sends a request and then blocks until a remote server sends a response. This approach is very similar to a well-known and well-understood mechanism referred to as a procedure call. Thus, the goal of a remote procedure call is to allow distributed programs to be written in the same style as conventional programs for centralised computer systems. This implies that RPC must be transparent. This leads to one of the main advantages of this communication technique: the programmer need not be aware that the called procedure is executing on a local or a remote computer.

When remote procedure calls are used a client interacts with a server by means of a call. To illustrate that both local and remote procedure calls look identical to the programmer, suppose that a client program requires some data from a file. For this purpose there is a read primitive in the program code.

In a system supported by a classical procedure call, the read routine from the library is inserted into the program. This procedure, when executing, firstly, puts the parameters into registers, and next traps to the kernel as a result of issuing a read system call. From the programmer point of view there is nothing special; the read procedure is called by pushing the parameters onto the stack and is executed. In a system supported by RPC, the read routine is a remote procedure which runs on a server computer. In this case, another call procedure, called a *client stub,* from the library is inserted into the program. When executing, it also traps to the kernel. However, rather than placing the parameters into registers, it packs them into a message and issues the send primitive, which forces the operating system to send it to the server. Next, it calls the receive primitive and blocks itself until the response comes back.

The server's operating system passes the arrived message to a *server stub,* which is bound to the server. The stub is blocked waiting for messages as a result of issuing the receive primitive. The parameters are unpacked from the received message and a procedure is called in a conventional manner. Thus, the parameters and the return address are on the stack, and the server does not see that the original call was made on a remote client computer. The server executes the procedure call and returns the results to the virtual caller, i.e., the server stub. The stub packs them into a message and issues a send to return the results. The stub comes back to the beginning of the loop to issue the receive primitive, and blocks waiting for the next request message.

The result message on the client computer is copied to the client process (practically to the stub's part of the client) buffer. The message is unpacked, the results extracted, and copied to the client in a conventional manner. As a result of calling read, the client process finds its data available. The client does not know that the procedure was executing remotely. The whole sequence of operations is illustrated in Figure 3.8.

As we could see above, the RPC mechanism can be used to provide an inter-process communication facility between a single client process and a single server process. Such a mechanism can be extended to a system of many clients and many servers. Furthermore, the RPC facility can be used in homogeneous as well as heterogeneous computer systems.

3.3.2 Basic Features and Properties

It is evident that the semantics of remote procedure calls is analogous to local procedure calls: the client is suspended when waiting for results; the client can pass arguments to the remote procedure; and the called procedure can return results. However, since the client's and server's processes are on different computers (with disjoint address spaces), the remote procedure has no access to data and variables of the client's environment.

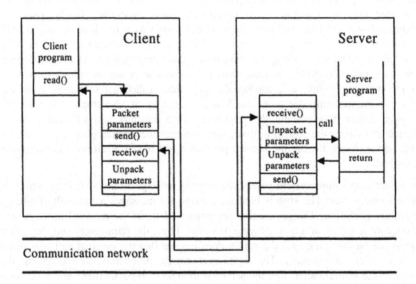

Figure 3.8: An RPC example: a read call

The difference between procedure calls and remote procedure calls is implied by the fact that the client and called procedure are in separate processes, usually running on separate computers. Thus, they are prone to the failures of computers as well as communication systems, they do not share the same address space, and they have separate lifetimes.

There is also a difference between message passing and remote procedure calls. Whereas in message passing all required values must be explicitly assigned into the fields of a message before transmission, the remote procedure call provides marshalling of the parameters for message transmission, i.e., the list of parameters is collected together by the system to form a message.

A remote procedure call mechanism should exhibit the following six properties [Nelson 1981], [LeBlanc 1982], [Hamilton 1984] and [Goscinski 1991]:

- The implementation of a transparent remote procedure call must maintain the same semantics as that used for local procedure calls.

- The level of static type checking (by the compiler) applied to local procedure calls applies equally to remote procedure calls.

- All basic data types should be allowed as parameters to a remote procedure call.

- The programming language that supports RPC should provide concurrency control and exception handling.

- A programming language, which uses RPC, must have some means of compiling, binding, and loading distributed programs onto the network.

- RPC should provide a recovery mechanism to deal with orphans when a remote procedure call fails.

3.3.3 Parameters and Results in RPCs

Parameter passing and the representation of parameters and results in messages are among the most important problems of the remote procedure call.

3.3.3.1 Representation of Parameters and Results

Parameters can be passed by value or by reference. By-value message systems require that message data be physically copied. Thus, passing value parameters over the network is easy: the stub copies parameters into a message and transmits it. If the semantics of communication primitives allow the client to be suspended until the message has been received, only one copy operation is necessary. Asynchronous message semantics often require that all message data be copied twice: once into a kernel buffer and again into the address space of the receiving process. Data copying costs can dominate the performance of by-value message systems. Moreover, by-value message systems often limit the maximum size of a message, forcing large data transfers to be performed in several message operations reducing performance.

Passing reference parameters (pointers) over a network is more complicated. In general, passing data by-reference requires sharing of memory. Processes may share access to either specific memory areas or entire address spaces. As a result, messages are used only for synchronisation and to transfer small amounts of data, such as pointers to shared memory. The main advantage of passing data by-reference is that it is cheap — large messages need not be copied more than once. The disadvantages of this method are that the programming task becomes more difficult, and it requires a combination of virtual memory management and inter-process communication, in the form of distributed shared memory.

A unique, a system wide pointer is needed for each object so that it can be remotely accessed. For large objects (e.g., files), some kind of capability mechanism could be set up using capabilities as pointers, but for small objects (e.g., integers, booleans) the overhead involved in creating a capability and sending it is too large, so that is highly undesirable. However, the data must be finally copied.

Linking both approaches, passing data by-value and passing data by-reference, can be the most effective solution. The representation of parameters and results in messages is natural for homogeneous systems. The representation is complicated in heterogeneous systems.

3.3.3.2 Marshalling Parameters and Results

Remote procedure calls require the transfer of language-level data structures between two computers involved in the call. This is generally performed by packing the data into a network buffer on one computer and unpacking it at the other site. This operation is called *marshalling*.

More precisely, marshalling is a process performed both when sending the call (request) as well as when sending the result, in which three actions can be distinguished:

- Taking the parameters to be passed to the remote procedure and results of executing the procedure;

- Assembling these two into a form suitable for transmission among computers involved in the remote procedure call; and

- Disassembling them on arrival.

The marshalling process must reflect the data structures of the language. Primitive types, structured types, and user defined types must be considered. In the majority of cases, marshalling procedures for scalar data types and procedures to marshal structured types built from the scalar ones are provided as a part of the RPC software. According to [Nelson 1981], the compiler should always generate in-line marshalling code for every remote call. This permits more efficient marshalling than interpretive schemes but can lead to unacceptably large amounts of code. However, some systems allow the programmer to define marshalling procedures for types that inplude pointers [Bacon and Hamilton 1987].

3.3.4 Client Server Binding

Usually, RPC hides all details of locating servers from clients. However, as we stated in Section 2.3, in a system with more than one server, e.g., a file server and a print server, the knowledge of location of files or a special type of printer is important. This implies the need for a mechanism to bind a client and a server, in particular, to bind an RPC stub to the right server and remote procedure.

Naming and addressing

[Birrell and Nelson 1984] identified two aspects of binding:

- The way a client specifies what it wants to be bound to — this is the problem of naming;

- The way of determination by a client (caller) of the computer address for the server and the specification of the procedure to be invoked — this is the problem of addressing.

The first aspect of binding, i.e., naming, was solved in [Birrell and Nelson 1984] in terms of interface names. In their proposal, individual procedures are identified by entry point numbers within an interface. Interface names are user created. The second problem is how to locate a server for a client. This issue was discussed in Section 2.6.

As discussed in Section 2.3.1, in a distributed system there are two different forms of cooperation between clients and servers. The first form assumes that a client requests a temporary service. The second form indicates that a client wants to arrange for a number of calls to be directed to a particular serving process. In the case of requests for a temporary service, the problem can be solved using broadcast and multicast messages to locate a process or a server. In the case that a solution is based on a name server this is not enough, because the process wants to call the located server during a time horizon.

This means that a special binding table should be created and registered containing established long term binding objects, i.e., client names and server names. The RPC run-time procedure for performing remote calls expects to be provided with a binding object as one of its arguments. This procedure directs a call to the binding address received. It should be possible to add new binding objects to the binding table, remove binding objects from the table (which in practice means breaking a binding), and update the table as well. In systems with name server(s), broadcasting is replaced by the operation of sending requests to a name server requesting a location of a given server and sending a response with an address of this server.

In summary, binding can be performed in two different ways: statically through the third party such as a name server; clients and servers are user processes, and dynamically this binding is between a client channel and a server process, and is controlled by the server which can allocate its server process to active channels.

Binding time

It is important to know when binding can take place. The construction and use of an RPC-based distributed application can be divided into three phases: compile time, link time, and call time [Bershad *et al.* 1987].

Compile time:

- The client and server modules are programmed as if they were intended to be linked together.

- A description of the interface implemented by a server is produced. It yields two stubs: client and server. The client stub, which looks to the client like a server, is linked with the client. The server stub, which looks to the server like a client, is linked with the server.

- The stubs shield the client and server from the details of binding and transport.

- Ideally the stubs are produced mechanically from the definition of the interface, by a stub generator.

Link time:

- A server makes its availability known by exporting (or registering) itself through the RPC routine support mechanism.

- A client binds itself to a specific server by making an import call to this mechanism.

- Calls can take place, once the binding process has been completed.

- It is expected that binding will be performed less frequently than calling.

Call time:

- In providing procedure call semantics by the inter-process communication facility of an operating system, the stubs employ some underlying transport layer protocol to transmit arguments and results reliably between clients and servers.

- The RPC facility should include some control information in each transport packet to track the state of a call.

3.4 Message Passing versus Remote Procedure Calls

The problem arises of deciding which of the two inter-process communication techniques presented above is better, if any, and whether there are any suggestions for when, and for what systems, these facilities should be used.

First of all, the syntax and semantics of the remote procedure call are the functions of the programming language being used. On the other hand, choosing a precise syntax and semantics for message passing is more difficult than for RPC because there are no standards for messages. Moreover, neglecting language aspects of RPC and because of the variety of message-passing semantics, these two facilities can look very similar. Examples of a message-passing system that looks like RPC are message passing for the V system (which in [Cheriton 1988] is called now the remote procedure call system), message passing for Amoeba [Tanenbaum and van Renesse 1985] and RHODOS [De Paoli *et al.* 1995].

Secondly, the RPC has an important advantage that the interface of a remote service can be easily documented as a set of procedures with certain parameter and result types. Moreover, from the interface specification, it is possible to automatically generate code that hides all the details of messages from a programmer. Note that a simplified structure that hides message details reduces the range of communication options available to applications programmers. On the other hand, a message-passing model provides flexibility not found in remote procedure call systems. However, this flexibility is at the cost of difficulty in the preparation of precisely documented behaviour of a message-passing interface.

The problem is, when these facilities should be used. The message-passing approach appears preferable when serialisation of request handling is required. The RPC approach appears preferable when there are significant performance benefits to concurrent request handling. RPC is particularly efficient for request-response transactions.

Inter-process communication is a distributed system facility whose performance has been extensively studied, in contrast to other facilities or issues. Unfortunately, these studies have been carried out mainly for one particular system [Cheriton 1988] [Rashid 1986] [Welch 1986]. This implies that it is very hard to say which form of inter-process communication offers the best performance.

3.5 Group Communication

When there is a need to send a request to a number of servers, group communication should be used for the performance and ease of programming reasons. The details of group communication will be presented in Chapter 9. In this section, we briefly introduce some basic concepts about group communication.

3.5.1 Basic Concepts

Distributed computing systems provide opportunities to improve the overall performance through parallel execution of programs on a cluster of workstations, decrease response time of databases using data replication, support synchronous distant meetings and cooperative workgroups, and increase reliability by service multiplication. In these cases many servers must contribute to the overall application. This implies a need to invoke multiple services by sending a simultaneous request to a number of servers, called a *group*.

The concept of a process group is not new. The V-system [Cheriton and Zwaenepoel 1985], Amoeba [Tanenbaum 1990], Chorus [Rozier *et al.* 1988], and RHODOS [Joyce and Goscinski 1997] all support this basic abstraction in providing process groups to applications and operating system services with the use of one-to-many communication pattern, called *group communication*.

A group is a collection of processes that share common features (described by a set of attributes) or application semantics, for instance file servers and printer servers. In general, processes are grouped in order to [Liang *et al.* 1990]:

- deal with a set of processes as a single abstraction;

- form a set of servers which can provide an identical service (but not necessary) of the same quality);

- provide a high-level communication abstraction to simplify user level programs in interacting with a group of receivers;

- encapsulate the internal state and hide interactions among group members from the clients, and provide a uniform interface to the external world;

52

- deliver a single message to multiple receivers thereby reducing the sender and receiving overheads; and

- construct larger systems using groups as their fundamental blocks.

There are several issues which allow us to set up a taxonomy of process groups: *group structure, group behaviour,* and *group types.*

3.5.1.1 Group Structures

Four group structures are often supported to provide the most appropriate policy for a wide range of user applications, as shown in Figure 3.9.

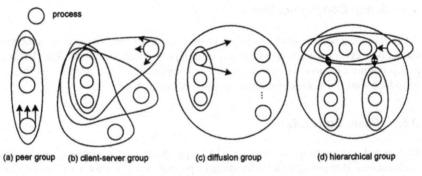

(a) peer group   (b) client-server group   (c) diffusion group   (d) hierarchical group

Figure 3.9: Group structures

- The *peer group* is composed of a set of member processes that cooperate for a particular purpose, see Figure 3.9(a). Fault-tolerant and load sharing applications dominate this type of group style. The major problem of the peer group style is that they do not scale very well.

- The *client-server group* is made from a potentially large number of client processes with a peer group of server processes, see Figure 3.9(b).

- The *diffusion group* is a special case of the client-server group, see Figure 3.9(c). Here, a single request message is sent by a client process to a full set of server and client processes.

- The *hierarchical group* is an extension to the client-server group, see Figure 3.9(d). In large applications with a need for sharing between large numbers of group members, it is important to localise interactions within smaller clusters of components in an effort to increase performance. In client-server applications with the hierarchical server, the client is bound transparently to a subgroup that accepts requests on its behalf. The subgroup is responsible for performing the mapping. However, the major problem with hierarchical groups is that they require a base group that may fail leaving the group inoperative.

3.5.1.2 Behaviour Classification of Process Groups

The application programmer must be aware of the behaviour of the application before a suitable policy can be formulated. According to the external behaviour, process groups can be classified into two major categories: deterministic and non-deterministic [Neufield et al. 1990] [Joyce and Goscinski 1997].

- *Deterministic groups:* a group is considered deterministic if each member must receive and act on a request. This requires the coordination and synchronisation between the members of the group. In a deterministic group, all members are considered equivalent. When receiving the same request in the same state, all members of the group will execute the same procedure and every member of the group will transfer to the same new state and produce the same response and external events.

- *Non-deterministic groups:* non-deterministic groups assume their applications do not require consistency in group state and behaviour, and they relax the deterministic coordination and synchronisation. Each group member is not equivalent and can provide a different response to a group request, or not respond at all, depending on the individual group member's state and function. Due to the relaxed group consistency requirements of the non-deterministic groups, the overheads associated with this group communication are substantially less than those of the deterministic groups.

3.5.1.3 Closed and Open Groups

In general, there are two group types of groups: closed or open [Tanenbaum 1990]. In the *closed group* only the members of the group can send and receive messages to access the resource(s) of the group. In the *open group* not only can the members of the group exchange messages and request services but non-members of the group can send messages to group members. Importantly, the non-members of the group need not join the group nor have any knowledge that the requested service is provided by a group.

Closed groups are typically used to support parallel processing where a group of process servers work together to formulate a result which does not require the interaction of members outside the group. Closed groups are often implemented in a peer group or diffusion group structure. Conversely, an open group would best suit a replicated file server where process members of the group should have the ability to send messages to the group members. A common group structure for the open group is the client-server or hierarchical group.

3.5.2 Group Membership Discovery and Operations

Group membership is responsible for providing a consistent view to all the members of the current group. Each member of the group must exchange messages amongst themselves to resolve the current status and membership of the group. The identification of the current members of the group is important in providing the specified message ordering semantics. Any change in group membership will require all members to be notified to satisfy the requested message requirements. For instance, if fault tolerance is required by the application program, not only must membership changes be provided to all group members before the next message, but all group members must be notified of the change at the same point in the message sequence of the group.

An extension to the group membership semantics is the dynamic and static group membership. Static group membership does not allow any members to leave or join the group after initiation of the group. On the other hand, dynamic group membership semantics allow processes to join and leave the group.

There are two different sets of primitives, the first used to support group membership discovery [Cristian 1991], and the second to support group association operations [Amir et al. 1993] [Birman and Joseph 1987] [Jia et al 1996]. Group membership discovery allows a process to determine a state of the group and its membership. However, as the requesting process has no knowledge of the group members location, network broadcast is required. The overheads associated with this method can be prohibitive if the network is large.

There are four operations that address group association: *create, destroy, join,* and *leave.* Initially a process requiring group communication creates the required group. A process is considered to be a group member after it has successfully issued a group join primitive, and will remain a member of the group until the process issues a leave group primitive. When the last member of the group leaves, the group will be destroyed.

Essential to the role of group operations is state management for its members. Whenever a process issues and completes a join group primitive, it will be provided with the complete state of the group. The groups' state will be provided from the current group members and will contain a copy of the current groups' view, delivered messages, and current message sequence. The state transferred must not violate the message ordering and reliability of the application messages.

Unfortunately, group membership is greatly complicated by network partitioning and process or computer failure. The group association primitives allow member processes to leave and join at any given time of the life of the group. Following network partitioning members of a group can be un-reachable for some period of time. This is further complicated as in an asynchronous environment, such as a distributed system, where it is almost impossible to distinguish between the slow response of a remote process to that of a partitioned network [Amir *et al.* 1992]. Hence, the group membership facility must provide the flexibility to maintain serviceable performance during network partitioning (although slightly degraded) by allowing a subgroup to form inside the communicating group. When the network partitions disappear the group membership support should allow the subgroups to join back into the original process group. This joining of the subgroups must re-synchronise the state of each member of the group to maintain consistency of the data and messages.

In fault tolerant applications, if a group member process terminates and leaves the group without notifying the current group members, the group will have to identify by its own means the terminated member. Once the group has come to an agreement on the member that has terminated, (i.e., the terminated process no longer responding to any incoming messages) the group membership state can be committed. Therefore, if the application requires consistent data between the members of the group, the terminated member may be removed from the group with the group membership support providing a consistent view of all the messages and events that have occurred. Depending upon the application, the group membership support must maintain the message ordering semantics requested by providing the appropriate state, message, and data consistency for all current group members.

3.6 Distributed Shared Memory

There are two basic paradigms for interprocess communication in distributed systems: one is the message-passing paradigm, which includes message-passing systems and remote procedure call (RPC) introduced above, the other is shared-memory paradigm. The message-passing paradigm uses two basic primitives, *Send* and *Receive* for interprocess communication, while the shared-memory paradigm provides processes in a system with a shared address space. Processes use this address space in the same way they use normal local memory. That is, processes access data in the shared address space through *Read* and *Write* primitives. This section introduces the distributed shared memory system.

3.6.1 What is a Distributed Shared Memory (DSM) System?

Distributed shared memory (DSM) is an abstraction used for sharing data between computers that do not share physical memory. Processes access DSM by reads and updates to what appears to be ordinary memory within their address space. However, an underlying run-time system ensures transparently that processes executing at different computers observe the updates made by one another. It is as if the processes access a single shared memory, but in fact the physical memory is distributed, as depicted in Figure 3.10, where processes running on each computer access the DSM as if they access a single shared memory; each computer is connected with one another through the network.

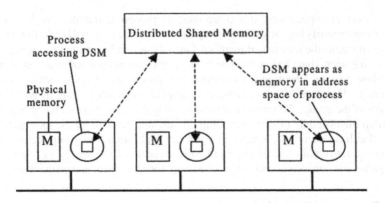

Figure 3.10: The distributed shared memory abstraction

The main point of DSM is that it spares the programmer the concerns of message passing when writing applications that might otherwise have to use it. DSM is primarily a tool for parallel and distributed (group) applications in which individual shared data items can be accessed directly. DSM is in general less appropriate in client-server systems, however, servers can provide DSM that is shared between clients.

As a communication mechanism, DSM is comparable with message-passing rather than with request-reply based communication (client-server model), since its application to parallel processing, in particular, entails the use of asynchronous communication. The DSM and message-passing approaches can be compared as follows:

Programming model: Under the message-passing model, variables have to be marshalled from one process, transmitted and unmarshalled into other variables at the receiving process. By contrast, with shared memory, the processes involved share variables directly, so no marshalling is necessary -- even of pointers to shared variables – and thus no separate communication operations are necessary.

Synchronization between processes is achieved in the message model through message passing primitives themselves, using techniques such as the lock server implementation. In the case of DSM, synchronization is via normal constructs for shared-memory programming such as locks and semaphores. Finally, since DSM can be made persistent, processes communicating via DSM may execute with non-overlapping lifetimes. A process can leave data in an agreed memory location for the other to examine when it runs. By contrast, processes communicating via message passing must execute at the same time.

Efficiency: Experiments show that certain parallel programs developed for DSM can be made to perform about as well as functionally equivalent programs written for message passing platforms on the same hardware [Carter et al 1991] – at least in the case of relatively small numbers of computers (ten or so). However, this result can not be generalized. The performance of a program based on DSM depends upon many factors, particularly the pattern of data sharing, such as whether an item is updated by several processes.

3.6.2 Design and Implementation Issues

There are several design and implementation issues concerning the main features that characterize a DSM system. These are the structure of data held in DSM; the synchronization model used to access DSM consistently at the application level; the DSM consistency model, which governs the consistency of data values accessed from different computers; the update options for communicating written values between computers; the granularity of sharing in a DSM implementation; and the problem of thrashing.

3.6.2.1 Structure

Structure defines the abstratc view of the shared-memory space to be presented to the application programmers of a DSM system. For example, the shared-memory space of one DSM system may appear to its programmers as a storage for words, while the programmers of another DSM system may view its shared-memory space as a storage for data objects. The three commonly used approaches for structuring the shared-memory space of a DSM system are as follows:

- *No structuring.* Most DSM systems do not structure their shared-memory space. In these systems, the shared-memory space is simply a linear array of words. An advantage of the use of unstructured shared-memory space is that it is convenient to choose any suitable page size as the unit of sharing and a fixed grain size may be used for all applications. Therefore, it is simple and easy to design such a DSM system. It also allows applications to impose whatever data structures they want on the shared memory.

- *Structuring by data type.* In this method, the shared-memory space is structured either as a collection of objects or as a collection of variables in the source language. The granularity in such DSM systems is an object or a variable. But since the sizes of the objects and data types vary greatly, these DSM systems use variable grain size to match the size of the object/variable being accessed by the application. The use of variable grain size complicates the design and implementation of these DSM systems.

- *Structuring as a database.* Another method is to structure the shared memory like a database. In this method, the shared-memory space is ordered as an associative memory (a memory addressed by content rather than by name or address) called a tuple space, which is a collection of immutable tuples with typed data items in their fields. A set of primitives that can be added to any base language (such as C or FORTRAN) are provided to place tuples in the tuple space and to read or extract them from tuple space. To perform updates, old data items in the DSM are replaced by new data items. Processes select tuples by specifying the number of their fields and their values or types.

Although this structure allows the location of data to be separated from its value, it requires programmers to use special access functions to interact with the shared-memory space. Therefore, access to shared data is non-transparent. In most other systems, access to shared data is transparent.

3.6.2.2 Synchronization Model

Many applications apply constraints concerning the values stored in shared memory. In order to use DSM, a distributed synchronization service needs to be provided, which includes familiar constructs such as locks and semaphores. Even when DSM is structured as a set of objects, the implementors of the objects have to be concerned with synchronization. Synchronization constructs are implemented using message passing. DSM implementations take advantage of application-level synchronization to reduce the amount of update transmission. The DSM then includes synchronization as an integrated component.

3.6.2.3 Consistency

A DSM system is a replication system and allows replication of shared data items. In such a system, copies of shared data items may simultaneously be available in the main memories of a number of nodes. In this case, the main problem is to solve the memory coherence that deals with the consistency of a piece of shared data lying in the main memories of two or more nodes. In other words, the issue of consistency arises for a DSM system which replicates the contents of shared memory by caching it at separate computers.

Consistency requirements vary from application to application. A consistency model besically refers to the degree of consistency that has to be maintained for the shared-memory data for the memory to work correctly for a certain set applications. It is defined as a set of rules that application must obey if they want the DSM system to provide the degree of consistency guaranteed by the consistency model. Several consistency models have been proposed in the literature. Of these, the main ones will be introduced in the next section.

3.6.2.4 Update Options

Applicable to a variety of DSM consistency models, two main implementation choices have been devised for propagating updates made by one process to the others: write-update and write-invalidate.

- *Write-update:* The updates made by a process are made locally and multicast to all other replica managers processing a copy of the data item, which immediately modify the data read by local processes. Processes read the local copies of data items without the need for communication. In addition to allowing multiple readers, several processes may write the same data item at the same time; this is known as *multiple-reader/multiple-writer sharing.*

- *Write-invalidate:* This is commonly implemented in the form of multiple-reader/single-writer sharing. At any time, a data item may either be accessed in read-only mode by one or more processes, or it may be read and written by a single process. An item that is currently accessed in read-only mode can be copied indefinitely to other processes. When a process attempts to write to it, a multicast message is first sent to all other copies to invalidate them and this is acknowledged before the write can take place; the other processes are thereby prevented from reading stale data (that is, data that are not up to date). Any processes attempting to access the data item are blocked if a writer exists. Eventually, control is transferred from the writing process, and other accesses may take place once the update has been sent. The effect is to process all accesses to the item on a first-come, first-served basis.

3.6.2.5 Granularity

An issue that is related to the structure of DSM is the granularity of sharing. Conceptually, all processes share the entire contents of a DSM. As processes sharing DSM execute, however, only certain parts of the data are actually shared and then only for certain times during the execution. It would be clearly very wasteful for the DSM implementation always to transmit the entire contents of DSM as processes access and update it. What should be the unit of sharing in a DSM implementation? That is, when a process has written to DSM, which data does the DSM run-time send in order to provide consistent values elsewhere?

In many cases, DSM implementations are page-based implementations. There are a few factors that influence the choice of unit (block size), such as paging overhead, directory size, thrashing and false sharing etc. The relative advantages and disadvantages of small and large unit sizes make it difficult for a DSM designer to decide on a proper block size. Therefore, a suitable compromise in granularity, adopted by several existing DSM systems, is to use the typical page size of a conventional virtual memory implementation as the block size of a DSM system. Using page size as the block size (unit) of a DSM system has the following advantages:

1. It allows the use of existing page-fault schemes (i.e., hardware mechanisms) to trigger a DSM page fault. Thus memory coherence problems can be resolved in page-fault handlers.

2. It allows the access right control (needed for each shared entity) to be readily integrated into the functionality of the memory management unit of the system

3. As long as a page can fit into a packet, page sizes do not impose undue communication overhead at the time of network page fault.

4. Experience has shown that a page size is a suitable data entity unit with respect to memory contention.

3.6.2.6 Thrashing

A potential problem with write-invalidate protocols is thrashing. Thrashing is said to occur where the DSM run-time spends an inordinate amount of time invalidating and transfering shared data compared with the time spent by application processes doing useful work. It occurs when several processes compete for the same data item, or for falsely shared data items. If, for example, one process repeatly reads a data item that another is regularly updating, then this item will be constantly transferred from the writer and invalidated at the reader. This is an example of a sharing pattern for which write-invalidate is inappropriate and write-update would be better.

3.6.3 Consistency Models

This section describes several most common used consistency models for DSM systems.

3.6.3.1 Sequential Consistency Model

The sequential consistency model was proposed by [Lamport 1978]. A shared-memory system is said to support the sequential consistency model if all processes see the same order of all memory access operations on the shared memory. The exact order in which the memory access operations are interleaved does not matter. That is, if the three operations read (r1), write (w1), read (r2) are performed on a memory address in that order, any of the orderings (r1, w1, r2), (r1, r2, w1), ... of the three operations is acceptable provided all processes see the same ordering. If one process sees one of the orderings of the three operations and another process sees a different one, the memory is not a sequentially consistent memory.

The consistency requirement of the sequential consistency model is weaker than that of the strict consistency model because the sequential consistency model does not guarantee that a read operation on a particular memory address always returns the same value as written by the most recent write operation to that address. As a consequence, with a sequentially consistent memory, running a program twice may not give the same result in the absence of explicit synchronization operations.

A DSM system supporting the sequential consistency model can be implemented by ensuring that no memory operation is started until all the previous ones have been completed. A sequentially consistent memory provides one-copy/single-copy semantics because all the processes sharing a memory location always see exactly the same contents stored in it. This is the most intuitively expected semantics for memory coherence. Therefore, sequential consistency is acceptable by most applications.

3.6.3.2 Weak Consistency Model

The weak consistency model is designed to attempt to avoid the costs of sequential consistency on multiprocessors, while retaining the effect of sequential consistency. This model takes advantage of the following two characteristics common to many applications:

1. It is not necessary to show the change in memory done by every write operation to other processes. The results of several write operations can be combined and sent to other processes only when they need it. For example, when a process executes in a critical section, other processes are not supposed to see the changes made by the process to the memory until the process exits from the critical section. In this case, all changes made to the memory by the process while it is in its critical section need be made visible to other processes only at the time when the process exits from the critical section.

2. Isolated accesses to shared variables are rare. That is, in many applications, a process makes several accesses to a set of shared variables and then no access at all to the variables in this set for a long time.

Both characteristics imply that better performance can be achieved if consistency is enforced on a group of memory reference operations rather than on individual memory reference operations. This is exactly the basic idea behind the weak consistency model.

The main problem in implementing this idea is determining how the system can know that it is time to show the changes performed by a process to other processes since this time is different for different applications. Since there is no way for the system to know this on its own, the programmers are asked to tell this to the system for their applications. For this, a DSM system that supports the weak consistency model uses a special variable called a synchronization variable. The operations on it are used to synchronize memory. That is, when a synchronization variable is accessed by a process, the entire (shared) memory is synchronized by making all the changes to the memory made by all processes visible to all other processes. Note that memory synchronization in a DSM system will involve propagating memory updates done at a node to all other nodes having a copy of the same memory addresses.

3.6.3.3 Release Consistency Model

In the weak consistency model the entire (shared) memory is synchronized when a synchronization variable is accessed by a process, and memory synchronization basically involves the following operations:

1. All changes made to the memory by the process are propagated to other nodes.

2. All changes made to the memory by other processes are propagated from other nodes to the process's node.

A closer observation shows that this is not really necessary because the first operation need only be performed when the process exits from a critical section and the second operation need only be performed when the process enters a critical section. Since a single synchronization variable is used in the weak consistency model, the system cannot know whether a process accessing a synchronization variable is entering a critical section or exiting from a critical section. Therefore, both the first and second operations are performed on every access to a synchronization variable by a process. For better performance and development of the weak consistency model, the *release consistency model* was designed to provide a mechanism to clearly tell the system whether a process is entering a critical section or exiting from a critical section so that the system can decide and perform only either the first or the second operation when a synchronization variable is accessed by a process. This is achieved by using two synchronization variables (called *acquire* and *release*) instead of a single synchronization variable. *Acquire* is used by a process to tell the system that it is about to enter a critical section, so that the system performs only the second operation when this variable is accessed. On the other hand, *release* is used by a process to tell the system that it has just exited from a critical section, so that the system only performs the first operation when the variable is accessed. Programmers are responsible for putting acquire and release at suitable places in their programs.

3.6.3.4 Discussion

There still are other consistency models including:

Causal consistency: Reads and writes may be related by the happened-before relationship. This is defined to hold between memory operations and when either (a) they are made by the same process; (b) a process reads a value written by another process; or (c) there exists a sequence of such operations linking the two operations. The model's constraint is that the value returned by a read must be consistent with the happened-before relationship.

Processor consistency: The memory is both coherent and adheres to the pipelined RAM model (see beblow). The simplest way to think of processor consistency is that the memory is coherent and that all processes agree on the ordering of any two write accesses made by the same process – that is, they agree with its program order.

Pipelined RAM: All processors agree on the order of writes issued by any given processor.

Among the consistency models described above, the most commonly used model in DSM systems is the sequential consistency model because it can be implemented, it supports the most intuitively expected semantics for memory coherence, and it does not impose any extra burden on the programmers. Another important reason for its popularity is that a sequential consistent DSM system allows existing multiprocessor programs to be run on multicomputer architectures without modification. This is because programs written for multiprocessors normally assume that memory is sequentially consistent. However, it is very restrictive and hence suffers from the drawback of low consistency. Therefore, several DSM systems are designed to use other consistency models that are weaker than sequential consistency.

Weak consistency, release consistency and some of the other consistency models weaker than sequential consistency and using explicit sunchronization variables appear to be more promising for use in DSM design because they provide better concurrency and also support the intuitively expected semantics. It does not seem to be a significant disadvantage of these consistency models that synchronization operations need to be known to the DSM run-time – as long as those supplied by the system are sufficiently powerful to meet the needs of programmers. Hence the only problem with these consistency models is that they require the programmers to use the synchronization variables properly. This imposes some burden on the programmers.

3.7 Summary

In this chapter we described two issues of the communication paradigm for the client-server cooperation. Firstly, the communication pattern, including one-to-one and one-to-many (group communication). Secondly, two techniques, message-passing and RPC, which are used to develop distributed computing systems. The message-passing technique allows clients and servers to exchange messages explicitly using the send and receive primitives. Various semantics, such as direct and indirect, blocking and non-blocking, buffered and unbuffered, reliable and unreliable can be used in message passing. The RPC technique allows clients to request services from servers by following a well-defined procedure call interface. Various issues are important in RPC, such as marshalling and unmarshalling of parameters and results, binding a client to a particular server, and raising exceptions. Two very important aspects are presented for group communication: semantics of message delivery and message response, and message ordering. These aspects strongly influence quality of and cost of programming and application development.

In addition to message-passing paradigm, we also discussed the distributed shared memory systems. Distributed shared memory (DSM) is an abstraction used for sharing data between computers that do not share physical memory. DSM is primarily a tool for parallel applications or for any distributed application or group of applications in which individual shared data items can be accessed directly. Various design and implementation issues about DSM have been discussed in this chapter. Among them, we focused on consistency models since a DSM system is a replication system and consistency is the most important concern in such a system. Several consistency models are presented, of these, the sequential consistency model is most commonly used.

64

Exercises

3.1.   What factors influence the performance of a communication facility? 3.1

3.2.   What are structured and unstructured messages? 3.2.1

3.3.   What are the basic message-passing primitives? Describe how they work. 3.2.2

3.4.   Discuss advantages and disadvantages of direct communication. 3.2.2

3.5.   Why is the message queue associated with a port finite length? 3.2.2

3.6.   What is the difference between blocking and nonblocking send primitives based on the first criterion? 3.2.2

3.7.   What are the buffered and unbuffered primitives? Compare their features. 3.2.2

3.8.   Describe the difference between at-least-once semantics and exactly-once semantics when dealing with multiple requests. 3.2.2

3.9.   What is the RPC? What features does it have? 3.3.1

3.10. What are called by-value parameter passing and by-reference parameter passing? 3.3.3

3.11. Describe how to marshal data from one computer to another computer. 3.3.3

3.12. What are the basic aspects of client server binding? 3.3.4

3.13. Compare the difference between message passing and RPC. 3.4

3.14. Why should we use a group? What structures do groups have in distributed computing? 3.5.1

3.15. What operations can be used in group memebership management? What happens if failures occur in a group? 3.5.2

3.16. What's a DSM system? What is its purpose?   3.6.1

3.17. Why do we use page size as the block size of a DSM system? 3.6.2

3.18. What problem may a DSM system with sequential consistency model have? 3.6.3

CHAPTER 4 INTERNETWORKING

As mentioned before, network software is arranged in a hierarchy of layers. Each layer presents an interface to the layers above it that extends the properties of the underlying communication system. Network functions are achieved through the layered protocols. This chapter discusses the communication protocols in a network, especially, TCP/IP protocols used on the current Internet. The next generation of Internet protocol – IPv6 is also addressed in the chapter.

4.1 Communication Protocol Architectures

4.1.1 The OSI Protocol Architecture

In the mid-1970s, different types of distributed systems (based on different types of computer networks) started to appear. As most of them were implemented using proprietary network models and protocols, it was very difficult to make machines and distributed systems from different vendors talk to each other. As a result, a range of standards started to be introduced.

The Open System Interconnection (OSI) Reference Model has been under development by the International Standards Organisation (ISO) since 1977. The reference model attempts to define a comprehensive set of protocols which will allow computers and other devices to communicate. Networks that are implemented using the model are "open" since they do not use proprietary protocols and therefore will not be restricted to use equipment that is supplied by a particular manufacturer. Once the OSI model has been fully defined and implemented, it is expected to dominate all inter-computer communications. It is therefore liable to have a profound effect on the way in which distributed programs will be structured.

The OSI reference model uses a layered protocol hierarchy, as illustrated in Figure 4.1. The following notations are applied to this model:

- Layer i offers an interface to users at layer $i+1$. The interface is the only point at which a user at layer $i+1$ can access the lower layers and is called the layer i protocol service access point (SAP).

- Layer i uses the interface provided by layer $i-1$ to implement its interface to layer $i+1$ and the layer i protocols. The data unit used in the layer i protocol is called the layer i protocol data unit (PDU).

- By convention, layer 0 is considered as primitive.

In order to specify the layer i protocol, we must precisely define the types of protocol data unit used in this layer's protocol entity. We also need to specify the operations (services) provided by this layer to transmit the PDUs of layer *i+1* to the peer protocol entity in a remote system. Of course, descriptions of the services used by this layer (provided by the layer *i-1*) are also needed.

Host A
Host B
i+1
Layer i SAP
i+1
Layer i+1
Layer i PDU
Layer i
Protocol
Entity
i
i
Layer i
Layer i Protocol
Layer i-1
i-1
Layer i-1 SAP
i-1

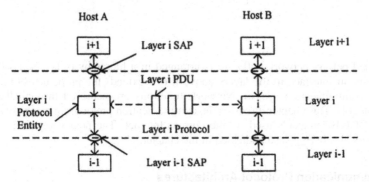

Figure 4.1: The layered protocol model

The approach taken in the OSI reference model is to identify a series of seven protocol layers. Each layer builds upon the services offered by the subordinate layers to offer an enhanced service to the upper layers, this policy is illustrated in Figure 4.2.

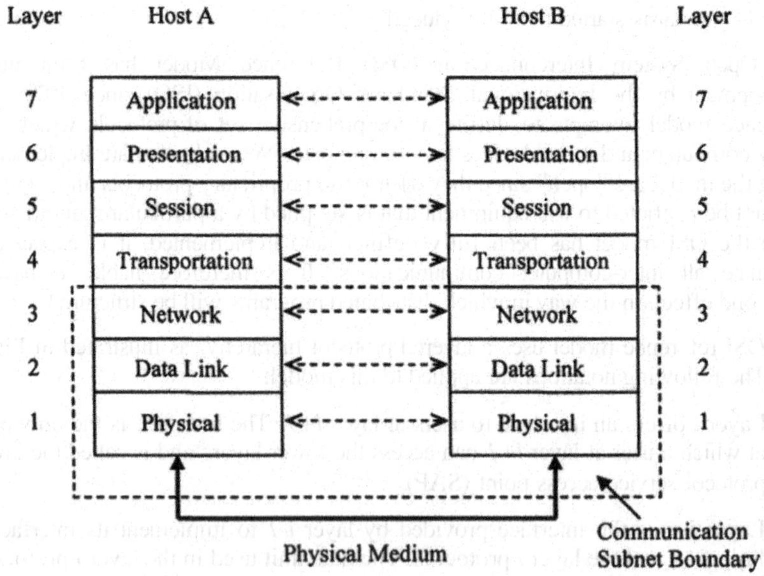

Layer
Host A
Host B
Layer
7
Application
Application
7
6
Presentation
Presentation
6
5
Session
Session
5
4
Transportation
Transportation
4
3
Network
Network
3
2
Data Link
Data Link
2
1
Physical
Physical
1
Communication
Subnet Boundary
Physical Medium

Figure 4.2: The OSI reference model

Programs that need to communicate with each other but reside on separate hosts may call upon the services offered by the top layer of protocol, or may use the protocol services offered by the same layer. This may depend on which layer the programs reside in (in terms of the OSI hierarchy). For example, assume program P_A on host A wants to communicate with program P_B on host B using the layer 7 application protocols. After P_A issues a PDU (message), the message is sent to the lower layers to process. Each layer of the protocol then processes the request and calls a series of lower-level operations that are provided by the subordinate layer. Eventually the bottom layer is reached and a series of message are physically transmitted to machine B by the communications hardware. At the destination machine B the messages are passed up the layers to the application layer and then delivered to P_B.

The operations provided by each layer of the OSI model are as follows:

- *Physical layer:* is concerned with transmitting raw (uninterpreted) bits over a communication channel. It mainly deals with mechanical, electrical, and procedural interfaces (such as RS232, RS449 and X.21), and the physical transmission medium.

- *Data link layer:* provides the protocols which control the flow of information over the link and makes the link appear free of transmission errors by using error correction or error detection and retransmission techniques. The PDUs used in this layer are usually called frames.

- *Network layer:* controls the operation of the subnet (communication system used by the network), implements higher level functions concerning the routing of packets (PDUs used by network layer) from one machine to another and the forwarding of packets between intermediary sites.

- *Transport layer:* implements a "transport service" which moves information from one machine to another. The services that are offered by this layer are independent of the underlying mechanisms that are used by the lower three layers to transmit information. Information may travel over a number of communications channels using different technologies, and the details should be hidden from the users of the transport layer. This layer is responsible for the end-to-end transmission of the data.

- *Session layer:* provides the protocols concerned with the establishment of sessions (dialogues) between users (or user programs). Example applications are remote login and file transfer.

- *Presentation layer:* implements the mapping between the representations of information used on different machines. The lower layers are concerned with the transmission of uninterpreted information between processes; the presentation layer is concerned with its meaning. The services provided by this layer range from the low-level mapping, such as from one character set to another, to the representations of higher level objects, such as arrays, records or graphical representations of information.

- *Application layer:* provides the higher level functions or utility services that are commonly needed when using computer networks, such as mail systems and directory services.

4.1.2 Internet Architecture

The current "Internet" can be defined as "the collection of all computers that can communicate, using the Internet protocol suite, with the computers and networks registered with the Internet Network Information Center (InterNIC)." This definition includes all computers to which one can directly send Internet Protocol packets (or indirectly, through a firewall).

Internet is the largest data network in the world and is actually an interconnection of several packet-switched networks. The Internet has a layered architecture: Figure 4.3 shows the comparison of Internet and OSI architectures.

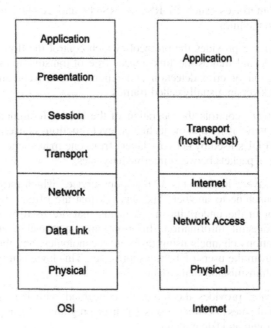

Figure 4.3: Comparison of Internet and OSI architectures

The functions of each Internet layer are as follows:

- *Network access layer:* This layer relies on the data link and physical layer protocols of the appropriate network and no specific protocols are defined.

- *Internet layer.* The Internet Protocol (IP) defined for this layer is a simple connectionless datagram protocol. It offers no error recovery and any error packets are simply discarded.

- *Transport layer:* Two protocols are defined: the Transmission Control Protocol (TCP) and the User Datagram Protocol (UDP). TCP is a connection-oriented protocol that permits the reliable transfer of data between the source and destination end users. UDP is a connectionless protocol that offers neither error recovery nor flow control.

- *User process layer (application):* This layer describes the applications and technologies that are used to provide end-user services.

Internet Protocol enables communication between computers on the Internet by routing data from a source computer to a destination computer. However, computer-to-computer communication only solves half of the network communication problem. In order for an application program, such as a mail program, to communicate with another application, such as a mail server, there needs to be a way to send data to specific programs within a computer.

Ports, or addresses within a computer, are used to enable communication between programs. An application server, such as a Web server or an FTP server, listens on a particular port for service requests, performs whatever service is requested, and returns information to the port used by the application program requesting the service. Popular Internet application protocols are associated with well-known ports. The server programs that implement these protocols listen on these ports for service requests. The well-known ports for some common Internet application protocols are shown in Table 4.1.

Table 4.1: Common Internet application protocols and their ports

Port	Protocol
21	File transfer protocol (ftp)
23	Telnet protocol (telnet)
25	Simple Mail Transfer Protocol (SMTP)
80	Hypertext Transfer Protocol (HTTP)

4.2 TCP/IP Protocol Suite

The ARPANET, sponsored by the Advanced Research Projects Agency (ARPA) and developed during late the 1960s and early 1970s, is a milestone for computer networks. In the early 1980s, a new family of protocols was specified as the standard for the ARPANET. Although the accurate name for this family of protocols is the "DARPA Internet protocol suite" it is commonly referred as the TCP/IP protocol suite, or just TCP/IP.

The *Internet domain sockets* on BSD UNIX use the TCP/IP protocol suite as the communication protocols among processes generally located on different computers across a network. We introduce the TCP/IP in this section.

4.2.1 Communication Protocols

Communications between computers connected by computer networks use well-defined protocols. A protocol is a set of rules and conventions agreed by all of the communication participants. As we have mentioned, in the OSI reference model, the communication protocols are modelled in seven layers. Layered models are easier to understand and make the implementation more manageable. A *protocol suite* is defined as a collection of protocols from more than one layer that forms a basis of a useful network. This collection is also called a *protocol family*. The TCP/IP protocol suite is an example.

There are many protocols defined in the TCP/IP protocol suite. We are going to describe three of them: the Transport Control Protocol (TCP), the User Datagram Protocol (UDP) and the Internet Protocol (IP). In the OSI reference model, the TCP and UDP protocols are Transport layer protocols, while the IP protocol is a Network layer protocol. Figure 4.4 illustrates the relationship of these protocols and their positions in the OSI reference model.

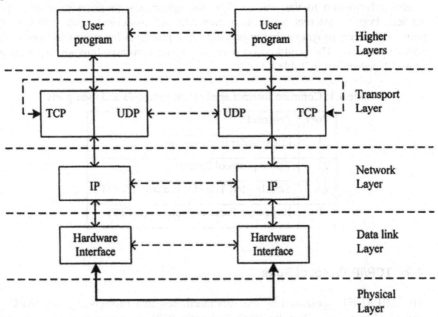

Figure 4.4: The Layered TCP/IP protocol suite

The TCP protocol is a connection-oriented protocol that provides a reliable, full-duplex, byte stream for interprocess communications. The UDP protocol, on the other hand, is a connectionless protocol that provides an unreliable datagram service: there is no guarantee that UDP datagrams ever reach their intended destinations. Acknowledgement must be used in order to provide reliable services when using the UDP protocol.

4.2.2 Network Layer Protocol: IP

The IP protocol is connectionless and unreliable. It is based on *internet datagrams*. The protocol takes a datagram from the transport layer (for example, from the TCP protocol). A datagram is up to 64K bytes long and it may be part of a longer message. Each datagram is transmitted over the network independently so the communication is connectionless. During transmission, a datagram may be lost or may be further fragmented into smaller units (called *IP packets*) as it goes through the protocol layers. When all the IP packets of a datagram finally arrive at the destination computer, they are reassembled to form the datagram and then transferred to the transport layer of the destination site. If any of the IP packets of a datagram are lost or corrupted, the entire datagram is discarded by the destination site so the IP protocol is therefore unreliable because it cannot guarantee the delivery of a datagram.

The IP datagram consists of a header and a text part. The header includes information such as the type of service, the length of the header, the length of the text part, the address of the source computer, the address of the destination computer, and other information.

4.2.2.1 IP Address

It is the IP layer that handles the routing through networks. The Internet address is used to identify networks and computers and is used in an IP datagram header to denote the source and destination computer addresses. An Internet address has 32 bits and encodes both a network ID number and a host ID number. Every host on a TCP/IP internet must have a unique Internet address. The network ID numbers are assigned by some kind of authority, e.g., the Network Information Center (NIC) located at SRI International, while the host ID numbers are assigned locally.

The common notation of an Internet address is to use 4 bytes, as shown in the following:

$$\texttt{field\_1.field\_2.field\_3.field\_4}$$

where $0 <= \texttt{field\_i} <= 255_{10}\ (FF_{16})$, $1 <= i <= 4$.

Depending on the network's class (described below), the network number can be `field_1`, or `field_1.field_2` or `field_1.field_2.field_3`. That means the host number can be `field_2.field_3.field_4`, `field_3.field_4`, or `field_4`.

Networks are classified into three classes, as listed in Table 4.2.

Table 4.2: Network classes

Class	Binary number of field₁	Network ID (decimal)
A	000 000 – 0111 111	0 - 126
B	1000 000 – 1011 1111	128 – 191.254
C	1100 0000 – 1101 1111	192 – 223.254.254

- *Class A* networks are the largest networks with more than 65,536 hosts. A class *A* network ID number is `field_1`.

- *Class B* networks are mid-size networks with host IDs ranging from 256 to 65,536. A class *B* network ID number is `field_1.field_2`.

- *Class C* networks are the smallest networks with up to 256 hosts. A class *C* network ID number is `field_1.field_2.field_3`.

Figure 4.5 illustrates the Internet address formats of these three network classes. For example, if we have an Internet address 98.15.12.63, we can tell that it is a class A network because **field₁** is within the range of 0 - 126. Its network ID number is 98 and host ID number is 15.12.63. If we have an Internet address 130.194.1.106, we can tell that it is a class B network because the **field₁.field₂** is within the range of 128 - 191.254. Its network ID number is 130.194 and host ID number is 1.106.

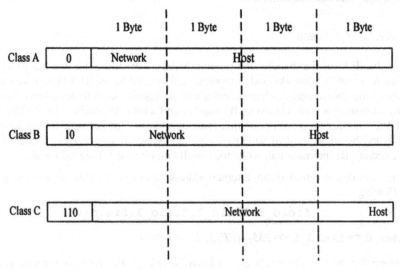

Figure 4.5: Internet network classes

Some IP addresses have significant meanings. For example, the address of 127.0.0.1 is the address of the local machine. It is used for allowing IP communications to the local machine so that sockets and other systems may run even when the machine is isolated from the network.

It is evident that an Internet address can only be assigned to one host. But a host can have several Internet addresses. This is because in some situations, we want a host to be connected to several networks.

4.2.2.2 Domain Name System

Although an Internet address clearly specifies the address of a host, few persons want to use Internet addresses directly: they are too hard to remember. Domain Name System (DNS) is used to name host addresses in more human-oriented ways and to find the Internet addresses corresponding to machine names.

The DNS is a hierarchical naming system: its name space is partitioned into sub-domains, which can themselves be further divided. The DNS is also a distributed system: the name space is delegated to local sites that are responsible for maintaining their part of the database. Programs called *name servers* manage the database.

The DNS name space can be represented as a tree, with the nodes in the tree representing *domain names*. A *fully qualified domain name* is identified by the components (nodes) of the path from the domain name to the root. A component is an arbitrary string of up to 63 octets in length; the length of a fully qualified domain name is limited to 256 octets. By convention, a domain name is written as a dot-separated sequence of components, listed right to left, starting with the component close to the root. The root is omitted from the name. Thus, *wan_res.cm.deakin.edu.au* is a fully qualified domain name. It is certainly easier to remember than the corresponding Internet addresses 139.130.118.102.

DNS name space is divided into *zones of authority,* and name servers have complete control of the names within their zones (domains). For easier management of domains, a large domain can be split into smaller sub-domains, and name servers can delegate authority to other name servers for sub-domains. For example, if *edu.au* represents the domain of all educational institutions in Australia, then *deakin.edu.au* and *anu.edu.au* are its two sub-domains. Queries for DNS information within sub-domain *deakin.edu.au* are first dealt with by the name server of this sub-domain. If this name server cannot answer a query, the query is then directed to the name server of *edu.au* domain. At last, the name server of the root can answer the query.

4.2.3 Transport Layer Protocol: TCP and UDP

As we have shown in Figure 4.3, user processes interact with the TCP/IP protocol suite by sending and receiving either TCP data or UDP data. To emphasise that the IP protocol is used, we sometimes refer to them as the TCP/IP or UDP/IP protocols. TCP provides a connection-oriented, reliable, full-duplex, byte-stream service, similar to a virtual circuit, to an application program. UDP, on the other hand, provides a connectionless, unreliable datagram service to an application program.

As we mentioned in the previous section, the Internet address is used to identify networks and computers. In order to let many processes use the TCP or UDP simultaneously (these processes may reside on any computers of a network), both protocols use 16-bit integer *port numbers* for identifying data associated with each user process. The association of port numbers and user processes last as long as the communication, so the following 5-tuple uniquely identifies a communication:

- The protocol (TCP or UDP);

- The local computer's Internet address;

- The local port number;

- The foreign computer's Internet address;

- The foreign port number.

For example, if we have a communication using TCP protocol. The server is on a host with domain name of *wan_res.cm.deakin.edu.au* (Internet address 139.130.118.102), using port number 5100. The client is on a host with domain name of *sky3.cm.deakin.edu.au* (Internet address 139.130.118.5), using port number 5101. The 5-tuple which uniquely defines the communication is:

{tcp, 139.130.118.102, 5100, 139.130.118.5, 5101}

Because the host name is easier to understand and there are some system calls to convert between a host name and its Internet address, the above 5-tuple can then be written as:

{tcp, wan_res.cm.deakin.edu.au, 5100, sky3.cm.deakin.edu.au, 5101}

Because *wan_res.cm.deakin.edu.au* and *sky3.cm.deakin.edu.au* are within the same sub-domain, we can even write the 5-tuple as:

{tcp, wan_res, 5100, sky3, 5101}

There are some restrictions in using port numbers. In TCP and UDP, port numbers in the range 1 through 255 are reserved. All well-known ports (some commonly used utilities use these ports) are in this range. For example, the File Transfer Protocol (FTP) server uses the well-known port number 21 (decimal). Some operating systems also reserve additional ports for privileged usages. For example, 4.3BSD reserves ports 1-1023 for superuser processes. Only port numbers of 1024 or greater can be assigned by user processes.

A TCP protocol entity accepts arbitrarily long messages from user processes, breaks them into datagrams of up to 64k bytes, and sends them to the IP layer. Before the real communication happens, a connection must be set up between the sender and the recipient. After the communication, the connection must be disconnected. The TCP protocol has a well-defined service interface. There are primitives used to actively and passively initiate connections, to send and receive data, to gracefully and abruptly terminate connections, and to ask for the status of a connection.

As the IP layer does not guarantee the proper delivery of a datagram, it is the responsibility of the transport layer to ensure that a datagram arrives at the destination properly using time-out and retransmission techniques. Also as datagrams are transmitted independently, the datagrams of a message may arrive at the destination out of order and it is also the TCP protocol's responsibility to reassemble them into the message in the proper sequence.

Each datagram submitted by the TCP to IP layer contains a TCP header and a data part. The whole TCP datagram is viewed by the IP as data only and an IP header is added to form an IP datagram. The TCP header contains the source port number, the destination port number, the sequence number, and other information.

A UDP protocol entity also accepts arbitrarily long messages from user processes, breaks them into datagrams of up to 64k bytes, and sends them to the IP layer. Unlike the TCP protocol, the UDP protocol has no connection involved to guarantee the delivery or sequencing of datagrams. In effect, UDP is simply a user interface to IP. A header is also added into a datagram by UDP, which contains the source port number and the destination port number.

4.3 The Next Generation Internet Protocol: IPv6

4.3.1 Why IPv6?

The current Internet protocol (IP) version is IPv4, which has been used for many years and also has critical limitations. Challenges faced by the current IPv4 can be summarized as follows:

- *Address spaces*
  - o Growth of the Internet. Maximum: 4 billion.
  - o When will addresses run out? Estimates: 2005.
  - o Single IP address for devices.
- *Mobile Internet*
  - o Internet services from everywhere.
  - o Removing location dependency.
- *Security*
  - o End-to-end encryption.

Data integrity and authentication requirements for the new protocol can be described as follows:

- Support billions of hosts.
- Reduce size of routing tables.
- Simplify protocol, process packets faster.

- Provide better security (authentication & privacy).

- Better QoS (particularly for real-time data).

- Aid multicasting, anycasting.

- Make it possible for a host to roam without changing its address.

The primary motivation for change from IPv4 to IPv6 is the limited address space. The 32-bit IPv4 address can only include just over a million networks on the Internet. At the current growth rate, each of the possible network prefixes will soon be assigned and no further growth will be possible.

The second motivation for change comes from requirements of new applications, especially applications that require real-time delivery of audio and video data. The current IP has limited capabilities for routing real-time data.

4.3.2 IPv6 Features

IPv6 retains many design features of IPv4, e.g., it still is connectionless. However, IPv6 also has many new features. It has practically unlimited address space, optional header fields (better support for options). It also simplifies packet header, provides authentication and privacy capability to make a network more secure, and pays more attention to type of service, e.g., Plug & Play, - better configuration options, etc. The new features of IPv6 can be summarized as follows:

- *Address size:* Instead of 32, each IPv6 address is 128 bits. The address space is large enough for many years of growth of Internet.

- *Header format:* The IPv6 header has a complete format compared to IPv4 headers.

- *Extension header:* Unlike IPv4, which uses a single header format for all datagrams, IPv6 encodes information into separate headers. A datagram of IPv6 contains a base header followed by 0 or more extension headers, and data.

- *Support for audio and video:* IPv6 includes a mechanism that allows a sender and receiver to establish a high-quality path through the underlying network and to associate datagrams with that path.

- *Extensible protocol:* Unlike IPv4, IPv6 does not specify all possible protocol features. Instead, the designers have provided a scheme that allows a sender to add additional information to a datagram. The extension makes IPv6 more flexible than IPv4.

- *Network management:* IPv6 has auto configuration ability. It can automate network address renumbering. DHCP support is mandated, i.e., every host can download its network configurations from a server at startup time. Auto-configuration allows hosts to operate in any location without any special support.

- *Auto address changes:* Address changes in IPv6 can also be automated. It has two ways to change an address:

  o Stateless: routers advertise prefixes that identify the subnet(s) associated with a link. Hosts generate an "interface token" that uniquely identifies an interface on a subnet. An address is formed by combining the above two.

  o Stateful: clients obtain address and/or configuration from a DHCP server. The DHCP server maintains the database and has a tight control over address assignments.

- *Mobility:* IPv6 was specifically designed to support mobility, which is based on core features of IPv6. Mobility is not an "Add-on" feature in IPv6. All IPv6 networks, LANs/Subnets, and nodes are mobile ready.

One of the questions in the IPv6 design is, why does IPv6 use separate extension headers? This can be explained from the following aspects:

- *Economy:* Partitioning the datagram functionality into separate headers is economical because it saves space. Having separate headers in IPv6 makes it possible to define a large set of features without requiring each datagram header to have at least one field for each feature.

- *Extensibility:* When adding a new feature, existing IPv6 protocol headers can remain unchanged. A new *next header* type can be defined as well as a new header format.

- *Advantage:* The chief advantage of placing new functionality in a new header lies in the ability to experiment with a new feature before changing all computers on the Internet.

4.4 Summary

Network architecture can have one of two types, one is defined by the OSI reference model and the other defined by the ARPANET model. The OSI reference model has seven protocol layers each of which builds upon the services offered by the subordinate layers to offer an enhanced service to the upper layers. The current Internet architecture was built on the ARPANET model which adopts four protocol layers. The main protocols used in the Internet architecture for network communication are TCP, UDP and IP protocols. IP protocol is a network layer protocol while TCP and UDP are transport layer protocols. The current IPv4 has a critical limitation, i.e., the limited address space so that it can not meet the demands of rapid growth of Internet. The study on the next generation of Internet protocol – IPv6 has been conducted for many years and will provide many new features as well as advantages compared with IPv4.

Exercises

4.1 What is the OSI reference model? What layers does it have? 4.1.1

78

4.2 How do programs residing on different computers communicate with each other in the OSI model? 4.1.1

4.3 What is the difference between the OSI architecture and the Internet architecture? 4.1.2

4.4 What method is used for application programs communication with each other on the Internet? 4.1.2

4.5 Describe how TCP/IP was evolved? 4.2.1

4.6 What is an IP address? Explain its meaning using examples. 4.2.1

4.7 What contents does an IP datagram have? 4.2.2

4.8 How does IP work? 4.2.2

4.9 How does TCP protocol overcome the unreliability of IP protocol? 4.2.2

4.10 What is a domain name system? 4.2.2

4.11 How to specify a communication uniquely? Give an example. 4.2.3

4.12 Why is UDP unreliable? 4.2.3

4.13 What is IPv6? Why do we need IPv6? 4.3

CHAPTER 5 INTERPROCESS COMMUNICATION USING MESSAGE PASSING

Processes in a distributed network system normally do not share common memory. Therefore, message passing is one of the effective communication mechanisms between these processes. In this chapter we discuss the most commonly used message-passing based interprocess communication mechanism, i.e., the socket API.

5.1 Developing Distributed Applications Using Message Passing

5.1.1 Communication Services in Message Passing

When talking about communications between different entities (computer hosts or programs) of a distributed software system, we can also view them as *connection-oriented* communications or *connectionless* communications. Transport protocols (TCP/UDP) are used to deliver information from one port to another using these two kinds of communication between application programs. TCP is a connection-oriented protocol, and UDP is a connectionless transport protocol. These communications can also be *reliable* or *unreliable*. We will discuss these forms of communication in this section.

5.1.1.1 Connection-Oriented and Connectionless Communications

For connection-oriented communications, the following three steps are needed:

* *Connection.* One of the communicating entities issues a connection call and a communication path between the two communicating entities is established before the real data exchange occurs.

* *Data exchange.* After the connection establishment, the two communicating entities can then exchange their data in any direction. The order of data packets is preserved.

* *Disconnection.* After the data exchange, one of the communicating entities may issue a disconnection call and disconnect the communication path.

In connectionless communications, no connection path is required before the real data exchange between two communicating entities. Any entity wanting to send a message can send it immediately to the underlying communication system. The message may carry some information other than the real message, such as the source identifier, the destination identifier, priority, etc. One of the characteristics of connectionless communication is that the message order may be different between the sender and the recipient.

Usually a connection-oriented service is more expensive than a connectionless service, because the former needs to establish, maintain, and disconnect the connection. The connection-oriented service is modeled like a telephone system. To talk to your correspondent, you pick up the phone and dial a number (connection), then talk (data exchange), then hang up (disconnection). The essential aspect of a connection is that it acts like a tube: the sender pushes messages into the tube at one end, and the receiver takes them out from the other end in the same order. The TCP connection-oriented protocol establishes a communication link between a source port/IP address and a destination port/IP address. The ports are bound together via this link until the connection is terminated and the link is broken.

In contrast, the connectionless service is modeled like a postal system. To send a letter (message) to your correspondent, you write the full destination address on the envelope, pack your letter into the envelope and drop it into the mail box. All these letters are routed through the postal system independently. It is possible that the letters arrive at the receiver's side in a different order to that sent. The UDP connectionless protocol differs from the TCP connection-oriented protocol in that it does not establish a link for the duration of the connection. When using UDP, an application program writes the destination port and IP address on a datagram and then sends the datagram to its destination.

5.1.1.2 Reliable Communication

A *reliable* communication service is one that never loses data. In this kind of service, usually an acknowledgement is sent back to the sender from the receiver indicating that a message has been correctly received. The acknowledgement introduces overhead and delay. Sometimes this is worthwhile, and sometimes this is not necessary. For example, during file transfer, the file owner wants every bit of the file to arrive at the destination in the same order as it is sent, and with no errors. In that case, a reliable connection-oriented communication service is appropriate. But if the application is digitised voice traffic, an unreliable connection-oriented service is appropriate: it is preferable for users to hear some noise on the line or lose a few words from time to time than to introduce a delay to await acknowledgement.

Reliable connection-oriented service has two minor variations: message sequences and byte streams. In the former, the message boundaries are preserved. This is appropriate when, for example, transferring a book over a network to a laser printer and these pages are sent as separated messages. In the latter, the connection is simply a stream of bytes, with no message boundaries. This is appropriate when, for example, the application is a remote login from a terminal to a mainframe.

A connectionless service can also be reliable or unreliable. An unreliable (meaning not acknowledged) connectionless service is often called a *datagram service,* by analogy with a telegram service, which also does not provide an acknowledgement back to the sender. An *acknowledged datagram service* provides a reliable and connectionless service. It is like sending a registered letter and requesting a return receipt. When the receipt comes back, the sender is absolutely sure that the letter was delivered to the intended correspondent.

The reliability of the TCP communication between the source and destination programs is ensured through error-detection and error-correction mechanisms that are implemented within TCP. TCP implements a connection as a stream of bytes from source to destination. This feature allows the use of the stream I/O classes provided by *java.io*. UDP is less reliable than TCP because there are no delivery-assurance or error-detection and error-correction mechanisms built into the protocol.

5.1.2 A Generic Framework for Distributed Applications

In a distributed application, there are usually a number of computers and processes managing some shared information, such as databases, files, or objects. User programs access these computers and processes to obtain the information the user needs, or to update the stored information through these computers and processes. Time, in a generic distributed application, is not as critical as in a distributed real-time application. Figure 5.1 is a generic framework of a distributed application.

According to Figure 5.1, a distributed application consists of several client programs and several server programs. Usually a server program is located on a remote computer and a client program is located on the user's (local) computer. A client program interfaces with the user, manages the local application process, and performs the communication between the client program and other related (remote) server programs. A server program usually manages an object (e.g., one part of a distributed database), performs the operations required by other programs, and manages the communications. Of course, the client program may also perform some operations directly on the local objects. This is not shown in the diagram because we want to emphasise the distributed characteristics of the application here. So, we can divide a distributed application into three parts:

- *User interface.* This deals with the interactions between the client program and the user.

- *Distributed frame.* This performs the communications among all the co-operative parts over the network.

- *Application modules.* They manage the objects and perform operations.

5.2 Sockets

TCP/IP networking software typically supports a number of different types of application programming interfaces (APIs) for communicating over an internet. However, many operating systems adopt the *socket API,* which originated as part of the BSD UNIX operating system. The socket interface provides an API for network

82

communication that is very close to the API provided for doing ordinary I/O with local devices. The socket interface has been implemented on a wide variety of UNIX and non-UNIX operating systems, and programs that access sockets can be used for implementing network communication in a heterogeneous environment in which hosts of all types must be able to communicate. The socket API is currently the most commonly used API for network programming in the TCP/IP environment and in other networking environments as well. We will introduce socket programming in this part.

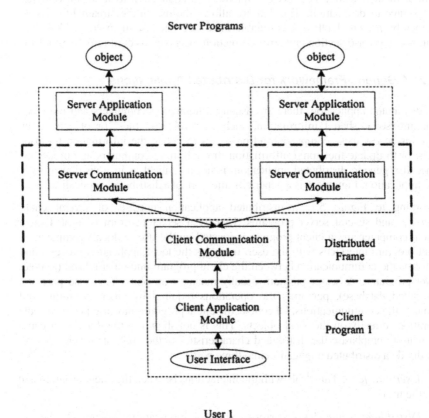

Figure 5.1: The distributed application model

5.2.1 Socket Abstraction

A socket is just another I/O abstraction. Figure 5.2 depicts a client-server system with socket API, where a client process in local UNIX domain requests a connection to a remote server process. The server process first creates a server socket and then listens to client requests. Once the client process creates its client socket which will request a connection to the server socket, the server will accept the request and establish the connection between the server and the client.

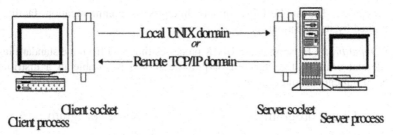

Figure 5.2: BSD interprocess sockets

Creating a socket is very much like opening a file, in that an integer "file handle" is returned to the caller. A program can read and write data to or from a socket by using the integer "file descriptor" in the same way it does I/O to a file, as shown in Figure 5.3. The difference is that the data written by one process is sent directly to a buffer in the process that owns the socket at the other end. Thus, a socket connection between two processes is like a bidirectional pipe.

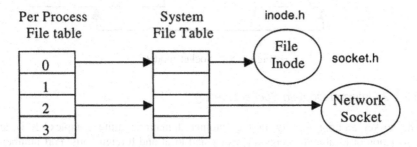

Figure 5.3: File and socket descriptors

5.2.2 BSD Internet Domain Sockets

The *Internet domain sockets* on BSD UNIX use the TCP/IP protocol suite as the communication protocols among processes generally located on different computers across a network.

5.2.2.1 Socket Model

The message-passing communication uses the socket model to implement the communication. The socket model consists of three parts: the socket layer, the protocol layer and the device layer, as depicted in Figure 5.4. This layered model is designed to support the following properties:

- *Transparency:* Communication between processes should not depend on whether or not the processes are on the same machine.

- *Efficiency.* The applicability of any interprocess communication facility is limited by its performance.

- *Compatibility:* Existing naive UNIX processes that read from the standard input file and write to the standard output file should be usable in a distributed environment without change.

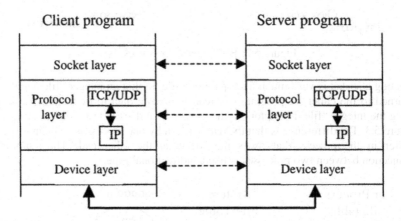

Figure 5.4: Socket model

5.2.2.2 Internet Domain Socket Naming

The socket naming facility in the Internet domain is quite complex. It is an association of local and foreign addresses, and local and foreign ports. Port numbers are allocated out of separate spaces for each Internet protocol. Associations (protocol, local address, local port, foreign address, and foreign port) must always be unique for each socket.

The definition of a socket name in the Internet domain is in *netinet/in.h:*

```
struct in_addr {
        union {
                struct { u_char s_b1,s_b2,s_b3,s_b4; } S_un_b;
                struct { u_short s_w1,s_w2; } S_un_w;
                u_long S_addr;
        } S_un;
#define s_addr S_un.S_addr/*can be used for most tcp & ip code*/
#define s_host S_un.S_un_b.s_b2    /* host on imp */
#define s_net  S_un.S_un_b.s_b1    /* network */
#define s_imp  S_un.S_un_w.s_w2    /* imp */
#define s_impno        S_un.S_un_b.s_b4    /* imp $ */
#define s_lh   S_un.S_un_b.s_b3    /* logical host */
};
/*
 * Socket address, internet style.
 */
struct sockaddr_in {
```

```
short    sin_family;
u_short         sin_port;
struct   in_addr sin_addr;
char     sin_zero[8];
};
```

This is quite complex, especially the *sin_addr* field. Fortunately we have some special system calls to deal with these fields and they can make the naming process much simpler. We will describe these system calls later. Actually, the name of an Internet Domain socket consists of two parts: a host name part and a port number part. As long as we know these two parts, we can use the socket.

Various types of socket addresses (e.g., the UNIX domain socket address, the Internet domain socket address as well as the XNS address) can be combined together into a uniform socket address, as defined in *sys/socket.h:*

```
struct sockaddr {
  u_short  sa_family;   /* address family: AF_XXX value */
  char sa_data[14];     /* up to 14 bytes of protocol-specific
                           address */
}
```

All the system calls that use a socket address as one of their parameters actually ask for a type *sockaddr* instead of individual types (such as *sockaddr_in*). However the best way to pass a parameter to socket-related system calls is to use the cast method in the C language. For example, no matter where *my_sock* is defined as a UNIX domain socket address *sockaddr_un*, or an Internet address *sockaddr_in*, we can use the following format for a connect call:

```
connect(sockDesc, (struct sockaddr *) &my_sock, sizeof(my_sock));
```

The *sockaddr* structure definition is also the reason that in some situations in the UNIX domain only 14 characters of a path name are recognised by the system. Because only 14 characters are defined in the *sockaddr's* protocol-specific address buffer, and the address types are usually cast to *sockaddr* type, only the first 14 characters are recognised.

5.2.2.3 Socket Types

Sockets are typed according to the communication properties visible to a user. Properties such as reliability, ordering, and prevention of duplication of messages are determined by types. Processes are presumed to communicate only between sockets of the same type. The basic set of socket types is defined in *sys/socket.h*, where five types of sockets are defined: *stream socket, datagram socket, raw socket, sequenced packet socket,* and *reliable-delivered message socket:*

```
/*
 * Types
 */
#define SOCK_STREAM    1        /* stream socket */
#define SOCK_DGRAM     2        /* datagram socket */
#define SOCK_RAW       3        /* raw-protocol interface */
#define SOCK_RDM       4        /* reliably-delivered message */
#define SOCK_SEQPACKET 5        /* sequenced packet stream */
```

A stream socket provides for the bi-directional, reliable, sequential, and unduplicated flow of data without record boundaries. It models connection-oriented virtual circuits. Sockets of type SOCK_STREAM are full-duplex byte streams, similar to pipes. A stream socket must be in a connected state before any data can be sent or received on it. A connection to another socket is created with a connect call (described later). Once connected, data can be transferred using *read* and *write* calls or some variant of the *send* and *recv* calls. When a session has been completed, a *close* may be performed.

The communication protocols used to implement a stream socket (SOCK_STREAM) type ensure that data is not lost or duplicated. If a piece of data for which the peer protocol has buffer space cannot be successfully transmitted within a reasonable length of time, then the connection is considered broken and calls will indicate that an error with -1 returns and with ETIMEDOUT as the specific code in the global variable *errno*. The protocols optionally keep sockets "warm" by forcing transmissions roughly every minute in the absence of other activity. An error is then indicated if no response can be elicited on an otherwise idle connection for an extended period (for example, 5 minutes). A SIGPIPE signal is raised if a process sends on a broken stream; this causes processes to interrupt their handling of the signal and then to exit.

A datagram socket (SOCK_DGRAM) supports bi-directional flow of data that is not promised to be sequential, reliable, or unduplicated. A *datagram* is defined as a connectionless, unreliable message of a fixed maximum length (typically small). So a process receiving messages on a datagram socket may find duplicated messages, and possibly in an order different from the order in which they were sent. An important characteristic of a datagram socket is that record boundaries in data are preserved. No connection is required to use a datagram socket and *sendto* and *recvfrom* calls are used to send and receive datagrams. This socket type closely models the facilities found in many contemporary packet switched networks.

A raw socket (SOCK_RAW) is used for unprocessed access to internal network layers. It has no specific semantics. These sockets are normally datagram-oriented. But their exact characteristics depend on the interface provided by the protocol. They have been provided mainly for further development and are now available only to the super-user.

The sequenced packet socket (SOCK_SEQPACKET) is similar to a datagram socket except that data are guaranteed to be received in the sequence that they are sent. These socket type also guarantees error-free data exchange. The reliably-delivered message socket (SOCK_RDM) is planned but not yet implemented.

As we usually only use stream and datagram sockets, we will not describe other socket types in this book.

5.3 Basic Socket System Calls

5.3.1 Some Special Functions

A number of functions have been provided by BSD UNIX for using sockets more easily. We are going to introduce some of them in this section.

When dealing with socket addresses, we usually need to do some operations on bit and byte strings. The following three functions are provided for this purpose:

```
bcopy(b1, b2, length)
char *b1, *b2;
int length;

bcmp(b1, b2, length)
char *b1, *b2;
int length;

bzero(b1, length)
char *b1;
int length;
```

These functions do not check the null byte for the end of a string, as is normally done in string operations. Instead, strings used here are treated as bit and byte strings. The *bcopy* function copies *length* bytes from string b1 to the string b2. The *bzero* function places length 0 bytes in the string b1. The *bcmp* function compares byte string b1 against byte string b2. Both strings are *length* bytes long, if they are identical a zero is returned, otherwise a nonzero value is returned.

Different computer architectures may have different byte orders. Byte orders are important when expressing Internet addresses, so the following functions are provided to convert values between host and network byte orders:

```
#include <sys/types.h>
#include <netinet/in.h>

netlong = htonl(hostlong);
u_long netlong, hostlong;

netshort = htons(hostshort);
u_short netshort, hostshort;

hostlong = ntohl(netlong);
u_long hostlong, netlong;

hostshort = ntohs(netshort);
u_short hostshort, netshort;
```

These functions convert 16-bit (short integer) and 32-bit (long integer) quantities between network byte order and host byte order. *htonl* is used to convert host-to-network, in long integer; *htons* is used to convert host-to-network, in short integer; *ntohl* is used to convert network-to-host, in long integer; *ntohs* is used to convert network-to-host, in short integer;

Sometimes it is very important to know on which host our program is executing. The following system call is used to obtain the local host name:

```
gethostname(name, namelen)
char *name;
int namelen;
```

The *gethostname* returns the standard host name for the current process in name, such as *sky3.cm.deakin.edu.au.* The parameter *namelen* specifies the size of the name array. The returned name is null-terminated unless insufficient space is provided. If the call succeeds, a value of 0 is returned. If the call fails, then a value of -1 is returned and an error code is placed in the global location *errno.*

As we mentioned in Section 5.2.3, a 5-tuple uniquely defines a communication:

```
{protocol, address(local), port(local), address(foreign),
port(foreign)}
```

where addresses are hosts' Internet addresses. A host Internet address data structure *hostent* is defined in the *netdb.h* header file containing host information. It is defined as:

```
struct    hostent {
   char    h_name;        / official name of host */
   char    **h_aliases;   /* alias list */
   int     h_addrtype;    /* address type */
   int     h_length;      /* length of address */
   char    **h_addr_list; /* list of addresses from name server */
#define    h_addr h_addr_list[0] /* address for backward compatibility
*/
};
```

The *h_name* field is the host's name string, the same as we obtained from *gethostname* call. The *h_aliases* field is a zero terminated array of alternate names for the host. The *h_addrtype* field currently is always AF_INET. The *h_length* field gives the length of the address (in bytes). The *h_addr_*list field is a pointer to the network address for the host. And the *h_addr* field is the host's first network address.

The following functions are used to get host information:

```
#include <netdb.h>
struct hostent *gethostbyname(name)
char *name;

struct hostent *gethostbyaddr(addr, len, type)
char *addr; int len, type;
```

The *gethostbyname* call returns the *hostent* data structure of the matching name. The name string can be obtained from call *gethostname.* The *gethostbyaddr* call returns the *hostent* data structure of the matching *addr, len* and *type.*

As we can see from the above description, the Internet address data structure is very complex. Fortunately, BSD UNIX has provided a group of functions for manipulating Internet addresses. They are described in *inet(3n)* of the BSD UNIX manual. We only describe the following call for our purpose:

```
#include <sys/socket.h>
#include <netinet/in.h>
#include <arpa/inet.h>

char *inet_ntoa(in)
struct in_addr in;
```

This call converts an Internet address to an ASCII string representing the address in "." notation (e.g., 139.130.118.102).

The following is a short program that prints out the host's information. It is named *phn.c* (print host name). By default it prints out the local host's information. If you specify a host name, it prints out the information for that host. The program is as follows:

```
/*
 * phn.c—print the host name and other information.
 * compile: cc -o phn phn.c
 * execution: phn
 *                phn hostname
 */

#include <stdio.h>
#include <sys/types.h>
#include <sys/socket.h>
#include <netinet/in.h>
#include <netdb.h>
#include <arpa/inet.h>   /* for inet_ntoa() */

#define MAXHOSTNAMELEN 32
main(argc, argv)
int argc;
char *argv[];
{
char hostName[MAXHOSTNAMELEN];
char *ptr;
struct hostent *hp;

    if (argc < 2) {
       if (gethostname(hostName, MAXHOSTNAMELEN) == -1)   /* get my host
name */
          exit(1);
    } else
       strcpy(hostName, argv[1]);
    /* get host's info */
    if ((hp = gethostbyname(hostName)) == NULL) {
       fprintf(stderr, "phn: %s: unknow host\n", hostName);
       exit(1);
    }

    printf("Host name: %s.\n", hp->h_name);
    while ((ptr = *(hp->h_aliases)) != NULL) {
       printf("   Alias: %s\n", ptr);
       hp->h_aliases++;
    }
    printf("Host address type: %d, address length=%d.\n", hp-
>h_addrtype,
          hp->h_length);
    if (hp->h_addrtype == AF_INET)
       pr_inet(hp->h_addr_list, hp->h_length);
    else
       printf(stderr, "phn: Unknown address type");
}

pr_inet(listptr, length)
char **listptr;
int length;
{
    struct in_addr *ptr;
    while ((ptr = (struct in_addr *) *listptr++) != NULL)
       printf("Internet address: %s\n", inet_ntoa(*ptr));
}
```

If you simply execute the program by typing in *phn,* then the information for the local host is printed out. One possible output could be:

```
Host name: sky3.cm.deakin.edu.au.
   Alias: sky3
Host address type: 2, address length=4.
Internet address: 139.130.118.5
```

If you execute the program by specifying a host name, such as *phn turin,* then the information of host *turin* will be printed out as:

```
Host name: turin.cm.deakin.edu.au.
Host address type: 2, address length=4.
Internet address: 128.184.82.150
```

5.3.2 Socket Creation

Several system calls are provided to create, use and manage sockets. Before using a connection-oriented socket, one must first create it, bind it to a name and connect it to another socket. For a server, after creation and binding, the socket may listen for a connection and accept it. All these are performed by a group of system calls. In most cases, three files will be included before using these calls, they are *sys/types.h, sys/socket.h* and *netinet/in.h.*

To create a socket, use the socket system call:

```
descriptor = socket(domain, type, protocol);
int descriptor;
int domain;
int type;
int protocol;
```

The *domain* is, of course, AF_INET. The *type* can be currently SOCK_STREAM, SOCK_DGRAM, or SOCK_RAW, whereas the *protocol* specifies a particular protocol to be used by the socket. If a 0 (zero) is specified in the protocol parameter, the system will select the proper protocol for you.

Normally only a single protocol exists to support a particular socket type using a given address format (domain). The most used protocols in the Internet domain are TCP (Transmission Control Protocol) and UDP (User Datagram Protocol), and they are used for sockets of type SOCK_STREAM and SOCK_DGRAM, respectively.

The returned value is actually a small integer which represents a socket, and the user may use it in the later system calls which operate on sockets.

5.3.3 Name Binding

After creation, generally a name will be bound to the socket so that the user can then use that socket. The bind call is used to assign a name to an unnamed socket:

```
bind(descriptor, name, namelen);
int descriptor;
struct sockaddr name;          / for Internet domain */
int namelen;
```

Internet domain socket naming is more complex than that of UNIX domain, but if you know the host name and the communication port (both are local), then the following fragment would be used (suppose the host name is *sky3,* the port is 5100 and we also want to bind the name to *descriptor*):

```
#include <netinet/in.h>
#include <netdb.h>
#define machine "sky3"
struct sockaddr_in my_sock;
struct hostent *hp;
hp = gethostbyname(machine);              /* get host's info */
bzero((char )&my_sock, sizeof(my_sock));/ clear my_sock to 0 */
my_sock.sin_family = hp->h_addrtype;   /* AF_INET domain */
my_sock.sin_port = htons(5100);                     /* set port */
bcopy(hp->h_addr, (char *)&my_sock. sin_addr, hp->h_length);
                /*get address */
if (bind(descriptor, (struct sockaddr *)&my_sock, sizeof(my_sock)) ==
-1)
                { /* error */}
```

5.3.4 *Connection Establishment*

In the Internet domain the following three system calls are used for socket connection: *listen, accept,* and *connect.*

Suppose we have socket *descriptorSer* in a server program and socket *descriptorCli* in a client program. If the server now is willing to offer its service, it uses a *listen* system call and then uses an *accept* system call that passively waits for the client to make connection. On the other hand, the *connect* system call is used by the client to initialise a connection. Please note, however, it is not necessary for UPD (connectionless) sockets to perform these steps.

The *listen* system call is quite simple:

```
listen(descriptorSer, 5);
```

where the last parameter is the maximum number of outstanding connections which may be queued waiting to be accepted by the server to accept, and 5 is the system limitation of maximum connection on any one queue.

After listening, the server uses the *accept* call to accept a connection:

```
int cliLen; struct sockaddr_in sockCli;   /* client socket address
*/
  cliLen = sizeof(sockCli);
  descriptorCom = accept(descriptorSer, (struct sockarrd *)&sockCli,
    &cliLen);
```

The returned value *descriptorCom* is a new socket and it is used in the input/output calls when needed. If the server wishes to find whom the client is, then several system calls can be applied to that socket, and they will return the client name *sockCli.*

The *connect* system call for a socket in the Internet domain looks like:

```
struct sockaddr_in sockSer;
```

```
connect(descriptorCli, (struct sockaddr *)&sockSer,
sizeof(sockSer));
```

In some situations the *connect* call may fail. These situations are very important when considering fault tolerance of the application system.

5.3.5 Transfer Data and Discard Sockets

Several system calls can be used to transfer data between connected sockets. The simplest group of such calls are *write* and *read* calls. They are identical to *write* and *read* for disk files:

```
char buf[BUFSIZE];
int msglen;
write(descriptor, buf, msglen);     /* send to correspondent */
read(descriptor, buf, sizeof(buf)); /* read from correspondent */
```

where *descriptor* is the socket created by the client in a client program and is the value returned from the server's *accept* call in a server program.

In a *write* call, the array *buf* contains the message to be sent and *msglen* gives the number of bytes to be sent. If a character string is to be sent, *strlen(buf)* can be used for the message length. By default, *write* does asynchronous writes. That is, after the data is written to a buffer cache, control returns to the program. The actual write to a device takes place after control returns. Upon successful completion, the number of bytes actually written is returned. Otherwise, a -1 is returned, and *errno* is set to indicate the error. The *errno* is the UNIX error number variable and is defined in *errno.h*. To use *errno,* the *errno.h* file must be included.

Upon successful completion, *read* returns the number of bytes actually read and placed in the array *buf.* The system returns the number of bytes requested *(sizeof(buf))* if the descriptor references a stream which has that many bytes left before the *end-of-file.* If the returned value is 0, then *end-of-file* has been reached. Otherwise, a -1 is returned and the global variable *errno* is set to indicate the error.

Alternatively, programs might use the *send* and *recv* system calls as follows:

```
int flags;
send(descriptor, buf, sizeof(buf), flags); /* send to correspondent
*/
recv(descriptor, buf, sizeof(buf), flags); /* receive from
        correspondent */
```

where *descriptor* in both server and client programs are the same as above. The *flags* can be 0 or can be specified explicitly. The most interesting flags are:

```
#define MSG_PEEK  0x1     /* look at data without reading */
#define MSG_OOB   0x2     /* process out-of-bound data */
```

A program can use the MSG_PEEK flag to look at the available data, without having the system discard the data after the *recv* call. The MSG_OOB flag specifies that the data to be sent or received is of type *out-of-bound* or *expedited*. With this type of data, we want the sending and receiving services to process these data before any other data that have been buffered. Out-of-bound type is only defined for stream sockets, and the UNIX domain stream sockets do not support it.

It is also possible to use the standard *stdio* to read the socket. In that case, an *fdopen* call can be used to open the socket for reading and the *fgetc* call can be used to read characters from the opened socked in the same manner as in file reading.

The above calls are generally used in connection-oriented communications. There are other data transmission calls that can be used at both connection-oriented and connectionless communication services. We mention the *sendto/recvfrom* pair here:

```
cc = sendto(descriptor, msg, len, flags, to, tolen)
int cc, descriptor;
char *msg;
int len, flags;
struct sockaddr_un *to;
int tolen;

cc = recvfrom(s, buf, len, flags, from, fromlen)
int cc, s;
char *buf;
int len, flags;
struct sockaddr *from;
int *fromlen;
```

In a *sendto* call, the address of the target is given by *to*, with *tolen* specifying the address size. The length of the message is given by *len*. If the message is too long to pass atomically through the underlying protocol, the error EMSGSIZE is returned, and the message is not transmitted.

The *sendto* call returns the number of characters sent, or -1 if an error occurred. Return values of - 1 only indicate some locally detected errors. If message space is unavailable at the socket to hold the message to be transmitted, *sendto* blocks, unless the socket has been placed in *nonblocking* I/O mode.

In a *recvfrom* call, if *from* is nonzero, the source address of the message is filled in on return. The *fromlen* is a value-result parameter, initialised to the size of the buffer associated with *from*, and modified on return to indicate the actual size of the address stored there. The length of the message is returned in *cc*. If the message is too long to fit in the supplied buffer, excess bytes can be discarded, depending on the type of socket sending the message. That is, if the sending socket is a sequenced packet stream socket, the excess bytes will be discarded.

If no messages are available at the socket, the *recvfrom* call waits for a message to arrive, unless the socket is *nonblocking*. If the socket is *nonblocking* then a *cc* of -1 is returned, and the global variable *errno* is set to EWOULDBLOCK.

Once a socket *descriptor* is no longer of use, it may be discarded by applying a *close* system call to the socket:

```
close(descriptor);
```
Upon successful completion, a value of 0 is returned. Otherwise, a value of -1 is returned, and the global variable, *errno*, is set.

If there are some data associated with a SOCK_STREAM type socket when the *close* call takes place, the system will continue to attempt to transfer the data.

94

However, if after about four minutes the data is still not delivered, it will be discarded. The *shutdown* system call can be used prior to a *close* call to discard the pending data if the user is not interested in it:

```
shutdown(descriptor, how);
int how;
```

Where *how* is 0 if the user is no longer interested in reading data, 1 if no more data will be sent, or 2 if no data is to be sent or received. Applying *shutdown* to a socket causes any data queued to be immediately discarded. A zero (0) is returned if the *shutdown* call succeeds, - 1 if it fails.

5.4 Examples in C

5.4.1 Using Stream Sockets: A Simple Example

In this example, two programs use connection-oriented Internet *stream* sockets to communicate with each other. The server program is supposed to be executed first. It creates an Internet stream socket and binds the socket to a name, then it listens to the socket and waits for a connection. If a connection request arrives, the server reads in a message from the client, displays it and writes back an acknowledgement to the client program. After that, the server program closes the socket and exits.

The server program is named ismpser.c indicating that it uses Internet domain sockets, and is a simple example of a server program. By default, it uses stream sockets. The listing is the following:

```
/* Simple example for Internet domain communications (stream socket)
   Server program (sequential)
   Compile: cc -o ismpser ismpser.c
   Execute: ismpser
   Note:    ismpser must be executed before ismpcli
*/

#include <stdio.h>
#include <sys/types.h>
#include <sys/socket.h>
#include <netinet/in.h>
#include <netdb.h>

#define MAXHOSTNAMELEN 32
#define SERVER_STREAM_PORT 5100
#define oops(msg) { perror(msg);   exit(-1); }

main()
{
int sockSer, sockPeer, cliLen;
int i;
struct sockaddr_in ser, cli;
char buf[BUFSIZ];
char myhostname[MAXHOSTNAMELEN];
struct hostent *hp;

    /* get server host's info */
    if (gethostname(myhostname, MAXHOSTNAMELEN) == -1)   /* get my host
name */
        oops("gethostname");
    if ((hp = gethostbyname(myhostname)) == NULL)
```

```
        oops("gethostbyname");    /* get host's network address */

    /* create an Internet domain, stream socket */
    if ((sockSer = socket(AF_INET, SOCK_STREAM, 0)) == -1)
        oops("socket");
    /* bind the server socket to an name */
    bzero((char ) &ser, sizeof(ser));    / empty name buffer */
    ser.sin_family = AF_INET;             /* Internet domain */
    ser.sin_port = htons(SERVER_STREAM_PORT);          /* port */
    bcopy(hp->h_addr, (char )&ser.sin_addr, hp->h_length); / host */
    if (bind(sockSer, &ser, sizeof(ser)) == -1)
        oops("bind");

    /* listen for connections */
    listen(sockSer, 5);
    /* accept connection from client */
    cliLen = sizeof(cli);
    if ((sockPeer = accept(sockSer, &cli, &cliLen)) == -1)
        oops("accept");
    /* accept data from the client */
    for (i=0; i<BUFSIZ; i++)  /* clean buf */
        buf[i] = '\0';
    if ((i = read(sockPeer, buf, sizeof(buf))) == -1)
        oops("read");
    printf("Server: Data received: %s. Length=%d.\n", buf, i);
    /* send data to the connected client */
    strcpy(buf, "This is the reply message from server program");
    if (write(sockPeer, buf, strlen(buf)) == -1)
        oops("write");
    printf("Server: Data sent: %s\n", buf);

    /* close the two sockets completely */
    if (close(sockSer) == -1 || close(sockPeer) == -1)
        oops("close");
    printf("Server: successful.\n");
}
```

The client program is supposed to be executed after the server program's execution. After the creation of an Internet stream socket, the client program initialises a connection to the server. If the connection succeeds, the client writes a message to the server and reads a reply from the server. The reply is then displayed and the client program exits.

The client program is named ismpcli.c indicating that it uses Internet domain sockets and is a simple example of a client program. By default, it uses stream sockets. The listing is the following:

```
/* Simple example for Internet domain communications (stream socket)
   Client program
   Compile: cc -o ismpcli ismpcli.c
   Execute: ismpcli
   Note:    ismpser must be executed before ismpcli
*/

#include <stdio.h>
#include <sys/types.h>
#include <sys/socket.h>
#include <netinet/in.h>
#include <netdb.h>

#define SERVER_STREAM_PORT 5100
#define SERVERHOSTNAME "berry.fcit.monash.edu.au"
#define oops(msg) ( perror(msg);  exit(-1); )

main()
```

```
{
int sockCli;
int i;
struct sockaddr_in ser;
char buf[BUFSIZ];
struct hostent *hp;

    /* get server host's network address */
    if ((hp=gethostbyname(SERVERHOSTNAME))==NULL)
      oops("gethostbyname");
    /* create an Internet domain, stream socket */
    if ((sockCli = socket(AF_INET, SOCK_STREAM, 0)) == -1)
      oops("socket");
    /* fill in the server address buffer */
    bzero((char ) &ser, sizeof(ser));     / empty name buffer */
    ser.sin_family = AF_INET;             /* Internet domain */
    ser.sin_port = htons(SERVER_STREAM_PORT);       /* port */
    bcopy(hp->h_addr, (char )&ser.sin_addr, hp->h_length); / host */

    /* connect to server, its name is in ser */
    if (connect(sockCli, &ser, sizeof(ser)) == -1)
      oops("connect");
    /* send a string to server */
    strcpy(buf, "This is a request message from client");
    if (write(sockCli, buf, strlen(buf)) == -1)
      oops("write");
    printf("Client: Data sent: %s\n", buf);
    /* read in data from the server */
    if ((i = read(sockCli, buf, sizeof(buf))) == -1)
      oops("read");
    printf("Client: Data received: %s. Length=%d.\n", buf, i);
    /* close the socket */
    if (close(sockCli) == -1)
      oops("close");
    printf("Client: successful.\n");
}
```

The communication can only be executed once by using the above two programs. In order to execute the communication many times, either a looping server or a concurrent server program would be used. We present a concurrent version of the server program here.

The concurrent version of the server program is named ismpsercon.c indicating that it uses Internet domain sockets and is a simple example of concurrent version of server program.

```
/* Simple example for Internet domain communications (stream socket)
   Server program (concurrent)
   Compile: cc -o ismpser ismpser.c
   Execute: ismpser
   Note:    ismpser must be executed before ismpcli
*/

#include <stdio.h>
#include <signal.h>
#include <sys/types.h>
#include <sys/socket.h>
#include <netinet/in.h>
#include <netdb.h>

#define MAXHOSTNAMELEN 32
#define SERVER_STREAM_PORT 5100
#define oops(msg) { perror(msg);   exit(-1); }

main()
```

```
{
int sockSer, sockPeer, cliLen;
struct sockaddr_in ser, cli;
char buf[BUFSIZ];
int mainPid, kidPid;
char myhostname[MAXHOSTNAMELEN];
struct hostent *hp;

  /* get server host's info */
  if (gethostname(myhostname, MAXHOSTNAMELEN) == -1)
    oops("gethostname");                    /* get my host name */
  if ((hp=gethostbyname(myhostname))==NULL)
    oops("gethostbyname");              /* get host's network address */
  /* create an Internet domain, stream socket */
  if ((sockSer = socket(AF_INET, SOCK_STREAM, 0)) == -1)
    oops("socket");
  /* bind the server socket to an name */
  bzero((char ) &ser, sizeof(ser));    / empty name buffer */
  ser.sin_family = AF_INET;                  /* Internet domain */
  ser.sin_port = htons(SERVER_STREAM_PORT);            /* port */
  bcopy(hp->h_addr, (char )&ser.sin_addr, hp->h_length); / host */
  if (bind(sockSer, &ser, sizeof(ser)) == -1)
    oops("bind");

  /* listen for connections */
  listen(sockSer, 5);
  while (1) {
    /* accept connection from client */
    cliLen = sizeof(cli);
    if ((sockPeer = accept(sockSer, &cli, &cliLen)) == -1)
      oops("accept");
    mainPid = getpid();   /* parent pid */
    /* communication processing */
    kidPid = commProc(sockPeer, mainPid, sockSer);

    /* parent process, ready to accept new connections */
    close(sockPeer);
  }
}

/*
 * Communication processing. Accept from client then reply.
 * If shutdown received, kill both child and parent processes.
 */
int commProc(sockDesc, mpid, sockSer)
int sockDesc;   /* peer socket descriptor */
int mpid;       /* parent's process pid */
int sockSer;    /* server socket descriptor */
{
  char buf[BUFSIZ];
  int i, kidPid;

  /* fork to two processes */
  if ((kidPid = fork()) != 0)
    return (kidPid);   /* return to parent */
  /* child process. Accept data from the client */
  for (i=0; i<BUFSIZ; i++)   /* clean buf */
    buf[i] = '\0';
  if ((i = read(sockDesc, buf, sizeof(buf))) == -1)
    oops("read");
  printf("Server: Data received: %s. Length=%d.\n", buf, i);
  if (strcmp(buf, "shutdown") == 0)
  { /* shutdown request */
    /* kill parent process */
    if (kill(mpid, SIGINT) == -1)
      perror("kill");

    /* close the two sockets completely */
```

```
    if (close(sockSer) == -1 || close(sockDesc) == -1)
      oops("close");
    /* kill child process */
    if (kill(kidPid, SIGINT) == -1)
      perror("kill");
    exit(0);
  }

  /* come here when it is a normal request message */
  /* send data to the connected client */
  strcpy(buf, "This is the reply message from server program");
  if (write(sockDesc, buf, strlen(buf)) == -1)
    oops("write");
  printf("Server: Data sent: %s\n", buf);
  exit(0);
}
```

The "shutdown" message can be sent by modifying the client program.

5.4.2 Using Datagram Sockets: A Simple Example

Next is an example of using Internet *datagram* sockets for simple communications. The example performs the same functions as the previous one. The main differences between using a datagram socket and using a stream socket are the socket creation and the data transfer calls. In this example program, we create datagram sockets and use *sendto/recvfrom* calls to transfer data between server and client programs.

The server program is named ismdser.c indicating that it uses Internet sockets and is a simple example of a server program using datagram sockets. The listing is the following:

```
/* Simple example for Internet domain communications (datagram socket)
   Server program (sequential)
   Compile: cc -o ismdser ismdser.c
   Execute: ismdser
   Note:    ismdser must be executed before ismdcli
*/

#include <stdio.h>
#include <sys/types.h>
#include <sys/socket.h>
#include <netinet/in.h>
#include <netdb.h>

#define MAXHOSTNAMELEN 32
#define SERVER_DGRAM_PORT 5200
#define oops(msg) { perror(msg);  exit(-1); }

main()
{
int sockSer, cliLen;
int i;
struct sockaddr_in ser, cli;
char buf[BUFSIZ];
char myhostname[MAXHOSTNAMELEN], forhostname[MAXHOSTNAMELEN];
struct hostent *hp;

  /* get server host's info */
  if (gethostname(myhostname, MAXHOSTNAMELEN) == -1)
    oops("gethostname");      /* get my host name */
  if ((hp = gethostbyname(myhostname)) == NULL)
    oops("gethostbyname");    /* get host's network address */
```

```
   /* create an Internet domain, datagram socket */
   if ((sockSer = socket(AF_INET, SOCK_DGRAM, 0)) == -1)
     oops("socket");
   /* bind the server socket to an name */
   bzero((char ) &ser, sizeof(ser));     / empty name buffer */
   ser.sin_family = AF_INET;                      /* Internet domain */
   ser.sin_port = htons(SERVER_DGRAM_PORT);              /* port */
   bcopy(hp->h_addr, (char )&ser.sin_addr, hp->h_length); / host */
   if (bind(sockSer, &ser, sizeof(ser)) == -1)
     oops("bind");

   /* accept data from the client */
   for (i=0; i<BUFSIZ; i++)  /* clean buf */
     buf[i] = '\0';
   bzero((char ) &cli, sizeof(cli));    / empty name buffer */
   cliLen = sizeof(cli);
   if ((i = recvfrom(sockSer, buf, sizeof(buf), 0, &cli, &cliLen)) == -
1)
     oops("recvfrom");
   /* get the client's host name and port */
   if ((hp = gethostbyaddr((char *)&cli.sin_addr, sizeof(struct
in_addr),
                    AF_INET)) == NULL)
     oops("gethostbyaddr");
   printf("Server: Request from: host: %s, port: %d.\n",
                    hp->h_name, ntohs(cli.sin_port));
   printf("Server: Received data: %s. Length=%d.\n", buf, i);

   /* send data to the corresponding client */
   strcpy(buf, "This is the reply message from server program");
   if (sendto(sockSer, buf, strlen(buf), 0, &cli, sizeof(cli)) == -1)
     oops("sendto");
   printf("Server: Data sent: %s\n", buf);
   /* close the socket completely */
   if (close(sockSer) == -1)
     oops("close");
   printf("Server: successful.\n");
}
```

The client program is named ismdcli.c indicating that it uses Internet domain sockets and is a simple example of a client program using datagram sockets. Its listing is as follow.

```
/* Simple example for Internet domain communications (datagram socket)
   Client program
   Compile: cc -o ismdcli ismdcli.c
   Execute: ismdcli
   Note:    ismdser must be executed before ismdcli
*/

#include <stdio.h>
#include <sys/types.h>
#include <sys/socket.h>
#include <netinet/in.h>
#include <netdb.h>

#define MAXHOSTNAMELEN 32
#define SERVER_DGRAM_PORT 5200
#define CLIENT_DGRAM_PORT 5201
#define SERVERHOSTNAME "berry.fcit.monash.edu.au"
#define oops(msg) { perror(msg);   exit(-1); }

main()
{
int sockCli;
int i;
struct sockaddr_in ser, cli;
```

```
char buf[BUFSIZ];
char myhostname[MAXHOSTNAMELEN];
struct hostent *hp;

    /* get client host's info */
    if (gethostname(myhostname, MAXHOSTNAMELEN) == -1)
        oops("gethostname");        /* get my host name */
    if ((hp = gethostbyname(myhostname)) == NULL)
        oops("gethostbyname");    /* get host's network address */
    /* create an Internet domain, datagram socket */
    if ((sockCli = socket(AF_INET, SOCK_DGRAM, 0)) == -1)
        oops("socket");
    /* bind the client socket to an name */
    bzero((char ) &cli, sizeof(cli));    / empty name buffer */
    cli.sin_family = AF_INET;                    /* Internet domain */
    cli.sin_port = htons(CLIENT_DGRAM_PORT);             /* port */
    bcopy(hp->h_addr, (char )&cli.sin_addr, hp->h_length); / host */
    if (bind(sockCli, &cli, sizeof(cli)) == -1)
        oops("bind");

    /* get server host's network address */
    if ((hp=gethostbyname(SERVERHOSTNAME))==NULL)
        oops("gethostbyname");
    /* fill in the server address buffer */
    bzero((char ) &ser, sizeof(ser));    / empty name buffer */
    ser.sin_family = AF_INET;                    /* Internet domain */
    ser.sin_port = htons(SERVER_DGRAM_PORT);             /* port */
    bcopy(hp->h_addr, (char )&ser.sin_addr, hp->h_length); / host */
    /* send a string to server */
    strcpy(buf, "This is a request message from client");
    if (sendto(sockCli, buf, strlen(buf), 0, &ser, sizeof(ser)) == -1)
        oops("sendto");
    printf("Client: Data sent: %s\n", buf);

    /* read in data from the server */
    if ((i = recvfrom(sockCli, buf, sizeof(buf), 0, (char *)0, (int
*)0)) == -1)
        oops("recvfrom");
    buf[i] = '\0';
    printf("Client: Received: %s. Length=%d.\n", buf, i);
    /* close the socket */
    if (close(sockCli) == -1)
        oops("close");
    printf("Client: successful.\n");
}
```

Similarly we have a concurrent version of the Internet datagram socket example. The concurrent server program is named ismdsercon.c as listed in the following:

```
/* Simple example for Internet domain communications (datagram socket)
    Server program (concurrent)
    Compile: cc -o ismdsercon ismdsercon.c
    Execute: ismdsercon
    Note:    ismdsercon must be executed before ismdcli
*/

#include <stdio.h>
#include <signal.h>
#include <sys/types.h>
#include <sys/socket.h>
#include <netinet/in.h>
#include <netdb.h>

#define MAXHOSTNAMELEN 32
#define SERVER_DGRAM_PORT 5200
#define oops(msg) { perror(msg);   exit(-1); }
```

```
main()
{
int sockSer, cliLen, i;
struct sockaddr_in ser, cli;
char buf[BUFSIZ];
int mainPid, kidPid;
char myhostname[MAXHOSTNAMELEN], forhostname[MAXHOSTNAMELEN];
struct hostent *hp;

  /* get server host's info */
  if (gethostname(myhostname, MAXHOSTNAMELEN) == -1)
    oops("gethostname");      /* get my host name */
  if ((hp=gethostbyname(myhostname))==NULL)
    oops("gethostbyname");    /* get host's network address */
  /* create an Internet domain, datagram socket */
  if ((sockSer = socket(AF_INET, SOCK_DGRAM, 0)) == -1)
    oops("socket");
  /* bind the server socket to an name */
  bzero((char ) &ser, sizeof(ser));     / empty name buffer */
  ser.sin_family = AF_INET;            /* Internet domain */
  ser.sin_port = htons(SERVER_DGRAM_PORT);           /* port */
  bcopy(hp->h_addr, (char )&ser.sin_addr, hp->h_length); / host */
  if (bind(sockSer, &ser, sizeof(ser)) == -1)
    oops("bind");

  while (1) {
    /* accept connection from client */
    cliLen = sizeof(cli);
    if ((i = recvfrom(sockSer, buf, sizeof(buf), 0, &cli, &cliLen)) ==
-1)
      oops("recvfrom");
    buf[i] = '\0';

    mainPid = getpid();  /* parent pid */
    /* communication processing */
    kidPid = commProc(sockSer, mainPid, buf, cli);

    /* parent process, ready to accept new connections */
  }
}

/*
 * Communication processing. Accept from client then reply.
 * If shutdown received, kill both child and parent processes.
 */
int commProc(sockDesc, mpid, bf, cli)
int sockDesc;   /* socket descriptor */
int mpid;       /* parent's process pid */
char *bf;

struct sockaddr_in cli;
{
  char buf[BUFSIZ];
  int kidPid;
  struct hostent *hp;

  /* fork to two processes */
  if ((kidPid = fork()) != 0)
    return (kidPid);  /* return to parent */
  /* child process */
  /* get the client's host name and port */
  if ((hp = gethostbyaddr((char *)&cli.sin_addr, sizeof(struct
in_addr),
                  AF_INET)) == NULL)
    oops("gethostbyaddr");
  printf("Server: Request from: host: %s, port: %d.\n",
                  hp->h_name, ntohs(cli.sin_port));
```

```
printf("Server: Received data: %s\n", bf);
if (strcmp(bf, "shutdown") == 0)
{ /* shutdown request */
  /* kill parent process */
  if (kill(mpid, SIGINT) == -1)
    perror("kill");
  /* close the two sockets completely */
  if (close(sockDesc) == -1)
    oops("close");

  /* kill child process */
  if (kill(kidPid, SIGINT) == -1)
    perror("kill");
  exit(0);
}

/* come here when it is a normal request message */
/* send data to the connected client */
strcpy(buf, "This is the reply message from server program");
if (sendto(sockDesc, buf, strlen(buf), 0, &cli, sizeof(cli)) == -1)
  oops("sendto");
printf("Server: Data sent: %s\n", buf);
exit(0);
}
```

5.5 Summary

Message passing is one of the most effective communication mechanisms between processes in a distributed network system. In this chapter we discussed the most commonly used message-passing based interprocess communication API for network programming - the socket API. TCP/IP networking software typically supports a number of different types of application programming interfaces (APIs) for communicating over a network. However, many operating systems adopt the socket API, which was originated as part of the BSD UNIX operating system. The socket interface provides an API for network communication that is very close to the API provided for doing ordinary I/O with local devices. In the chapter we mainly discussed the BSD Internet domain sockets. A number of issues, such as naming, types, and system calls about the BSD sockets were addressed. Two examples in C were also presented to demonstrate how to write socket programming.

Exercises

5.1   What are connection-oriented communication and connectionless communication? Give examples. 5.1.1

5.2   How can one achieve a reliable communication? 5.1.1

5.3   Describe the purposes of client and server programs in the distributed application system. 5.1.2

5.4   What is a socket? Why is it important? 5.2.1

5.5   Why do we divide a socket model into three parts? 5.2.2

5.6   What does a socket name consist of? 5.2.2

5.7 What is the best way to pass a parameter to socket-related system calls? Give an example. 5.2.2

5.8 What is a stream socket? How does one send and receive data using it? 5.2.2

5.9 What is a datagram socket? How does one send and receive data using it? 5.2.2

5.10 How do you convert values between host and network byte order? 5.3.1

5.11 How do you get host information? Run the program *phn.c* on your machine to get your host information. 5.3.1

5.12 Suppose there are two sockets located in a server and a client program respectively. Write a simple program using *listen, accept* and *connect* calls to connect them. 5.3.4

5.13 What system calls mentioned in the book can be used at both connection-oriented and connectionless communication services? Explain them briefly. 5.3.5

5.14 Understand programs ismpser.c and ismpcli.c for both stream socket and datagram socket. Compile and run them on your machine. Describe what is the difference between stream socket programming and datagram socket programming. 5.4

This page intentionally left blank

CHAPTER 6 TCP/UDP COMMUNICATION IN JAVA

Chapter 5 discussed the BSD Internet socket, which is currently the most commonly used API for network programming. The BSD Internet domain sockets use the TCP/IP (or UDP/IP) protocol suite as the communication protocols among processes. In this chapter we want to address the TCP/UDP programming in Java, since the Java language is currently the most commonly used language to implement a distributed computing system. Java provides the reliable stream-based communication for TCP as well as the unreliable datagram communication for UDP.

6.1 Java Sockets

The socket API in Java is provided in the *java.net* package which has several classes supporting socket-based client/server communication.

6.1.1 Java Net Package

Client and server sockets for connection-oriented and connectionless communication are implemented by the *Socket, ServerSocket, DatagramSocket,* and *MulticastSocket* classes in the *java.net* package. In addition to these socket related classes, the *java.net* package also contains other classes that can help the communication. In particular, the *InetAddress* class encapsulates Internet IP addresses and supports conversion between dotted decimal addresses and host names. The *DatagramPacket* class is used to construct UDP datagram packets. The *SocketImpl* and *DatagramSocketImpl* classes and the *SocketImplFactory* interface provide hooks for implementing custom sockets.

High-level browser-server Web connections are implemented through the *URL, URLConnection, HttpURLConnection,* and *URLEncoder* classes. The *ContentHandler* and *URLStreamHandler* classes are abstract classes that can be used for the implementation of Web content and stream handlers. They are supported by the *ContentHandlerFactory* and *URLStreamHandlerFactory* interfaces. The *FileNameMap* interface is used to map filenames to MIME types.

The classes in the *java.net* package can be listed as follows:

The Classes

- ContentHandler
- DatagramPacket

- DatagramSocket
- DatagramSocketImpl
- HttpURLConnection
- InetAddress
- MulticastSocket
- ServerSocket
- Socket
- SocketImpl
- URL
- URLConnection
- URLEncoder
- URLStreamHandler

The Interfaces

- ContentHandlerFactory
- FileNameMap
- SocketImplFactory
- URLStreamHandlerFactory

Exceptions

- BindException
- ConnectException
- MalformedURLException
- NoRouteToHostException
- ProtocolException
- SocketException
- UnknownHostException
- UnknownServiceException

In this section we mainly discuss the *Socket* and *ServerSocket* classes. Other classes such as *DatagramSocket* and *DatagramPacket* etc. are discussed later.

6.1.2   The Socket Class

Connection-based sockets for clients are implemented through the *Socket* class. These sockets are used to develop client applications that utilize services provided by connection-oriented server applications.

The access methods of the *Socket* class are used to access the I/O streams (a stream is a high level abstraction representing a Java connection channel, a file, or a memory buffer, and is the basis for most Java communications) and connection parameters associated with a connected socket. Here are some access methods for the Socket class:

- Methods for accessing the socket information. The *getInetAddress()* and *getPort()* methods get the IP address of the destination host and the destination host port number to which the socket is connected. The *getLocalPort()* method returns the source host local port number associated with the socket. The *getLocalAddress()* method returns the local IP address associated with the socket.

- Methods for I/O. The *getInputStream()* and *getOutputStream()* methods are used to access the input and output streams associated with a socket.

- Other interesting methods. The *close()* method is used to close a socket. The *toString()* method returns a string representation of the socket.

6.1.3 The ServerSocket Class

A server works like a receptionist. She sits in the front desk of a company and waits for customers. She has no idea who will come or when they come. However, once a customer comes in, the receptionist will normally arrange a suitable staff of the company to actually work on the customer's request. After that, the receptionist will then wait for the next customer to arrive, or to serve the next waiting customer. Java provides the *ServerSocket* class to allow programmers to write servers that behave like a receptionist.

A TCP server socket is implemented by the *ServerSocket* class. Once a Java *ServerSocket* is established, it runs on a server and listens on a particular port of the server machine for incoming TCP connections. When a client *Socket* on a remote host attempts to connect to the port, the server tries to accept the connection request, negotiates the connection between the server and the client, and opens a regular *Socket* between the two hosts for the regular communication between the client and the server. The *ServerSocket* cannot be used for regular communications.

Only one client can connect to a server's *ServerSocket* any time. Multiple clients trying to connect to the same port on a server at the same time will be queued up. However, once the server has established a regular *Socket* for client and server communicaiton, the next queued client will be served. Incoming data is distinguished by the server port to which it is addressed, the client host and the client port from which it came.

Similarly, no more than one server socket can listen to a particular port on a host at one time. Therefore, since a server may need to handle many connections at once, server programs tend to be heavily multi-threaded. Generally speaking, a server socket listening on a port will only accept connections (just like the receptionist). It then passes off the actual processing of connections to a separate thread (just like an actual staff to serve the customer request).

The *ServerSocket* has three constructors that specify a paort to which the server socket is to listen for incoming connection requests, an optional maximum connection request queue length, and an optional Internet address. The Internet address argument allows *multihomed* hosts (that is, hosts with more than one

Internet address) to limit connections to a specific interface. These three constructors are listed as follows:

```
public ServerSocket(int port) throws IOException, BindException
public ServerSocket(int port, int queueLength) throws IOException,
  BindException
public ServerSocket(int port, int queueLength, InetAddress
  bindAddress) throws IOException
```

The operating system stores incoming connection requests addressed to a particular port in an FIFO (first-in-first-out) queue. The default length of the queue is normally 50 (this can vary from operating system to operating system). Incoming connections are refused if the queue is already full and the operating system is responsible for anaging the incoming. The default queue length can be changed by using the above constructors (up to the maximum length set by the operating system). Most medium size applications set the default queue length between 5 and 50.

Normally you only need to specify a port you want to listen on in the constructor of a *ServerSocket,* as shown below:

```
try {
    ServerSocket ss = new ServerSocket(80);
}
catch (IOException e) {
  System.err.println(e);
}
```

The newly created *ServerSocket* object will attempt to bind to the port on the local host given by the port argument (80 in the above example). However, if the port is already occupied by server, then a *java.net.BindException,* a subclass of *java.io.IOException,* is thrown, as no more than one process or thread can listen to a particular port at a time. This includes non-Java processes or threads. For example, if there is already an HTTP server running on port 80 (the default port for an HTTP server), the above program segment will not be able to bind to port 80. On Unix systems (but not Windows or the Mac) users' programs must be running as root to bind to a port between 1 and 1023.

Port number zero (0) is a special number. It lets the operating system to pick an available port. The details of the allocated port can be found out by using the *getLocalPort()* method. This is useful if the client and the server have already established a separate channel of communication over which the chosen port number can be communicated.

The methods provided by the *ServerSocket* include:

- The *accept()* method. It is used to cause the server socket to listen and wait until an incoming connection is established. It returns an object of class *Socket* once a connection is made. This *Socket* object is then used to carry out a service for a single client.

- The information methods. The *getInetAddress( )* method returns the address of the host to which the socket is connected. The *getLocalPort( )* method returns the port on which the server socket listens for an incoming connection.

- Other interesting methods. The *toString( )* method returns the socket's address and port number as a string in preparation for printing. The *close( )* method closes the server socket.

6.2 Building TCP Clients and Servers

6.2.1 Essential Components of Communication

The Java client-server communication shows some basic steps that are needed to establish a TCP communication connection. The essential components of any communication are:

- The underlying communication protocol. In this instance, the TCP.

- The application's communication protocol.

- The client program.

- The server program.

In a TCP communication, the following steps are needed:

- Create the server socket and listen to client connection request.

- Create the client socket and issue a connection request to the server.

- The server accepts the connection. The communication channel is then established and communications between the client and the server can be carried out using the application's communication protocol.

The application's protocol is like the following in the simplest case:

- The client sends a "Hello, Server" string to the server.

- The server replies a string "You have connected to the Very Simple Server.".

- Both client and server exit.

6.2.2 Implementing a TCP Client Program

The following steps are carried out when implementing our example TCP client program:

- Create a socket for communicating with the server on a specific port.

- Create an *InputStream,* in our case, a *BufferedReader,* to receive responses from the server.

- Create an *OutputStream,* in our case, a *PrintWriter,* to send messages to the server.

- Write to the *OutputStream.*

- Read from the *InputStream.*

- Close the *InputStream,* the *OutputStream,* and the socket before the client exits.

The client program, named C.java, is as follows.

```java
import java.io.*;
import java.net.*;
public class C {
  public static final int DEFAULT_PORT = 6789;
  public static void usage() {
    System.out.println("Usage: java C [<port>]");
    System.exit(0);
  }
  public static void main(String[] args) {
    int port = DEFAULT_PORT;
    Socket s = null;
    // parse the port specification
    if ((args.length != 0) && (args.length != 1)) usage();
    if (args.length == 0) port = DEFAULT_PORT;
    else {
      try {
        port = Integer.parseInt(args[0]);
      }
      catch(NumberFormatException e) {
        usage();
      }
    }
    try {
      BufferedReader reader;
      PrintWriter writer;
      // create a socket to communicate to the specified host and port
      s = new Socket("localhost", port);
      // create streams for reading and writing
        reader = new BufferedReader(new
        InputStreamReader(s.getInputStream()));
    writer = new PrintWriter(new
OutputStreamWriter(s.getOutputStream()));
      // tell the user that we've connected
      System.out.println("Connected to " + s.getInetAddress() +
        ":" + s.getPort());
      String line;
    // write a line to the server
      writer.println("Hello, Server");
    writer.flush();
      // read the response (a line) from the server
      line = reader.readLine();
      // write the line to console
      System.out.println("Server says: " + line);
    reader.close();
    writer.close();
    }
    catch (IOException e) {
      System.err.println(e);
    }
```

```
// always be sure to close the socket
finally {
  try {
    if (s != null) s.close();
  }
  catch (IOException e2) { }
  }
}
}
```

The program assumes that the server runs on the "local host" (i.e., with an IP address of 127.0.0.1) and uses a default port number of 6789. The statement

```
System.out.println("Connected to
"+s.getInetAddress()+":"+s.getPort());
```

displays the server host IP address and the port number that the client has connected to.

6.2.3 Implementing a TCP Server Program

When implementing the example TCP server, the following steps are carried out:

- Create a server socket to listen and accept client connection requests.

- Create an *InputStream,* in our case, a *BufferedReader,* to read messages from the client.

- Create an *OutputStream,* in our case, a *PrintWriter,* to send replies to the client.

- Read from the *InputStream.*

- Write to the *OutputStream.*

- Close the *InputStream,* the *OutputStream,* and the socket before the server exits.

The server program, named S.java, is as follows:

```
import java.net.*;
import java.io.*;
public class S {
  public final static int DEFAULT_PORT = 6789;
  public static void main (String args[]) throws IOException {
    Socket client;
    if (args.length != 1)
      client = accept (DEFAULT_PORT);
    else
      client = accept (Integer.parseInt (args[0]));
    try {
      PrintWriter writer;
      BufferedReader reader;
        reader = new BufferedReader(new
        InputStreamReader(client.getInputStream()));
        writer = new PrintWriter(new
        OutputStreamWriter(client.getOutputStream()));
      // read a line
```

```
      String line = reader.readLine();
      System.out.println("Client says: " + line);
      // write a line
         writer.println ("You have connected to the Very Simple
Server.");
      writer.flush();
      reader.close();
      writer.close();
      } finally { // closing down the connection
        System.out.println ("Closing");
        client.close ();
      }
   }
   static Socket accept (int port) throws IOException {
     System.out.println ("Starting on port " + port);
     ServerSocket server = new ServerSocket (port);
     System.out.println ("Waiting");
     Socket client = server.accept ();
     System.out.println ("Accepted from " + client.getInetAddress ());
     server.close ();
     return client;
   }
}
```

The server uses a default port of 6789 for communication. When a connection request is accepted, the server uses the following statement to display the IP address of the client computer:

```
System.out.println ("Accepted from " + client.getInetAddress ());
```

6.3   Examples in Java

The above simple communication example is of no practical use at all. A number of issues need to be addressed in order to improve the simple example for practical use:

- The exchange of multiple messages between the client and the server.

- The ability to run the server and the client programs on any Internet host.

- The ability for the server to deal with multiple client connections simultaneously.

6.3.1   Exchange of Multiple Messages

The first issue is to define the application's communication protocol to allow multiple exchanges of messages. Here is an example:

The server:

- After establishing the connection, the server sends an initial message to the client.

- The server waits for the client's messages.

- When the message arrives, the serve responds with an "OK" to the clients and then displays the message. If the incoming message is "Server Exit", then the server exits. Otherwise, it returns to the waiting step.

The client:

- After a successful connection, the client displays the initial response from the server.

- The client reads a line from the keyboard, and sends it to the server. Then the client reads the response from the server and displays it.

- The input string from the keyboard is checked. The client exits if the keyboard input string is "Server Exit" or the server is disconnected. Otherwise, it returns to the previous step.

The server program, named S1.java, is as follows:

```
import java.net.*;
import java.io.*;
public class S1 {
  public final static int DEFAULT_PORT = 6789;
  public static void main (String args[]) throws IOException {
    Socket client;
    if (args.length != 1)
      client = accept (DEFAULT_PORT);
    else
      client = accept (Integer.parseInt (args[0]));
    try {
      PrintWriter writer;
      BufferedReader reader;
        reader = new BufferedReader(new
        InputStreamReader(client.getInputStream()));
        writer = new PrintWriter(new
        OutputStreamWriter(client.getOutputStream()));
      writer.println ("You are now connected to the Simple Echo
Server.");
      writer.flush();
        for (;;) {
        // read a line
        String line = reader.readLine();
          // and send back ACK
        writer.println("OK");
        writer.flush();
        System.out.println("Client says: " + line);
        if (line.equals("Server Exit")) {
          break;
          }
        }
      reader.close();
      writer.close();
    } finally {
      System.out.println ("Closing");
      client.close ();
    }
  }
  static Socket accept (int port) throws IOException {
    System.out.println ("Starting on port " + port);
```

```
    ServerSocket server = new ServerSocket (port);
    System.out.println ("Waiting");
    Socket client = server.accept ();
    System.out.println ("Accepted from " + client.getInetAddress ());
    server.close ();
    return client;
  }
}
```

The client program, named C1.java, is as follows:

```
import java.io.*;
import java.net.*;
public class C1 {
public static final int DEFAULT_PORT = 6789;
public static void usage() {
    System.out.println("Usage: java C1 [<port>]");
    System.exit(0);
  }
  public static void main(String[] args) {
    int port = DEFAULT_PORT;
    Socket s = null;
    int end = 0;
    // parse the port specification
    if ((args.length != 0) && (args.length != 1)) usage();
    if (args.length == 0) port = DEFAULT_PORT;
    else {
      try {
        port = Integer.parseInt(args[0]);
      }
      catch(NumberFormatException e) {
      usage();
      }
    }
    try {
      PrintWriter writer;
      BufferedReader reader;
      BufferedReader kbd;
      // create a socket to communicate to the specified host and port
      //InetAddress myhost = getLocalHost();
      s = new Socket("localhost", port);
      // create streams for reading and writing
      reader = new BufferedReader(new
InputStreamReader(s.getInputStream()));
    OutputStream sout = s.getOutputStream();
    writer = new PrintWriter(new
OutputStreamWriter(s.getOutputStream()));
      // create a stream for reading from keyboard
      kbd = new BufferedReader(new InputStreamReader(System.in));
      // tell the user that we've connected
      System.out.println("Connected to " + s.getInetAddress() +
        ":" + s.getPort());
      String line;
      // read the first response (a line) from the server
      line = reader.readLine();
      // write the line to console
      System.out.println(line);
      while (true) {
        // print a prompt
        System.out.print("> ");
        System.out.flush();
        // read a line from console, check for EOF
        line = kbd.readLine();
        if (line.equals("Server Exit")) end = 1;
        // send it to the server
        writer.println(line);
```

```
        writer.flush();
        // read a line from the server
        line = reader.readLine();
        // check if connection is closed, i.e., EOF
        if (line == null) {
          System.out.println("Connection closed by server.");
          break;
        }
        if (end == 1) {
            break;   }
        // write the line to console
        System.out.println("Server says: " + line);
      }
      reader.close();
      writer.close();
    }
    catch (IOException e) {
      System.err.println(e);
    }
    // always be sure to close the socket
    finally {
      try {
        if (s != null) s.close();
      }
      catch (IOException e2) { }
    }
  }
}
```

6.3.2 Executing the Programs on Internet Hosts

The first requirement to execute the client-server programs on Internet hosts is to know the IP addresses or/and the host names of the computers. The following program, named InetExample.java, from the text book displays the details of a host:

```
import java.net.*;
import java.io.*;
public class InetExample {
  public static void main (String args[]) {
    printLocalAddress ();
    Reader kbd = new FileReader (FileDescriptor.in);
    BufferedReader bufferedKbd = new BufferedReader (kbd);
    try {
      String name;
      do {
        System.out.print ("Enter a hostname or IP address: ");
        System.out.flush ();
        name = bufferedKbd.readLine ();
        if (name != null)
          printRemoteAddress (name);
      } while (name != null);
      System.out.println ("exit");
    } catch (IOException ex) {
      System.out.println ("Input error:");
      ex.printStackTrace ();
    }
  }
  static void printLocalAddress () {
    try {
      InetAddress myself = InetAddress.getLocalHost ();
```

```
      System.out.println ("My name : " + myself.getHostName ());
      System.out.println ("My IP : " + myself.getHostAddress ());
      System.out.println ("My class : " + ipClass (myself.getAddress
()));
    } catch (UnknownHostException ex) {
      System.out.println ("Failed to find myself:");
      ex.printStackTrace ();
    }
  }
  static char ipClass (byte[] ip) {
    int highByte = 0xff & ip[0];
    return (highByte < 128) ? 'A' : (highByte < 192) ? 'B' :
      (highByte < 224) ? 'C' : (highByte < 240) ? 'D' : 'E';
  }
  static void printRemoteAddress (String name) {
    try {
      System.out.println ("Looking up " + name + "...");
      InetAddress machine = InetAddress.getByName (name);
      System.out.println ("Host name : " + machine.getHostName ());
      System.out.println ("Host IP : " + machine.getHostAddress ());
      System.out.println ("Host class : " +
                          ipClass (machine.getAddress ()));
    } catch (UnknownHostException ex) {
      System.out.println ("Failed to lookup " + name);
    }
  }
}
```

The *main( )* method first calls the *PrintLocalAddress( )* method to display the local host name and IP address. Then it sits in a loop that reads host names from the keyboard and uses the *PrintRemoteAddress()* method to display the *InetAddress* information about the host.

To allow our client-server program to run on any host, we only need to change the client program; the server program can remain the same. Here is the new client program, named as C2.java:

```
import java.io.*;
import java.net.*;
public class C2 {
  public static final int DEFAULT_PORT = 6789;
  public static void usage() {
    System.out.println("Usage: java C2 <serverhost>");
    System.exit(0);
  }
  public static void main(String[] args) {
    int port = DEFAULT_PORT;
    String address = "";
    Socket s = null;
    int end = 0;
    // parse the port specification
    if ((args.length != 0) && (args.length != 1)) usage();
    if (args.length == 0) {
      port = DEFAULT_PORT;
    address = "localhost";
    } else {
        address = args[0];
    }
    try {
```

```java
      PrintWriter writer;
      BufferedReader reader;
      BufferedReader kbd;
      // create a socket to communicate to the specified host and port
      s = new Socket(address, port);
      // create streams for reading and writing
        reader = new BufferedReader(new
        InputStreamReader(s.getInputStream()));
    OutputStream sout = s.getOutputStream();
    writer = new PrintWriter(new
OutputStreamWriter(s.getOutputStream()));
      // create a stream for reading from keyboard
      kbd = new BufferedReader(new InputStreamReader(System.in));
      // tell the user that we've connected
      System.out.println("Connected to " + s.getInetAddress() +
        ":" + s.getPort());
      String line;
      // read the first response (a line) from the server
      line = reader.readLine();
      // write the line to console
      System.out.println(line);
      while (true) {
        // print a prompt
        System.out.print("> ");
        System.out.flush();
        // read a line from console, check for EOF
        line = kbd.readLine();
        if (line.equals("Server Exit")) end = 1;
        // send it to the server
        writer.println(line);
        writer.flush();
        // read a line from the server
        line = reader.readLine();
        // check if connection is closed, i.e., EOF
        if (line == null) {
          System.out.println("Connection closed by server.");
          break;
        }
        if (end == 1) {
        break;
      }
        // write the line to console
        System.out.println("Server says: " + line);
      }
    reader.close();
    writer.close();
    }
    catch (IOException e) {
      System.err.println(e);
    }
    // always be sure to close the socket
    finally {
      try {
        if (s != null) s.close();
      }
      catch (IOException e2) { }
    }
  }
}
```

In this version, we use a variable

```
String address = "";
```

to store the IP address entered from the keyboard. The socket is then created using the following statement:

```
s = new Socket(address, port);
```

6.3.3 Supporting Multiple Clients

To support multiple clients, only the server program needs to be changed; the client program remains the same. When the server is initialized, we obtain the server socket and wait for client connection requests. When a client connection request is accepted, we use a thread to deal with the accepted incoming client connection. The server then goes back to wait for new connection requests. Clients can issue two commands during this time, one is a "Client Exit" command, telling the server that the current client is willing to disconnect. The other is the "Server Exit" command, in which the whole program exits.

```
import java.net.*;
import java.io.*;

public class S3 extends Thread {
  public final static int DEFAULT_PORT = 6789;
  private Socket client = null;

  public S3(Socket inSock) {
    super("echoServer");
    client = inSock;
  }

  public void run() {
    Socket cSock = client;
    PrintWriter writer;
    BufferedReader reader;
    try {
    String line;
        System.out.println ("Accepted from " +
cSock.getInetAddress());
        reader = new BufferedReader(new
        InputStreamReader(cSock.getInputStream()));
        writer = new PrintWriter(new
        OutputStreamWriter(cSock.getOutputStream()));
        writer.println ("You are now connected to the Simple Echo
Server.");
      writer.flush();
        for (;;) {
      // read a line
      line = reader.readLine();
        // and send back ACK
      writer.println("OK");
      writer.flush();
      System.out.println("Client says: " + line);
      if (line.equals("Server Exit") || line.equals("Client Exit"))
break;
      }
```

```
      System.out.println ("Closing the client " +
cSock.getInetAddress());
      reader.close();
   writer.close();
      cSock.close ();
   if (line.equals("Server Exit")) {
      System.out.println ("Closing the server");
      // server.close ();
      System.exit(0);
   }
   } catch (IOException e1) {
      System.err.println("Exception: " + e1.getMessage());
   System.exit(1);
   }
 }

 public static void main (String args[]) {
   ServerSocket server = null;
   try {
      server = new ServerSocket(DEFAULT_PORT);
      System.out.println ("Starting on port " + DEFAULT_PORT);
   } catch (IOException e) {
      System.err.println("Exception: could't make server socket.");
   System.exit(1);
   }
   while (true) {
      Socket incomingSocket = null;
      // wait fot a connection request
      System.out.println("Waiting...");
      try {
        incomingSocket = server.accept();
        // call a thread to deal with a connection
        S3 es = new S3(incomingSocket);
        es.start();
      } catch (IOException e) {
        System.err.println("Exception: could't make server socket.");
        System.exit(1); }
   }
 }
}
```

6.4   A More Complex Example - A Java Messaging Program using TCP

In this section we use connection-oriented mechanism (TCP) to build a simple "messaging" system. The system consists of a server program and a client program. The client has two basic functions: a message sending function and a message receiving function. Using the message sending function, one user (the sender) can send a message addressed to another user (the receiver) to the system The server will then store the message for the receiver until the receiver uses the message receiving function of the client to retrieve his/her messages from the server. Then the received message is deleted from the server. Also, the sender should be able to accept simultaneous connections from multiple clients and should be able to send the same message to a number of receivers simultaneously.

6.4.1 The Design

The system is divided into a server component and a client component. The action sequence of the server is as follows:

- Wait for a client to connect and build a connection when accept request from client

- Create a new server thread object to handle the connection

- Receive the username from the sender and store it in the username list

- Broadcast the username list to all users

- Receive the message addressed to specified users (receiver) from the client and store the message for those users respectively.

- Send back to client all messages stored for a particular user when required.

The action sequence of the client is as follows:

- Set up an interface for the user to interact with the system

- Connect to the server

- Send own username to the server

- Receive username list from the server and show it in the system

- Get the message from the user's input

- Get the selection of receivers from the username list. The specified message will be addressed to all selected receivers

- Send the message to the server

- Retrieve all messages for the user from the server

- Close the connection to the server

For better scalability and modularity, the client program is divided into two classes. One class, MessageClient, provides functions for connecting to the server; storing a message and retrieving messages. Another class, MessageApplet, provides the graphical user interface to the user and invokes functions in MessageClient to carry out the communication to the server. To achieve this, a MessageApplet is associated with a MessageClient.

The server program also has two classes: MessageServer and MessageServerThread. The MessageServer class uses a username list to store the names for all users.. The MessageServerThread class, which is used to handle interaction with individual MessageClient, needs to store the messages belong to the client. The MessageServer also has a list of MessageServerThread. According to the creation and destroy of threads, MessageServer constantly updates its username list and MessageServerThread list.

6.4.2 The Implementation

To launch a server, a user can choose a port number to run the server on a machine. When the port number is not specified, a default port number (6789) is used. The user can also specify the Internet address and the port number of the server to run the client java application. When the address of the server is not provided, a default value is set to localhost.

A simple application protocol is designed to enable the communication between the client and the server: Any messages passing through the system is started with a number at the range of 1 to 4.

- Number 1 indicates storing message. It is used only from the client to the server. Following the number 1, is a number indicating the number of receivers. Then follows an index list of receivers. After that is the message.

- Number 2 indicates retrieval of messages for a particular user. When the client requests its messages from the server, it merely sends a number 2. The response of the server also starts with a number 2. After that, a number indicating the number of messages is sent, followed by the messages one by one.

- Number 3 indicates the query and answer of a message. The server sends a number 3 to the client at the start of a connection session. The client replies with its username following a number 3.

- Number 4 indicates the broadcast of the username list. It is only used by the server: a server sends a number 4 to the client indicating the following messages is the username list. Firstly, the number of usernames is sent. Then, the usernames are sent one by one.

Empty strings are not permitted to be stored on the server. When the client runs in java applet inside a web page, the Java policy needs to be set to allow the client machine to trust the server program. The general method to set this is through the running of the policytool on the client machine and to add socket permission into the permission list. A message without a receiver cannot be sent.

The username is contained in the Applet parameter from the HTML file. If it is not specified, the username will be set to the IP address and port number of the client machine in the format of xxx.xxx.xxx.xxx:yyy.

To launch the server, type in java MessageServer [portno] in the command line and the server will up on the specified port. If port number is not provided, the server will use the default port number of 6789. The server prints a message and awaits until a client requests a connection. For every message stored the server prints out the received message. For a client retrieving messages, the server prints out a message to indicate the event. When a client quits the program, the server prints out the information indicating the corresponding username is removed from the username list.

The MessageApplet class is an applet runs in a web page or appletviewer. Files message1.html, message2.html and message3.html are created with different value of username parameters. Type `appletviewer message[1-3].html` will start the applet with a particular username. Three parameters, the host name, the port number and the username, can be set as parameters in the HTML file. If they are not specified, the system will use the default values, which are localhost and 6789. A textfield is placed on the upper part of the applet with a store button on its right. Type message in the textfield and click the store button then the message will be sent to the server. The textfield is then cleared. Underneath the textfield, there is a textarea that supports multiple lines. Right to the textarea is a button called retrieve. By clicking this button, messages are retrieved from the server and displayed in the textarea. The textarea is not editable. The messages will stay in the textarea until next retrieval. At the bottom, there is a List showing all the usernames of clients currently connected to the server. To send a message addressing to particular users, the username should be selected and shown in highlighted color. The list will be updated automatically during the execution of the program.

6.4.3 The Programs

The MessageServer.java program is shown below:

```
// MessageServer.java
import java.io.*;
import java.net.*;
import java.util.Vector;

class MessageServer {
  Vector threadlist=new Vector();
  Vector userlist=new Vector();
  ServerSocket welcomesocket;
  Socket connectionsocket;
  int port=6789;
  public void run(String[] argv) {
    if((argv.length<1)) {
      System.err.println("No port number is given! using default");
    } else {
      if((argv.length>2)) {
        System.err.println("Usage: java MessageServer port");
        ystem.exit(0);
      } else {
        try {
          port=Integer.parseInt(argv[0]);
        } catch(Exception e) {
          System.err.println("Usage: java MessageServer port");
          System.exit(0);
        }
      }
    }
    try {
      welcomesocket=new ServerSocket(port);
      while(welcomesocket!=null) {
        connectionsocket=welcomesocket.accept();
        if(connectionsocket!=null) {
          System.out.println("Connection built to"
            +connectionsocket.getInetAddress().toString()
            +": "+connectionsocket.getPort());
        }
        MessageServerThread mst=new
MessageServerThread(connectionsocket,this);
```

```
                threadlist.add(mst);
                mst.getUsername();
                mst.start();


          }
     }catch(Exception e){System.out.println("Failed to provide
service");}
   }

   public void addMessages(int[] index,String themessage) {
      for(int i=0;i<index.length;i++) {
         MessageServerThread
mst=(MessageServerThread)threadlist.elementAt(index[i]);
         mst.addMessage(themessage);
      }
   }

   public void addUser(String username) {
      System.out.println("add a user into the list");
      userlist.add(username);
      broadcastUserlist();
   }

   public void removeUser(MessageServerThread mst) {
      System.out.println("Remove a user who exited");
      int i=threadlist.lastIndexOf(mst);
      threadlist.removeElement(mst);
      userlist.removeElementAt(i);
      broadcastUserlist();
   }

   public void broadcastUserlist() {
      for(int i=0;i<threadlist.size();i++) {
         MessageServerThread
mst=(MessageServerThread)threadlist.elementAt(i);
         mst.sendUserlist(userlist);
      }
   }

   public static void main(String[] args) {
      MessageServer ms=new MessageServer();
      ms.run(args);
   }
}
```

Here is the MessageServerThread.java program:

```
// MessageServerThread.java
import java.util.*;
import java.net.*;
import java.io.*;

public class MessageServerThread extends Thread
{
   MessageServer server;
   Socket socket;
   DataInputStream dis; // input communication channel from client
   DataOutputStream dos; // output communication channel to client
   Vector clientmessages=new Vector();
   String clientmessage="";

   public MessageServerThread(Socket localSocket, MessageServer
localServer)
   {
      server = localServer;
      socket = localSocket;
      try {
         dis = new DataInputStream(socket.getInputStream());
```

```
        dos = new DataOutputStream(socket.getOutputStream());
    }`catch(Exception e)`{
      System.err.println("exception at ServerThread");
      dis=null;
      dos=null;
    }
}

public void getUsername() {
    try {
      dos.writeInt(3);
      dos.flush();
      String readusername=dis.readUTF();
      System.out.println(readusername+" has join the system");
      server.addUser(readusername);
      }catch(Exception e) {}
    }

// waits for input from the client - either insert or delete
public void run()
{
    while(true) {
      try {
        int a=dis.readInt();
        if(a==1) {
          int noofusers=dis.readInt();
          int[] index=new int[noofusers];
          for(int i=0;i<noofusers;i++) {
            index[i]=dis.readInt();
          }
          clientmessage=dis.readUTF();
          server.addMessages(index,clientmessage);
          System.out.println("Recieved message: "+clientmessage);
        } else if(a==2) {
          dos.writeInt(2);
          dos.writeInt(clientmessages.size());
          dos.flush();
          for(int i=0;i<clientmessages.size();i++) {
            dos.writeUTF((String)clientmessages.elementAt(i));
            dos.flush();
          }
          clientmessages.removeAllElements();
          System.out.println("Message retrieved and reset");
        }
      } catch(Exception e) {
        System.out.println("Client closed the connection");
        server.removeUser(this);
        break;
      }
    }
}

public void addMessage(String themessage) {
    clientmessages.add(themessage);
}

public void sendUserlist(Vector ulist)
{
    String s;
    try {
      dos.writeInt(4);
      dos.writeInt(ulist.size()); // tell user number of usernames
      for(int i = 0; i < ulist.size(); i++) {
        dos.writeUTF((String)ulist.elementAt(i));
      }
      dos.flush(); // flush to ensure sending data
    } catch(Exception e){System.out.println("exception at sending user
list"+e);}}
```

```
      }
}
```

The MessageApplet.java program contains the source code of both the MessageApplet class and the MessageClient class. It is shown below:

```java
// MessageApplet.java
import java.io.*;
import java.net.*;
import java.applet.*;
import java.awt.*;
import java.awt.event.*;

public class MessageApplet extends Applet implements ActionListener{
   TextField sendmessage=new TextField(40);
   TextArea returnmessage=new TextArea(15,40);
   List userlist=new List(10,true);
   Button store=new Button("  Store  ");
   Button retrival=new Button("Retrival");
   String message;
   String[] messages;
   MessageClient mc;
   String hostname;
   InetAddress thehost;
   int portno;
   String username="";

   public void init()
   {
     try {
       username=getParameter("username");
       hostname=getParameter("server");
       portno=Integer.parseInt(getParameter("port"));
     }catch(Exception e){
       System.out.println("Missing parameters! using default");
       hostname="localhost";
       portno=6789;
     }
     try {
       InetAddress thehost=InetAddress.getByName(hostname);
       mc=new MessageClient(thehost,portno,this);
       mc.start();
     }catch(Exception ee){
       showStatus("Cannot connect");
       System.out.println("Cannot connect");
     }
     setSize(400,450);
     store.addActionListener(this);
     retrival.addActionListener(this);
     returnmessage.setEditable(false);
     add(sendmessage);
     add(store);
     add(returnmessage);
     add(retrival);
     add(userlist);
   }

   public void actionPerformed(ActionEvent e)
   {
     if(e.getSource()==store) {
       if((sendmessage.getText().length()>=1)
         &&(userlist.getSelectedIndexes().length>0)) {
         mc.addMessage(userlist.getSelectedIndexes(),
           sendmessage.getText());
         sendmessage.setText("");
       }
     } else if(e.getSource()==retrival) {
```

```
      mc.getMessage();
    }
  }

  public void updateMessageBoard(String[] messages) {
    returnmessage.setText("");
    for(int i=0;i<messages.length;i++)
    returnmessage.append(messages[i]+"\n");
  }

  public void updateUserlist(String[] users) {
    userlist.removeAll();
    for(int i=0;i<users.length;i++)
    userlist.add(users[i]);
  }
}

class MessageClient extends Thread{
  DataInputStream infromserver;
  DataOutputStream outtoserver;
  MessageApplet ma;
  Socket clientsocket;
  public MessageClient(InetAddress host,int port,MessageApplet ma)
  {
    this.ma=ma;
    try {
      clientsocket=new Socket(host,port);
      System.out.println("Connection has been built to the server
        at "+host+":"+port);
    } catch(Exception e)
      {System.out.println("Cannot connect to the specified
        server!"+host+":"+port);}
    try {
      outtoserver=new
        DataOutputStream(clientsocket.getOutputStream());
      infromserver=new DataInputStream(clientsocket.getInputStream())
    } catch(Exception e) {System.out.println("Input or Output
      denied!");}
  }

  public void run()
  {
    try {
      while(infromserver!=null) {
      int a=infromserver.readInt();
      switch(a) {
        case(2):
          int num=infromserver.readInt();
          String[] returnvalue=new String[num];
          for(int i=0;i<num;i++)
            returnvalue[i]=infromserver.readUTF();
            ma.updateMessageBoard(returnvalue);
            break;
        case(3):
          if(ma.username.compareTo("")!=0)
            outtoserver.writeUTF(ma.username);
          else
            outtoserver.writeUTF(
              clientsocket.getLocalAddress().getHostAddress()
              +":"+clientsocket.getLocalPort());
          outtoserver.flush();
          break;
        case(4):
          int num1=infromserver.readInt();
          String[] returnvalue1=new String[num1];
          for(int i=0;i<num1;i++)
            returnvalue1[i]=infromserver.readUTF();
          ma.updateUserlist(returnvalue1);
```

```
        break;
      }
    }
  }catch(Exception e) {System.out.println("Failed to receive
    data"+e);}
}

public void addMessage(int[] indexes,String themessage)
{
  try {
    outtoserver.writeInt(1);
    outtoserver.writeInt(indexes.length);
    for(int i=0;i<indexes.length;i++) {
      outtoserver.writeInt(indexes[i]);
    }
    outtoserver.writeUTF(themessage);
    outtoserver.flush();
  }catch(Exception e) {System.out.println("Failed to save message
    to server!"+e);}
}

public void getMessage()
{
  try {
    outtoserver.writeInt(2);
    outtoserver.flush();
  }catch(Exception e) {System.out.println("Failed to recieve message
    from server!"+e);}
}

public void destory()
{
  try {
    clientsocket.close();
  }catch(Exception e) {System.out.println("Failed to close the
    connection!"+e);}
}
}
```

File message1.html is listed below:

```
<!DOCTYPE HTML><HTML><HEAD></HEAD><BODY>
<APPLET CODE="MessageApplet.class" CODEBASE="." WIDTH=400 HEIGHT=300>
<PARAM name="server" value="localhost">
<PARAM name="port" value="6789">
<PARAM name="username" value="User 1">
</APPLET>
</BODY></HTML>
```

The other two files, message2.html and message3.html, are almost the same as the message1.html file, except that the "username" is changed to "User 2" and "User 3", respectively.

6.5 Datagram Communications in Java

6.5.1 Why Datagram Communication ?

For many applications the convenience of the TCP sockets outweighs the overhead required. However, for certain applications it is much more efficient to utilize datagrams: small, fixed-length messages sent between computers of a network.

A TCP connection carries a number of overhead factors. First, one needs to go through several steps to open a connection. This takes a certain time. Once a connection is open, sending and receiving data involves several steps. The final step is to tear down the connection after the communication. If one is to send a large amount of data that must be reliably delivered, then the TCP protocol is suitable. However, if one only needs to send a short, simple message quickly, then all these steps may not be worthwhile.

The difference between datagram and TCP connections is like the difference between post offices and telephones. With a telephone, you make a connection to a specific telephone number, if the person on the destination answers the phone, you two are able to talk for a certain period of time, exchanging an arbitrary amount of information, and then you close the connection. With a post offices, you typically send a letter with the destination address on the envelope. Because of errors in sorting, transportation and delivery and delays you cannot be certain if or when the person addressed receives the letter. The only way to know is to request and receive some kind of acknowledgement. You may retry several times if you get no response, then give up.

On an IP network such as the Internet, the UDP (User Datagram Protocol) is used to transmit fixed-length datagrams. This is the protocol that Java taps with the *DatagramSocket* class.

6.5.2 Java Datagram-based Classes

Datagrams have the following advantages:

- *Speed.* UDP involves low overhead since there is no need to set up connections, to maintain the order and correctness of the message delivery, or to tear down the connections after the communication.

- *Message-oriented instead of stream-oriented.* If the message to be sent is small and simple, it may be easier to simply send the chunk of bytes instead of going through the steps of converting it to and from streams.

Two *java.net* classes define the heart of datagram-based messaging in Java: they are the *DatagramSocket* and the *DatagramPacket* classes. A *DatagramSocket* is an interface through which *DatagramPackets* are transmitted. A *DatagramPacket* is simply an IP-specific wrapper for a block of data.

The *DatagramSocket* class provides a good interface to the UDP protocol. This class is responsible for sending and receiving *DatagramPacket* via the UDP protocol. The most commonly used *DatagramSocket* methods are listed below:

- *DatagramSocket().* Constructor comes in two formats: one is used to specify the local port used and the other picks an ephemeral local port for you.

- *receive()*. Receive a *DatagramPacket* from any remote server.

- *send()*. Send a *DatagramPacket* to the remote server specified in the *DatagramPacket*.

- *close()*. Tear down local communication resources. After this method is called, the object involved is released.

- *getLocalPost()*. Return the local port this *DatagramSocket* is using.

Note that there are two flavors of *DatagramSocket:* those created to send *DatagramPackets,* and those created to receive *DatagramPackets.* A "send" *DatagramSocket* uses an ephemeral local port assigned by the native UDP implementation. A "receive" *DatagramSockect* requires a specific local port number.

A *DatagramPacket* represents the datagram transmitted via a *DatagramSocket.* The most frequently used methods of *DatagramPacket* are:

- *DatagramPacket()*. Constructor comes in two formats: a "send" packet and a "receive" packet. For the *send* packet, you need to specify a remote *InetAddress* and a port to which the packet should be sent, as well as a data buffer and length to be sent. For the *receive* packet, you need to provide an empty buffer into which data should be stored, and the maximum number of bytes to be stored.

- *getAddress()*. This method allows one to either obtain the *InetAddress* of the host that sends the *DatagramPacket,* or to obtain the *InetAddress* of the host to which this packet is addressed.

- *getData()*. This method allows one to access the raw binary data wrapped in the *DatagramPacket.*

- *getLength()*. This method allows one to determine the length of data wrapped in the *DatagramPacket* without getting a reference to the data block itself.

- *getPort()*. This method returns either the port of the server to which this packet will be sent, or the port of the server that sends this packet, depending on whether the packet was built to be sent or built to receive data.

It is also possible to exchange data via datagrams using the *Socket* class. To do so, you must use one of the *Socket* constructors that includes the Boolean *useStream* parameter, as in,

```
Socket(InetAddress address, int port, Boolean useStream)
```

and set *useStream* to *false.* This tells *Socket* to use the faster UDP. The advantage to using this interface is that it provides a stream interface to a datagram. Also, there is no need to instantiate and maintain a separate *DatagramPacket* to hold the data.

But there are significant disadvantages as well. First, there is no way to detect if a particular datagram sent does not arrive at the destination. Your stream interface can lie to you. Second, you still have to go through the hassle of setting up the connection.

UDP ports are separate from TCP ports. Each computer has 65,536 UDP ports as well as its 65,536 TCP ports. You can have a ServerSocket bound to TCP port 20 at the same time as a DatagramSocket is bound to UDP port 20. Most of the time it should be obvious from context whether or not I'm talking about TCP ports or UDP ports.

6.6 Building UDP Servers and Clients

6.6.1 Sending and Receiving UDP Datagrams

To send data to a particular server, you must first convert the data into byte array. Next you pass this byte array, the length of the data in the array (most of the time this will be the length of the array), the local *InetAddress* and the port to which you wish to send it, into the *DatagramPacket* constructor. For example,

```
try {
  InetAddress turin = new InetAddess("turin.cm.deakin.edu.au");
  int chargen = 19;
  String s = "My second UDP Packet";
  byte[] b = s.getBytes();
  DatagramPacket dp = new DatagramPacket(b, b.length, turin, chargen);
}
catch (UnknownHostException e) {
  System.err.println(e);
}
```

Next you create a *DatagramSocket* object and pass the packet to its *send()* method. For example,

```
try {
  DatagramSocket sender = new DatagramSocket();
  sender.send(dp);
}
catch (IOException e) {
  System.err.println(e);
}
```

To receive data sent to you, you construct a *DatagramSocket* object with a port on which you want to listen. Then you pass an empty *DatagramPacket* object to the *DatagramSocket*'s *receive()* method.

```
    public  synchronized  void  receive(DatagramPacket  dp)  throws
IOException
```

The calling thread blocks until a datagram is received. Then the datagram dp is filled with the data from that datagram. You can then use *getPort()* and *getAddress()* to tell where the packet came from, *getData()* to retrieve the data, and *getLength()* to see how many bytes were in the data. If the received packet was too long for the buffer, then it's truncated to the length of the buffer. For example,

```
try {
  byte buffer = new byte[65536]; // maximum size of an IP packet
  DatagramPacket dp = new DatagramPacket(buffer, buffer.length);
  DatagramSocket ds = new DatagramSocket(2134);
  ds.receive(dp);
  byte[] data = dp.getData();
  String s = new String(data, 0, data.getLength());
```

```
  System.out.println("Port " + dp.getPort() + " on " + dp.getAddress()
    + " sent this message:");
  System.out.println(s);
}
catch (IOException e) {
  System.err.println(e);
}
```

6.6.2 Datagram Server

The steps for setting up a datagram server are as follows:

- Create a *DatagramPocket* for receiving the data, indicating the buffer to hold the data and the maximum length of the buffer.

- Create a *DatagramSocket* on which to listen.

- Receive a packet from a client.

Here is a simple server example (DatagramReceive.Java).

```
import java.net.*;
public class DatagramReceive {
  static final int PORT = 7890;
  public static void main( String args[] ) throws Exception {
    String theReceiveString;
    byte[] theReceiveBuffer = new byte[ 2048 ];

    // Make a packet to receive into...
    DatagramPacket theReceivePacket =
      new DatagramPacket( theReceiveBuffer, theReceiveBuffer.length );

    // Make a socket to listen on...
    DatagramSocket theReceiveSocket = new DatagramSocket( PORT );

    // Receive a packet...
    theReceiveSocket.receive( theReceivePacket );

    // Convert the packet to a string...
    theReceiveString =
      new String( theReceiveBuffer, 0, theReceivePacket.getLength() );

    // Print out the string...
    System.out.println( theReceiveString );

    //  Close the socket...
    theReceiveSocket.close();
    }
}
```

The *main()* method first builds an empty *DatagramPacket* object using a designated buffer. Then it creates a *DatagramSocket* using the default port. The *DatagramSocket* will receive a *DatagramPacket* which will fill the previous *DatagramPacket*. Then the program extracts the string from this datagram packet and prints it out.

6.6.3 Datagram Client

The steps of setting up a datagram client are as follows:

- Find the destination's IP address.

- Create a *DatagramPacket* based on the destination address and the data to be sent.

- Create a *DatagramSocket* for sending the packet.

- Send the *DatagramPacket* over the *DatagramSocket*.

Here is the program named DatagramSend.java:

```java
import java.net.*;
import java.io.IOException;

public class DatagramSend {
  static final int PORT = 7890;
  public static void main( String args[] ) throws Exception {
    String theStringToSend = "I'm a datagram and I'm O.K.";
    byte[] theByteArray = new byte[ theStringToSend.length() ];
    theByteArray = theStringToSend.getBytes();

    // Get the IP address of our destination...
    InetAddress theIPAddress = null;
    try {
      theIPAddress = InetAddress.getByName( "localhost" );
    } catch (UnknownHostException e) {
      System.out.println("Host not found: " + e);
      System.exit(1);
    }

    // Build the packet...
    DatagramPacket thePacket = new DatagramPacket( theByteArray,
      theStringToSend.length(),
      theIPAddress,
      PORT );

    // Now send the packet
    DatagramSocket theSocket = null;
    try {
      theSocket = new DatagramSocket();
    } catch (SocketException e) {
        System.out.println("Underlying network software has failed:
                            + e);
        System.exit(1);
    }
    try {
      theSocket.send( thePacket );
    } catch (IOException e) {
      System.out.println("IO Exception: " + e);
    }
    theSocket.close();
    }
}
```

The *main()* method first designs a string "I'm a datagram and I'm O.K." and translates it into a byte array. It also gets the local IP address using the *InetAddress* class and then builds a *DatagramPacket* object using the above byte array, the length of the string, the IP address and the default port. Then it creates a sending *DatagramSocket* and sends out the *DatagramPacket* built before by invoking the *send()* method. After that, the program closes the *DatagramSocket.*

6.7 Summary

As mentioned in Chapter 5, the BSD Internet domain sockets use the TCP/IP (or UDP/IP) protocol suite as the communication protocols among processes. TCP is a connection-oriented protocol and it implements a connection as a stream of bytes from source to destination, while UDP is a connectionless transport protocol and uses datagrams to implement its communication. In this chapter we discussed the datagrams for the TCP/UDP communications. Java provides the reliable stream-based communication for TCP as well as the unreliable datagram communication for UDP. The stream-based communication is like a telephone system which has the connection built first, whereas datagram communication is like a mail system which has no fixed connection. Java various input/output streams allow application programs to input and output various data, such as bytes, string, file etc. The Java socket API provides the basis of TCP/UDP communication. Various examples presented in the chapter have been a great help for readers in writing Java TCP/UDP programs of their own.

Exercises

6.1 How does one build a connection between a Java socket and a Java server socket? Write a program. 6.2

6.2 How does one close a socket? Give an example. 6.2

6.3 How does one write a TCP server program? Give an example. 6.3.3

6.4 Write a client/server program using *stream* communication to implement the following functions: 6.4

   1. The server can accept multiple clients and they can exchange multiple messages.

   2. The server can send a message to all clients simultaneously.

   Hint: use a separate thread to manage each connection and use *suspend()* and *resume()* methods of *Thread* class.

6.5 Compile the three programs in the chat example (6.4) and test run the server on one machine, the client instances on at least two machines. If possible, form a group to test run the chat program (the server runs on one site and the client is run on multiple sites).

6.6 Discuss the advantages and disadvantages of TCP and UDP. 6.5.1

134

6.7 Is it possible to exchange data via datagrams using the *Socket* class? How? 6.5.2

6.8 How does one write a datagram client program? 6.6.3

6.9 Write a client/server program using *datagram* communication to implement the following functions: the server can communicate with multiple clients and print out each client's message. Hint: use *getAddress()* to get a client address. 6.7

CHAPTER 7 INTERPROCESS COMMUNICATION USING RPC

When using message passing for interprocess communications, a programmer is aware of the passing of messages between the two processes. However, in a remote procedure call situation, passing of messages is invisible to the programmer. Instead, a language-level concept, the procedure call, is used to mask the actual communication between two processes. In this chapter we discuss two commonly used RPC tools, the DCE/RPC and the SUN/RPC. We have developed an RPC tool, called the Simple RPC tool, which will be described in the chapter.

The idea of RPC has been extended to develop interprocess communication mechanisms for object-oriented paradigm, notably the Remote Method Invocation (RMI) in Java. We also introduce this mechanism in the chapter.

7.1 Distributed Computing Environment (DCE)

Open Software Foundation's Distributed Computing Environment (DCE) [OSF 1990] is a vendor-neutral platform for supporting distributed applications. DCE is a standard software structure for distributed computing that is designed to operate across a range of standard Unix, VMS, OS/2, and other operating systems. It includes standards for RPC, name (binding) services, time (synchronisation) services, security services, and thread services all sufficient for client-server computing across heterogeneous architectures. DCE/RPC is based on Apollo's Network Computing System (NCS) and can be used in several programming language environments (e.g., C and Pascal).

DCE is based on the client-server model. It uses the client-server model to support its infrastructure and transparent services. All DCE services are provided through servers. By using DCE, application programmers can avoid considerable work in creating supporting services, such as creating communication protocols for various parts of a distributed program, building a directory service for locating those pieces, and maintaining a service for providing security, in their own program. They can rely on DCE for providing these services.

7.1.1 The Architecture of DCE

The architecture of DCE masks the physical complexity of the networked environment by providing a layer of logical simplicity. The layer is composed of a set of services that can be used separately or in combination to form a comprehensive distributed computing system. Figure 7.1 shows the architecture of DCE. Servers that provide DCE services usually run on different computers, so do clients and servers of a distributed application program that uses DCE.

DCE is based on a layered model which integrates a set of fundamental technologies. To applications, DCE appears to be a single logical system with two broad categories of services [Chappell 1994], [OSF 1992]:

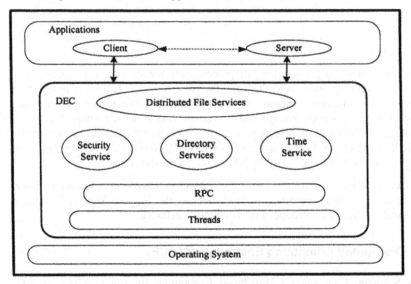

Figure 7.1: DCE architecture

The DCE Core Services

These services provide tools with which software developers can create end-user applications and system software products for distributed computing. These services include:

- *Threads:* DCE supports multithreaded applications;

- *RPC:* The DCE/RPC is the fundamental communication mechanism and is used in building all other services and applications. It masks differences in data representation on different hardware platforms and thus allows distributed programs to work transparently across heterogeneous systems;

- *Security Services:* The DCE Security Service provides the mechanism for writing applications that support secure communication between clients and servers;

- *Directory Services:* The DCE Cell Directory Service (CDS) provides a mechanism for logically naming objects within a DCE cell (a group of client and server computers). DCE cells can also participate in a world-wide directory service using the DCE Global Directory Service (GDS), which is based on the X.500 standard, or the Internet-style Domain Name Service (DNS);

- *Time Services:* The DCE Distributed Time Service (DTS) provides a way to synchronise the clocks on different computers in a distributed computing system.

DCE Data-Sharing Services

In addition to the core services, DCE provides important data-sharing services, which require no programming on the part of the end user and facilitate the better use of shared information. These services include:

- *Distributed File Services:* The DCE Distributed File Service (DFS) provides a high- performance, scalable, secure method for sharing remote files;

- *Enhanced File Services:* The Enhanced File Service provides features which greatly increase the availability and further simplify the administration of DFS.

DCE is a highly integrated package and its components depend on one another for correct functioning. Some pairs of components (e.g., Security Service and RPC) have mutual dependencies. For example, the Security Service is implemented using RPC, and it requires the use of the Security Service to make RPCs secure.

In a typical distributed environment, most clients perform their communication with only a small set of servers. In DCE, computers that communicate frequently are placed in a single cell. A cell's size and geographical location are determined by the people administering the cell. Cells may exist along social, political, or organisational boundaries and may contain up to several thousand computers. Although DCE allows clients and servers to communicate in different cells, it optimises for the more common case of intra-cell communication. One computer can belong to only one cell at a time.

A user is authenticated within one local cell. All other cells to which a particular user has access are considered *foreign cells*. If a cell is configured to participate in a global naming service, users from foreign cells which also participate in the global naming service may be permitted to access data in the local cell.

7.1.2 The Role of RPC

DCE RPC is based on the Apollo's Network Computing System (NCA/RPC). RPC fits very naturally into the client-server model. The components of DCE RPC can be split into the following two groups according to the stage of their usage:

- *Used in development.* They include IDL (Interface Definition Language) and the idl compiler. The IDL is a language used to define data types and operations applicable to each interface in a platform independent manner. The idl compiler is a tool used to translate IDL definitions into code (usually in C) which can be used in distributed applications;

138

- *Used in runtime.* They include RPC runtime library, *rpcd* (RPC daemon), and *rpccp* (RPC control program).

To build a basic DCE application, the application developer has to supply the following three files:

- *The interface definition file.* It defines the interfaces (data structures, procedure names, and parameters) of the remote procedures that are offered by the server;

- *The client program.* It defines the user interfaces, the calls to the remote procedures of the server, and the client side processing functions;

- *The server program.* It implements the calls offered by the server.

The first step for building a DCE application is to compile the interface definition file using the idl compiler to produce the interface header file, and the client and the server stubs. Then the client program and server program are compiled with their related stub files and the interface header. Finally, the client and server executables are generated by linking these object files with the RPC runtime library. Figure 7.2 shows these operations.

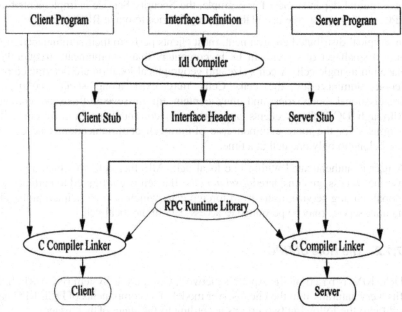

Figure 7.2: Build a DCE application

DCE uses threads to improve the efficiency of RPCs. A *thread* is a 'lightweight' process that executes a portion of a program, cooperating with other threads concurrently executing in the same address space of a process. Most of the information that is a part of a process can then be shared by all threads executing within the process' address space. By sharing common information, the overhead incurred in creating and maintaining the information, and the amount of information that needs to be saved when switching between threads of the same program is reduced significantly.

The thread facility can be provided by the operating system or DCE, but in both cases DCE specifies an application programming interface (API) to access thread services from applications. The API routines allow programmers to create and terminate threads, have one thread waiting for another to complete, and perform thread synchronisation. To provide a service, for example, a separate server can be used to interface with a group of clients and a separate thread within a particular server can be used to process an RPC from a client (Figure 7.3(a)). In this case, a server can serve many clients from many groups simultaneously. Within a client, a separate thread can be used to perform an RPC, allowing several RPCs to be executed at the same time (Figure 7.3(b)).

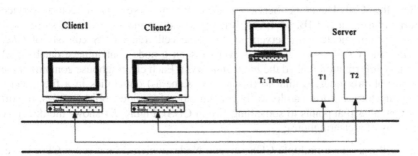

(a) A server communicates with multiple clients using threads

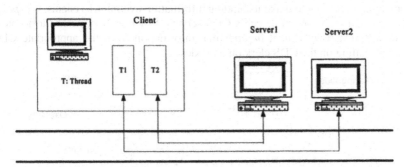

Figure 7.3: Using threads in a client-server application

7.1.3 The DCE Services

All the high-level DCE services, such as directory services, security services, time services, and distributed file services, are provided by relevant servers. This section briefly discusses these services and servers.

7.1.3.1 Directory Services

The main job of the directory services is to help clients find the locations of appropriate servers. To let clients access the services offered by a server, the server has to place some binding information into a directory. As mentioned in Chapter 2, to access the services of a server, a client needs to acquire that server's binding information from the directory and to bind the information with the client. The client can then access the server directly.

A *directory* is a hierarchically structured database that stores dynamic system configuration information. The directory is a realisation of the naming system. Each name has attributes associated with it, which can be obtained via a query using the name.

Each cell in a DCE distributed computing system has its own directory service, called the Cell Directory Service (CDS), which stores the directory service information for a cell [Bond 1995]. It is optimised for intra-cell access, since most clients communicate with servers in the same cell. Each CDS consists of *CDS servers* and *CDS clerks*. A CDS server runs on a node containing a database of directory information (called the *clearinghouse*). Each clearinghouse contains some number of directories, similar to (but not the same as) directories in a file system. Each directory, in turn, can logically contain other directories, object entries, or soft links (an alias that points to something else in CDS). Figure 7.4 shows the directory hierarchy of a clearinghouse.

Each cell may have multiple CDS servers. Nodes which do not run a CDS server must run a CDS clerk. A CDS clerk acts as an intermediary between a distributed application and the CDS server on a node not running a CDS server.

When a server wishes to make its binding information available to clients, it *exports* that information on one of its cell's CDS servers. When a client wishes to locate a server within its own cell, it *imports* that information from the appropriate CDS server by calling on the CDS clerk on its node.

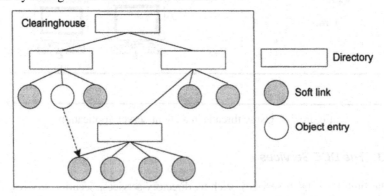

Figure 7.4: The CDS directory hierarchy

DCE uses the Domain Name System (DNS) or Global Directory Service (GDS, based on the X.500 standard) to enable clients to access servers in foreign cells. To access a server in a foreign cell, a client gives the cell's name and the name of the desired server in that cell. A CDS component called a Global Directory Agent (GDA) extracts the location of the named cell's CDS server from DNS or GDS, then a query is sent directly to this foreign server. Figure 7.5 shows the components of the DCE directory service.

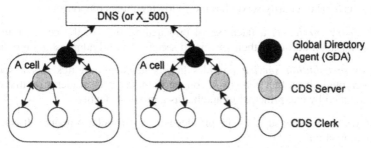

Figure 7.5: Components of the DCE directory service

CDS supports replication of its information. Replication is done at the directory level, so any directory and the objects it contains can be copied by a cell administrator and kept in two or more CDS servers running concurrently within a cell. There are two types of directory replicas: *master replicas* and *read-only replicas*. Master replicas can accept any directory service operations (such as read and update operations) whereas read-only replicas can only accept read operations.

All the update operations happen on a master replica [Rosenberg *et al.* 1992], [Bond 1995]. There are two methods for maintaining data consistency between a master replica and its read-only replicas: immediate propagation and skulking. With immediate propagation, a change to the master replica causes the change to be immediately applied to all of its read-only replicas. However, if read-only replica is not available during the propagation, the change is simply not made to that replica. With skulking, the changes are carried out on a periodical basis. The skulking operation ensures that when a failed replica restarts its information will be consistent with other replicas.

7.1.3.2 Security Services

DCE provides the following four security services:

- *Authentication.* When a client requests some service from a server, it must identify itself and must provide some information to prove its true identity;

- *Authorisation.* Once a client's identity has been authenticated, the next question is whether the client has the right to perform the service it is requesting;

- *Data integrity.* This service guards against the alteration of data during the transmission of the data. It allows a recipient of a message to determine whether the data has been tampered with;

- *Data privacy.* It ensures that data sent between clients and servers cannot be read by anyone but the parties involved in the communication.

A security server (it may be replicated) is responsible for providing these services within a cell. The security server has the following three components:

- *Registry service* is a database of principal (a user of the cell), group, and organisation accounts, their associated secret keys and administration policies.

- *Key distribution service* provides tickets to clients. A ticket is a specially encrypted object that contains a conversation key and an identifier that can be presented by one principal to another as a proof of identity.

- *Privilege service* supplies the privileges of a particular principal. It is used in authorisation.

The security server must run on a secure computer, since the registry on which it relies contains a secret key, generated from a password, for every principal in the cell.

DCE security services are based on the Kerberos V5.0, created by the MIT/Project Athena [MIT 1994], and DCE extends Kerberos version 5 by providing authorisation services [Chappell 1994].

7.1.3.3 Time Services

Distributed time service (DTS) of DCE is designed to keep a set of clocks on different computers synchronised. DTS uses the usual client-server structure: DTS clients, daemon processes called *clerks,* request the correct time from some number of servers, receive responses, and then reset their clocks as necessary to reflect this new knowledge. How often a clerk resynchronises, and thus how accurate that system's clock will be, is configured by the system administrator.

Time in DTS is expressed as an *interval* (a time plus or minus an inaccuracy). A new time interval is calculated as the intersection of all the received intervals. For example, as shown in Figure 7.6, if a clerk receives four time intervals from time server 1, 2, 3, and 4, then the time synchronisation of the clerk is performed (the value returned by time server 3 is regarded to be faulty since it does not intersect with the majority, and is ignored). As a result, the clerk's time is set to be the intersection of time intervals from time server 1,2, and 4.

There are several components that comprise the DCE DTS:

- *Time clerk* is the client side of DTS. It runs on a client computer and keeps the computer's local time synchronised by asking a time server for the correct time and adjusting the local time accordingly.

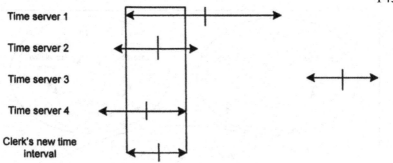

Figure 7.6: Time synchronisation using intervals

- *Time servers* are of three types. The local time server maintains the time synchronisation of a given LAN. The global time server and courier time servers are used to synchronise time among interconnected LANs. A time server synchronises with other time servers by asking these time servers for correct times and adjusts its time accordingly.

- *DTS API* provides an interface where application programs can access time information provided by the DTS.

Figure 7.7 shows the time synchronisation among time servers and clerks within a cell with multiple LANs. Within LAN 3, the time clerk synchronises its time by receiving (the dashed lines) time intervals from three time servers (time servers on computer 1, computer 2 and computer 3). The new time interval of the time clerk is then calculated from these received time intervals. Time synchronisation between the interconnected LANs (LAN 1, LAN 2 and LAN 3) are carried out by the global time servers within each LAN (the solid lines). An application (in Computer 4) accesses time information through the API provided by the DTS.

7.1.3.4 Distributed File Services

DCE uses its distributed file services (DFSs) to join the file systems of individual computers within a cell into a single file space. A uniform and transparent interface is provided for applications to accessing files located in the network. DFS is derived from the Andrew File System (AFS) [Satyanarayanan 1989]. It uses RPC for client-server communication, uses threads to enhance parallelism, relies on the DCE directory to locate servers, and uses DCE security services to protect from attackers.

DFS uses the client-server model. DFS clients, called cache managers, communicate with DFS servers using RPC on behalf of user applications. There are two types of DFS servers:

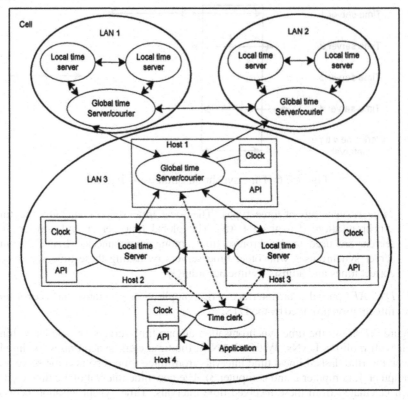

Figure 7.7: Time synchronisation within a multi-LAN cell

- A fileset location server which stores the locations of system and user files in DFS;

- A file server which manages files.

When a file is first accessed by an application from a computer, that computer's cache manager copies the file's first chunk (the default size is 64K bytes, so many files will be copied in their entirety) to its local disk (cache). Applications on that computer are then free to read and write the data on the cache. If multiple computers are caching the same chunk of a file, a somewhat elaborate token mechanism is used to maintain consistency among their caches.

A typical interaction between various components of DFS is shown in Figure 7.8, where the number represents steps:

Step 1: At first, the application issues a file request call to the cache manager in its computer;

Step 2: If the requested file is located in the local cache, the request is served using the local copy of the file. Otherwise, the cache manager locates the fileset location server through the CDS server (cell directory service, see Section 7.1.1);

Step 3: The location of the file server that stores the requested file is found through the fileset location server;

Step 4: Finally, the cache manager calls the file server and the file data is accessed.

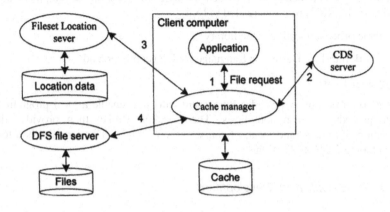

Figure 7.8: Interactions between DFS components

7.2 The DCE/RPC

In an application developed using DCE/RPC, a user accesses a distributed application program by interacting with a client program and the client program interacts with a server program (probably through the underlying structure) to perform the user's tasks. Usually a client program may have direct access to network brokers and server support tools, but may have no direct access to the underlying basic heterogeneous interconnect. A dashed line is used to mark the interaction between client programs and the basic heterogeneous interconnect.

The server programs are designed to perform specific functions and they can be located in any of the hosts of a computer network. Similar to a client program, a server program usually has direct access to network brokers and server support tools, but may have no direct access to the underlying basic heterogeneous interconnect.

The network brokers are used for locating server locations. At the beginning of a server program's execution, the server usually registers itself with location brokers. A client program then uses the location brokers to locate a server that it needs to communicate with. By using these location brokers, it is possible that server locations are transparent to user (client) programs.

The server support tools provide some facilities for simplifying distributed application programming and the heterogeneous interconnect provides the basic interconnection between heterogeneous computing systems.

7.2.1 DCE/RPC Facility

The following components are provided by DCE to assist the development and execution of the RPC programs related to DCE:

- Remote procedure call runtime library,

- Network Interface Definition Language (NIDL) compiler, and

- Location Broker.

The RPC runtime library provides the system calls that enable a local program to execute procedures on remote hosts. The Location Broker then provides the information of remote (and local, of course) servers. The NIDL compiler is a tool for developing DCE applications.

7.2.1.1 DCE Application Development

The process of a typical DCE application development might be as follows. At first, the programmer uses the NIDL language to write an *interface definition file* which defines all of the remote service interfaces (procedures). The programmer then compiles this definition using the NIDL compiler. In general, there are four output files for an interface definition, where two of them are client stubs (one is called a client stub and the other a client switch. We will describe them more fully later), one is a server stub, and the last one is an include file for the use of both client and server programs. The programmer then builds the server program, which implements the remote interfaces described in the interface definition, and the client program, which makes use of the remote procedures and other application functions (as well as providing a user interface). The formats for the remote procedure calls in the client program are defined in the interface definition. Finally, the server program is linked with the server stub and the client program is linked with the client stubs. Now the server program can run on a remote host and the client program running on a local host can execute the remote procedures in the same way as it requests local procedures.

The above process is for developing "non-replicated" client/server programs, that is, only one server is responsible for managing an object (eg, a database file). If we want to replicate a very important object in several locations, we need to develop "replicated" servers to manage these replicated objects. As these replicated servers need to communicate with each other to maintain the consistency of the replicated objects, a replicated server will have the function of both a server and a client program. That is, a replicated server needs to be linked with stub files provided for both server and client programs. This will cause naming conflicts between stub routines because the same procedure (service interface) names are defined in both server and client stub files.

The method used in DCE to solve this problem is to use two client stub files, one is called the client stub and the other the client switch [Kong 1990]. The client switch contains "public" procedure names (the same names defined in the interface definition file and can be referenced by client programs), while the client stub contains only "private" procedure names (these procedures have the same function as the public procedures) that are not visible outside the stub program.

To build an ordinary (non-replicated) client, both the client stub and client switch files are linked with the client program. An RPC call in the client program will then go to the client stub, the client switch, and then to the particular procedure. To build a replicated server, only the client stub (of course, the server stub as well) needs to be linked with the server program. An RPC call in the server program will then go to the client stub directly, and then to the particular procedure.

7.2.1.2 Location Broker

Note that we did not mention the Location Broker above. A small and specific application needn't have recourse to the Location Broker because the client program knows where the remote services are located. The Location Broker is very useful in general, however. Usually, a server program must register all of its services with the Location Broker. The client program can then find the service through the Location Broker. After the client finds the location of the service, it then calls the service directly. This is called *unbound* (or *allocated*) calling. DCE also supports other calling semantics, such as *bound-to-host* and *fully bound* calls [Kong 1990].

There are two kinds of location brokers, one called the *Global Location Broker* (GLB) and the other called the *Local Location Broker* (LLB), respectively. The LLB provides the services information for its local host, and the GLB provides the services information for the whole network. When the difference between these location brokers is not important, we will use the term *Location Broker* (LB) to refer to them. There are some system calls provided by DCE to manage the location brokers. Because there may be many services registered in a Location Broker, a unique naming facility called the Universal Unique Identifier (UUID) is employed. Each service has to be assigned a UUID before it is registered with the LB. These UUIDs are used by DCE to distinguish one service from another.

7.2.1.3 RPC Handle

In DCE, an object is an entity manipulated by well-defined operations. Each object is identified by an object UUID. On the other hand, the RPC runtime library is implemented on the basis of sockets. When a client makes a remote procedure call, requesting that a particular operation be performed on a particular object, the RPC runtime library needs some information about the object and server. This information is represented by an *RPC handle*. DCE provides several system calls to create and manage handles. After a handle is bound to a server, the client can use this handle to access the server. An RPC handle can be in three states:

- Unbound (or allocated).

- Bound-to-host.

- Bound-to-server (or fully bound).

If a client knows an object's UUID (and, of course, its interface operations), but does not know its location, an unbound handle can be used. When the client uses this handle to make a remote procedure call to request a particular operation on the object, the runtime library broadcasts a message to all hosts on the local network. Any host which supports the operation on the object may respond to the request. The caller runtime library then accepts the first response as the one it requested. After that, the handle becomes fully bound to that server.

If a client knows an object's UUID and the host on which it is located, a bound-to-host handle can be used. When the client uses this handle to make a remote procedure call, the runtime library sends a message to the host's Location Broker. If the requested interface is registered on the Location Broker, the proper server will get this message and respond to the client. Again, the handle becomes fully bound after this call.

If a client knows an object's UUID, its host, and its server address, then a fully bound handle can be used. When the client uses this handle to make a remote procedure call, the runtime library sends a message directly to the socket address of the handle.

7.2.1.4 Concurrent Programming Support

In addition to the RPC runtime library, NIDL compiler, and Location Broker, the Apollo also provides a Concurrent Programming Support (CPS) software tool to support the execution of DCE. This tool consists of four classes of system calls:

- *Task* programming calls that create and manage multitasking environments.

- *Eventcount* system calls that create and manage eventcounts for synchronising programming events.

- *Mutex* programming calls that provide applications with mutual exclusion, resource-sharing and synchronisation

- *Pfm* programming calls that control signals, faults, and exceptions for faults.

A distributed program in DCE can be functionally divided into two parts: the server part and the client part. Each part can be located on any host in the network. Usually, a server part manages an object, and a client part accesses the object by using the remote procedures provided by the server. An RPC-oriented program (in short, an *RPC program*) may consist of several servers and clients, and all these parts of the program work together concurrently on the programmer's task. A server or client can fork to several processes if necessary.

After a programmer compiles his interface definition with the NIDL compiler, the source code for the server and client stubs are generated, and their object files linked with the server and client programs respectively. When a remote procedure call is issued in the client program, it actually goes to the client stub, which then communicates with the server stub (if the server's address is known). Then the procedure implementing the required service is called by the server stub, and the return data are transferred through the server and client stubs back to the client program. The RPC runtime library contains the routines, tables, and data that support the communication of remote procedure calls between server and client stubs.

7.2.2 Related Tools

In DEC workstations running the Ultrix operating system (similar to BSD UNIX), the DCE/RPC tools are located in the /etc/ncs directory. We will first describe how to set up location brokers and then describe the use of the lb_admin and uuid_gen tools.

Usually the global and local location brokers are set up by system programmers. On a LAN, there can be more than one global location broker and on each workstation there should be a local location broker. As the DEC's Ultrix system only uses non-replicated global location brokers, this means only one global location broker can be set up in a LAN. A global location broker can be executed on any host of the LAN. The non-replicated global location broker is invoked by

> /etc/ncs/nrglbd

and the local location broker is invoked by

> /etc/ncs/llbd

These programs are better invoked when the system is booted.

A tool called lb_admin is used to manage the information stored in these location brokers. UUIDs are used in these brokers for identifying different server objects. Actually, a server object is uniquely identified to location brokers by:

> (object, type, interface, socket address)

where object, type and interface are UUIDs and socket address consists of a host name and a port number.

With lb_admin, you can select to use either global or local location brokers. After you selected this (default is local), the location broker remains unchanged until your next selection. The tool is invoked by

> /etc/ncs/lb_admin

Then the tool prompts lb_admin: and waits for your command. The main commands are:

```
r[egister]                register a server object
u[nregister]              delete a server object
us[e_broker]              change location broker (local or global)
l[ookup]                  look up the stored objects
q[uit]                    exit
h[elp]                    help
```

The uuid_gen program is used to generate a UUID. It is useful when programming a server's NIDL interface definition file. In that case, you may need to specify the UUIDs for your server object. It is invoked by

> /etc/ncs/uuid_gen

The program then prints out a new UUID.

7.2.3 Exception Handling

In each RPC call, there is a parameter used specially for the return status (usually it is the last parameter). It is a data type of status_$t, defined as follows:

```
typedef union {
  struct {
    unsigned fail : 1,
             subsys : 7,
             mode : 8;
    short    code;
  } s;
  long all;
} status_$t;
```

Usually only the all field is considered. It reports the return status of the remote procedure call. If this field is not equal to status_$ok, an internal defined constant, then there may have been something wrong during the call. A client program may receive the following three classes of errors when using RPCs:

- Communication errors.

- Server-failure errors.

- Interface mismatch errors.

When the underlying communication facility fails, the client's remote call may fail to reach the server or may fail to receive the response from the server. This failure is indicated by the rpc_$comm_failure status in the status return of the call. To overcome this, the client program may try to find another server with the same service.

If a server process crashes while handling a remote call, a failure status is returned to the calling client. In this case, the error is signalled in the same manner as if the server had been locally linked with the client.

If the version of an interface used to generate the server stub file is not identical to the version of the interface used to generate the client stub and switch files, an interface mismatch error occurs. This is because in the NIDL interface definition, one can set a version number to indicate a change in the interface. After a change, new server and client stubs are generated and should be linked with both server and client programs. One cannot recover from this error. The only remedy is to re-build the out-of-date client or server.

Apart from checking status returned, one can use *cleanup handlers* to catch RPC errors. The RPC runtime library always signals a failure if an error occurs during a remote procedure call. This signal invokes the topmost cleanup handler on a handler stack set up by the user program.

The pfm_$cleanup system call is used to set a cleanup handler. If the operating system detects a fault while a cleanup handler is set, it first "unwinds" the process stack to the most recent pfm_$cleanup call and releases that cleanup handler. The system then returns from the pfm_$cleanup call with the status value for the error that caused the failure. Program execution then continues with the code immediately following the pfm_$cleanup call. This will usually be code that handles the fault.

The code should first test the return value of the pfm_$cleanup call to see if the handler is set. If it is not set (that is, this cleanup handler has been released by the operating system), some error must have occurred and the error handling code can be executed. If an RPC call is successful, a pfm_$rls_cleanup call should be used to release the cleanup handler set before the RPC call. In that case the previous cleanup handler will become the topmost one, and will be invoked if a subsequent RPC call fails. It is good practice to enclose all important RPC calls with the pfm_$cleanup and pfm_$rls_cleanup calls.

7.3 SUN/RPC

Sun RPC was designed for client-server communication in the Sun NFS network file system. Sun RPC is sometimes called ONC (Open Network Computing) RPC. It is supplied as a part of the various Sun and other UNIX operating systems and is also available with other NFS insallations.

7.3.1 Interface Definition Language

The Sun RPC system provides an interface language called XDR and an interface compiler called *rpcgen* which is intended for use with the C programming language.

The Sun XDR language, which was originally designed for specifying external data representations, was extended to become an interface definition language. It may be used to define a service interface for Sun RPC by specifying a set of procedure definitions together with supporting type definitions. The features of the Sun XDR language can be summarized as follows:

• Most languages allow interface names to be specified, but Sun RPC does not - instead of this, a program number and a version number are supplied. The program numbers can be obtained from a central authority to allow every program to have its own unique number. The version number changes when a procedure signature changes. Both program and version number are passed in the request message, so that client and server can check that they are using the same version.

- A procedure definition specifies a procedure signature and a procedure number. The procedure number is used as a procedure identifier in request messages. It would be possible for the interface compiler to generate procedure identifiers.

- Only a single input parameter is allowed. Therefore, procedures requiring multiple parameters must include them as components of a single structure.

- The output parameters of a procedure are returned via a single result.

- The procedure signature consists of the result type, the name of the procedure, and the type of the input parameter. The type of both the result and the input parameter may specify either a single value or a structure containing several values.

The interface definition language provides a notation for defining constants, typedefs, structures, enumerated types, unions and programs. Typedefs, structures and enumerated types use the C language syntax. The interface compiler *rpcgen* can be used to generate the following from an interface definition:

- Client stub procedures;

- Server main procedure, dispatcher and server stub procedures;

- XDR marshalling and unmarshalling procedures for use by the dispatcher and client and server stub procedures.

A client stub file that contains one stub procedure for each procedure defined in the interface definition file can be created by *rpcgen*. A client stub procedure name is the name of the procedure given in the interface definition, converted to lowercase and with an underscore and the version number appended. The name of the client stub file is formed by taking the base name of the input file to *rpcgen* and adding a *_clnt.c* suffix.

A server stub file that contains the *main* routine, the *dispatcher* routine, and one stub procedure for each procedure defined in the interface definition file plus a null procedure can be generated by *rpcgen*. The *main* routine creates the transport handles and registers the service. The default is to register the program on both the UDP and TCP transports. However, a user can select which transport to use with a command-line option to *rpcgen*. The *dispatcher* routine dispatches incoming remote procedure calls to the appropriate procedure. The name used for the dispatch routine is formed by mapping the program name to lowercase characters and appending an underscore followed by the version number. The name of the server stub file is formed by taking the base name of the input file to rpcgen and adding a *_svc.c* suffix.

An XDR filters file can be produced by *rpcgen* to contain XDR marshalling and unmarshalling procedures. These procedures are used by the client and server stub procedures. The name of this file is formed by taking the base name of the input file to *rpcgen* and adding a *_xdr.c* suffix.

Now using the files generated by *rpcgen,* an RPC application is created in the following steps:

1. The application programmer manually writes the client program and server program for the application.

2. The client program file is compiled to get a client object file.

3. The server program file is compiled to get a server object file.

4. The client stub file and the XDR filters file are compiled to get a client stub object file.

5. The server stub file and the XDR filters file are compiled to get a server stub object file.

6. The client object file, the client stub object file, and the client-side RPC runtime library are linked together to get the client executable file.

7. The server object file, the server stub object file, and the server-side RPC runtime library are linked together to get the server executable file.

7.3.2 *Security Services*

Sun RPC supports the following three types of authentication (often referred to as *flavors*):

- *No authentication.* This is the default type. In this case, no attempt is made by the server to check a client's authenticity before executing the requested procedure. Consequently, clients do not pass any authentication parameters in request messages.

- *UNIX-style authentication.* This style is used to restrict access to a service to a certain set of users. In this case, the uid and gid of the user running the client program are passed in every request message, and based on this authentication information, the server decides whether to execute the requested procedure or not.

- *DES-style authentication.* Data Encryption Standard (DES) is an encryption technique. In DES-style authentication, each user has a globally unique name called *netname.* The *netname* of the user running the client program is passed in encrypted form in every request message. On the server side, the encrypted *netname* is first decrypted and then the server uses the information in *netname* to decide whether to execute the requested procedure or not.

The DES-style authentication is recommended for users who need more security than UNIX-style authentication. RPCs using DES-style authentication are also referred to as *secure RPC.*

Clients have the flexibility to select any of the above three authentication flavors for an RPC. The type of authentication can be specified when a client handle is created. It is possible to use a different authentication mechanism for different remote procedures within a distributed aplication by setting the authentication type to the flavor desired before doing the RPC.

7.3.3 Some Issues

7.3.3.1 Call Semantics

Sun RPC supports at-least-once semantics. After sending a request message, the RPC runtime library waits for a timeout period for the server to reply before retransmitting the request. The number of retries is the total time to wait divided by the timeout period. The total time to wait and the timeout period have default values of 25 and 5 seconds, respectively. These default values can be set to different values by the users. Eventually, if no reply is received from the server within the total time to wait, the RPC runtime library returns a timeout error.

7.3.3.2 Exception Handling

The RPC runtime library of Sun RPC has several procedures for processing detected errors. The server-side error-handling procedures typically send a reply message back to the client side, indicating the detected error. However, the client-side error-handling procedures provide the flexibility to choose the error-reporting mechanism. That is, errors may be reported to users either by printing error messages to *stderr* or by returning strings containing error messages to clients.

7.3.3.3 Client-Server Binding

Sun RPC does not have a networkwide binding service for client-server binding. Instead, each node has a local binding agent called *portmapper* that maintains a database of mapping of all local services (as mentioned earlier, each service is identified by its program number and version number) and their port numbers. The *portmapper* runs at a well-known port number on every node.

When a server starts up, it registers its program number, version number, and port number with the local *portmapper*. When a client wants to do an RPC, it must first find out the port number of the server that supports the remote procedure. For this, the client makes a remote request to the *portmapper* at the server's host, specifying the program number and version number. This means that a client must specify the host name of the server when it imports a service interface. In effect, this means that Sun RPC has no location transparency.

The procedure clnt_create is used by a client to import a service interface. It returns a client handle that contains the necessary information for communicating with the corresponding server port, such as the socket descriptor and socket address.

The client handle is used by the client to directly communicate with the server when making subsequent RPCs to procedures of the service interface.

7.3.4 Critiques of Sun RPC

In spite of its popularity, some of the criticisms made against Sun RPC are as follows:

1. Sun RPC lacks location transparency because a client has to specify the host name of the server when it imports a service interface.

2. The interface definition language of Sun RPC does not allow a general specification of procedure arguments and results. It allows only a single argument and a single result. This requirement forces multiple arguments or return values to be packaged as a single structure. While DCE RPC IDL allows a completely general specification of procedure arguments and results.

3. Sun RPC is not transport independent and the transport protocol is limited to either UDP or TCP. However, a transport-independent version of Sun RPC, known as TI-RPC (transport-independent RPC), has been developed by Sun-soft, Inc. TI-RPC provides a simple and consistent way in which transports can be dynamically selected depending upon user preference and the availability of the transport.

4. In UDP, Sun RPC messages are limited to 8 kilobytes length.

5. Sun RPC supports only at-least-once call semantics, which may not be acceptable for some applications. DCE RPC supports at-most-once semantics.

6. Sun RPC does not have a networkwide client-server binding service, while DCE RPC does.

7. Sun RPC does not include any integrated facility for threads in the client or server, although Sun OS has a separate threads package.

7.4 The Simple RPC

One of the problems of existing RPC systems is that they are very complex and not easy to use. A programmer has to get many preparations before he can make use of an RPC system for his distributed programming. This is typically true when an RPC system is been used for teaching purpose. The Simple RPC (SRPC) was developed by one of our authors in 1992 to overcome the complexity problem. Its source can be downloaded from: http://www.it.deakin.edu.au/~wanlei/srpcv1_1.tar.Z.

7.4.1 An Introduction of SRPC

SRPC is a simple remote procedure call (RPC) system. The main design purpose is to understand basic RPC principles and to serve as a tool for further research and development. The system is small, simple, expandable and concise. It is easy to understand and easy to use. The SRPC only contains the essential features of an RPC system, such as a location server and a stub generator, among other things. Two features are left for further expanding: the concurrent processing of client calls within a server, and the use and representation of complex data types and structures.

Apart from simplicity, another interesting feature of SRPC system is that, the stub compiler (we call it *stub and driver generator,* or SDG in short) not only produces the server and client stubs, but also creates remote procedures' framework, *makefile,* and driver programs for both server and client. So, after using this make utility, a user can test the program's executability by simply executing the server and client driver programs.

The client/server model is used in SRPC programs. So an SRPC program has two parts: a server part and a client part. The server part is composed of a server driver, a stub, and a file which implements all the remote procedures (called *procedure file*). The server part (or a server program as it is sometimes called) is a "forever" running program which resides on a host and awaits calls from clients.

The client part (or a client program) consists of a driver and a stub. It runs on a host (usually a different host from the server's host) and makes calls to the server by using the remote procedures exported by the server.

When the client driver makes a call, it goes to the client stub. The client stub then makes use of the Internet entity of the client host for sending the calling message to the Internet entity of the server's host. At the server side, the Internet entity will send the calling message to the server stub. The server stub then reports the call to the server and an appropriate procedure defined in the procedures file is executed. The result of the call follows the calling route in reverse, through the server stub, the Internet entity of the server host, the Internet entity of the client host, and the client stub, and backs to the client driver.

The pre-condition of the above calling is that the client knows the address of the server before the call. With the help of a location server (LS), the run-time address of a server can be easily accessed.

One typical scenario of SRPC programs using LS can be described below: When the server is started, it first registers its location to the LS and then waits for clients' calls. The clients know the server by a name (character string) defined by the user. When a client is invoked, it consults the LS for the server's location. After the location is found, the client then can make any number of RPC calls to that server by using the obtained location. If a "shutdown" call is issued by a client program, the server un-registers itself from the LS and exits from the system.

SRPC is implemented by using Internet socket. So it can be used on any BSD-like operating systems, such as BSD4.2, BSD4.3, Ultrix and other similar UNIX systems.

7.4.2 Installation

The distributed version is the SRPC version 1.1. It consists of a compressed file called `srpcv1_1.tar.Z`. The following steps can be used to install it:

1. Make a sub-directory called `srpc` (or whatever you want to call it). Copy the compressed file `srpcv1_1.tar.Z` into this directory. Also make a `lib` sub-directory (at the same level as `srpc`) if you have no such directory.

2. Uncompress the file:

   ```
   uncompress -v srpcv1_1.tar
   ```

3. Un-tar the file:

   ```
   tar -xf srpcv1_1.tar
   ```

4. Make library files:

   ```
   make_lib
   ```

5. Make stub and driver program generator:

   ```
   make -f mkdrpc
   ```

6. Make Location Server (LS):

   ```
   make -f mkloc
   ```

Now the SRPC system is ready to use.

7.4.3 The SRPC System Architecture

SRPC version 1.1 has three components: a library, a Location Server and a Stub and Driver Generator.

7.4.3.1 The System Library

One of the advantages of using RPC systems is that a user does not need to know the implementation details of remote procedures. The user only needs to call a pre-defined remote procedure like he/she calls a local procedure.

The system library is one way to achieve the transparency. The library contains all the low-level and system-oriented calls. Its main function is to make the low-level facilities transparent to the upper-level programs. So the stub and driver programs of both server and client will not deal with their Internet entities directly.

The library is named `asIsc.a` and is located in the `lib` directory. It must be linked to the server and client programs respectively.

There are three source files:

> `asI.h` Header file

`asIsc.c` Main source file

`make_lib` Shell file for making the library

All the library calls can be divided into the following call levels (in the up-down order):

- *SRPC Level* is the highest level. It contains calls that deal with RPC-related operations.

- *Remote Operation Level* contains calls that deal with remote operations. These remote operations follow the definitions of OSI Application level primitives.

- *Socket Level* contains calls that deal with socket level operations.

- *Utility Level* contains all the utility calls used in different levels.

The System Calls section of the SRPC Programmer's Manual lists all the library calls.

7.4.3.2 The Location Server

Another way of hiding the implementation details is the use of the Location Server (LS). LS is used to hide server locations from a user. It is executed before any other SRPC program is started. After that, it resides on a host and awaits calls from servers and clients.

A location of a server in SRPC can be expressed in a triple:

`(host, port, protocol)`

where the `host` is the host name or address on which the server is running, the `port` is the socket port number of the server and the `protocol` is the protocol used in client-server communication. The host name and address is assigned by system programmers. The port number can be an integer greater than 1024 (lower port numbers are reserved by the operating system and other system utilities). The protocols used in SRPC are Internet stream and Internet datagram.

LS uses a "well-known" address. By default, it is assigned to

`(137.132.87.2, 5010, "Internet_stream").`

A maintenance tool is also provided to maintain the location database of the location server. It provides calls to register, to un-register, and to locate an entry of the database. It also can be used to list all the database entries and shut down the location server.

LS is also implemented by using the SRPC system. Following files are related to the location server:

`loc.def`	LS server definition file (refer to next section for the details of server definition files)
`loc.h`	LS header file
`locSer.c`	LS server driver program

```
locStubSer.c  LS server stub
locOps.c      LS remote procedures
locCli.c      LS client driver program
locStubCli.c  LS client stub
mkloc         LS make file
```

After using command:

```
make -f mkloc
```

two executable files are created:

```
locSer        LS server
locCli        LS maintenance program
```

By default, `locSer` must be executed on host 137.132.87.2 (`sun.iscs.nus.sg`), but this can be changed by editing the LS header file `loc.h` and library call header file `asI.h,` and re-compile the library and location server by using the above commands. You can change the following two definitions in both `loc.h` and `asI.h` files to suit your own needs:

```
#define LOCATIONSERVERHOST "137.132.87.2"
#define LOCATIONSERVERPORT 5010
```

In order to register to the LS, a server has to provide its location to the LS, with the port number as an optional. If the registering server has no port number, the LS will assign it one. The assignment range is from 5050 to 9999. Each time one number is assigned, the LS adds 1 to the number. If the number reaches 9999, the next number will start again from 5050.

Usually there should be one LS (or equivalent entity) running on each host for most existing RPC systems. In that case the LS's location can also be hidden from users. Also, multiple LSs may have the potential of offering a fault-tolerant system. We only use one LS in SRPC because the simplicity is one of our design priorities. We feel the sacrifice is not too much because the SRPC only needs to be installed once on a network and that is the only place that one has to know the location of the LS.

7.4.4   The Stub and Driver Generator

7.4.4.1 Syntax

The purpose of the stub and driver program generator is to generate stubs and driver programs for server and client programs according to Server Definition Files (SDF). Listing 7.1 is the syntax of a server definition file:

Listing 7.1: Server definition file syntax

```
<SDF> ::= BBEGIN
<HEADER>
[ <CONST> ]
<FUNCS>
BEND
```

```
<HEADER> ::= Server Name: variable ;
Comment: string ;
Communication Protocol: variable ;
[ Client Port: integer ;]
[ Server Host: string ;
Server Port: integer ;]
<CONST> ::= constant
<FUNCS> ::= RPC Functions: <RPCS>
<RPCS> ::= <RPC> { <RPC> }
<RPC> ::= Name: string ; <PARAMS>
<PARAMS> ::= { <PARAM> }
<PARAM> ::= Param: <CLASS>: declarator ;
<CLASS> ::= in | out
```

We use a modified BNF to denote the syntax of definition files. In this notation, non-terminals are denoted in brackets < and > , and terminals are denoted as in normal font, while the symbol ::= denotes "defined as". Three operators are involved, namely:

1. the construct { x } means that x is replaced an arbitrary number of times,

2. the construct [x] means that x is optional, and

3. the construct x | y means that one of the items is selected.

The following notes apply to Listing 7.1.

1. The "variable", "integer", and "string" have the same meanings as in the C programming language.

2. The "constant" and "declarator" have the same meaning as in the C programming language (only character strings are allowed now).

3. Comments are allowed in the definition file. They are the same as in the C programming language (using /* and */).

7.4.4.2 Semantics

A server definition file is defined as a <HEADER> part followed by a <FUNCS> part. The <HEADER> includes a server's name, a comment string, a communication protocol, a client port number, a server host name or address, and a server port number. The last two parts are optional.

The server's name is defined as a variable in the C language. This name will be used in many places. For example, when a client asks the LS to locate a server, it provides the server's name defined here. The name is also used as a prefix in naming all the files generated by the SDG.

The comment string usually specifies what the server is going to do. The comment string is stored with the server registering message. By looking at this string, one can determine the purpose of the server.

The communication protocol part is used to define which communication protocol is to be used. Currently only Internet stream and Internet datagram protocols are allowed.

The client port is necessary only if the Internet datagram protocol is defined. For Internet stream protocol, this part is not used. A port number of greater than 5050 is recommended if the client port part is to be defined.

The server host part, together with the server port number part, is optional. It defines on which host the server is going to run. It can be defined as a host name (such as sun.iscs.nus.sg) or a host address (such as 137.132.87.2).

The server port part defines on which port the server is going to listen. It is usually larger than 1024 and less than, say, 10000. Note that the port number 5010 is reserved by the LS server. For safety reasons, the users are suggested to use port numbers that are larger than 5050.

The <CONST> part is optional. It defines constants used in remote procedures. The format is the same as in C language.

The <FUNCS> part defines the remote procedures of the server. At least one remote procedure must be defined. Each remote procedure is defined as a name part and a parameter (<PARAMS>) part. The name of a remote procedure is simply a variable. There can be zero or several parameters, each consisting of a class and a declaration. The class can be *in* or *out,* which tells the SRPC system that the parameter is used for input or output, respectively. The declaration part is the same as in the C language. In this version, only a simple character string is allowed in parameter definitions.

7.4.5   Implementation

The generator has the following five source files:

sersers.h	Header file.
autopre.h	Header file.
autopre.c	Pre-processing module.
autodp.c	Main module of the generator.
mkdrpc	Make file.

When executing command

```
make -f mkdrpc
```

the generator's executable file "autodp" will be created.

After a programmer sends a server definition file to the generator, the generator first does syntax checking. If no errors are found, several program source files and a makefile are generated.

The subsequent processing is specified by the makefile. That is, when using the make utility, the executable files of both the server and client will be generated. By default, if there is no Server Host and Server Port definition in an SDF file, the SDG generated server driver will register itself to the LS at the beginning and un-register itself before exiting from the system. The SDG generated client driver then will locate the server through the LS before making an RPC call. If there are above definitions in an SDF file, the SDG generated server driver will not register itself to the LS server and therefore there will be no un-registering before it exits. For the corresponding client driver, there will be no locating operation before calling. It will call the RPC directly because the client driver knows the server address already.

7.4.6 An Application Example

For example, suppose we have a server definition file called sf.def (it is included with the distribution). It defines a "send-and-forward" system in that the server acts as a message storage and the client acts as both message sender and receiver. Listing 7.2 is the server definition file:

Listing 7.2: Server definition file example

```
/* Store and forward program's server definition file */
/* An example for SRPC system */
BEGIN
Server Name: sf;
Comment: Store and forward system;
Communication Protocol: internet_stream;
#define MAXNAMELEN 64
#define MAXMSGLEN 500
#define MAXSTRLEN 80
RPC Functions:
Name: storeMsg;
Param: in receiver: char receiver[MAXNAMELEN];
Param: in msg: char msg[MAXMSGLEN];
Param: out stat: char stat[MAXSTRLEN];
Name: forwardMsg;
Param: in receiver: char receiver[MAXNAMELEN];
Param: out msg: char msg[MAXMSGLEN];
Name: listMsg;
END
```

Three remote procedures are defined in this SDF file. As there are no Server Host and Server Port definitions, the server program is going to run on any host and the LS will be responsible for assigning a server port to the server during the server's registration. The following command will produce the appropriate stub and driver files:

```
autodp sf.def
```

The generated files are:

sf.h	Header file, must be included by both server and client stubs.
sfSer.c	Server driver file.
sfStubSer.c	Server stub file.
sfOps.c	Frameworks of server procedures file.

sfCli.c	Client driver file.
sfStubCli.c	Client stub file.
makefile	Make file.

After using the make utility (simply use "make" command), two executable files are created:

sfSer	Server program.
SfCli	Client program.

Note that the sfOps.c file only defines the frameworks of the remote procedures. Their details are to be programmed by the programmer. A sample programming of these remote procedures is listed in file sfops.c. So you can simply copy this file to sfOps.c.

The server driver is simple. It does the initialisation first. Then it loops "forever" to process incoming calls until the client issues a "shutdown" call. In that case the server exits. The incoming calls are handled by the server stub and underlying library functions.

The generated client driver can execute the server's remote procedures one-by-one. If the server driver is running and the client driver is invoked, the client driver then first lists all the remote procedures provided by the server, and asks the user to choose from the list. After the selection, the input parameters of the named remote procedure are then input from the keyboard. After that, the driver program does some initialisation and the remote procedure is executed and the returned results are displayed. The actual calling and displaying are handled by the client stub and underlying library functions.

The termination of the server program also needs to be mentioned. After the server program is started, it will run forever unless the programmer kills its process or there exists a facility to terminate the server. Here we provide a facility to do that job. We add a "remote shutdown" procedure into the server, and allow the remote shutdown of the server in the server program. Hence when the client driver calls the remote shutdown procedure of the server, the server will shut down itself and exit from the system.

7.5 Remote Method Invocation (RMI)

7.5.1 RMI Architecture

Java Remote Method Invocation (RMI) is a simple, yet powerful, Java-based framework for distributed object design and implementation. A remote invocation is a form of the RPC, where procedures can be invoked from remote machines. Java RMI extends the RPC further to the distributed objects' world, that is, RMI permits executing methods of objects residing on remote machines, with results returned to the calling environment.

RMI is a higher level abstraction than servers. In client-server computing, we typically develop an application level protocol to communicate between Java clients and servers, but with RMI we do not need to do this as RMI takes care of communication details for us. Using RMI is as simple as invoking a method of an object.

Figure 7.9 shows the RMI architecture in which a Java client invokes a remote Java server object.

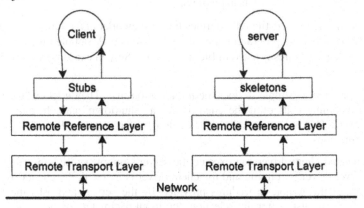

Figure 7.9: The RMI architecture

A client RMI call invokes the client-side stub (the proxy of the remote method that resides on the client's machine). The stub uses *Object Serialization* to marshal the arguments, i.e., render argument object values into a stream of bytes that can be transmitted over a network. The stub then passes control to the Java Virtual Machine's RMI layer. The skeleton on the server side dispatches the call to the actual remote object after unmarshaling the arguments into variables in memory. The stub and skeleton programs are generated by the *rmic* compiler.

The Remote Reference layer permits various protocols for remote invocation, such as unicast point-to-point (the one currently has been implemented).

Before a remote object can be accessed, it has to be registered into the naming server. The RMI framework provides a simple naming service. Remote objects can register to the naming server using the *java.rmi.Naming* class with a URL-like naming scheme.

7.5.2 RMI Implementation

The key interfaces and classes in RMI are:

- *Remote* is an interface in the *java.rmi* package. It defines all remote interfaces.

- RMI server functions are provided by the *RemoteObject* and its subclasses.

- *RemoteServer* is a subclass of *RemoteObject.*

- *UnicastRemoteObject* is a subclass of *RemoteObject* in the *java.rmi.server* package.

- *RemoteException* is a class in the *java.rmi* package, used for RMI to throw exceptions at runtime.

The RMI implementation involves the following steps:

- Defining the remote interface. This is the interface through which remote clients will access the server and is done by extending the *Remote* interface and defining methods that can be invoked remotely.

- Implementing the remote interface. Remote method calls will ultimately be made upon their implementations. The interface is normally implemented via the extending of the *UnicastRemoteObject* class. The *UnicastRemoteObject* class defines a remote object which is valid when the server is running. This object hides the implementation of the interface from the public interface and can contain some methods that are not visible through the interface. Any remote object passed as an argument to RMI must also be defined as an interface.

- Creating stubs and skeletons using *rmic* compiler.

- Compiling the remote interface and implementation file using *javac* compiler.

- Creating a client program, either a pure Java application or an applet and the HTML page to invoke the server services.

A Simple RMI Example

This example creates a simple date server to provide the date and time information to clients. The first step is to define the server interface, named `DateServer`, that lists all methods a client can call. In this example, only one method is defined. Here is the Java program `DateServer.java`:

```
import java.rmi.Remote;
import java.rmi.RemoteException;
import java.util.Date;

public interface DateServer extends Remote {
  public Date getDate () throws RemoteException;
}
```

Note that the *getDate()* method must throw a *RemoteException* to allow the program to detect problems occurred in remote invocation. The second step is to implement the remote object interface, through the program `DateServerImpl.java`:

```
import java.rmi.*;
import java.rmi.server.*;
import java.util.Date;

public class DateServerImpl extends UnicastRemoteObject implements
DateServer {
```

```
  public DateServerImpl () throws RemoteException {
  }

  public Date getDate () {
    return new Date ();
  }

  public static void main (String[] args) throws Exception {
    DateServerImpl dateServer = new DateServerImpl ();
    System.out.println("Registering to Name Server");
    Naming.bind ("Date Server", dateServer);
    System.out.println("Registered!");
  }
}
```

All remote object implementations must extend *RemoteObject* or one of its subclasses (such as the *UnicastRemoteObject,* provided by the JDK for implementing TCP-based client-server programs). The *getDate()* method simply returns the date information of the server host. The *main()* method creates a new *DateServerImpl* named *dateServer* and registers it to the RMI naming registry using the name of "Date Server". If the name is already registered, then an *AlreadyBoundException* will be raised. To overcome this, we could use the *rebind()* method instead of the *bind()* method.

The third step is to generate the stub and the skeleton programs:

```
        rmic DateServerImpl
```

The two classes *(DateServerImpl_Stub.class* and *DateServerImpl_Skel.class)* will be generated after the compilation.

The fourth step is to create the client program to access the services provided by the server. The client is named DateClient.java:

```
import java.rmi.Naming;
import java.util.Date;

public class DateClient {
  public static void main (String[] args) throws Exception {
    if (args.length != 1)
      throw new IllegalArgumentException ("Syntax: DateClient
<hostname>");
    DateServer dateServer = (DateServer) Naming.lookup
      ("rmi://" + args[0] + "/Date Server");
    Date when = dateServer.getDate ();
    System.out.println (when);
  }
}
```

The client program uses the *lookup()* method of *java.rmi.Naming* to get the information of the "Date Server" from the registry. The *lookup()* method has two parameters, one provides the location of the registry and the other provides the name of the server.

The last step of using this simple RMI program is to run it via the following executions:

- Start the registry: *rmiregistry*

- Start the server: *java DateServerImpl*

- Start the client: *java DateClient localhost*

7.5.3 Interfaces and Classes

The main packages for the RMI framework are: *java.rmi, java.rmi.server, java.rmi.registry, java.rmi.dgc,* and *java.rmi.activation* (Java 1.2).

- *java.rmi:* provides the *Remote* interface, a class for accessing remote names, the *MarshalledObject* class, and a security manager for RMI.

- *java.rmi.registry:* provides classes and interfaces that are used by the remote registry.

- *java.rmi.server:* provides the classes and interfaces used to implement remote objects, stubs, and skeletons, and to support RMI communication. This package implements the bulk of the RMI API.

- *java.rmi.activation:* supports persistent object references and remote object activation.

- *java.rmi.dgc:* provides classes and interfaces that are used by the RMI distributed garbage collector.

7.6 An Interesting RMI Application

In this section we re-implement the messaging system of Section 6.4 using the RMI method.

Here we do not need to provide the application protocol in the messaging system when we use the RMI for the implementation. The client side application or applet save or retrieve messages simply through access to the remote object. Because the abstraction provided by RMI is at a higher level, the client can invoke the methods just like accessing the local object. This could simplify both server and client side program.

Generally, the RMI is treated as a service provided by the server to the clients. The service is named and bound to an object in the implementation. That is, a server is mainly provided by a single object, even though there are many service requests. Moreover, the clients of the messaging system need to interact in terms of addressing messages to each other. The server needs to provide depository to all the messages for all the clients rather than store a single message queue for a single user. As a result, users will be identified by an ID or username. This ID or username will be provided when a client enters the system or retrieves messages. Also, the client has to provide the list of recipients while the client wants to address a message to multiple users.

The message storage and retrieval is rather a passive service, that is, the server responses only after the client sends the request. The service is passive so that the service does not need to be implemented in threads. On the other hand, a client of the system has to update the username lists constantly because it needs to send messages to other users via the server. The service of query and retrieve of the latest username list have to be invoked constantly. Because the service is passive, the server cannot automatically send the username list to all users. However, the username list retrieval can be seen as a service. A client can invoke the service in every time frame, such as a tenth second. Therefore, a client should have a thread to handle the username list.

The interface remains the same as the implementation of multiple threads message server described in section 6.4. A text field is used for entering a message by the user. A text area is used to show the retrieved messages. A list is used to show the latest user list. Two buttons are used to store (send) message and retrieve messages, respectively.

There are three program files: RMIMessageClient.java, RMIMessageServer.java and RMIMessageServerImpl.java.

The file RMIMessageServer.java is the interface of remote objects and also the source of stub and sketch class.

```java
// RMIMessageServer.java
import java.io.*;
import java.net.*;
import java.util.Vector;
import java.rmi.*;

public interface RMIMessageServer extends Remote{
    public static final String REGISTRY_NAME="Message_Server";
    public int addUser(String username) throws RemoteException;
    public boolean userlistChanged() throws RemoteException;
    public String[] getUserlist() throws RemoteException;
    public void addMessage(String themessage,int[] recipients) throws
RemoteException;
    public String[] retrieveMessage(int recipient) throws
RemoteException;
    public void removeUser(int recipient) throws RemoteException;
}
```

The RMIMessageServerImpl.java is an implementation of RMIMessageServer.java, which carries out the actually functionalities.

```java
// RMIMessageServerImpl.java
import java.io.*;
import java.net.*;
import java.util.Vector;
import java.rmi.*;
import java.rmi.server.*;

public class RMIMessageServerImpl extends UnicastRemoteObject
implements RMIMessageServer{
    private int usernumber=0;
    private Vector messages=new Vector();
    private Vector userlist=new Vector();

    public RMIMessageServerImpl() throws RemoteException {
    }
```

```
public static void main(String[] argv) throws RemoteException{
    RMIMessageServerImpl messageserver=new RMIMessageServerImpl();
    try {
        Naming.rebind(REGISTRY_NAME,messageserver);
    }catch(Exception e){}
}

public int addUser(String username) throws RemoteException {
    System.out.println("new user joins in: "+username);
    userlist.add(new Integer(usernumber));
    userlist.add(username);
    Vector v=new Vector();
    messages.add(v);
    usernumber++;
    return(usernumber-1);
}

public boolean userlistChanged() throws RemoteException{
    return(true);
}

public String[] getUserlist() throws RemoteException{
    int size=userlist.size();
    String[] result=new String[size];
    for(int i=0;i<size;i=i+2)
        result[i]=((Integer)userlist.elementAt(i)).toString();
    for(int i=1;i<size;i=i+2)
        result[i]=(String)userlist.elementAt(i);
    return(result);
}

public void addMessage(String themessage,int[] recipients) throws
RemoteException{
    System.out.println("Received message: "+themessage);
    System.out.print("for users: ");
    for(int i=0;i<recipients.length;i++) {
        Integer usernumber=new Integer(recipients[i]);
        System.out.print(usernumber+" ");
        int index=userlist.indexOf(usernumber)/2;
        Vector v=(Vector)messages.elementAt(index);
        v.add(themessage);
    }
    System.out.println("");
}

public String[] retrieveMessage(int recipient) throws
RemoteException{
    System.out.println("Received request for message retrival,
user id "+recipient);
    Integer usernumber=new Integer(recipient);
    int index=userlist.indexOf(usernumber)/2;
    Vector v=(Vector)messages.elementAt(index);
    int size=v.size();
    String[] result=new String[size];
    for(int i=0;i<size;i++) {
        result[i]=(String)v.elementAt(i);
        System.out.println(result[i]);
    }
    System.out.println("Messages queue reset");
    v.clear();
    return(result);
}

public void removeUser(int recipient) throws RemoteException{
    Integer usernumber=new Integer(recipient);
    int index=userlist.indexOf(usernumber)/2;
    messages.remove(index);
```

```
         System.out.println("Remove user
"+(String)userlist.elementAt(index*2+1)+" from the list...");
         userlist.remove(index*2+1);
         userlist.remove(index*2);

    }
}
```

The RMIMessageClient.java is a Java application with graphical user interface provided by the frame.

```
// RMIMessageClient.java
import java.net.*;
import java.awt.*;
import java.awt.event.*;
import java.rmi.*;
import java.rmi.registry.*;

public class RMIMessageClient extends Frame implements Runnable,
ActionListener{
  TextField sendmessage=new TextField(40);
  TextArea returnmessage=new TextArea(15,40);
  List userlist=new List(10,true);
  Button store=new Button("  Store  ");
  Button retrival=new Button("Retrival");
  int id;
  String host,username;
  RMIMessageServer server;
  Thread thread;
  int[] idlist;
  String[] namelist;
  boolean firsttime=true;

  public RMIMessageClient(String host,String username) throws
Exception,NotBoundException {
    super("RMIMessageService--"+host+" Username:"+username);
    this.host=host;
    this.username=username;
    setLayout(new FlowLayout());
    add(sendmessage);
    add(store);
    add(returnmessage);
    add(retrival);
    add(userlist);
    store.addActionListener(this);
    retrival.addActionListener(this);
    pack();
    setSize(410,480);
    show();
    setVisible(true);
    this.addWindowListener(new WindowAdapter() {
      public void windowClosing(WindowEvent ev) {
        stop();
        dispose();
      }
    });
    server=(RMIMessageServer)Naming.lookup("rmi://"+host
      +"/Message_Server");
    thread=new Thread(this);
    thread.start();
    id=server.addUser(username);
    System.out.println(id);
  }

  public void run() {
    while(thread!=null) {
      try {
```

```
      String[] userliststring=server.getUserlist();
      int num=userliststring.length;
      boolean changed=true;
      if(firsttime) {
        firsttime=false;
      } else {
        if(num==(idlist.length)*2) {
          changed=false;
          for(int i=0;i<num-1;i+=2)
            changed=changed
              ||(idlist[i/2]!=Integer.parseInt(userliststring[i]));
        } else {
          changed=true;
        }
      }
      if(changed) {
        changed=true;
        userlist.removeAll();//retain selection on the list!
        idlist=new int[num/2];
        namelist=new String[num/2];
        for(int i=1;i<num;i+=2) {
          namelist[(i-1)/2]=userliststring[i];
          userlist.add(userliststring[i]);
        }
        for(int i=0;i<num-1;i+=2)
          idlist[i/2]=Integer.parseInt(userliststring[i]);
      }
      Thread.sleep(1000);
    }catch(Exception e){System.out.println(e);}
  }
}

public synchronized void stop() {
  try {
    server.removeUser(id);
  }catch(Exception e) {System.out.println(e);}
  if(thread!=null) {
    System.out.println("stop");
    thread.interrupt();
    thread=null;
    server=null;
  }
}

public void actionPerformed(ActionEvent e) {
  if(e.getSource()==store) {
    try {
      if((sendmessage.getText().length()>=1)
          &&(userlist.getSelectedIndexes().length>0)) {
        int[] tmplist=userlist.getSelectedIndexes();
        int[] tmpidlist=new int[tmplist.length];
        for(int i=0;i<tmplist.length;i++)
        tmpidlist[i]=idlist[tmplist[i]];
        server.addMessage(sendmessage.getText(),tmpidlist);
        sendmessage.setText("");
      }
    }catch(Exception ee) {System.out.println(ee);}
  } else if(e.getSource()==retrival) {
    try {
      returnmessage.setText("");
      String[] messages=server.retrieveMessage(id);
      for(int i=0;i<messages.length;i++)
      returnmessage.append(messages[i]+"\n");
    }catch(Exception ee){System.out.println(ee);}
  }
}

public static void main(String args[]) throws Exception {
```

```
    if(args.length!=2)
      throw new IllegalArgumentException("Syntax: java
        RMIMessageClient <host> <username)");
    RMIMessageClient client=new RMIMessageClient(args[0],args[1]);
  }
}
```

The following steps are used to compile the programs:

- Compile the server stub: javac RMIMessageServer.java

- Create the stub and the sketch classes: rmic RMIMessageServerImpl

- Compile the server implementation: javac RMIMessageServerImpl.java

- Compile the client application: javac RMIMessageClient.java

The following steps are used to run the system:

1. Run registry for RMI: rmiregistry

2. Start the server implementation: java RMIMessageServerImpl

3. Start the client application: java RMIMessageClient <host> <username>

7.7 Summary

In this chapter we discussed two commonly used RPC tools, the DCE/RPC and the SUN/RPC, and the Remote Method Invocation (RMI) in Java. First, we described applications of the client-server model in the development of an advanced distributed computing environment, DCE. DCE is built on top of existing operating systems and it hides the heterogeneity of underlying computers by providing an integrated environment for distributed computing. DCE consists of many integrated services, such as thread and RPC services, security services, directory services, time services, and distributed file services, that are necessary in performing client-server computing in a heterogeneous environment. Most of these services are implemented as individual servers or groups of co-operating servers. Application processes, that act as clients of DCE servers, obtain services from DCE servers. DCE RPC makes use of all the DCE features.

Sun RPC was designed for client-server communication in the Sun NFS network file system. It is supplied as a part of the various Sun and other UNIX operating systems. Despite its popularity, Sun RPC has some disadvantages most of which DCE RPC can overcome. Therefore, DCE RPC and Sun RPC are most commonly used RPC tools. In the chapter, we also introduced the SRPC system, which can overcome the complexity problem of existing RPC systems. The SRPC only contains the essential features of an RPC system, but is easy to understand and use.

We also introduced the Java Remote Method Invocation (RMI) in the chapter, because it is a simple, yet powerful, Java-based framework for distributed object design. A remote invocation is a form of the RPC, where procedures can be invoked from remote machines. Java RMI extends the RPC further to the distributed objects' world.

Exercises

7.1 What services can a DCE provide? 7.1.1

7.2 What is a cell in DCE? What are foreign cells? 7.1.1

7.3 How does one build a basic DCE application? 7.1.2

7.4 What is a CDS? What components does it have? Explain their purposes. 7.1.3

7.5 What services can a security server provide in DCE? 7.1.3.2

7.6 How does one calculate a DTS interval? Give an example. 7.1.3.3

7.7 How does one develop a replicated DCE program? Describe the process. 7.2.1

7.8 What types of handle does an RPC have? Explain their functions. 7.2.1

7.9 What is the lb_admin tool in DCE Ultrix system? 7.2.2

7.10 How does one use the `pfm_$cleanup` call to handle a failure in DCE? 7.2.3

7.11 How does one create a Sun RPC application using *rpcgen*? 7.3.1

7.12 What method is used in Sun RPC for building a client-server binding? 7.3.2

7.13 Can a Sun RPC system use a transport protocol rather than TCP and UDP? Why? 7.3.4

7.14 How many components does an SRPC have? How do they work? 7.4.1

7.15 What mechanism is used in an SRPC to achieve the call transparency? 7.4.3.1

7.16 How many location servers are there in an SRPC? 7.4.3.2

7.17 How does one use SDF and SDG to make an SRPC application and run it? 7.4.5-7.4.6

7.18 Re-write the server definition file in Listing 7.2 giving the specific server host and server port in order to run the server program on a particular machine. 7.4.6

7.19 What is an RMI? How does one implement it? 7.5.1-7.5.2

7.20 What are steps to write a client/server program using RMI? Design an RMI program in which the server provides the weekly course information to clients. 7.5.2

7.21 What components and their functions does the Java RMI package have? 7.5.3

7.22 Design an RMI application in which clients can calculate Math questions. 7.6

This page intentionally left blank

CHAPTER 8 GROUP COMMUNICATIONS

Group communication is highly desirable for maintaining a consistent state in distributed systems. Many existing protocols are quite expensive and of limited benefit for distributed systems in terms of efficiency. This chapter describes concepts and design techniques of group communication protocol including message ordering, dynamic assessment of membership and fault tolerance. The protocol ensures total ordering of messages and atomicity of delivery in the presence of communication failures and site failures, and guarantees that all operational members belonging to the same group observe a consistent view of ordered events. The dynamic membership and failure recovery algorithms can handle: site failures and recovery; group partitions and merges; members' dynamic join and leave procedures.

8.1 Introduction

Distributed systems providing overall services need careful design and implementation in order to preserve consistency of shared information among the cooperative processes and servers (such as mirror sites of web servers). Group communication is used to increase the availability of the systems. The key idea is to replicate system data/servers running on distributed computers. Achieving the correct function of the replicated servers requires all the members to have a consistent view of cooperative tasks in a group of servers. However, the underlying communication and distributed systems are imperfect and they are subject to a number of possible failures, such as site crashes and communication failures. The unreliable Internet communication medium may lose messages or reorder the messages. For example, the network may be partitioned into separate segments. Currently, the most practical systems use reliable multicast protocol to achieve a consistent view among operational processes. In this chapter, we focus on the local area network server group and we use a "Process" to denote such a member server process that runs the protocol on a site.

To see the usefulness of the reliable multicast protocol, consider, for example, a well-known "transaction commit problem" which arises in distributed database systems. The problem is for all the data manager processes that have participated in a particular transaction to agree on whether to install the transaction results in the database or discard them. Whatever decision is made, all data manager processes must make the same decision in order to preserve the consistency of the database. Reliable multicast, in contrast to *unicast* communication which involves a single source and a single destination, refers to a single source and a set of destinations. A multicast group is a collection of members that are the destinations of the same sequence of messages. The multicast protocol guarantees the following properties:

- *Ordering.* A sequence of delivered messages is identical at all operational receivers.

- *Atomicity.* A message issued by a sender either correctly reaches all operational receivers in a group or none of them.

- *Termination.* All non-faulty processes will finally deliver its messages within a finite number of message transmissions (this issue is difficult and we refer the interested readers to [Fischer et al 1985]).

A well-known approach to achieving a consistent view in a cooperating group in spite of failures is provided by the concept of reliable broadcast protocols [Chang and Maxemchuk 1984] [Birman et al 1991]. These protocols guarantee delivery of a sequence of messages to the group members in a specific order (e.g., total order). Multicast protocols can be exploited on all system levels. To demonstrate the usefulness of reliable group protocols on the application level, consider, for example, a parallel application. Typically, a number of processes cooperate to compute a single result. If one of the processes finds a partial result (e.g., a better bound in a parallel branch and bound program) it is desirable that this partial result is multicasted immediately to the other processes. By receiving this partial result as soon as possible, the other processes do not waste cycles on outdated computions.

8.2   Features of Group Communication

Group communication is an operating system abstraction that supports the programmer by offering convenience and clarity. This operating system abstraction must be distinguished from the message transmission mechanisms such as multicast (one-to-many physical entities connected by a network) or its special case broadcast (one-to-all physical entities connected by a network).

In group communication, a client sends a request to a group of servers which share a common group name and provide the desired services. This request is delivered following the semantics of an agreed primitive. The primitive should be constructed such that there is no difference between invoking a single server or a group of servers. This means that communication pattern transparency is provided to the programmer.

Thus, groups should be named in the same manner single processes are named. Each group is treated as one single entity; its internal structure and interactions are not shown to the users. The mapping of group names on multicast addresses is performed by an interprocess communication facility of an operating system and supported by a naming server. However, if multicast or even broadcast are not provided, group communication could be supported by one-to- one communication at the network level.

Communication groups are dynamic. This means that new groups can be created and some groups can be destroyed. A process can be a member of more than one group at the same time. It can leave a group or join another one.

In summary, group communication shares many design features with message passing and RPC. However, there are some issues which are very specific, and their knowledge could be of great value to the programmer of distributed computing systems and applications. Furthermore, group communication is characterised by basic policies and mechanisms to allow the programmer to implement an application. The following issues are of primary importance in group communication: *message delivery, response,* and *ordering.*

8.2.1 Message Delivery Semantics

Message delivery semantics relate to the successful delivery of a message to processes in a group. There are four choices of delivery semantics [Joyce and Goscinski 1997] [Wang and Zhou 1998a]:

- *Single (unreliable) delivery.* Single delivery semantics require that only one of the current group members needs to receive the message for the group communication successfully;

- *K-delivery.* In the k-delivery semantics, at least k members of the current group will receive the message successfully;

- *Quorum (best effort) delivery.* With quorum delivery semantics, a majority of the current group members will receive the message successfully;

- *Atomic delivery.* With atomic delivery all current members of the group successfully receive the message or none does. This delivery semantic is the most stringent as processes can and do fail and networks may also partition during the delivery process of the request messages, making some group members un-reachable.

Note that group communication should provide all these semantics in an effort to support a wide range of applications. Importantly, the policy of an application is supported by the transport protocol used by the group communication.

8.2.2 Message Response Semantics

By providing a wide range of message response semantics the application programmers are capable of applying flexible group communication to a variety of applications. The message response semantics specify the number and type of expected message responses. There are five broad categories for response semantics:

- *No responses.* By providing no response to a delivered request message the group communication facility is only able to provide unreliable group communication;

- *Single response.* The client process expects (for successful delivery of a message) a single response from one member of a group;

- *K-responses.* The client process expects to obtain k responses for the delivered message from the members of a process group. By using k response semantics the group resilience can be defined [Kaashoek and Tanenbaum 1994]. The resilience of a group is based on the minimum number of processes that must receive and respond to a message;

- *Majority response.* The client process expects to receive a majority of responses from the members of a process group;

- *Total response.* The client process requires all members of a group to respond to the delivery of a request message.

Importantly, the response semantics are based on the services a group is attempting to supply. With these message delivery and response semantics the group communication facility is capable of providing communication support to a wide range of applications. For example, a file update operation in a distributed file service will require all members of a group to receive messages and respond to the requesting process with an acknowledgment message stating the success or failure of the operation.

8.2.3 Message Ordering in Group Communication

The ordering of message delivery in group communication has become a hotly debated topic [Birman 1993] [Birman 1994] [Cheriton and Skeen 1993]. The reason is that, the semantics of message ordering are an important factor in providing better application performance and reduction in the complexity of distributed application programming. This is of critical importance for reliable processing in distributed systems. The order of message delivery to members of a group will dictate the type of group it is able to support.

There are four possible message ordering semantics [Joyce and Goscinski 1997]:

- *No ordering.* This semantic implies that all request messages will be sent to the current group of processes in no apparent order, as soon as they arrive at a workstation. No ordering is easy but makes application programmers work harder as they have to cope with their own message ordering protocol.

- *FIFO ordering.* This semantic implies that all request messages transmitted by a client process to the current members of a group will be delivered in the first in first out (FIFO) order. FIFO ordering ensures that all messages issued by a sender will be delivered to the members in the same order. For example, if a site multicasts a message *m* before it multicasts a message *m'*, then no correct site delivers *m'* unless it has previously delivered *m*. However, messages coming from different workstations can arrive out of order.

- *Causal ordering.* The causal ordering semantic is defined in [Lamport 1978] to reflect the logical ordering of messages. Causal order is the reflexive transitive closure of the message order relation. This implies that if the sending of a message *m'* causally follows the delivery of a message *m*, then each process in the group receives *m* before *m'*. Three rules define the relations of message *m*, *m'* and *m"* as below:

(i)   Message *m* causally precedes message *m'* if a site *S* sends *m* before it sends *m'* and this relation is denoted as *m->m'*, as depicted in Figure 8.1(a);

(ii) Message *m* causally precedes message *m'* if a site *S* receives *m* before it sends *m'* and is denoted as *m->m'*, as depicted in Figure 8.1(b);

(iii) If *m->m'* and *m'->m"*, then *m->m"* (transitive closure);

(iv) If *m* and *m'* do not have the above relation, then they are called the concurrent message, denoted as *m || m'*.

Causal ordering has been motivated by Lamport's definition of the ordering of events in a distributed system. This is often referred to as the "happen before" relationship [Lamport 1978].

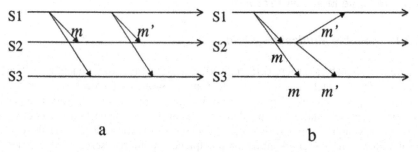

a   b

Figure 8.1: Causal ordering rule (Group G={S1, S2, S3})

- *Total ordering.* Total ordering semantic implies that all messages are reliably delivered in sequence to all members of a group. Also, total ordered semantic guarantees that all group members see the same order of messages. All messages arriving at all workstations are ordered. Total ordering is the most stringent ordering as all message transfers between all members of the group are in order. This implies that all processes within the group perceive the same total ordering of messages. In causal ordering we are concerned with the relationship of two messages while in total ordering we are concerned with seeing the same order of messages for all group member processes.

Total ordering ensures that each correct member delivers all messages in the same relative order. Of course, the total ordering must not violate the causal ordering, i.e., the property of total ordering is stronger than causal ordering. There are differences between the casual and total ordering. To illustrate the difference, assume a server replicates objects for client processes to increase availability and reliability. It guarantees that all the replicas are consistent. If a client may only update its own

180

objects, it is sufficient that all messages from the same client will be ordered. If a client may update any of the objects, the causal order is not sufficient since the order of messages may be different between any two clients even though the causal order is guaranteed for each individual client. More specifically, we use the following figure to indicate the difference of the two kinds of ordering. In Figure 8.2, assume group $G = \{S2, S3\}$, and messages a and b are concurrent messages; a and b do not obey the total ordering in the left and do obey it in the right.

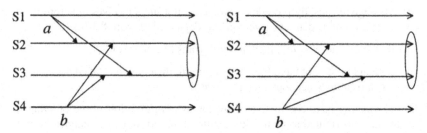

Figure 8.2: Causal ordering and total ordering

8.3　Reliable Multicast Protocol

8.3.1　Reliable Multicast System

Figure 8.3 depicts a group communication system providing reliable multicast services. In this architecture, each site runs a multicast protocol server process which accepts multicast requests from its local application. A server accepts requests via a submittal queue and delivers messages to its application via a delivery queue. For simplicity, we assume the queues never overflow. Whenever there is a local request (message) in either of the queues, both the server and the local application will process them as soon as they can.

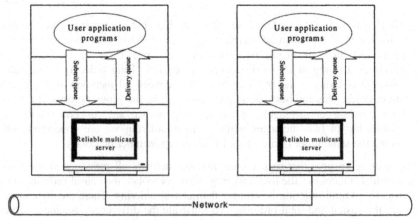

Figure 8.3: Reliable multicast system architecture

Communication among the sites is achieved by exchanging broadcast or point-to-point messages. User group application processes running on the upper level of the system access the common resources (e.g., file, shared objects and database systems) and share common information. Assume the continued executions of the multicast servers in a group of processors. The application on one of the processors works as follows. In case of needing the reliable multicast service, it opens a port (e.g., TCP stream socket) to the server. The server listens to the connection request and accepts the connection. Upon building the connection, the application is able to send a message to other applications of the group via its server by entrusting the message into the port. On receiving a multicast message from its server, the application is sure that the message is totally ordered and received by all the other members in the group (atomicity) even in the presence of message lost or site crash.

Each site in the system is connected to the network via a *network interface*. The interface monitors the network and copies messages identified with its address code into a buffer that can be accessed by a connected site. Unfortunately, there is no guarantee that a site will receive every message addressed to it. For example,

- the buffer might be full when a message is received by the interface;

- the interface might not monitor the network at the time the message is delivered;

- in a contention network, an undetected collision that affects certain network interfaces could cause them to miss a message;

- a site may suddenly halt, killing all the processes that are executing there and losing all its volatile states. Consequently, no message from this site is ever received by all others.

We here abstract two kinds of failure scenario:

(1) *Lost message.* Messages may be lost because of a buffer overflow or they may be discarded due to a transmission error. An arbitrary number of messages may be lost; however, all of the messages received at a site are free of transmission errors (Ethernet properties [MB76]);

(2) *Fail stop.* When a site fails, the site simply stops processing. It does not send malicious messages or perform any incorrect action.

8.3.2 Design Issues

To identify the characteristics of the reliable multicast protocol and how it is designed, several design issues have to be considered: *acknowledgement, addressing, ordering, reliability, delivery semantics,* and *dynamic group*:

- Acknowledgement: two styles of acknowledgement systems exist in the current group multicast protocol designs, namely, positive acks and negative acks. In the positive acks, upon receiving a message, the receiver explicitly sends back a message to acknowledge the reception. For the negative acks, the message sender (source) assigns a sequence number to each message. It is not necessary for the receivers to explicitly acknowledge the messages. Lost messages can be detected when a higher sequence number than expected is received, and retransmissions of the lost messages can be requested. Therefore, the negative acks can be used to reduce the packet transmission and synchronization overhead.

- Multicast addressing: two methods are used to indicate the multicast addressing. The simplest one is allowing a sender to explicitly indicate the destinations to which a message should be delivered. The second one is using one single address for a group of sites (IP address). In this case, a sender can issue a message for a single address even though the sender does not know who are the members in the group. This method saves bandwidth and simplifies communication design.

- Ordering: ordering is an important criterion for the design of multicast communication. Most group communication systems categorized the ordering as no ordering, FIFO, causal, and total ordering with increasing strength. They have been introduced in the previous section.

- Reliability: reliability deals with recovering from communication and site failures, such as buffer overflows, distorted packets, missed packets and site crashes, and even more serious failures such as network partitions. Reliability is more difficult to implement for group communication than for point-to-point communication.

- Delivery semantics: this semantics involves successfully delivering a message to a group. There are four common choices: 1-delivery, k-delivery, quorum delivery, and atomic delivery, which have been introduced before.

- Dynamic group membership: this allows the group size (membership) changes dynamically without interfering message ordering and reliability. The change also should not suspend normal operation for a long time. All the group members view a join/leave event in a consistent way. A newly joined member is able to transfer its state to reflect the group communication.

8.4 Multicast Approaches

A number of algorithms has been published recently, addressing reliable atomic message multicast. In the following, we summarize three typical reliable multicast approaches and restrict our discussions mainly to the algorithms that are designated for asynchronous computing environments. For a detailed comparision of our protocol with related work, the interested reader is referred to [Jia et al 1996].

8.4.1 Centralized Approach

The typical protocols of this approach were the algorithms of Chang and Maxemchuk [Chang and Maxemchuk 1984]. They have described a family of protocols that achieve totally ordered broadcasts determined by a "token site". A sender broadcasts a message to all recipients. If the token site receives the message, it broadcasts an acknowledgement message containing the message *id* and a timestamp (total order, see Figure 8.4). A message may be committed only when the token has been passed around some of the sites in the token list to achieve message fault tolerance.

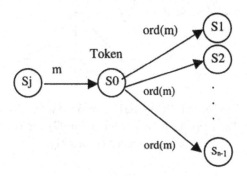

Figure 8.4: A group comprises of $n+1$ sites. Member $S_j, j \in \{0, ..., n\}$, transmits its multicast request m to S_0, the token site S_0 orders m and multicasts it over the group (S_0 and S_j can be identical).

Kaashoek and Tanenbaum have simplified the approach of Chang and Maxemchuck's protocol by using a fixed sequencer [Kaashoek and Tanenbaum 1991]. Whenever the sequencer receives a point-to-point message, it allocates the next sequence number and broadcasts the message with the sequence number. Lost messages can be detected by a gap in the sequence numbers. However, the sequencer still could become a bottleneck in a large group.

Garcia-Molina et al. [Garcia-Molina and Spauster 1991] have proposed an approach to solve the multiple overlapped group message-ordering problem. In their protocol, a tree is superimposed on the set of processes in the system. To transmit a broadcast, the message is forwarded to the least common ancestor of the destination processes, which in turn uses a reliable FIFO protocol to handle the message delivery (Figure 8.5). Other logical token ring algorithms were developed by [Amir et al 1993] and [Rajagopalan and McKinley 1989], which involve token passing explicitly from process to process in order to achieve fault-tolerance. Only the process holding the token can broadcast or retransmit messages. The token needs to be transmitted at least two rounds in a group in order to achieve fault tolerance (Figure 8.6).

The advantages of the centralized approach are their simplicity and efficiency of establishing the total order of messages. However, there are some drawbacks related to this senario: concurrent multicast requests must be blocked until they are ordered. To achieve a multicast resilience to a degree r, i.e., a multicast message will not be lost even to r site failures, the token is required to rotate over r member sites where $r < n$ to ensure that at least one of the members will have the copy of the message in case of r site failures simultaneously.

184

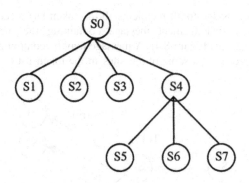

Figure 8.5: Groups $G_1=\{S_0, S_1, S_2, S_3, S_4\}$, $G_2=\{S_1, S_5, S_6, S_7\}$, and $G_3=\{S_0, S_1\}$ yield a tree and site S_0 orders the messages for groups G_1 and G_3, site S_1 orders the messages in related G_2 and G_3.

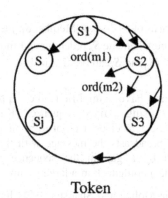

Token

Figure 8.6: A group of n members form a logical token ring. Member S_1 and S_2 have multicast ordered messages m_1 and m_2. The token is transmitted to S_3. S_3 transmits the token to the next site without multicasting any message.

Tolerating failure of the token holder requires some expensive election and reformation algorithms. Moreover, the token holder failure during the token message transmission may cause the token information to be lost, as a consequence, no member in the group is able to recover the token information. For example, consider that a token keeps a record of the acknowledgements from other sites and, the record must be transmitted to the next member. Before the token transmission, the token holder fails. Consequently, the record gets lost and is unrecoverable since no member other than the token holder knows exactly how many acknowledgements were collected by the failed token holder before its failure. Furthermore, the token transmissions introduce extra packets into the network and may incur considerable latency for delivering messages to the applications. In case of a fixed token holder (a single token holder), the token holder could become a bottleneck when a burst of multicast requests are in a large group. Typically, the approach must handle the issue of data and control flow of the message buffers.

8.4.2 Symmetrical Approach (Decentralized)

By symmetries we mean for a group of sites, there is no site playing a role of "token" or "sequencer". In contrast to the centralized algorithm, for a specific multicast message, a member determines the message (delivery) order and its atomicity only after gathering enough acknowledgements with the subsequent multicast messages. The subsequent multicast messages form a partial order [Melliar-Smith et al 1990] (or a context graph [Peterson et al 1989]), carrying the positive or negative *acks* for the previous received messages. Based on the partial order (context graph), a site sees a multicast followed by which, therefore, it is able to determine a total order or atomic (stable) multicasts within the partial order.

This approach reduces synchronous overhead and enables more parallelism within a system. However, it is complicated compared with its centralized counterpart. Because a site has to maintain a partial order (graph) for a set of multicasts it received, the overhead is high. In order to achieve enough information for ordering and atomicity of a message, the site waiting subsequent multicasts may incur a longer delay. In case of sparse message transmissions, an even longer time is needed to gather enough acknowledgement information.

8.4.3 Two-phase Approach

The ISIS system developed by Birman et al. proposes a family of protocols and implements them using the causal broadcast (CBCAST) primitive and atomic broadcast (ABCAST) [Birman and Joseph 1987] primitive. CBCAST is used to enforce a delivery ordering when desired with minimal synchronization. ABCAST achieves total ordering of message and operates by the 2-phase approach (recent versions have adopted a token-passing group). [Veríssimo et al 1989] also described a 2-phase protocol *AMP*.

The two-phase approach works as follows. Independently, a site issuing a multicast message controls the order and (atomic) delivery of the message. In the first phase, a message is multicasted and all potential receivers send back a locally assigned priority order [Birman and Joseph 1987] (or an acknowledgement [Veríssimo et al 1989]). In the second phase, if all receivers have returned their ordering (or affirmative reply messages), the sender multicasts a final order (or a decision message such as *commit*). This scheme is simple and can greatly shorten the time needed for a multicast message delivery (order), however, many packets are transmitted in the network and consume network bandwidth. Because the sender has to wait for the acknowledgements, further delay is introduced if there is any message lost or a receiver site failure before issuing an acknowledgement message.

8.5 Multicast in Java

The *java.net* package provides a class called *MulticastSocket,* which enables programmers to write multicast communication in Java. A *MulticastSocket* is a *DatagramSocket* with additional capabilities for joining groups of other multicast hosts on the Internet. The *DatagramSocket* class is used to create UDP socket connections. It sends and receives data using packets, which are represented as *DatagramPacket* objects. In order for two programs to talk to each other over a UDP connection, they both have to have *DatagramSocket* connected to a port on their machines. This can be done by creating a *DatagramSocket* object.

Data is sent over a *DatagramSocket* using *DatagramPacket,* and each *DatagramSocket* contains a data buffer, the address of the remote host to send the data to, and the port number the server is listening on. Thus, for a client to send a buffer of data to a server listening on port 5555 on machine "purejava", we would write something like this:

```
byte buf[] = {'h', 'e', 'l', 'l', 'o'};
InetAddress address = InetAddress.getByName("purejava");
DatagramSocket ds = new DatagramSocket();
DatagramPacket packet = new DatagramPacket(buf, buf.length,
address, 5555);
ds.send(packet);
```

The remote server can receive the data request from the client as follows:

```
byte buf[] = new byte[256];
DatagramPacket packet = new DatagramPacket(buf, buf.length);
ds.receive(packet);
```

Note that the *DatagramPacket* constructor used in the server's code requires only two arguments: a byte array that contains client-specific data and the length of the byte array. However, when we are constructing a *DatagramPacket* to send over the *DatagramSocket* as shown above, we have to provide the Internet address and port number of the packet's destination.

The *MulticastSocket* is used on the client side to listen for packets that the server broadcasts to multiple clients. A multicast group is identified by a class D (those in the range 224.0.0.1 to 239.255.255.254) IP address. Broadcasting packets to multiple recipients is analogous to radio and television broadcasting. A practical use of multicast IP is for broadcasting audio and video over the Internet.

A process that wants to listen on the multicast address creates a *MulticastSocket* and then joins the multicast session by calling the *joinGroup()* method. For example, to join a group and send the group a greeting, we would write something like the following:

```
byte msg[] = {'h', 'i', ',', 't', 'h', 'e', 'r', 'e'};
InetAddress group = InetAddress.getByName("229.2.56.29");
MulticastSocket ms = new MulticastSocket(6666);
Ms.joinGroup();
DatagramPacket greetings = new DatagramPacket(msg, msg.length, group,
6666);
```

```
ms.send(greetings);
```

Once the connection to the multicast session is established, a client can read data being broadcasted on the channel as follows:

```
byte buf[] = new byte[1024];
DatagramPacket packet = new DatagramPacket(buf, buf.length);
ms.receive(packet);
```

Once the broadcast is over, or when we want to stop listening, we can disconnect by leaving the group using the leaveGroup() method:

```
ms.leaveGroup(group);
```

Example: The following two programs implement the multicast communication between two sub-networks. The Courier.java program receives packets from a sub-network and then forwards them to the Publisher.java program, which will publish these packets to another sub-network. The two programs first establish multicast communication between each other and then receive/send packets. The Courier.java program is listed as follows:

```
import java.net.*;
import java.io.*;

public class Courier {

    DatagramPacket receivePacket, sendPacket;
    DatagramSocket sendSocket;
    MulticastSocket receiveSocket;
    int sendPort = 4100;
    int receivePort = 4000;
    InetAddress local = null;
    InetAddress remote = null;

    public Courier()
    {
        try {
            local = InetAddress.getByName("ALL-SYSTEMS.MCAST.NET");
            remote = InetAddress.getByName("sky60.cm.deakin.edu.au");
        }
        catch (UnknownHostException uhe) {
            System.err.println(uhe);
        }
        catch (Exception e) {
            System.err.println(e);
        }

        try {
        sendSocket = new DatagramSocket();
        receiveSocket = new MulticastSocket(receivePort);
        receiveSocket.setTTL((byte) 1);
        receiveSocket.joinGroup(local);
        }
        catch (SocketException se) {
        System.err.println(se);
        }
        catch (IOException ioe) {
        System.err.println(ioe);
```

```
      }
   }

   public void forwardPackets()
   {
      // set up packet to receive data into
      byte[] buffer = new byte[30];
      receivePacket = new DatagramPacket(buffer, buffer.length);

      while (true) {
        try {
          receiveSocket.receive(receivePacket);
          byte[] data = receivePacket.getData();
        sendPacket   =   new   DatagramPacket(data,   data.length,   remote,
sendPort);
        sendSocket.send(sendPacket);
          }
      catch (IOException ioe) {
        System.err.println(ioe);
      }
       }
   }

   public static void main(String[] args)
   {
      Courier c = new Courier();
      c.forwardPackets();
   }
}
```

The Courier constructor first gets the local and remote (the publisher) machine addresses, then creates a DatagramSocket object as the sending socket and a MulticastSocket object as the receiving socket. The sending socket will send packets to the publisher while the receiving socket receives packets from a multicast group, thus the receiving socket has to join the group. In order to avoid packets being flooded onto other networks, Java multicast datagrams include a TTL (Time To Live) field in the header to reduce packets unnecessarily circulating and congesting networks. In Courier.java we invoke the MulticastSocket's *setTTL()* method to set TTL to 1, which means all the members on the *same subnet* receive datagrams from a sender.

The publisher.java is listed as follows.

```
import java.net.*;
import java.io.*;

public class Publisher {

   DatagramPacket receivePacket, sendPacket;
   DatagramSocket receiveSocket;
   MulticastSocket sendSocket;
   int sendPort = 4000;
   int receivePort = 4100;
   InetAddress local = null;

   public Publisher()
   {
```

```
    try {
local = InetAddress.getByName("ALL-SYSTEMS.MCAST.NET");
    }
    catch (UnknownHostException uhe) {
System.err.println(uhe);
    }
    catch (Exception e) {
System.err.println(e);
    }

    try {
receiveSocket = new DatagramSocket(receivePort);
sendSocket = new MulticastSocket();
sendSocket.setTTL((byte) 1);
    }
    catch (SocketException se) {
System.err.println(se);
    }
    catch (IOException ioe) {
System.err.println(ioe);
    }
}

public void multicastPackets()
{
    // set up packet to receive data into
    byte[] buffer = new byte[30];
    receivePacket = new DatagramPacket(buffer, buffer.length);

    while (true) {
       try {
          receiveSocket.receive(receivePacket);
          byte[] data = receivePacket.getData();
       sendPacket =    new   DatagramPacket(data,    data.length,   local,
sendPort);
       sendSocket.send(sendPacket);
       }
    catch (IOException ioe) {
       System.err.println(ioe);
    }
    }
}

public static void main(String[] args)
{
    Publisher p = new Publisher();
    p.multicastPackets();
}
}
```

The Publisher constructor first gets the local machine address, then creates a
DatagramSocket object as the receiving socket and a MulticastSocket object as the
sending socket. The receiving socket will receive packets from the Courier while
the sending socket sends packets to a multicast group. Similarly, in order to avoid
packets being flooded onto other networks, the Publisher sets TTL to 1, which
means all the members on the *same subnet* receive datagrams from a sender. The

Publisher provides a *multicastPackets()* method to receive packets from the
courier, and then multicasts them to another subnet.

8.6   Total Ordered Multicast Protocol based on a Logical Ring

From the discussion above, we have found that the logical ring is a simple and
efficient approach for the design of a reliable multicast protocol: discrete broadcasts
of many distributed members are reduced to one token holder multicast at one time.
This method substantially simplifies the synchronous requirements of the
applications. This section discusses the design of Reliable Multicast Protocol (called
RMP) in the aspects of *ordering, atomicity, membership,* and *fault-tolerance.*

8.6.1   Achieving Total Ordering

Let a group comprising a set of sites be denoted as $G = \{S_i\}$ and $n = |G|$ is the size
of the group. The core idea of RMP protocol is to organize a group of sites into a
logical ring. During the ring construction, the protocol assigns each member a
unique index which is a one-to-one mapping of the site identity *(sid)* on which the
member resides. We assume a *sid* is unique and never changed or lost no matter
whether the site crashes or recovers. The members are arranged in an increasing
order of their indices so as to form a logic ring. At any given time there is only one
member on the ring serving as the token holder and multicasting a total ordered
message. After dispatching such a message, the token position implicitly circulates
to the next member on the ring. Each member maintains a local sequence number
which comes from the previous correct multicast message.

To predict the current token holder's position, each member computes the token
holder's index via its local sequence number plus 1 modulo the size of the ring
(group). All the members send their requests to or expect a multicast from the
current token holder. More precisely, after starting the protocol in a group, one
member will become the coordinator of the logical ring formation via competition.

Assume a ring (group) comprises members $S_0, S_1, ..., S_{n-1}$ and each member
maintains a consistent logical ring $R = (id(S_0), id(S_1), ..., id(S_{n-1}))$ which is a member
list corresponding to each member state. Given the consistent logical ring R, when
the protocol starts the normal operation, S_0 is the coordinator of the ring and S_1
serves as the current token holder, transmitting the first multicast message, then S_2,
S_3 and so forth. Each member on the logical ring periodically takes its turn to serve
as the token holder and multicast an ordered message. Define $s \oplus 1 = (s + 1)\ mod\ n$.
All members, upon reception of a correctly ordered message, assign the message
sequence number *m.s* as their sequence number s, compute the next token holder
(id) via the ring element $R[s \oplus 1]$ and expect the next multicast message with total
order $s+1$ from member $R[s \oplus 1]$. This guarantees that a receiver can order the
messages from the token holder correctly in case they arrive out of order (see Figure
8.7).

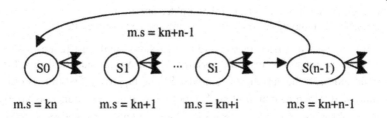

Figure 8.7: Logical token ring structure and normal operations. Site $S_{i \oplus 1}$ multicasts a message with order $kn + i+1$ if all the messages m, $m.s \leq kn + i$, have been received by $S_{i \oplus 1}$, where $k = \{0, 1, 2,...\}$ and $0 \leq i \leq n - 1$.

In order to ensure the proper normal operations of the protocol, all the members on the logical ring are required to comply with the following rules:

Rule 1: A member S cannot send its multicast request to a site which is not assumed as the next token holder by S, i.e., S sends its multicast request to S' if and only if S has received the ordered multicast messages sent by the member which is the predecessor of S' on the logical ring.

Rule 2: A member S cannot assume itself to be the current token holder without receiving all the prior multicasts from the predecessor token holders in the ring.

Rule 3: A member S cannot deliver a multicast m to its applications if $m.s$ is greater than its local sequence number s, namely, S can deliver m (not necessarily) if $m.s \leq s+1$.

In the normal case, **Rule 1** ensures that a sender will either send a request to the correct token holder or detect and complete the lost messages. **Rule 2** prevents a member from multicasting a wrong order message. **Rule 3** emphasises that all multicast messages that can be delivered to the applications are totally ordered. A non-token holder may wait a random time for sending a multicast request to the current token holder to avoid request collisions. The use of $m.s$ (order) is two fold: if m is a point-to-point message, the source S_i of m acknowledges all the previously received messages by assigning its sequence number s_i to $m.s$. A token holder multicasts a total ordered $m.s$ which implicitly acknowledges any previous multicast and request messages. Consequently, no explicit acknowledgement messages are required during the normal operations of the protocol and the lost message can be effectively detected by the existence of the gap of a receiver sequence number s and the incoming message order $m.s$. The token holder takes the other multicast requests as acknowledgement messages because the requests carry on their sender sequence numbers, however, it has a priority to multicast its own request if it has one.

This approach prevents message starvation in case of request collisions. If the token does not receive any request during a specific time interval, it multicasts an ordered *NULL* (heart-beat) message to keep the protocol alive and to facilitate the commitment of the atomic messages without further delay. Every token holder is obliged to multicast one message no matter whether there is a request or not. A site

192

may not realize that it is the current token holder due to not receiving the previous message(s). This can be detected by an incoming request or timeout.

There are two cases that need message retransmissions: multicast request collision and messages missing. For example, assume S_i and S_j simultaneously send their requests m_i and m_j to the current token holder S_k, and m_j arrives first thus is ordered and multicasted. Upon reception of m_j, S_i modifies s_i, $m_i.s$ and retransmits m_i to the next token holder $S_{k \oplus 1}$. Since $S_{k \oplus l}$ never receives mj, it buffers m_i and requests S_k for the lost message m_j. On receiving the retransmission, m_i is ordered and multicasted as depicted in Figure 8.8.

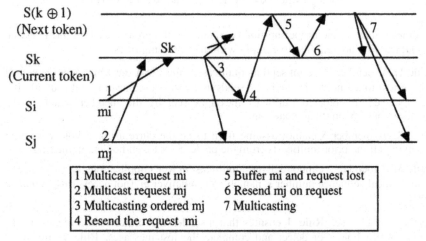

1 Multicast request mi	5 Buffer mi and request lost
2 Multicast request mj	6 Resend mj on request
3 Multicasting ordered mj	7 Multicasting
4 Resend the request mi	

Figure 8.8: Message retransmission example

8.6.2 Atomic Message Delivery

RMP provides consistent order and atomic deliveries. *Consistent order delivery* is defined to mean that a message m is delivered by a process P on R in a consistent order if it keeps total ordering of messages and ring version. For instance, if a member receives two messages m and m' with $m.s < m'.s$ but $m'.version < m.version$, even in this case, total order is preserved between m and m', but the consistent order is still violated. *Atomic delivery* means that if a correct process P delivers m in the consistent order and knows that all operational processes on R have received m it will deliver it. In addition to the total ordering delivery, RMP, encompasses three mechanisms for achieving atomic message delivery:

Simple type

It requires no extra effort of the protocol. Once all the members receive a multicast message m originating from the token holder S, they wait until the token transfers through the entire ring R and back to S. At this moment, all members have seen the token, thus implicitly acknowledging their receptions of m. Consequently, every member on R knows all other members have received m. This method is simple, however, it requires up to n-1 multicast delay times before a message can be safely committed.

Speed-up type

High level applications may specify an emergency message and require the protocol to commit all received messages. RMP provides a speed-up delivery service for this purpose. After a token holder has multicasted such a message m, on receiving m from the current token holder, each non-faulty member (except the token holder) immediately multicasts a short acknowledgement message. Thus, all members send their *ack* messages almost simultaneously. This short *ack* message has nothing to do with ordering. Any operational member on the ring, upon reception of the n-2 (for the token holder, n-1) *ack* messages, delivers the uncommitted messages prior to (including) m to their applications. This approach is fast but invokes too much load on the network and also consumes extra bandwidth. The trade-off can be decided by the high level applications.

Safe parameter approach

The safe parameter [JKN95, KT91] can be computed as the low water-marker of the total order of messages received by all members known to the token holder. The approach is simple: a site S maintains an array K, recording the total order sequence numbers corresponding to all the members. Before a message m is multicasted by S (it is the token holder), S computes a safe parameter as $m.k = min(K[1], ..., K[n])$, which represents the "all-received-up-to" message sequence number. It indicates that the messages with order number less than or equal to $m.k$ had been received by every member on the ring.

Note that the safety parameter can be piggybacked onto the normal multicast message and the sequence number $m.s$ is also taken as an *ack* of the message originator about reception of previous multicast messages. A token holder is interested in receiving such acknowledgments for establishing the safety parameter. For any two successive multicasts m and m', if $m.k < m'.k$, the uncommitted (not delivered) message m'' with order number $m.k < m''.s \le m'.k$ can be safely committed. One of the important properties of a safety parameter is that every member, on receiving a multicast message, can capture the current global view, i.e., the total order of messages received by every member in the group without additional communication overhead. Although, the computation may increase the token processing time, the advantage of the global view on the ring seen by each of the members outweighs this computation cost.

Also note that the token process in a ring R will not block itself from waiting for the *ack* message which may not come due to stop of a member process. In order to keep the protocol alive, the token process still transfers an ordered message even though the atomicity of previous multicast messages cannot be met at the moment. The token transferring to the failed member will trigger the fault tolerant mechanism of RMP and the atomicity of the messages will be finally achieved, exclusive of the failed member, as illustrated in the next section.

More on the system level, multicast protocols are used in fault-tolerant storage services [BSS91]. A reliable storage service can be built by replicating data objects on n processors each with its own disk. If an object needs to be updated, the service either has to send the new object value to all processes or invalidate all other copies of the updated object. It is obvious that multicast is more efficient and reliable than a sequence of low-level point-to-point messages.

8.6.3 Membership

Group membership change is very important to the consistency of a group. There are two issues related to the membership: *membership construction* and *dynamic membership*.

8.6.3.1 Membership Construction

Membership construction involves constructing a logical ring (membership list). Intuitively, any site S wishing to create a logical ring for a group of n sites opens a ring list R and inserts its entity as the first element of R by $R[0] = id(S)$. It also proposes a ring version with 1 (denote $R.version = 1$) and broadcasts a reformation message to invite the specific members to join the ring. A member S' that agrees with the invitation of S sends a *positive* acknowledgement message to it. The S, as the coordinator, inserts $id(S')$ as $R[i] = id(S')$ upon receiving such an *ack,* until the completion of the ring R. Then S multicasts a message containing R to all members in R. Upon reception of further acknowledgement from each member in R, a consensus is achieved and S multicasts a *resume* message to start the normal operations.

Receiving the *resume* message (including S itself) enables all the members to set the final official R and commit R to the user applications. As a result, reaching the consensus allows S to broadcast a message containing a $Gid = \{version, coord, size(G)\}$ to the overall network. This enables the members to be noticed by the members outside the group that may request the group service or join the group later on. Note that a group cannot be destroyed or deleted by a single message. When the last member leaves the group, the group ceases to exist. Should S ever receive a negative response, it terminates ring configuration and waits for another ring invitation.

It is possible that multiple sites may claim the function of the ring coordinator. A competition then occurs and every site stays in an initial state, voting itself as the coordinator and attempting to form a logical ring. To avoid the competition to some extent, our membership algorithm employs three criteria for the coordinator candidate selection and authorization. Let sites S_1 and S_2 invite each other:

- **Criterion 1 (C1):** If $S_1.version > S_2.version,$ then S_1 is chosen as the candidate;

- **Criterion 2 (C2):** If $S_1.version = S_2.version$ and $S_1.s > S_2.s$ (the total sequence numbers) then S_2 votes S_1 as the candidate;

- **Criterion 3 (C3):** If $S_1.version = S_2.version$, $S_1.s = S_2.s$ and $sid(S_1) > sid(S_2)$, (the site *ids*) then S_1 is considered as the candidate.

As the results of applying **C1** through **C3**, S_2 answers a positive message to S_1 and inversely, S_1 sends a negative response to S_2. Given the selection rules, when the protocol starts initially, each site waits a random time interval for an invitation. Through our experiments in applying the selection rules **(C1)** - **(C3)** on the coordinator voting, we have found that one of the sites will prevail and be quickly elected as the coordinator, thereby, reducing the reformation time and avoiding a race. After the election, the coordinator constructs a token ring based on the positive response members and delivers the ring across the group as described previously.

8.6.3.2 Dynamic Membership

Dynamic membership allows a site to join or leave a ring dynamically. A scheme is devised to enable a newly started site (*restart_ID* = 0) to detect a current executing operational ring, so as to join the ring. Let a site S be outside a ring R; it can detect R by listening to a message from R actively. Once S receives a message m, it checks $m.version$. If it is greater than its own version, S picks $m.coord$ which is the id of another member S' as its own coordinator and sends a new member "join" request to the coordinator. The ring coordinator responds to the "join" request with the current ring status.

There are two ways for the coordinator to handle the new member join request: (1) it starts a reformation phase immediately or (2) it waits until it is the token holder and then starts the reformation. A problem arises when method (1) is deployed: if the coordinator immediately broadcasts an invitation message and enters in a reformation phase while some other sites are multicasting their normal ordered messages, the messages will be interfered with by the normal operation of the multicast, because some messages will have been received before the invitation and some will be received after. Consequently, there is an inconsistent order of seeing the membership change interleaved with the normal multicast messages.

To avoid such interference, we employ the second method: the coordinator keeps in mind the "join" request and waits until the token goes to it. At this moment, there is no other site transmitting normal messages and all members are expecting an ordered message from the coordinator (which is the token holder too). Subsequently, it starts a reformation procedure and includes applicants. This method will have the applicants wait for up to $n-1$ multicast transmission time with non-interference. An example is given in Figure 8.9. Notice that a new started site is too impatient to wait for the reformation response of the coordinator and transmits its own ring invitation message; upon receiving such an invitation, the existing ring coordinator will respond with a negative point-to-point message to the site that forces it to give up the invitation.

In case a member voluntarily leaves the group, it simply multicasts a *quit* message then leaves the group without having permission from any other member. On receiving the *quit* message, the current token holder leads the other members to form a new ring. In general, those *join/leave* algorithms will change the size of the group.

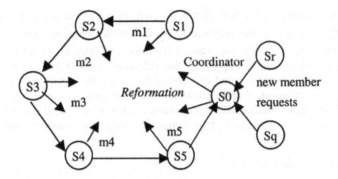

Figure 8.9: Dynamic membership. Sites S_q and S_r apply to coordinator S_0 for a membership. When S_0 is the current token holder, it starts a reformation phase to integrate these applicants.

8.6.4 Fault Tolerance

Group communication requires resilience in the sense that even if any fault/failure occurs to a message or a site, the group is able to proceed with its operation. Identification of a fault is considered from two aspects:

- Fault occurrence: in normal operation, a single member P_i may fail at any time. But RMP treats the logical failure time as that it happens when P_i turns to serve as the current token process, and no multicast message is ever received by any of the members on R after expiring certain timer.

- Fault detection: when timeout is reached, the remaining members are able to detect a failure of P_i. Even if P_i is a logical failure, during the ring reformation, the remaining processes will see that P is still alive and it can be included in the new ring.

This section considers fault tolerance of the protocol from three aspects: (1) tolerating a single site fault; (2) recovering from multiple site faults and (3) dealing with network partitions.

8.6.4.1 Single Member Failure

Each token holder is supposed to send at least one "heart-beat" message. Therefore, it is relatively easy for a group member to detect a failure of the current token holder when the token holder is not heard by the other receivers for a certain time period. In the presence of a single site fault, most existing protocols deal with the fault by electing a coordinator to form a new group. Normally, the reformation overhead is very high. To authorize a reformation coordinator, several tests such as majority, sequence and resilience must be undertaken [CM84]. It may happen that if a single member fails, repetitively, several members compete to be the coordinator, try to form a new membership list and give up the reformation attempt when none of them can reform a majority of members. Substantial delay is introduced.

To overcome the delay case, a more efficient algorithm for handling such a "single fault" is proposed. The philosophy of the algorithm is to have the prior token holder on the old ring as a pre-authorized coordinator, leading the surviving members to form a new ring when the current token holder fails. Therefore, it will save the efforts to elect and authorize a coordinator. More precisely, assume the failure of token holder S is detected by some other members, those members will probe into S and report the fault to S_i, piggybacking their state (sequence number etc.) while S_i is the predecessor of S on R. If S_i does agree with the fault reports, it starts a reformation algorithm to construct a new ring. There are several reasons to choose S_i as the coordinator: (1) S_i has the highest probability of being alive since it just transmitted a message; (2) If S fails before its transmission, S_i is up-to-date (with the highest sequence number and safe parameter); and (3) S_i can be reached by the other members with higher probability because they have just received a message from it. Under the assumption of single failure of S, S_i is the defaut choice to be, without elections, the coordinator among the correct members.

Reformation procedure

The reformation procedure works as follows. First of all, S_i collects the reports of all other members about S (in fact, nearly all the surviving members send their opinions about "S is down" to S_i simultaneously, because every member is monitoring S with the same time-out setting). If S does not stop, after learning such probe message, S_i should retransmit its multicast messages immediately, or if any member had received a multicast message from S before, it also should help to retransmit the multicast message originally from S. In either case, the algorithm aborts. During the report collection, lost messages can be retransmitted.

Secondly, to reform a new ring, S_i must have a consensus of the alive members. Since we assumed only one site fault, S_i will finally achieve such consensus to ensure that every operational member in the group agrees with the failure and receives the same set of messages (failure and message atomicity). Those messages sent by the old ring should be committed despite ring reformation. S_i constructs a new ring containing the operational members, increments the ring version and multicasts the new ring to the group with an up-to-date safe parameter $m.k$. On receipt of the reformation message, all members on the new ring update their R, commit the messages in the reception queue and acknowledge S_i. When S_i receives all *acks,* it multicasts a "resume" command, instructing all the members to resume normal operation. As soon as the resume message is received, all members on the new ring deliver the new ring to the application processes, informing users of the change in the membership.

However, any member may fail during the reformation phase. If a member, other than the coordinator, fails, the coordinator just eliminates the failed member out of the new ring. If the coordinator fails or is not reachable by the majority of members, a complete recovery algorithm is invoked (see below).

8.6.4.2 Multiple Failures

A recovery algorithm has to be developed for multiple faults. Assume the network does not partition. When multiple sites fail (or in case of the simultaneous failures of the token holder and the pre-authorized coordinator holder), the single failure algorithm is no longer applicable. The surviving members have to enter a complete reformation mode to elect a coordinator for the ring reconfiguration. The complete recovery algorithm follows the coordinator selection criteria **C1-C3** as shown in the previous subsection.

The recovery algorithm runs in two phases. In the first phase, the algorithm detects which members are alive and chooses one member as the coordinator to handle the second phase, e.g., a site S. Upon detecting such failures, S multicasts a message attaching its sequence number, claiming to be the coordinator and inviting other survived sites in the group to join a new ring. On receipt of such an invitation message, a site wishing to join the new ring responds with its sequence number to the inviter. Possible lost messages can be compensated. **C1 - C3** are applied if a member receives more than one invitation or if a coordinator invites another coordinator. When a coordinator has finally invited the majority members of the group and there is no additional join site by a certain timeout, it constructs a new ring, increments the ring version and multicasts the ring attaching the up-to-date safe parameter to the group (broadcasts new *Gid* to the network as well). A ring without a majority of members must block until some new sites join or all its members join another ring.

The second phase of the algorithm is similar to the single fault tolerance algorithm above. Since we have assumed that a network does not partition, one of the coordinators will finally form a ring with majority members and the protocol can continue its normal operation.

8.6.4.3 Network Partitioning

When a network partitions, a group may be segmented into several small subgroups. The following two cases must be considered:

Case 1. There is a subgroup with majority membership of the original group and it will form a new ring. Any entering site can join the subgroup as long as the subgroup is *reachable,* that is, the communication paths exist between the join site and the operational subgroup. To cope with the reformation, a coordinator must be chosen:

- If the current token holder does not crash and can be reached by the majority members, the token holder is the reformation coordinator;

- If the token holder crashes or is no longer reachable, the immediate prior token holder is the coordinator;

- Recall that the majority membership is a necessary condition for the group reformation. When the above two cases do not apply, the surviving members have to elect a coordinator to reconfigure a new ring in cooperation with the majority members.

Those three algorithms are nearly the same as the reformation algorithms mentioned before. Hence, we do not discuss them in detail.

Case 2. There is no subgroup with majority membership; all the members in the subgroups are blocked. The coordinators in the subgroups periodically broadcast an invitation message. Once the communication paths are reestablished and the small rings can merge (by join) into a large ring containing the majority members of the group, then the protocol can resume normal operation. The merging is similar to the algorithm of the two coordinators inviting each other. Again, they are omitted here.

8.6.5 Efficiency

We have discussed the design of RMP in the above. The efficiency of such RMP can be addressed in the following aspects:

- Fast locating the token site and ordering multicasts. RMP has minimized the control message overhead: for each ordered multicast message, normally, one point-to-point message is needed to transmit the request from a source site to the token holder. If the token holder transmits a message from its own application process, this message can be directly multicasted without any extra point-to-point delay. In case of multiple senders, one of the senders may have to retransmit its requests up to n–1 times (until its turn to be the token holder) but the request still can be taken as an acknowledgement message.

- Efficient message validity checking. Attaching the sequence number of each source site to every message transmission regardless of the message type (an ordered multicast, a multicast request or a reformation message) makes the lost message detection very efficient because a receiver is able to check the order of an incoming message against its own sequence number. In addition, RMP has provided an ordered message with a ring version, enabling a destination of the message to decide if its communication party is on the same ring. Therefore the receiver detects effectively between itself and the message sender that the sender is a valid member of the ring.

- Quick snapshot of the global state. With safe parameters, one round of token rotation time is needed at most to reflect the maximum delay of the atomic delivery. Before the token rotates the n-1 members, if every member has sent a request or multicasted a message, the delay times can be further reduced. Therefore, the safe delivery latency is less than n-1 multicast delay times. However, n-1 multicast delay can be taken as the upper-bound delay of RMP. Even so, to achieve the total ordering by piggybacking the safe parameter with each ordered multicast message, RMP entails the minimal overhead to capture the (global) snapshot of the instantaneous state of the overall group.

- Flexible change of membership. A site can join the logical ring at any point of time and the membership mechanism reacts to a new member join request quickly without interfering with the normal order message multicast. On the other hand, the fault tolerance mechanism of the protocol is deterministic and guarantees failure-notice atomicity. During a normal operation, every correct member is waiting for some multicast messages from the current token holder. Therefore, they are unanimously monitoring the activity of the token holder. Suppose a site stops after it just transmitted an ordered multicast message; this failure will be detected by up to n-1 subsequent ordered multicast messages. Every alive member sees the failure at the same time, likewise, a coordinator forms a new ring after reaching the consensus of the surviving members. All the members will see the ring (membership) change simultaneously.

- Scaling. As the group size becomes large, the group communication performance is affected because more control messages and longer delay are needed for committing safe (atomic) messages to applications. In terms of control messages and delivery delay for an ordered, reliable multicast message, most existing protocols do not scale well. RMP deals with the problem in two ways: (1) with a small size group and lower frequency of messages (message cycle time), each member on the ring waits until its turn to be the token holder, then multicasts the messages generated from its applications. If there is no application message, it transmits a NULL packet (heart-beat) as a live message and acknowledges previous multicasts it received; (2) for a large size group, if the cycle time is long, a member that wants to send a message rapidly sends the message to the current token holder. The second method introduces only one extra point-to-point control message, enabling a member to fast multicast its message without waiting a longer time. But in terms of the atomic delivery, RMP still entails some delay.

8.7 Implementation Issues

This section discusses the implementation of reliable multicast protocol (RMP) based on a logical token ring. The logical token ring has been considered as a simple and efficient approach in the design of multicast protocol because the discrete multicast messages of many distributed processes are reduced to one process holding the token and multicasting a totally-ordered message at one time. RMP is implemented based on the UNIX 4.3 BSD operating system which provides a rich set of distributed program facilities. These facilities could be easily used in supporting resource sharing in a distributed environment. The initial implementation intends to implement RMP using sockets on a local area network connected to a 10 M Ethernet.

Both connection and connectionless sockets have been used between client processes and RMP processes. UNIX domain sockets are used for passing connection byte streams whereas datagram sockets are used to transmit messages across networks that model potentially unreliable, connectionless packet communication. The datagram socket *id* of each endpoint of communication is defined prior to transmission of any data, and is maintained at each process so that it can be presented at any time.

8.7.1 System Structure and Communication Assumptions

Figure 8.10 illustrates the system structure which consists of a group of sites, i.e., self-contained computers including high level application software. The sites are loosely coupled by a network and each RMP server process, *process* or *member* for short, accepts multicast requests from its local application via a submittal queue *QSUB* and delivers messages to the application via a delivery queue *QCMT*. Note that a process interacts with its applications through TCP connection. Once *QSUB* is full, the process ceases accepting messages and the applications are blocked. As long as the process has made a room from *QSUB,* it is able to receive the message request from its applications. The user application processes running on the upper level of the system access common resources, e.g., files, shared objects and database systems etc., and share the common information via resource managers.

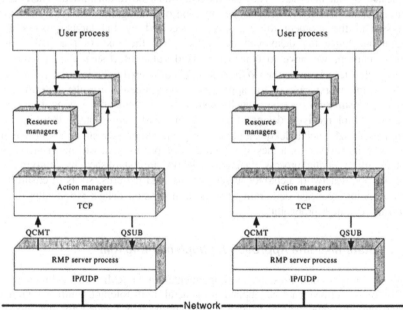

Figure 8.10: System structure

The strongest assumption that can be made about inter-process communication is that any message sent by an alive member to another (alive) member is always received within a given delay - the so-called *synchronous communication* assumption. The nice property of this assumption is that one member can reliably detect whether another member is alive just by sending a query and waiting a bounded time period for a response. Unfortunately, in a system where members must communicate over a shared network, such perfection is guaranteed only with certain probability, by using multiple communication paths and/or message retransmissions. It is even impossible to give a probabilistic guarantee, since the actual load on the network is unpredictable.

The opposite approach is to consider that there is no predefined limit on the time it takes for a message to reach its destination. Protocols designed without knowledge of time limits could be easily ported from one environment to another, since they would operate correctly whatever the performance of the network. With such *asynchronous communication,* a member cannot decide whether another member has crashed or whether its query or the expected response is still on its way going through the network. In practice, it is essential to introduce some notion of time so that members know how long to wait for an expected response before suspecting that the originator of the response might have failed.

For the implementation of RMP, we have used the datagram communication in an asynchronous network, which provides cheap means for any member to send a message to any other members. The datagram message packet may be lost, duplicated or out of order. The lost message must be retransmitted. There is an arbitrary random delay δ between the emission of a datagram message by a source process and the moment the message is received by the target process at a destination. Since the delay can be variable, for the sake of practical system implementation, we have to consider a fixed value of δ such that a datagram message that travels more than δ time units is considered to be lost. Therefore, δ is taken as the worst case or an approximate measurement for the point-to-point message transmission over an asynchronous network. Similarly, among a group of processes which receive a datagram message multicast from a source, there is also a random delay Δ. Such a delay should be designated to prevent situations in which a process waits forever for a message from another process that will never arrive due to the failure of the process. Datagram delays are established by studying the statistics about network behavior under various load patterns, so as to ensure that point-to-point/broadcast datagram message transmission delays are smaller than δ (Δ) with very high probability.

8.7.2 State Machine Approach for Implementing RMP

Although this section presents an implementation of RMP, the techniques and algorithms described can be applied to general fault-tolerant multicast protocol design and implementation. State machine approach is applied for the modular design and implementation of RMP. Therefore, RMP is taken as the modular composition of sub-protocols that work cooperatively in achieving message ordering, reliability and system fault-tolerance. This is similar to the microprotocol approach in [HS91, RB93]. To better understand the structure of RMP, the modular hierarchy is shown in Figure 8.11. RMP is a composition of *total ordering, atomicity, fault-tolerant* and *membership* protocols which achieve services as described in the previous sections. In RMP, the total order respects the causal order of Lamport. Message *receive* and *delivery* is distinguished. Message receive means that a message is received by RMP process while message delivery means that a message is committed to high level applications by the process.

The total ordering protocol guarantees the message multicast and delivery to applications in the same relative order. If a message desires atomic delivery, the atomic protocol is invoked. During the normal message multicast, by the *timeout* mechanism, if any fault is suspected, the fault-tolerant protocol is invoked to perform fault detection and fault location. Any membership change of the process group due to fault recovery or dynamic group is conducted by the membership protocol to handle the member join/leave, merge of two partitioning segments etc. The membership protocol forming a new group must guarantee membership change atomicity and have a consensus among the operational members. Since we have presented the design of these protocols in the previous section, we only discuss some issues about ordering protocol and membership protocol in this section.

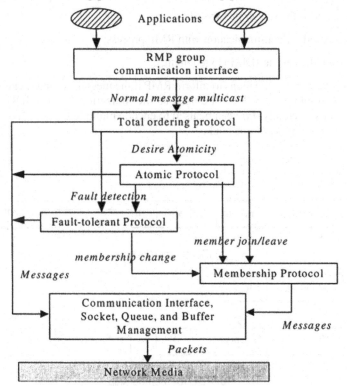

Figure 8.11: RMP hierarchy structure

8.7.3 *Message Packet and Control Information*

To implement message packets, one must define their types. RMP classifies the messages as *up-stream* and *down-stream*. A message received/delivered by a

204

process from/to upper application is defined as an information data unit (IDU); and a message sent/received by a process to/from network is defined as a packet data unit (PDU). A process attaches a PDU header to an IDU and makes it a PDU for network transmission. Likewise, a PDU can be stripped of its PDU header to become an IDU for delivery. Their formats are further given below:

IDU. There are two types of IDUs. One is the data IDU and another the membership IDU. The data IDU is used for data message passing between applications and processes. Membership IDU is delivered by a process to notify the applications of membership change. The format of the membership IDU is shown in Figure 8.12(a) in which sid_i is the id of a member process (or a member internet id) in a group; variable vi is used to inform applications about whether a member is new ($vi = 0$) or old ($vi > 0$) in G. RMP defines an IDU_HEADER for the use and information of high level applications. It consists of $sender\_id, port, length, flag,$ where

- $sender\_id$ is the sender process $id;$

- $port$ is used for communication with RMP process;

- $length$ indicates the IDU in byte length;

- $flag$ is used by applications to inform RMP if the message is an urgent message. For example, $flag = 1$ can be used as the indication that the IDU requires atomicity. Actually, $flag$ can be used to encode multiple types of IDU and this is out of the scope of this book.

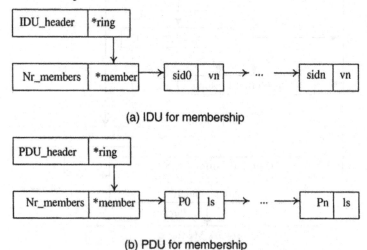

(a) IDU for membership

(b) PDU for membership

Figure 8.12: Packet for logical ring

PDU. In general, RMP control information is included in a PDU header with type PDU_HEADER. Its instance is attached to an IDU before sending it to a network. It is denoted as *header = (protocolID, version, sender, mid, s, k, code, len, coordinator),* where

- *protocolID* is the *id* of RMP which is currently running;

- *version* is the version of *R;*

- *sender* is *sid* of the PDU sender (or internet address);

- *mid = (sid, ls)* is a unique message *id* in which *sid* is the originator *sid* of the PDU[1]; *ls* is the local sequence number of the originator for this PDU;

- *s* is a sequence number denoting a total order of PDU if it is a multicast message; otherwise, it represents an acknowledgment of the sender about the previous message received;

- *k* is called a safe parameter, showing the sender's view of maximum order of the messages received by every member on the ring;

- *code* denotes the type of *m* and it is interpreted by the RMP as external events;

- *len* is the length of the PDU in bytes;

- *coordinator* is *sid* of ring coordinator.

There are three kinds of PDUs, namely *control, data,* and *ring* PDUs. A control PDU only has a *header;* A data PDU is a pair of *(header, *data)* where **data* is the pointer to IDU; a ring PDU is structured as in Figure 8.12(b) in which P_i is the member *sid* and *ls* is the local message sequence number of P_i.

8.7.4 Ordering Protocol

The value of total order for a multicast message in *R* is recorded in a sequence number *S*. There is a virtual token rotating in *R*. At one time, there is only one member holding the token, multicasting a total ordered message, and incrementing *S* by 1. The token implicitly circulates to the next process on *R*. Each member uses *S* for checking the message total ordering it received. All members expect the totally-ordered incoming message from the token holder. Each member predicts the id of the token holder by value of *S* plus 1 modulo the size of *R* which is denoted as *S⊕1*. A member wishing to multicast data messages can wait until it holds the token. If it has an urgent message, it can send the message to the current token holder, requesting the holder to multicast on behalf of it. If the token holder does not have a data message to send, it has to multicast a *NULL* message to let the token go to the next process on *R*, as shown in Figure 8.13.

---

* In general *sender = mid.sid*. In case that the PDU is a delegate message, the sender is different from the packet originator, then *sender not= mid.sid*.

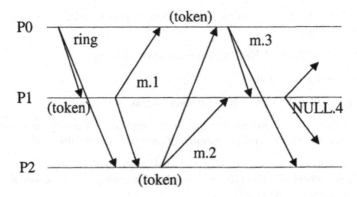

Figure 8.13: Ordered multicast

In this figure, a group consists of 3 members. P_0 multicasts ring R to all the processes and informs the membership and passes the token to P_1. P_1 then transmits $m.1$ and piggybacks the token to P_2 implicitly. P_2 then multicasts $m.2$. Upon receiving $m.1$, the receivers advance their S by $S := S+1$ and know that P_2 is the second token holder, and so forth. If P_{n-1} has multicasted the $(n-1)$th message, the token transfers to P_0 again for the multicast of the nth message. If the token holder has nothing to send, a *NULL* message is transmitted.

It may happen that different members have inconsistent values of S. This indicates that the members with a lower value of S may lose some ordered multicast messages. The member, upon reception of an ordered multicast message, can detect the lost messages via the gap between its S and the incoming message order. As a result, retransmission of the lost messages are immediately carried out without further delay. In RMP, a receiver initiates the message retransmission. Assume that P receives m and detects the missed messages via $S < m.s$, it sends a request to *m.sender*, asking for the retransmission of messages with order between $m.s$ - S. On the other hand, if $S > m.s$, P retransmits the messages with order in S - $m.s$ to *m.sender*. Intuitively, using S to monitor the token holder seems to cause problems because of inconsistent values of S. In fact, this scheme helps individual members to monitor the expected incoming message efficiently.

Multicasting a message from a user application to a network until it is received by group members requires message picketing and sending to the network. A user application on top of process P_i calls the RMP interface function *rmp_multicast (data)*, which generates an IDU header and inserts the IDU into the RMP port by calling Unix system call *write(rmp_port, IDU, idu_length)*. Figure 8.14 depicts the steps taken for a data message IDU received by a RMP and multicasted to the network. In the figure, the RMP uses Unix call *recv* to receive the IDU (step 1). The IDU is converted into a PDU by adding a PDU header with order S and it is queued in *QSUB* for multicast (step 2 and 3). On receiving, and therefore holding the token, P_i multicasts the PDU to the network; if not, the flag of the IDU is checked to see if it is *fast* or *atomfast*. In the latter case, the PDU is forwarded to the current token holder anticipated by P_i where $i = S_i \oplus 1$.

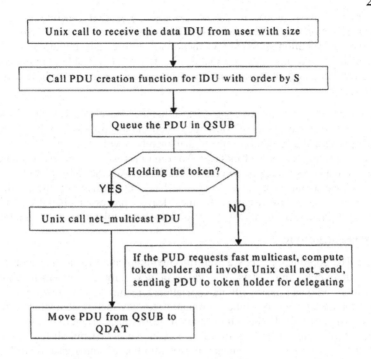

Figure 8.14: Steps taken for RMP to multicast an ordered message

Reception of a multicast message m requires P_i to save the sender information in the corresponding membership, say $R[j]$ where $m.sender = P_j$. The information includes the sender's local sequence number. The $m.s$ is checked to see if it is in the expected message order, i.e., if $m.s = S_i+1$. If so, m is queued in $QDAT$ for delivery. Otherwise, m is queued in $QSUS$ until it is in the total order in terms of P_i and it is linked to $QDAT$. In case that the flag of m requires atomic delivery, atomic protocol is invoked as described in the next subsection.

8.7.5 Membership Protocol

Dynamic membership protocol allows a process to join or leave R dynamically even when the process is not known in advance. Actually, RMP uses Ethernet broadcast to implement multicast. The dynamic membership change algorithm has been described in Section 8.6.3.2. Here we want to discuss some issues in the presence of faults.

Failure during membership change

When a new process wants to join a group, there are two cases that must be considered: (1) the "join" request is lost, and (2) the coordinator fails during the process join. In the first case, the new process normally sets a special timer to monitor the response of the coordinator. On expiration of the timer, the new process can retransmit its requests. In the second case, if several timeouts are reached without reception of a response from the coordinator, the new process will broadcast an invitation message. As mentioned before, this invitation forces the processes in the existing ring to respond. The new process is able to join the group eventually along with the group reformation, as shown in the 2-phase algorithm described below.

When a member wants to leave, one issue is that the "leave" message may be lost. If the coordinator misses a "leave" message, when the token moves to the position of the left process, the remaining operational members will detect its leave because they are expecting an ordered message from the process. In this circumstance, the process is treated as a stopped process and RMP invokes the fault-tolerant protocol. Therefore, we assume the "leave" message has been received by the coordinator. Membership change in response to the "leave" process is handled with the following 2-phase algorithm, which is similar to that in tolerating single site failure.

Two-phase algorithm

Phase1: The coordinator sends a "reform" invitation message to all members and collects their *acks* and orders, i.e., value of *ack.s,* for an agreement about the reformation. In fact, nearly all the operational members send their *acks* to the coordinator simultaneously. If the coordinator sees any inconsistency between *ack.s* and its own *S,* it will do the retransmission of messages. Therefore, lost messages can be retransmitted. If the coordinator receives the *acks* from all the operational members or the majority of members, it goes into Phase2, otherwise, RMP loops in this phase until the majority condition is met.

Phase2: The coordinator constructs a new logical token ring R' in terms of the members acknowledged. It forms a message, containing the new ring, multicasts the message and piggybacks an up-to-date safety parameter to inform all the members to replace R and increment their ring version. Note that the messages sent in R should be committed despite the reformation. On receipt of R', all members on R' commit the messages in accordance with the safety parameter. The coordinator multicasts a resume message to the members in R'. As soon as the resume message is received, all members deliver R' to their application processes, inform users of the change of membership and resume normal operations.

Note that the consensus of membership change is achieved approximately among the operational processes. A coordinator who fails to recruit the majority of members must block all processes until some new processes join it or all members join another ring. The blocked processes remain in the old ring in case several partitions occur. RMP allows users to decide if a minority ring can continue to operate. In practice, as long as the majority of members are alive, the coordinator will finally form a ring with the majority of members and RMP can continue its normal operations.

Failure during the reformation

Any member may fail during the reformation phase. Suppose a member, other than the coordinator, fails before sending its *ack.* The coordinator can detect this failure by time-out, i.e., the coordinator is expecting an *ack* message from the process. On expiration of the timer, the coordinator eliminates the failed process from the new ring. If the process fails after it sent out the *ack,* the coordinator cannot detect the failure. The failed process will be included in the new ring. But this causes no trouble because normal execution of RMP in the new ring will circulate the virtual token to the failed process eventually. The failure thus can be detected by the fault-tolerant protocol described earlier.

If the coordinator fails or is not reachable by the majority of members, a new coordinator must be elected according to rules (**C1 – C3**) described in Section 8.5.3.1. The rules are applied if a process receives more than one invitation or if a candidate invites another candidate. As long as the coordinator is elected, the two-phase reformation algorithm can be performed again.

8.8 Summary

Group communication is highly desirable for maintaining a consistent state in distributed systems. Most underlying communication and distributed systems are subject to a number of possible failures, such as site crashes and communication failures. Currently, most practical systems use reliable multicast protocols to achieve a consistent view among the operational processes. Group communication is achieved through reliable multicast protocols. A reliable multicast protocol (RMP) guarantees the properties such as ordering and atomicity. This chapter discussed the design and implementation of an RMP based on a logical token ring for the general distributed asynchronous systems. The RMP based on a logical token ring has very simple structure. The novelty of the RMP is to rotate the token position implicitly on the ring while multicasting an ordered message at the same time. The protocol requires a minimum number of control messages and transfers the token responsibility among the processes on a logical ring, placing total orders on each multicast message and ensuring the messages are received by all correct processes in the same order. The RMP has provided efficient algorithms for reliable message delivery and for failure detection and recovery of ordering. In addition, it offers flexibility of dynamic group membership changes, requiring the minimum resources of the underlying communication networks. In respect to message atomicity, the RMP has minimized control messages and communication costs while incurring a short delay. It is superior to the existing token based protocols and is competitive with the two-phase method in terms of safe delivery delay. The significant contributions of the RMP lies in its global optimization of the modular design and implementation for total message ordering, atomicity, dynamic group configuration and fault-tolerance.

Exercises

8.1   What is unicast communication? What is multicast communication? 8.1

8.2   What features does group communication have? 8.2

8.3   What is quorom delivery? What is its other name? 8.2.1

8.4   What is the difference between causal ordering and total ordering? 8.2.3

8.5   Given the following figure, specify which messages conform to FIFO and Causal ordering. Does it meet total ordering? 8.2.3

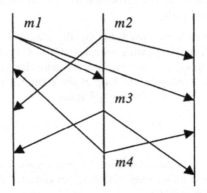

8.6   What kind of failures may occur in the multicast communication system? 8.3.1

8.7   How does one understand using negative acknowledgment systems to reduce the packet transmission and synchronization overheads? 8.3.2

8.8   How does one achieve a multicast resilience to the degree r in the centralized multicast approach? 8.4.1

8.9   Design two programs to achieve: (1) a client sends packets to a multicast group; (2) a group member receives the packets and displays the packet contents. 8.5

8.10   What is a logical ring? How is it formed? 8.6.1

8.11   How does one calculate a current token holder's position? Give an example. 8.6.1

8.12   What is the safe parameter approach? 8.6.2

8.13   How is the coordinator selected during membership construction? 8.6.3.1

8.14   How is a member "join" request handled? 8.6.3.2

8.15   In the tolerating single site failure algorithm, why choose the prior token holder as the coordinator? 8.6.4.1

8.16   In the same algorithm, what are the purposes of two phases for reformation? 8.6.4.1

8.17   What are results of network partitioning in terms of group communication? 8.6.4.2

8.18   Why can RMP minimize the control message overhead? 8.6.5

8.19   What is asynchronous communication? How does one deal with it? 8.7.1

8.20   How is RMP constructed? 8.7.2

8.21 How are the lost messages in RMP transmitted? 8.7.5

8.22 Compare the differences between two 2-phase algorithms used in tolerating single site failure and membership protocol. 8.7.8, 8.6.4.1

This page intentionally left blank

CHAPTER 9 RELIABILITY AND REPLICATION TECHNIQUES

A computer system, or a distributed system consists of many hardware/software components that are likely to fail eventually. In many cases, such failures may have disastrous results. With the ever increasing dependency being placed on distributed systems, the number of users requiring fault tolerance is likely to increase. The design and understanding of fault-tolerant distributed systems is a very difficult task. We have to deal with not only all the complex problems of distributed systems when all the components are well, but also the more complex problems when some of the components fail. This chapter introduces the basic concepts and techniques that relate to fault-tolerant computing.

9.1 Basic Concepts

Each component in a computer system is generally constructed from a collection of other software and hardware components, some of which may fail from time to time. There are two approaches to increasing system reliability: *fault avoidance* and *fault tolerance*. The goal of fault avoidance is to reduce the likelihood of failures (by using conservative design practices, high-reliability components, etc.) while the goal of fault tolerance is to ensure correct operation even in the presence of faults. In this section, we introduce the basic concepts about system reliability, such as fault, failure, reliability, availability, and so on.

9.1.1 Fault Tolerance

Before we introduce the concept of system reliability, there are some other concepts about fault tolerant computing that need to be classified.

- *System/specification.* A system is defined as an identifiable mechanism that maintains an observable behaviour at its interface with its environment. The system's behaviour is defined by a finite set of specifications that describes the inputs to and responses from the system, and system's states and state transitions. Figure 9.1 shows a system decomposition.

- *Faults/errors/failures.* A fault is a source that has the potential of generating errors. An error is the manifestation of a fault within a program, a data structure, a component, or a system; errors can occur some distance from the fault location. A failure occurs when the delivered services deviate from the specified services. Failures are caused by errors. Figure 9.2(a) depicts the relationship of fault, error, and failure.

214

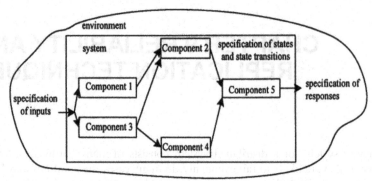

Figure 9.1: A system

- *Permanent/intermittent/transient failures.* Faults, errors, and failures can be further classified as *permanent* (that is, continuous and stable; in hardware, permanent failure reflects an irreversible physical change), *intermittent* (that is, only occasionally present due to unstable hardware or varying hardware or software state, such as a function of load or activity), and *transient* (that is, resulting from temporary environmental conditions).

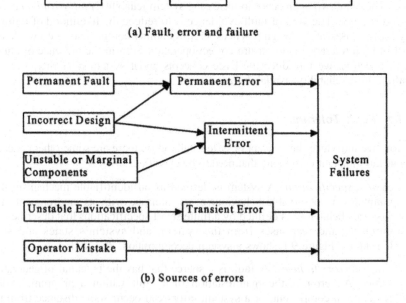

Figure 9.2: Fault, error, and failure

Transient and intermittent faults are a major source of error in systems; 80-90% of electronic failures in computers are transient and intermittent. Figure 9.2(b) shows the source of errors.

- *Failure Rate.* Failure Rate is defined as the expected number of failures of a type of device or system per a given time period. For example, a 32K RAM chip may have a failure rate of 7 failures per million hours.

Sometimes it is convenient to define the *failure rate function* as a function of time. From the failure rate function we can calculate the failure rate (failures per unit of time) in a given time. The commonly accepted relationship between the failure rate function and time for electronic components is called the *bathtub curve,* as shown in Figure 9.3. Here λ is the failure rate and is normally expressed in units of failures per hour (or per million hours).

Failure rate

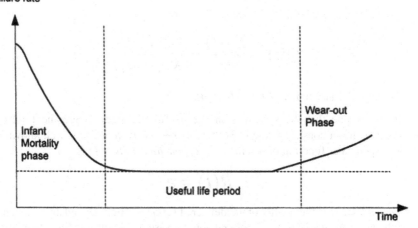

Figure 9.3: The bathtub curve

- *Fault coverage.* Fault coverage is a measure of a system's ability to perform fault tolerance. There are four primary types of fault coverage: fault detection, fault location, fault containment, and fault recovery coverage, respectively. They are measures of a system's ability to detect, locate, contain, and recover from faults. The fault recovery coverage is the most commonly considered, and the general term "fault coverage" is often used to mean fault recovery coverage. It is mathematically defined as the conditional probability that, given the existence of a fault, the system recovers:

$$C = P(fault\ recovery \mid fault\ existence).$$

9.1.2 *Reliability and Availability*

Reliability is a conditional probability that a system survives for the time interval [0, t], given that it was operational at time $t=0$. That is, the reliability R of a system is a function of time t:

$$R(t) = Pr \{0 \text{ failures in } [0, t] \mid \text{no failure at } t = 0\}.$$

Let $N_o(t)$ be the number of components that are operating correctly at time t, $N_f(t)$ be the number of components that have failed at time t, and N be the number of components that are in operation at time t:

$$R(t) = \frac{N_o(t)}{N} = \frac{N_o(t)}{N_o(t) + N_f(t)}$$

Similarly, we can define the *unreliability* Q as:

$$Q(t) = \frac{N_f(t)}{N} = \frac{N_f(t)}{N_o(t) + N_f(t)}$$

Of course, at any time t, $R(t) = 1.0 - Q(t)$.

If we assume that the system is in the useful-life stage where the failure rate function has a constant value of λ, then the *reliability function* is well known to be an exponential function of parameter λ *(exponential failure law)*:

$$R(t) = e^{-\lambda t}$$

Dependability is the quality of the delivered services. High dependability means that reliance can justifiably be placed on a system. Fault-tolerant computing is concerned with the method of achieving computer system dependability.

Availability is the intuitive sense of reliability. A system is reliable if it is able to perform its intended function at the moment the function is required. Formally, it is the probability that the system is operational at the instance of time t. To understand the availability, we have to classify the following concepts:

- *Mean time to failure (MTTF):* MTTF is the expected time that a system will operate before the *first* failure occurs.

$$MTTF = \frac{\sum_{i=1}^{N} t_i}{N}$$

where N is the number of identical systems measured, t_i is the time that system i operates before encountering the first failure, and the start time is t (=0). If the reliability function obeys the exponential failure law, then

$$MTTF = \int_0^\infty e^{-\lambda t} dt = \frac{1}{\lambda}$$

- *Mean time to repair (MTTR):* MTTR is the average time required to repair a system. If the ith of N faults requires a time t_i to repair, the MTTR is estimated as:

$$MTTR = \frac{\sum_{i=1} t_i}{N}$$

The MTTR is normally specified in terms of a *repair rate* μ, which is the average number of repairs that occur per time period (hour):

$$MTTR = \frac{1}{\mu}$$

- *Mean time between failure (MTBF):* MTBF is the average time between failures of a system. For example, if there are N systems and each of them is operated for some time T and the number of failures encountered by the ith system is recorded as n_i. The average number of failures is computed as

$$n_{avg} = \sum_{i-1}^{N} \frac{n_i}{N}$$

Finally, the MTBF is

$$MTBF = \frac{T}{n_{avg}}$$

If we assume that all repairs to a system make the system perfect once again just as it was when it was new, the relationship between the *MTTF* and *MTBF* is: *MTBF = MTTF + MTTR*, as illustrated in Figure 9.4.

9.1.3 Failure Classification

[Cristian 1991] gives the following classification of failures that might happen in the distributed systems with respect to services provided by servers.

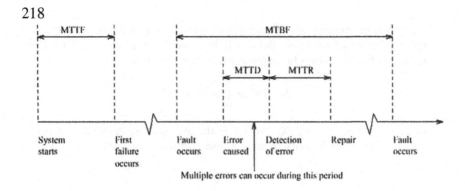

Figure 9.4: Relationships between MTBF, MTTF, and MTTR.

- *Omission failure:* a failure occurs when a server omits to respond to an input. This kind of failure could be due to lost requests from clients.

- *Timing failure:* a failure occurs when a server's response is functionally correct but untimely. Timing failures can be either early or late. The cause of this kind of failure might be that the server is busy with a high priority job, the heavy traffic of network, queuing problem, and so on.

- *Response failure:* a failure occurs when a server responds incorrectly. This failure could be caused by design errors incurred in implementing the server, or the protocol used to communicate between clients and the server.

- *Crash failure:* a crash failure occurs when a server stops running. This failure could be a hardware failure, the machine being switched off deliberately, or a detected error, possibly non-recoverable, that brings the system to a fail-stop.

9.2   Techniques to Achieve Reliability

There are a number of techniques used to build reliable distributed network systems: *redundancy, fault avoidance techniques, fault detection techniques,* and *fault tolerance techniques.*

9.2.1   Redundancy

Redundancy is the basic requirement in any technique to achieve reliability. Redundant elements are those system components that can be removed without affecting the performance of a system (assuming that the remaining system is fault free). Redundancy provides information about the state of the system and the components that are needed for recovery from failures.

In terms of using resources, there are space and time redundancies respectively:

- *Space redundancy:*

  o Hardware redundancy: uses extra gates, memory cells, bus lines, functional modules, and other hardware to supply recovery information.

  o Software redundancy: uses alternate or independent versions of algorithms to provide recovery information.

- *Time redundancy:* uses extra computing or execution by the same or different methods to retry the failed operation and provide a basis for subsequent action.

Redundancies can also be classified as:

- *Static redundancy:* employs redundant components to mask the effects of hardware or software failures within a given module. The output of the module remains unaffected, i.e., error free, as long as the protection due to redundancy is effective. This module assumes that failures of redundant elements are independent, not related.

- *Dynamic redundancy:* allows errors to appear at the output of modules. When a fault is detected, a recovery action eliminates or corrects the resulting error. Dynamic redundancy implies a requirement for fault detection, fault location and recovery processes.

In response to a failure, a redundant system may take the following steps:

- *Fault confinement:* limiting the spread of fault effects to one area of the system, thereby preventing contamination of other areas.

- *Fault detection:* detecting faults, e.g., checking parity, consistency, protocol violation, etc. But they cannot be perfect and fault latency (the delay from the manifestation of the fault to the detection of the fault) exists.

- *Fault masking or static redundancy:* using techniques to hide the effects of failures. Majority voting is an example of fault masking.

- *Retry:* in many cases a second attempt of an operation may be successful. This is particularly true with a transient fault that causes no physical damage.

- *Diagnosis:* obtaining information about a failure's location and/or properties.

- *Reconfiguration:* replacing the failed component or isolating it from the rest of the system, or "graceful degradation".

- *Recovery:* after the elimination of errors, the system operation is normally backed up (rolled back) to some point in its processing that proceeded the fault detection, usually using backup files, checkpointing, etc.

- *Restart:* when recovery is impossible or if the system is not designed for recovery.

  o "Hot" restart: resumption of all operations from the point of fault detection.

  o "Warm" restart: only some of the processes can be resumed without loss.

o "Cold" restart: complete reload of the system, with no processes surviving.

- Repair: repairing the faulty component diagnosed.

- Reintegration: reintegrating the repaired module into the system.

9.2.2 Fault Avoidance Techniques

Fault avoidance techniques are used to reduce the probability of failure and are intended to decrease the possibility of transient faults by manipulating factors that affect the failure rates. Environmental changes, quality changes, and complexity changes due to component integration level are three fault avoidance techniques whose goal is to obtain a lower system failure rate.

- *Environmental changes:* e.g., the use of a cooling system to control the (junction) temperature.

- *Quality changes:* e.g., testing, debugging, verification, and in-house screening to eliminate weak hardware/software components.

- *Complexity changes:* e.g., higher integration/abstraction/modelling levels permit designs with fewer chips, fewer solder joints, less board space, fewer functions/procedures, fewer modules, fewer interactions, and thus reduce failure rates.

9.2.3 Fault Detection Techniques

The first step in tolerating faults is to detect faults. Therefore, fault detection techniques are an integrated part of fault tolerant techniques. Fault detection techniques recognise the inevitability of eventual failure, no matter how well the system is designed. The key to fault detection is redundancy. Fault detection techniques include the following:

- *Duplication:* applicable to all areas and levels of computer design. Two identical copies are employed. When a failure occurs in one copy, the two copies are no longer identical and a simple comparison detects the fault.

  Duplication can detect all non-overlapping, single faults except faults in the comparison unit. Identical faults from identical modules are not detectable because both copies are in agreement.

- *Error-Detection Code:* e.g., Parity, Checksums, or Cyclic Codes (Cyclic Redundancy Check, CRC). They are the systematic application of redundancy to information.

- *Self-Checking and Fail-Safe (Fail-Stop):* a self-checking system checks its own behaviour against some pre-specified specifications to ensure that it is doing the right thing. A fail-stop system stops functioning (no more input to and output from the system) as long as a fault occurs.

- *Watchdog Timers and Timeouts:* watchdog timers provide a simple and inexpensive way to keep track of proper process functioning. A timer is maintained as a process separated from the process it checks. If the timer is not reset before it times out, it is indicative that the corresponding process failed in some way. It is assumed that any failure in the checked process will cause it to miss, resetting its watchdog timer. Coverage is limited, however, because data and results are not checked, and because the process may fail partially yet still be able to reset its timer. This technique can be used in both hardware and software designs.

  Timeouts are different from the watchdog timers in that they provide a finer check of control flow. They are based on the principle that certain operations should complete within a prespecified maximum time.

- *Consistency and Capability Checking:* consistency checking is performed by verifying that intermediate or final results are within a reasonable range either on an absolute basis or as a function of the inputs.

  Capability checking is usually part of the operating system, but it can also be implemented in hardware. This technique guarantees that access to objects is limited to users with proper authorisation.

9.2.4   Fault Tolerance Techniques

Fault tolerance techniques can be categorised into *static redundancy* and *dynamic redundancy,* according to their use of redundant components.

Static redundancy techniques

Static redundancy uses redundancy to provide fault tolerance by either isolating or correcting faults before the faulty results reach module outputs. Once the redundant copies of an element are connected in the circuit or embedded into the program, they remain fixed. The errors resulting from faulty components are "masked" by the presence of other copies of those components. No fault detection is provided (but can be added in). The static redundancy technique has the following methods:

- *Voting:* one common technique of static redundancy is the N-modular redundancy with voting (NMR): eg., Triple Modular Redundancy (TMR). By using majority voting (two out of three), a failure in any one of these three copies can be masked.

  This concept can be extended to include "N" copies with majority voting at the outputs (NMR). Normally N is an odd number. The cost of NMR is N times the basic hardware / software cost, plus the cost of the voter.

  In digital systems, majority voting is normally performed on a bit-by-bit basis. Voting can be applied at any level in the system: gate level, module level, bus level, software level (N-version programming).

- *Error-Correcting Codes:* this is the most commonly used means of static redundancy. Many use Hamming single-error-correcting (SEC) codes. These codes are inexpensive in terms of both cost and performance overheads (with 10-40% redundancy and very small decoding and encoding delays). These codes are widely used in RAM designs (RAMs contribute 60-70% of system failure rates).

Dynamic redundancy techniques

Dynamic redundancy techniques involve the reconfiguration of system components in response to failures. The reconfiguration prevents failures from contributing their effects to the system operation. If static redundancy is used as part of the dynamic redundancy scheme, the removal of failed components may be postponed until enough failures have accumulated to threaten an impending unmaskable failure. The dynamic redundancy techniques include the following:

- *Reconfigurable duplication:* two units (A and B) run simultaneously, and their outputs are always compared. However, the output of only one unit goes to the external hardware. The other unit (standby unit) functions in parallel with the active unit, but it is not connected to the outputs. When a comparison detects a failure, diagnosis will determine which of the units is bad and the good unit will be switched on-line so that its outputs supply the external components. The other unit will be switched off-line. Figure 9.5 shows the architecture of a reconfigurable duplication system.

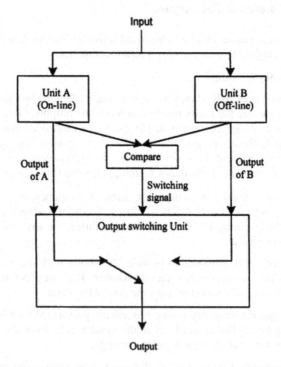

Figure 9.5: Reconfigurable duplication architecture

Following is a list of some possible diagnostic methods that can be used in the *Compare* and *Output Switching Unit* of Figure 9.5.

o   Run a diagnostic program.

o   Include self-checking capabilities in each module.

υ   Use a watchdog timer.

o   Use an outside arbiter.

- *Reconfigurable N-module-redundancy (NMR):* one of the drawbacks of NMR with voting is that the fault-masking ability deteriorates as more copies fail. The faulty modules eventually out-vote the good modules. However, an NMR can still function if the known bad modules could be disconnected in the vote.

- *Hybrid redundancy:* combine NMR with voting and backup sparing techniques. A core of N identical modules is in use at any one time, with their outputs voted upon to produce the system output. When a disagreement is detected, the module (or modules) in the minority are considered to have failed and are replaced by an equivalent number of spare modules. Hybrid system reliability is greatly dependent on the switch complexity.

- *Adaptive voting:* to modify the voting process dynamically as the system deteriorates. For example, in an NMR/simplex system, the initial configuration is conventional NMR. When one module fails, it and one other module are removed from the system, leaving an (N-2) modular redundancy system. The removal of two modules preserves the property that all votes are unambiguous: no tie is possible. Eventually, the system deteriorates into a simplex system.

- *Graceful degradation:* graceful-degradation techniques use the redundant components as part of the system's normal resources at all times.

- *Recovery:* recovery techniques can restore enough of the system state to allow process execution to recommence, without a complete restart and with little or no loss of acquired information. Recovery techniques are usually implemented in software, but may have some hardware bases as well.

   o   Backward Error Recovery Techniques: process execution is restarted at (rolled back to) some point before the occurrence of the error.

   o   Retry techniques: are the fastest and conceptually the simplest.

   o   Checkpoint techniques: back up the process to an earlier point in its execution. Checkpointing is often implemented in software and requires little or no hardware, but it requires extra time.

- *Journaling:* a technique in which a copy of the initial data is stored as a process begins. As the process executes, it makes a record of all transactions that affect the data. Thus, if the process fails, its effect can be recreated by running a copy of the backup data through the transactions a second time, after any failures have been repaired.

- *Forward Error Recovery Techniques:* attempt to continue operation with the system state at hand, even though it may be faulty. These techniques are usually highly application dependent.

- *Masking:* is a commonly used fault-tolerant method. Hierarchical failure masking and group failure masking are two end points of a continuum of failure masking techniques. With hierarchical failure masking, servers at the higher level of abstraction will mask the failure of the lower-level servers. With group failure masking, by employing a group of redundant servers, if some of these fail, the rest of the servers will provide the services.

A key issue in designing multi-layered fault-tolerant systems is how to balance the amounts of failure detection, recovery, and masking redundancy used at various abstraction levels of a system, in order to obtain the best possible overall cost/performance results. Thus, a small investment at a lower level of abstraction for ensuring that lower-level servers have a stronger failure semantics can often contribute to substantial cost savings and speed improvements at higher levels of abstraction and can result in a lower overall cost.

9.3 Software Fault Tolerance

Why do we require fault tolerance in software? Software does not degrade physically as a function of time or environmental stresses. A program that has once performed a given task as specified will continue to do so provided that none of the following change: the input, the computing environment, or user requirements.

However, the above factors do change. So, past and current failure-free operation cannot be taken as a dependable indication that there will be no failures in the future. Failure experience in current software has shown that existing software products exhibit a fairly constant failure frequency. *Fault density* has been defined as the number of faults per 1000 lines of code. It ranges 10-50 for "good" software and 1-5 after intensive testing.

Software failures usually differ in their impact on the operations of an organisation. Therefore, we need to classify them by severity and come up with the failure intensity or reliability for each classification. At least three classification criteria are in common use: *cost impact, human impact,* and *service impact.*

Difficulties in software test and verification:

- Difficulties in testing: testing can be used to show the presence of bugs, but never show their absence. Complete testing of any practical programs is impossible because of the vast number of possible input combinations.

- Difficulties in verification: formal verification has been applied on an experimental basis and usually to small programs (too formal, difficult to use, expensive in handling large programs, difficult in real-time program verification, and difficult in translating a natural language specification into a formal specification).

9.3.1 Techniques for Software Fault-tolerance

Design techniques for software fault tolerance include *N-version programming* and *recovery blocks.*

N-version programming. The independent generation of N *(>=2)* functionally equivalent programs, called *versions,* from the same initial specification.

When $N=2$, N-version programming can be expected to provide good coverage for error detection but may be found wanting in assuring continued operation of the software. Upon disagreement among the versions, three alternatives are available:

- Retry or restart (in this case fault containment rather than fault tolerance is provided);

- Retransmission to a "safe state," possibly followed by later retries;

- Reliance on one of the versions, either designed in advance as more reliable or selected by a diagnostic program.

For $N >= 3$, a majority voting logic can be implemented. $N=3$ is the most commonly used method. A 3-version programming requires:

1. Three independent programs, each furnishing identical output formats.

2. An acceptance program that evaluates the output of requirement 1.

3. A driver (or executive segment) that invokes requirements 1 and 2 and furnishes the results to other programs.

Recovery block. A recovery block consists of three software elements:

- A primary routine, which executes critical software functions;

- An acceptance test, which tests the output of the primary routine after each execution;

- An alternate routine, which performs the same function as the primary routine (but may be less capable or slower), and is invoked by the acceptance test upon detection of a failure.

A recovery block is a block in the normal programming language sense, except that, at the entrance to the block, it is an automatic recovery point and at the exit it is an acceptance test. The acceptance test is used to test if the system is in an acceptable state after the first execution of the block, or primary module as it is often called. The failure of the acceptance test results in the program being restored to the recovery point at the beginning of the block and the second alternative module being executed. If the second module also fails the acceptance test, then the program is restored to the recovery point and yet another alternative module is executed. If all the alternatives are exhausted, the system fails. Therefore, the recovery must take place at a higher level. The recovery block is used for safely accessing critical data. It also detects errors through the acceptance test after running each alternative. It could be designed to detect further errors by thoughtfully designing alternatives.

The structure of a recovery block can be described as follows:

```
Structure:
Ensure T
    By P
    Else by Q
Else Error
```

where T is the acceptance test condition that is expected to be met by successful execution of either the primary routine P or alternate routine Q. The structure is easily expanded to accommodate several alternates $Q_1, Q_2, ..., Q_n$.

Error Recover. Error recovery is a mechanism which brings a system to an error-free state. There are two approaches to recovery: *backward recovery* and *forward recovery*. The backward recovery restores the system to a prior state, which is referred to as a *recovery point*. The forward recovery attempts to continue from an erroneous state by making selective corrections to the system state. The act of establishing the recovery point is the *checkpointing* which is a process of checking and saving the current system state for recovery. Rollback is one of the backward recovery mechanisms. Rollback is often employed by database systems to return the system state from the unfinished transaction to the previous consistent state by undoing all the steps that have been done since the transaction was started.

To be able to recover, it is necessary to store the system's state at the recovery point to a stable storage, such as a hard disk, so recovery needs *space*. Also recovery takes *time*, and the whole process has to stop from proceeding by executing a recovery algorithm instead. In a real-time system, because of the tight time constraint to reach a certain state, recovery mechanisms might not be a possible solution to the detected errors.

Domino effect. If two concurrent processes are interacting with each other, one process that rolls back to its recovery point might cause the other one to roll back to its recovery point as well. This procedure could go on until the whole system returns to its original state. This phenomenon is called the *domino effect*. The cause of this phenomenon is that each process is designed to have its own recovery point which does not consider others' recovery points. By carefully designing a consistent recovery point among all processes that are interacting with each other during the execution, this problem can be avoided.

Logging. Logging (or audit trail) is a way used to keep track of modifications or operations since last checkpointing, so the system can be able to roll back to the latest consistent state. There are various logging mechanisms designed to suit a variety of applications. Logs are saved to permanent storage (disk files) to survive any crashes.

9.4 Reliability Modelling

We have introduced the basic concepts of reliability and fault-tolerance above. In this section we discuss how to build a model to properly describe system reliability.

9.4.1 Combinatorial Models

Series systems

Our discussion of reliability modelling starts from a *series system*. A series system is one in which each element is required to operate correctly for the system to operate correctly (no redundancy). Figure 9.6 depicts a series system.

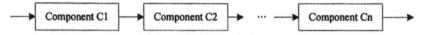

Figure 9.6: Reliability block diagram of a series system

Let $C_{iw}(t)$ represent the event that component C_i is working properly at time t, $R_i(t)$ is the reliability of component C_i at time t, and $R_{series}(t)$ is the reliability of the series system. The reliability at any time t is the probability that all N components are working properly:

$$R_{series}(t) = P(C_{1w}(t) \cap C_{2w}(t) \cap ... \cap C_{Nw}(t))$$

Assume that the events $C_{iw}(t)$ are independent, then

$$R_{series}(t) = R_1(t)R_2(t)...R_N(t) = \prod_{i=1}^{N} R_i(t)$$

Suppose each component C_i satisfies the exponential failure law such that the reliability of each component is $R_i(t) = e^{-\lambda_i t}$. Then

$$R_{series}(t) = e^{-\lambda_1 t}...e^{-\lambda_N t} = e^{-\lambda_{system} t}$$

where $\lambda_{system} = \sum_{i=1}^{N} \lambda_i$ and corresponds to the failure rate of the system.

Example: Figure 9.7 shows a simple aircraft control system. Each element of the system is required if the system is to perform correctly. There is no redundancy.

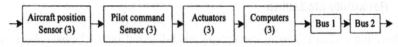

Figure 9.7: The example reliability block diagram

Assume that all six sensors have the same reliability $R_s(t)$, each of the three actuators has the reliability $R_{act}(t)$, and each computer has the reliability $R_c(t)$. Also let the computer interconnection bus have the reliability $R_{bus1}(t)$ and the primary control bus have the reliability $R_{bus2}(t)$; then

$$R_{system}(t) = R_s^6(t)R_{act}^3(t)R_c^3(t)R_{bus1}(t)R_{bus2}(t)$$

and

$$\lambda_{system} = 6\lambda_s + 3\lambda_{act} + 3\lambda_c + \lambda_{bus1} + \lambda_{bus2}$$

Parallel systems

A parallel system is one in which only one of several elements must be operational for the system to perform its functions correctly, as depicted in Figure 9.8.

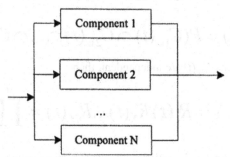

Figure 9.8: Reliability block diagram of the parallel system

The unreliability of a parallel system can be computed as the probability that all the N elements fail. Let $C_{if}(t)$ represent the event that element i has failed at time t, $Q_{parallel}(t)$ be the unreliability of the parallel system, and $Q_i(t)$ be the unreliability of the ith element. Then

$$Q_{parallel}(t) = P(C_{1f}(t) \cap C_{2f}(t) \cap ... \cap C_{Nf}(t))$$

$$= Q_1(t)Q_2(t)...Q_N(t) = \prod_{i=1...N} Q_i(t)$$

So the reliability of the parallel system is:

$$R_{parallel}(t) = 1.0 - Q_{parallel}(t) = 1.0 - \prod_{i=1...N} Q_i(t) = 1.0 - \prod_{i=1...N}(1.0 - R_i(t)).$$

The above equations assume that the failures of the individual elements that make up the parallel system are independent.

Example: Figure 9.9 depicts a simple aerospace control system. The system has two identical units of devices, and it requires that at least one of the units work properly for the system to perform its function. Once a unit has failed, it is assumed that another unit automatically resumes the functions of the failed unit.

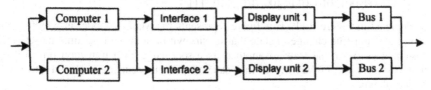

Figure 9.9: Example reliability block diagram

A parallel organisation can be reduced to a series element with the same reliability. So the reduced reliability diagram for the system is

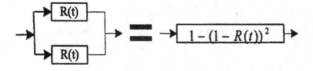

Figure 9.10: Reduced reliability block diagram

where $R_c(t)$ is the reliability of one computer, $R_{if}(t)$ is the reliability of one interface unit, $R_d(t)$ is the reliability of one display unit, and $R_b(t)$ is the reliability of one bus. So

$$R_{system} =$$

$$(1-(1-R_c(t))^2)(1-(1-R_{if}(t))^2)(1-(1-R_d(t))^2)(1-(1-R_b(t))^2).$$

The reliability of the system after one hour given $R_c(1) = R_{if}(1) = R_b(1) = 0.9$ will be $R_{system}(1\,hour) = 0.96.$

9.4.2 Markov Models

Example: The analysis of the *Triple-Modular Redundancy (TMR)* model. Three identical modules are used to execute a task. Their results are compared through a majority voting (two out of three). Thus a failure in any of these modules can be masked.

Let states be $S = (S_1, S_2, S_3)$, where $S_i = 1$ if module i is fault free and $S_i = 0$ if module i is faulty. The *TMR* has eight states:

$$000, 001, 010, 011, 100, 101, 110, 111$$

as depicted in Figure 9.11. This figure represents the Markov model in which each state transition (the change of state that occurs within a system; as time passes, the system goes from one state to another) is associated with a transition probability that describes the probability of that state transition occurring within a specified period of time.

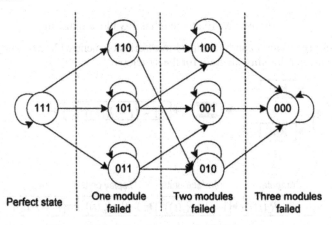

Figure 9.11: State diagram of a TRM system

The states 000, 001, 010, 100 in Figure 9.11 represent states in which the system has ceased to function correctly. Assume that the system does not contain repair and that only one failure will occur at a time. The above states can be partitioned into three categories: the *perfect state* (111); the *one-failed states* (110), (101), and (011), the *system failed states* (100), (001), (101), and (000). They can be used to reduce the Markov model.

Reduced Markov Model: Let state 3 correspond to the state in which all three modules are functioning correctly; state 2 is the state in which two modules are working correctly; state 1 is the failed state in which two or more modules have failed. Figure 9.12 shows the reduced Markov model. In this model,

$$R_{TMR}(t) = 3e^{-2}\lambda t - 2e^{-3}\lambda t.$$

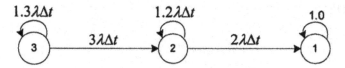

Figure 9.12: Reduced state diagram of a TMR system

9.4.3 Fault Coverage and Its Impact on Reliability

Consider a simple parallel system consisting of two identical modules shown in Figure 9.13.

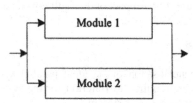

Figure 9.13: Reliability block diagram of a simple parallel system

Assume that module 1 is the primary and module 2 is switched in if module 1 fails. But this depends on the ability to detect and handle the faults. So,

$$R_{system}(t) = R_1(t) + (1 - R_1(t))C_1 R_2(t)$$

where C_1 is the fault coverage of module 1, $R_i(t)$ $(i = 1,2)$ is the reliability of module i. If the reliabilities and fault coverage factors of the two modules are the same, then

$$R_{system}(t) = R(t) + (1 - R(t))CR(t).$$

This is a linear function between the system reliability R and the fault coverage C, as depicted in Figure 9.14. It is observed that with the increase of C, the system is more and more reliable. From Figure 9.14, we can see:

If $C = 1.0$ (perfect parallel system), then

$$R_{system}(t) = 2R(t) - R(t)^2 = 1 - (1 - R(t))^2.$$

If $C = 0.0$, the reliability expression reduces to the reliability of one module.

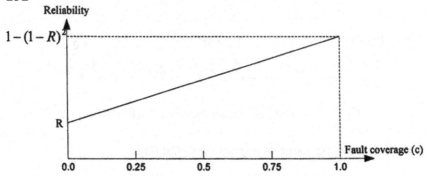

Figure 9.14: Impact of the fault coverage

9.4.4 M-of-N Systems

M-of-N systems is the generalisation of the ideal parallel system, where M of the total N identical modules are required to function for the system to function. TMR (triple module redundancy) is a 2-of-3 system.

Suppose that we have a TMR system. If we ignore the reliability of the voter, then

$$R_{TMR} = R_1(t)R_2(t)R_3(t) + R_1(t)R_2(t)(1 - R_3(t))$$
$$+ R_1(t)(1 - R_2(t))R_3(t) + (1 - R_1(t))R_2(t)R_3(t)$$

where $R_i(t)$ is the reliability of the ith module. If $R_1(t) = R_2(t) = R_3(t)$, then

$$R_{TMR} = R^3(t) + 3R^2(t)(1 - R(t)) = 3R^2(t) - 2R^3(t).$$

Comparison of the reliabilities of TMR and a single module is shown in Figure 9.15.

It is easy to find the crossover point: $R_{TMR} = 3R^2 - 2R^3 = R$, which implies the quadratic equation

$$R^2 - \frac{3}{2}R + 0.5 = 0.$$

The two solutions of this function are 0.5 and 1.0.

This example also shows that a system can be tolerant of faults and still have a low reliability. We can also calculate the reliability of a general M-of-N system:

$$R_{M-of-N} = \sum_{i=0}^{N-M} \binom{N}{i} R^{N-i}(t)(1 - R(t))^i$$

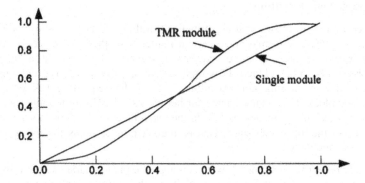

Figure 9.15: Reliability comparison of TMR and a single module

where

$$\binom{N}{i} = \frac{N!}{(N-i)!i!}.$$

For example, the TMR system reliability can be derived from the above formula:

$$R_{TMN} = \sum_{i=0}^{1}\binom{3}{i}R^{3-i}(t)(1-R(t))^{i} = 3R^{2}(t) - 2R^{3}(t).$$

9.5 Fault Tolerant Distributed Algorithms

9.5.1 Distributed Mutual Exclusion

The problem of mutual exclusion frequently arises in distributed systems whenever concurrent access to shared resources by several sites/processes is involved. For correctness, it is necessary to ensure that the shared resource be accessed by a single site/process at a time. This requires that concurrent access to a shared resource by several uncoordinated user-requests be serialised to secure the integrity of the shared resource. It requires that the action performed by a user on a shared resource must be *atomic*. That is, if several users concurrently access a shared resource, then the actions performed by a user, as far as the other users are concerned, must be instantaneous and indivisible. Hence the net effects on the shared resource is the same as if the actions were executed serially, as opposed to an interleaved manner. Mutual exclusion is a fundamental issue in the design of distributed systems and provides an efficient and robust technique for their viable design.

Mutual exclusion algorithms

Distributed mutual exclusion can be formalized in the following system model. At any instant, a site/process may have several requests for the *critical section* (CS). The site/process queues up these requests and serves them one at a time. A site/process can be in one of the following three states: *requesting CS, executing CS,* or *idle* (neither requesting nor executing CS). In the requesting CS state, the site/process is blocked and cannot make further requests for CS. In the idle state, the site/process is executing outside its CS. In the token-based algorithms, a site/process can also be in the idle token state. That is, the site/process holds the token and is executing outside the CS.

The primary objective of a mutual exclusion algorithm is to guarantee that only one request accesses the CS at a time. In addition, the following characteristics are considered important in a mutual exclusion algorithm:

- *Freedom from deadlocks.* Two or more sites/processes should not endlessly wait for messages that will never arrive.

- *Freedom from starvation.* A site/process should not be forced to wait indefinitely to execute CS while other sites/processes are repeatedly executing CS. That is, in a finite time, all requesting sites/processes should have an opportunity to execute the CS.

- *Fairness.* Fairness implies freedom from starvation (but not vice-versa). It requires that requests are executed in a certain order (e.g., the order in which they arrive at the CS, or in which they were issued).

- *Fault tolerance.* A mutual exclusion algorithm is fault-tolerant if in the wake of a failure, it can reorganise itself so that it continues to function without any (prolonged) disruptions.

In a simple solution to distributed mutual exclusion, a site/process, called the control site/process, is assigned the task of granting permission for the CS execution. To request the CS, a site/process sends a REQUEST message to the control site/process. The control site/process queues up the requests for the CS and grants them permission one by one.

This naive, centralised solution has several drawbacks. First, there is a single point of failure in the control site/process. Second, the control site/process and the communication links to it are likely to become bottlenecks. Third, the performance of the algorithm is poor because of the synchronisation delays imposed by the control site/process.

Token-based and non-token-based algorithms

During the 1980s and 1990s, the problem of mutual exclusion received considerable attention and several algorithms to achieve mutual exclusion in distributed systems were proposed. They tend to differ in their network topology (e.g., bus, tree, ring, etc.) and in the amount of information maintained by each site/process about other sites/processes. These algorithms can be classified into the following two groups:

- *Token-based*: a unique token (also known as the PRIVILEGE message) is shared among the sites/processes. A site/process is allowed to enter CS if it possesses the token and it continues to hold the token until the execution of the CS is over. These algorithms essentially differ in the way a site/process carries out the search for the token.

- *Non-token-based (time ordering)*: they require two or more rounds of message exchanges among the sites/processes. These algorithms are assertion based because a site/process can enter its CS when an assertion defined on its local variable becomes true. Mutual exclusion is enforced because the assertion becomes true only at one site/process at any given time.

Depending upon the way a site/process carries out its search for the token, there are numerous token-based algorithms. The simplest token-based algorithm is the generic token ring algorithm presented in most text books. In this algorithm all sites/processes are ordered in a unidirectional ring. Each site/process awaits the arrival of the token from its predecessor, enters the CS (if it wants to) when the token arrives, and then passes the token to its successor. Two problems must be solved here. The first is the loss of the token, and the second is the broken ring (as the result of a failed site/process, for example). Two algorithms are proposed to deal with these problems.

Other token-based algorithms do not order the sites/processes. For example, in the Suzuki and Kasami algorithm, if a site/process (say, A) attempting to enter the CS does not have the token, it broadcasts a REQUEST message for the token to all the other sites/processes. A site/process (say, B) that possesses the token sends the token to A upon receiving the REQUEST message if B is not using the CS. Otherwise the token is sent to A after B exits from the CS. The main design issues of this algorithm are to distinguish outdated REQUEST messages from current REQUEST messages and to determine which site/process has an outstanding request for the CS.

Many token-based algorithms use sequence numbers to order requests for the CS and to resolve conflicts between simultaneous requests for the CS. Every request for the token contains a sequence number and the sequence numbers of sites/processes advance independently. A site/process increments its sequence number counter every time it makes a request for the token. A primary function of the sequence number is to distinguish between old and current requests.

In non-token-based mutual exclusion algorithms, a site/process communicates with a set of other sites/processes to arbitrate who should execute the CS next. For a site/process S_i, requesting set R_i contains IDs of all those sites/processes from which site/process S_i must acquire permission before entering the CS.

Non-token-based algorithms use timestamps to order requests for the CS and to resolve conflicts between simultaneous requests for the CS. Logical clocks, instead of physical clocks, are used. Each request for the CS gets a timestamp, and smaller timestamp requests have priority over larger timestamp requests.

9.5.2 Election Algorithms

An election algorithm carries out a procedure to choose a site/process from a group, for example, to take over the role of a failed site/process. The main requirement is that a unique site/process is elected, even if several sites/processes call elections concurrently.

Basically, there are two types of election algorithms: one is the *ring-based election algorithms* and the other is the *broadcast election algorithms*. The ring-based election algorithms assume that an order (a physical or logical ring) exists among all the sites/processes and the election messages flow along the ring. A site/process (say, i) wanting to be elected sends a message of (REQ, i) along the ring. Another site/process (say, j) forwards the request to its successor if $i > j$ (or *equivalently, $i <$ j*). Otherwise, the message (REQ, j) is sent instead. At the end of the message circulation, the site/process with the highest (lowest) number will be elected and the message of (ELECTED, k) (k is the highest (lowest) number among all sites/processes) is sent to all sites/processes.

The broadcast election algorithms assume that a site/ process knows the identifiers and addresses of all other sites/processes. A site/process (say A) begins an election by sending an *election* message to those sites/processes that have a higher identifier. If none of the sites/processes return an answer message within a certain time, A considers itself as elected. A then sends a coordinator message to all sites/processes with a lower identifier and these sites/processes will treat A as elected. If a site/process (say, B) receives an *election* message from A (that means A has a lower identifier than B), B sends back an answer message to A and then B starts another round of election.

9.5.3 Deadlock Detection and Prevention

In a distributed system, a process can request and release local or remote resources in any order and a process can request some resources while holding others. If the sequence of the allocation of resources to processes is not controlled in such environments, deadlock can occur.

A set of processes is deadlocked if each process in the set is waiting for an event that only another process in the set can cause. Because all the processes are waiting, none of them will ever cause any events that could wake up any of the other members of the set, and all the processes continue to wait forever.

A resource allocation graph (a directed graph) can be used to model deadlocks. In such a graph:

- Circles represent processes.

- Squares represent resources.

- An arc from a resource node to a process node means that the resource previously has been requested by, granted to, and is currently held by that process.

- An arc from a resource node to a process node means that the resource previously has been requested by, granted to, and is currently held by that process.

- An arc from a process node to a resource node means that the process is currently blocked or waiting for that resource.

Figure 9.16 shows a deadlock using a resource allocation graph, where process A holds resource R_1 and is requesting resource R_2. At the same time, process B holds resource R_2 and is requesting resource R_1.

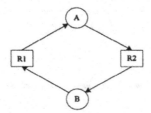

Figure 9.16: Deadlock

9.5.3.1   Distributed Deadlock Detection

Centralised algorithm. A central coordinator maintains the resource graph for the whole system (the union of all the individual graphs on each site). Whenever there is a change in a local graph, the coordinator must know this by some message-passing facility. When the coordinator detects a cycle, it kills off one process to break the deadlock.

Because of the message delays, *false deadlock* may occur. Figure 9.17 shows a false deadlock example. At a particular time, the resource allocation graphs on Sites 1, 2, and 3 are shown in Figure 9.17 (a), (b) and (c), respectively. Now assume that two messages are sent by Site 1 and Site 2 to the coordinator:

- *Msg_0*: Site 1 sends a message to the coordinator announcing the release of R_2 by B;

- *Msg_1*: Site 2 sends a message to the coordinator announcing that B is waiting for resource R_3.

A false deadlock occurs if *msg_1* arrives first. Figure 9.17 (d) shows the false deadlock.

Distributed algorithm. Suppose that processes are allowed to request multiple resources simultaneously. The Chandy-Misra-Haas algorithm works as follows:

1. When a process has to wait for some resources held by other process(es), a probe message is generated and sent to the process(es) holding the needed resources. The message consists of three numbers: the process that is just blocked, the process sending the message, and the process to whom it is being sent.

238

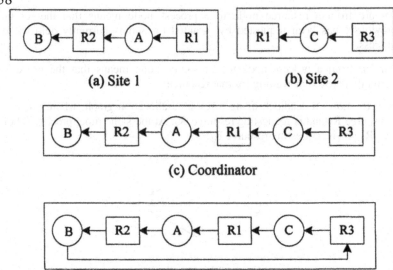

(a) Site 1   (b) Site 2

(c) Coordinator

(d) Coordinator where msg1 arrives and msg0 is delayed

Figure 9.17: False deadlock

2. When the message arrives, the recipient checks to see if it itself is waiting for any processes. If so, the message is updated, keeping the first field but replacing the second field by its own process number and the third one by the number of the process it is waiting for. The message is sent to the process on which it is blocked. If it is blocked on multiple processes, all of them are sent messages.

3. If a message goes all the way around and comes back to the original sender, that is, the process listed in the first field, a cycle exists and the system is deadlocked.

Example: Figure 9.18 shows an example of the deadlock detection algorithm.

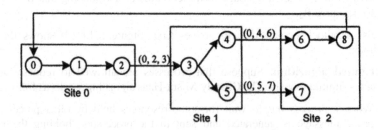

Figure 9.18. Distributed deadlock detection

Probe messages:

1st msg: process 0 to process 1: (0, 0,1)
process 1 to process 2: (0, 1,2)
process 2 to process 3: (0,2, 3), cross sites
process 3 to process 4: (0, 3,4)
process 3 to process 5: (0,3, 5)
process 4 to process 6: (0,4, 6), cross sites
process 5 to process 7: (0, 5,7), cross sites
process 6 to process 8: (0,6, 8)
process 8 to process 0: (0, 8, 0), cross sites
DEADLOCK!

Break a deadlock:

1. Let the process that initiated the probe commit suicide. Problem: if several processes simultaneously invoke the algorithm, overkill may happen.

2. Let each process add its identity to the end of the probe message, so that when it returns to the initial sender, the complete cycle will be listed. The sender can then see which process has the highest number, and kill that one, or send it a message asking it to kill itself.

9.5.3.2 Distributed Deadlock Prevention

To prevent the deadlock, a system is carefully designed so that deadlocks are structurally impossible. Some possible techniques are:

- A process can only hold one resource at a time.

- All processes must request all their resources initially.

- Processes must release all resources when asking for a new one.

- All resources are ordered and processes acquire them in strictly increasing order. So a process can never hold a high resource and ask for a low one, thus making cycles impossible.

With global time and atomic transactions, two other practical algorithms are possible. Both are based on the idea of assigning each transaction a global timestamp at the moment it starts (two transactions are not assigned the same timestamps).

When one process is about to block waiting for a resource that another process is using, a check is made to see which one has a larger timestamp (younger). We can then allow the wait only if the waiting process has a lower timestamp (older) than the process waited for. So, following any chain of waiting processes, the timestamps only increase, so cycles are impossible. Alternatively, we can use higher timestamps (older).

9.6 Replication and Reliability

High-speed networks make it possible to run distributed software on multiple machines efficiently. With the ever-growing dependency being placed on distributed computing systems, the requirement for their reliability has is increased enormously. A number of techniques have been proposed for the construction of reliable and fault-tolerant systems. One of these techniques is to replicate critical system service on multiple machines connected by networks so that if one copy (replica) fails, other replicas can still provide the continuing service.

When failures occur in hardware/software, the system may generate incorrect results or may simply stop before finishing the intended computation. Therefore, failures in distributed systems can have different semantics, and in turn, they require individual treatments [Cristian 1991]. Distributed systems are typically subject to two kinds of failures: site failure and communication link failure, which can result in the following failure semantics:

- *Fail-stop failure* [Schlichting and Schneider 1983]. Fail-stop failure is used to describe a process/processor which either works correctly, or simply stops working without taking any incorrect action. The fail-stop process/processor has the property of informing others by a notification service upon the failure or remaining in a state that the failure is detectable to others. There is also another term *Fail-silent failure* [Power 1994] used in the literature. Fail-silent failure exhibits the same halt-on-failure semantics as the fail-stop failure. But the failed process/processor may not have the capability of notifying others, nor is able to be detectable to others.

- *Network link failure* [Tanenbaum 1996]. This refers to the breakdown of a communication link between sites. The link failure makes it impossible to send or receive messages over the failed links. Also messages in transmission can be lost.

- *Network partition failure* [Birman 1996]. Network link failures can lead to partition failure, where a group of sites involved in a distributed system is partitioned into a set of subgroups, of which members of the same subgroup can communicate but not with members of different subgroups.

- *Timing failure* [Johnson 1989]. This refers to a violation of assumed temporal property of the system, such as clock drift bound between machines, or a message transmission delay between sites linked by networks.

- *Byzantine failure* [Lamport et al 1982]. This refers to any violation of the system behavior. In particular, it is used to refer to corrupted messages, such as malicious messages, that give wrong instructions, and as a result, may bring down the system.

To be able to detect the failure of a process/processor, failure-detecting techniques are needed. Traditionally, a technique often used is that the detecting process sends a message asking "Are you alive?" to the remote process/processor to check whether the remote process/processor is operating or not. If the remote process/processor responds within a predetermined time period, it indicates the aliveness of the remote process/processor; otherwise, the detecting process will time out and assume that the remote process/processor is dead. This method is based on a pre-assumption that the system is a synchronous distributed system. A synchronous distributed system has an upper-bound for message transmission delay [Mullender 1993]. Therefore, the time-out can be set statically to a value larger than the upper-bound.

On the contrary, an asynchronous distributed system does not have such an upper-bound. Thus, the time-out can not be used as a criterion for detecting the failure of a process/processor. The asynchronous distributed environment is close to reality where a message transmission can be delayed indefinitely. However, such a system is hard to implement because of the uncertainty of message transmission delay. An implementation that works for an asynchronous distributed system should work for a synchronous system [Cristian 1991, 1996].

Most techniques for achieving fault-tolerance rely on introducing extra redundant components to the system in order to detect and recover from component failures. Employing redundant components is a common concept in real life. An aircraft has four engines so that if any of the engines shuts down, the remaining engines can still keep the craft in the air and land safely. Computer hardware systems often employ duplicated parts (i.e., dual processors) to survive partial failures as well.

The client/server distributed computing model cannot be regarded as a reliable model, as the server is the single processing point. In the face of a site failure or a communication link failure, the server becomes inaccessible. Distributed replication is then a technique to solve this problem. With a large number of powerful machines available on the network, it becomes possible to duplicate a critical server on multiple machines so that if one server fails, the failure can be masked by its replicas. In turn, the service is continued. Distributed replication systems make three major contributions: increasing the availability, achieving fault-tolerance, and improving the performance.

- *Increasing the availability.* Availability refers to the accessibility of a system service. For a non-replicated server system, if the server breaks down, the service becomes unavailable. With a replicated server system, high availability can be achieved by software and/or data being available on multiple sites. Thus, if one server is down, the remaining replicas can still provide the service.

- *Fault tolerance.* The ability to recover from component failures to a system consistent state without performing incorrect actions is said to be fault-tolerance. In a distributed replication system, the failure of one replica due to a process/processor crashing can be tolerated (masked) by its replicated counterparts. However, some synchronisation among the remaining replicas has to be performed to reach a consistent system state in the event of a crash. Then an illusion of continuous service can be presented as if nothing has happened. Availability and fault tolerance are very closely related issues. Availability requires service being available, whereas fault tolerance imposes failures being tolerable.

- *Enhanced performance.* Replication is also a key to providing better performance. As now the service is running at multiple sites, clients do not have to line up at one site, instead, they can line up at different sites. If the replicated service is shared by a large community of clients, the response time can be dramatically improved.

9.7 Replication Schemes

There are two major styles of replication schemes presented in the literature, namely the *primary-backup replication scheme* [Budhiraja et al 1993], and the *active replication scheme* [Guerraoui and Schiper 1997] [Schneider 1990]. Their characteristics, advantages and drawbacks are different. The two schemes can also be combined in an integrated replication scheme that can accommodate the active replication scheme, as well as the primary-backup scheme in a unified form. The integrated scheme is based on the active replication, but is configurable to the primary-backup scheme.

Before starting detailed discussions, some terminology used hereafter needs to be clarified so that ambiguity can be avoided. A list of terms we like to differentiate in the distributed system context are: service/application, server, client, replica/member and replica/server group.

- *Service/application.* A service in a distributed system provides a set of well-defined operations exported to clients. The set of operations is often defined by an abstract service interface. The service is also referred to as an application in this book, as the service represents the application-level functions.

- *Server.* A server is a software entity running on an autonomous machine. The server implements the set of operations exported to clients. The implementation details of the service can be hidden from clients, and clients only see the abstract service interface that defines the set of operations.

- *Client.* A client is the user of a service. It typically invokes the operations provided by the server. Often, the client and the server are running on different machines, in turn their communications have to go through the underlying networks.

- *Stateful versus stateless server* [Birman 1996] [Zhou and Goscinski 1997]. If a server maintains some form of data on behalf of clients, we refer to it as a stateful server. A notorious example of this stateful server is the database server. On the contrary, if no client requests have any effect on the state of a server, whether the server does or does not maintain any data, this kind of server is referred to as a stateless server. A good example of the stateless server is the WWW (World Wide Web) server, where the server manages WWW pages, but WWW clients (browsers) cannot change the content of WWW pages (browsers can only retrieve the pages).

- *Replica/member* and *replica/server group*. A replica is a software entity representing the replicated server. The functionality of a replica is two-fold:

providing the service and implementing the underlying replication control protocol. A collection of replicas forms a *replica group,* and replicas are assumed to be identical copies in this book. We also call a replica in a replica group a member, and call a replica group a server group as well.

* *Query* versus *update operation.* Operations exported by a server can be categorised as either query or update operations. A query operation does not change the state of the data maintained by the server, but an update operation does. An operation invoked by a request contains the name of the operation and a list of actual parameters.

Next we introduce several replication schemes mentioned before.

9.7.1 Case Study 1: The Primary-Backup Scheme

The primary-backup scheme has been researched extensively by many researchers [Borg et al 1989] [Budhiraja et al 1992, 1993] [Powell 1994] [Jalote 1994] [Mehra et al 1997]. Figure 9.19 depicts the general architecture of this scheme. In essence, it is a simple scheme especially used in tolerating a process/processor failure by crashing. However, the primary-backup scheme can become complicated when employing multiple backups. The complexity derives from keeping the consistency among backups: (1) When the primary propagates its state to backups, the atomicity property, i.e., either all of backups receive a propagation or none of them receives it, should be guaranteed. (2) When the primary crashes, the backups have to elect a new primary. The election algorithm has to run a consensus protocol to guarantee that only one candidate satisfies as the primary.

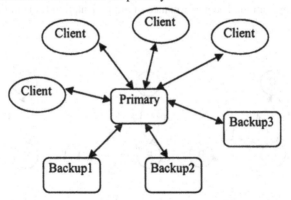

Figure 9.19: The Primary-Backup Replication Scheme

Replicas in a primary-backup scheme are distinguished as either the primary or a backup. At any time, there is only one replica acting as the primary. In other words, there is not a time when two replicas are the primary. Clients send requests to the primary only, backups do not receive any request directly from clients. The data-consistency between the primary and backups is preserved by the primary propagating state changes (or updates directly) to backups. The scheme exhibits a

244

fail-over time that is a time period between the primary crashing and the new primary taking over the process. During the fail-over time period, no replica is operating.

According to how often state changes are propagated to backups, the primary-backup scheme is further divided into the *hot* (every state change is sent to the backup/backups right away), the *warm* (a collection of state changes is sent out at a time interval), and the *cold* (no state change is sent to backups while the primary is operating) strategies [Wellings 1996]. Obviously, different strategies affect the *fail-over* time. In general, the more frequently the propagation is performed, the shorter the fail-over time incurs.

Also the choice of propagation strategies can be affected by the environment within which a primary-backup system is running. For example, in an environment where all replicas can access the same file system, the primary can save the update requests to a log file to allow the backups access instead of sending requests directly to backups, thus the cold strategy is enough. In fact, the cold strategy is most suitable to a server providing only read-like service, in other words, no state changes. Cold strategy is considered to be the simplest propagation strategy of all.

The hot strategy is most applicable to a system that requires a real-time fail-over period so that when the primary crashes, the switch-over time (the fail-over time) is minimum. But the hot strategy can affect the response time depending on how the hot propagation is implemented. Figure 9.20 describes three different implementations. In the implementation (a), the response time for an update request is the worst compared with implementation (b) and (c). The implementation (b) gives the best response time as it executes the request and sends a reply to the client before the propagation. The performance of implementation (c) is in the middle.

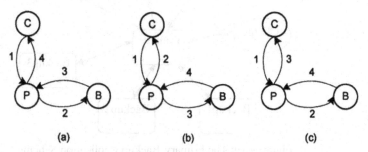

Figure 9.20. Hot replication implementations -- P represents the primary; B represents the backup; and C represents the client. *In (a), 1, 2, 3 and 4 denote requests, propagations, acknowledgements and replies respectively; In (b), 1, 2, 3 and 4 denote requests, replies, propagations and acknowledgements respectively;In (c), 1, 2, 3 and 4 denote requests, propagations, replies and acknowledgements respectively.*

The warm strategy follows the implementation of Figure 9.20 (b), but the propagation is not sent out per update. This strategy is often applicable to business-oriented servers, such as database servers where fast responses have a higher priority. The propagation frequency is determined by the semantics of the business application domain.

In summary, choosing a right propagation strategy (hot/warm/cold) depends on the requirement of the fail-over time and the environment in which a replication system is running.

The primary-backup scheme has been described as the passive replication in the literature [Budhiraja et al 1992, 1993] for the reason that backups sit back and passively react to state changes without being involved in any interaction with clients. The scheme is also labelled as easily implementable, less redundant processing, thus, less costly and more prevalent in practice.

However, the major drawback of the scheme is that the primary becomes the communication bottleneck due to the fact that all requests are sent to the primary. Other downsides of this scheme are: (1) In the event of the primary's failure, there exists a fail-over time during which there is no server available. (2) There can be request losses when the primary fails, e.g., the requests received by the primary but not yet being propagated are lost. The request loss problem is solvable, however, it needs to introduce some extra handling at the client side (see next chapter about the discussion of how a client switches to a new replica).

9.7.2 Case Study 2: The Active Replication Scheme

The active replication scheme is proposed to give rise to system performance by letting different replicas execute client requests concurrently. The performance can be improved enormously when most requests are queries. The scheme is based on an architecture in which each replica receives and processes requests. In contrast to the primary-backup scheme, this scheme is named *active* for the reason that all replicas are actively involved with clients, process requests and send replies. Figure 9.21 depicts this architecture.

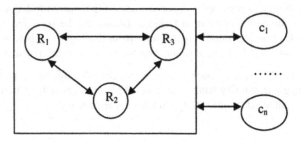

Figure 9.21. The active replication scheme -- R_1, R_2, R_3 represent an active replica group, whereas c_1, ..., c_n represent a set of clients. *A client can send its requests to any replica or some replicas. Replicas that receive the request will send the reply back to the client.*

The active scheme mainly has the advantage of masking server failures automatically over the primary-backup scheme. Active replication can be used to mask the server crashing automatically, provided that a request is sent to multiple replicas by a client. As long as one reply comes back, the client will not notice the failure of other replicas. The client often takes the earliest reply, and drops late ones. If an update request is not sent to full membership of a replica group, then the replicas receiving the update have to propagate the update to other members. Often this is done by competing, where multiple replicas propagate the request at the same time.

A common method proposed in [Powell 1994] to reduce unnecessary message transmissions is that, if a replica is about to send a reply to a client, it checks if there is any propagation of the request being received from other competitor replicas; if there is, it stops sending such a propagation; otherwise this replica sends the reply together with the original request to the client and all replicas, which will in turn stop their competitors sending their replies and propagations. Competing propagation and redundant replies can generate tremendous network traffic, and congest the network eventually, if the percentage of the update operations issued by clients is high. Another proposed approach is to let the client be responsible for sending an update to the full membership so that replicas are free from propagating requests. However, this can be a problem when the client fails during the procedure. The failure can leave the group in an inconsistent state whereby some replicas receive the request, some do not.

Another advantage of the active scheme over the primary-backup scheme is no fail-over time. As long as one replica is operating, the service remains available.

Ordering Constraints

The active scheme seems to solve the bottleneck problem very well. But, it introduces a subtle problem known as request ordering [Birman 1993]. Since clients send requests concurrently, the order of requests arriving at each replica may be different due to the network bandwidth/traffic and different speeds of sites. Figure 9.22 depicts this scenario. Therefore, executing the same set of operations in different orders at replicas may result in divergent states of replicas.

According to the data semantics of a service application, arriving request orders can be constrained. In other words, an ordering constraint can be specified, such as first-in-first-out (FIFO) order, causal order (came from the happened-before relationship defined by [Lamport 1978]), total order, and total+causal order [Birman 1993].

On the contrary, the primary-backup scheme handles the ordering very well. In fact, ordering is done intrinsically simply because all requests go to the primary. Backups. merely get the same set of ordered updates from the primary.

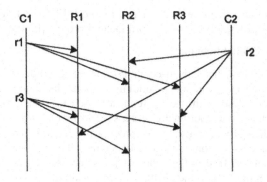

Figure 9.22. The scenario of requests arriving in different orders -- R_1, R_2 and R_3 represent replicas; c_1 and c_2, represent clients; and r_1, r_2, and r_3 represent messages. *Two clients, c_1 and c_2, send requests to all replicas; c_1 sends r_1 and r_3, and c_2 sends r_2. But $\{r_1, r_2, r_3\}$ arrives at R_1, R_2 and R_3 in the orders of, $<r_1, r_3, r_2>$, $<r_2, r_1, r_3>$ and $<r_1, r_2, r_3>$ respectively.*

Deterministic Processes

If data consistency is based on the propagation strategy among replicas, then all replicas have to be assumed to be *deterministic processes*. A deterministic process is one that, when starting from the same initial state and executing the same sequence of operations, it ends up with the same state and generates the same sequence of outputs. Therefore replica consistency can be easily preserved by executing the same set of ordered operations. This scheme is also described as the state machine approach [Schneider 1990], which provides a framework for understanding and designing replication control protocols. Many software systems involve replication techniques derived from the state machine approach. In essence, a state machine is used to model each replica as a deterministic process. Thus, the consistency issue turns out to be how to deliver the same set of operations in a relative order to each replica in a concurrent (replicas receive requests concurrently) and failure-prone (the failures of senders and receivers) environment.

Compared to the active scheme, the primary-backup scheme does not require determinism as a pre-assumption since the non-deterministic factor can be decided by the primary and passed on to backups.

9.7.3 Case Study 3: Two Particular Replication Schemes

The preceding sections presented general structures for the primary-backup and the active replication schemes, their key characteristics, advantages and drawbacks. This section takes a look at two particular replication schemes that have appeared in the literature. They are based on either the primary-backup or the active scheme.

The coordinator-cohort scheme was developed by the ISIS project, and the leader-follower scheme was developed by the Esprit Delta-4 project [Powell 1994].

The Coordinator-Cohort Scheme

The coordinator-cohort scheme is used in ISIS as an example of testing group communication services to support building reliable distributed systems. This scheme is relatively close to the active replication scheme. The basic idea is, for each request, a team of one coordinator and a subset of replicas (being cohorts) out of the whole replica group is formed to process the request. The coordinator is responsible for processing the request and sending the reply, whereas cohorts monitor the coordinator. One of the cohorts takes over when the coordinator fails. When sending the reply back to the client, the coordinator also sends the reply to the cohorts as well so that cohorts are informed of the completion of the request. If the cohots have not received the expected reply from the coordinator after a time-out, they conclude that the coordinator has failed and then take a corresponding action by selecting a new coordinator who takes over the process. ISIS uses its atomic multicast primitive for this purpose, and the destinations of the multicast include all cohorts and the caller.

This scheme seems to be able to perform requests concurrently between replicas, however, when a member is involved in a coordinator-cohort group, it can not accept another request nor be in another coordinator-cohort group. The performance of the coordinator-cohort scheme is very questionable due to this reason. Also, since the coordinator-cohort group has to be formed up-front before executing each request, the response time can be considerably long.

The Leader-Follower Scheme

The leader-follower scheme developed in the project Esprit Delta-4 [Powell 1994] is rather closer to the primary-backup scheme than the active one. The general idea is that in a replica group, one replica is assigned as the leader and others as followers. All replicas receive requests and execute requests autonomously, but only the leader generates replies.

This scheme is designed with treating group non-determinism in mind. In the situation of a non-deterministic event arising, the leader makes a decision and informs followers about it so that all members can reach the same state even if they execute requests autonomously. Non-deterministic factors considered are process preemption and time-related operations. The request ordering issue is included as a non-deterministic factor by the scheme.

- *Request ordering.* The request order is decided by the leader which sends notification messages to indicate to followers in what order requests are to be executed. This order is the same as the leader's.

- *Process preemption.* Process preemption may cause inconsistency between replicas even when requests are ordered. To solve this problem, a set of preemption points has to be defined within the server. When the leader process is preempted during an execution of a request, the leader rolls back to the last preemption point and instructs followers to roll back to the same preemption point. Solving process preemption is not an easy task. It is doubtful this method will work in general, as a preemption point may not be easily definable.

- *Time-related operations.* If a request involves an operation reading the local clock time in the calculation, then the leader needs to pass the reading as an extra parameter to followers so that the same request will result in the same state between the leader and the followers.

The leader-follower scheme does not solve the communication bottleneck problem, as requests are queued up at the leader for results. This scheme is basically a primary-backup scheme. The only saving is that no request propagations between the leader and followers, instead, notification messages are sent from the leader to followers. The saving is based on the assumption that notification messages are smaller than propagation messages. However, sending a request to all replicas is then shifted to the client side where the client is responsible for sending requests to the full membership of the replica group.

9.8 The Primary-Peer Replication Scheme

Although the primary-backup is relatively easy to implement, its bottleneck problem prevents it from being an advanced replication approach. The active scheme improves the performance but it brings great complexity which has to be restrained. For the two particular schemes, the coordinator-cohort has the problem of forming a group upon each request and may result in a long response time. The leader-follower scheme is very close to the primary-backup scheme that requests are lined up at the leader site, i.e., no concurrency at all. Therefore, to overcome these drawbacks, we propose a new scheme called *primary-peer replication scheme (PPRS),* based on the above schemes.

9.8.1 Description of the Scheme

A solution is to integrate the two schemes together [Wang and Zhou 1998a]. The scheme is called a primary-peer replication scheme (PPRS). It is based on the idea of an active architecture by restraining some design options in order to simplify communications among clients and replicas. Furthermore, it has the flexibility of being configurable to the primary-backup scheme. This is done simply by letting all updates go to the primary of a group and leaving other members (now backups) only receiving propagations. Figure 9.23 depicts the architecture of the PPRS.

Here we outline its design ideas and features:

- The PPRS allows each replica to take requests so that concurrent execution can be performed. This will give rise to a better system throughput as we have discussed.

- A client is connected with one replica at a time. The client sends all its requests to the connecting replica only. Upon the failure of the connecting replica, the client shifts to another replica. It can also switch to a different replica when the currently connecting replica becomes very slow. Clients are no longer involved in sending requests to multiple replicas. Thus, clients become lightweight software entities. Designing a lightweight client has become the trend of client/server systems nowadays [Linthicum 1997].

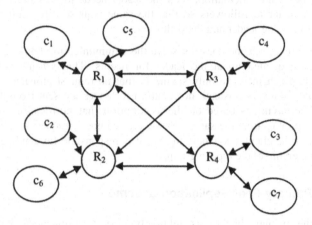

Figure 9.23. The Primary-Peer Replication Scheme — R_1, R_2, R_3, R_4 represent a 4-replica system, whereas c_1, ..., c_7 represent seven clients connected to the replica system.

- The PPRS retains the idea of designating a replica as the primary. The primary is depicted in Figure 9.23 by the blank-filled circle. In addition to being a general member, the designated primary is responsible for making decisions on behalf of the group in certain situations, such as initiating relevant replication control protocols due to external events (group membership changes), coordinating the execution of the protocols, and informing other members about the decision. Also non-deterministic factors can be resolved if any.

- For each update request, only one replica will involve propagations. This removes the possibility of competitive propagations between multiple replicas, which happens in the active scheme. Propagations now only happen between replicas without involving clients. This reduces the design complexity and simplifies the implementation.

However, the imperfection of the PPRS is that clients will observe the replica failure, and the fail-over time is not avoidable. The fail-over happens when a replica fails so that clients connected to the failed replica have to switch to other replicas and may need to re-send their last requests. But this fail-over time should not be very significant as requests sent to the new replica can be processed right away.

9.8.2 Replication Transparency

To be able to connect to a replica in the group, a client needs to know who are in the group, i.e., the references of all replicas. If replicas reside at permanent sites, clients can be hard wired to the references of the replicas. However, replicas may crash and leave voluntarily, a new replica may join the group to re balance the load, or due to some administration reasons, a replica has to be moved to a new site, then the references that clients kept become stale.

There are generally two methods to solve this problem. First, every replica keeps a copy of the current membership. When a replica is added to the group, each replica updates its membership to reflect the change. Then the replica piggybacks the new membership to its connecting clients. By doing so, the clients can track the membership changes. However, the drawbacks of this design are: (1) The replica has to keep records of all connecting clients so that the membership changes can be passed to them. (2) The replica group is not transparent to clients, i.e., clients see the internal structure of the group.

The second method uses a group naming service (GNS) to set up separately on a stable site to manage membership changes. A replica group is registered to the GNS under a unique group name, and any membership change is sent to the GNS by the primary member of the replica group. Clients only need to contact with the GNS to get the reference to a replica.

This approach provides a set of methods to create a group, add, delete or remove replica members from a group. When a group of replicas is created, the primary of the group registers to the GNS (invoking *createGroup( )*). The primary is also responsible for updating the GNS with any membership changes (invoking *addMember( )* or *deleteMember( )*). When a replica crashes, the primary invokes *deleteMember* (group, backup) to remove the crashed replica. When a new replica joins the group, the primary invokes *addMember* (group, backup) to add the new replica. Whereas *bind* (group_name) is invoked by clients to get a reference to an operating replica. For an active scheme, all replicas form a ring. Upon receiving a binding request, the GNS will return the next operating replica in the ring to the client so that each replica is connected with a roughly even number of clients, thus, loads are split over replicas. For a primary-backup group, the GNS always returns the reference to the primary.

9.9 Replication Consistency

Distributed replication provides high availability, fault-tolerance and enhanced performance. But these features come at a price: replication adds great complexity to the system development. Most important of all, replication jeopardises data consistency. In turn mechanisms have to be employed to enforce data consistency. Maintaining data consistency is very expensive, a common practice is then to relax the data consistency level as low as possible to give rise to better system performance.

Data replication in the transactional model has been researched extensively. Data replication mechanisms developed for the transactional model are very strict since one-copy serialisability [Attiya and Welch 1994] is often required in order to maintain the ACID (Atomicity, Consistency, Isolation and Durability) property. Basically, a write operation (i.e., an update) has to be performed on most replicas synchronously before the result is returned to the client. Therefore, a long response time may incur and a low system throughput rate is achieved.

Not all replication systems require such a strong transactional semantics [Zhou and Goscinski 1999]. Update ordering is an alternative data consistency model which has weaker semantics than that of the one-copy serialisability. The basic idea of the update-ordering model is to let replicas execute the same set of update requests in a sensible order. This order meets the requirements of both the clients and the data semantics of a replicated service application. Compared to the data replication in the transactional context, the update ordering model generally gives a better response time and a high system throughput rate because it allows updates to be executed concurrently at different replicas. Update ordering is adopted as the general data consistency model for maintaining the data consistency in a replication system built upon the PPRS structure.

A PPRS replica group can be configured in two major styles: either a primary-backup group or a primary-peer group. For a primary-backup group, ordering is not an issue of concern, as we have discussed before that requests are ordered at the primary intrinsically. Therefore, the update-ordering data consistency model applies to the primary-peer group only.

The update ordering data consistency model requires placing ordering constraints on update operations so that updates arriving at replicas are ordered. Generally, if solely from the replica group point of view, as long as updates are executed at all replicas in the same order, the data consistency is guaranteed among replicas. However, from the client point of view, it may require updates sent from the same client to be executed in the sending order at all replicas, or updates having a happened-before [Lamport 1978] relation to be executed at all replicas by keeping that happened-before relation.

Formally, update ordering is categorised in terms of FIFO, causal, total, and total+causal to reflect data consistency requirements from both clients and the replica group. Ordering constraints have different levels of strength. FIFO is the weakest one and total+casual is the strictest. The system performance, especially the system throughput, is largely affected by the strength level of the ordering constraint being placed on a replica group.

Adopting a strict data consistency model is very expensive, and it may not be needed for a service application. Depending on the data semantics of the application domain, the strength level of the data consistency model should be relaxed as much as possible to give rise to the system efficiency.

9.10 Summary

A computer system, or a distributed system consists of many hardware/software components that are likely to fail eventually. In this chapter we introduced the basic concepts and techniques that relate to fault-tolerant computing. First, we presented the concepts of the reliability of a distributed system and techniques for achieving it. We classify the basic techniques used to build reliable distributed network systems: redundancy, fault avoidance techniques, fault detection techniques, and fault tolerance techniques. Also we described several system models to build the reliability functions properly so that we can get the reliabilities of several typical systems. Then we discussed the distributed mutual exclusion, which frequently arises in distributed systems whenever concurrent access to shared resources by several sites/processes is involved. Mutual exclusion is a fundamental issue in the design of distributed systems and an efficient and robust technique for the viable design of distributed systems.

The client/server distributed computing model can not be regarded as a reliable model, as the server is the single processing point. In the face of a site failure or a communication link failure, the server becomes inaccessible. Distributed replication is then a technique to solve this problem. Distributed replication systems make three major contributions: increasing the availability, achieving fault-tolerance, and improving performance. There are two major styles of replication schemes presented in the literature, namely the primary-backup replication scheme, and the active replication scheme. In the chapter we addressed these two schemes as well as two other schemes: the coordinator-cohort scheme developed by the ISIS project and the leader-follower scheme developed by the Esprit Delta-4 project. Though these schemes are extremely useful, they all have drawbacks. To overcome these, we propose a new scheme called primary-peer replication scheme (PPRS), based on integration of the above schemes.

Exercises

9.1   What are two major approaches to increase system reliability? 9.1

9.2   What is the bathtub curve? What does it mean in this book? 9.1.1

9.3   What is the MTBF? What relationship is between MTBF, MTTF, and MTTR? 9.1.2

9.4   How does a redundant system handle a failure? 9.2.1

9.5   What are the commonly used techniques for static redundancy? 9.2.4

9.6   What is the N-version programming approach? 9.3.1

9.7   How does one calculate the reliability R(t) of a series system and a parallel system? 9.4.1

9.8   How does one calculate the reliability R(t) of a 4 of 6 system? 9.4.4

9.9   What are two major types of distributed mutual exclusion algorithms? 9.5.1

254

9.10   What purpose is the election algorithms? 9.5.2

9.11   When would process deadlocks happen? How are them detected? 9.5.3

9.12   What contributions does a distributed replication system make? 9.6

9.13   What strategies does the primary-backup scheme have? How is one chosen? 9.7.1

9.14   Compare the advantages and disadvantages of the primary-backup scheme and the active replication scheme. 9.7.2

9.15   What is the PPRS? What features does it have? 9.8.1

9.16   What data consistency model is used in the PPRS? 9.9

CHAPTER 10 SECURITY

There is a pervasive need for measures to guarantee the privacy, integrity and availability of resources in distributed network systems. Designers of secure distributed systems must cope with exposed service interfaces and insecure networks in an environment where attackers are likely to have knowledge of the algorithms used and how to deploy computing resources. In this chapter we talk about security issues of distributed network systems, such as integrity mechanisms and encryption techniques.

10.1   Secure Networks

10.1.1   What is a Secure Network?

A work on any type of networking is not complete without a discussion of network security. Networks cannot be simply classified as secure or not secure since the term "secure" is not absolute: each group of users may define the level of security differently. For example, some organizations may regard the stored data as valuable and require that only authenticated users gain access to these data. Some organizations allow outside users to browse their data, but prevent the data from being altered by outside users. Some organizations may regard communication of the data as the most important issue in network security and require that messages be kept private and that senders and recipients be authenticated. Yet many other organizations need some combination of the above requirements. Therefore, the first step for an organization in building a secure network is to define its security policy. The security policy specifies clearly and unambiguously the items that are to be protected.

A number of issues need to be considered in defining a security policy. They include an assessment of the value of information within an organization and an assessment of the costs and benefits of various security policies. Generally speaking, the following three aspects of security can be considered:

- *Data integrity* refers to the correctness of data and protection from changes.

- *Data availability* refers to protection against disruption of services.

- *Data confidentiality and privacy* refer to protection against snooping or wiretapping.

10.1.2 Integrity Mechanisms and Access Control

The techniques used to ensure the integrity of data against accidental damage are the checksums and cyclic redundancy checks (CRC). To use such techniques, a sender computes a small, integer value as a function of the data in a packet. The receiver re-computes the function from the data that arrives, and compares the result to the value that the sender computed.

However, the checksums or the CRC cannot absolutely guarantee data integrity. For example, a planned attacker can alter the data and then can create a valid checksum for the altered data.

The password mechanism is used in most computer systems to control access to resources. This method works well in a conventional computer system but may be vulnerable in a networked environment. If a user at one location sends a password across a network to a computer at another location, anyone who wiretaps the network can obtain a copy of the password. Wiretapping is easy when packets travel across a LAN because many LAN technologies permit an attached station to capture a copy of all traffic. In such a situation, additional steps must be taken to prevent passwords from being reused.

10.2 Data Encryption

10.2.1 Encryption Principles

Encryption is a method that transforms information in a way that it cannot be understood by anyone except the intended recipient who possesses a secret method to decrypt the message. Figure 10.1 depicts the encryption process, in which the sender uses an encryption function $c = f(k, p)$ to encrypt the plain text p with a key k and produces a cyphered text c. The cyphered text c is then transmitted over the network. When c is received, the receiver uses a decypher function $p = f'(k, c)$ to obtain the plain text file via the same key k and the received cyphered text c. The encryption process should guaranttee that, without the key and the correct function, it is very difficult to obtain the original plain text from the cyphered text.

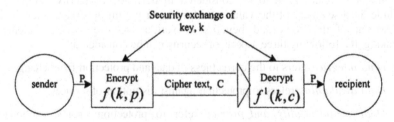

Figure 10.1. Single (private) key encryption

The fundamental theory of data encryption is cryptographics, which is to provide a mechanism for two people to communicate without any other person being able to read messages. The word *cryptography* is derived from the Greek words which means hidden, or secret, writing.

Private key schemes

The encryption process can use either a public key or a private key. With a private key scheme, the key is known only to the two communicating parties. This key can be fixed or can be passed from the two parties over a secure communication link (perhaps over the postal network or a leased line). The two most popular private key techniques are DES (Data Encryption Standard) and IDEA (International Data Encryption Algorithm).

DES is a block cipher scheme which operates on 64-bit block sizes. The private key has only 56 useful bits as eight of its bits are used for parity. This gives 2^{56} or 10^{17} possible keys. DES uses a complex series of permutations and substitutions; the result of these operations is computed in exclusive-OR (XOR) with the input. This is then repeated 16 times using a different order of the key bits each time. DES is a very strong code and has never been broken, although several high-powered computers are now available and could crack the code using brute force. A possible solution is 3DES (or triple DES) which uses DES three times in a row. First to encrypt, next to decrypt and finally to encrypt. This system allows a key-length of more than 128 bits.

IDEA is similar to DES. It operates on 64-bit blocks of plain text and uses a 128-bit key. IDEA operates over 17 rounds with a complicated mangler function. During decryption this function does not have to be reversed and can simply be applied in the same way as during encryption (this also occurs with DES). IDEA uses a different key expansion for encryption and decryption, but every other part of the process is identical. The same keys are used in DES decryption but in the reverse order. The key is devised in eight 16-bit blocks: the first six are used in the first round of encryption and the last two are used in the second run. It is free for use in a non-commercial version and appears to be a strong cipher.

The problem with the private key schemes is the secured exchange of the key k: how can we be sure the key is known only by both authorized parties (the postal network and the leased line are not safe)? A key distribution server sometimes is used to supply secret keys to clients. Figure 10.2 illustrates an example of a key distribution server. Here user A needs to communicate with user B. A key is needed for both parties.

Public key encryption

A well-known encryption method is the *public key encryption*. It uses two different keys (encryption key K_e and decryption key K_d): K_e is known to the sender and K_d the recipient. K_e can be made known publicly for use by anyone who wants to communicate, while K_d is kept secret. The RSA (after its inventors Rivest, Shamir, and Adleman) technique is one of the most popular public key encryption techniques and is based on the difficulty of factoring large numbers. It is secure for

258

key-length of over 728 bits. Compared with DES it is relatively slow but it has the advantage that users can choose their own code whenever they need one.

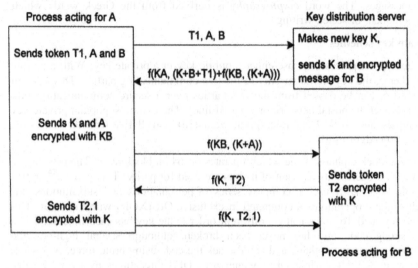

Figure 10.2. Key distribution server

Here is an example: *A* (the receiver) requires some secret information from *B* (the sender). *A* generates a pair of keys K_e and K_d. K_d is kept secret and K_e is sent to *B*. *B* uses $c = E(K_e, p)$ to encrypt the message and sends *c* to *A*. *A* then decrypts the message *c* using $p = D(Kd, c)$. Figure 10.3 depicts this process.

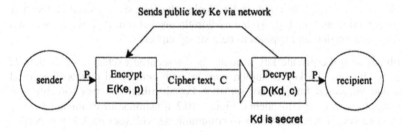

Figure 10.3. Public key encryption

The following steps can be used to generate the public and private keys used in the above encryption:

1. Select two large prime numbers, *a* and *b* (each will be roughly 256 bits long). The factors *a* and *b* remain secret and *n* is the result of multiplying them together. Each of the prime numbers is of the order of 10^{100}.

2. Choose the public key. To do this a number e is chosen so that e and $(a-1)'(b-1)$ are relatively prime. Two numbers are relatively prime if they have no common factor greater than 1. The public-key is then $<e, n>$ and is 512 bits long.

3. Choose the private key. Next the private key for decryption, d, is computed so that

$$d = e^{-1} \ mod \ [(a-1)'(b-1)].$$

This then gives a private key of $<d, n>$. The values p and q can then be discarded (but should never be disclosed to anyone).

The encryption process of message, m, to ciphertext, c, is then defined by

$$c = m^e \ mod \ n.$$

The message, m, is then decrypted with

$$m = c^d \ mod \ n.$$

It should be noticed that the message block m must be less than n. When n is 512 bits then a message which is longer than 512 bits can be broken up into blocks of 512 bits.

10.2.2 Basic Encryption Techniques

Basic encryption techniques include code shifting, code mapping, key application, and bit shifting.

10.2.2.1 Code Shifting

Code shifting is a simple encryption technique in which encrypted letters are used to replace the letters of the plain text with a shifted equivalent alphabet. For example moving the letters four places from the right to the left gives:

```
ABCDEFGHIJKLMNOPQRSTUVWXYZ
WXYZABCDEFGHIJKLMNOPQRSTUV
```

Thus a message:

```
LET US MEET AT THE ROYAL PLAZA
```

would become:

```
HAP QO IAAP WP PDA NKUWH LHWVW
```

This code has the problem of being reasonably easy to decode, as there are only 26 different code combinations. The first documented use of this type of code was by Julius Caesar who used a 3-letter shift.

10.2.2.2 Code Mappings

Another simple encryption technique is the code mapping, which uses a codebook to represent the characters, often known as a monoalphabetic code. Code mappings have no underlying mathematical relationship. An example could be:

Input: abcdefghijklmnopqrstuvwxyz

Encrypted: tapyrbdzwiuoxvmfkeljnhcqgs

The number of different character maps can be determined as follows:

- Take the letter 'A' then this can be mapped to 26 different letters.

- If 'A' is mapped to a certain letter then 'B' can only map to 25 letters.

- If 'B' is mapped to a certain letter then 'C' can be mapped to 24 letters.

- Continue until the alphabet is exhausted.

Thus, in general, the number of combinations will be:

26*25*24*23…4*3*2*1

Thus the code has 26! different character mappings (approximately $4.03*10^{26}$). It suffers from the fact that the probabilities of the mapped characters will be similar to those in normal text. Thus if there is a large amount of text, then the character having the highest probablity will be either an 'e' or a 't'. The character with the lowest probability will tend to be a 'z' or a 'q' (which is also likely followed by the character map for a 'u').

A code mapping encryption scheme is easy to implement but unfortunately, once it has been "cracked", it is easy to decrypt the encrypted data. Normally this type of code is implemented with an extra parameter which changes its mapping, such as changing the code mapping over time depending on the time of day and/or date. Only parties that are allowed to decrypt the message know the mappings of the code to time and/or date. For example each day of the week may have a different code mapping.

10.2.2.3 Key Application

To make it easy to decrypt, a key is normally applied to the text. This makes it easy to decrypt the message if the key is known but difficult to decrypt the message if the key is not known. An example of a key operation is to take each of the characters in a text message and then exclusive-OR (XOR) the character with a key value. For example the ASCII character 'A' has the bit pattern:

100 0001

and if the key had a value of 5 then 'A' exclusive-OR'ed with 5 would give:

```
'A'       100 0001
Key (5)   000 0101
```

```
Ex-OR    100 0100
```

The bit pattern 100 0100 would be encrypted as character 'D'.

10.2.2.4 Bit Shifting

A typical method used to encrypt text is to shift the bits within each character. For example ASCII characters only use the lower seven bits of an 8-bit character. Thus, shifting the bit positions one place to the left will encrypt the data to a different character. For a left shift a 0 or a 1 can be shifted into the least significant bit; for a right shift the least significant bit can be shifted into the position of the most significant bit. When shifting more than one position a rotate left or rotate right can be used. Note that most of the characters produced by shifting may not be printable, thus a text editor (or viewer) cannot view them. For example, in C the characters would be processed with:

```
ch=ch << 1;
```

which shifts the bits of ch one place to the left, and decrypted by:

```
ch=ch >> 1;
```

which shifts the bits of ch one place to the right.

10.3 Cracking the Code

10.3.1 Cracking Organizations

Many institutions and individuals read data that is not intended for them. They include:

- Government agencies. Traditionally governments around the world have reserved the rights to tap into any communication they think may be against the national interests.

- Spies who tap into communication for government and industry information.

- Individuals who like to read other people's messages.

- Individuals who hack into systems and read sensitive information.

- Criminals who intercept information in order to use it for crime, such as intercepting PIN numbers on bank accounts.

For example, the US government has proposed to beat encryption by trying to learn everyone's encryption key with the Clipper chip. The US government keeps a record of all the series numbers and encryption keys for each Clipper chip manufactured.

No matter how difficult an encryption is, every code is crackable and the measure of the security of a code is the amount of time it takes persons (not addressed in the code) to break the code. Normally to break a code, a computer tries all the possible keys until it finds the match. Thus a 1-bit code only has two keys. A 2-bit code would have 4 keys, and so on. For a 64-bit code it has 18,400,000,000,000,000,000 different keys. If one key is tested every 10μs, then it would take $1.84*10^{14}$ seconds (or 5,834,602 years).

However, as the improvement of computer power and techniques in parallel processing, the time used to crack a code may decrease dramatically. For example, if we think 1 million years would be safe for a code and we assume an increase of computer power of a factor of 2 every year, then it would take only 500,000 years by the next year. The same code would then be cracked in 1 year after 20 years. If we use parallel processing techniques, then the code would be cracked much sooner.

10.3.2 Cracking Methods

A cryptosystem converts plaintext into ciphertext using a key. There are several methods that a hacker can use to crack a code, including:

- Known plaintext attack. Where the hacker knows part of the ciphertext and the corresponding plaintext. The known ciphertext and plaintext can then be used to decrypt the rest of the ciphertext.

- Chosen ciphertext. Where the hacker sends a message to the target, this is then encrypted by the target's private-key and the hacker then analyses the encrypted message. For example, a hacker may send an email to the encryption file server and the hacker spies on the delivered message.

- Exhaustive search. Where the hacker uses brute force to decrypt the ciphertext and tries every possible key.

- Active attack. Where the hacker inserts or modifies messages.

- Man in the middle. Where the hacker is hidden between two parties and impersonates each of them to the other.

- The replay system. Where the hacker takes a legitimate message and sends it into the network at some future time.

- Cut and paste. Where the hacker mixes parts of two different encrypted messages and, sometimes, is able to create a new message. This message is likely to make no sense, but may trick the receiver into doing something that helps the hacker.

- Time resetting. Some encryption schemes use the time of the computer to create the key. Resetting this time or determining the time that the message was created can give some useful information to the hacker.

Another way to crack a code is to exploit a weakness in the generation of the encryption key. The hacker can then guess which keys are more likely to occur.

This is known as a *statistical attack*. Many programming languages use a random number generator based on the current system time (such as *rand( )*). This method is not good in data encryption as the hacker can simply determine the time when the message was encrypted and the algorithm was used.

An improved source of randomness is the time between two keystrokes (as used in PGP – pretty good privacy). However this system has been criticized as a hacker can spy on a user over a network and determine the time between keystrokes. Other sources of true randomness have also been investigated, including noise from an electronic device and noise from an audio source.

10.4 Security Mechanisms on the Internet

10.4.1 Digital Signatures

Digital signatures are widely used on the Internet to authenticate the sender of a message. To sign a message, the sender encrypts the message using a key known only to the sender. The recipient uses the inverse function to decrypt the message. The receiver knows who sent the message because only the sender has the key needed to encrypt the message. A public key technique can be used in such a situation.

A sender uses a private key to encrypt the message. To verify the signature, the recipient looks up the user (sender)'s public key and uses it to decrypt the message. Because only the user knows the private key, only the user can encrypt a message that can be decoded with the public key.

Interestingly, two levels of encryption can be used to guarantee that a message is both authentic and private. First, the message is signed by using the sender's private key to encrypt it. Second, the encrypted message is encrypted again using the recipient's public key. Here is the expression:

```
X = encrypt(public-rec, encrypt(private-sen, M))
```

where *M* denotes a message to be sent, *X* denotes the string results from the two-level encryption, *private-sen* denotes the sender's private key, and *public-rec* denotes the recipient's public key.

At the recipient's side, the decryption process is the reverse of the encryption process. First, the recipient uses the private key to decrypt the message, resulting in a digitally signed message. Then, the recipient uses the public key of the sender to decrypt the message again. The process can be expressed as follows:

```
M = decrypt(public-sen, decrypt(private-rec, X))
```

where *X* is the encrypted message received by the recipient, *M* is the original message, *private-rec* denotes the recipient's private key, and *public-sen* denotes the sender's public key.

If a meaningful message results from the double decryption, it must be true that the message was confidential and authentic.

10.4.2 Packet Filtering

To prevent each computer on a network from accessing arbitrary computers or services, many sites use a technique known as *packet filtering*. A packet filter is a program that operates in a router. The filter consists of software that can prevent packets from passing through the router on a path from one network to another. A manager must configure the packet filter to specify which packets are permitted and which should be blocked. Figure 10.4 illustrates such a filter.

Packet filter in router

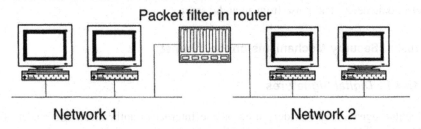

Network 1   Network 2

Figure 10.4. Packet filter in a router

A packet filter is configured to examine the packet header of each packet in order to decide which packets are allowed to pass through from one network to another. For example, the source and destination fields of a packet are examined to determine if the packet is to be blocked or not. The filter can also examine the protocol of each packet or high-level service to block the access of a particular protocol or service. For example, a packet filter can be configured to block all WWW access but allow for email packets.

10.4.3 Internet Firewall

A packet filter can be used as a firewall for an organization to protect its computers from unwanted Internet traffic, as illustrated in Figure 10.5.

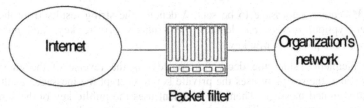

Figure 10.5. Internet firewall

Like a conventional firewall, an Internet firewall is designed to keep problems on the Internet from spreading into an organization's computer network. Without a firewall, an organization has to make all its computers secure to prevent unwanted Internet traffic. With a firewall, however, the organization can save money simply by installing the firewall and configuring it to meet the requirements.

10.5   Distributed Denial of Service Attacks

According to [Pfleeger 2003], Denial-of-Service (DoS) attack is an availability attack, since a DoS attack is characterized by an explicit attempt from an attacker to prevent legitimate users of a service from using the desired resource [CERT 2001b] [Householder et al. 2001] [Lau et al. 2000]. The attackers are not going to thieve, modify or remove the information exchanged on networks, but they attempt to impair a network service, thus to block legitimate users from accessing the service. The Distributed Denial-of-Service (DDoS) attacks are network flooding attacks from multiple machines, simultaneously. In order to launch a DDoS attack, the attacker first scans millions of machines for vulnerable service and other weakness, then gains access and compromises these zombie (or slave) machines. These infected machines can recruit more zombies. When the assault starts, the real attacker hides his identity and sends orders to zombies to perform the attacks [Xiang et al. 2004].

The attacks, together with the growing awareness of cyber-terrorism [Blane 2003], make researchers think of possible defense approach against them. However, there is still "a long way to go" to reach an appropriate balance between system safety and threats [Ware 1998]. Nowadays DDoS attacks become more sophisticated and more difficult to defeat. Most of current defense systems are passive, which means the defense actions are taken only after the DDoS attacks are launched. Thus, more or less, the target host or network is harmed before the attack source(s) can be found and controlled.

In order to suppress the attack as early as possible, we need an active DDoS defense system. Defenders must use new tactics and launch active countermeasures to fight against aggressors [Strassman 2003].

10.5.1   Launching a DDoS Attack

Figure 10.6 shows a hierarchical model of a DDoS attack. The most common attacks involve sending a large number of packets to a destination, thus causing excessive amounts of endpoint, and possibly transit, network bandwidth to be consumed [Householder et al. 2001]. The attack usually starts from multiple sources to aim at a single target. Multiple target attacks are less common; however, there is the possibility for attackers to launch such a type of attack.

To launch a DDoS attack, the attacker first scans millions of machines for vulnerable service and other weakness that permits penetrations, then controls and compromises these machines so called handlers, and zombies. After being installed the malicious scripts, such as scanning tools, attack tools, root kits, sniffers, handler and zombie program, and lists of vulnerable and previously compromised hosts, etc., these infected machines can recruit more machines. This propagation phase is quite like the spreading phase of computer viruses.

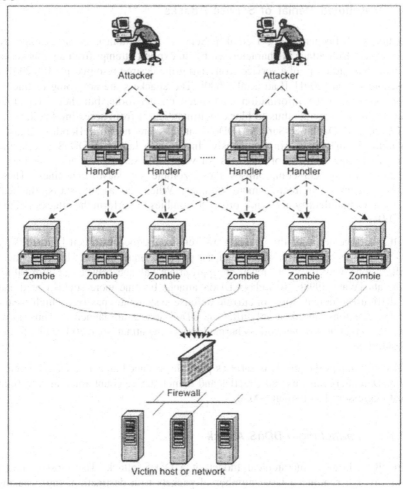

Figure 10.6. A hierarchical model of a DDoS attack

Then the communication channels between the attacker and the handlers, and between the handlers and zombies are established. These control channels are designed to be secret to public, in order to conceal the activity of attacker. TCP, UDP, ICMP, or a combination of these protocols is used to perform the communication. Recently, some attack tools exploit the existing infrastructure of Internet Relay Chat (IRC) networks, which are not as easily discovered as earlier versions, because they do not present a new open port that could be found by a scan or audit scheme [Houle and Weaver 2001].

Staying behind the scenes of attack, the real attacker sends a command to the handlers to initiate a coordinated attack. When the handlers receive the command, they transfer it to the zombies under their control. Upon receiving attack commands, the zombies begin the attack on the victim [Lau et al. 2000]. The real attacker is trying to hide himself from detection, for example, by providing spoofed IP addresses. It makes difficult to trace the real source of attacker and filter malicious packets from the legitimate traffic.

The Internet has grown without an overall architectural design [Neumann 2000]. This architecture paradigm is beneficial to the rapid growth of the Internet. However, such architecture opens several security issues that provide opportunities for the attackers. The fundamental characteristic of the Internet that allures DDoS attack is that the Internet security is highly interdependent [Houle and Weaver 2001]. DDoS attacks are commonly launched from systems that are subverted by an intruder via a security-related compromise rather than from the intruder's own system or systems. Thus no matter how well secured the victim system may be, its susceptibility depends on the state of security of the rest global environment. It is easy for attackers to hide their identities from tracing back in different networks.

Another characteristic of the Internet comprising of limited and consumable resources is also an inherent reason attracts attacks. Bandwidth, processing power, and storage capacities are all targets of attacks. Each host or network has limited resources that can be exhausted by a sufficient number of users.

Moreover, the Internet provides a target rich environment [Zaroo 2002]. There are millions of hosts and networks in the Internet with vulnerabilities that can be exploited to launch an attack. With the well developed DDoS tools, even an unexperienced user can start an attack easily.

10.5.2 Evolution of DDoS Attacks

In February 1996, CERT Coordination Centre issued an advisory on UDP port Denial of Service attack [CERT 1996a]. At the same year, advisories on TCP SYN flooding attacks and DoS attack via ping were also reported [CERT 1996b] [CERT 1996c]. Two DoS attack tools, 'Teardrop' and 'Land', are reported in 1997. These tools are being used to exploit two vulnerabilities in the TCP/IP protocol and they enable a remote user to cause a Denial of Service [CERT 1997]. A smurf IP DoS attacks is reported in 1998 [CERT 1998]. In the next year, two distributed tools 'Trinoo' (or Trin00) and 'Tribe Flood Network' (TFN) are firstly reported in CERT advisory and incident note [CERT 1999a] [CERT 1999b]. DDoS tools began to be deployed in this year, such as, Trinoo, TFN, and Stacheldraht. Stacheldraht combined features of Trinoo and TFN and added encrypted communications between attacker and handlers. However, unfortunately, the public were not ready to defense these vicious attacks.

Then in February 2000, Yahoo becomes the first website hit by a series of high-profile attacks in a three-day period. During the next hours, Amazon.com, eBuy, CNN.com, Buy.com, ZDNet, E*Trade, Excite.com were all subject to total or regional outages by DDoS attacks. In some cases, the servers were flooded by even 1 gigabit per second of incoming data, which caused them to go offline for several hours [Garber 2000]. Actually, the first reported large-scale DDoS attack via the public Internet occurred in August 1999 at the University of Minnesota [ANML

2001]. But only in February 2000 accidents make people be aware of the danger of DDoS. Some defense mechanisms are researched in this year, such as filtering [Ferguson and Senie 2000] [Park and Lee 2000], overlay defense network [Stone 2000], link testing traceback [Stone 2000] [Burch and Cheswick 2000], messaging traceback [Bellovin 2000] and so on. However, attack tools were becoming even harder to defeat. Packet amplification using name servers [CERT 2000e], 'mstream' featured TCP packets with randomized source information and randomized destination port [CERT 2000f], attacks to Kerberos and ISC BIND software [CERT 2000b] [CERT 2000c], were rapidly developed in the year. In [Dietrich et al. 2001], a well developed tool 'Shaft' is analysed in detail. It is shown that this tool has some capability to resist the counter measures to DDoS attacks. 'Carko' tool is reported in 2001 [CERT 2001a]. Other intruder tool such as worm were improved in this year, for instance, 'ramen', 'erkms', 'li0n', 'Code Red' and so on [Houle and Weaver 2001].

In order to avoid being tracked, DDoS attackers structure their attack traffic to use reflectors [Paxson 2001]. It is a modification to the conventional attack mode, where the zombies use reflectors to amplify the attack traffics enormously. Since there is a very large number of reflectors, it is very difficult to locate all the zombies, say nothing of tracing back and controlling the real attacker.

In another area, there is possibility that the DDoS attacks invade the wireless Internet including the Wireless Extended Internet, the Wireless Portal Network, and the Wireless Ad Hoc network [Geng et al. 2002]. Both mobile phone virus [Dennis 2000] and SMS flooder [Sherriff 2000] show that wireless world is the future DDoS targets. Today the widespread deployment of IEEE 802.11-based wireless network is highly susceptible to DDoS attacks targeting its management and media access protocols [Bellardo and Savage 2003].

Nowadays there is a trend toward non-disclosure within the intruder communities. So new attack tools are often kept private to the outside world. Thus, when public awareness of a DDoS rises, the method or tool is already in some degree of widely spread use [Houle and Weaver 2001]. The evolvement and development towards sophisticate, automated, intelligent, highly distributed features of DDoS tools are still going on. The DDoS tools today include a self-upgrade mechanism [Levy 2003b] and have tremendous spread capability [Moore et al. 2003].

10.5.3   Classification of DDoS Attacks

According to [CERT 2001b], modes of attack include consumption of resources, destruction or alteration of configuration information, and physical destruction or alteration of network components. In [Mirkovic et al. 2002a], the attacks are classified by degree of automation, exploited vulnerability, attack rate dynamics, and impact. Here from the technical point of view we classify the attacks by attacking methods as below. The resources consumed by attacks include network bandwidth, disk space, CPU time, data structures, even printers, tape devices, network connections, etc.

SYN flood – Any system providing TCP-based network services is potentially subject to this attack. The attackers use half-open connections to cause the server exhaust its resource to keep the information describing all pending connections. The result would be system crash or system inoperative [CERT 1996b].

TCP reset – TCP reset also exploit the characteristics of TCP protocol. By listening the TCP connections to the victim, the attacker sends a fake TCP RESET packet to the victim. Then it causes the victim to inadvertently terminate its TCP connection [Mohiuddin 2002].

ICMP attack – Smurf attack sends forged ICMP echo request packets to IP broadcast addresses. These attacks lead large amounts of ICMP echo reply packets being sent from an intermediary site to a victim, accordingly cause network congestion or outages [CERT 1998]. ICMP datagram can also be used to start an attack via ping. Attackers use the 'ping' command to construct oversized ICMP datagram to launch the attack [CERT 1996c].

UDP storm – This kind of attack can not only impair the hosts' services, but also congest or slow down the intervening network. When a connection is established between two UDP services, each of which produces a very high number of packets, thus cause an attack.

DNS request – In this attack scenario, the attack sends a large number of UDP-based DNS requests to a name server using a spoofed source IP address. Then the name server, acting as an intermediary party in the attack, responds by sending back to the spoofed IP address as the victim destination. Because of the amplification effect of DNS response, it can cause serious bandwidth attack [CERT 2000e].

CGI request – By simply sending multiple CGI request to the target server, the attacker consumes the CPU resource of the victim. Then the server is forced to terminate its services.

Mail bomb – A mail bomb is the sending of a massive amount of e-mail to a specific person or system. A huge amount of mail may simply fill up the recipient's disk space on the server or, in some cases, may be too much for a server to handle and may cause the server to stop functioning. This attack is also a kind of flood attack [SearchSecurity 2003].

ARP storm – During a DDoS attack, the ARP request volume can become very massive, and then the victim system can be negatively affected.

Algorithmic Complexity Attacks – It's a class of low-bandwidth DoS attacks that exploit algorithmic deficiencies in the worst case performance of algorithms used in many mainstream applications. For example, both binary trees and hash tables with carefully chosen input can be the attack targets to consume system resources greatly [Crosby and Wallach 2003].

10.5.4   Some Key Technical Methods of DDoS Tools

Although so many protocols and system vulnerabilities are exploited by DDoS attacks as it is shown above, the attack tools need some key technical methods to launch an attack successfully, such as scanning, propagation, and communication, as it is illustrated in figure 10.7. These measures are utilized before the real attack starts. Therefore, they are also the key issues in active defense mechanism against DDoS attacks. It is beneficial to understand these issues clearly to build an active defense system.

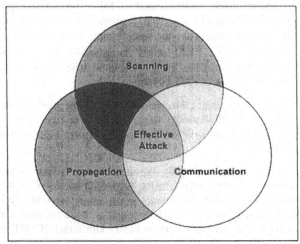

Figure 10.7. Key methods used before making an effective DDoS attack

Scanning is the first step to intrude other systems. Only after the vulnerabilities of other systems are found can the malicious scripts be installed to recruit more handlers or zombies and start an attack. Some attacks use random scanning strategy. By using different seeds, the comprised host probes random IP address to find the potential targets. Some virus attacks, such as Code Red, use this strategy and sometimes cause network congestion for the high traffic volume. Upon that this deployment phase becomes the attack phase. Other scanning strategies such as hit list scanning, topological scanning, permutation scanning, and local subnet scanning are also popular or potential in deployment of DDoS attacks [Weaver 2002] [Mirkovic et al. 2002a]. It is noticeable that the hit list scanning produces a great propagation speed due to exponential spread and no collisions during the scanning phase. If we could find and control the malicious scanning actions of attackers, we could guard our systems on the first step.

Today the propagation mechanism of DDoS tools is quite automated. Without manual intervention by an intruder, the malicious code can propagate at a very high speed. Central source propagation model, back-chaining model and autonomous model are three main models of propagation [Houle and Weaver 2001]. In central source model, the attack code is stored in a central server or set of servers. After an agent machine is compromised, the code is downloaded from the central source. In back-chaining propagation model, the infected machine is the source for next propagation approach. While more efficient, the autonomous model just injects attack instructions directly into the target host during the exploitation. The propagation methods are developed well; even the offline infrastructure world could be affected seriously by propagation of online 'pests' [Levy 2003a].

Although some attacks do not need human to issue commands to start the onset, or the handlers can autonomously control the zombie army, the communication channel is important to the attack scheme. Early DDoS tools open service port to communicate with each other. Some tools employ encryption technology to conceal the control channels, such as the Stacheldraht tool. As it is mentioned before, Internet Relay Chat (IRC) networks is widely used by the attackers. Both public and private IRC servers are used to serve as the communications backbone for DDoS networks. Because they do not present a new open port that could be found by a scan or audit, it is more difficult to identify the DDoS networks.

10.6   Passive Defense against DDoS Attacks

10.6.1   Passive Defense Cycle

Passive defense actions are taken only after the DDoS attacks are launched. Hence, the target host or network is harmed to some certain extents before the attack source(s) can be located and handled. Traditional passive defense mechanism includes a protect-detect-react cycle [Householder et al. 2001]. That is after attack actions are detected, then some reacting steps are taken, such as traffic limiting, blocking, and filtering. This method has advantages over the poor "lesson learned" experience, which responses only after the accident is over. However, it is far from enough. We need an active defense system with a surveillance-trace-control cycle, which will be present in detail in the later part of this chapter.

By deploying the passive defense system, an attack is usually detected by monitoring of inbound traffic volumes and other performance metrics. But ironically, the first signal of attack often comes from the external customer's report that shows the service is no longer reachable, instead of the alarm of detection system. Then apparently it is too late to protect the victim from the attack.

10.6.2   Current Passive Defense Mechanisms

Passive defense mechanisms can be classified into two categories, one is detecting mechanism, and the other is reacting mechanism. The common detection method includes monitoring traffic volumes and source IP addresses, and resource accounting. However, usually simply monitoring of the traffic volume can't tell accurately the real attack, because some time Internet flash crowds also cause network congestion [Jung et al. 2002]. So this method can't differentiate legitimate requests or malicious requests. According to the characteristic of IP spoofing

272

techniques of DDoS attack, monitoring of source IP addresses is a feasible measure to discover the attack. Detecting mechanisms of passive defense systems are introduced later.

After detecting the malicious actions of DDoS attacks, the passive defense system turns into reacting stage. Filtering out the attack traffic stream is one of the simple and straightforward methods to counter DDoS attacks. But it relies on an ingenious and sensitive detection system, otherwise it will drop the legitimate packets as well, and in that case it also falls in a denial of service. Reconfiguration [Mirkovic et al. 2002a] is another measure to defeat attacks. It changes the topology of the victim or the intermediate network to either add more resource to the victim, or to isolate the attack machines.

An apparent symptom of the DDoS attacks is network congestion. Network traffic congestion control is a popular measure to alleviate the harm of DDoS attacks. Congestion control is a mechanism for a router to identify and restrict flows that are using a disproportionate share of bandwidth in times of congestion.

Another DDoS defense mechanism is IP traceback. With the ability to trace IP packets to their origins, it provides the defense system to identify the true source of the packets causing a DDoS, in order to stop the attacks. Later in this chapter we will introduce current research on filtering, congestion control, and passive IP traceback.

Table 10.1 Summary of current passive defense mechanisms

Defense mechanism		Main features	Advantages	Disadvantages
Detecting mechanism	Traffic volume monitoring [Paxson 1999] [Estan and Varghese 2001] [Cisco 2003] [Gil and Poletto 2001]	Detect attacks by monitoring the changes of traffic volume. Detectable features of traffic are required.	• Easy to deploy • Simple and fast algorithm	• Can not differentiate flash crowd and the real attack • Ineffective when the DDoS attack doesn't have high traffic volume
	Source IP address monitoring [Jung et al. 2002] [Peng et al. 2003a] [Peng et al. 2003b] [Peng et al. 2004]	Detect attacks by monitoring the incoming packets' IP addresses.	• Can differentiate flash crowd and the spoofed IP addresses attack • To some degree it can detect the attack pattern using reflectors	• Invalid when the attacks come from real IP addresses • Less effective for the high traffic volume attacks
	Packet content analysis [Papadopoulos et al. 2003]	Detect attacks by analysing the features of packet content such as ramp up, spectral content, etc.	• Have good logical, precise pertinence to some certain attack patterns	• Current coarse granularity analysis introduces errors • The computation work may be too complex to deploy
Reacting mechanism	Filtering [Ferguson and Senie 2000] [Park and Lee 2000] [Park and Lee 2001b] [Kargl et al. 2001] [Li et al. 2002]	Dropping the unwanted packets in routers.	• Can filter out the spoofed IP packets • Potential to defend the highly	• Only effective when it is deployed globally • Can not defend the attack using real IP addresses

[Thompson et al. 2003] [Jin et al. 2003]		distributed attacks	
Congestion control [Floyd and Jacobson 1993] [Floyd 1994] [Lin and Morris 1997] [Stoica et al. 1998] [Ott et al. 1999] [Mahajan et al. 2001] [Yau et al. 02] [Mahajan et al. 2002] [Kohler et al. 2004]	Regulate the traffic behaviours by analysing flows. It is a method aiming at solving the congestion problem, instead of radically solving the DDoS problem.	• Can avoid overall network congestion • Not only DDoS can be controlled, but also other misbehaviours can be adjusted	• May have some unfairness effects • Ineffective when the attack is a low bandwidth attack • Can not detect the discontinuous attack flows • May block some legitimate traffic
Passive traceback [Stone 2000] [Burch and Cheswick 2000] [Bellovin 2000] [Mankin et al. 2001] [Wang and Schulzrinne 2003]	Identify the real source of the packets causing a DDoS. The passive traceback process starts after the attack begins.	• Compatible with current network protocols • Easy to implement	• Can only find the malicious hosts sending attack packets • Needs a long time and heavy computation load to establish the real path • Not suitable for distributed defense scheme
Replication [Yan et al. 2000]	Prepare the spare resource for consuming of attacks, which is a typical passive method.	• It can absorb some attack flood and provide resources to legitimate users • No computation burden	• Expensive installation of spare resources • The resources still may be exhausted by DDoS attacks

The main features, advantages and disadvantages of current passive defense mechanisms are listed in table 10.1. In the later part of this chapter, each mechanism will be discussed in detail.

Because of the popular occurrence of SYN flood attacks in the Internet, the mechanism of it and its countermeasure are studied for a long time. So as a special issue, we will introduce passive defense against SYN DDoS attacks in section 10.6.5.

10.6.3 Detecting Mechanisms

Detecting mechanisms for the defense against DDoS attacks include: Traffic Volume Monitoring, Source IP Address Monitoring, and Monitoring Other Features.

Traffic Volume Monitoring

DDoS attacks usually cause a high volume of network traffic, so one of the DDoS attack signals is the sudden growth of traffic volume. The Internet traffic patterns and characteristics are studied by Thompson [Thompson 1997] in terms of packet sizes, flow duration, volume, and percentage composition by protocol and application. Traffic volume is the main feature used by the early network intrusion detection systems (IDS) to detection abnormal network actions.

Bro [Paxson 1999] is a general-purpose network intrusion detection system (IDS) that passively monitors a network link over which the intruder's traffic transits. Bro is divided into an "event engine" that reduces a kernel-filtered network traffic stream into a series of higher-level events, and a "policy script interpreter" that interprets event handlers written in a specialized language used to express a site's security policy. In some situations, it becomes the attack target and is suffered from the DDoS attacks [Crosby and Wallach 2003].

In flow granularity, some traffic flows in the Internet are looked as large and malicious flows. Cristian Estan proposed two algorithms for identifying the large flows, one is sample and hold, the other is multistage filters [Estan and Varghese 2001]. Some methods of traffic measurement, for example, Cisco's NetFlow [Cisco 2003], are usually slow by using of DRAM and inaccurate by random sampling. It is impossible to keep the state for every flow because of the scaling problem. Compared with NetFlow, sample and hold method needs less flow memory. If M is the available amount of memory, the errors of this method can be represented as an variable proportional to $1/M$ (where NetFlow's error is proportional to $1/\sqrt{M}$), so it introduces less errors compared with NetFlow. Multistage filters method is to hash a packet of a certain flow by using hash function into a stage table, and hash other packets in the same way. Each table entry contains a counter that is incremented by the packet size. If all the hashed counters are above the threshold, this flow is passed to the flow memory for individual observation. Their solution may be a practical way to identify the heavy hitters.

A MUti-Level Tree for Online Packet Statistics (MULTOPS) is proposed in [Gil and Poletto 2001], which relies on the assumption that the packet rate of traffic going in one direction is proportional to the packet rate of traffic going in the opposite direction. This assumption makes this method unsuitable for asymmetric routers; especially in some real video stream network, the monitored traffic from server to client is much higher than from client to server, thus it introduces detection error. MULTOPS is a tree structure to detect ongoing bandwidth attacks. However, when the attack is launched from distributed sources, it fails to detect it. Besides, IP spoofing also affects the capability of MULTOPS.

Traffic volumes monitoring is a simple way to detect the attack, however, some time in the Internet flash crowds also cause a high volume of traffic. So by just merely monitoring the traffic volume usually can't tell exactly the real malicious traffics. And some attacks don't have the feature of high traffic volume, which is classified as low-bandwidth attacks. So volume monitoring also can't differentiate legitimate packets or malicious packets.

In order to evade punishment, many attacks have the characteristic of IP spoofing techniques, so monitoring of source IP addresses is a feasible measure to mitigate the attack.

Source IP Address Monitoring

In order to determine the attack, one of the passive approaches is to monitor the number of new coming source IP address, rather than the traffic volume. In [Jung et al. 2002], it is found that during some DDoS attacks, most source IP addresses are new to the victim.

In [Peng et al. 2003b] and [Peng et al. 2004], Source IP address Monitoring (SIM) is used to detect DDoS attacks. The advantage of IP address monitoring is it can effectively differentiate the traffics by flash crowd or DDoS attack; because in a flash crowd situation, the source IP addresses usually appeared to the victim before, while in DDoS attacks, IP addresses are new to the victim. By the reason of that the attack traffic from distributed sources may be small compared to normal background traffic, an accumulated traffic monitoring is used to identify attacks. To some degree, it could detect the attack pattern of DDoS using reflectors [Paxson 2001], which employs reflectors to make attacks.

In [Peng et al. 2003a], machine learning is also used to find the attack patterns. Sharing the distributed beliefs method let distributed defense agents communicate with each other to detect attacks. As the experiment data, the traffic data from University of Auckland is used to evaluate the performance. However, they only use two agents to evaluate performance, which is not enough to simulate the real situation; another problem of it is that the communication cost between agents may be huge if the number of agents increases.

Monitoring Other Features

Besides volume and IP address monitoring, there are also other features of DDoS attacks could be detected, such as IP header content, ramp up behaviour for multi-source attacks, and spectral content [Hussain et al. 2003]. The application of this technique is COSSACK, which is to suppress the distributed and coordinated attacks [Papadopoulos et al. 2003]. It is a distributed architecture combines multicast communications, traditional IDS systems and novel blind detection techniques. However, this approach's effectiveness still need further study, because spectral analysis is a coarse granularity analysis.

The goal of SOS [Keromytis et al. 2002] infrastructure is to distinguish between authorized and unauthorized traffic. The drawback of SOS is it precludes casual access to a web server by anonymous, yet benign users. As an extension of SOS, WebSOS [Morein et al. 2003] uses a combination of Graphic Turing tests and cryptographic protocols for data origin authentication, thus defeats automated attack zombies. To some degree, it could only protect web servers. And because it implements authentication in application layer, it will loss efficiency or itself will become the attack target.

10.6.4   Reacting Mechanisms

Reacting mechanisms for the defense against DDoS attacks include: Filtering, Congestion Control, Passive Traceback, and Replication.

Filtering

One of the simple and straightforward methods to counter DDoS attacks is to filter out the attack stream completely. Filtering is to drop the unwanted packets in certain routers. Although some DDoS attacks use packets that request legitimate services from the victim, which is called non-filterable attacks [Mirkovic et al. 2002a], filtering helps the victim to defend the spoofed IP packets attacks.

From the point of view of deployment, filtering can be classified as ingress filtering and egress filtering. Ingress filtering is deployed on the external interface of a network and drops all spoofed incoming packets, for instance, the IP addresses that belong to its internal network, which is the obvious case. On the other hand, egress filtering is applied on the internal interface of a network to deal with the packets going out. In the same way, egress filtering drops all the packets that do not have their local network addresses. It would be an efficient defense scheme against DDoS attacks if these filtering mechanisms are widely accepted and deployed, because it could perfectly stop all spoofed packets travelling through the Internet. Furthermore, it helps to traceback any packet's original source, since it forces users to send true IP addresses. Traceback is another measure to defeat DDoS attack, which will be introduced in the later section. However, these mechanisms are not widely deployed by the ISPs or even resisted because of the liability problems.

Ingress filtering is initially proposed in RFC2267, which is replaced by a newer version RFC2827 [Ferguson and Senie 2000]. In order to achieve better result in countering distributed attacks, Park and Lee [2000] [2001b] propose a router-based Distributed Packet Filtering (DPF). However, in current Internet environment, it is infeasible to cover the whole network by such a defense system, although in a theoretically perfect situation, it can prevent all the forged IP addresses. Another way of filtering is proposed in [Kargl et al. 2001] by using Class-Based Queuing on a web load-balancer to identify misbehaving IP packets and put them to lower priority queues. But if the attacks use spoofed IP addresses from time to time, it is difficult to classify the packets.

The requirement of global deployment is also essential to the Source Address Validity Enforcement Protocol (SAVE) [Li et al. 2002]. In a distributed fashion, the SAVE protocol maintains an incoming table at each participating router, which indicates the router's proper incoming interface for packets from all sources. Each router sends SAVE updates to all destinations in its forwarding table, sending a new update when routing to a destination is changed. Then all routers have sent such updates to their destinations, each router will have a complete set of legitimate sources of each incoming interface. How it works well with the existed network protocols is still an open question. Furthermore, the authentication and computational overhead also need further study.

Similarly, Roshan Thomas proposed a legitimacy-based DDoS filtering scheme, NetBouncer [Thomas et al. 2003]. It maintains a legitimacy list to differentiate malicious packets and legitimate packets. If the packets are not in the list, it will proceed to administer a variety of legitimacy tests to challenge the client to prove its legitimacy. However, it is not tested in real network environment.

Another filtering mechanism is proposed as Hop-Count Filtering [Jin et al. 2003]. The idea is that although the attacker can forge any field in IP header, the number of hops an IP packet takes to reach its destination can't be falsified. So Hop-Count Filtering (HCF) could be mainly applied to filter the spoofed IP packets. It extracts the TTL information from the IP head to compute the hop-count, then by comparing the computed hop-count with the stored hop-count, the likely spoofed packets are identified. Because this method still has some certain false positive rate, it takes no action to defend attacks until in the action state. Steven J. Templeton also found that the final TTL values from an IP address are generally clustered around a single value [Templeton and Levitt 2003], but no solution provided.

In the Internet there may be a single IP address that has multiple valid hop-counts at the same time, so the result of this method becomes less creditable. If the computation burden of the system is well solved, it may be a feasible filtering solution against DDoS attacks, and more realistic deployments are needed to proof the effectiveness.

Congestion Control

From the view of traffic flow (instead of packet), congestion control regulates the behaviours of flows in the Internet. Routers deployed on the Internet nowadays have a best-effort manner, which introduces potentially negative impacts. Sally Floyd argues that router mechanisms are needed to identify and restrict the flows that are using a disproportionate share of the bandwidth in times of congestion [Floyd and Fall 1999]. Random Early Detection (RED) and the RED-related techniques are one of the main streams of congestion control.

Random Early Detection (RED) [Floyd and Jacobson 1993] helps to avoid the congestion in packet-switched networks. By computing the average queue size, the RED gateway can detect incipient congestion. The gateway could notify connections of congestion either by dropping packets arriving at the gateway or by setting a bit in packet headers. When the average queue size exceeds a preset threshold, the gateway drops or marks each arriving packet with a certain probability, where the exact probability is a function of the average queue size. It randomly chooses packets to be marked during congestion, to identify which connections belong to misbehaving users.

In order to reduce the unfairness effects of RED, Flow Random Early Drop (FRED) is proposed in [Lin and Morris 1997], which provides selective dropping based on per-active-flow buffer counts. It discards packets to protect flows that are using less than their fare share and prevent aggressive flows from monopolizing buffer space and bandwidth. It introduces parameters of the minimum and maximum number of packets each flow should be allowed to buffer. It needs collect or analyse the state information for every individual flow. When DDoS attacks come from different sources, and traffic from these sources are small, then this method is of no effect.

Stabilized Random Early Drop (SRED) [Ott et al. 1999] pre-emptively discards packets with a load-dependent probability when a buffer in a router seems congested. The idea is to compare the packet arrives at some buffer with the randomly chosen packet that proceeded before. If the two packets are of the same flow, it is said 'hit'. The sequence of hits is used to find candidates for misbehaving flow, because hits are more likely to occur in this kind of flow. If there is a hit with a high count and a high total occurrence, the flow then has a high probability of being a misbehaving flow. This method can only detect the continuous and durative misbehaving traffic flow from a same source, which has the same problem as FRED.

Ratul Mahajan, et al. proposed a mechanism named RED with Preferential Dropping (RED-PD) [Mahajan et al. 2001], which keeps partial flow state for the high-bandwidth flows. It uses the packet drop history at the router to detect high-bandwidth flows in times of congestion and preferentially drops packets from these flows. By restricting high-bandwidth flows, it improves the performance of low-bandwidth flows. However, if the attacks are low-rate TCP-targeted DDoS attacks, both RED and RED-PD become less effective to detect the attacks [Kuzmanovic and Knightly 2003]. Compared with high-rate DDoS attacks, Low-rate attacks are more difficult to detect. It exploits TCP's retransmission time-out mechanism and then throttle TCP flows to a small fraction of their ideal rate while eluding detection.

Today there are other approaches on solving the congestion problem of a network, such as Explicit Congestion Notification (ECN) [Floyd 1994], Core-Stateless Fair Queuing (CSFQ) [Stoica et al. 1998], Datagram Congestion Control Protocol (DCCP) [Kohler et al. 2004], Max-min fairness control [Yau et al. 2002], and Aggregate-based Congestion Control (ACC) [Mahajan et al. 2002]. Some network congestion is caused by DDoS attacks, but not all the congestions are triggered by DDoS attacks. Here we only introduce some congestion control methods related to DDoS attacks.

Aggregate-based Congestion Control (ACC) [Mahajan et al. 2002] is to minimize the immediate damage done by high-bandwidth aggregates. It includes a detecting mechanism, aggregate controlling mechanism, and a cooperative pushback mechanism in which a router can ask upstream routers to control an aggregate. However, in fact it doesn't aim to block the attack traffics, or to find the sources of attacks.

To some degree, both filtering-based and congestion control techniques will alleviate the anguished symptom of DDoS attacks, but they may inevitably block some legitimate traffic, the more effective methods still need further research.

Passive Traceback

IP traceback is the ability to trace IP packets to their origins [Aljifri 2003]; it provides the defense system with the ability to identify true source of the packets causing a DDoS, thus possibly to stop the attacks. The aim of traceback is to construct the path of each router traversed by the attack packet on its journey from source to the victim [Snoeren et al. 2002]. Under a real DDoS attack scenario, the source addresses of attack packets usually are counterfeited and looked like having nothing to do with the attackers themselves. With IP spoofing techniques, header of source address is manipulated and falsified. Therefore, these addresses are of no use to identify the attackers. We must trace its real source by other measures through the network.

We classify current traceback approaches into two categories, one is passive and the other is active. Passive measures start the traceback process in response to an attack. It depends on the active attack; because when the attack stops, it can't effectively follow up the clue of attack. Active traceback helps the defense system actively finding the attack source, not only the attack zombies and handlers, but also the real attacker who issues commands. Currently traceback methods fall into the following categories [Aljifri 2003]: link testing [Stone 2000] [Burch and Cheswick 2000], messaging [Bellovin 2000] [Mankin et al. 2001] [Wang and Schulzrinne 2003], logging [Duffield and Grossglauser 2000] [Snoeren et al. 2001] [Baba and Matsuda 2002], and packet marking [Savage et al. 2000] [Savage et al. 2001] [Park and Lee 2001a] [Song and Perrig 2001] [Dean et al. 2001] [Adler 2002] [Waldvogel 2002] [Yaar et al. 2003]. Most of them are currently applied in traditional passive defense scheme, while the later two can be used in active defense systems.

♦ Link testing

Link testing methods include input debugging [Stone 2000] and controlled flooding methods [Burch and Cheswick 2000]. The main idea of it is to start from the victim to find the attack from upstream links, and then determine which one carries the attack traffic. CenterTrack [Stone 2000] is an example of hop-by-hop tracking through an overlay network. By capturing the attack signature in some routers, the system tries to find which previous hop the attack is coming from or through. It uses IP tunnels to reroute interesting datagram directly from edge routers to special tracking routers. The tracking routers then determine the ingress edge router by observing tunnels.

By the assumption that in the Internet most routes are largely symmetric, Hal Burch [Burch and Cheswick 2000] introduced another link testing method of controlled flooding. It applies a brief bust of load to every link attached to the victim, by using UDP chargen service. If the loaded link is perturbed by the controlled flood, then it is probably the path from the source end to the victim end. However, paradoxically, itself may be a kind of DoS attack, because it will introduce network congestion to the legitimate users.

Although link testing has some advantages such as compatibility with existing protocols, routers and network infrastructure, it also has some significant limitations. First, it consumes a great deal of time to establish the attack path that may include multiple branch points, however, the attack doesn't often last for an enough long time for traceback. Second, if the attack comes from within the backbone itself, or, a backbone router is a victim, it is not suitable for this method to reconstruct the attack path. Third, if the attack is a large scale of DDoS attack, it is less effective. Moreover, if some attack only needs a single packet, instead of flows of packets, this method can not handle the attacks at all.

♦ Messaging

Another traceback technique is messaging. Bellovin proposed an ICMP message to find the source of forged IP packets [Bellovin 2000]. In this scheme, routers send ICMP messages to the destinations, for every 20000 packets passing through. For a high volume flow, the victim will eventually receive ICMPs from all the routers along the path back to the source, revealing its location. However, if each zombie of the attack contributes only a small amount of the total attack traffic, it's difficult for this method to rebuild the real path. Moreover, ICMP packets are often treated or filtered by routers with a low priority, in order to reduce the additional traffic. Thus it also makes this method less effective. Allison Mankin modified this method by proposing an intension-driven ICMP traceback [Mankin et al. 2001]. It introduces an extra bit in the routing and forwarding process, to help the ICMP traceback more useful. ICMP scheme is vulnerable to attackers with falsified ICMP messages. So to alleviate the problem, iCaddie, with the authentication feature, is proposed in [Wang and Schulzrinne 2003]. A caddie message is an extra ICMP message generated by a router or an application, attached with the entire packet routing history of one randomly selected packet, which is called ball packet. This method avoids the forging problem, however, in general, messaging schemes introduce additional network traffic, and can't handle the highly distributed attacks, although it is simple to deploy in the existed network infrastructure.

Replication

Replication is to use redundant resources of the same nature to cope with sudden surge of demand. This idea is also applied in defending against DDoS attacks. Some researchers propose the replication scheme to defeat DDoS attacks. The XenoService [Yan et al. 2000] is a distributed network of web hosts that respond to an attack on any one web site by replicating it rapidly and widely. So the server can absorb a packet flood and continue trading. However, some attack traffic volume reaches several gigabytes, and then this method may not absorb such huge attack traffic well. Moreover, replication itself consumes many resources, which is also vulnerable to the attacks.

10.6.5 SYN Attacks and Its Countermeasures

SYN flooding attacks are among the most commonly used attacks [CERT 1996b]. The passive approaches to defeat SYN flooding attacks usually include deployment of defense mechanism at the firewall for victim or inside the victim host. The first step to defend is to detect the SYN attack. There are lots of features of SYN attack for detect. A simple method is to detect the number of received SYN segments per second by a given TCP port [Mutaf 1999]. When the number exceeds the acceptable critical value, it decides there is an attack and acts accordingly. This method is simple but with less accuracy. Without reside in the victim machine, the method of Wang et al. [2002] doesn't monitor the victim server, but detect SYN flooding attacks at leaf routers that connect end hosts to the Internet. It applies non-parametric Cumulative Sum (CUSUM) method [Pollak 1986], which is an instance of Sequential Change Point Detection method, to detect the abrupt change of SYN segments. First it identifies different packets of TCP SYNs, FINs and RSTs, then by detecting the abruptly increasing discrepancy between the numbers of SYNs and FINs, it finds the SYN flooding. But if the attacker sends flooding packets of a mixture of SYNs and FINs (RSTs), then itself is unprotected to attacks.

Other practical defense measures include SYN cache and SYN cookie, although both have flaws such as causing infinite queue and consuming host resources [Lemon 2002]. In [Schnackenberg et al. 1997], a software tool named Synkill to defeat SYN flooding attacks is proposed. It monitors the packets and classifies them into different categories as follows, never seen (null), correctly behaving (good), potentially spoofed (new), most certainly spoofed (bad), administratively good (perfect) and administratively bad (evil). When it finds bad or evil packets, it just sends RST packets to the connection, or helps to complete the three-way handshake. The key part lies in the classification process that may introduce false positive and false negative. Attackers may "teach" Synkill what are good addresses that are in fact spoofed. So it becomes less effective. It is also vulnerable to attacks because in order to finish the process it consumes a great lot of resources of victim machine.

Another way to defeat SYN flood is for a server always to accept a new connection request and put the pending requests to a cache [Ricciulli et al. 1999], with a random drop scheme to get space for new coming requests. This solution allows flexible trade-off defense effectiveness with resource requirements, but it only guarantees service in a probabilistic manner. Thus, an attacker may still occasionally affect connections requested by legitimate clients.

Current Linux kernels include a facility called TCP SYN cookies to counter the SYN flooding attacks. The rationale is to keep the connection state in the SYN cookie, but outside its memory. Zuquete [2002] proposed an improved method of SYN cookies. The key idea is to exploit a kind of TCP connection called simultaneous connection initiation in order to lead client hosts to send together TCP options and SYN cookies to a server being attacked. However, it causes some problems in Windows client systems or firewall protected client systems.

10.6.6   Limitation of Passive Defense

As we mentioned before, passive defense mechanism includes a protect-detect-react cycle [Householder et al. 2001]. The passive defense system just waits for the possible attacks, then after the attack actions are detected, the reacting steps such as traffic limiting, blocking, filtering and traceback are taken. For more effective defense, today's passive defense architectures evolve toward distributed and coordinated.

However, most of the current passive systems are not automated and often with high detection false positive. In industry area, Cisco routers have some features to defend DDoS attacks, such as access lists, access list logging, debug logging and IP accounting [Cisco 1999]. However, it mainly describes how to detect the attack manually when the router is the ultimate target of Smurf attacks and SYN floods, or used as a Smurf reflector. So the main limitation of passive defense system is that it can only detect and react after attack is launched. Other limitations of passive defense are listed as follows.

1. Response is always lagging behind the attack, thus it is not a potent defense method inherently.

2. It is hard to deploy an automated and intelligent passive system, because most of the methods rely on manual configuration and other defense action.

3. It can't effectively avoid network congestion, since the flood has already arrived, congestion control can only be the rescue after the event.

4. If attackers continue their attack for a limited time, being traced by the passive system becomes impossible.

5. The "ultimate" source may in fact be a compromised computer, but not the real attacker, so passive traceback becomes less effective, because the huge number of sources could overwhelm the trace system.

From the discussion above we can see that new approaches, such as the active defense, are critically needed to strike down DDoS attacks.

10.7 Active Defense against DDoS Attacks

10.7.1 Active Defense Cycle

In section 10.5 we outline some key methods used before making an effective DDoS attack, for example, scanning, propagation and communication. If we can block these basic actions of scanning, propagation and communication on the early stage of attacks, then we are able to minimize the damage as much as possible. Here we introduce the original idea of active defense cycle, a surveillance-trace-control cycle, as shown in Figure 10.8 [Xiang et al. 2004].

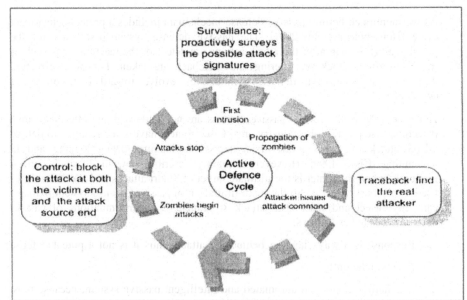

Figure 10.8. Active defense cycle

In this active defense cycle, surveillance is one of the important chains. It is different from the passive monitoring actions, which is just waiting for the attack signals. Surveillance is to deploy distributed sensors through out the protected network, which proactively surveys the possible attack signatures. Here attack signatures not only include some patterns which can be used to help distinguish malicious packets from normal traffic [Stone 2000], but also the scanning signatures, propagation patterns and communication patterns of the masters, handlers, and zombies.

Traceback may be an effective method to find the real attacker. Passive traceback usually can't locate the real attacker, but it detects thousands of attack zombies, which exhausts the capability of a defense system. The aim of active traceback is not just find the zombies, but to dig out the wire-puller behind curtain. Current traceback techniques such as logging and packet marking can be applied in active DDoS defense systems.

Control stage of the active defense cycle is to block attack packets not only near the victim side, but also close to the attack source end. Pushback [Ioannidis and Bellovin 2002] is a promising way to control and punish the attack. It is a cooperative mechanism in which routers can ask adjacent routers to clog an aggregate upstream, in order to penalize the source attacker.

Compared with the passive defense cycle, which is a protect-detect-react cycle, the active defense cycle covers all the DDoS attack stages. It has its features such as surveying in advance, active traceback and source end control. We also acknowledge that active defense cycle may not always suitable and effective for all kinds of DDoS attacks. In some situation, we should still need passive react, to assist the active system, or even degrade or shut down services, although this is the worst case.

10.7.2   Objectives of Active Defense

The aim of the active defense system is to control the attack as soon as possible, and reduce the damage to the minimum degree. Only a global deployment will protect against DDoS attacks [Geng and Whinston 2000]. Listed below are four design objectives of the active defense system.

1. Finding malicious actions during the DDoS deployment period.

2. Sharing attacking information such as communication signatures between coordinated systems.

3. Recording the clues of malicious actions for later analysing, learning and forensic purposes.

4. A scalable architecture to protect the network resources, for future deploying distributed security infrastructure.

To realize the above objectives, some current techniques can be applied to build the active defense system. Jelena Mirkovic proposed the idea of source-end DDoS defense [Mirkovic et al. 2002b] [Mirkovic et al. 2003], which is also trying to depress the attack as soon as possible. Active traceback and protocol-based defense mechanisms may be other methods to control the attack forcefully. We will introduce these techniques in the following sections, as well as some theoretical methods to support them.

10.7.3   Current Techniques Applicable in Active Defense

Current active defense mechanisms include source end defense, active traceback which is classified into logging traceback and packet marking traceback, and protocol-based defense. In Table 10.2, the main features, advantages and disadvantages of each method are analysed. Then in the later sections, each method will be discussed in detail.

Table 10.2 Summary of current active defense mechanisms

Defense mechanism	Main features	Advantages	Disadvantages
Source end defense [Mirkovic et al. 2002b] [Mirkovic et al. 2003]	Both detection components and defeating components are deployed at the source end of attacking	• Detect DDoS attack as soon as possible • Avoid overall network congestion	• Lack of coordination • Less sensitive to catch the attack signals • Liability problems
Logging traceback [Duffield and Grossglauser 2000] [Snoeren et al. 2001] [Baba and Matsuda 2002]	Gather (sample) packets in the network to reconstruct the path of attack traffic	• Can find the source of attack packets even when there is only very limited number of packets • Can be exploited to trace the real attacker who sends attack commands	• Large storage of logging data • Some times needs excessive processing time • Less scalability compared with other traceback methods
Packet marking traceback [Savage et al. 2000] [Savage et al. 2001] [Peng et al. 2002a] [Peng et al. 2002b] [Park and Lee 2001a] [Adler 2002] [Dean et al. 2001] [Yaar et al. 2003]	Insert traceback data in to IP packet for marking the packet on its way through the various of routers	• No extra storage is needed since it puts mark in IP header • Can also be used in packet filtering • May be suitable for distributed attacks	• Can only track back in a probabilistic manner • Encounters difficulties when the number of attack sources increases • The system must collect a minimum number of packets to perform the task
Protocol-based defense [Kent and Atkinson 1998a] [IPSec 2004] [Leiwo 1997] [Leiwo et al. 2000] [Aura et al. 2000] [Eronen 2000] [Matsuura 2000a] [Matsuura and Imai 2000b] [Aiello et al. 2002]	Modify current protocols or propose new protocols in order to solve the current security problems	• If the limitation of current network protocols can be fixed, DDoS problem can be controlled fundamentally	• Depends on the wide acceptance and deployment of new protocols

Source End Defense

DDoS attacks consume resources such as host computing capability, storage, and network bandwidth at the victim end. The direct assault prevention measure is victim end defense. However, some attacks should be controlled as close to the attack source as possible, because it may save the response time to defend against the attack, thus performs an active defense. Source end defense has lots of advantages over victim end defense [Mirkovic et al. 2002b] [Mirkovic et al. 2003]. For example, source end defense could avoid network congestion by restraining streams near the source and let the spare network free from congestion. And because there are fewer hops from the detection point to the attack source, it is easier to traceback. Moreover, since routers near the source are likely have less traffic burden therefore can dedicate more of their resources to deploy more complex detection strategies.

D-WARD [Mirkovic et al. 2002b] [Mirkovic et al. 2003] is a DDoS defense system deployed at source end network, which autonomously detects and defeats attacks originating from these networks. It includes observation and throttling components, which can be a part of source router, or be a separate unit to interact with the source router to obtain traffic statistics and install rate limiting rules. The observation component monitors two-way traffic at a flow granularity to detect the attack. Flow classification, connection classification, TCP normal traffic model, ICMP normal traffic model, UDP normal traffic model are used to differentiate the malicious flow and the legitimate flow. Once the attack flow is found, the misbehaviour flow is under the control of rate limiting rules.

D-WARD can detect some attacks at the source edge network and it attempts to determine outgoing attack traffic. But since there is no any coordination among instances of agents, the detection may be error prone. Moreover, the detection of UDP attacks and asymmetric routes still need further study, because it can't work well with such conditions.

Source end defense is a promising scheme that can be applied in the active defense system. However, it faces lots challenges such as detection sensitivity, agent coordination, and liability. When the defense system is deployed in the source end, there are fewer strong signals to indicate the attack than at victim end, at which there are usually apparent signals such as high volume of network traffic. So a high sensitivity is essential for source end defending.

To protect more networks, every system should have good scalability. When the system is deployed through out a large scale of networks, how to coordinate the defense agents is an open research problem. If the agents are compromised by attackers, the defense system will become less effective or even cause more damage to the victim network. They must avoid being attack targets.

Just like egress filtering, source end defense also has the problem of liability. Because direct benefit of the system is usually felt by the victim, but not by the deploying network, there should be a common security understanding over the Internet society.

Active Traceback

Passive traceback spends a large amount of resources to traceback and identify individual zombies and handlers, which is ineffective in stopping the real attacker. To defend in advance, active traceback may be one of the main directions of active DDoS defense methods. Current traceback techniques, such as logging and packet marking, can be utilized in active defense. Sally Floyd, Steven Bellovin and John Ioannidis proposed a concept of pushback, traceback working together with congestion control [Floyd et al. 2001] [Ioannidis and Bellovin 2002]. Pushback [Bellovin 2001] is a cooperative mechanism in which routers can ask adjacent routers to block an aggregate upstream. In a network environment, upstream routers are notified to drop malicious packets on the request of downstream routers.

◆ Logging

Logging may be the most direct detection method for analysing the traffic pattern. Although to store all the data in the network is impossible, probabilistic sampling or storing transformed information is still feasible. For example, Duffield and Grossglauser [2000] used trajectory sampling to measure the network traffic, and Alex C. Snoreren [Snoeren et al. 2001] proposed a hash-based traceback method.

The key idea of trajectory sampling measurement is to base the sampling decision on a deterministic hash function over the packet's content. This method can be applied to trace the real attack source because trajectories provide the actual path that packets are taking to reach the victim despite the false source address information. This method critically relies on a statistically representative sampling hash function to be selected. Therefore, it may be suitable for some network traffic observation, but not for all. It can only collect trajectory samples and construct the paths within the measurement domain, but if DDoS attacks come from different sources, it's difficult to deploy such measurement system in a large scale.

Source Path Isolation Engine (SPIE) [Snoeren et al. 2001] records sets of hashes of packets traversing a given router, which is digest input. Then a victim can find the path of a given packet by querying routers within a domain for the set of hashes corresponding to the packet. The main advantage of this method is that it can even find the source of a single packet with relative low storage requirement. In [Sanchez et al. 2001], hardware support for SPIE in high speed routers (OC-48 and faster) is discussed.

Baba and Matsuda [2002] proposed another logging approach. The tracing agents (tracers) are deployed in the network to log the attack packets, and are coordinated by the managing agents. Different fields in an IP packet are used in these logging schemes. In [Baba and Matsuda 2002] the IP data is stored from the first byte up to 20 bytes, in order to save storage resources.

Although it needs excessive processing and storage requirements, logging traceback may be a promising choice in active defense system. When the DDoS attack signature or deployment signature is detected, we can require the logging traceback to find the real source of attacker, because it provides relatively precise detection and doesn't need a large amount attack packets. Then it is possible to protect the victim before the suffering occurs.

♦ Packet marking

The idea of packet marking is to insert traceback data into the IP packet for marking the packet on its way through the various routers from the attack source to the destination. Then markings in individual packets can be used to deduce the path of the traffic.

Probabilistic Packet Marking (PPM) [Savage et al. 2000] [Savage et al. 2001] is the main method of packet marking. The assumption of PPM is that the attacking packets are much more frequent than the normal packets. It lets routers mark the packets with path information probabilistically and let the victim reconstruct the attack path using the marked packets. The PPM encodes the information in rarely used field within the IP header. In order to save storage in IP header field, compressed edge fragment sampling method is used. It requires less traffic volume than ICMP traceback, but it encounters computational difficulties as the numbers of attack sources increases. Because the number of packets needed to reconstruct the attack path depends on the number of packets which are marked by the further router in the attack path. In order to reduce the number of packets needed to reconstruct the attack path, [Peng et al. 2002a] [Peng et al. 2002b] proposed an adjusted PPM. To some degree it solved the problem of vulnerabilities of PPM [Park and Lee 2001a], which is easy to be affected by spoofed marking field. In [Adler 2002], the effectiveness and the tradeoffs of PPM are investigated. And an alternative packet marking with less packet header bits requirement is proposed. However, to perform a successful traceback, enough packets must be collected to reconstruct each edge of the attack path and then the full attack graph. Moreover, PPM is vulnerable to some attack of adding falsified information to the packets, for example, Groups Of Strongly Similar Birthdays (GOSSIB) [Waldvogel 2002].

Dean et al. [Dean et al. 2001] proposed an alternative marking scheme using polynomial reconstruction to build the path. An algebraic approach is used to encode the path information into the fragment identification field of an IP packet. The number of packets needed to rebuild the path is quadratic to the number of attack sources. Thus when there are multiple attackers this method becomes less effective.

By storing a hash of each IP address instead of the address itself, Song and Perrig [2001] proposed an advanced and authenticated marking scheme for IP traceback. It is supposedly more efficient and accurate than others for the path reconstruction under DDoS attacks. And it prevents a compromised router from forging other uncompromised routers markings by authentication scheme. Yaar et al. [2003] proposed Path Identifier (Pi), with an ability of filtering any incoming packets that match known attacker markings, which is a per-packet deterministic mechanism. Each router in the packet traverse path uses the TTL value to index into the IP identification field to insert its marking.

Packet marking may be suitable for active defense against distributed attacks. However, the system must collect a minimum number of packets, and it could produce a high false positive rate. Currently there is no single effective traceback technique to trace the attack source in real time and precisely. Both existed network protocols and hardware should be improved for security concerns.

Protocol-based Defense

Today many protocols are designed to remove ambiguities and provide better security features. Many of the protocols are related to the Internet Protocol Version 6 (IPv6). It is designed to be a simple, forward-compatible upgrade to the existing IPv4, which is intended to resolve all the weakness that IPv4 is currently manifesting [Sportack 1999], such as security. The new security suite protocols include IP Security (IPSec) [Kent and Atkinson 1998a] [IPSec 2004], which works with Authentication Header (AH) [Kent 1998b], Encapsulating Security Payload (ESP) [Kent 1998c], Internet Key Exchange (IKE) [Harkins and Carrel 1998], [Kerberos 2004], and others. From the view of active defense, protocol-based defense scheme can efficiently prevent DDoS attacks. As we know, it is the protocols' limitations that permit DDoS attacks, so if this problem is fixed, the DDoS problem can also be cleared up. However, it largely depends on the wide acceptance and deployment of new protocols.

Today some protocols are proposed to protect networks or hosts from DDoS attacks. The early protocols are to solve the resource allocation DoS attacks, mainly rely on authentication techniques. The idea is to allocate resources of targets only after the requests have been authenticated [Leiwo 1997] [Leiwo et al. 2000] [Aura et al. 2000] [Eronen 2000]. In [Aura et al. 2000], client puzzles are used to authenticate the legitimate users. When server receives request from a new client side, it creates a puzzle for client. Then client commits its resources into solving the puzzle and feed back the solution. After server verifies the solution, it commits resources to expensive parts of the authentication.

From the analysis above we can see that these approaches are high level prevention, so only suitable to defend some kinds of attacks such as SYN flood. Moreover, it needs high computation capability if the server receives a heavy load, then the authentication process may also be the attack target, thus causing DoS.

Before secured data can be exchanged, a security agreement between two computers must be established. To build this agreement between the two computers, the IETF has established a standard method of security association and key exchange resolution named Internet Key Exchange (IKE). Because IKE is computationally expensive, which is vulnerable to DoS attacks, attacks can abuse the resources of servers. In order to protect IKE, Kanta Matsuura [2000a] gives an estimation of servers' performance that depends on the number of on-going processes. It uses a protection strategy called Falling-Together (FT) mechanism, which can improve IKE. In [Matsuura and Imai 2000b], the author also provides a modification version to improve the IKE protocol. In [Aiello et al. 2002], Just Fast Keying (JFK) is another protocol proposed to protect IKE from DoS attacks. In [Kaufman et al 2003], a UDP-based protocol to defend DoS attacks is proposed. All these approaches aim at keeping IKE from DoS attacks.

Because today's Internet has the best-effort characteristic and can introduce forged IP packets, it's difficult to perfectly achieve the goal of prohibiting malicious actions in the Internet. In the next generation protocols, DDoS should be an important issue to be addressed.

Theoretical Detection Methods

An example to detect and forecast possible attacks by analysing certain variables is the MIB analysis. In [Cabrera et al. 2001], Management Information Base (MIB) traffic variables are collected to detect attacks. The Network Management System (NMS) collected 91 MIB variables for analysing purpose. Once the key variables at the target are determined, the correlations between the key variables and others are also determined. Following the detection of correlations, the precursors to attacks can be found by the jumps of statistical absolute values of the variables. Currently Statistical and other mathematical methods, neural network, and data mining may be applied to detect such abnormal characteristics.

♦ Statistical methods

By observing the normal network traffic pattern and comparing it with the ongoing traffic is a simple and fast method. Ming Li et al proposed a decision making mechanism based on a statistical model [Li et al. 2003]. The assumption of this method is the traffic variables obey Normal Distribution. Therefore they introduce detection probability *Pd*, false alarm probability *Pf*, and missing probability *Pm* as follows.

$$P_d = \int_{\frac{V-\mu_\xi}{\sigma}}^{\infty} \frac{1}{\sqrt{2\pi}} e^{-\frac{t^2}{2}} dt \qquad P_f = \int_{\frac{V}{\sigma}}^{\infty} \frac{1}{\sqrt{2\pi}} e^{-\frac{t^2}{2}} dt \qquad P_d = \int_{-\infty}^{\frac{V-\mu_\xi}{\sigma}} \frac{1}{\sqrt{2\pi}} e^{-\frac{t^2}{2}} dt$$

Where V is the threshold of distance variable ξ, which means the distance between the experimental value and the mean value. And μ_ξ is the mean of ξ and σ is the standard deviation of ξ.

Statistical method is faster than other methods because it consumes less computational resource. However, it is not flexible and adaptable to all the patterns, so the detection criteria should be amended from time to time.

♦ Change point methods

The DDoS attacks usually cause some sudden change of variables of the network, so the change point detection methods are currently widely used in finding the attacks. The non-parametric Cumulative Sum (CUSUM) method [Basseville and Nikiforov 1993] and the Shiryaev-Pollak [Pollak 1986] methods are two major sequential change-point detection algorithms.

The CUSUM is applied in [Wang et al. 2002] [Peng et al. 2004], for SYN segments monitoring and source IP address monitoring. It detects changes based on the cumulative effect of the changes made in the random sequence instead of using a single threshold to check every variable. The basic idea of CUSUM is to compare the cumulative sum and an adaptive threshold.

Rudolf B. Blazek et al. [2001] develops adaptive sequential and batch-sequential methods for an early detection of DDoS attacks. It is also based on the change point detection theory, and it is to detect a change in statistical models as soon as possible. It gathers statistical analysis data from multiple layers of the network protocol for detection of very subtle traffic changes, which are typical for the attacks. But in this paper it doesn't propose a defense model, only the algorithm is shown.

◆ Neural network

The function of the neural network is to receive input patterns and produce a pattern on its output which is correct for that class [Picton 2000]. In a large number of cases it is possible to reduce a problem to pattern classification. So it may be achievable to apply neural network techniques to find patterns of DDoS attacks or their prophase signals.

The two significant features of neural network is the ability to learn and generalize. After leaning and training, the system could get the capability to recognise certain patterns and give the correct output response to them. And it also is able to generalize from the examples shown during training.

Compared with the statistical method, this method may be less rigid and suitable for more DDoS attack patterns. After training and adjustment, the error could be reduced to adapt some certain patterns. In our future work, we will apply this method to test if it could generate satisfactory detection results.

◆ Data mining

When the detection data is huge, for instance, traffic logging is used to analyse the possible DDoS attack signatures, data mining may be a feasible method to process the decision making work. Data mining is defined as the automatic or semi-automatic process of discovering patterns in data [Witten and Frank 2000]. According to Roiger and Geatz [2003], data mining is to employ one or more computer learning techniques to automatically analyse and extract knowledge from data. The purpose of a data mining session is to identify trends and patterns in data.

So data mining may help detect the possible attack patterns, not only the existed attack patterns, but also the new patterns. Before training, we should establish a database for data mining. It could be all raw traffic logging data, or the extracted signature data of attacks and normal traffics. This method may be a practical way to judge the attack action, but the possible false positive rate should be an important issue we concern.

10.7.4   Comparison between Passive and Active Defense

According to the discussion above, both active mechanism and passive mechanism offer advantages and disadvantages to DDoS defense. In table 10.3, the comparison between passive and active defense is listed. From this table, we find active DDoS defense approach has lots of advantages over the traditional passive system, although it faces lots of challenges.

Table 10.3 Comparison between passive and active defense

	Passive Defense	Active Defense
Defense cycle	Protect-Detect-React	Surveillance-Trace-Control
Main features	• Defense actions are taken only after the DDoS attacks are launched • Defense system is waiting for attacks • The target host or network is harmed before the attack source(s) can be found and controlled	• Protect victim end before the attacks start • Actively finding the possible attacks • Traceback the real attacker
Current mechanisms	• Traffic volume monitoring • Source IP address monitoring • Packet content analysis • Filtering • Congestion control • Passive traceback • Replication	• Source end defense • Logging traceback • Packet marking traceback • Protocol-based defense
Advantages	• Easy to find the attack signals • Inexpensive deployment	• Prevent possible attacks in advance • Find and control the real source who starts DDoS attacks • Provide more resources available for legitimate users • Prevent large scale and highly distributed DDoS attacks
Disadvantages	• Response is always lagging behind the attack, so it can't protect victim in time • It is hard to deploy an automated and intelligent passive system • It can't effectively avoid network congestion • Traceback process is difficult • Can only defeat parts of zombie attacks instead of real attacker	• The pre-attack signatures and communication before the attack is difficult to detect • Difficulty in liability during the deployment stage

First, this system monitors the crime signatures of DDoS attacks by intrusion surveillance system. Therefore by the greatest extent it controls the possibility of malicious scanning, and propagation of zombies. Unfortunately, passive defense system totally omits this mechanism.

Second, intrusion surveillance system also monitors the communication between the attacker and the compromised machines. Although some communications are encrypted, this system still can find some characteristics of attacks, by learning the communication patterns or data mining techniques. Except in some attacks, intruders use private IRC channels to communicate, which are secret from public and hard to be found.

Since an active system can detect the attack before the real damage occurs by the surveillance system and attack control system, it can control the attack sources as early as possible, thus avoids overall network congestion and provides more resources available for legitimate users. Besides, it is beneficial to trace back to attack source and prevents large scale and highly distributed DDoS attacks, especially it is deployed near the attack sources.

10.7.5 Major Challenges of Active Defense

Active approach offers several advantages to the defense. However, some key issues in active defense are still unresolved. According to the surveillance-trace-control defense cycle, intrusion signature detection, active traceback, and coordinated active defense system are three major challenges of active defense against DDoS attacks.

First, today the DDoS attack tools become more sophisticated and difficult to detect. So how to detect the minus intrusion signature becomes a key challenge in active defense approach. For example, some attacks just compromise a huge number of hosts and use their legitimate IP address to start a well organized assault. So there is no signal of deluge of forged IP addresses during the attack. We must find other mechanisms to detect the possible intrusion signature. Many network Intrusion Detection System (IDS) use byte sequences as signatures to detect malicious network traffics. To improve the preciseness, Sommer and Paxson [2003] propose a method to detect signatures with context detection. It provides both regular expressions context matching and Bro's [Paxson 1999] protocol context matching. Context analysis may be a feasible method to detect the early signature of malicious scanning, propagation of attack tools, and communication between the attacker, handlers and zombies.

Second, how to trace back the real attacking source and punish the attacker is another main challenge in active defense. Current research proves active traceback is an effective countermeasure against DDoS attacks. However, the prevalent traceback methods can only probabilistically trace every attack host, in another word, the zombie, but not the real attacker. So if there are thousands of zombies launch a single attack, the traceback will become totally ineffective. Therefore, at present traceback is not panacea to DDoS attack. It needs further research to provide a solution to traceback the real attacker.

Finally, coordinated active defense is another main challenge of active defense. Because the active defense system should be deployed through out the protected network, at both victim end and source end, the defense sensors, coordinators, and controllers should have a secure channel to communicate with each other, and avoid possible DoS attacks. Moreover, the communication and computation load of the system should be controlled in a modest scale; otherwise it will cause new DoS to the rest of the network.

10.8 Summary

A work on any type of networking is not complete without a discussion of network security. The first step for building a secure network is to define its security policy. The security policy specifies clearly and unambiguously the items that are to be protected. In many cases these items are data integrity, data availability, and data confidentiality and privacy. To protect these, data encryption is necessary. Cryptography provides the basis for the authentication of messages as well as their secrecy and integrity; carefully designed security protocols are required to exploit it. Public key cryptography makes it easy to distribute cryptography keys but its performance is inadequate for the encryption of bulk data. Secret key cryptography is more suitable for bulk encryption tasks. Hybrid protocols such as SSL (Secure Sockets Layer) establish a secure channel using public key cryptography and then use it to exchange secret keys for use in subsequent data exchanges. Digital information can be signed, producing digital certificates. Certificates enable trust to be established among users and organizations. DDoS is a serious availability attack in the Internet and wireless network or other infrastructure as well. Currently the defense mechanisms are mainly passive, in that the target host or network is impaired before the attack source(s) can be found and controlled. The concept of active defense against DDoS attacks is a new direction of mitigating the infamous DDoS attacks in the Internet. As we have seen, it has lots of advantages over conventional passive defense mechanisms. We discuss the objectives of active defense, key issues in this area, current techniques that can be applied in this defense scheme, and the main challenges of it. However, this is only the first step toward realizing the secure Internet paradigm.

Exercises

10.1 What is the first step in building a secure network? What security issues have to be addressed? 10.1.1.

10.2 What is data encryption? Give an example to describe the encryption process. 10.2.1.

10.3 Understand the DES technique. Use your own words to describe it. 10.2.1.

10.4 How many keys are used in public key encryption? 10.2.1.

10.5 Use the code shifting technique by moving the letters of the alphabet five places from right to left to encrypt the message "This is my Java". 10.2.2.

10.6 Use XOR to encrypt the same message in 10.5 (key value is 5). 10.2.2.

10.7 What is the statistical attack used by a hacker to crack a code? 10.3.2.

10.8 How can one achieve digital signatures on the Internet, i.e., how does one encrypt and decrypt a message on the Internet? 10.4.1.

10.9 What is DDoS attack? 10.5.1

10.10 Why DDoS attacks are relatively easy to launch but difficult to defeat? 10.5.2

10.11 What are the key technical methods used in DDoS attacks? 10.5.4

10.12 What are the major passive defense mechanisms against DDoS attacks? 10.6

10.13 Briefly describe the passive defense cycle. 10.6

10.14 What are the major active defense mechanisms against DDoS attacks? 10.7

10.15 Briefly describe the active defense cycle. 10.7

10.16 What are the limitations of passive defense against DDoS attacks? 10.6.6

10.17 What are the major challenges of active defense against DDoS attacks? 10.7.

CHAPTER 11 A REACTIVE SYSTEM ARCHITECTURE FOR FAULT-TOLERANT COMPUTING

Most fault-tolerant application programs cannot cope with constant changes in their environments and user requirements because they embed fault-tolerant computing policies and mechanisms together so that if policies or mechanisms are changed the whole programs have to be changed. This chapter presents a reactive system approach to overcoming this limitation. The reactive system concepts are an attractive paradigm for system design, development and maintenance because it separates policies from mechanisms. In the chapter we propose a generic reactive system architecture and use group communication primitives to model it. We then implement it as a generic package which can be applied in any distributed applications. The system performance shows that it can be used in a distributed environment effectively.

11.1 Introduction

As mentioned previously, it is essential to build distributed network systems that can tolerate component failures. However, the development of distributed and fault-tolerant computing systems is a very difficult task. One of the reasons is that, in normal practice, most fault-tolerant computing policies and mechanisms are deeply embedded into application programs. If one of the policies and mechanisms is to be changed the whole programs have to be changed as well, therefore these applications cannot cope with changes in environments, policies and mechanisms [Zhou 1999]. To build better fault-tolerant distributed applications that can adapt to constant changes in environments and user requirements, it is necessary to separate fault-tolerant computing policies and mechanisms from application programs.

In this chapter we propose a novel approach – the reactive system approach to achieving this goal. The reactive system concepts are an attractive paradigm for system design, development and maintenance because they can separate policies from mechanisms [Chen and Zhou 2000a]. Reactive systems were defined by Harel and Pnueli as systems that maintain ongoing interactions with their environments, rather than producing some final results on terminations [Caspi et al 1994][Harel and Pnueli 1985]. Such systems are often concurrent and distributed. Much research has been done on the development of reactive systems since the 1990s (partly see [Boasson 1998][Bounabat et al 1999] [Boussinot 1991][Harel and Shtul-Trauring 1990][Quintero 1996][Systa 1996]), but most of them are concentrated on process control (such as controlling a robot) and also lack of modularity. They mainly stress system controllers' behaviors and have no emphasis on the mechanisms for

296

obtaining information or responding to outside events. If the control algorithms for a system are changed, the whole system has to be changed. Thus, these methods can not provide a flexible system architecture to tolerate component failures.

We propose that a reactive system consists of three layers: policies, mechanisms and applications. The system managements implement the policies and sensors/actuators are used to implement the mechanisms. Objects in the environment implement the applications. This reactive architecture model can separate fault-tolerant computing policies and mechanisms when applied in fault-tolerant computing. We will use the Agent [Bounabat et al 1999] [Bussmann and Demazeau 1994] and Actor [Agha 1986] [Hewitt 1977] concepts to build the reactive modules. The model is constructed with group communication mechanisms and implemented as a generic package with the Java language. We also evaluate the system performance to demonstrate its effectiveness and potential benefits when used in a distributed environment.

11.2 The Reactive System Model

11.2.1 The Generic Reactive System Architecture

A reactive system is composed of a number of components, such as controllers, sensors, actuators, and physical objects in its environment, which may run in parallel [Boasson 1996]. Sensors are used to acquaint the environment information, which will be sent to its controllers. The controllers make certain decisions based on predefined policies and the information received from sensors. To maintain the interaction with its environment, the system uses actuators to react to its environment by changing the states of application objects according to decisions received from the controllers. Therefore, we can say that a reactive system uses sensors and actuators to implement the mechanisms that interact with its environment or applications; its controllers, we call them decision-making managers (DMMs), are used to implement the policies regarding control of the applications [Boasson 1993]. Hence we obtain a generic reactive system architecture, as depicted in Figure 11.1,

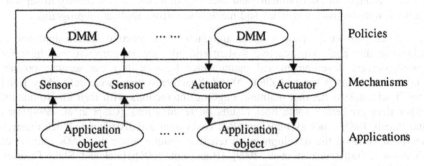

Figure 11.1: The generic reactive system architecture

where DMMs represent decision-making managers; sensors and actuators connect with the DMMs and application objects by receiving inputs or sending outputs of the system.

In this model, sensors can be attached to applications to obtain their states (or equivalently, to monitor events about the applications). These events are sent to DMMs which will make certain decisions and react to them by using actuators to change the states of the applications. This model represents a generic reactive system and consists of three levels: policies, mechanisms and applications:

- **Policies:** The policy level deals with the system policies regarding to the control of application objects. For example, in fault-tolerant computing, it may determine what strategies are used in detecting component failures, what information is to be collected from the application programs, and what techniques are used in masking and/or tolerating component failures. These policies are implemented through DMMs.

- **Mechanisms:** The mechanism level deals with all mechanisms for implementing policies such as fault-tolerant computing strategies. For example, it deals with mechanisms used in detecting and reporting component failures, and mechanisms used in masking and recovering from component failures. These mechanisms are implemented through sensors and actuators.

- **Applications:** The application level deals with issues about fault-tolerant computing application objects, such as database servers, replicas, network routers, etc.

The major advantage of this model is the separation of policies and mechanisms, i.e., if a policy is changed it may have no impact on related mechanisms and vice versa. For example, if a decision making condition based on two sensors was "AND" and now is changed to "OR", the sensors can still be used without any changes required, i.e., the mechanism level can remain unchanged. This advantage will lead to a better software architecture and has great significance in developing fault-tolerant and distributed computing applications since it can separate fault-tolerant computing policies and mechanisms from applications [Chen and Zhou 2000a][Zhou 1999].

11.2.2 Reactive Modules

The reactive system model we proposed above mainly consists of DMMs, sensors, actuators and application objects. Since these components are all active (they form the nature of the reactive system), we introduce the *Actor* concept, which was originally proposed by Hewitt [Hewitt 1977], and later developed by Agha [Agha 1986], to model them. An actor is the basic concept in the Real-time Object-Oriented Modelling (ROOM) and it can be used to model reactive components [Selic et al 1994]. In general, an actor represents an active object that has a clearly defined purpose. It may have its own execution thread and can, therefore, operate concurrently with other active objects in its domain.

However, a DMM in a reactive system is more like an agent. It has knowledge-based abilities to make decisions and change the state of the system, thus DMMs can be considered as decisional agents. Therefore, in this paper we model a reactive system as a distributed computing system consisting of DMM agents and sensor/actuator actors.

11.2.2.1 DMM Agents

The purpose of a DMM agent is to make decisions according to the predefined policies and the collected information from sensors and then send the decisions to actuators. The model of DMM agents is built on the decisional model [Bussmann and Demazeau 1994] allowing the representation of objects according to their behavioral aspects and their degree of intelligence.

Definition 1. A DMM agent is a 5-tuple <E, S, D, P, dec>, where

- E: set of external states received from sensors. Each one represents at any given time an object state from the environment.

- S: set of signaling received by the agent. Each signaling reflects at any given time the state of the controlled tools or objects used to achieve a specific goal.

- D: set of decisions generated by the agent. Each decision is a solution concerning process behavior in the future.

- P: agent's control policies. Each decision is made according to the predefined policies.

The sets above indicate the received events (E, S), the emitted (output) events (D), and the internal events (P). The decisional function dec is described as follows.

Decisional function. *dec* is a decisional function that defines the behavior of a DMM agent.

$$dec: E \times S \times P \to D, \ (e, s, p) \to d \ \text{with}$$

$$dec(e, s, p) = d \Rightarrow [e \wedge s \wedge p \leftrightarrow d]$$

where $\to$ stands for "leads to" and $\leftrightarrow$ means "simultaneous" (same as the following). This means that depending on a predefined policy p, and as soon as the receipt of an external object state e and a signaling s, a corresponding decision d is instantaneously produced by the function *dec*, as shown in Figure 11.2.

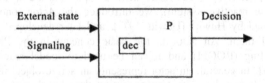

Figure 11.2: A DMM agent

11.2.2.2 Sensor Actors

We can model sensors/actuators as actors. Each actor has a clearly defined purpose, which is an abstraction, or distillation, of its various functional capabilities. This is both implied and enforced by the *encapsulation shell* of the actor. This shell suggests that the contained functionality is to be viewed as a conceptual unit.

The purpose of a sensor is to capture the state information of application objects and then report them to its subscribers. For instance, it may either report to its subscribers immediately once an event occurs (called *event sensor*), or periodically check the state of an application and then report to the subscribers (called *polling sensor*). A generic sensor actor has a main function: *sen*

$$sen: A \rightarrow E, \quad a \rightarrow e \ \text{ with } \ sen(a) = e \Rightarrow [a \leftrightarrow e]$$

where

- A: set of actions exerted on the system and captured by the sensor. Each action is undergone by an outside object.

- E: set of external states delivered by the sensor. Each one represents at any given time an object state from the environment.

This means that depending on an outside action a, a corresponding state e (of external objects) is instantaneously produced by the function *sen*.

11.2.2.3 Actuator Actors

The purpose of an actuator is to perform actions according to decisions received from DMMs. For instance, it may perform the task of setting a value, or activating a buddy server, or switching a light, etc. A generic actuator actor can be described by a function: *act*

$$act: D \rightarrow A, \quad d \rightarrow a \ \text{ with } \ act(d) = a \Rightarrow [d \leftrightarrow a]$$

where

- D: set of decisions received from DMM agents. Each decision is a solution concerning process behavior in the future.

- A: set of actions emitted by the actuator. Each action will be carried out to change the states of the controlled tools or objects.

This means that depending on a decision d made by a DMM, corresponding action a is instantaneously produced by the function *act*.

11.2.2.4 Communication Protocols

Each agent or actor provides one or more openings or interface components, which we call *ports*, to communicate with other entities in its environment. The message exchange between these ports complies with access protocols. We give the protocols on the DMM's ports in the following. Sensors and actuators' protocols are similar to these.

A DMM agent has a set of ports to communicate with other objects. The access protocols on the input and output ports are defined as follows:

protocol class Input

> **in:** {{signal, Message}, {error, ErrorCode}}
> **out:** {{enable, Command}, {disable, Command}}

protocol class Output

> **in:** {done, Message}
> **out:** {{decision, Policy}, {exstate, Message}, {error, ErrorCode}}

where "Input" and "Output" are protocol class names, and the pairs {signal, data-type} specify individual message data. The first parameter represents the content of the appropriate data object, and the last one represents the name of the appropriate data type.

11.2.3 *Simple and Composite Entities*

Sensors and actuators can be simple or composite. A simple sensor (actuator) can only be directly attached to one application. Figure 11.3 (a) shows a simple sensor/actuator architecture. Here the simple sensor *S* is attached to the application *AP1* and reports some state changes of *AP1* to the DMM. The DMM receives reports from *S*, makes certain decisions according to some predefined policy, and uses the simple actuator *A* to change the state of the application *AP1* when necessary. A composite sensor (actuator) can consist of multiple sensors (actuators) from multiple applications. For example, Figure 11.3 (b) shows that the DMM uses a composite *Sc* to monitor state changes of two applications *AP1* and *AP2*, and uses a composite actuator *Ac* to change some state of *AP1* and *AP2* when necessary. The composite sensor *Sc* consists of two simple sensors *S1* and *S2* that monitor the state changes of *AP1*, and another simple sensor *S3* that monitors the state changes of *AP2*. Similarly, the composite actuator *Ac* consists of three simple actuators *A1*, *A2*, and *A3*.

A composite sensor (actuator) can be decomposed into multiple independent simple sensors (actuators). For example, the composite sensor *Sc* in Figure 11.3 (b) is composed of three independent simple sensors *S1*, *S2* and *S3*. *S1* and *S2* are attached to the same application *AP1*, while *S3* is attached to application *AP2*. They all report to the DMM, and they can be seen as independent simple sensors (actuators). For simplicity, we discuss only the simple sensor and actuator. Also, a simple sensor/actuator can be implemented as an embedded entity or a stand-alone entity.

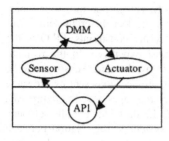

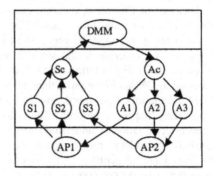

(a) A simple sensor/actuator   (b) A composite sensor/actuator

3: Sensors and actuators

11.3 Group Communication Services

In the reactive system model, a DMM may subscribe to multiple sensors and actuators, and a (simple) sensor/actuator may report to (or receive from) multiple DMMs as well (but attached to one application only). Therefore, the communication between these reactive modules is very complicated. The different arrival ordering of messages from sensors to DMMs (or from DMMs to actuators) may cause the system to generate different results, for instance, in a traffic light control system, different orders of vehicle arrival in an intersection will have different effects on the decision making. Component failure is another issue that has to be addressed to make fault-tolerance possible in a reactive system itself. The correctness of the reactive system model is, therefore, subject to component failures and different ordering of message delivery.

To solve these problems we can use group communication services such as message ordering and multicast service, which provide a useful infrastructure for fault tolerance in distributed applications [Birman and Renesse 1994]. A reactive system is a proper candidate for using group communication primitives, since reports originated from sensors need to be multicasted to a group of DMMs, and so do decisions from DMMs to a group of actuators.

11.3.1 Ordering Constraints

Without a mechanism to ensure ordered delivery of messages, when two originators multicast to a group at about the same time, their messages may not arrive in the same relative order at members of the group. For instance, this may happen if one of the messages is dropped by one of the recipients and has to be retransmitted. This is the result of different network latencies on communication links between the members and different speeds of machines on which the group members are running.

As discussed in Chapter 9, ordering constraints can be categorised into four types: FIFO, causal, total and total+causal [Birman 1993] to reflect different semantical requirements of message delivery. Among these ordering constraints, FIFO is the least and total ordering is the strictest and also most expensive. In the reactive system model, FIFO ordering means that reports sent by the same sensor are to be processed in DMMs in the order they are sent, and so are decisions sent by the same DMM in actuators. Causal ordering means that, if two messages have the nature of a cause-effect (happened-before) relation, this relation should be kept at all members. Cause-effect relation is understood in the reactive system as the relation between decisions and related reports based on which these decisions were made. Since decisions (sent to actuators) and reports (sent to DMMs) never reach the same component, we do not consider this ordering in the reactive system model. Total ordering in the model means that all messages from different sensors are delivered to every DMM in the same order, or all decisions from different DMMs are delivered to every actuator in the same order.

To ensure the correct semantics of the reactive system, a sensible arrival order of message delivery has to be assigned and enforced over the reactive components group, in other words, message delivery among DMMs, sensors and actuators should have ordering constraints. At least (constraint) the FIFO ordering should be the default constraint among them. This is to guarantee that all DMMs get the correct information, and applications get the correct responses to their inputs. Since the order of messages from different sensors may be a fatal factor affecting DMMs to make decisions and since the order of decisions is crucial to actuators as well, it is necessary to apply the **total ordering** in the reactive system model.

A reactive system mainly has two communication groups for multicasting, one is a sensor-to-DMM group for sensors multicasting reports to the groups of DMMs, and the other is a DMM-to-actuator group for DMMs multicasting decisions to the groups of actuators. We apply these two groups with the total ordering constraint, i.e., all messages from different sensors are delivered to every DMM in the same order, or all decisions from different DMMs are delivered to every actuator in the same order. This constraint will be achieved by implementing the corresponding ordering protocol addressed in Section 11.4.

11.3.2 Fault Tolerance in the Reactive System

The objective of our reactive system model is to develop fault-tolerant computing applications. We have to make the reactive system model itself fault-tolerant, i.e., the system must continue to work and maintain correctness even in the presence of component failures. We give the following resolutions in the case of DMM, sensor or actuator failures:

- *A DMM crash.* A DMM is most likely attached to a server replica or runs independently on a host. Since most reactive systems are distributed systems and the replication technology is widely used in such systems, we can assume that there are at least two DMMs (including a replica) running in a reactive system. If a DMM crashes, its function will be replaced by another DMM attached to a replica until it recovers. In the actuator group it is assigned to, certain protocol has to be invoked to ensure all the actuators receive the complete decisions.

- *A sensor/actuator crash.* A sensor/actuator is either running independently with an application object or directly embedded into the application. If it is embedded into the application, the sensor/actuator fails only when the application crashes. In this case, the system has a predefined policy for dealing with application object failures. If the sensor/actuator is a stand-alone entity, we have the following policy to deal with its failure. We choose a DMM as a coordinator in the system and attach an embedded sensor/actuator which has the same function with the stand-alone sensor/actuator to each application object. These embedded sensors/actuators are subscribed by the coordinator only, i.e., they report to the coordinator DMM only (the coordinator performs its normal functions). Therefore, once a stand-alone sensor/actuator fails, its subscribers will notify the coordinator and then it will activate the embedded sensor/actuator attached to the application. Then the DMMs subscribing to the failed sensor/actuator will communicate with the embedded sensor/actuator via the coordinator until the failed sensor/actuator recovers. Of course, certain protocol has to be invoked to ensure the subscribers receive the complete information from the failed sensor.

By using these strategies we can assure that the system continues to work even in the case of a DMM, a sensor or an actuator failure. To maintain the system consistency, we have to ensure complete communication between the failed component and the all other components in all cases.

11.3.3 Atomic Multicast Service

A component failure may lead to incomplete communication in the system, for example, if a sensor fails during the transmission of its report, some DMMs may receive its report whereas some may not. This may lead to a conflict situation if those DMMs receiving the report are making decisions whereas other DMMs are not. Similar situations happen when a DMM fails while sending its decisions to actuators. Therefore, complete communication must be guaranteed in the case of component failures. We define the completeness requirement as follows: if a DMM receives a report from a sensor, all other DMMs that subscribe to this sensor should receive it as well; Similarly, all actuators that are appointed by a DMM should receive a decision from the DMM if any one of them receives it.

This property is to guarantee that all DMMs receive the same set of reports from a sensor so that they all can have this information to make decisions, and all actuators can receive the same decision from their DMM, even in the case of component failures. This property is achieved through the atomic multicast service.

The current TCP communication channels guarantee messages transmitted in the right ordering, no message duplication or loss. However, sending a message down to multiple channels is still error-prone, as the sending component may fail in the middle of the sending process, as a result, some components will receive the message, some will not. Therefore it is crucial to ensure a multicast primitive that either sends messages to all receivers or none of them, i.e., a property known as *multicasting atomicity* or *atomic multicast* [Birman et al 1991].

An atomic multicasting protocol has to guarantee all-or-none semantics. It is a protocol that tolerates the sender's failure in the middle of multicasting. The protocol should guarantee two properties: (1) in the absence of sender's failure, a multicast is received by all operational members; (2) in the presence of sender's failure, a multicast is either received by all operational members or by none of them. Note that we use the term operational members instead of members to ensure that the multicasting will proceed despite any receiver's failure during the transmission. We will implement the multicasting atomicity protocol in the reactive system model to guarantee the complete communication in Section 4.

11.3.4 Membership Management

Both reliable and ordered multicast services are implemented through the group membership management. Membership is the information about a group that shows who are currently in the group, in other words, who are apparently operational. It can be changed by members *leaving* or *joining*, especially by *crash leaving*. When the membership changes, the system may suffer from incorrect scenarios. For example, a sensor crash failure leads to a membership change and causes its subscribers to receive incomplete reports and the system to generate errors. Therefore, it is necessary to develop relevant protocols to maintain the system consistency when the membership changes. The group membership management is a mechanism to make the system consistent and fault-tolerant.

Group construction is very cumbersome in a reactive system. In many cases, each sensor is subscribed by all DMMs and each DMM appoints to all actuators thus there are only two groups in the system, one is the sensor-to-DMM group and the other is the DMM-to-actuator group. However, in the case that different sensors are subscribed by different DMMs, or different DMMs appoint different actuators, we have to build a number of groups based on each sensor and its subscribers, or each DMM and its actuators. Sensors subscribed by same DMMs will form a sensor-to-DMM group, and DMMs appointing to same actuators will form a DMM-to-actuator group. In each of these groups, the group members are not equally weighted, i.e., only some of the group members are senders multicasting messages to the rest of the members which are only receivers. It is, therefore, essential to differentiate the group members when membership changes.

We use an object *view* to represent the membership. The *view* is initialised to contain a set of initial members $\{g_1, ..., g_n\}$, and is encapsulated with two basic operations, *leaveGroup()* and *joinGroup()*, to remove or add a member from (or to) the *view*, respectively. View change events are delivered in *total order* at all members. Members start from the same initial view: $view_0$. The i-th view is $view_i$, $i = 0, 1, 2, ...$; $view_i$ and $view_{i+1}$ are different only by an addition or a deletion of one member. A view update event (join/leave) is sent to the group coordinator first, from where the event is multicasted to other members by the coordinator with $view_{i+1}$ replacing $view_i$, i.e. changing $view_i$ to $view_{i+1}$. This will ensure the same set of view change operations to be delivered in total order at all members. [Wang 1999] presents the detailed protocols for membership changes by a join/leave event including a crash leaving.

11.4 Implementation Issues

The implementation of the reactive system model includes implementing three reactive modules: DMM, sensor and actuator, respectively. Their design given above is very generic so we can implement them as generic classes using the Java language. Java virtual machines, which are rapidly becoming available on every computing platform, provide a virtual, homogeneous platform for distributed and parallel computing on a global scale [Arnold and Gosling 1996] [Gosling 1997].

The implementation of the reactive classes involves the reactive control protocols and the network application programming interfaces (API). The network API often includes the primitives to both reliable and unreliable point-to-point network communications. Java provides these two communication primitives: multicast data-gram and stream-based communications, therefore we will implement the generic DMM, sensor and actuator classes with these two communication patterns.

The reactive control protocols include all protocols used to implement group communication services discussed in Section 3. They are implemented as objects based on the network API primitives, and embedded in the generic classes. The generic Java classes also include a number of utility objects which are at the lowest layer and manage basic resources such as group views, communication channels and threads etc. Thus the Java reactive classes can be understood as composite objects consisting of multi-layered objects.

11.4.1 Multicast Datagram Communication

The multicast datagram method is a communication mechanism used in the UDP protocol and the group communication. It uses multicast datagrams to implement communication between entities within a single thread entity. Using the single thread of control, a datagram can be sent out onto a subnet, where a group of entities are located and receiving, with an address reserved for multicasting, whenever a specific event occurs. Other entities can connect to the subnet simply by creating a multicast socket and join in the group.

In order to avoid packets being flooded onto other networks, Java multicast datagrams include a TTL (Time To Live) field in the header to reduce packets unnecessarily circulating and congesting networks. The programmer can increase the TTL allowing the packet to travel further, for example, the TTL could be:

- 0: all subscribers on the *same host machine* receive datagrams from a sensor.

- 1: all subscribers on the *same subnet* receive datagrams from a sensor.

- 32: all subscribers located on *any of the subnets* to receive packets from sensors also located on any of the subnets (not necessarily on the same subnet).

However, many routers provide only limited support for multicasting. Packets are allowed to be multicasted within a subnet, but not to pass through the router into other subnets. This may become a problem in the case that a DMM subscribes to multiple sensors or a sensor reports to multiple DMMs, where multiple entities are located on different subnets. To overcome this, a tunnelling approach has been invoked, as shown in Figure 11.4. The tunnelling approach builds a tunnel between two subnets and establishes two software entities, one located on a subnet, and another on a remote subnet. On the first subnet, a *courier* joins the multicast group, and retransmits the locally multicasting packets using either datagrams or sockets to another remote subnet. At the other end of the tunnel, a *publisher* receives these packets and multicasts them onto the remote subnet using the same address/port as the class.

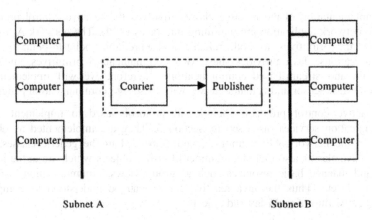

Subnet A   Subnet B

Figure 11.4: Tunnelling multicast packets between subnets

Two variations of tunnelling have been implemented, one using datagrams and the other using stream-based communication. As the packets are being transmitted through several networks in some cases, the stream-based method has the advantage of providing reliable communication. However, it does suffer from an additional overhead of converting datagrams into stream and vice versa at the other end.

11.4.2 Stream-based Communication

The stream-based communication can provide reliable communication between entities. Current TCP protocol used in Internet adopts this communication method; Since each stream-based communication is dedicated to one connection between two entities, a stream-based class must be implemented as a multi-threaded entity to handle multiple connections with a group of entities. Using the Java multiple threads, a message is sent out to each receiver using dedicated connections established between a sender and receivers. Each connection is handled by its own thread of execution. Other entities can subscribe to this sender by simply requesting a connection to it, which will be handled by a new thread.

It is required that a sensor (or DMM) class sends its reports (or decisions) to its multiple subscribers (or actuators) simultaneously. In order to achieve this in the stream-based sensor or DMM class, we invoke the *ThreadGroup* method from Java. This method uses a ThreadGroup object to place and control a number of threads in a class, i.e., each DMM or sensor creates a ThreadGroup object, into which each new thread created to handle a connection is placed so that it can control the processing of these threads. Using this method, the sensor (or DMM) can invoke each thread in the group to send reports (or decisions) to its subscribers (or actuators) at the same time, rather than the threads having to send to them individually and asynchronously. Figure 11.5 depicts the architecture of a stream-based sensor class.

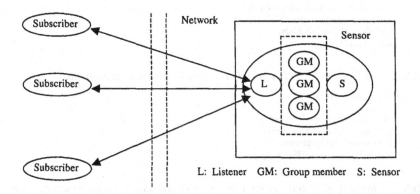

Figure 11.5: The generic sensor architecture

11.4.3 Total Ordering Protocol

There are generally two algorithms used to implement total ordering. One is to generate a unique sequence number (USN) for each message delivery [Birman and Renesse 1994]. Thus, messages can be processed in a unique sequential order group wide. The other one is the token-ring algorithm. The USN algorithm has two approaches as well: centralised approach and distributed approach. We adopt the simple approach: the *centralised sequencer* for implementing the total ordering of message delivery.

Centralised sequencer is a straightforward technique that allows one member to be the USN generator (named sequencer). When a message is originated from a component, the component sends a USN request to the sequencer. The sequencer simply keeps a USN counter that increases by 1 each time a USN request is received. The value of the USN counter is then returned to the component. Then the component attaches the USN to the message which is sent to other components later on.

We use a supervisory DMM as the sequencer. To be able to decide that a total-ordering operation is deliverable, each member keeps a variable of USN major in its local space to record the maximum USN executed so far. If a received total-ordering operation holds the next USN, then this operation is ready to be executed. Otherwise the operation is deferred until lower USN operations are performed. Here we give the full algorithm for the centralised sequencer method:

Listing 1. Assigning the USN Protocol

Rule 1: *Acquiring a USN from the sequencer.* At each member site:

```
while (true) {
    receive (application, m); //m is a total-ordering message.
    send (the sequencer, USN-request);
    receive (the sequencer, USN-reply);
    m.USN := USN-reply.USN;
    multicast (m);
}
```

Rule 2: *Assigning the USN to a member's request.* At the sequencer site:

```
int USN counter := 0;
while (true) {
    receive (member, USN-request);
    USN counter := USN counter+1;
    USN-reply := USN counter;
    send (the member, USN-reply);
}
```

Rule 3: *Checking if a totally-ordered message is executable.* At each member site:

```
int USN major := 0;
while (true) {
    receive (member, m);
    if m.USN == USN major+1
        m is executable;
    else  m is deferred;
}
```

11.4.4 Multicasting Atomicity Protocol

The atomic multicast protocol is used to ensure complete communication between group members even in the case of member crashes. It is implemented by letting a sender multicast sequentially, i.e., one multicast after another. The sender ensures that before starting a new multicast, the previous one is confirmed to have reached all operational members. We refer to a multicast that may not be received by all receivers as an *unstable* multicast, and a *stable* multicast means that the multicast is received by all operational members. The implementation is based on the assumption that a reliable FIFO communication can be established between group members. This is achievable by creating a TCP/IP reliable channel between any two members.

The basic idea of achieving multicasting atomicity is to let operational receivers exchange their latest multicast received from the crashed member. The atomic multicast protocol only deals with sender's failures. We first choose a DMM as a coordinator in a group (sensor-to-DMM or DMM-to-actuator). Let $G = \{g_1, ..., g_n\}$ $(n>2)$ be the membership of the group. At the member g_i, $i = 1, ..., n$, it keeps a vector of the latest multicast from every sender: $mcast[g_1, ..., g_m]$, where $mcast[g_k]$ is the latest multicast message from g_k, $k = 1, ..., m$; $m < n$. If g_i is a sender, its vector is null. Upon the reception of a message $m_i^{g_k}$ from site g_k at g_i, $mcast[g_k] := m_i^{g_k}$.

When a member first detects the failure of a sender g_k (not receiving any message from it within a maximum time frame), it sends an $m_{atom}(g_k)$ message indicating the failure of g_k to the coordinator. Upon receiving this message, the coordinator initiates the multicasting atomicity protocol by multicasting this message to the group. Each group member that receives messages from g_k will reply to the coordinator by attaching its latest message received from g_k after receiving the $m_{atom}(g_k)$ from the coordinator. The coordinator then collects these messages that each member received from g_k. Since multicasts are sent in a sequential order, the collected messages will be either the $m_i^{g_k}$ or the $m_{i+1}^{g_k}$. Based on this information, the coordinator is able to conclude that the $m_{i+1}^{g_k}$ is the unstable message, and finally multicast it to all of these operational members. Then these operational members receive the latest multicast from the failed member g_k. We give the full multicasting atomicity protocol as follows. The protocol starts when the first member detects the crash of g_k and then sends an $m_{atom}(g_k)$ message to the coordinator.

Listing 2. Atomic Multicasting Protocol

Step 1: The coordinator initializes the protocol by multicasting the $m_{atom}(g_k)$ to all group members.

Step 2: Upon receiving the $m_{atom}(g_k)$ from the coordinator, each non-coordinator member g_i, that has a communication channel with g_k and receives messages from it, replies with an $m_{atom\text{-}reply}(g_i, mcast[g_k])$ message to the coordinator. $mcast[g_k]$ is the latest multicast received from g_k and kept at g_i.

Step 3: Upon receiving messages of $m_{atom\text{-}reply}(g_i, mcast[g_k])$ from all non-coordinator members, the coordinator concludes that the unstable multicast is the $(m_{i+1}^{g_k})$ from the crashed member, and multicasts an $m_{atom\text{-}commit}(m_{i+1}^{g_k})$ message to the group.

Step 4: Upon receiving the $m_{atom\text{-}commit}(m_{i+1}^{g_k})$ from the coordinator, each non-coordinator member that received messages from g_k adds the $m_{i+1}^{g_k}$ to its message buffer.

The advantage of this protocol is that, in the absence of failure, no extra message is needed for preventing the sender failure, except an n-vector is used at each member to store the latest multicasts received from other group members.

11.4.5 DMM Classes

The generic DMM class implements the following functions: first, it subscribes to sensors by establishing connections with the sensors and then waits for reports from them; Upon receiving reports from sensors, it will process them and make decisions according to the predefined policy. The decisions will then be sent to the related actuators to change the relevant applications' states. The generic DMM class leaves reports processing and decision making empty, that will be implemented by specific DMMs.

Both the multicast DMM and stream-based DMM classes are implemented. The multicast DMM uses one major thread of control to achieve the above functions while the stream-based DMM class will be implemented as a multi-threaded entity consisting of multiple objects each of which handles a specific task. Utility objects in the DMM include the following:

- **Communication handler.** This object sets up the connections between this DMM and the sensors/actuators in the groups it subscribes to. Multicasting primitives are methods encapsulated in this object.

- **Group manager.** A group object managing the local views of an operational component. It basically provides two methods, leaveGroup() and joinGroup(), to remove a group member when it leaves and to add a member when a new one joins respectively.

- **USN and USNAssignor.** USNAssignor assigns the USN to each decision sent to different actuators. The USN checks the deliverability of each report received from sensors. These two objects implement the USN protocol described by Listing 4.1.

The DMM class also has some mini-protocol objects which are based on utility objects to implement relatively smaller protocols, such as multicast atomicity protocol, member joining and leaving protocols for membership management, etc.

- *StateTransfer* implements the state transfer protocol. The protocol guarantees a new member joining the group in a consistent way.

- *CrashAtomicity* performs the crash atomicity protocol (Listing 4.2) that guarantees the atomic multicasting property when a member crashes. It also updates each member's local view to remove the crashed component.

- *VoluntaryLeave* performs the voluntary leave protocol and updates each member's local view to remove the voluntarily leaving member.

The root DMM object is constructed by aggregating and initializing the necessary lower layer objects which are instantiated from their classes, and linking the main service of DMM such as information processing and decision making etc.

11.4.6 Sensor/Actuator Classes

The generic Java sensor class implements the functions of monitoring events and reporting to DMMs. It can be subscribed by many other entities and is capable of reporting to them simultaneously. The Java sensor first builds connections with its subscribers and then monitors for events and reports to its subscribers once events occur. The generic sensor class will leave information capturing empty that will be implemented by specific sensors.

The generic Java actuator class implements the functions of receiving decisions from DMMs and then performing actions to change the states of applications. It can be subscribed by multiple DMMs and is able to receive decisions from them and execute them one by one. In the actuator class, there is no need to deal with the synchronization problem.

Both multicast and stream-based sensor/actuator classes are implemented. They are similar to the DMMs, i.e., they have the same objects as it does and only the contents of these objects are different.

11.4.7 Discussion

We have conducted a series tests to evaluate the performance of the reactive system implemented above, and obtained the following results. Multicast datagram communication is a common unreliable communication service which does not guarantee any reliability. Messages sent by using such a service may get lost, duplicated or delivered out of order. When the message delivery is applied with the ordering constraint, a big overhead occurs on the system. Therefore, multicast datagrams may have limited applications in distributed systems covering multiple subnets. However, from our test results we found that within a local subnet, multicasting communication is the fastest way to respond to events. On a local machine or covering multiple remote subnets, multicasting communication is faster than stream-based communication to respond to events when the number of DMMs increases to a certain number.

Stream-based communication is more reliable and may be more suited to distributed systems than multicast datagrams. When message delivery in such a communication is applied with an ordering constraint, there is only a slight increase of the time occurred for the system. The stream-based DMMs and sensors/actuators running in a distributed environment are more effective than those running in a centralized system. They do not have tunneling overhead when covering multiple subnets. Thus we recommend stream-based communication as the implementation method for a distributed computing system covering multiple subnets.

11.5 A Fault-Tolerant Application

In a distributed computing environment, two types of failure may occur: a process/processor at a given site may fail (referred to as a site failure), and

312

communication between two sites may fail (referred to as a link failure) [Cristian 1991] [Jalote 1994]. A site failure results in fail-silent or crash failure semantics, i.e., a process/processor either works correctly or simply stops working without taking any incorrect action [Schlichting and Schneider 1983]. A link failure may result in network partitioning, which is a major threat to the reliability of distributed systems and to the availability of replicated data [Tanenbaum 1996]. When these failures occur the system may generate incorrect results or may simply stop before finishing the intended computation so that the system cannot provide intended services. Therefore, it is essential to build distributed systems that can tolerate these failures. In this section we apply the reactive approach proposed above in a replicated database system to deal with two types of failure: crash failure and network partitioning failure, for the purpose of demonstrating the potential benefits of the reactive system model.

11.5.1 The Replicated Database System

In order to tolerate various failures, most fault-tolerant techniques rely on introducing extra redundant components to a system. Replication is such a technology making fault-tolerance possible in a distributed database system. Replication is the maintenance of on-line copies of data and other resources by using replicas. It is a key to the effectiveness of distributed systems, in that it can provide enhanced performance, high availability and fault-tolerance [Helal et al 1996].

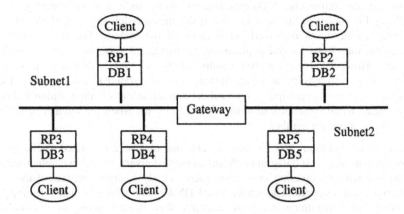

Figure 11.6: A distributed replication system

A distributed replication system within a wide area network (WAN) is composed of several subnets located several or thousands of miles away and connected by gateways [Davidson 1984]. Replication produces replicas of database servers. At each subnet, there is one or more database server groups, which are comprised of replicas running on each workstation, as depicted in Figure 11.6. For simplicity, we only include two subnets connected by one gateway in the network configuration.

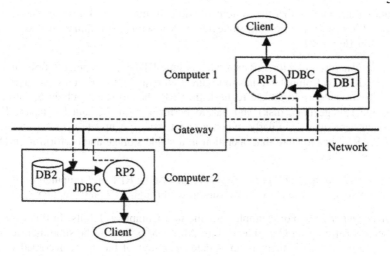

Figure 11.7: Replication manager and database server

In Figure 11.6, each workstation has a database server and a replication manager running respectively. All database servers (or replicas) store identical information initially and each of them can accept client requests that read or update stored information independently. A replication manager can access the local database server and other replicas through JDBC. A client connects to a replication manager and issues transaction requests through it to obtain database services. Figure 11.7 shows two workstations located on two subnets, where RP stands for a replication manager; DB represents a database server.

The task of the replicated system is to maintain data consistency among all the replicas throughout the whole network, even in the case of site or link failures. If a client requires a read-only operation, this request can be served by the local replication manager reading from the local database server. If a client wants to perform an update operation, the operation has to be performed in all database servers. This can be done if all the replicas are running well without faults. However, site or link failures may occur in the system, and it would be a problem to perform an update operation on the replica(s) located on a fault site or a partitioned subnet. In these cases, some strategies have to be invoked to maintain the data consistency. We discuss the failure scenarios next.

11.5.2 Failure Scenario

11.5.2.1 Crash Failure

Crash failures in a replicated database system include a database server failure, a replication manager failure, or a computer (workstation) failure. They may cause the data to be inconsistent and the system to provide incorrect services. The fault-tolerant requirement is that the system should continue to work even in the case of failures. We have the following strategies to deal with crash failures in the system depicted in Figure 11.7:

- A *database server fails.* For example, assume DB1 on Computer 1 fails. In this case, RP1 on Computer 1 has to re-direct all requests to DB2 on Computer 2. If such a request is an update request, then RP1 has to store such an update in a stable storage (e.g., disk) and has to perform it on the failed database DB1 when it recovers. Similarly, when a client issues an update operation through RP2, RP2 has to store that operation in a stable storage and perform it on DB1 when it recovers.

- A *replication manager fails.* For example, assume RP1 on Computer 1 fails. In that case, all requests have to be submitted through RP2 on Computer 2.

- A *computer fails.* For example, assume that Computer 1 fails. In this case, all servers running on Computer 1 fail. All requests have to be submitted to RP2 on Computer 2. If there is an update operation, it has to be recorded in the stable storage and has to be performed on DB1 when Computer 1 recovers (and DB1 recovers as well).

In cases 2 and 3, it is easy for a client to know whether a replication manager is alive or not through the program interface. If the local replication manager fails, a client can submit his (her) requests to another replication manager. Hence it is simple to deal with a replication manager failure. In cases 1 and 3, it is essential for a replication manager to know if a database server is alive or not. How to detect and deal with a database server failure remains a problem. If the failure detecting mechanism and the failure processing policy are all embedded into the replication manager, once the detecting mechanism is changed the replication manager has to be changed as well. Thus this strategy lacks flexibility and cannot adapt to constant changes.

11.5.2.2 The Network Partitioning Failure

Network partitioning occurs when link failures fragment the network into isolated sub-networks called partitions, such that sites or processes within a given partition are able to communicate with one another but not with sites or processes in other partitions. If processes continue to operate in the disconnected partitions, they might perform incompatible operations and make the application data inconsistent [Davidson 1985].

In the replicated database system we talked about above, network partitioning failure happens when the gateway between two subnets fails. This leads to a situation where replication managers and server group members distributed in different subnets cannot communicate with one another and may stop processing a client transaction request, for instance, an update operation cannot be performed on another partitioned subnet. Therefore, it is essential for the replication managers within each subnet to know whether a partitioning happens so that they can take certain measures to process clients' requests in the case of this failure [Birman 1996].

A number of diverse solutions have been proposed to solve the network partitioning problem [Davidson 1984]. But most strategies on network partitioning require that the failure initially be recognized. They assume that the partitioning failure detection has already been done, thus they may have some restrictions due to different failure detection strategies. We attempt here to use the reactive system approach to solve this problem and provide a solution for failure detection, analysis and resolution.

11.5.3 Fault Detection

We can use the Java reactive system modules introduced above to deal with crash failures and network partitioning failures that occur in the replicated database system. We use sensors to detect the possible failures of various system objects and DMMs to implement various fault-tolerant policies.

11.5.3.1 Crash Failure

As discussed earlier, a replication manager crash or a computer crash is simple to deal with. We only discuss a database server failure here. When a database server crashes, it is essential for replication managers to know it so that they can take certain measures to further process client requests. To achieve this, we run a Java DMM, a Java sensor and a Java actuator on each computer respectively. Each DMM will subscribe to all sensors and actuators running on all computers. Due to different types of reactive module we can have several choices:

- *Using stand-alone DMMs:* Stand-alone DMMs can run independently on each host and operate concurrently with other objects. Actuators are embedded into replication managers for transmitting decisions from DMMs to the replication managers. To detect a database server failure, we also have two options of using sensors: polling sensors and event sensors.

    1. *Using polling sensors.* A polling sensor can be run on each computer independently to check the status (liveliness) of the database server periodically and then report to the DMMs subscribing to it, as depicted in Figure 11.8, where we only include two workstations located on two subnets. Once a database server fails, the polling sensor monitoring it will report to both DMMs. In this case, DMMs and polling sensors are running independently on Computer 1 and 2, while actuators are embedded into RPs.

    2. *Using event sensors.* We may want to know the failures of database servers immediately once they occur. In this case we can use event sensors instead of polling sensors running on each computer. The DMMs and actuators are the same as above, but two event sensors are attached to RP1 and RP2 respectively to report the failure of the connection between RP1 and DB1

316

or between RP2 and DB2, as depicted in Figure 11.9. If a database server fails the connection between this replica and the relevant replication manager fails as well. Thus the corresponding event sensor will catch this event and report to both DMMs immediately.

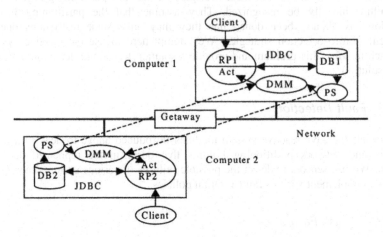

Figure 11.8: Using polling sensors – PS stands for a polling sensor; Act is an actuator.

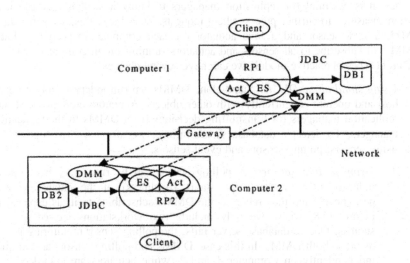

Figure 11.9: Using event sensors – ES stands for an event sensor; Act is an actuator.

- *Using embedded DMMs:* We can also use embedded DMMs to implement the above functions. In this case, a DMM is embedded into the replication manager on each computer, thus we do not need actuators since the DMMs can instruct the replication managers directly, as depicted in Figure 11.10. Sensors in this case are polling sensors which run independently on each computer. Once a database server fails, the polling sensor monitoring it will report to both DMMs.

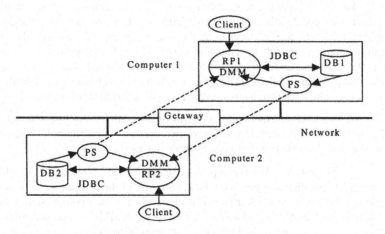

Figure 11.10: Using embedded DMMs

In all cases above, both DMMs will receive the reports from the sensors about the failures of database servers if they occur. Then they will make certain decisions (as described earlier) and use the actuators to instruct RP1 and RP2 to process clients' requests promptly.

Detecting strategy

Let S be a sensor. We use S_r to denote the sensor report about the state of a replica r that S monitors, or the connection state between a replica r and a replication manager. For a polling sensor, if S_r is true, that means the replica r is alive; whereas for an event sensor, if S_r is true, that means a connection failure between the replica r and the related replication manager occurs. We use "¬" to denote that no event occurs. Hence we have

$$\text{if } \neg S_r, \text{ then r is faulty, where S is a polling sensor, and} \qquad (1)$$

$$\text{if } S_r, \text{ then r is faulty, where S is an event sensor.} \qquad (2)$$

The time interval for evaluating "¬" in (1) is set to be greater than the polling time interval of S. Formulas (1) and (2) are the strategies used by DMMs to detect the fault existence.

11.5.3.2 Network Partitioning Failure

To detect and analyze partitioning failures, we add a dedicated decision making manager (DMM) as a server group component in each subnet for failure handling and help in transaction processing. Each of these DMMs will subscribe to multiple

318

sensors/actuators attached to each server member on different subnets to detect the partition existence. The idea of detecting a partitioning failure is described as follows. A DMM in one subnet regularly receives reports from sensors attached to all server members, some of which may not be reachable if a partitioning occurs. If the DMM does not receive the reports from some sensors within a maximum time frame, the DMM decides that the gateway might be down by noticing that those unreachable members are all located in the same subnet. To confirm that the partitioning happened, the DMM sends a message to the other DMMs in that subnet to see if they are reachable. If it does not receive the replied message within a maximum time from another DMM, the gateway between the two DMMs is assumed down, which leads to the two subnets being partitioned from each other.

Similarly, we can have several choices in terms of using different sensors/actuators, or different DMMs to do that. Here we give two options, one using polling sensors and the other using timer sensors, to demonstrate our method.

- *Using polling sensors.* We run a polling sensor on each host across the whole network to periodically report the connection state of the host it monitors to the DMMs subscribing to it, as depicted in Figure 11.11. Each polling sensor runs on a host independently and is subscribed by all DMMs located on different subnets. Actuators are embedded into each replication manager on a host and used to instruct them to process clients' requests according to decisions made by the DMMs.

- *Using timer sensors.* We can also use timer sensors to report each host's state. In this case, a timer sensor is attached to a host by being embedded into the replication manager to monitor the connection state of this host to the network, as depicted in Figure 11.12, where the DMMs and actuators are the same as above. Once a connection failure occurs the timer sensor will report it to the DMMs subscribing to it.

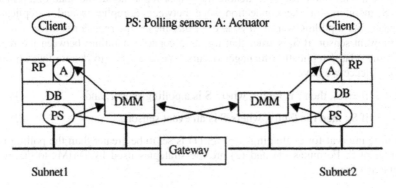

Figure 11.11: Using polling sensors for network partitioning

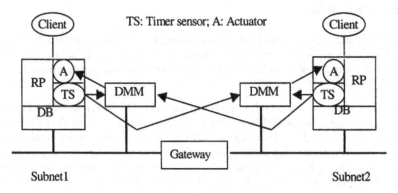

Figure 11.12: Using event sensors for partition-tolerant applications

In both cases, the DMMs will decide whether a partition happens according to the reports received from the sensors and then make decisions to instruct the RPs how to process clients' transactions using the actuators. In this solution, the RPs deal with transaction processing while the DMMs deal with failure handling.

Partition detecting and notifying

Assume that there are m subnets in the network environment and the maximum number of replicas on each subnet is n. We use S_{ij} ($i=1, 2, ..., m; j=1, 2, ..., n$) to denote the sensor attached to the jth replica in the ith subnet; D_k ($k=1, 2, ..., m$) denotes the DMM in the kth subnet. S_{ij} will report to all D_k periodically about the connection state (or liveliness) of the replica it is attached to. Hence, if $\neg S_{ij} . D_k$, $i \neq k$, then the jth replica in the ith subnet is faulty to D_k, i.e., faulty to the kth subnet. Therefore we have,

$\forall k, \exists i, i \neq k$, for all j ($= 1, 2, ..., n$)

if $\neg S_{ij} . D_k$ then the ith subnet may be partitioned with the kth subnet. (3)

To confirm that the partitioning happened, two DMMs located in the partitioned subnets send a message to each other to see if they are reachable, i.e.,

For i, k in (3)

if $\neg D_k . D_i$ then the ith subnet must be partitioned with the kth subnet. (4)

The time interval for "$\neg$" is set to be greater than the longer time interval of polling S and timer S. Formula (3) and (4) are the strategies for each DMM located in a subnet to detect a partition existence. Once a network partitioning has been detected, one of the DMMs from two subnets will use actuators to notify all the server groups about the partition situation to save unnecessary network communication overheads caused by some server members trying to contact the other partitioned subnet. The DMM is also responsible to notify all parties once the crashed gateway is up and the partition no longer exists.

11.5.4 Fault Tolerance

Once a database server crash failure has been detected, the fault tolerance is simple. The policy for a replication manager to process a client's requests in the case of the failure has been described in Section 5.1. We mainly discuss partitioning tolerance in the following.

In this section we use a relatively centralized method with the Primary/Non-Primary replication control protocol [Paris 1992] to deal with the network partitioning problem. The method is described as follows. A client transaction request can consist of different sub-transactions each of which is to be served by a group of servers or replicas. Replication managers which receive the requests from clients divide the transactions into sub-transactions and pass them onto the different replicas. Among one group of replicas, a Primary Replica leads other Non-primary Replicas. The transaction processing policy for the system is to treat the Primary Replica for every sub-transaction, or service, as the checkpoint for a *fully commit* mode. Any replica can execute a service freely but a *partial commit* mode is returned if it is a Non-primary Replica. Only those transactions checked by Primary Replicas will be finalized by either being upgraded to a fully commit mode or downgraded to an abort if conflict exists. Coordination among replica groups is carried out by replication managers to finalize transactions after collecting results from different service executions [Chen and Zhou 2000b].

During network partitioning, the main problem is that a client could issue a transaction request which involves server members in different partitioned subnets so that the continued transaction processing could result in inconsistent data in different replicas. To solve this problem, we assume that all the Primary sites for one such transaction are located in the same subnet, which is the common case for most transactions. Hence, network partitioning could happen in two cases:

- One is when a P site sends a transaction to an NP site in the partitioned subnet.

- The other is when an NP site sends a transaction to a P site in the partitioned subnet for checking and finalising it from a partial commit mode.

Our solution is that, in either case, a DMM is running on each subnet respectively and each DMM will decide whether a partitioning happens according to formulas (3) and (4). If a transaction is sent to the partitioned subnet, the replication manager on the P/NP site will send it to the relevant DMM located on the same subnet for recording and further processing. When a DMM receives a transaction record during the partitioning, it identifies its type, whether initialized by the P or NP site, and then stores it in different object lists. After the partitioning is repaired, these DMMs exchange their knowledge of transactions and then send their transaction lists to the relevant replication managers on the same subnet. A DMM will then use actuators to instruct the replication managers to perform these transactions.

For the transactions from P sites for compulsory execution, the replication managers execute them and then check the result to ensure whether it conflicts with the present state. If the conflict exists, the replication managers notify the DMM to invoke certain conflict resolving programs such as a backout strategy. For the transactions from NP sites for checking and finalising, the replication managers check them to see whether they can be executed. If they can, the replication managers will check the result to see if it conflicts with the present state. If the conflict does exist, a notification should be made to the DMM and it will abort these transactions and notify the original NP sites to roll back. If no conflicts are detected, the DMM will contact the original NP to finalise the transactions. This is the primary first policy which guarantees the primary site interest.

We give the full algorithms used by DMMs and replication managers for partition detection and transaction execution in Listing 3 and 4 respectively.

Listing 3: Algorithm used by DMMs for partition detection

```
partition_detecting()
{
  int checkFlag = 0;
  while (true) {
    /* receive reports from sensors. */
    check and evaluate the reports sent by the sensors;
    if  the formula (3) == true {
        find the possible partitioned subnet no. i and the DMM address in that subnet;
        /* set that DMM as the message sending target */
        send out checking message to the DMM and wait for reply;
        if the formula (4) == true {
            checkFlag = 1; /* confirms the partition really occurs */
            broadcast the partition to all server members and other DMMs;
            while (checkFlag ==1) {
                if a transaction is sent to the partitioned subnet i {
                    /* receive it from the replication manager */
                    identify and store it in a different list according to its type;
                }
                check and evaluate the reports received from the sensors;
                if any report from the partitioned subnet i {
                    checkFlag = 0; /* partition is repaired */
                }
            }
        }
        else   /* no partitioning occurs */
           continue; /* go back to while */
    }
    else   /* no partitioning occurs */
       continue; /* go back to while */

    /* transaction exchanging */
    send the transaction lists to other DMMs;
    wait for reply messages from other DMMs;
    if  a reply message is the confirmation of receiving transactions
        delete the transaction object list including those transactions;
    else
        if a reply message includes the transaction lists initialised by other P/NP sites
            store the transactions and send confirmation to the sending DMM;
    /* endif */

    /* instruct RPs to process transactions */
    send the transaction lists to RPMs on the same subnet for execution.
  } /* end of while */
}
```

Listing 4: Algorithm used by RPs for transaction execution

```
transaction_execution()
{
    int checkFlag = 0;   /* conflict flag;
    /* receive the transaction lists from the DMM for execution.
    while(true) {
        execute a transaction and check the result whether conflict with the present
        state and then return checkFlag;
        if checkFlag == 0   /* the transaction result no conflict with the present state
        {
            if the transaction from NP site
                inform the NP site to finalise the transaction;
            else /* from P site
                continue; /* go back to while;
        }
        else /* conflict exists;
        {
            if the transaction from P site
                notify the DMM to decide a strategy (backout) to resolve the conflict;
            else /* the transaction from NP site;
                abort this transaction and notify the original NP site to
            roll back;
        }
        checkFlag = 0;
    }
}
```

In the case where network partitioning results in different P sites involved in one transaction being located in different partitions, the replication managers in the P sites cannot fully execute the whole transaction. We propose two options: one is to let the client abort the transaction and the other is to store the transaction and re-execute it after the network partitioning is recovered. The detailed implementation of this application can be referred to [Chen and Zhou 2000b].

11.5.5 Remarks

We have used the reactive modules to resolve the database server failure and the network partitioning failure above. The crash failure is simple, while the network partitioning problem is dealt with by the Primary/Non-Primary replica model. Compared with other fault-tolerant strategies, our method has a flexible system architecture which can adapt to constant changes in user requirements. In the resolution we used different DMMs and sensors to implement the fault-tolerant policies and the failure detection mechanisms, for example, we used the same DMMs but different sensors, i.e., polling sensors, event sensors and timer sensors respectively, while the system performs the same functions. It shows that the sensors are changed while the DMMs remain unchanged and vice versa. This is the advantage of separation of policies and mechanisms.

However, one may argue that a relatively centralized DMM used in each subnet for the network partitioning problem is fault prone. This situation could be made very rare by placing DMMs in stable sites. While the possibility does exist, transactions recorded by DMMs should be backed up in non-lost devices when they are sent by other P/NP sites.

11.6 Summary

This chapter has presented the design, implementation and evaluation of the reactive system model for building better fault-tolerant distributed applications. The main advantage of reactive system concepts is the separation of mechanisms and policies in software development. To build and design this model, we introduced group communication mechanisms which provide fault-tolerance in the reactive system. The implementation of the model is based on multicast datagram communication and stream-based communication, respectively, provided by Java. Three reactive modules: DMM, sensor and actuator are implemented as generic Java classes which can be applied in distributed applications. The performance evaluation shows that the model with stream-based communication is more reliable and effective when running in a distributed environment.

The reactive system model we designed in this chapter is flexible, reliable and fault-tolerant. The separation of policies and mechanisms makes the model very flexible and can be used to develop better fault-tolerant distributed applications. The model is also fault-tolerant, since its group communication services guarantee correctness and complete communication even in the case of component failures. The application of the reactive system model in the replicated database system provides a fault-tolerance solution to deal with crash failures and network partitioning failures. The main advantage of the reactive system concepts is the separation of mechanisms and policies in software development. In the solution, we separate the DMMs and the sensors/actuators, i.e., we separate the fault-tolerant policies and the mechanisms. The DMMs stay the same no matter what sensors and actuators are or what changes they have, and vice versa. Their main task is to make decisions according to the reports from the sensors they subscribed, and the main task of sensors is to monitor state events. This separation makes the system maintenance easier, and provides a flexible system architecture which can cope with constant changes in environments and user requirements.

Exercises

11.1   What is a reactive system? 11.1

11.2   What components does a reactive system consist of? How do they implement three layers: policies, mechanisms and applications? 11.2.1

11.3   What is the advantage of the reactive system model? 11.2.1

11.4   What is an Actor? What is its encapsulation shell? 11.2.2

324

11.5 Why does the reactive system model need group communication services? 11.3

11.6 How do we understand the FIFO ordering in the reactive system model? 11.3.1

11.7 What is total ordering in the reactive system? Why should total ordering be ensured in the system? 11.3.1

11.8 How does one deal with a sensor failure? 11.3.2

11.9 What is the multicast atomicity in the reactive system? 11.3.3

11.10 How does one implement multicast communication between subnets? 11.4.1

11.11 How does one achieve synchronization in the sensor class? 11.4.2

11.12 What is the centralized sequencer method? 11.4.3

11.13 How does one achieve multicast atomicity in the reactive system? 11.4.4

11.14 Compare multicast communication and stream-based communication. 11.4.7

11.15 What failure scenario can occur in a distributed computing system? 11.5

11.16 What is the most used technique to make fault-tolerance? 11.5.1

11.17 What is the task of a replicated database system? 11.5.1

11.18 What is the network partition failure? 11.5.2

11.19 What is the main problem of network partition? How is it solved using the reactive system approach? 11.5.4

CHAPTER 12 WEB-BASED
DATABASES

World Wide Web has changed the way we do business and research. It also brings a lot of challenges, such as infinite contents, resource diversity, and maintenance and update of contents. Web-based database (WBDB) is one of the answers to these challenges. In this chapter, we classify WBDB architectures into three types [Lan et al. 2001]: two-tier architecture, three-tier architecture, and hybrid architectures, according to WBDB access methods. Then the existing technologies used in WBDB are introduced as various generations, i.e., the traditional Web (generation 1), fast and more interactive Web (generation 2), Java-based Web (generation 3), and a new generation combining the techniques of XML and mobile agents. Based on the introduction, we provide the challenges and some solutions for current WBDB. Finally we outline a future framework of WBDB.

12.1   Introduction

Internet Computing

The Web is a collection of resources including Gopher, FTP, HTTP, Telnet, Usenet, WAIS, and others, which can be accessed via a Web browser. It consists of a lot of Web pages, which are interactive pages of text, graphics and other forms of data and multimedia such as sounds and movies that Internet users can access at any time [Wodaski 1997].

There are a lot of challenges for the current Web. The Web is almost infinite at the current time and contains every aspect of society. On the Web today, content is king. Any site that successfully attracts repeated visitors has to have fresh and constantly updated content. Moreover, users feel comfortable only if they can get the valuable, fresh information rapidly. The problem is how can we satisfy the demands from users.

An effective web site is big and constantly changing, such as many product pages and a lot of updates each month. So as a web site grows one may run into two problems: the web site has so much information that visitors cannot quickly find what they want. Also it is desirable that the visitors be able to enter data and make the site interactive. The problem is that the people providing the content for a site are not the same people handling its design. Oftentimes, the content provider doesn't even know HTML.

Maintenance of a content-driven site can be a real pain, too. Many sites are locked into a dry, outdated design because rewriting those hundreds of HTML files to reflect a new design would take forever. Server-side can help ease the burden a little, but one still ends up with hundreds of files that need to be maintained should one wish to make a fundamental change to the site.

Finally, the Web today consists of various information resources, such as texts, pictures, and other forms of multimedia [Cruickshank 1998]. How can the Web query the contents and publish them on the Web pages? How can the Web realize dynamic data publishing?

One solution to these challenges is database-driven site design [Zhou 2000] [Ioannidis 2000]. By achieving complete separation between the design of a site and the content the site presents, one can work with each without disturbing the other. Instead of writing an HTML file for every page of a site, one only needs to write a page for each kind of information one wants to be able to present. Instead of endlessly pasting new content into the tired page layouts, it would be more efficient to create a simple content management system that allows the writers to post new content themselves without a lick of HTML [Ashenfelter 1999].

The World Wide Web is just about the best way ever to distribute information – it is fast, nearly ubiquitous, and depends on no particular computer platform. And databases are just about the best way to store and access information - they are structured and searchable. A database is a structured format for organizing and maintaining information that can be easily retrieved. The database management system is a closed system in the sense that all operations on the data managed by the DBMS will be stored back to the database. Obviously in this context we are limiting ourselves to the digital world where possible formats span the range from plain text files to complex object-oriented databases. Therefore, we can combine these two technologies, both for Web publishers who need to post up-to-the-minute pages and for web users who want to obtain valuable updated information quickly. A Web-based database is a key component of many applications, such as applications in electronic commerce, information retrieval, and multimedia.

Web-Based Database

After Web and databases are incorporated together, a new term "Web-based database" (WBDB) arises. Generally speaking, a web-based database is a database that resides entirely on an Internet server. Access to the database is through a web browser and usually utilizes a password system that allows for restricted access to users depending on the privileges they have been given.

Web-based databases can be used for a range of functions, some examples are

- Creation of product catalogues.

- A back end for e-commerce allowing for instant update of prices, product details etc.

- Frequently updateable newsletters, company activities, minutes of meetings etc.

- Maintenance of client or user details for email, reference etc.

Web-based databases possess a number of advantages [Winslett 1997]:

- *Maintenance and updating.* A Web-based database separates content (database) from presentation (an HTML page). It means that the owner of a site is able to update the content of the site without constantly having to go through its webmaster or designer. Creating a Web template once and merging it with new content (database) is a more reliable way than publishing information with a consistent layout.

- *Reusability and modularity.* By designing additional templates, one can easily reuse content on another Web site or modify it to fit a new design. For users, databases make site searches more accurate: they can be limited to certain fields, returning better-quality hits than full-text searches.

- *Distribution of data update.* With the right interface, even a novice user can go into the database to update information; the Web publishing system can then send out the changes immediately.

- *Security.* Databases help ensure that contents are accessed by authorized users.

Wide ranges of features are available for most Web-based databases. Some of the more common ones include:

- Password access and privilege-based restrictions.

- Ability to download database files as text or tab delimited files that can be read by a database or spreadsheet program on the local computer.

- Ability to include images, email links and hyperlinks to other web pages in the database output.

In addition, some new functions can be developed using the combined features from Web-based databases, such as [Ramakrishman 2000]:

- Keeping track of the origin and modification history of each article by the use of a DBMS;

- Obtaining valuable new data by tracking and logging user activity and user contribution in the process of interaction;

- Dynamically personalizing (or at least fine-tuning) the downloaded Web pages according to the information about the current page and user's experience.

So Web-based database is JUST in time, and already works in many fields. The researchers' tasks are to make it evolve rapidly and satisfy the user's requirement by developing new methods, languages, and frameworks.

A Web-based database system is considered to be a large distributed database system and at the same time, it is different from a distributed database system in the following:

- *Number of users:* For traditional database a limited number of users is served where as in Web-based database system the number of users is very large. Therefore, a Web-based database system should be able to support large number of transactions with reasonable response time. Large number of users in a Web-based database affects the overall performance of the system. For example, in an online reservation system the database servers should be scalable to handle large volume of database requests. This becomes more critical when there are more write requests like booking of a passenger seat or updating customer details. Recovery of the lost transactions in these systems, therefore, is an important task for reliable performance.

- *Transaction processing:* Another aspect where traditional DBMS is different from Web-based database system is transaction processing. In traditional DBMS locking mechanism is used to provide concurrency control. Locking mechanism provides lock on data items for write transaction. The other write transactions has to wait until the transaction holding lock on data items is complete (commit) or abort. One major characteristics of debit-credit type transaction is that it will not hold lock for a long time. For web-based databases, even a simple transaction may hold lock for a period of time that is long enough to degrade the performance of the system due to communication failure. For example, in the online reservation system a client cannot hold lock on data items for long time while making the reservation. Therefore, a modified model of transaction processing for Web-based database system is required.

- *Delivery of query results:* Two important cases should be considered. A complex query and query with large result size. In the first case, long execution time is needed and in the latter case long result retrieval time is needed. In traditional DBMSs, result is delivered after the query execution is complete. In a Web-based database system, however, long waiting time cannot be tolerated. In such a system, when the first page of result is available it is sent to the user immediately. The database server continues to process the original query concurrently while the server transmits the available data over the internet. The problem arises when database server fails during the transmission of result to the user. Recovery techniques should be available to recover the lost result pages after the availability of server.

12.2 Architectures of WBDB

Architecture is a subject of design and implementation and reflects the spatial arrangement of application data and the spatial-temporal distribution of computation. There are different WBDB frameworks according to various technologies and requirements. Generally speaking, WBDB can be considered as a single huge database as well as multiple data sources. There are a lot of technologies that can be used for WBDB. Languages for web applications and web servers are Java, PHP, Perl, HTML, DHTML, XML, SQL and so forth. Access technologies include CGI, JavaScript, Servlet, JDBC, and ODBC. Common enterprise databases include Oracle, Sysbase, Informix, DB2, m-SQL, mySQL, SQL-Server, and Butler-SQL [Gould 1998] [Dragan 1997]. We generally classify WBDB architectures into the following types: two-tier architecture, three-tier architecture, and hybrid architectures.

12.2.1 Two-tier Architecture of WBDB

The minimal spatial configuration of a WBDB is the two-tier architecture. The basic framework is shown in Figure 12.1.

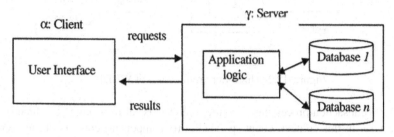

Figure 12.1. Two-tier architecture of WBDB

It closely resembles the traditional client-server paradigm. But there are still some differences between them. The two-tier architecture includes client (we called it α), and server (we called it γ), here α and γ are used to represent the different parts in WBDB. The two-tier solution clients are thin, and are lightweight applications responsible only for rendering the presentation. Application logic and data reside on the server side [Fraternali 1999]. Technologies involved in a two-tier architecture are JDBC, XML, and SQL.

12.2.2 Three-tier Architecture of WBDB

The three-tier architecture is a popular model, which contains generally client (we called it α), application server (we called it β), and data server (we called it γ), see Figure 12.2. A full-fledged WBDB requires these three essential components although they can represent various types of technologies. In the following, we discuss some current three-tier architectures of WBDB.

In the three-tier model of a database gateway, the three components are client API library, server API library, and glue [Rennhackkamp 1997]. The α component is the client API library, which consists of client-side APIs. They determine the format and meaning of the requests that the client applications may issue. Glue is the β component, which owns translation and mapping mechanisms. It transforms the client API to the DBMS (Database Management System) server's API, and vice versa for the data returned to the clients. The server API library on the database server-side is the γ component. It manages the database service available to the clients. The services change in terms of authentication from the DBMS.

330

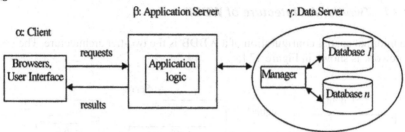

Figure 12.2. Three-tier architecture of WBDB

The TP (transaction-processing) monitor model is also a kind of three-tier architecture. In this context, client application (α component) consists of the user-interface functions, such as screen logic, screen handling, input handling, and some validation functions. Application server (β component) provides all of the details of application services. Resource managers (γ component) can provide all of the lower-level services, such as communication between the database and the application services.

The extended client/server model is a typical three-tier architecture. In such a model, the client Web browser (α component) sends requests to the Web server (β component). The Web server transfers the requests to a database server (γ component). After the database server processes the requests, the results are retrieved to the client Web browser by the reverse pathway. In the transition, the web server can handle the results from the database [Hightower 1997].

In the multi-distributed databases (MDBS) scenario, the Web server (β) requests the MDBS (γ) to retrieve the required data [Ramakrishman 00]. The γ server does this by issuing a global-level SQL query to the MDBS. The MDBS then decomposes the whole query and generates the local queries according to various features of engaging database servers. Then these local queries can be issued to corresponding database servers that may be managed by the DBMS servers. But these DBMS servers can be accessed through all sorts of database access technologies. The MDBS integrates the local results it receives from all the database servers and finally presents a global result to the web server. In this case, the MDBS handles all the operations including data locating, interrelating, and integrating. The web server just sends the requests from clients, which is different from the typical client/server model.

All the technologies can be used in the three-tier architecture according to different user requirements. The three-tier or even n-tier models are essential models to structure a WBDB. We discuss them in Section 3 in more detail.

12.2.3 Hybrid Architecture of WBDB

There are several ways of combining various technologies into the Web or a database to enhance the performance of WBDB. A general architecture is to apply agent-based computing concepts in building WBDBs [Bouchaib et al 1999], see Figure 12.3. Restrictedly speaking, however, it also is the three-tier architecture.

In an agent-based scenario, a client (α) sends either data or data and programs over the Web server that activates the agent (φ). The agent then processes the requested data using its own programs or using the received programs. After the completion of the preliminary processing, the agent will send the data/program/medium result to the application server (β) for further processing. Then the Web server communicates with the database, and the database server (γ) finishes the manipulation to the database and transfers the results to the Web server. The Web server will return the results back to the client directly or via the agent.

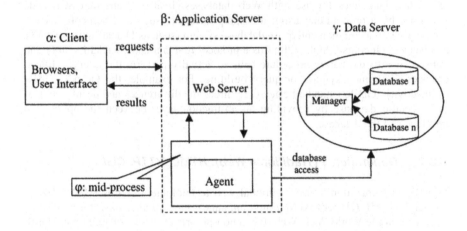

Figure 12.3. Hybrid architecture of WBDB (agent-based)

12.3 Web Based Database Access Technologies

Building WBDBs involves many technologies, such as database, Web server, Web browser, application server, SQL, CGI, JAVA and so on [Wreden 1997]. Some technologies work for the interface; others may deal with the database access, or glue everything together, or just applications. The questions are: how do they work in a real scenario? What are the advantages and drawbacks of different technologies? In order to give a satisfactory answer, we present an implementation framework and then analyze them respectively.

We borrow the term "Generation" from [Kutz and Ramakrishnan 1999] with which the author classified the different stages in the development of web-based database application technologies. Here "Generation" means a change in technology that "rewrites" web application design guidelines by overcoming significant limitations of the previous generation. The existing technologies used in WBDB can be classified as technologies for the traditional Web (generation 1), fast and more interactive Web (generation 2), and Java-based Web (generation 3) [Kutz and Ramakrishnan 1999]. The properties of three generations will be described next. We then propose a novel generation, although it is not a full-fledged one.

12.3.1 Generic SQL

In the following discussion, almost all technologies use SQL or other query languages based on SQL to manipulate all types of databases. Virtually all commercial (relational) database products understand SQL, though most also have their own special dialects. This means that for most DB technologies, database queries developed for use with a particular database are portable from one product or tool to another. This means that developers rarely have to spend time learning proprietary languages for use with Web databases. It also means that SQL code developed by a programmer using a desktop database (such as Microsoft Access) can be used on a common enterprise database system (such as Oracle) with virtually no changes. Of course, SQL still needs a protocol that can take standard syntax and translate it into the native procedure calls to actually perform the query, while it provides a common syntax for query building. For example, the Open Database Connectivity (ODBC) standard effectively hides the differences and peculiarities of each specific database by providing an abstraction layer between the application interface and the database.

12.3.2 Generation 1 (Traditional Web): HTML, HTTP, CGI

WDBDs in Generation 1 use traditional web technologies such as HTML, HTTP, and CGI. HTML (HyperText Markup Language) is the *lingua franca* for publishing hypertext on the World Wide Web. It is a non-proprietary format based upon SGML [W3C 2001]. HTML has a fixed set of element types and uses a form of tagging called structural markup. It can be published on the Web by the Web browser. HTTP is a set of standards used by computers to transfer hypertext files (web pages), which are generally written in HTML, across the Internet.

CGI is a standard interface between Web servers and outside applications. It is one of the early techniques for integrating databases into a Web environment. Running a CGI script from a Web browser lets developers create Web pages that return data based on user input, calling a compiled program such as C or VB or Perl script to access databases.

Generally speaking, the CGI-based framework of WBDB can be viewed as a three-tier architecture. According to Section 12.2 in this chapter, we regard it as a hybrid architecture metaphor to an agent model. This can help us compare the performance of the technology with other technologies. The basic process steps are shown in Figure 12.4. A user opens a Web page and fills in a form containing CGI parameters. The form request is wrapped in an HTTP request to the Web server.

333

After the client connects to the Web server, the Web server finds the CGI request and initiates a CGI process to handle the form request. Then the CGI program can access the database by ODBC (Open Database Connectivity) or native drivers from special databases such as Oracle [Linthicum 1997]. The CGI program receives the data from the database and generates HTML documents. These documents are transferred to the Web browser by the Web server and published on the Web pages.

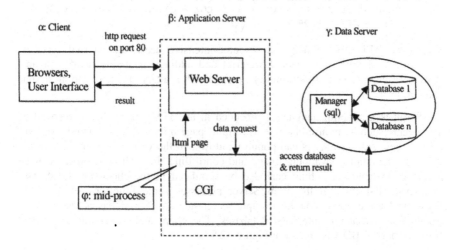

Figure 12.4. Generation 1 framework (CGI-based) of WBDB

The main advantages of the CGI-based framework are its simplicity, language independence, Web server independence, and its wide acceptance. It is flexible for the Web server to work without relying on the CGI program. CGI's easy programming features make it a widely used technology in building WBDBs.

Despite these advantages, the CGI approach has some problems. The main problem is that the Web server has to generate a new process for each CGI script. For a large popular website that can have thousands of access users simultaneously, this procedure will result in serious resource waste and make the communication between clients and servers very slow. The second problem is that the communication through a Web server can possibly cause a bottleneck [Zhou and Zhang 2000]. For every request that is exchanged, the Web server has to convert data from or to an HTML document. This necessary conversion process adds significant overhead when processing a database query. The third problem is that every query submitted to the CGI is regarded as a new encounter. As a result, the database server has to perform the same logon and logout procedure, even if the same user submits multiple queries.

Due to its easy usability and the popularity of Generation 1 WBDBs, CGI is widely adopted by many developers, especially in developing small-size WBDB.

334

12.3.3 Generation 2 (Faster and More interactive Web): JavaScript, Server-side API

Netscape's Server API (NSAPI) and Microsoft's Internet Server API (ISAPI) are two alternatives to CGI. So is JavaScript. We can view Generation 2 as:

```
Generation 2 = Generation 1 -- CGI + ServerSide API or
Generation 2 = Generation 1 -- CGI + Client and Server-side
JavaScript + Frames.
```

Server-side APIs offer much less resource-intensive access to external services. Replacing CGI with server-side JavaScript and adding client-side JavaScript and frames (user interface functionality) significantly alters the application design domain.

JavaScript is a scripting language embedded in an HTML page. It can respond to user events such as mouse clicks, form input, page navigation, and validation and alerts. Client-side JavaScript can popup windows. In the windows, some functions, such as calculations, swapping image and controlling the GUI components can be executed. Database searching can also be simulated in the client-side JavaScript. JavaScript that runs in the Web Server processes some functions of the Web Browser. Unlike client-side JavaScript, server-side JavaScript has access to host resources, external programs and databases. The client and server-side JavaScript framework of WBDB is shown in Figure 12.5.

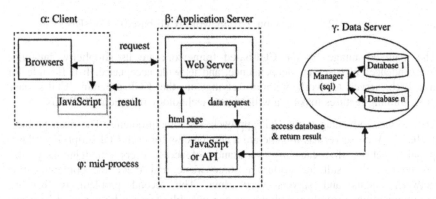

Figure 12.5. Generation 2 framework (Client and Server-side JavaScript) of WBDB

Compared with the CGI-based framework, the JavaScript/API approach works more efficiently. The transportation speed is fast. Its shorter server-side response time allows for designs of novel Web user interface that programmers would never even consider with CGI. The same language on client and server made communication and programming easier.

There are also some shortcomings for Generation 2. Due to the limitation of GUI features, user interface of Generation 2 is still HTML. It must run inside a browser. It requires the use of frames in order to maintain a persistent visual user interface context while updating another GUI control using values from a database. It cannot send the user interface an unsolicited message from the server.

12.3.4 Generation 3 (Java-based Web): Java, JDBC

Technologies of Generation 3 are popular in current applications. These technologies include Java, JDBC, Servlet and so forth.

12.3.4.1 JAVA and JDBC

The JDBC-based framework of WBDB is shown in Figure 12.6.

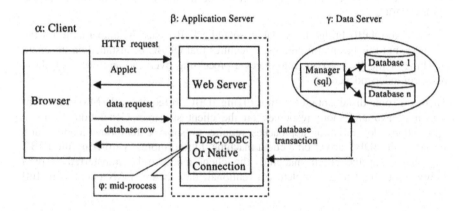

Figure 12.6. Generation 3 (JDBC-based) framework of WBDB

Java is an object-oriented, secure, architectural neutral, portable language. The unique feature of Java lies in the fact that it combines both compiled and interpreted codes [Yang et al 1998]. The Java executable code (called bytecode) is generated by platform-dependent compilers and runs on any platform as long as its operating system is running the Java Interpreter (JVM) or any Java enabled Web browser. The Java bytecode represents the instructions for a virtual microprocessor (JVM) [Papastavtou 1998]. Another key characteristic of Java is the small size of its compiled code, which enables Java compiled class to travel efficiently through the Web. A typical example is a Java applet. A Java applet can run within the context of a Java enabled Web browser [Bouguettaya et al 1999]. The other features of Java are Exception handling, Automatic garbage collection, GUI components, and Application interactivity, Bypass HTTP interaction.

Based on the above features, a Java program can run almost everywhere once it is written. It can be used by both client-side and server-side programs. Its GUI interface makes the interactivity more effective. By building the new user interface classes or components, the communication is more interactive. The applet can run entirely in its own window even if delivered via an HTML page.

The Java database connectivity (JDBC) is the Java standard specification for accessing and manipulating databases. The JDBC consists of two layers: the JDBC API and the JDBC driver API [Papastavtou 1998]. The JDBC API provides a standard interface to allow applet programmers to access and manipulate information in databases, regardless of which DBMS is being used. The JDBC driver API is a set of pure Java classes that provide access to data of many different types. This lets programmers create a standard applet that would allow anyone, regardless of the location or the computer they are using, to see the data they want. A client that employs the JDBC API must first download a JDBC driver to its environment before accessing a particular database. For a high-level Java edition, sometimes a JDBC driver is required from the database vendor or one must use JDBC/ODBC.

A JDBC-to-ODBC bridge is available, should a JDBC class be unavailable for the database, but this has its limitations. It requires that ODBC be installed on the client machine or the Web server, introduces a processing overhead and does not allow platform independence.

There are some disadvantages with utilizing JDBC. It requires a JVM on the client side like Java and more resources on the client site than Generation 1 and 2 applications do. Existing approaches require to some extent downloading and initiating the JDBC driver on a client machine. Furthermore, by utilizing the JDBC API classes at the client machine, the client tends to be transferred from a lightweight client to a complete conventional, data-aware, LAN client with full functionality.

12.3.4.2 Servlet

Servlets are small pieces of Java code that serve HTTP requests and dynamically generate HTML documents. They combine Java strengths (mentioned above) on the server side with the accessibility of HTML clients to deliver database applications [Pour 1998]. The Framework for accessing the database through servlets is shown in Figure 12.7.

Servlets act on the server side like applets on the client side. Using servlets has the following advantages. Servlets can interact with a back-end database via JDBC for storing and accessing user accounts. Servlets can keep data persistent between requests. A pool of database connections can be shared by multiple requests and frequently requested information can be cached [Bergsten 1998]. Unlike CGI scripts to create a new process for each request, all servlet requests are handled in the same process by separate threads. Servlets deliver the same functionality as CGI scripts but they are faster, cleaner, easier to use. Additionally, servlets provide a Java-based solution that addresses the problems associated with server-side programming.

The tradeoff of servlets exists in its middleware characteristic in the client/server architecture. Programmers must create their own command formats in order to marshal and de-marshal the parameters [Pour 1998]. It also does not support a scalable server-side component infrastructure. Implemented as CORBA or RMI objects, servlets involved in an interaction must take place through a generic API.

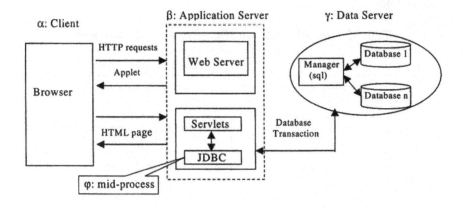

Figure 12.7. Servlet-based framework of WBDB

12.3.5 A New Generation: XML, Client/Mobile Agents/Server

12.3.5.1 XML-based WBDB

There is a trend to use XML to map with database at present [Petrou et al. 1998]. Its simplest form is a two-tier architecture as shown in Figure 12.8. Concurrently, some systems only utilize XML's strengths to make original architecture more scalable.

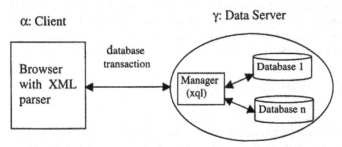

Figure 12.8. XML–based two-tier framework of WBDB

XML is currently in the process of replacing HTML as a standard document markup language for the Web. For database researchers, XML improves over HTML along two main directions of interest of our research community, i.e., providing data semantics and data independence [Cheung et al. 2000] [Bouguettaya 2000]. Generally speaking, XML has the following advantages: (1) XML can define its own tags using DTD (Document Type Definition); (2) XML document structures can be nested to any level of complexity; (3) Any XML documents can contain an optional description of its grammar for the use of application that is required to perform structural validation; (4) XML documents can map with databases such as those in Table 12.1.

Table 12.1. Mapping between SQL query and XML document

SQL query	XML document
Column names	Element tag names
Scalar value names	Elements
Attributes	Sub-element
Collection	List of elements

Further XML data can be stored in a database in various ways. Oracle 8I provides such ways as large objects storage and objected-relational storage. Additionally, the XML documents can be stored as structured, unstructured or hybrid formats according to different data types [Banerjee et al 1998] [Zaniolo et al 2000].

To achieve XML for current needs a new query language XQL has been proposed and widely accepted [Prescod 1997]. XQL supports the notions of hierarchy, sequence, and position. Elements and attributes can be searched, based on their context and content. XQL also provides means to compose and combine XML documents on the fly. XQL delivers XML as a result of all queries. There are already some applications of XML such as Tamino (an Internet Database System) [Sipe 2000].

For various aims, XSL (Extensible Stylesheet Language) also has been developed to transform structured XML documents into formatted, scrollable, searchable documents with tables of contents, indexes, footnotes, and other navigational tools [Rennhackkamp 1997].

12.3.5.2 Mobile Agent Involved Architecture

Mobile agents are processes dispatched from a source computer to accomplish a specific task [Bouchaib et al 1999]. After its submission, a mobile agent proceeds autonomously and independently of the sending client. When it reaches a server, it is delivered to an agent execution environment. Then if the agent possesses necessary authentication credentials, its executable parts are started. To accomplish its task, the mobile agent can transport itself to another server, spawn new agents, and interact with other agents [Hara et al. 2000]. Upon completion, the mobile agent delivers the results to the sending clients or another server.

There are obvious interests in mobile agents applied in Internet applications. Some of them are:

• Bandwidth savings because they can move computation to the data;

• Flexibility because they do not require the remote availability of specific code;

• Suitability and reliability for mobile computing because they do not require continuous network connections [Cabri et al 2000].

The infrastructure involved with mobile agents can work as in Figure 12.9. It can utilize the advantages of mobile agents and eliminate the overhead between the client and the database. The strength of mobile agents is that they do not rely on certain Web/database servers and can move autonomously to new destinations, compared with servlets. Another strong point of mobile agents is that they can be delivered many times to achieve various goals. The key problems are the mobile agents' coordination and security.

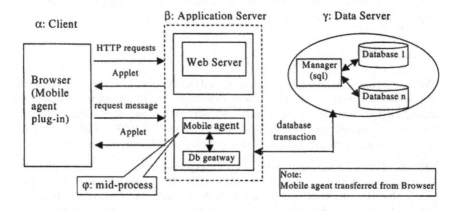

Figure 12.9. Mobile agent involved framework of WBDB

12.3.6 Other Useful Techniques

Due to the enormous market for WBDBs, there are all sorts of technologies developed to satisfy the actual requirements. Here CORBA and RMI are two useful ones as the middleware for WBDB.

12.3.6.1 CORBA

CORBA is an extremely large and complex collection of specifications and protocols. The CORBA's infrastructure provides mechanisms to deal with platform heterogeneity, transparent location and implementation of objects, interoperability and communication between software components of a distributed object environment [Bouguettaya et al 1999]. The interface language for CORBA programs is the Interface Definition Language (IDL). CORBA is language neutral in the sense that clients and servers may be implemented in any of the supported languages, including C, C++, Smalltalk, Ada, Cobol, and Java.

The object manager for CORBA is the Object Request Broker (ORB). The ORB enables objects to send and receives message from objects without regard to whether they are local or remote. CORBA has both static and dynamic means for a server to provide remote objects. The static method involves client "stub" and server "stub" (also server "skeleton"). A stub links an object to the ORB on its machine and is typically generated from IDL. The static use of stubs needs to create and compile the remote objects before it is implemented. To avoid this problem, a Dynamic Invocation Interface (DII) is provided. CORBA also has the ability to communicate with ORBs on different LANs using the Internet Inter-Orb Protocol (IIOP), which extends TCP/IP.

Generally, CORBA is probably the best choice for implementing middleware to serve the database's information to distributed clients if legacy databases are involved [Buss and Jackson 1998].

12.3.6.2 RMI

RMI is contained in Java Development Kit (JDK) devoted to identifying a remote object (via a "marker" interface) and throwing remote exceptions, registering remote objects, serving remote objects, and performing remote garbage collection. RMI is an object-oriented type of Remote Procedure Call (RPC). RMI is designed to minimize the disparities between using ordinary (local) and remote objects.

RMI is Java-centric, and shares Java's specifications, involving platform independence, JVM run-time environment. The RMI approach also implements remote objects in the same manner as CORBA including the client-side stub and the server-side skeleton. An important aspect of RMI is the security manager that is used to implement a security policy. The tradeoff of RMI being Java-based technology is that it is not cross-language. Interoperability to non-Java must be done via JNI. On the other hand, Java's inherent cross-platform capabilities substantially increase the number of platforms on which the distributed application may be run. In addition, several technologies such as JavaBeans and JDBC provide object and database access services. These functions enforce the implementations based on RMI in the context of WBDB.

For situations in which much of the implementation is new or Java interfaces and future application, RMI is the superior choice due to its tighter relationship with the implementing language and the superiority of Java as an Object-Oriented language.

12.4 Challenges

With the growing popularity of the Internet and the Web, there is a fast growing demand for access to database management systems from the Web. World Wide

Web is a gigantic database with enormous potential applications in business, science, engineering, and education. As a consequence, the number of potential users of Web-based databases is very large.

As we discussed above, a complete WBDB consists of user interfaces generally displayed on the Web browser, Web application server, and database server responsible for data manipulation. In this section, we will discuss the challenges based on WBDB in these three aspects.

12.4.1 User Interfaces

Current problems about user interfaces are shown in various aspects [Nielsen 1999], such as:

- How to decide the writing style to make the content more obvious. Users universally despise gratuitous animation and scrolling text field because they distract from the content, and the worst is, slow down the use of the Web. These factors usually make users give up surfing on the Web since they cannot get the most interesting contents. After all, only the contents are what users want ultimately. On the other hand, the UI should balance the trade-off between pictures and contents since a small picture may carry many more messages than a ten-page text.

- How to make user interfaces simple. Intuitive and simple query interfaces are needed to provide access for users with a wide variety of needs and usually with limited database skills.

- How to deal with the device diversity on the Web. The recommended way is to separate presentation and content and encode the presentation-specific instructions in style sheets that can be optimised for each platform.

In order to make navigation or browsing more easily understood, some useful methods can be used [Nielsen 1999] [Zhang and Xu 2000]:

- *Aggregation.* Aggregation is a process by which the properties of a collection are described in terms of the sums of the properties of the units contained in that collection. The most elementary aggregative procedure is counting and a frequency obtained by counting represents the properties of a set by numbers rather than the list of elements it contains. Aggregation in the same site is easy to achieve due to the consistency of the data, whereas how to realize aggregation across sites is not a well-solved problem regards of data diversity.

- *Summarization.* Summarization is the process of condensing a source text into a shorter version while preserving its information content. The strong points of this method exist in enriching search results, and getting a fast overview of document collections.

- *Filtering* (eliminating the stuff the user doesn't care about). Collaborative filtering and quality-based filters should work well. The key problem is to find ways to focus on the most valuable information instead of a complete set of relevant documents. For example, show only contents that other people have found to be valuable or that are published within a short time period. One interesting approach to guiding users to good documents is the PHOAKS project at AT&T Research [Nielsen 1999]. This system is based on a collaborative filtering system that recognizes and reuses recommendations other than ratings-based systems that are built on the assumption of role uniformity.

12.4.2 Application Server

An application server is mainly responsible for providing access services for WBDB. The WBDB access services include connection and resource management, connected and disconnected sessions, local cache, connectionless updatability, navigation (scrolling, filtering and ordering), binding from programming language, and distributed queries, distributed transactions [Blakeley and Deshpande 2000]. The main problems are:

- *Access diversity.* How can users use one program intelligently to access distributed diverse databases when they search/query data?

- *Cache management.* How to identify the valuable information to cache? When a connection is broken, the server should cache results from databases and return it to users after the connection is available again [Park et al. 2000] [Lin and Ye 2000] [Francis and Sato 1997].

- *Agent process.* Some specific agents should reside on the server, which can be triggered by users. The functions consist of access databases, re-constructed contents to adapt to client display equipment, filtering and ordering, and distributed transactions. These agents sometimes can receive from users as mobile agents.

- *Server programming.* A programmer should take a lot of aspects into account when he selects a programming language for server services. A programmer, in order to assure effectiveness, must consider independence of the operating system, consistency with the UI, easy operation, scalability, and component-based reusability.

- *Security.* WBDB server-side security is based on name services. If a hostile party gains control of the name service, any security depending solely on correlating names and network addresses will be for naught [Rubin and Geer 1998].

12.4.3 Database Server

Databases are often called the back-end of a client-server application. They provide the invisible, but essential, core functionality of data storage and manipulation. After a database is merged with the Web, the main challenges exist in the following:

- *Integration with information retrieval.* A database server deals with precise queries on structured information, but information retrieval mostly deals with unstructured textual information and imprecise queries. How can we add more power to text processing considering that text databases have become more popular recently?

- *Handling diversity* (ease of publishing and querying on the Web). A database server can help the trade-off between ease of publishing and ease of querying on the Web if we can find more effective and general ways to handle diversity. The traditional problems are how to deal with different processors, different operating systems, and different language pales, in comparison to the data diversity.

- *Integrating and extending the query mechanism.* The most pressing database problem on the Web is how to integrate different query mechanisms. A demand is how to make search facilities attached with searching results so that we can search further in present contents. Another problem is how we can provide query mechanisms that can simultaneously handle several types of data such as numeric, textual, and spatial information?

- *Collecting data and doing research on the Web.* How can we comprehensively collect diverse information from many resources? How can we utilize the resources on the Web to do research?

- *Consistency.* Some of the research questions are how to define consistency problems on the Web, how to detect them, and how to integrate systems of different levels of consistency requirements.

- *Interaction with users.* Supporting the paradigm of customer-centric e-business, we not only have to track what users visit a Web site, but also to enable them to offer opinions and contribute to the content of the Web site in various ways. In order to personalize a user's experience, a site must dynamically construct (or at least fine-tune) each page as it is delivered, taking into account information about the current page. In a word, as web-based databases go beyond a passive collection of pages to be browsed and seek to present users with a personalized, interactive experience, the role of the database management system becomes central. Supporting feedback, hand holding, customizing on the fly, adapting to user preferences and history, and visualizing progress are some of the issues that will need to be addressed. After that, the website even can provide useful searching & feedback results from other users according to certain relationships among the demands or keywords

12.4.4 Other Challenges

In addition to these problems or limitations, there are other general challenges for WBDB.

- *Security.* One research effort attempts to extend the capabilities of current authorization models of relational DBMSs to WBDBs so that a wide variety of application authorization policies can be directly supported, and to extend the relational model to incorporate mandatory access controls. The other direction concerns the development of adequate authorization models for advanced DBMSs, like object-oriented DBMSs or active DBMSs. With regard to WBDB, the protection of information is difficult because of the peculiarity of the hypertext paradigm and the distribution at different sites. There are several issues related to access control in WBDB, such as formulation of an authorization model for a hypertext system, model extension to take distribution aspects into consideration, and investigation of different policies for the administration of authorizations.

- *Reliability.* It is essential to manipulate WBDB successfully. This will involve the classical approaches such as fault avoidance and fault tolerance. In a WWW environment, realizing the reliability is more complicated due to unpredictable factors. New models and techniques are required when taking transactions through the Web into account.

- *Transaction.* Transaction management deals with the problems of always keeping the database in a consistent state even when concurrent access and failure occur. There are lock-based and timestamp-based concurrency control algorithms and deadlock management. Again, a lot of research into this aspect of WBDB is required.

12.5 A Layered Framework for WBDBs

A WBDB should own the functions and avoid/reduce the problems described in Section 12.4. Considering the whole scenario, a WBDB can have a framework as shown in Figure 12.10.

12.5.1 Description of Layers

α-Client

This layer should contain several agents to resolve the client-side issues. A main agent (e.g., user agent) is the intelligent interactive interface (IAFace). It assists a user in formulating queries and displaying the results of queries in a manner sensitive to the user's context [Bayardo et al 1997]. It can trigger specific agents to process individual specifications in terms of the user's profile. The functions of this layer include outlining the good contents, generating optimal designs for different devices to avoid animation, and scrolling text fielding, filtering useless materials for certain domains in favor of the most valuable information.

In some cases some sub-agents are required. For instance, to realize optimal designs, the XML parser agent is necessary. The content will need to be encoded with much-enhanced structure and meta-information beyond current HTML. XML-based databases should be a suitable option for this goal since XML documents may comply with a *document type definition* (DTD), a specification that is given separately from the document, or a sort of document schema.

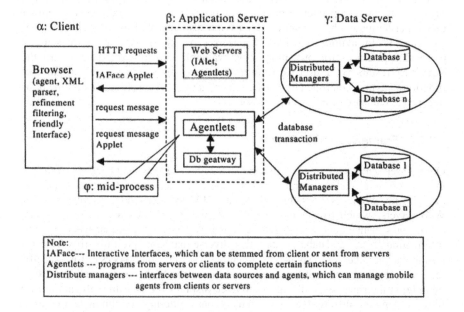

Figure 12.10. Intelligent interactive framework of WBDB

β-Application

β-Application is the most important layer in the whole framework. Agentlets - programs from servers or clients to complete certain functions - are main components that can perform the meditative functions. On the one hand, the broker agent accepts queries and sends them to semantic agents in terms of the domain-independent rules. After semantic queries are generated, the broker agent diverts the tasks to semantic corresponsive agents. The special execution agents communicate with the databases by calling the suitable access database gateways. They also process or analyze the generated results to satisfy the user requirements, such as performing or pre-processing aggregation and summarization from selected information. The results will be fed back to the user interface through further analysis by the ubiquitous filtering agent.

On the other hand, IAFace can also get the relative URLs or links of execution agents from the broker agent (effectively, a cache of metadata). Some server work was done on the client-side programs (client-side agents) which can trigger the server Agentlets to communicate with databases directly.

γ-Database

Distributed managers, interfaces between data sources and agents from both the β-**application** server layer and the **γ-database** layer, are the main components of the **γ-database,** which can also manage mobile agents from clients or servers. They also support agents to extend functions. For example, agents can record data rating according to an independent domain, and provide recommendations for similar users. Furthermore, the recommendations are also recorded as specifications for later queries. In addition, database managers can call an agent to record a user's personal experiences for presenting more valuable contents and later return the experience results to the user for forming the user's preference document. Another function of agents controlled by database managers is to do sub-queries on the basis of concrete database or information resources.

12.5.2 Framework Workflow

Once a user sends requests to Web servers, the Web servers send back an IAFace to the user so as to realize interactive activities with each other. Generally, the user provides his whole requests through IAFace. IAFace can send the requests to the Web servers, which trigger an Agentlet to analyze requests and to distract sub-queries or semantic queries to different databases managers. The managers integrate information from the databases and other diverse databases preliminarily. The raw results arrive the corresponsive Agentlets to do mid-process for specific requirements. If the current connection is broken, the Web servers cach the results by judging their necessity. The user interface displays the valuable information for him by running different agents such as ones filtering to eliminate the extra contents.

Some useless or valueless information can also be thrown away by the Web servers or database managers according to the user's established demands. Meanwhile, the Web servers or client browsers, depending on the capacity of the clients' equipment, can process the requirements for a diverse display. Of course, a user can adjust his requirements through the interactive interface. The proposed architecture uses a number of current technologies, such as XML, Java Servlet, Enterprise JavaBean, JDBC, Java and so forth.

12.6   Developing Web-Based Databases

Java network programming opens the possibility of building Web-based distributed databases. A Web-based distributed database is a key component of many Internet-related applications, such as applications in electronic commerce, information retrieval, and multimedia.

The current wisdom on databases is that information stored in databases is owned by the database management systems (DBMS) that manage the databases. The DBMS is a closed system in the sense that all operations on the data managed by the DBMS will be stored back to the database. A further development on distributed databases and heterogeneous databases allows information to be stored in different databases using various formats and to be shared among participating databases. However, a distributed heterogeneous database system is still a closed system that is managed by a distributed database management system (DDBMS).

The Web-based database approach represents a deviation from this traditional mode of thinking. It allows data to be represented in objects (consisting of data and methods that manipulate the data) and the access of these objects is open to anyone with the correct access rights. Information stored in a Web-based database is independent of any particular software (such as the DBMSs in the traditional database approach). Access to the Web-based database can be easily integrated into any user interface, such as a conventional WWW browser or a particular application program. Web-based databases have a great potential in electronic commerce, information retrieval and multimedia applications.

12.6.1 The Java Database Connectivity (JDBC) Package

The JDBC package is a set of Java classes that can be used by applications to make database calls. It specifies the interfaces between Java and databases (based on SQL2). All implementation of JDBC drivers is done by third party companies with special expertise. A change of a driver will not change the program. The major advantages of using JDBC are the cross-platform independence and the possibility of delivering database functionality using Java applets through the Internet.

JDBC's classes are contained in the *java.sql* package. It includes the following major classes:

- *DriverManger:* the *DriverManager* object is used to facilitate the use of multiple database drivers in a single application. Each JDBC driver can be used to connect to a different data source.

- *Connection:* after a JDBC driver has been registered with the *DriverManager,* a data source, user ID, password, or other pertinent information can be specified to create a connection to a database. This *Connection* object is used in later calls to specify to which databases the calls should be placed. JDBC supports having multiple *Connection* objects open at any given time.

- *Statement:* the *Statement* object mimics the SQL statement that the application wants to apply against a database.

- *ResultSet:* after a call is made by a *Statement* object, the results of the query are put into a *ResultSet* object. This object can then be traversed to retrieve multiple rows as well as multiple columns.

- *ResultSetMetaData:* the *ResultSetMetaData* object can be used to inquire about the contents of a *ResultSet* object.

- *DatabaseMetaData:* the *DatabaseMetaData* object can be used to query the support options for a given database.

- *SQLException:* this exception is used to capture most problems that are returned from database systems. In addition, the JDBC offers an *SQLWarning* class that returns information which is not as severe as the *SQLException* class does.

A JDBC program initially invokes the *DriverManager* class's *getConnection( )* method to establish a connection to the database. Once the connection is established, the program calls either the *createStatement( ), prepareStatement( ),* or *prepareCall( )* method of the *Connection* object and prepares for executing the SQL statements. SQL statements can be executed by invoking the *Statement* object, or via the *PreparedStatement* object or the *CallableStatement* object.

Next, the program either calls the *executeQuery( ), executeUpdate( ),* or *execute( )* method of the *Statement, PreparedStatement,* or *CallableStatement* object. The *executeQuery( )* method is used when only one *ResultSet* is needed, and the *execute( )* method is used when more than one *ResultSet* is returned. The *executeUpdate( )* method is used if no *ResultSet* is needed and the SQL statement contains an UPDATE, INSERT, or DELETE. The *next( )* method of the *ResultSet* object can be used to process multiple rows of data.

12.6.2 Steps for Developing Web-based Databases

12.6.2.1 Preparing the Database

The first step in developing a web-based database using JDBC is to prepare the database for JDBC connection. We use an Access database as an example. First, a blank database, named dbtest.mdb, is created. Second, the following steps are used to prepare the database for JDBC access:

- From the *Start* menu select the *Settings*;

- Click the Control Panel, then the ODBC Data Source (32bit);

- Click *System DSN,* then *Add*;

- Select Microsoft Database Driver (*.mdb);

- Type in data source name and use *"Select"* to find the database "dbtest.mdb"; Use *"Options"* to set the username and password.

12.6.2.2 Creating the Database Tables

Assume that the database contains three tables: CUSTOMER, PRODUCT, and TRANSACTIONS.

The following Java program "CreateCustomer.java" creates the customer table with four columns (C_NAME, C_ID, C_ADDR, and C_PHONE):

```
import java.sql.*;
public class CreateCustomer {
    public static void main(String args[]) {
        String url = "jdbc:odbc:dbtest";
        Connection con;
        String createString;
        createString = "create table CUSTOMER "
```

```
                  "(C_NAME varchar(30), " +
                  "C_ID int, " +
                  "C_ADDR varchar(50), " +
                  "C_PHONE varchar(12) )";
            Statement stmt;
            try {

        Class.forName("sun.jdbc.odbc.JdbcOdbcDriver").newInstance();
            } catch(Exception e) {
                System.err.print("ClassNotFoundException: ");
                System.err.println(e.getMessage());
            }
            try {
                con = DriverManager.getConnection(url, "admin", "admin");
                stmt = con.createStatement();
                stmt.executeUpdate(createString);
                stmt.close();
                con.close();
            } catch(SQLException ex) {
                System.err.println("SQLException: " + ex.getMessage());
            }
        }
    }
}
```

Now, you can compile the program and run it. After that, check the database to see if the table is created.

The creation of the PRODUCT table (with five columns of P_NAME, P_DESC, P_CODE, P_UNIT, and P_STOCK) is similar. The Java program "CreateProduct.java" is listed below:

```
import java.sql.*;
public class CreateProduct {
    public static void main(String args[]) {
        String url = "jdbc:odbc:dbtest";
        Connection con;
        String createString;
        createString = "create table PRODUCT " +
            "(P_NAME varchar(20), " +
            "P_DESC varchar(40), " +
            "P_CODE varchar(8), " +
            "P_UNIT_PRICE float, " +
            "P_STOCK int )";
        Statement stmt;
        try {

    Class.forName("sun.jdbc.odbc.JdbcOdbcDriver").newInstance();
        } catch(Exception e) {
            System.err.print("ClassNotFoundException: ");
            System.err.println(e.getMessage());
        }
        try {
            con = DriverManager.getConnection(url, "admin", "admin");
            stmt = con.createStatement();
            stmt.executeUpdate(createString);
            stmt.close();
            con.close();
        } catch(SQLException ex) {
            System.err.println("SQLException: " + ex.getMessage());
```

```
        }
    }
}
```

You can also compile the program, run it, and check the database to see if the table is created.

The creation of the TRANSACTION table (with column of T_ID, C_ID, P_CODE, T_NUM, T_TOTAL_PRICE, and T_DAATE) is also similar. The following Java program "CreateTransaction.java" completes such a task:

```
import java.sql.*;
public class CreateTransaction {
    public static void main(String args[]) {
        String url = "jdbc:odbc:dbtest";
        Connection con;
        String createString;
        createString = "create table TRANSACTION " +
            "(T_ID int, " +
            "C_ID int, " +
            "P_CODE varchar(8), " +
            "T_NUM int, " +
            "T_TOTAL_PRICE float, " +
            "T_DATE date )";
        Statement stmt;
        try {

    Class.forName("sun.jdbc.odbc.JdbcOdbcDriver").newInstance();
        } catch(Exception e) {
            System.err.print("ClassNotFoundException: ");
            System.err.println(e.getMessage());
        }
        try {
            con = DriverManager.getConnection(url, "admin", "admin");
            stmt = con.createStatement();
    stmt.executeUpdate(createString);
            stmt.close();
            con.close();
        } catch(SQLException ex) {
            System.err.println("SQLException: " + ex.getMessage());
        }
    }
}
```

You should also compile the program, run it, and check the database to see if the table is created.

12.6.2.3 Populating the Tables

We populate the three tables using the following programs, named InsertCustomer.java, InsertProduct.java, and InsertTransaction.java, respectively:

```
// "InsertCustomer.java"
import java.sql.*;
public class InsertCustomer {
```

```java
    public static void main(String args[]) {
        String url = "jdbc:odbc:dbtest";
        Connection con;
        Statement stmt;
        String query = "select * from CUSTOMER";
        try {
            Class.forName("sun.jdbc.odbc.JdbcOdbcDriver");

        } catch(java.lang.ClassNotFoundException e) {
            System.err.print("ClassNotFoundException: ");
            System.err.println(e.getMessage());
        }
        try {
    con = DriverManager.getConnection(url, "admin", "admin");
            stmt = con.createStatement();
            stmt.executeUpdate("insert into CUSTOMER " +
            "values('John Smith', 100, '123 King St.', '03-9123
4567')");
            stmt.executeUpdate("insert into CUSTOMER " +
            "values('Alex Lee', 101, '234 Queen St.', '03-9234
5678')");
            stmt.executeUpdate("insert into CUSTOMER " +
            "values('Anne Wong', 102, '345 Yarra Ave.', '03-9345
6789')");
            stmt.executeUpdate("insert into CUSTOMER " +
            "values('Tanya Foo', 103, '456 Irving Rd.', '03-9456
7890')");

            ResultSet rs = stmt.executeQuery(query);
            System.out.println("C_NAME C_ID C_ADDR C_PHONE");
            while (rs.next()) {
             String s = rs.getString("C_NAME");
             int i = rs.getInt("C_ID");
             String s1 = rs.getString("C_ADDR");
             String s2 = rs.getString("C_PHONE");
             System.out.println(s + "    " + i + "    " + s1 + "    " + s2);
            }
            stmt.close();
            con.close();
        } catch(SQLException ex) {
            System.err.println("SQLException: " + ex.getMessage());
        }
    }
}

// "InsertProduct.java":
import java.sql.*;
public class InsertProduct {
    public static void main(String args[]) {
        String url = "jdbc:odbc:dbtest";
        Connection con;
        Statement stmt;
        String query = "select * from PRODUCT";
        try {
            Class.forName("sun.jdbc.odbc.JdbcOdbcDriver");

        } catch(java.lang.ClassNotFoundException e) {
            System.err.print("ClassNotFoundException: ");
            System.err.println(e.getMessage());
        }
```

352

```java
        try {
            con = DriverManager.getConnection(url, "admin", "admin");
            stmt = con.createStatement();
            stmt.executeUpdate("insert into PRODUCT " +
                "values('TV', 'Philip, 68cm, flat screen', 'T0010',
1200.00, 10)");
            stmt.executeUpdate("insert into PRODUCT " +
                "values('VCR', 'Sony, Mid-Drive', 'V100', 500.00, 15)");
            stmt.executeUpdate("insert into PRODUCT " +
                "values('TV', 'Tohisba, 34cm, remote control',
'T0012', 300.00, 20)");
            stmt.executeUpdate("insert into PRODUCT " +
"values('PC', 'Dell, 256M RAM, 10GHD, 17\" monitor', 'P0012', 2400.00,
12)");

            ResultSet rs = stmt.executeQuery(query);
            System.out.println("P_NAME  P_DESC  P_CODE  P_UNIT_PRICE
P_STOCK");
            while (rs.next()) {
             String s = rs.getString("P_NAME");
             String s1 = rs.getString("P_DESC");
             String s2 = rs.getString("P_CODE");
             float f = rs.getFloat("P_UNIT_PRICE");
             int i = rs.getInt("P_STOCK");
             System.out.println(s + "   " + s1 + "   "
+ s2 + "   " + f + "   " + i);
            }
            stmt.close();
            con.close();
        } catch(SQLException ex) {
            System.err.println("SQLException: " + ex.getMessage());
        }
    }
}

// "InsertTransaction.java":
import java.sql.*;
public class InsertTransaction {
    public static void main(String args[]) {
        String url = "jdbc:odbc:dbtest";
        Connection con;
        Statement stmt;
        String query = "select * from TRANSACTION";
        try {
            Class.forName("sun.jdbc.odbc.JdbcOdbcDriver");

        } catch(java.lang.ClassNotFoundException e) {
            System.err.print("ClassNotFoundException: ");
            System.err.println(e.getMessage());
        }
        try {
            con = DriverManager.getConnection(url, "admin", "admin");
            stmt = con.createStatement();
            stmt.executeUpdate("insert into TRANSACTION " +
                "values(500, 100, 'T0010', 1, 1200.00, #1/8/2000#)");
            stmt.executeUpdate("insert into TRANSACTION " +
                "values(501, 101, 'V100', 2, 1000.00, #2/20/2000#)");

            ResultSet rs = stmt.executeQuery(query);
```

```
            System.out.println("T_ID  C_ID  P_CODE  T_NUM
T_TOTAL_PRICE  T_DATE");
            while (rs.next()) {
                int i = rs.getInt("T_ID");
                int i1 = rs.getInt("C_ID");
                String s = rs.getString("P_CODE");
                int i2 = rs.getInt("T_NUM");
                float f = rs.getFloat("T_TOTAL_PRICE");
                Date d = rs.getDate("T_DATE");
                System.out.println(i + "   " + i1 + "   " + s +
                    "   " + i2 + "   " + f + "   " + d);
            }
            stmt.close();
            con.close();
        } catch(SQLException ex) {
            System.err.println("SQLException: " + ex.getMessage());
        }
    }
}
```

You can compile the programs, run them, and check the database to see if the tables are populated.

12.6.2.4 Printing the Columns of Tables

The following Java program "PrintColumns.Java" prints all contents of the CUSTOMER table:

```
import java.sql.*;
class PrintColumns  {
    public static void main(String args[]) {
        String url = "jdbc:odbc:dbtest";
        Connection con;
        String query = "select * from CUSTOMER";
        Statement stmt;
        try {
            Class.forName("sun.jdbc.odbc.JdbcOdbcDriver");
        } catch(java.lang.ClassNotFoundException e) {
            System.err.print("ClassNotFoundException: ");
            System.err.println(e.getMessage());
        }
        try {
            con = DriverManager.getConnection(url, "admin", "admin");
            stmt = con.createStatement();
            ResultSet rs = stmt.executeQuery(query);
            ResultSetMetaData rsmd = rs.getMetaData();
            PrintColumnTypes.printColTypes(rsmd);
            System.out.println("");
            int numberOfColumns = rsmd.getColumnCount();
            for (int i = 1; i <= numberOfColumns; i++) {
                if (i > 1) System.out.print(",  ");
                String columnName = rsmd.getColumnName(i);
                System.out.print(columnName);
            }
            System.out.println("");
            while (rs.next()) {
                for (int i = 1; i <= numberOfColumns; i++) {
```

```
            if (i > 1) System.out.print(",  ");
            String columnValue = rs.getString(i);
            System.out.print(columnValue);
          }
          System.out.println("");
        }
        stmt.close();
        con.close();
      } catch(SQLException ex) {
        System.err.print("SQLException: ");
        System.err.println(ex.getMessage());
      }
    }
}
```

The program uses a Java class called *PrintColumnTypes,* to identify the types used in the database and JDBC. The program (called `PrintColumnTypes.Java`) is shown below:

```
import java.sql.*;
public class PrintColumnTypes  {
    public static void printColTypes(ResultSetMetaData rsmd)
        throws SQLException {

        int columns = rsmd.getColumnCount();
        for (int i = 1; i <= columns; i++) {
            int jdbcType = rsmd.getColumnType(i);
            String name = rsmd.getColumnTypeName(i);
            System.out.print("Column " + i + " is JDBC type " +
jdbcType);
            System.out.println(", which the DBMS calls " + name);
        }
    }
}
```

You should compile the program, run it, and check if the table is printed properly.

To print the columns of the PRODUCT and the TRANSACTION tables, only one line of the above program needs to be changed:

```
String query = "select * from CUSTOMER";
```

Just change CUSTOMER into PRODUCT or TRANSACTION, then it will print the contents of these tables, respetively.

12.6.2.5 Select Statements (one table)

The following Java program "`SelectStatement.java`" executes the following SQL statement:

```
select P_DESC, P_STOCK
       from PRODUCT
       where P_NAME like 'TV';
```

You can execute other SQL statements by simply changing the corresponding statement in the program.

```
import java.sql.*;
public class SelectStatement  {
    public static void main(String args[]) {
        String url = "jdbc:odbc:dbtest";
        Connection con;
        String query = "select P_DESC, P_STOCK " +
            "from PRODUCT " +
            "where P_NAME like 'TV'";
        Statement stmt;
        try {
            Class.forName("sun.jdbc.odbc.JdbcOdbcDriver");
        } catch(java.lang.ClassNotFoundException e) {
            System.err.print("ClassNotFoundException: ");
            System.err.println(e.getMessage());
        }
        try {
            con = DriverManager.getConnection(url, "admin", "admin");
            stmt = con.createStatement();
            ResultSet rs = stmt.executeQuery(query);
            ResultSetMetaData rsmd = rs.getMetaData();
            int numberOfColumns = rsmd.getColumnCount();
            int rowCount = 1;
            while (rs.next()) {
                System.out.println("Row " + rowCount + ":   ");
                for (int i = 1; i <= numberOfColumns; i++) {
                    System.out.print("   Column " + i + ":   ");
                    System.out.println(rs.getString(i));
                }
                System.out.println("");
                rowCount++;
            }
            stmt.close();
            con.close();

        } catch(SQLException ex) {
            System.err.print("SQLException: ");
            System.err.println(ex.getMessage());
        }
    }
}
```

You should compile the program, run it, and check the database to see if the result is selected properly.

12.6.3 Developing A JDBC Application

In this section we use an example to show how to develop a JDBC application. This example has a database that stores data, a server that manages the access of the database, and a client that interfaces with users. The client uses a Java applet to access the server and the server uses JDBC to access the database.

Prepare the Access database and the HTML file

We use the Access database, "dbtest.mdb", created in the previous section. It includes three tables: CUSTOMER, PRODUCT, and TRANSACTION.

The first step is to prepare the following HTML file, named `Applet.html`, to use the applet:

```
<HTML>
<title>Database Operations</title>

<applet code="ClientApplet.class"
    width=600 height=350>
</applet>
</HTML>
```

Prepare the Java applet programs

Create the main applet program, "ClientApplet.java". This program implements the user interface. You should change the IP address in the program to a proper IP address.

```java
import java.awt.*;
import java.awt.event.*;
import java.applet.Applet;
import java.io.*;

public class ClientApplet extends Applet {
    private static final String host= "192.168.0.1";
    TextArea ta;
    ClientComm cc;
    ClientCommExit cce;
    ClientCommSQL ccs;
    TextField sqlcommand;

    public void init () {
        Panel p1 = new Panel(new BorderLayout(10, 10));
        Button p1b1 = new Button ("Resulsts Returned");
        p1.add (p1b1, BorderLayout.NORTH);
        ta = new TextArea ();
        ta.setEditable(false);
        p1.add (ta, BorderLayout.CENTER);
        sqlcommand = new TextField ("", 50);
        p1.add (sqlcommand, BorderLayout.SOUTH);
        add (p1);

        Panel p2 = new Panel (new FlowLayout());
        Button p2bCus = new Button ("All Customers");
        p2.add (p2bCus);
        p2bCus.addActionListener (new ActionListener() {
            public void actionPerformed (ActionEvent e) {
                ByteArrayOutputStream bao = new ByteArrayOutputStream();
                cc = new ClientComm(host, 0, 1, bao);
                ta.setText (bao.toString()+"Returned by the <All Customer>
request");
            }
        };

        Button p2bPro = new Button ("All Products");
        p2.add (p2bPro);
        p2bPro.addActionListener (new ActionListener() {
            public void actionPerformed (ActionEvent e) {
                ByteArrayOutputStream bao = new ByteArrayOutputStream();
                cc = new ClientComm(host, 0, 2, bao);
```

```
              ta.setText (bao.toString()+"Returned by the <All Product>
request");
          }
      };

      Button p2bTra = new Button ("All Transactions");
      p2.add (p2bTra);
      p2bTra.addActionListener (new ActionListener() {
        public void actionPerformed (ActionEvent e) {
          ByteArrayOutputStream bao = new ByteArrayOutputStream();
          cc = new ClientComm(host, 0, 3, bao);
          ta.setText (bao.toString()+"Returned by the <All Transaction>
request");
          }
      };

      Button p2bSQL = new Button ("SQL Command");
      p2.add (p2bSQL);
      p2bSQL.addActionListener (new ActionListener() {
        public void actionPerformed (ActionEvent e) {
          ByteArrayOutputStream bao = new ByteArrayOutputStream();
          ccs = new ClientCommSQL(host, 0, 4, sqlcommand.getText(),
bao);
          ta.setText (bao.toString()+"Returned by the <SQL Command>
request");
          }
      };

      Button p2bExit = new Button ("ShutDown Server");
      p2.add (p2bExit);
      p2bExit.addActionListener (new ActionListener() {
        public void actionPerformed (ActionEvent e) {
          ByteArrayOutputStream bao = new ByteArrayOutputStream();
          cce = new ClientCommExit(host, 0, bao);
          ta.setText (bao.toString()+"Returned by the <ShutDown Server>
request");
          //System.exit(0);
          }
      };

      add (p2);
    }
}
```

Create the Java program that implements the *ClientComm* class used in the applet: ClientComm.java. This program deals with the major communication work between the applet and the server.

```
import java.io.*;
import java.net.*;

public class ClientComm {
  public static final int DEFAULT_PORT = 6789;
  private String host = "";
  private int port = 0;
  private OutputStream os = null;
  boolean DEBUG = true;

  public ClientComm (String h, int p, int choice, OutputStream o) {
    host = h;
```

```
    port = ((p == 0) ? DEFAULT_PORT : p);
    os = o;
    Socket s = null;
    PrintWriter out = new PrintWriter (os, true);
    if (DEBUG) {
      System.out.println("Applet about to create a socket on "
          + host + " at port " + port);
    }

    try {
      // create a socket to communicate to the specified host and port
      s = new Socket(host, port);
      // create streams for reading and writing
      BufferedReader sin = new BufferedReader(new
InputStreamReader(s.getInputStream())));
      PrintStream sout = new PrintStream(s.getOutputStream(), true);
      if (DEBUG) {
        System.out.println("Applet has created sin and sout ");
      }

      // tell the user that we've connected
      out.println("Connected to " + s.getInetAddress() +
        ":" + s.getPort());

      if (DEBUG) {
        System.out.println("Applet has connected to "+
s.getInetAddress() +
            ":" + s.getPort());
      }

      String line;
      // read the first response (a line) from the server
      line = sin.readLine();
      if (DEBUG) {
        System.out.println("Applet has read a line: " + line);
      }

      // write the line to the user
      out.println(line);
      out.flush();
      // send the command choice to the server
      if (choice <=3) {
        sout.println(choice);
      } else {
        sout.println("Wrong command");
      }
      if (DEBUG) {
        System.out.println("Applet has sent sout the choice: "+
choice);
      }

      // read a line from the server
      line = sin.readLine();
      if (DEBUG) {
        System.out.println("Applet has read a line: " + line);
      }

      out.println(line);
      // check if connection is closed, i.e., EOF
      if (line == null) {
```

```
      out.println("Connection closed by server.");
    }
    while (true) {
      line=sin.readLine();
      if (DEBUG) {
        System.out.println("Applet has read a line: " + line);
      }

    out.println(line);
    if (line.equals("EndOfRecord")) break;
  }
  }
  catch (IOException e) {
    System.err.println(e);
  }
  // always be sure to close the socket
  finally {
    try {
      if (s != null) s.close();
    }
    catch (IOException e2) { }
  }
  }
}
```

Create the Java program that implements the *ClientCommExit* class used in the applet: `ClientCommExit.java`. This program deals with the special applet command of "Server Exit".

```
import java.io.*;
import java.net.*;

public class ClientCommExit {
  public static final int DEFAULT_PORT = 6789;
  private String host = "";
  private int port = 0;
  private OutputStream os = null;
  boolean DEBUG = true;

  public ClientCommExit (String h, int p, OutputStream o) {
    host = h;
    port = ((p == 0) ? DEFAULT_PORT : p);
    os = o;
    Socket s = null;
    PrintWriter out = new PrintWriter (os, true);
    if (DEBUG) {
      System.out.println("Applet about to create a socket on "
                    + host + " at port " + port);
    }

    try {
      // create a socket to communicate to the specified host and port
      s = new Socket(host, port);
      // create streams for reading and writing
      BufferedReader sin = new BufferedReader(new
InputStreamReader(s.getInputStream()));
      PrintStream sout = new PrintStream(s.getOutputStream(), true);
      if (DEBUG) {
        System.out.println("Applet has created sin and sout ");
      }
```

```
      // tell the user that we've connected
      out.println("Connected to " + s.getInetAddress() +
        ":" + s.getPort());

      if (DEBUG) {
        System.out.println("Applet has connected to "+
s.getInetAddress() +
            ":" + s.getPort());
      }

      String line;
      // read the first response (a line) from the server
      line = sin.readLine();
      if (DEBUG) {
        System.out.println("Applet has read a line: " + line);
      }

      // write the line to the user
      out.println(line);
      out.flush();
      // send the command choice to the server
      sout.println("Server Exit");
      if (DEBUG) {
        System.out.println("Applet has sent sout the command: Server
Exit");
      }
    }
    catch (IOException e) {
      System.err.println(e);
    }
    // always be sure to close the socket
    finally {
      try {
        if (s != null) s.close();
      }
      catch (IOException e2) { }
    }
  }
}
```

Create the Java program that implements the *ClientCommSQL* class used in the applet: ClientCommSQL.java. This program deals with the special applet commands for SQL statements.

```
import java.io.*;
import java.net.*;

public class ClientCommSQL {
  public static final int DEFAULT_PORT = 6789;
  private String host = "";
  private int port = 0;
  private OutputStream os = null;
  boolean DEBUG = true;

  public ClientCommSQL (String h, int p, int choice, String cmd,
OutputStream o) {
    host = h;
    port = ((p == 0) ? DEFAULT_PORT : p);
```

```
    os = o;
    Socket s = null;
    PrintWriter out = new PrintWriter (os, true);
    if (DEBUG) {
      System.out.println("Applet about to create a socket on "
          + host + " at port " + port);
    }

    try {
      // create a socket to communicate to the specified host and port
      s = new Socket(host, port);
      // create streams for reading and writing
      BufferedReader sin = new BufferedReader(new
InputStreamReader(s.getInputStream())));
      PrintStream sout = new PrintStream(s.getOutputStream(), true);
      if (DEBUG) {
        System.out.println("Applet has created sin and sout ");
      }

      // tell the user that we've connected
      out.println("Connected to " + s.getInetAddress() +
        ":" + s.getPort());

      if (DEBUG) {
        System.out.println("Applet has connected to "+
s.getInetAddress() +
            ":" + s.getPort());
      }

      String line;
      // read the first response (a line) from the server
      line = sin.readLine();
      if (DEBUG) {
        System.out.println("Applet has read a line: " + line);
      }

      // write the line to the user
      out.println(line);
      out.flush();
      // send the command choice to the server
      if (choice ==4) {
        sout.println(choice);
        sout.println(cmd);
      } else {
        sout.println("Wrong command");
      }
      if (DEBUG) {
        System.out.println("Applet has sent sout the choice/SQL: "+
choice+ "/"+cmd);
      }

      // read a line from the server
      line = sin.readLine();
      if (DEBUG) {
        System.out.println("Applet has read a line: " + line);
      }

      out.println(line);
      // check if connection is closed, i.e., EOF
      if (line == null) {
```

```
            out.println("Connection closed by server.");
        }
    while (true) {
        line=sin.readLine();
        if (DEBUG) {
          System.out.println("Applet has read a line: " + line);
        }

      out.println(line);
      if (line.equals("EndOfRecord")) break;
    }
    }
    catch (IOException e) {
      System.err.println(e);
    }
    // always be sure to close the socket
    finally {
      try {
        if (s != null) s.close();
      }
      catch (IOException e2) { }
    }
  }
}
```

Prepare the main server program

Create the main server program, SDB.java. This program accepts applet connections and user commands and then dispatches the commands to individual processing programs accordingly.

```
import java.net.*;
import java.io.*;

public class SDB {

    public static void main (String args[]) throws IOException {
      Socket client;
      int port = 0;
      int end = 0;
      BufferedReader in;
      PrintStream out;

      if (args.length != 1)
        port = 6789;
      else
        port = Integer.parseInt(args[0]);

      try {
        while (end == 0) {
          client = accept (port);
          in = new BufferedReader(new
InputStreamReader(client.getInputStream())));
          out = new PrintStream(client.getOutputStream());
          out.println ("You are now connected to the Simple Database
Server.");
        // read a line
        String line = in.readLine();
          // and send back ACK
```

```
    // out.println("OK");
    System.out.println("Received: " + line);
      if (line.equals("1")) DispCus.DispCus(out);
      else if (line.equals("2")) DispPro.DispPro(out);
      else if (line.equals("3")) DispTra.DispTra(out);
      else if (line.equals("4")) {
      out.println("OK");
      line = in.readLine();
        System.out.println ("Received: " + line);
        ExeSQL.ExeSQL(out, line);
      }
    if (line.equals("Server Exit")) {
        end = 1;
        }
        client.close();
      }
  } finally {
    System.out.println ("Closing");
  }
}

  static Socket accept (int port) throws IOException {
    System.out.println ("Starting on port " + port);
    ServerSocket server = new ServerSocket (port);

    System.out.println ("Waiting");
    Socket client = server.accept ();
    System.out.println ("Accepted from " + client.getInetAddress ());

    server.close ();
    return client;
  }
}
```

Prepare the database access programs

Create the Java program, DispCus.java, to display the customer table.

```
import java.net.*;
import java.io.*;
import java.sql.*;
public class DispCus {
    public static void DispCus(PrintStream out) {
        String url = "jdbc:odbc:dbtest";
        Connection con;
        String query = "select * from Customer ";
        Statement stmt;
        try {
            Class.forName("sun.jdbc.odbc.JdbcOdbcDriver");
        } catch(java.lang.ClassNotFoundException e) {
            System.err.print("ClassNotFoundException: ");
            System.err.println(e.getMessage());
        }
        try {
            con = DriverManager.getConnection(url, "admin", "admin");
            stmt = con.createStatement();
            ResultSet rs = stmt.executeQuery(query);
            ResultSetMetaData rsmd = rs.getMetaData();
            int numberOfColumns = rsmd.getColumnCount();
            int rowCount = 1;
```

364

```
            while (rs.next()) {
                out.println("Row " + rowCount + ":   ");
                for (int i = 1; i <= numberOfColumns; i++) {
                    out.print("   Column " + i + ":   ");
                    out.println(rs.getString(i));
                }
                out.println("");
                rowCount++;
            }
            out.println("EndOfRecord");
            stmt.close();
            con.close();

        } catch(SQLException ex) {
            System.err.print("SQLException: ");
            System.err.println(ex.getMessage());
        }
    }
}
```

Create the Java program, DispPro.java, to display the product table.

```
import java.net.*;
import java.io.*;
import java.sql.*;
public class DispPro  {
    public static void DispPro(PrintStream out) {
        String url = "jdbc:odbc:dbtest";
        Connection con;
        String query = "select * from Product ";
        Statement stmt;
        try {
            Class.forName("sun.jdbc.odbc.JdbcOdbcDriver");
        } catch(java.lang.ClassNotFoundException e) {
            System.err.print("ClassNotFoundException: ");
            System.err.println(e.getMessage());
        }
        try {
            con = DriverManager.getConnection(url, "admin", "admin");
            stmt = con.createStatement();
            ResultSet rs = stmt.executeQuery(query);
            ResultSetMetaData rsmd = rs.getMetaData();
            int numberOfColumns = rsmd.getColumnCount();
            int rowCount = 1;
            while (rs.next()) {
                out.println("Row " + rowCount + ":   ");
                for (int i = 1; i <= numberOfColumns; i++) {
                    out.print("   Column " + i + ":   ");
                    out.println(rs.getString(i));
                }
                out.println("");
                rowCount++;
            }
            out.println("EndOfRecord");
            stmt.close();
            con.close();

        } catch(SQLException ex) {
            System.err.print("SQLException: ");
            System.err.println(ex.getMessage());
```

```
            }
        }
}
```

Create the Java program, `DispTra.java`, to display the transaction table.

```java
import java.net.*;
import java.io.*;
import java.sql.*;
public class DispTra {
    public static void DispTra(PrintStream out) {
        String url = "jdbc:odbc:dbtest";
        Connection con;
        String query = "select * from Transaction ";
        Statement stmt;
        try {
            Class.forName("sun.jdbc.odbc.JdbcOdbcDriver");
        } catch(java.lang.ClassNotFoundException e) {
            System.err.print("ClassNotFoundException: ");
            System.err.println(e.getMessage());
        }
        try {
            con = DriverManager.getConnection(url, "admin", "admin");
            stmt = con.createStatement();
            ResultSet rs = stmt.executeQuery(query);
            ResultSetMetaData rsmd = rs.getMetaData();
            int numberOfColumns = rsmd.getColumnCount();
            int rowCount = 1;
            while (rs.next()) {
                out.println("Row " + rowCount + ": ");
                for (int i = 1; i <= numberOfColumns; i++) {
                    out.print("   Column " + i + ": ");
                    out.println(rs.getString(i));
                }
                out.println("");
                rowCount++;
            }
            out.println("EndOfRecord");
            stmt.close();
            con.close();

        } catch(SQLException ex) {
            System.err.print("SQLException: ");
            System.err.println(ex.getMessage());
        }
    }
}
```

Create the Java program, `ExeSQL.java`, to execute an SQL statement.

```java
import java.net.*;
import java.io.*;
import java.sql.*;
public class ExeSQL {
    public static void ExeSQL(PrintStream out, String sqlstr) {
        String url = "jdbc:odbc:dbtest";
        Connection con;
        Statement stmt;
        try {
            Class.forName("sun.jdbc.odbc.JdbcOdbcDriver");
```

```
        } catch(java.lang.ClassNotFoundException e) {
            System.err.print("ClassNotFoundException: ");
            System.err.println(e.getMessage());
        }
        try {
            con = DriverManager.getConnection(url, "admin", "admin");
            stmt = con.createStatement();
            ResultSet rs = stmt.executeQuery(sqlstr);
            ResultSetMetaData rsmd = rs.getMetaData();
            int numberOfColumns = rsmd.getColumnCount();
            int rowCount = 1;
            while (rs.next()) {
                out.println("Row " + rowCount + ":   ");
                for (int i = 1; i <= numberOfColumns; i++) {
                    out.print("   Column " + i + ": ");
                    out.println(rs.getString(i));
                }
                out.println("");
                rowCount++;
            }
            out.println("EndOfRecord");
            stmt.close();
            con.close();
        } catch(SQLException ex) {
            System.err.print("SQLException: ");
            System.err.println(ex.getMessage());
            out.println("No result.");
            out.println("EndOfRecord");
        }
    }
}
```

Compile and test the programs

The following steps are used to compile and execute the example:

- Compile all the Java programs.

- Execute the server program *SDB* class first.

- Execute the applet via the `applet.html` using the *appletviewer* browser.

Note that the server's host IP address is hard-coded into the `Client-Applet.java` program. It can be changed to any host address that the server is running. Of course, the applet program has to be re-compiled. This address can be easily entered as a parameter of the program.

12.7 Summary

In this chapter, we introduced the Web-based database (WBDB) concepts and classified the WBDB architecture into two-tier architecture, three-tier architecture, and hybrid architecture according to the database access methods. Then the existing tecnologies used in WBDB were introduced as different generations, i.e., technologies for the traditional Web (Generation 1), the fast and more interactive Web (Generation 2), the Java-based Web (Generation 3), and a new generation.

Based on these introductions, we discussed the challenges and provided some solutions for current WBDB. We also pictured a future framework of WBDB, which serves interaction and valuable data retrieval, and presented function descriptions of three layers. Through describing the services of three layers in the later framework, we proposed that the intelligent or semantic queries will be the new trend on the basis of a semantic Web. Besides, agent-based services occupy more and more important roles in the WBDB areas of scalability and extensibility. Finally, we addressed how to develop WBDB applications using JDBC. The JDBC package is a set of Java classes that can be used by applications to make database calls on the Internet. Examples presented in the chapter show that the development of WBDB using JDBC is quite interesting and convenient.

Exercises

12.1   What challenges are faced by the Web? 12.1.1

12.2   What functions does the WBDB achieve? 12.1.2

12.3   What components compose the three-tier architecture of WBDB? Describe their functions. 12.2.2

12.4   Describe the advantages and disadvantages of the CGI approach. 12.3.2

12.5   What is the Generation 2 technology for WBDB? Describe its process step. 12.3.3

12.6   What is JDBC? How does it work? 12.3.4.1

12.7   What is XQL? What is it for? 12.3.5.1

12.8   Why can we use mobile agents in Internet applications? 12.3.5.2

12.9   Why does the author say that CORBA is probably the best choice for implementing middleware in the WBDB applications? 12.3.6.1

12.10 What challenges are faced by WBDB access services? 12.4.2

12.11 What are Agentlets? What can they do? 12.5.1

12.12 What components are included in the JDBC package? 12.6.1

12.13 Re-write the program in 12.6.2 to create the database *'dbtest.db'* again by adding a MANUFACTURER table and a column of P_MANUFACTURER in the table PRODUCT. The columns of MANUFACTURER table are M_NAME, M_ADDR, M_PRODUCTS and M_NUMBER.

12.14 Use the updated database to rewrite the JDBC application in 12.6.3

This page intentionally left blank

CHAPTER 13 MOBILE COMPUTING

Mobile computing requires wireless communication, mobility and portability. In the past few years, we have seen an explosion of mobile devices over the world such as notebooks, multimedia PDA and mobile phones. The rapidly expanding markets for cellular voice and limited data service have created a great demand for mobile communication and computing. Mobile communications applications include mobile computing and wireless communications. Many of the advances in communications involve the use of Internet Protocol (IP), Asynchronous Transfer Mode (ATM), and ad hoc network protocols. Recently much focus has been directed at advancing communication technology in the area of mobile wireless networks especially on the IP based wireless networks. This chapter focuses on two major issues: Mobile IP and mobile multicast and anycast applications.

13.1   Introduction

It is known that IP nodes - hosts and routers - use their routing table to make packet forwarding decisions based on the packet header network prefix of the IP destination address. This implies that all nodes with interfaces on a given link must have identical network-prefix portions of their IP addresses on those interfaces.

To see the problem with this scenario, let us examine what happens if a host whose network-prefix has been assigned to one link, disconnects from that link and then connects to a new link, which has been assigned a different network-connection as shown in Figure 13.1 below:

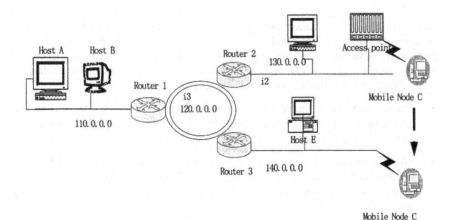

Figure 13.1. Example of Mobile Applications

Now suppose mobile node C has been moved from LAN 130.0.0 to 140.0.0. At this moment, host A initiates a packet to mobile node C. Following the IP routing procedure, the following steps are taken:

1. A sends a packet destined to router 1 with network-prefix = 120.0.0 (i.e., destination address 120.0.0.4) and IP source address (110.0.0.1).

2. Router 1 finds an entry of the destination with network-prefix 120.0.0. in the row of its routing table, which specifies a next-hop of Router 2 (130.0.0) via interface "i3".

3. Router 2 has a direct route in its routing table for the destination with network prefix equal to 120.0.0, so Router 2 transmits the packet via interface i2 to LAN 2. However, the packet cannot be delivered based upon the network prefix as mobile node C has been disconnected from the LAN 2. Router 2 will then send an ICMP Host Unreachable error message back to the source of the packets - Host A.

Methods to solve the problem

By host-specific routes: Solving this problem by changing all routers' specific routes. This may require all routers on the routes for a mobile host to change their routing tables. The solution is not scalable and thus not feasible as the changing routes cost too much. If there are many mobile hosts roaming on the Internet, each of the mobile nodes needs a specific route, then there are thousands of such modifications for each router. Besides the cost, the change of the routes is not secure and not robust.

Just changethe the mobile node's IP address: This approach does not solve the problem. Once a mobile node moves from one lihk to another, the "foreign link" must assign a new address to the mobile node with the network prefix identical to the local network prefix. But there are several problems associated: how does a host, once it wants to transmit a message to a mobile node, know the new IP address of the node. When the mobile node keeps changing, the problem gets even more serious.

Only need nomadicity: Like mobile phones, if all the communications are initiated by users, the users do not mind restarting the applications. Then in this case, the nomadicity is indeed sufficient and mobility is not absolutely necessary. However, there are many applications that must not be re-started when a mobile node changes links. Many of them involve the virtues of using a fixed IP address:

• Many applications have configuration databases, which depend on IP addresses, as opposed to hostnames. In the presence of rapidly changing IP, addresses, those applications would break down.

• There is sufficient reason to believe that servers, not just clients, would need to become mobile (such as military, remote medicine and remote mine detection and disaster relief etc). Apparently, those servers cannot be allowed to stop service during mobility.

- Some application vendors provide network-licensing systems, which restrict access to only those nodes possessing specific ranges of IP addresses. Without mobile IP, a nomadic node, which changes link and IP addresses, will no longer be able to obtain a license over the network to use these applications.

- Some security mechanisms provide access-privileges to nodes based upon their IP address. Mobile nodes employing Mobile IP allow such mechanisms to work in the presence of node mobility.

- Maintaining a pool of addresses for assignment to nomadic nodes can be difficult, and in some cases no assignment mechanism might be available [Soloman 1998].

Mobile IP

Mobile IP provides an efficient, scalable mechanism for node mobility within the Internet. Using Mobile IP, nodes may change their point-of-attachment to the Internet without changing their IP address. This allows them to maintain transport and higher-layer connections while moving. Node mobility is realized without the need to propagate host-specific routes throughout the Internet routing fabric. The protocol is documented in Proposed Standard IETF Working Group RFC documents [Perkins 1996b]. The physical constraints of mobile communications typically include low bandwidth of link layer connection, high error rates, and temporary disconnection.

This section discusses the applicability Mobile IP to provide host mobility on the Internet. In particular, the key features of Mobile IP based on [Solomon 1996] is described. Mobile IP allows transparent routing of IP packets to mobile nodes on the Internet. Each mobile node is always identified by its home address, regardless of its current point of attachment to the Internet. While situated away from its home, a mobile node is also associated with a care-of address (to be discuss later), which provides information about its current point of attachment to the Internet. The protocol provides for registering the care-of address with a home agent. The home agent sends datagrams destined for the mobile node through a tunnel to the care-of address. After arriving at the end of the tunnel, each datagram packet (we use packet and datagram interchangeably in this chapter) is then delivered to the mobile node [Perkins 1996b].

13.2 Overview of Mobile IP

Mobile IP executes the function of the network layer, Layer 3 of the Open Systems Interconnection (OSI) Model. The network layer is responsible for dynamically selecting a path from the original source of a packet to its ultimate destination. On the Internet, the network layer protocol is named Internet Protocol (IP), which relies on typical routing protocols to move the packet from one place to another. Examples of routing protocols include Open Shortest Path First (OSPF), the Routing Information Protocol (RIP), and the Border Gateway Protocol (BGP). As a network layer protocol, Mobile IP is completely independent of the media over which it runs. Thus a mobile node using Mobile IP can move from one type of medium to another without losing connectivity.

The requirements of Mobile IP are as follows:

1. A mobile node must be able to communicate with other nodes after changing its link-layer point-of-attachment to the Internet.

2. A mobile node must be able to communicate using only its home (permanent) IP address, regardless of its current link-layer point-of-attachment to the Internet.

3. A mobile node must be able to communicate with other computers that do not implement the Mobile IP mobility functions.

4. A mobile node must not be exposed to any new security threats over and above those to which a fixed node on the Internet is exposed.

In brief, Mobile IP routing works as follows. Packets destined to a mobile node are routed first to its home network—a network identified by the network prefix of the mobile node's (permanent) home address. At the home network, the mobile node's home agent intercepts such packets and tunnels them to the mobile node's most recently reported care-of address. At the endpoint of the tunnel, the inner packets are decapsulated and delivered to the mobile node. In the reverse direction, packets sourced by mobile nodes are routed to their destination using standard IP routing mechanisms [Soloman 1998].

Thus, Mobile IP relies on protocol tunneling to deliver packets to mobile nodes that are away from their home network. The mobile node's home address is hidden from routers along the path from the home agent to the mobile node due to the presence of the tunnel. The encapsulating packet is destined to the mobile node's care-of address, a topologically significant address, to which standard IP routing mechanisms can deliver packets.

The Mobile IP protocol defines the following: an authenticated registration procedure by which a mobile node informs its home agent(s) of its care-of address(es); an extension to ICMP Router Discovery [Deering 1991] which allows mobile nodes to discover prospective home agents and foreign agents; and the rules for routing packets to and from mobile nodes, including the specification of one mandatory tunneling mechanism [Perkins 1996a] and several optional tunneling mechanisms [Perkins 1994] [Hanks etal 1994].

Tunneling: A tunnel is the path followed by a first packet while it is encapsulated within the payload portion of the second packet, as shown in Figure 13.2.

The Mobile IP protocol places no additional constraints on the assignment of IP addresses. That is, a mobile node can be assigned an IP address by the organization that owns the machine. This protocol assumes that mobile nodes will not change their point of attachment to the Internet more frequently than once per second. This protocol assumes that IP unicast datagrams are routed based on the destination address in the datagram header (for example, by source address) [Perkins 1996b].

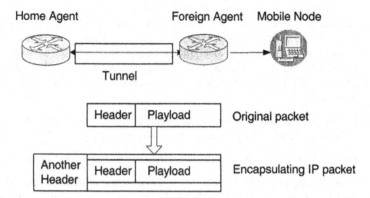

Figure 13.2. IP Tunneling

Mobile IP is intended to enable nodes to move from one IP subnet to another. It is just as suitable for mobility across homogeneous media as for mobility across heterogeneous media. Mobile IP introduces the following new functional entities:

- *Mobile Node:* A host or router that changes its point of attachment from one network or sub-network to another. A mobile node may change its location without changing its IP address; it may continue to communicate with other Internet nodes at any location using its (constant) IP address, assuming link-layer connectivity to a point of attachment is available.

- *Home Agent:* A router on a mobile node's home network, which tunnels datagrams for delivery to the mobile node when it is away from home, and maintains current location information for the mobile node.

- *Foreign Agent:* A router on a mobile node's visited network, which provides routing services to the mobile node while registered. The foreign agent de-tunnels and delivers datagrams to the mobile node that were tunneled by the mobile node's home agent. For datagrams sent by a mobile node, the foreign agent may serve as a default router for registered mobile nodes.

A mobile node is given with a long-term IP address on a home network. This home address is administered in the same way as a "permanent" IP address provided to a stationary host. When away from its home network, the mobile node is associated with a "care-of address" which reflects the mobile node's current point of attachment. The mobile node uses its home address as the source address of all IP datagrams that it sends.

To understand mobile IP well, we classify the following concepts:

- Agent Advertisement: An advertisement message constructed by attaching a special Extension to a router advertisement [Deering 1991] message.

- Authentication: The process of verifying (using cryptographic techniques, for all applications in this specification) the identity of the originator of a message.

- Care-of Address: The termination point of a tunnel toward a mobile node, for datagrams forwarded to the mobile node while it is away from home. The protocol can use two different types of care-of address: a "foreign agent care-of address" is an address of a foreign agent with which the mobile node is registered, and a "co-located care-of address" is an externally obtained local address which the mobile node has associated with one of its own network interfaces.

- Correspondent Node: A peer with which a mobile node is communicating. A correspondent node may be either mobile or stationary.

- Foreign Network: Any network other than the mobile node's Home Network.

- Home Address: An IP address that is assigned for an extended period of time to a mobile node. It remains unchanged regardless of where the node is attached to the Internet.

- Home Network: A network, possibly virtual, having a network prefix matching that of a mobile node's home address. Note that standard IP routing mechanisms will deliver datagrams destined to a mobile node's Home Address to the mobile node's Home Network.

- Link: A facility or medium over which nodes can communicate at the link layer. A link underlies the network layer.

- Link-Layer Address: The address used to identify an endpoint of some communication over a physical link. Typically, the Link-Layer address is an interface's Media Access Control (MAC) address.

- Mobility Agent: Either a home agent or a foreign agent.

- Mobility Binding: The association of a home address with a care-of address, along with the remaining lifetime of that association.

- Mobility Security Association: A collection of security contexts, between a pair of nodes, which may be applied to Mobile IP protocol messages exchanged between them. Each context indicates an authentication algorithm and mode, a secret (a shared key, or appropriate public/private key pair), and a style of replay protection in use. Security Parameter Index (SPI): An index identifying a security context between a pair of nodes among the contexts available in the Mobility Security Association. SPI values 0 through 255 are reserved and must not be used in any Mobility Security Association. Nonce: A randomly chosen value, different from previous choices, inserted in a message to protect against replays. Security issues will not be discussed in this chapter. Readers are referred to [Perkins 1998] for details.

- Node: A host or a router.

- Tunnel: The path followed by a datagram while it is encapsulated. The model is that, while it is encapsulated, a datagram is routed to a knowledgeable decapsulating agent, which decapsulates the datagram and then correctly delivers it to its ultimate destination.

- Virtual Network: A network with no physical instantiation beyond a router (with a physical network interface on another network). The router (e.g., a home agent) generally advertises reachability to the virtual network using conventional routing protocols.

- Visited Network: A network other than a mobile node's Home Network, to which the mobile node is currently connected.

- Visitor List: The list of mobile nodes visiting a foreign agent.

Mobile IP, in essence, is a way of doing three relatively separate functions [Perkins 1998]:

1. *Agent discovery:* Home agent and foreign agents may advertise their availability on each link for which they provide service. Thus a mobile node has to determine if it is currently connected to its home link or foreign link. A newly arrived mobile node must solicit an agent if one is present to provide connection service.

2. *Registration:* When a mobile node is away from its home network or it detects that it has changed its link of attachment from one network to another. Depending on its method of attachment, the mobile node will register either directly with its home agent or through a foreign agent, which will forward the registration to the home agent.

3. *Routing (tunneling):* The specific mechanisms by which packets are routed to and from a mobile node. In order for datagrams to be delivered to the mobile node when it is away from home, the home agent has to *tunnel* the datagrams to the care-of address.

The following steps provide a rough outline of operation of the Mobile IP protocol:

1. Mobility agents (i.e., foreign agents and home agents) advertise their presence via Agent Advertisement messages. A mobile node may optionally solicit an Agent Advertisement message from any locally attached mobility agents through an Agent Solicitation message.

2. A mobile node receives these Agent Advertisements and determines whether it is on its home network or a foreign network.

3. When the mobile node detects that it is located on its home network, it operates without mobility services. If returning to its home network from being registered elsewhere, the mobile node deregisters with its home agent, through exchange of a Registration Request and Registration Reply message with it.

4. When a mobile node detects that it has moved to a foreign network, it obtains a care-of address on the foreign network. The care-of address can either be determined from a foreign agent's advertisements (a foreign agent care-of address), or by some external assignment mechanism such as DHCP [Droms 1997] (a co-located care-of address).

5. The mobile node operating away from home then registers its new care-of address with its home agent through exchange of a Registration Request and

Registration Reply message with it, (possibly) via a foreign agent ([Perkins 1996b]).

6. Datagrams sent to the mobile node's home address are intercepted by its home agent, tunneled by the home agent to the mobile node's care-of address, received at the tunnel endpoint (either at a foreign agent or at the mobile node itself), and finally delivered to the mobile node.

7. In the reverse direction, datagrams sent by the mobile node are generally delivered to their destination using standard IP routing mechanisms, not necessarily passing through the home agent.

8. When away from home, Mobile IP uses protocol tunneling to hide a mobile node's home address from intervening routers between its home network and its current location. The tunnel terminates at the mobile node's care-of address. The care-of address must be an address to which datagrams can be delivered via conventional IP routing. At the care-of address, the original datagram is removed from the tunnel and delivered to the mobile node.

Mobile IP provides two alternative modes for the acquisition of a care-of address:

• A "foreign agent care-of address" is a care-of address provided by a foreign agent through its Agent Advertisement messages. In this case, the care-of address is an IP address of the foreign agent. In this mode, the foreign agent is the endpoint of the tunnel and, upon receiving tunneled datagrams, decapsulates them and delivers the inner datagram to the mobile node. This mode of acquisition is preferred because it allows many mobile nodes to share the same care-of address and therefore does not place unnecessary demands on the already limited IPv4 address space.

• A "co-located care-of address" is a care-of address acquired by the mobile node as a local IP address through some external means, which the mobile node then associates with one of its own network interfaces. The address may be dynamically acquired as a temporary address by the mobile node such as through DHCP [Droms 1997], or may be owned by the mobile node as a long-term address for its use only while visiting some foreign network. When using a co-located care-of address, the mobile node serves as the endpoint of the tunnel and itself performs decapsulation of the datagrams tunneled to it.

The mode of using a co-located care-of address has the advantage that it allows a mobile node to function without a foreign agent, for example, in networks that have not yet deployed a foreign agent. It does, however, place additional burden on the IPv4 address space because it requires a pool of addresses within the foreign network to be made available to visiting mobile nodes. It is difficult to efficiently maintain pools of addresses for each subnet that may permit mobile nodes to visit. It is important to understand the distinction between the care-of address and the foreign agent functions. The care-of address is simply the endpoint of the tunnel. It might indeed be an address of a foreign agent (a foreign agent care-of address), but it might instead be an address temporarily acquired by the mobile node (a co-located care-of address). A foreign agent, on the other hand, is a mobility agent that provides services to mobile nodes.

For example, Figure 13.3 illustrates the routing of packets to and from a mobile node away from home, once the mobile node has registered with its home agent. In Figure 13.4, the mobile node is using a foreign agent care-of address, not a co-located care-of address.

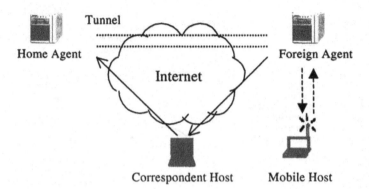

Figure 13.3. Operation of Mobile Node under Mobile IP

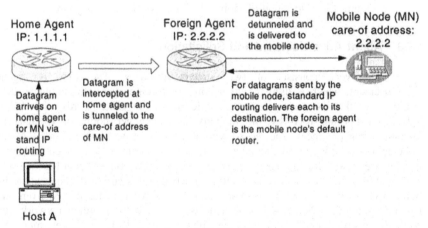

Figure 13.4. Operation of Mobile IP on care-of address

Similarly, a mobile node and a prospective or current foreign agent are able to exchange datagrams without relying on standard IP routing mechanisms; that is, those mechanisms that make forwarding decisions based upon the network-prefix of the destination address in the IP header. This requirement can be satisfied if the foreign agent and the visiting mobile node have an interface on the same link. In this case, the mobile node and foreign agent simply bypass their normal IP routing mechanism when sending datagrams to each other, addressing the underlying link-layer packets to their respective link-layer addresses. Other placements of the

378

foreign agent relative to the mobile node are also possible using other mechanisms to exchange datagrams between these nodes.

If a mobile node is using a co-located care-of address (as described in (2) above), the mobile node must be located on the link identified by the network prefix of this care-of address. Otherwise, datagrams destined to the care-of address would be undeliverable. As shown in the below figure:

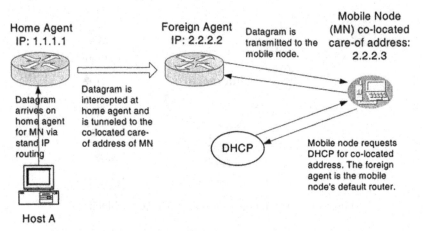

Figure 13.5. Operation of Mobile IP on collocated care-of address

13.3 Agent Advertisement and Solicitation

Agent Discovery consists of two simple messages. The first is Agent Advertisement, which is used by either home or foreign agents to announce their ability to make the connection to mobile nodes. In other words, the Agent Advertisements are used by the mobility agents (either home or foreign) to announce their presences. The second type of message of Agent Discovery is Agent Solicitation which is sent by mobile nodes that want to connect to an agent and have no paitence to wait for the next periodic advertisement to come. Agent Discovery is a method by which a mobile node determines whether it is currently connected to its home network or to a foreign network, and detects when it has moved from one network to another. When a mobile node is connected to a foreign network, the methods specified in this section also allow the mobile node to determine the foreign agent care-of address offered by each foreign agent on that network [Soloman 1998] [Perkins 1998].

Mobile IP extends ICMP Router Discovery [Deering 1991] as its primary mechanism for Agent Discovery. An Agent Advertisement is formed by including a Mobility Agent Advertisement Extension in an ICMP Router Advertisement message. An Agent Solicitation message is identical to an ICMP Router Solicitation, except that its IP TTL (time-to-live field) must be set to 1. This section describes the message formats and procedures by which mobile nodes, foreign agents, and home agents cooperate to realize the Agent Advertisement and

Solicitation may not be necessary for link layers that already provide this functionality.

```
+-+-+-+-+-+-+-+-+-+-+-+-+-+-+-+-+-+-+-+-+-+-+-+-+-+-+-+-+-+-+-+
|                  IP Header   Figure 13.6                    |
+-+-+-+-+-+-+-+-+-+-+-+-+-+-+-+-+-+-+-+-+-+-+-+-+-+-+-+-+-+-+-+
|    Type=9     |    Code      |        Checksum              |
+-+-+-+-+-+-+-+-+-+-+-+-+-+-+-+-+-+-+-+-+-+-+-+-+-+-+-+-+-+-+-+
|   Num Addrs   |Addr Entry Size|        Lifetime             |
+-+-+-+-+-+-+-+-+-+-+-+-+-+-+-+-+-+-+-+-+-+-+-+-+-+-+-+-+-+-+-+
|                   Router Address[1]                         |
+-+-+-+-+-+-+-+-+-+-+-+-+-+-+-+-+-+-+-+-+-+-+-+-+-+-+-+-+-+-+-+
|                  Preference Level[1]                        |
+-+-+-+-+-+-+-+-+-+-+-+-+-+-+-+-+-+-+-+-+-+-+-+-+-+-+-+-+-+-+-
|                            .                                |
|                            .                                |
|                            .                                |
+-+-+-+-+-+-+-+-+-+-+-+-+-+-+-+-+-+-+-+-+-+-+-+-+-+-+-+-+-+-+-+
|    Type=16    |    Length    |      Sequence Number         |
+-+-+-+-+-+-+-+-+-+-+-+-+-+-+-+-+-+-+-+-+-+-+-+-+-+-+-+-+-+-+-+
|   Registration Lifetime      |R|B|H|F|M|G|r|T|   reserved   |
+-+-+-+-+-+-+-+-+-+-+-+-+-+-+-+-+-+-+-+-+-+-+-+-+-+-+-+-+-+-+-+
|                zero or more Care-of Addresses               |
|                            ...                              |
```

Figure 13.6. ICMP Router Advertisement and Mobility Agent Advertisement
Extension Message [Deering 1991] [Perkins 1996b]

```
 0                   1                   2                   3
 0 1 2 3 4 5 6 7 8 9 0 1 2 3 4 5 6 7 8 9 0 1 2 3 4 5 6 7 8 9 0 1
+-+-+-+-+-+-+-+-+-+-+-+-+-+-+-+-+-+-+-+-+-+-+-+-+-+-+-+-+-+-+-+-+
| Vers=4 |  IHL   |Type of Services|        Total Length        |
+-+-+-+-+-+-+-+-+-+-+-+-+-+-+-+-+-+-+-+-+-+-+-+-+-+-+-+-+-+-+-+-+
|       Identification           |Flags|     Fragment Offset   |
+-+-+-+-+-+-+-+-+-+-+-+-+-+-+-+-+-+-+-+-+-+-+-+-+-+-+-+-+-+-+-+-+
|Time to Live=1  |Protocol=ICMP  |       Header Checksum        |
+-+-+-+-+-+-+-+-+-+-+-+-+-+-+-+-+-+-+-+-+-+-+-+-+-+-+-+-+-+-+-+-+
|       Source address = Mobile node's home address            |
+-+-+-+-+-+-+-+-+-+-+-+-+-+-+-+-+-+-+-+-+-+-+-+-+-+-+-+-+-+-+-+-
| Dest. address = 255.255.255.255 (bcast) or 224.0.0.2 (mcast) |
+-+-+-+-+-+-+-+-+-+-+-+-+-+-+-+-+-+-+-+-+-+-+-+-+-+-+-+-+-+-+-+-+
|    Type=10     |  Code=0       |         Checksum             |
+-+-+-+-+-+-+-+-+-+-+-+-+-+-+-+-+-+-+-+-+-+-+-+-+-+-+-+-+-+-+-+-+
|                          Reserved                            |
+-+-+-+-+-+-+-+-+-+-+-+-+-+-+-+-+-+-+-+-+-+-+-+-+-+-+-+-+-+-+-+-+
```

Figure 13.7. ICMP Router Solicitation Message [Deering 1991]

Agent Advertisements are transmitted by a mobility agent to advertise its services on a link. Mobile nodes use these advertisements to determine their current point of attachment to the Internet. An Agent Advertisement is an ICMP Router Advertisement that has been extended to also carry a Mobility Agent Advertisement Extension and, optionally, a Prefix-Lengths Extension, One-byte Padding Extension, or other Extensions that are defined in [Perkins 1996b]. Figure 13.6 depicts such a message and Figure 13.7 depicts a solicitation message.

In these messages, there are two types of fields listed as follows:

IP Fields:

- Source Address: An IP address belonging to the interface from which this message is sent.

- Destination Address: The configured Advertisement Address or the IP address of a neighboring host.

- Time-to-Live = 1 if the Destination Address is an IP multicast address; at least 1 otherwise.

ICMP Fields:

- Code = 0;

- Checksum: The 16-bit checksum is the complement sum of the ICMP message, starting with the ICMP Type. For computing the checksum, the Checksum field is set to 0.

- Addrs: The number of router addresses advertised in this message.

- Addr Entry Size: The number of 32-bit words of information per each router address (2, in the version of the protocol described here).

- Lifetime: The maximum number of seconds that the router addresses may be considered valid.

The ICMP Router Advertisement portion of the Agent Advertisement may contain one or more router addresses. An agent only puts its own addresses, if any, in the advertisement. Whether or not its own address appears in the Router Addresses, a foreign agent must route datagrams it receives from registered mobile nodes.

The Mobility Agent Advertisement Extension follows the ICMP Router Advertisement fields. It is used to indicate that an ICMP Router Advertisement message is also an Agent Advertisement being sent by a mobility agent. The Mobility Agent Advertisement Extension is defined as follows:

- Length = (6 + 4*N), where 6 accounts for the number of bytes in the Sequence Number, Registration Lifetime, flags, and reserved fields, and N is the number of care-of addresses advertised.

- Sequence Number: The count of Agent Advertisement messages sent since the agent was initialized [Perkins 1996b].

- Registration Lifetime: The longest lifetime (measured in seconds) that this agent is willing to accept in any Registration Request. A value of 0xffff indicates infinity. This field has no relation to the "Lifetime" field within the ICMP Router Advertisement portion of the Agent Advertisement.

- R: Registration required. Registration with this foreign agent (or another foreign agent on this link) is required even when using a co-located care-of address.

- B: Busy. The foreign agent will not accept registrations from additional mobile nodes.

- H: Home agent. This agent offers service as a home agent on the link on which this Agent Advertisement message is sent.

- F: Foreign agent. This agent offers service as a foreign agent on the link on which this Agent Advertisement message is sent.

- M: Minimal encapsulation. This agent implements receiving tunneled datagrams that use minimal encapsulation [Perkins 1994].

- G: GRE encapsulation. This agent implements receiving tunneled datagrams that use GRE encapsulation [Hanks et al 1994].

- r : Sent as zero; ignored on reception. Not allocated for any other uses.

- T: Foreign agent supports reverse tunneling.

- Reserved: Sent as zero; ignored on reception.

- Care-of Address(es): The advertised foreign agent care-of address(es) provided by this foreign agent. An Agent Advertisement must include at least one care-of address if the 'F' bit is set. The number of care-of addresses presented is determined by the Length field in the Extension.

13.3.1 Foreign Agent and Home Agent

Any mobility agent, which cannot be discovered by a link-layer protocol, must send Agent Advertisements. An agent, which can be discovered by a link-layer protocol, should also implement Agent Advertisements. However, the Advertisements need not be sent, except when the site policy requires registration with the agent (i.e., when the 'R' bit is set), or as a response to a specific Agent Solicitation. All mobility agents must process packets that they receive addressed to the Mobile-Agents multicast group, at address 224.0.0.11. A mobile node may send an Agent Solicitation to 224.0.0.11. All mobility agents should respond to Agent Solicitations.

The same procedures, defaults, and constants are used in Agent Advertisement messages and Agent Solicitation messages as specified for ICMP Router Discovery [Deering 1991]. The following exception must be considered:

- A mobility agent must limit the rate at which it sends broadcast or multicast Agent Advertisements; the maximum rate should be chosen so that the Advertisements do not consume a significant amount of network bandwidth.

- A mobility agent that receives a Router Solicitation must not require that the IP Source Address be the address of a neighbor (i.e., an address that matches one of the router's own addresses on the arrival interface, under the subnet mask associated with that address of the router).

- A mobility agent may be configured to send Agent Advertisements only in response to an Agent Solicitation message.

If the home network is a virtual network, the home network has no physical realization external to the home agent itself. In this case, there is no physical network link on which to send Agent Advertisement messages advertising the home agent. Mobile nodes for which this is the home network are always treated as being away from home.

Home agents and foreign agents must support tunneling datagrams using IP in IP encapsulation [Perkins 1996a]. Any mobile node that uses a co-located care-of address must support receiving datagrams tunneled using IP in IP encapsulation. Minimal encapsulation [Perkins 1994] and GRE encapsulation [Hanks et al 1994] are alternate encapsulation methods, which may optionally be supported by mobility agents and mobile nodes. The use of these alternative forms of encapsulation, when requested by the mobile node, is otherwise at the discretion of the home agent.

13.3.2 Mobile Node Considerations

Every mobile node must implement *Agent Solicitation*. Solicitations are sent in the absence of Agent Advertisements and when a care-of address has not been determined through a link-layer protocol or other means. The mobile node uses the same procedures, defaults, and constants for Agent Solicitation as specified for ICMP Router Solicitation messages [Deering 1991], except that the mobile node may solicit more often than once every three seconds, and that a mobile node that is currently not connected to any foreign agent may solicit more times than MAX_SOLICITATIONS.

The rate at which a mobile node sends Solicitations must be limited by the mobile node. The mobile node may send three initial Solicitations at a maximum rate of one per second while searching for an agent. After this, the rate at which Solicitations are sent is reduced so as to limit the overhead on the local link. Subsequent Solicitations must be sent using a binary exponential backoff mechanism, i.e., doubling the interval between consecutive Solicitations, up to a maximum interval. The maximum interval should be chosen appropriately based upon the characteristics of the media over which the mobile node is soliciting. This maximum interval should be at least one minute between Solicitations.

While still searching for an agent, the mobile node must not increase the rate at which it sends Solicitations unless it has received a positive indication that it has moved to a new link. After successfully registering with an agent, the mobile node should also increase the rate at which it will send Solicitations when it next begins searching for a new agent with which to register. The increased solicitation rate may revert to the maximum rate, but then must be limited in the manner described above. In all cases, the recommended solicitation intervals are nominal values. Mobile nodes must randomize their solicitation times around these nominal values as specified for ICMP Router Discovery [Deering 1991].

Mobile nodes have to process received Agent Advertisements. A mobile node can distinguish an Agent Advertisement message from other uses of the ICMP Router Advertisement message by examining the number of advertised addresses and the IP Total Length field. When the IP total length indicates that the ICMP message is longer than needed for the number of advertised addresses, the remaining data is interpreted as one or more Extensions. The presence of a Mobility Agent Advertisement Extension identifies the advertisement as an Agent Advertisement.

If there is more than one advertised address, the mobile node should pick the first address for its initial registration attempt. If the registration attempt fails with a status Code indicating rejection by the foreign agent, the mobile node may retry the attempt with each subsequent advertised address in turn.

Note that the mobile node receives an Agent Advertisement with the 'R' bit set; the mobile node should register through the foreign agent, even when the mobile node might be able to acquire its own co-located care-of address. This feature is intended to allow sites to enforce visiting policies (such as accounting), which require exchanges of authorization.

If formerly reserved bits require some kind of monitoring/enforcement at the foreign link, foreign agents implementing the new specification for the formerly reserved bits can set the 'R' bit. This has the effect of forcing the mobile node to register through the foreign agent, so the foreign agent could then monitor/enforce the policy.

13.3.3 Move Detection

Two primary mechanisms are provided for mobile nodes to detect when they have moved from one subnet to another. Other mechanisms may also be used. When the mobile node detects that it has moved, it should register (next subsection) with a suitable care-of address on the new foreign network. However, the mobile node must not register more frequently than once per second on average. The following algorithm is presented for the move detection:

> The first method of move detection is based upon the Lifetime field within the main body of the ICMP Router Advertisement portion of the Agent Advertisement. A mobile node should record the Lifetime received in any Agent Advertisements, until that Lifetime expires. If the mobile node fails to receive another advertisement from the same agent within the specified Lifetime, it should assume that it has lost contact with that agent. If the mobile node has previously received an Agent Advertisement from another agent for which the Lifetime field has not yet expired, the mobile node may immediately attempt registration with that other agent. Otherwise, the mobile node should attempt to discover a new agent with which to register.

384
13.3.4 Returning Home

A mobile node can detect that it has returned to its home network when it receives an Agent Advertisement from its own home agent. If so, it should deregister with its home agent. Before attempting to deregister, the mobile node should configure its routing table appropriately for its home network.

13.4 Registration

Mobile IP registration provides a flexible mechanism for mobile nodes to communicate their current reachability information to their home agent. A mobile node registers whenever it detects that its point-of-attachment to the network has changed from one link to another. Registration is a process by which a mobile node

- Requests datagram routing service from a foreign agent of a foreign link;

- Informs its home agent of its care-of address for the specified Lifetime;

- Renews a registration which is due to expire; and

- Deregisters when it returns to its home network.

Furthermore registration creates or modifies a mobility binding at the home agent, associating the mobile node. Several other (optional) capabilities are available through the registration procedure, which enables a mobile node to:

- Discover its home address, if the mobile node is not configured with this information;

- Maintain multiple simultaneous registrations, so that a copy of each datagram will be tunneled to each active care-of address;

- Deregister specific care-of addresses while retaining other mobility bindings, and

- Discover the address of a home agent if the mobile node is not configured with this information.

13.4.1 Registration Overview

Mobile IP defines two different registration procedures, one via a foreign agent that relays the registration to the mobile node's home agent, and one directly with the mobile node's home agent. The following rules determine which of these two registration procedures to use in any particular circumstance:

- If a mobile node is registering a foreign agent care-of address, the mobile node must register via that foreign agent.

- If a mobile node is using a co-located care-of address, and receives an Agent Advertisement from a foreign agent on the link on which it is using this care-of address, the mobile node should register via that foreign agent (or via another foreign agent on this link) if the 'R' bit is set in the received Agent Advertisement message.

- If a mobile node is otherwise using a co-located care-of address, the mobile node must register directly with its home agent.

- If a mobile node has returned to its home network and is (de)registering with its home agent, the mobile node must register directly with its home agent.

Both registration procedures involve the exchange of Registration Request and Registration Reply messages. When registering via a foreign agent, the registration procedure requires four messages as shown below as well as in Figure 13.8.

1. The mobile node sends a Registration Request to the prospective foreign agent to begin the registration process.

2. The foreign agent processes the Registration Request and then relays it to the home agent.

3. The home agent sends a Registration Reply to the foreign agent to grant or deny the Request.

4. The foreign agent processes the Registration Reply and then relays it to the mobile node to inform it of the disposition of its Request.

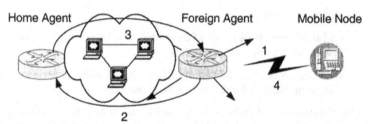

Figure 13.8. The mobility agents (either home or foreign) multicast Agent Advertisement. 1 means that mobile node sends Registration Request to home agent via foreign agent; 2 represents that the foreign agent passes the request to the home agent; 3 is that home agent send back Registration Reply via foreign agent; 4 is that the final reply is sent to the mobile node about success or denial of the request.

When the mobile node registers directly with its home agent, the registration procedure requires only the following two messages:

1. The mobile node sends a Registration Request to the home agent.

2. The home agent sends a Registration Reply to the mobile node, granting or denying the Request.

13.4.2 Responses to Registration Request and Authentication

Foreign Agent

In Figure 13.8, it is assumed that the mobile node is registering through a foreign agent; otherwise, it just registers directly through the home agent. The foreign agent, upon reception of the request, will perform validity checks on the request (like UDP packet check, see [Perkins 1998]). The foreign agent can also reject the request by sending Registration Reply directly to the mobile node with a *Code* field indicating the cause of the rejection. The reasons and the Codes are listed in Table 13.1.

Home Agent

Upon receipt of a Registration Request, a home agent performs a set of validity checks. Mostly, the *authentication checks* may invalidate the Registration Request if the authentication fails. In this case, the home agent also responds to the request by sending back a Registration Reply with appropriate code as listed in Table 13.1.

If the Registration Request (RR) is valid, the home agent updates the mobile node's binding entry(s) according to specified Care-of Address, Mobile Node's Home Address, Lifetime and S fields (Figure 13.9) depending on the request. The action of the home agent is illustrated below (as Table 5-2 of [Soloman 1998]):

1. If RR-filed Care-of Address $\neq$ home address then

2.   If Lifetime > 0 then

3.   If S-bit = 0 then Replace all of the mobile node's existing bindings (if any) with the specific care-of address;

4.   else Create a binding for the specified care-of address, leaving any other existing binding for the mobile node unmodified.

5.   else (Lifetime = 0) If S-bit = 1 then delete the mobile node's binding for the specified care-of address, leaving any other existing binding unmodified.

6.   else (RR-filed Care-of Address = home address)

7.   Delete all of the mobile node's bindings.

Authentication

Each mobile node, foreign agent, and home agent must be able to support a mobility security association for mobile entities, indexed by their SPI and IP address. In the case of the mobile node, this must be its Home Address. Registration messages between a mobile node and its home agent must be authenticated with an authorization-enabling extension, e.g. the Mobile-Home Authentication Extension (see [Perkins 1996b]).

13.4.3 Registration Related Message Format

There are mainly two types of message related to registration: *registration request* and *registration reply*.

13.4.3.1 Registration Request

A mobile node registers with its home agent using a Registration Request message so that its home agent can create or modify a mobility binding for that mobile node (e.g., with a new lifetime). The Request may be relayed to the home agent by the foreign agent through which the mobile node is registering, or it may be sent directly to the home agent in the case in which the mobile node is registering a co-located care-of address. Source Port can be any variable and Destination Port = 434. The UDP header is followed by the Mobile IP fields shown below:

```
 0                   1                   2                   3
 0 1 2 3 4 5 6 7 8 9 0 1 2 3 4 5 6 7 8 9 0 1 2 3 4 5 6 7 8 9 0 1
+-+-+-+-+-+-+-+-+-+-+-+-+-+-+-+-+-+-+-+-+-+-+-+-+-+-+-+-+-+-+-+-+
| Vers=4 | IHL   |Type of Services|      Total Length           |
+-+-+-+-+-+-+-+-+-+-+-+-+-+-+-+-+-+-+-+-+-+-+-+-+-+-+-+-+-+-+-+-+
|      Identification           |Flags|      Fragment Offset    |
+-+-+-+-+-+-+-+-+-+-+-+-+-+-+-+-+-+-+-+-+-+-+-+-+-+-+-+-+-+-+-+-+
|Time to Live   |Protocol=UDP   |       Header Checksum         |
+-+-+-+-+-+-+-+-+-+-+-+-+-+-+-+-+-+-+-+-+-+-+-+-+-+-+-+-+-+-+-+-+
|                      Source address                           |
+-+-+-+-+-+-+-+-+-+-+-+-+-+-+-+-+-+-+-+-+-+-+-+-+-+-+-+-+-+-+-+-|
|                   Destination  address                        |
+-+-+-+-+-+-+-+-+-+-+-+-+-+-+-+-+-+-+-+-+-+-+-+-+-+-+-+-+-+-+-+-+
|        Source Port            |   Destination Port = 434       |
+-+-+-+-+-+-+-+-+-+-+-+-+-+-+-+-+-+-+-+-+-+-+-+-+-+-+-+-+-+-+-+-+
|        Lengt                  |         Checksum               |
+-+-+-+-+-+-+-+-+-+-+-+-+-+-+-+-+-+-+-+-+-+-+-+-+-+-+-+-+-+-+-+-+
|    Type=1     |S|B|D|M|G|r|T|x|           Lifetime             |
+-+-+-+-+-+-+-+-+-+-+-+-+-+-+-+-+-+-+-+-+-+-+-+-+-+-+-+-+-+-+-+-+
|                      Home Address                             |
+-+-+-+-+-+-+-+-+-+-+-+-+-+-+-+-+-+-+-+-+-+-+-+-+-+-+-+-+-+-+-+-+
|                      Home Agent                               |
+-+-+-+-+-+-+-+-+-+-+-+-+-+-+-+-+-+-+-+-+-+-+-+-+-+-+-+-+-+-+-+-+
|                   Care-of Address                             |
+-+-+-+-+-+-+-+-+-+-+-+-+-+-+-+-+-+-+-+-+-+-+-+-+-+-+-+-+-+-+-+-+
|                   Identification                              |
+-+-+-+-+-+-+-+-+-+-+-+-+-+-+-+-+-+-+-+-+-+-+-+-+-+-+-+-+-+-+-+-+
| Optional Extensions ...                                       |
+-+-+-+-+-+-+-+-+-+-+-+-+-+-+-+-+-+-+-+-+-+-+-+-+-+-+-+-+-+-+-+-+
|    Type=32    |    Length     |    Security Parameter ...      |
+-+-+-+-+-+-+-+-+-+-+-+-+-+-+-+-+-+-+-+-+-+-+-+-+-+-+-+-+-+-+-+-+
|    ... Index (SPI)            |                                |
|        Authenticator (Default equals Keyed MD5) [RFC2002]     |
+-+-+-+-+-+-+-+-+-+-+-+-+-+-+-+-+-+-+-+-+-+-+-+-+-+-+-+-+-+-+-+-+
```

Figure 13.9. The message format of Registration Request and Mobile-Foreign Authentication Extension. This Extension may be included in Registration Requests and Replies in cases in which a mobility security association exists between the mobile node and the foreign agent.

Illustration of the message fields:

- S: Simultaneous bindings. If the 'S' bit is set, the mobile node is requesting that the home agent retain its prior mobility bindings, as described before.

- B: Broadcast datagrams. If the 'B' bit is set, the mobile node requests that the home agent tunnel to it any broadcast datagrams that it receives on the home network.

- D: Decapsulation by mobile node. If the 'D' bit is set, the mobile node will itself decapsulate datagrams which are sent to the care-of address. That is, the mobile node is using a co-located care-of address.

- M: Minimal encapsulation. If the 'M' bit is set, the mobile node requests that its home agent use minimal encapsulation [Perkins 1994] for datagrams tunneled to the mobile node.

- G: GRE encapsulation. If the 'G' bit is set, the mobile node requests that its home agent use GRE encapsulation [Hanks et al 1994] for datagrams tunneled to the mobile node.

- r: Sent as zero; ignored on reception, should not be allocated for any other uses.

- T: Reverse Tunneling requested; see [RFC3024].

- x: Sent as zero; ignored on reception.

- Lifetime: The number of seconds remaining before the registration is considered expired. A value of zero indicates a request for deregistration. A value of 0xffff indicates infinity.

- Home Address: The IP address of the mobile node.

- Home Agent: The IP address of the mobile node's home agent.

- Care-of Address: The IP address for the end of the tunnel.

- Identification: A 64-bit number, constructed by the mobile node, used for matching Registration Requests with Registration Replies, and for protecting against replay attacks of registration messages.

- Extensions: The fixed portion of the Registration Request is followed by one or more of the Extensions. An authorization-enabling extension must be included in all Registration Requests. See [Perkins 1996b] for further information on the relative order in which different extensions appear.

13.4.3.2 Registration Reply

A mobility agent returns a Registration Reply message to a mobile node, which has sent a Registration Request message. If the mobile node is requesting service from a foreign agent, that foreign agent will receive the Reply from the home agent and subsequently relay it to the mobile node. The Reply message contains the necessary codes to inform the mobile node about the status of its Request, along with the lifetime granted by the home agent, which may be smaller than the original Request. The foreign agent must not increase the Lifetime selected by the mobile node in the Registration Request, since the Lifetime is covered by an authentication extension which enables authorization by the home agent. Such an extension contains authentication data which cannot be correctly (re)computed by the foreign agent. The home agent must not increase the Lifetime selected by the mobile node in the Registration Request, since doing so could increase it beyond the maximum Registration Lifetime allowed by the foreign agent. If the Lifetime received in the Registration Reply is greater than that in the Registration Request, the Lifetime in the Request must be used. When the Lifetime received in the Registration Reply is less than that in the Registration Request, the Lifetime in the Reply must be used. The UDP header is followed by the Mobile IP fields shown below:

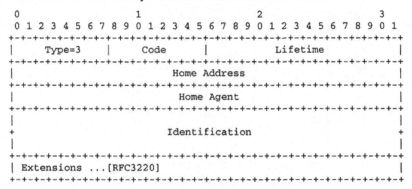

Figure 13.10. The message format of Registration Reply

Illustration of the message:

- Code: A value indicating the result of the Registration Request. See Table 13.1 for a list of currently defined code values.

- Lifetime: If the Code field indicates that the registration was accepted, the Lifetime field is set to the number of seconds remaining before the registration is considered expired. A value of zero indicates that the mobile node has been deregistered. A value of 0xffff indicates infinity. If the Code field indicates that the registration was denied, the contents of the Lifetime field are unspecified and must be ignored on reception.

- Home Address: The IP address of the mobile node.

- Home Agent: The IP address of the mobile node's home agent.

- Identification: A 64-bit number used for matching Registration Requests with Registration Replies, and for protecting against replay attacks of registration messages. The value is based on the Identification field from the Registration Request message from the mobile node, and on the style of replay protection used in the security context between the mobile node and its home agent (defined by the mobility security association between them, and SPI value in the authorization-enabling extension).

- Extensions: The fixed portion of the Registration Reply is followed by one or more of the Extensions listed [RFC3220].

The following table defines usage within the Code field.

Table 13.1. The Code field of Registration Reply

0	Registration accepted;
1	Registration accepted, but simultaneous mobility bindings unsupported
	Registration denied by the foreign agent:
64	Reason unspecified
65	Administratively prohibited
66	Insufficient resources
67	Mobile node failed authentication
68	Home agent failed authentication
69	Requested Lifetime too long
70	Poorly formed Request
71	Poorly formed Reply
72	Requested encapsulation unavailable
73	Reserved and unavailable
77	Invalid care-of address
78	Registration timeout
80	Home network unreachable (ICMP error received)
81	Home agent host unreachable (ICMP error received)
82	Home agent port unreachable (ICMP error received)
88	Home agent unreachable (other ICMP error received)
	Registration denied by the home agent:
128	Reason unspecified
129	Administratively prohibited
130	Insufficient resources
131	Mobile node failed authentication
132	Foreign agent failed authentication
133	Registration Identification mismatch
134	Poorly formed Request
135	Too many simultaneous mobility bindings
136	Unknown home agent address

13.5 Mobile Routing (Tunnelling)

The previous two subsections discussed the two important issues: (1) How a mobile node to know to which agent it can attach (Agent Discovery) and (2) How the mobile node informs its home agent of its current location using the registration procedure described in the Registration section. This section describes how mobile nodes, home agents, and (possibly) foreign agents cooperate to route datagrams to/from mobile nodes that are connected to a foreign network.

13.5.1 Packet Routing when Mobile Node is at Home

This case is simple, when connected to its home network, a mobile node operates without the support of mobility services. The packets are routed to the mobile node's home link just like the normal IP routing to the network prefix. Thus no special routing procedure is required in order to deliver the datagram packets to the mobile node when it is at home.

Some mobile node routing implementations store a copy of the mobile node's "home routing table entries" in the routing table but it must be noted when the network topology changes, the routing table may not be able to quickly respond to the change of default router for the mobile nodes. That is, it operates in the same way as any other (fixed) host or router does.

13.5.2 Packet Routing when Mobile Node is on a Foreign Link

13.5.2.1 Unicast Datagram Routing

This method is used when the mobile node is away from home and using a care-of address or co-located care-of address. The procedure of routing a packet to the mobile node that is connected to the foreign link is summarized as follows:

1. A router on the home link, possibly the home agent, sends *Agent Advertisement,* advertising reachability to the network-prefix, which equals the mobile node's home address.

2. Packets destined to the mobile node's home address are routed to its home link, specifically to its home agent.

3. The home agent intercepts packets destined to the mobile node, assuming the mobile node has registered one or more care-of addresses, and tunnels a copy to each such care-of address.

4. At each care-of address, i.e., an address of a foreign agent or an address collocated within the mobile node itself, the original packet is extracted from the tunnel and delivered to the mobile node.

When registered on a foreign network, the mobile node chooses a default router. There are two cases: mobile node on the foreign link with care-of address and collocated care-of address:

1. If the mobile node is registered using a foreign agent *care-of address,* it may use its foreign agent as a first-hop router. The foreign agent's address can be learned from *Agent Advertisement.* Otherwise, the mobile node must choose its

default router from among the Router Addresses advertised in the ICMP *Router Advertisement* portion of that *Agent Advertisement* message.

2. If the mobile node is registered directly with its home agent using a co-located care-of address, then the mobile node should choose its default router from among those advertised in any ICMP Router *Advertisement* message that it receives for which its externally obtained care-of address and the Router Address match under the network prefix. If the mobile node's externally obtained care-of address matches the IP source address of the Agent Advertisement under the network prefix, the mobile node may also consider that IP source address as another possible choice for the IP address of a default router.

Home Agent Routing

Both cases require the home agent to tunnel/de-tunnel the packet to/from the mobile node. Whenever the home agent receives a packet destined to the mobile node, it encapsulates an outer header (as shown in Figure13.2) destined with the (collocated) care-of address learnt from the registration of the mobile node and tunnels the packet to the default router of the mobile node. More specifically, when a home agent receives a datagram packet, intercepted for one of its mobile nodes registered away from home, the home agent examines the datagram to check if it is already encapsulated. If so, special rules apply in the forwarding of that datagram to the mobile node:

*   If the inner (encapsulated) Destination Address is the same as the outer Destination Address (the mobile node), then the home agent also examines the outer Source Address of the encapsulated packet (the source address of the tunnel). If this outer Source Address is the same as the mobile node's current care-of address, the home agent has to discard that packet in order to prevent a likely routing loop. If, instead, the outer Source Address is not the same as the mobile node's current care-of address, then the home agent will forward the packet to the mobile node. In order to forward the packet in this case, the home agent may simply alter the outer Destination Address to the care-of address, rather than re-encapsulating the packet.

*   Otherwise (the inner Destination Address is not the same as the outer Destination Address), the home agent should encapsulate the packet again (nested encapsulation), with the new outer Destination Address set equal to the mobile node's care-of address. That is, the home agent forwards the entire packet to the mobile node in the same way as any other packet (encapsulated already or not).

Foreign Agent Routing

Upon receipt of an encapsulated packet sent to its advertised care-of address, a foreign agent compares the inner destination address to those entries in its visitor list (whenever a mobile node registers successfully, the home address of the mobile node is bounded in the list). When the destination does not match the address of any mobile node currently in the visitor list, the foreign agent does not forward the packet without modifications to the original IP header (because otherwise a routing loop is likely to result). The packet is discarded. Otherwise, the foreign agent forwards the decapsulated packet to the mobile node.

Each foreign agent also supports the mandatory features for reverse tunneling [RFC3024] to home network. In this case, the home agent must assume the mobile node is at home and simply forwards the packet directly onto the home network. For multi-homed home agents, the source address in the outer IP header of the encapsulated packet must be the address sent to the mobile node in the home agent field of the registration reply. That is, the home agent cannot use the address of some other network interface as the source address. Nodes implementing tunneling also implement the "tunnel soft state" mechanism [RFC2003], which allows ICMP error messages returned from the tunnel to correctly be reflected back to the original senders of the tunneled packets.

If the Lifetime for a given mobility binding expires before the home agent has received another valid Registration Request for that mobile node, then that binding is deleted from the mobility binding list. The home agent does not send any Registration Reply message simply because the mobile node's binding has expired. The entry in the visitor list of the mobile node's current foreign agent will expire naturally, probably at the same time as the binding expired at the home agent. When a mobility binding's lifetime expires, the home agent must delete the binding, but it must retain any other (non-expired) simultaneous mobility bindings that it holds for the mobile node.

Broadcast Datagram Packets

When a home agent receives a broadcast packet, it must not forward the packet to any mobile nodes in its mobility binding list other than those that have requested forwarding of broadcast packets. A mobile node may request forwarding of broadcast packets by setting the 'B' bit in its Registration Request message (Figure 13.9). For each such registered mobile node, the home agent should forward received broadcast packets to the mobile node, although it is a matter of configuration at the home agent as to which specific categories of broadcast packets will be forwarded to such mobile nodes.

If the 'D' bit was set in the mobile node's Registration Request message, indicating that the mobile node is using a co-located care-of address, the home agent simply tunnels appropriate broadcast IP packets to the mobile node's care-of address. Otherwise (the 'D' bit was not set), the home agent first encapsulates the broadcast packet in a unicast packet addressed to the mobile node's home address, and then tunnels this encapsulated packet to the foreign agent. This extra level of encapsulation is required so that the foreign agent can determine which mobile node should receive the packet after it is decapsulated. When received by the foreign agent, the unicast encapsulated packet is detunneled and delivered to the mobile node in the same way as any other datagram. In either case, the mobile node decapsulates the packet it receives in order to recover the original broadcast packet.

13.5.2.2 Multicast Datagram Packets Routing

As mentioned previously, a mobile node that is connected to its home network functions in the same way as any other (fixed) host or router. Thus, when it is at home, a mobile node functions identically to other multicast senders and receivers. This section therefore describes the behavior of a mobile node that is visiting a foreign network.

In order to receive multicasts, a mobile node must join the multicast group in one of two ways. First, a mobile node may join the group via a (local) multicast router on the visited subnet. This option assumes that there is a multicast router present on the visited subnet. If the mobile node is using a co-located care-of address, it should use this address as the source IP address of its IGMP [Deering 1989] messages. Otherwise, it may use its home address.

Alternatively, a mobile node which wishes to receive multicasts may join groups via a bi-directional tunnel to its home agent, assuming that its home agent is a multicast router. The mobile node tunnels IGMP messages to its home agent and the home agent forwards multicast packets down the tunnel to the mobile node. For packets tunneled to the home agent, the source address in the IP header should be the mobile node's home address. The rules for multicast packet delivery to mobile nodes in this case are identical to those for broadcast packets. If the mobile node is using a co-located care-of address (the 'D' bit was set in the mobile node's Registration Request), then the home agent tunnels the packet to this care-of address; otherwise, the home agent first encapsulates the packet in a unicast packet addressed to the mobile node's home address and then must tunnel the resulting packet (nested tunneling) to the mobile node's care-of address. For this reason, the mobile node must be capable of decapsulating packets sent to its home address in order to receive multicast packets.

A mobile node that wishes to send packets to a multicast group also has two options: (1) send directly on the visited network; or (2) send via a tunnel to its home agent. Because multicast routing in general depends upon the IP source address, a mobile node which sends multicast packets directly on the visited network must use a co-located care-of address as the IP source address. Similarly, a mobile node which tunnels a multicast packet to its home agent uses its home address as the IP source address of both the (inner) multicast packet and the (outer) encapsulating packet. This second option assumes that the home agent is a multicast router.

13.5.3 Mobile Routers and Networks

A mobile node can be a router that is responsible for the mobility of one or more entire networks moving together, perhaps on an airplane, a ship, a train, an automobile, a bicycle, or a kayak. The nodes connected to a network served by the mobile router may themselves be fixed nodes or mobile nodes or routers. In this document, such networks are called "mobile networks".

A mobile router may act as a foreign agent and provide a foreign agent care-of address to mobile nodes connected to the mobile network. Typical routing to a mobile node via a mobile router in this case is illustrated by the following example:

1) A laptop computer is disconnected from its home network and later attached to a network port in the seat back of an aircraft. The laptop computer uses Mobile IP to register on this foreign network, using a foreign agent care-of address discovered through an Agent Advertisement from the aircraft's foreign agent.

2) The aircraft network is itself mobile. Suppose the node serving as the foreign agent on the aircraft also serves as the default router that connects the aircraft network to the rest of the Internet. When the aircraft is at home, this router is attached to some fixed network at the airline's headquarters, which is the router's home network. While the aircraft is in flight, this router registers from time to time over its radio link with a series of foreign agents below it on the ground. This router's home agent is a node on the fixed network at the airline's headquarters.

3) Some correspondent node sends a packet to the laptop computer, addressing the packet to the laptop's home address. This packet is initially routed to the laptop's home network.

4) The laptop's home agent intercepts the packet on the home network and tunnels it to the laptop's care-of address, which in this example is an address of the node serving as router and foreign agent on the aircraft. Normal IP routing will route the packet to the fixed network at the airline's headquarters.

5) The aircraft router and foreign agent's home agent there intercepts the packet and tunnels it to its current care-of address, which in this example is some foreign agent on the ground below the aircraft. The original packet from the correspondent node has now been encapsulated twice: once by the laptop's home agent and again by the aircraft's home agent.

6) The foreign agent on the ground decapsulates the packet, yielding a packet still encapsulated by the laptop's home agent, with a destination address of the laptop's care-of address. The ground foreign agent sends the resulting packet over its radio link to the aircraft.

7) The foreign agent on the aircraft decapsulates the packet, yielding the original packet from the correspondent node, with a destination address of the laptop's home address. The aircraft foreign agent delivers the packet over the aircraft network to the laptop's link-layer address.

This example illustrates the case in which a mobile node is attached to a mobile network. That is, the mobile node is mobile with respect to the network, which itself is also mobile (here with respect to the ground). If, instead, the node is fixed with respect to the mobile network (the mobile network is the fixed node's home network), then either of two methods may be used to cause packets from correspondent nodes to be routed to the fixed node.

A home agent may be configured to have a permanent registration for the fixed node that indicates the mobile router's address as the fixed host's care-of address. The mobile router's home agent will usually be used for this purpose. The home agent is then responsible for advertising connectivity using normal routing protocols to the fixed node. Any packets sent to the fixed node will thus use nested tunneling as described above.

Alternatively, the mobile router may advertise connectivity to the entire mobile network using normal IP routing protocols through a bi-directional tunnel to its own home agent. This method avoids the need for nested tunneling of packets.

13.6 Case Study: Mobile Multicast using Anycasting

This section presents a novel and efficient multicast algorithm that aims at reducing delay and communication cost for the registration between mobile nodes and mobility agents and solicitation for foreign agent services based on Mobile IP. The protocol applies anycast group technology to support multicast transmissions for both mobile nodes and home/foreign agents. Mobile hosts use anycast tunneling to connect to the nearest available home/foreign agent where an agent is able to forward the multicast messages by selecting anycast route to a multicast router so as to reduce the end-to-end delay. The performance analysis and experiments demonstrated that our algorithm is able to enhance the performance over existing remote subscription and bi-directional tunneling approaches regardless of the locations of mobile nodes/hosts.

IP multicast [Deering 1989] provides unreliable multicast delivery for wired networks. In mobile multicast communications, two issues are primary important: One is for mobile nodes and mobility agents to discover each other's presence and another is the datagram routing efficiency. Traditional multicast research considered reliability of message delivery in the multicast group in guaranteeing the properties such as total ordering, atomicity, dynamic group membership and fault-tolerance etc [Jia et al 1996].

There have been some well-known wireless multicast systems developed. Forwarding pointers and location independent addressing to support mobility has been discussed in [Patridge et al 1993], but the multicast service is unreliable. However, it does not allow dynamic group membership. Multicast tunneling is proposed to forward multicast packets from one foreign network to another when the mobility agent receives packets addressed to mobile nodes that are nomadic.

13.6.1 Problems with Mobile IP

Mobile IP defined three approaches to support mobile connection and multicast: (1) Agent discovery: Home agents and foreign agents (HA and FA) may advertise their availability on each link for which they provide service. A newly arrived mobile node can send a solicitation on the link to learn if any prospective agents are present. (2) remote subscription: When a mobile node is away from home, it registers its care-of address (an IP address at the mobile node's current point of attachment to the Internet when it is not attached to the home network) with its home agent. Depending on its method of attachment, the mobile node will register either directly with its home agent or through a foreign agent, which forwards the registration to the home agent. (3) bi-directional tunneling multicast: Unicast tunnels are used to encapsulate and to send multicast packets over the Internet when the intermediate routers cannot handle multicast packets. In order for multicast datagrams to be delivered to the mobile node when it is away from home, the home agent has to tunnel the datagrams to the care-of address. A mobile node is addressed on its home network that is called home address. Agent discovery may require more advertisements solicitations messages. Remote subscription is inefficient for dynamic membership and location change of mobile nodes. Bi-directional tunneling multicast may cause tunnel convergence problems with packet duplication (Figure 13.11).

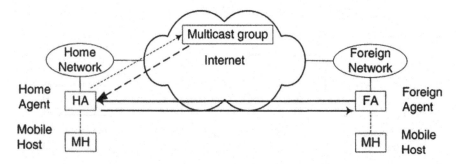

Figure 13.11. Bi-directional Tunneled Multicast Method

Motivation of MMP

Anycast address and service have been defined for Internet Protocol version 6 (IPv6) [Deering and Hinden 1995]. It is a communication for a single sender sending to the "nearest" member in a group of receivers, preferably only one of the servers that supports the anycast address [Johnson and Deering 1999]. It uses unicast address and the router can register the anycast address for its interface. Anycast is useful when a host requests a service from a server in a group but does not care which server is used. Anycast can simplify the task of finding an appropriate server. For example, users can use the anycast address to choose the mirrored FTP sites and to connect to the nearest (available) server.

To improve the efficiency in terms of Mobile IP on multicast communication, particularly in terms of the three issues mentioned above, we propose a novel efficient mobile multicast protocol (MMP), taking advantage of anycast routing technology. MMP targets two purposes: (1) mobility agents (MAs: both home/foreign agents) anycast group to facilitate flexible connections for mobile nodes. Using a well-known anycast address, the home agents need not multicast/broadcast router advertisements and the mobile nodes may register directly through the well-known anycast address of the anycast agent groups so as

398

to reduce the connection cost for the mobile nodes. (2) An anycast address is configured by a group of multicast routers on the subnet that are designed to support a specific multicast group. Using anycast can dynamically select the paths to the multicast router to reduce the end-to-end multicast delay.

13.6.2 Mobile Multicast Protocol (MMP)

Before proceeding with the description of the protocol, the following assumptions are made (see Figure 13.12 for an example of MMP topology):

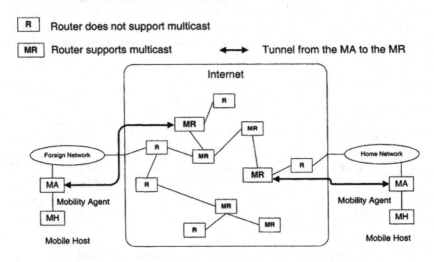

Figure 13.12. MMP topology and Mobile Connections

- A set of hosts and mobile nodes forms a multicast group G. Each individual mobile node has knowledge of the multicast group id to which it is interested in transmission and reception of multicast messages.

- Both home agent and foreign agent (denoted as Mobility Agent-MA) are special routers that provide service for the attachment of mobile nodes.

- There is at least one MA in each subnet.

Multicast routers can configure its interface to route both multicast and anycast packets (see [Jia et al 2000]). Each MA maintains four lists for the dynamic memberships of mobile nodes in multicast group G: (1) Membership list: ML(G) contains the ids of members in group G; (2) Visitor-list: VL(G) records the ids of foreign mobile nodes that belong to G that visit this MA; (3) Away-list: AL(G) keeps a record of the ids of mobile nodes in G that went away (or disconnected) from this MA; (4) Tunneling list: TL(G) records the ids of foreign agents that are interested in transmission/reception of multicast packets for G. MMP was designed in three major phases that work interactively:

- Initialization phase: Configurations of multicast and anycast group for routers, mobility agents and mobile nodes.

- Registration and membership phase: Registrations and reformation for the dynamic membership of mobile nodes.

- Multicast transmission phase: Multicast packet transmissions and deliveries for the group of members including station hosts and mobile nodes.

The three phases are detailed below:

Phase1: Initialization

1. Membership Initialization for a given group of G: An individual MA sets $ML(G) = VL(G) = AL(G) = TL(G) = \{ \}$.

2. Multicast Tree Formation: Core-based Tree (CBT) technique is used to build a multicast propagation tree for the routers (called a CBT tree). One router is selected as the core (or root) of the tree. To establish such a tree, Mobility Agents that provide multicast service for G must join the CBT tree by linking itself to the core (see [Ballardie 1997] for details). All routers including MAs in the tree are called ontree routers.

3. Mobility Agent Anycast Group Configuration: The mobility agents that offer attachment for mobile nodes in G form an anycast group [Jia et al 2000]. All the mobility agents that provide connections for G can register through the groups well-known reserved anycast address GA [Johnson and Deering 1999] and configure one of its interfaces to accept the registration for home/foreign mobile nodes. Our protocol mandates that the agents in the same anycast group GA will share the same authentication for mobile node registrations, i.e., $MA1 \in GA$ and $MA2 \in GA$ imply that both MA1 and MA2 agree to delegate each other on connection authentication and multicast packet delivery for the mobile nodes that previously attached to another party.

4. Ontree Router Anycast Group Configuration: For the group G, virtual anycast address TA is assigned to and configured by all routers in the shared tree for group G [Jia et al 1999]. The router configurations are classified as ontree and offtree:

   - Ontree Router Configuration: For a multicast group G, when the shared multicast tree is built, all ontree routers (including the core) are selected to join an anycast group with anycast address TA which is advertised to the network (broadcast by the core). TA may be considered as some "temporary" anycast address as long as the CBT tree exists. For any ontree router, there is a Forwarding Information Base (FIB) used as its multicast routing table [Jia et al 2000]. An entry of the FIB has the form of

     <G, input-interface, output-interfaces>.

   - Off tree Router Configuration: Upon reception of address TA broadcast from the core in the shared tree, the off-tree routers, including those foreign agents, that are interested in transmitting multicast packets to G will assign TA as an interface entry by configuring with <TA, G> mappings in the routing table. The anycast routing table enables the router to dynamically select a "better" path to reach the CBT tree among multiple paths even in the presence of link/hop failure.

Phase 2: Dynamic Member Registration and Connection

With the proposed anycast group, a mobile node may learn the existing agents by caching the anycast address through DHCP or SLP services [Droms 1993] [Veizades et al 1997]. In the register message of mobile node, normally the D-bit is set to enable the mobile node to receive/de-capsulate incoming multicast packets. MMP allows membership changes to be made to a multicast group G. A mobile node is allowed to join or leave a multicast group at will. To join a multicast group G in the home network, a mobile node must register through the home agent. In current Mobile IP, a mobility agent must also broadcast advertisement messages periodically (similar to ICMP advertisement messages) and the mobile node has to send a solicitation message to contact the agent when it hears no advertisement for a certain period of time. This phase is designed to reduce the cost of advertisement using anycast group by the following steps:

1. Mobile Node Home Registration: A mobile node MN must register through its home agent and join G for multicast message transmission. The registration can be accomplished through anycast connection by using GA to connect to the "nearest" MA in its home network. Upon establishment of the connection between MA and Mn, two cases must be considered:

   • Case 1: The MA is an ontree router of G: Similar to Mobile IP, the MA performs the corresponding authentication and mobility binding such as care-of address (CA) assignment to Mn (denoted as CA(Mn)) and calls Insert(CA(Mn), ML(G)) to insert CA of Mn into membership list ML(G).

   • Case 2: The MA is an offtree router. Similar to Case 1, the MA must first check authentication of MN, then calls *Insert(CA(Mn), ML(G))*. The following sub-cases must be considered:

      • Sub-case 1: The MA is a multicast router and uses GA to join the CBT tree for G by sending join-request to the "nearest" on-tree router in TA.

      • Sub-case 2: The MA is not a multicast router. It builds an anycast tunnel to the "nearest" on-tree router so that a single "tree trunk" is grafted on the CBT tree (see [Jia et al 1999] for detail).

2. Mobile Node-Visit a Foreign Network: A mobile node MN originally registered in MA1∈GA in Subnet 1 and moves to foreign network Subnet 2 to connect with MA2. Two cases must be considered:

   • Case 1: MA2∈GA, since both MA1 and MA2 are in GA, they are in the same authentication group. Mn may use address GA to contact MA2 for registration. Upon checking authentication and acceptance for Mn, MA2 executes *Insert(CA(Mn), VL(G))*. On the other hand, MA1 calls *Move(CA(Mn), ML(G), AL(G))* to move CA of Mn from membership list ML(G) to away-list AL(G).

- Case 2: **MA2∉GA,** MA2 does not provide service for multicast group G. Thus, MA2 applies a bi-directional tunneling approach similar to Mobile IP. Upon acceptance of the visiting MN, MA2 calls *Insert(CA(Mn), VL(G))*. Since MA2 is not an ontree router, it sets a tunnel to MA1 and then calls *Insert(id(MA2), TL(G))* to record the tunneling information for MA2.

4. Mobile Node Leaves: When a mobile node leaves its home network, it should notify its home agent MA by sending a de-registration message. The latter calls *Move(CA(Mn), ML(G), AL(G))*. In case ML(G) = VL(G) = TL(G)={ }, i.e., the MA does not have any mobile node attached to G nor any tunnel for visitor members in G, then the MA uses an IGMP message to notify its up-link node until the core is reached from the shared tree [Fenner 1997].

5. Foreign Mobile Node/Agent Leaves: An MA may set up a specific timeout for the foreign mobile nodes in list VL(G). When the timer expires, the MA just deletes the node id from its VL(G). A similar approach can be applied for the management of list TL(G).

Phase 3: Multicast Transmission Phase

1. Multicast transmission: A mobile node may generate a multicast message m, intending to send to G. Message m is thus transmitted to home agent MA. When MA receives m, it first encapsulates m with a multicast header and then imbeds m with an anycast address TA into an anycast packet mA. The packet is then routed to the address TA using dynamic anycast routing algorithms (refer to [Jia et al 2000] for details). When a router in TA receives the anycast packet, it strips m from mA, i.e., strips off the anycast header of mA, and propagates it across group G. For a visited mobile node Mn, if it wants to send the multicast packet, the packets can be forwarded through the foreign agents. Like Mobile IP, a co-located care-of address on the foreign network is required and used as the source address for multicast packets to group G.

2. Multicast packet reception-delivery: When an MA receives an encapsulated multicast packet m from a router on the CBT tree, it strips-off the multicast header from the packet and makes the packet delivery to the ids in ML(G) and VL(G). The packet is also tunneled and retransmitted to the agents in TL(G) when TL(G) is not empty.

Note that if the mobile node is using a colocated care-of address, it should use this address as the source IP address of its IGMP [Fenner 1997] (membership) messages; otherwise, it is required to use its home address for multicast transmissions.

13.6.3 Performance

This section presents the performance analysis for the MMP protocol and demonstrates experimental results to show availability of the protocol by simulation results. In particular, we compare the complexity of MMP with remote subscription (RS) and bi-directional (BD) approaches in terms of number of broadcast/multicast packets and end-to-end delay of multicast.

13.6.3.1 Analysis

To analyze the performances of the MMP protocol, we use the following metrics for the comparison of MMP with methods proposed in Mobile IP:

- Number of Messages (m/bcasts): the number of messages (including multicast and broadcast) required for the corresponding operation.

- Delay: total delays in seconds to accomplish the operation and D is used to measure a single multicast/broadcast (minimum) transmission delay.

Table 13.2. Performance comparisons

Operations	Protocols	# of Messages (m/bcasts)	Delay (sec)
Agent Discovery	Mobile IP	1	1
	MMP	0	0
Registration on HA	RS	2	$1+2\Delta$
	MMP	2	2Δ
Registration on FA	BD	4	$1+4\Delta$
	MMP	2	2Δ

According to Mobile IP, the agent discovery requires the MA to send broadcasts for agent advertisement. Mobile nodes use these advertisements to determine their current point of attachment to the Internet. The advertisement is sent at max rate of once every second (so the delay). Therefore, for a mobile node, it has to wait for the advertisement and then it learns of the presence of a mobile agent. With MMP, in the presence of anycast address GA, mobile nodes already have knowledge of the presence of MA. Thus no agent advertisement is required.

For registration of a mobile node, we differentiate the registration on the home agent (HA) from that on the foreign agent (FA). If the registration is on the HA, in terms of message number, MMP is the same as the protocols based on mobile IP. But delay is shorter as MMP does not wait for the advertisements of HA. Only the transmission delay of two messages is taken into account.

Mobile IP makes use of bi-directional tunneling for a mobile node to register to a foreign network under the assumption that its home agent is a multicast router. The mobile node tunnels IGMP messages to its home agent and the home agent forwards multicast datagrams down the tunnel to the mobile nodes. It is known that four messages are required: one is the request from a mobile node to FA, then FA relays the request to HA. HA, in turn, sends back a message of acceptance or denial to FA and then FA relays the final status to the mobile node. While in MMP, if the FA is in the same anycast group as that of HA, only two messages are required: the registration through FA is the same as through HA. For the delay analysis, the reason is similar to the above argument.

13.6.3.2 Simulation Model

In the simulation, we consider 16 local area networks with a maximum of 90 mobile nodes and each LAN has two mobility agents (i.e., one home and one foreign agent). All mobile nodes are allowed to roam in the network at random. The residency time for each mobile node to stay at a network (home or foreign) is drawn from an exponential distribution with a mean of r time-units. The travel time for going between subnets is exponentially distributed with a mean of (r/0.9)*0.1 time-units. Thus, mobile nodes spend 10 percent of their time in transition, and 90 percent of their time connected to an LAN. In addition, each mobile node has a probability p of losing the connection with a local mobility agent.

We assume that each multicast group has only one source for generating multicast messages in ratio of 1 time-units. The delivery of each multicast message to the group recipients is done by scheduling from the source to a mobility agent, and then to the mobile nodes. To simplify the simulation, the topology of LANs is located on an x-y coordinate as shown in Figure 13.13. The network topology between the LANs is not drawn, for simplicity.

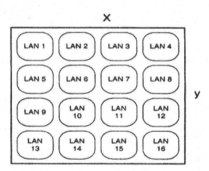

Figure 13.13. Network Topology of the Simulation

The simulation experiments were conducted using a multi-factor experimental design. The warm-up period used for the simulations was 20 percent of the simulation time t, which is an input parameter. After the warm-up period, the simulator collects simulation statistics relating to mobile multicast until the end of

404

the simulation. We execute 10 simulations for each set of workload parameters and achieve the mean value.

13.6.3.3 Simulation Results

The experiment compares the effectiveness of multicast delivery of MMP to bi-directional tunneling in terms of message delivery delay and number of delivered messages. The simulation considers one multicast group with up to 90 (mobile) nodes across 9 LANs, and 8,500 multicast messages are generated within 2500 seconds.

Figure 13.14 shows that our protocol can provide a better multicast service to mobile nodes as the message delivery delay is lower than that of bi-directional tunneling. The high delay demonstrates the transmission overhead in the tunnel from home network to foreign network of bi-directional tunneling. Figure 13.15 shows that about 90 percent of the generated messages were delivered to the mobile nodes by MMP and about 50 percent of the generated message were delivered by bi-directional tunneling protocol. For MMP, two situations may affect the delivery of multicast messages to the mobile nodes: (1) the node may be in transit state and (2) the node may be attached to a network with poor link connection due to the noise environments. The unsuccessful deliveries in bi-directional tunneling may be caused by inconsistent information in a home network about the location of its mobile nodes.

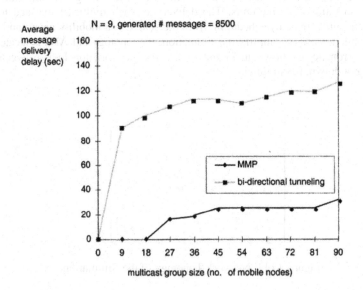

Figure 13.14. Message delivery delays.

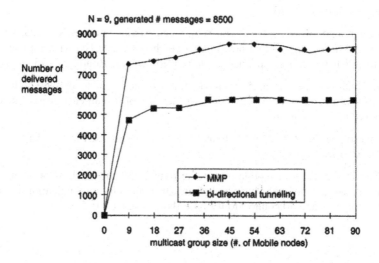

Figure 13.15. Number of delivered messages.

13.7 Summary

MMP extends the Mobile IP with anycast address group technology for agent discovery, registration of mobile nodes and delivery of multicast packets. The utilization of anycast addresses for the mobility agent group can reduce the cost and delay when the mobile nodes register with mobility agents between subnets, without impacting its performance. In contrast to bi-directional tunneling and remote subscriptions, MMP is more efficient in terms of delivery delay and throughput of multicast packets. The cost of the employing anycast address/group is that the multicast routers involved in the group have to manage the anycast addresses. This management may be taken as setup cost and will not compromise the (runtime) dynamic performance of MMP. In this sense, MMP provides a performance extension for Mobile IP, especially when multicast services are desired.

Exercises

13.1 Give the routing table for Router 1 in Figure 13.1. 13.1

13.2 What are the differences between *care-of address* and *collocated care-of address*? 13.2.

13.3 What are the three major functions that Mobile IP must facilitate? 13.2.

13.4 Give the packet header structure of *Agent Advertisement, Agent Solicitation* and *Agent Reply.* 13.3.

13.5 Illustrate the importance of tunneling in the role of datagram routing. 13.3.1

13.6 Describe the routing action for home, and foreign agents in cases of unicast, multicast and broadcast. 13.5

13.7 Design a protocol to solve the problem when a mobile node MN is attached to a foreign link F1 where another host in F1 (which is local to F1) wishes to send a packet to MN using MN's home address (so called Triangle Routing). 13.5.

13.8 Evaluate the performance overhead for a home agent to deliver multicast datagram to a mobile node MN which is a member of a multicast group but has been moved to a foreign link. 13.5

13.9 Investigate the RFC documents and list the concepts used in the chapter and their relationship. 13.3-4.

13.10 Consider a group of mobile routers residing in a team of ships or airplanes. Design a protocol (approach) by which they can maintain communication in case not every router is able to connect to the base (home) agent. 13.5-6.

CHAPTER 14 DISTRIBUTED NETWORK SYSTEMS: CASE STUDIES

In the previous chapters we have discussed various aspects of distributed network systems. Distributed network systems are now used everywhere, especially on the Internet. In this chapter we study several well-known distributed network systems, as examples of our discussion.

14.1   Distributed File Systems

The client-server model has changed the image of computing and has allowed the establishment of distributed computing. in particular, the client-server model has been used to develop distributed software, including network and distributed operating systems as well as applications. The first step in this direction was made when inexpensive diskless personal computers connected by inexpensive and simple local networks were forced to share a file service or a printer service.

In this section we present one of the most important achievements of the 1980s, which is still in use now, a network file system based on the client-server model. It is Sun Microsystems' Network File System, known as NFS [Sandberg *et al.* 1985]. NFS is an example of a distributed file system.

14.1.1   What is a Distributed File System

A distributed file system is a key component of any distributed computing system. The main function of a distributed file system is to create a common file system that can be shared by all clients running on autonomous computers in a distributed computing system. The common file system should store programs and data and make them available as needed. Since files can be stored anywhere in a distributed computing system, this means that a distributed file system should provide location transparency. This means, users, regardless of their physical location, can access files without knowing their location.

To achieve such a goal a distributed file system usually follows the client-server model. A distributed file system typically provides two types of services: the file service and the directory service, which are implemented by the file server and the directory server distributed over the network, respectively. These two servers can also be implemented as a single server. The file server provides operations on the contents of files such as read, write, and append. The directory server provides operations, such as directory and file creation and deletion, for manipulating directories and file names. The client application program interface (client API, usually in the form of a process or a group of processes) runs on each client computer and provides a uniform user-level interface for accessing file servers. Figure 14.1 shows the structure of a distributed file system based on the client-server model.

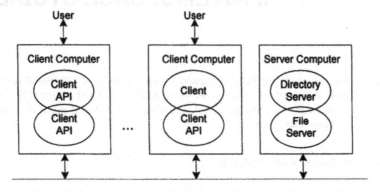

Figure 14.1. A distributed file system structure

14.1.2 A Distributed File System Example -- NFS

Sun Microsystems' Network File System is a typical example of the application of the client-server model in the development of a distributed file system. The rest of this section describes briefly the architecture and implementation of NFS.

NFS was developed by Sun Microsystems and introduced in late 1984 [Sandberg *et al.* 1985]. Since then it has been widely used in both industry and academia. NFS was originally developed for use on Unix workstations. Currently, many manufacturers support it for other operating systems (e.g., Microsoft Windows operating systems). Here, NFS is introduced based on the Unix system.

To understand the architecture of NFS, we need to define the following terms used in NFS:

- INODE. This is a data structure that represents either an open file or directory within the Unix file system. It is used to identify and locate a file or directory within the local Unix file system;

- RNODE (the remote file node). This is a data structure that represents either an open file or directory within a remote file system (a file system that is not located on the local computer);

- VNODE (the virtual file node). This is a data structure that represents either an open file or directory within the virtual file system (VFS);

- VFS (the virtual file system). This is a data structure (linked lists of VNODEs) that contains all necessary information on a real file system that is managed by the NFS. Each VNODE associated with a given file system is included in a linked list attached to the VFS for that file system. For example, if the real file system managed by the NFS is a Unix file system, then an open file in this file system is represented by a VNODE containing a pointer (called the private data pointer) that points to an INODE data structure. If the real file system is a remote file system, the private data pointer of the VNODE points to an RNODE data structure.

The NFS server integrates functions of both a file server and a directory server and the NFS clients use a uniform interface, the VFS/VNODE interface, to access the NFS server. The VFS/ VNODE interface abstraction makes it possible to achieve the goal of supporting multiple file system types in a generic fashion. The VFS and VNODE data structures provide the linkage between the abstract uniform file system interface and the real file system (such as a Unix file system or an MS Windows file system) that accesses the data. Further, the VFS/VNODE interface abstraction allows NFS to make remote files and local files appear identical to a client program.

The NFS clients and servers communicate using the remote procedure call (RPC) technique. An external data representation (XDR) specification is used to describe RPC protocols in a machine and system independent way. This design strategy has helped NFS to be ported from the original Unix platform to various non-Unix platforms. Figure 14.2 illustrates the NFS structure.

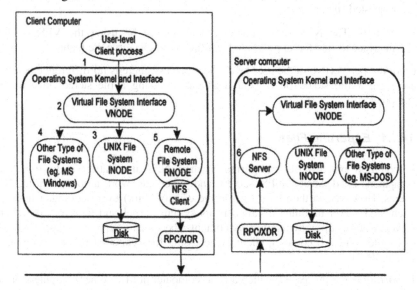

Figure 14.2. NFS structure

14.1.3 Processing User Calls

NFS provides transparent access to files of a distributed computing system for client processes. In NFS, a client process accesses files through the normal operating system interface. All operating system calls that manipulate files or file systems are modified to perform operations on VFSs/VNODEs. The VFS/VNODE interface hides the heterogeneity of underlying file systems and the location of these file systems. Based on Figure 14.2, the steps of processing a user-level file system call can be described as follows:

- Step 1. The user-level client process makes the file system call through the normal operating system interface;

- Step 2. The request is redirected to the VFS/VNODE interface. A VNODE is used to describe the file or directory accessed by the client process;

- Step 3. If the request is for accessing a file stored in the local Unix file system, the INODE pointed by the VNODE is used. The Unix INODE interface is used and the request is served by the Unix file system interface;

- Step 4. If the request is for accessing a file stored locally in other types of file systems (such as an MS Windows file system), a proper interface of the particular file system is used to serve the request;

- Step 5. If the request is for accessing a file stored remotely, the RNODE pointed by the VNODE is used and the request is passed to the NFS client. Some messages following RPC to the remote NFS server that stores the requested file are sent;

- Step 6. The NFS server processes the request by using the VFS/VNODE interface to find the appropriate local file system to serve the request.

From the perspective of the user-level client process, there is no difference between accessing a file stored on a local disk and accessing a file stored on a remote computer.

14.1.4 Exporting Files

A common practice of configuring a large NFS installation is to use some computers as dedicated NFS servers and others as workstations running NFS clients. However, in theory (at least in the case of Unix) every computer has NFS client and server modules installed in its system kernel and therefore the client-server relationship is symmetric. A computer becomes a server by exporting some of its files and it becomes a client by accessing files exported by other computers [Stern 1991].

Exporting is the process by which a local computer notifies other computers on the network of the availability of specific file systems (directories) for sharing. In this case, the local computer becomes the NFS server that manages the exported file systems, and other computers become NFS clients that access the specific file systems.

In the case of Unix, a system file (called *dfstab*) is used to store the names of directories (as well as some access rights) that the server is willing to share with other computers. An NFS client accesses files on the NFS server by *mounting* the server's exported directories. During the mounting process, a client requests the appropriate remote server or servers to provide access to the directories that the client has specified in another system file (called *vfstab*). The server receives the request and determines if the requested file system is available to the client, by checking its *dfstab* file. If it is, the file system can then be mounted. In that case, the client creates a VFS data structure and a mounted-on VNODE data structure. The VNODE also contains a pointer to an RNODE. The RNODE is also created by the client and it contains the information about the remote file system.

14.1.5 The Role of RPC

The communication between NFS clients and servers is implemented as a set of RPC procedures that use XDR for the purpose of passing parameters between NFS clients and servers. These operations are performed on RNODEs only. NFS daemons (server processes), called *nfsd* daemons, run on NFS servers and accept RPCs from clients. Another NFS server daemon, called *mountd* daemon, handles file system mount requests and some pathname translation. On an NFS client, the *biod* daemon is usually run to improve NFS performance, but it is not required.

NFS servers are designed to be *stateless,* meaning that there is no need to maintain information (such as whether a file is open, the position of the file pointer, etc.) about past requests. The client keeps track of all information required to send requests to the server. Therefore NFS RPC requests are designed to completely describe the operation to be performed. Also, most NFS RPC requests are *idempotent,* meaning that an NFS client may send the same request one or more times without any harmful side effects. The net result of these duplicate requests is the same. NFS RPC requests are transported using the unreliable User Datagram Protocol (UDP). NFS servers notify clients when an RPC completes by sending the client an acknowledgment, also using UDP.

The stateless protocol minimises the burden of crash recovery. A stateless server does not need to restore its previous main memory image or any other information regarding which clients it was interacting with before crashing. It simply restarts to recover after crashing.

An NFS client process sends its RPC requests to an NFS server one at a time. Although a client computer may have several NFS RPC requests in progress at any time, each of these requests must come from a different client process. When a client makes an RPC request, it sets a timeout period during which the server must service and acknowledge it. If the server does not acknowledge during the timeout period, the client retransmits the request. This may happen if the request is lost along the way, or if the server is too slow because of overloading. Since the RPC requests are idempotent, there is no harm if the server executes the same request twice. If the client gets a second acknowledgment from the request, the client simply discards it.

14.1.6 Remarks

In this section we describe a system, the Sun's Network File System that applies the client-server model in its implementation. NFS lets users in various locations access files stored in the network transparently. The NFS server manages files stored in the network, whereas NSF clients request file services from the server using RPCs. NFS is the most widely used file system in local area networks nowadays.

14.2 Network Operating Systems: Unix/Linux

UNIX describes a family of computer operating systems developed at Bell Laboratories. The UNIX system includes both the operating system and its associated commands. The operating system manages the resources of the computing environment by providing a hierarchical file system, process management and other functions. The commands provided include basic file and data management, editors, assemblers, compilers and text formatters.

Linux is a UNIX type of operating system, originally created by Linus Torvalds in 1991, that has been enhanced by developers around the world. Linux is an independent POSIX (Portable Operating System Interface) implementation and is compliant with X/Open and POSIX standards. Linux features include true multitasking, multiuser support, virtual memory, shared libraries, demand loading, proper memory management, TCP/IP networking, shell, file structure, utilities, and applications that are common in many UNIX implementations. In this section, we briefly introduce the main features of UNIX and Linux.

14.2.1 UNIX System Concepts

14.2.1.1 The File System

A file system in UNIX allows users to store information by name. Protection from hardware failures can be provided and security from unauthorized access is also available. The UNIX file system is simple; there are no control blocks, devices are hidden, and there is a uniform interface for all input-output. Within the file system three types of files are distinguished:

- An ordinary file contains characters of a document or program. Executable programs (binary files) are also stored as ordinary files. No record structure is imposed on files; a file consists of a sequence of characters. A newline character may delimit records as required by applications.

- A directory holds the names of other files or directories. A user may create sub-directories to group files related to a project. Consequently, the file system is a hierarchy. A directory can be read, but not written, as if it were an ordinary file.

- Special files correspond to input or output devices. The same interface as ordinary files is available; however, information is not kept in the file system, it is provided directly by the device. The same access protection is available for special and ordinary files.

The file system provides a hierarchical naming structure. Each directory contains the names of files or further directories. There is no formatting of the file contents; each file consists simply of a sequence of characters. It is convenient to establish conventions for formatting files but this is left to individual programs. The UNIX system knows about the file format used by executable programs (a.out files).

14.2.1.2 Process Management

All user work in the UNIX system is carried out by processes. A process is a single sequence of events and consists of some computer memory and files being accessed. A process is created by a copy of the process being made. The two processes are only distinguished by the parent being able to wait for the child to finish. A process may replace itself by another program to be executed. This mechanism is both elegant and effective.

A UNIX kernel uses processes to manage the execution of applications. The process construct allows the kernel to control the use of system resources so that

- All currently active applications have reasonable access to system resources.

- Applications cannot inadvertently or deliberately interfere with one another's access to the resources.

The more detailed process management will be discussed in the next section.

14.2.1.3 The Shell

The UNIX system is simple and elegant and provides an attractive programming environment. The facilities and tools in UNIX are made available to users via a command language that provides the interface between users and the UNIX operating system. This program is called the *shell* and programs written in this language are sometimes referred to as shell scripts.

The shell provides notation for directing input and output from commands and control flow mechanisms. The shell executes commands that are read either from a terminal or a file. Files containing commands may be created, allowing users to build their own commands. These newly defined commands have the same status as system commands. In this way, a new environment can be established reflecting the requirements or style of an individual or a group.

Pipes allow processes to be linked together so that the output from one process is the input to the next. The shell provides a notation enabling pipes to be used with a minimum of effort.

14.2.2 The UNIX Processes

14.2.2.1 Process Address Spaces

When a program is compiled, the compiler creates the program's executable files, also referred to as the *executable image*. The kernel uses this file to create a *logical address space* that contains the following sections of data:

- The program's text section, which contains the executable instructions.

- The program's initialized data. This data is global data, which will be accessible to the program's main routine and all of the subroutines defined in the program and in any libraries that the program references.

- The program's uninitialized data. The compiler allocates storage for this data, but the data is not initialized until runtime. This data is also global data.

The executable file also includes a header, which specifies the location and size of each of the data sections. When the program is being prepared for execution, the system's program loader uses the header information to set up the process's virtual address space.

When the process's address space is set up, it contains a text section, and an initialized data section, an uninitialized data section, and two additional sections: the process's heap, and the process's user stack. The heap contains memory that the process explicitly acquires during its execution. Typically, a process uses heap memory to store dynamically required data structures. When a new data structure is required, the process executes a call to *malloc()* to allocate the memory. When the data structure is no longer needed, the process can execute a call to *free()* to free the memory. Like the initialized and uninitialized data, the heap data is global.

In contrast to the data contained in the heap, the data contained on the stack is local data, which is accessible only to the process's currently active routine. A process's user stack grows and shrinks dynamically as needed.

14.2.2.2 Process Management System Calls

The UNIX kernel provides a set of process management system calls that allow processes to create other processes, to manage the execution of related processes, and to terminate themselves or the processes they control. These include *fork()*, *exec()*, *wait()*, and *exit()*.

Processes use the *fork( )* and *exec( )* system calls to create processes and execute new programs, respectively. The *fork( )* system call creates a new process by duplicating the address space of the calling process. The calling process is referred to as the parent process and the new process is referred to as the child process. Upon successful completion of *fork( )*, the parent and child have duplicate address spaces and are executing the same program.

The *exec( )* system call allows a process to execute a new program by loading the program into the process's address space. Generally, a child process that is to execute a new program issues a call to *exec( )* after the call to *fork( )*. A parent process may choose to wait for its child to complete execution before resuming execution itself. For example, the shell does this when executing commands in the foreground. The user enters a command to the shell, the shell uses *fork( )* to create a new process, the new process calls *exec( )* to load the command's program, and the shell waits for the program to complete execution.

A process that needs to wait in this fashion does so using the *wait( )* system call. This system call suspends the calling process's execution until the child process either terminates or suspends itself. It is called with a status argument that the system uses to inform the waiting process about the exit or suspend status of the child process. When the child exits or suspends itself, the system copies its status to the status variable and allows the parent process to resume execution. The parent can examine the status variable to determine what happended to the child.

When a process wants to explicitly terminate its execution, it does so using the *exit( )* system call. This system call releases all of the process's system resources and may send a signal to the process's parent process to indicate that the child has exited.

14.2.2.3 Process Context and Context-Switching

A CPU always executes instructions within the context of the current process. In general, a process's context is specified by its memory map and by its computational state. A process's computational state is specified by the contents of the CPU's registers as the CPU executes the process. The detailed characteristics of a CPU's registers are hardware-specific, but in general, CPUs include the following types of registers:

- *Program counter:* this register is the means by which the CPU finds the next instruction to execute. A CPU's behavior with respect to this register is hardware-dependent, but many CPUs increment this register at the time they are loading the current instruction so that when the current instruction has been executed, the CPU can find and load the next instruction.

- *Stack management registers:* the CPU uses these registers to locate and manipulate the process's stacks. In UNIX systems, a user process has two stacks: a user stack and a kernel stack. When a process executes in user mode, variables are stored on the user stack. When the process executes a system call, the system call's variables are stored on the kernel stack. Stack management is highly machine-dependent. The CPU must be able to determine which stack is currently active, and it must be able to locate variables on the stacks.

- *General registers:* these registers are used to store variables that the CPU needs to access quickly. Usually, the general registers hold operands that are being manipulated by the process's current state of execution. For example, if a process is executing a for loop that increments and tests a variable before looping, that variable is probably being stored in a general register.

A process's computational state is highly dynamic. The program counter changes with each instruction, and the stack management registers change each time the process executes a system call or subroutine.

Any of a number of events can interrupt a process's execution. When an interruption occurs, the kernel must save the process's computational state so that when the process resumes execution, it executes from the point of interruption. When the kernel schedules a new process for execution, it switches the CPU's context from the previous process to the new process. The kernel saves the first process's register state in memory, purges the CPU's registers and MMU, and then loads the new process's register state into the CPU.

14.2.3 Linux as a UNIX Platform

Like other UNIX systems, Linux is a multiuser, multitasking operating system, which means that Linux allows multiple users to log in and run more than one program at the same time.

Linux is designed to comply with IEEE Std 1003.1-1990 (POSIX). This standard defines the functions that applications written in the C programming language use to access the services of the operating system, for tasks ranging from opening a file to allocating memory. In 1996, Linux version 1.2.13, packaged by Open Linux Ltd., was validated conforming to the POSIX standard. Along with POSIX conformance, Linux includes many features of other UNIX standards, such as the System V Interface Document (SVID) and the Berkeley Software Distribution (BSD) version of UNIX. Linux takes an electic approach, picking the most-needed features of several standard flavors of UNIX.

The main features of Linux can be summarized as follows:

- *Virtual memory.* It is possible to add up to 16 swapping areas during runtime, each of which can hold 128 MB and can be used for a total of 2 GB swap space.

- *Development languages.* Linux supports most common languages including C, C++, Java, Ada95, Pascal, FORTRAN, etc.

- *UNIX commands and tools.* It supports most UNIX commands such as Is, tr, sed, awk, etc. and tools such as gcc, gdb, make, bison, flex, perl, rcs, cvs, and prof.

- *UNIX source/binary compatibility.* Linux is compatible with most POSIX, System V, and BSD at the source level. Through iBCS2-compliant emulation, it is compatible with many SCO, SVR3, and SVR4 at the binary level.

- *Graphical environments.* It provides X11R5 and X11R6 techniques for graphical uses. Motif is available separately.

- *Shells.* It supports all three common shells. The default Linux shell is called *Bash,* which stands for *Bourne-Again Shell* – a reference to the *Bourne shell,* which has been the standard UNIX shell since its early days.

- *LAN support.* It supports Appletalk server and NetWare client and server.

- *Internet communications.* It supports TCP/IP networking including FTP, Telnet, etc.

- *File systems.* Linux file system supports file systems of up to 4 TB and names up to 255 characters long. Also it supports NFS and System V. Transparent access to MS-DOS FAT partition via a separate file system. Partition looks like a normal UNIX file system.

14.2.4 Linux Networking

14.2.4.1 TCP/IP

Linux supports the TCP/IP protocol suite and includes all common network applications, such as telnet, ftp, and rlogin. At the physical network level, Linux includes drivers for many Ethernet cards. Token-ring is also an integral part of the Linux kernel source; all you have to do is to rebuild the kernel and enable support for token-ring.

Linux also includes the Berkeley Sockets (so named because the socket interface was introduced in Berkeley UNIX around 1982) – a popular interface for network programming in TCP/IP networks. For those with C programming experience, the Sockets interface consists of several C header files and several C functions that you call to set up connections and to send and receive data.

You can use the Berkeley Sockets programming interface to develop Internet tools such as WWW browsers. Because most TCP/IP programs (including those that are available for free at various Internet sites) use the Sockets programming interface, it is easy to get these programs up and running on Linux, because Linux includes the Sockets interface.

14.2.4.2 PPP and SLIP

When you access the Internet through a server over a phone line and a modem, the server runs either of two protocols:

- Serial Line Internet Protocol (SLIP)

- Point-to-Point Protocol (PPP)

Both protocols support TCP/IP over a dial-up line. SLIP is a simpler and older protocol than PPP, which has more features for establishing a connection. However, nearly everyone uses PPP nowadays. To establish a connection, your system must run the same protocol as the ISP's system.

Linux supports both SLIP and PPP for dial-up Internet connections. You can also turn your Linux system into a SLIP or PPP server so that other computers can dial into your computer and establish a TCP/IP connection over the phone line.

14.2.4.3 File Sharing with NFS

In DOS and Windows, users see the file server's disk as being just another drive, with its own drive letter (such as U). In PC networks, file sharing typically is implemented with Novell NetWare or Microsoft Windows networking protocols. The concept of file sharing exists in UNIX as well. The Network File System (NFS) provides a standard way for a system to access another system's files over the network. To the user, the remote system's files appear to be in a directory on the local system.

NFS is available in Linux; you can share your Linux system's directories with other systems that support NFS. The other systems that access your Linux system's files via NFS do not necessarily have to run UNIX; in fact, NFS is available for DOS and Windows as well. Therefore, you can use a Linux PC as the file server for a small workgroup of PCs that run DOS and Windows.

14.2.4.4 UUCP

An old but important data-exchange protocol is UUCP (UNIX-to-UNIX Copy). For some systems, this protocol continues to be a means of exchanging electronic mail and news. Usenet news – the bulletin-board system (BBS) of the Internet – originated with UUCP. Computers that were connected to one another over phone lines and modems used UUCP to exchange mail messages, news items, and files. Essentially, the messages and news were relayed from one computer to another. That system was a low-cost way to deliver news and mail. Although today much of the e-mail and news travels over permanent network connections of the Internet, UUCP still allows many distant systems to be part of the Internet community, as far as Usenet news and e-mail go.

Linux includes UUCP. If your Linux system has a modem, and if you want to exchange files with another system via a dial-up connection, you can use UUCP.

However, with the proliferation of Internet service providers, chances are good that you will probably connect your Linux PC to the Internet through an ISP.

14.2.5 Software Development in Linux

Of all the potential uses of Linux, software development fits Linux perfectly. Software-development tools such as the compiler and the libraries are included in Linux because they are needed to rebuild the Linux kernel. As far as the development environment goes, you have the same basic tools (such as an editor, a compiler, and a debugger) that you might use on other UNIX workstations, such as those from Hewlett-Packard (HP), Sun Microsystems, and IBM. Therefore, if you work by day on one of the mainstream UNIX workstations, you can use a Linux PC at home to duplicate that development environment at a fraction of the cost. Then you can either complete work projects at home or devote your time to software that you write for fun and then share on the Internet.

14.3 CORBA

14.3.1 What is CORBA?

Common Object Request Broker Architecture (CORBA) is a middleware design that allows application programs to communicate with one another irrespective of their programming languages, their hardware and software platforms, the networks they communicate over and their implementors. In other words, CORBA is a specification of architecture and interface that allows an application to make requests of objects (servers) in a transparent, independent manner, regardless of language, platform, operating system or locale considerations. The CORBA programming paradigm combines distributed client-server programming and object-oriented programming methodologies.

Applications are built from CORBA objects, which implement interfaces defined in CORBA's interface definition language, IDL. Clients access the methods in the IDL interfaces of CORBA objects by means of RMI. The middleware component that supports RMI is called the Object Request Broker or ORB. ORB is the message bus that facilitates object communications across distributed heterogeneous computing environment.

The specification of CORBA has been sponsored by members of the Object Management Group (OMG). Many different ORBs have been implemented from the specification, supporting a variety of programming languages. ORB is also a component of the Object Management Architecture (OMA). The OMA provides fundamental models on which CORBA and other standard interfaces are based.

The Object Management Architecture (OMA) has the following key features:

- *The Core Object Model:* defines concepts that allow distributed application development to be facilitated by an Object Request Broker (ORB). The

420

concepts include: objects, operations, non-object types, interfaces and substitutability.

- *The Reference Architecture:* provides standardised interfaces for supporting application development. They include: the ORB, object services, domain interfaces, common facilities, application interfaces.

Figue 14.3 illustrates the OMA Reference Architecture.

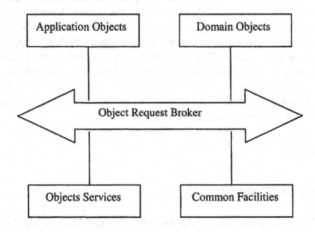

Figure 14.3. OMA Reference Architecture

14.3.2 The CORBA Architecture

As mentioned above, CORBA supports client-server programming. It has the following concepts:

- *Client:* makes requests to other components in a distributed application.

- *Server:* provides an implementation of a component that a client uses. A server can also act as a client to other servers.

- *Interface definition:* describes the functionality of a CORBA object. Clients of CORBA objects rely only on the interfaces.

- *CORBA servers:* they are programs that provide the implementation of one or more CORBA objects.

Figure 14.4 illustrates the client-server interaction in CORBA. CORBA provides location transparency and programming language transparency via the use of OMG's Interface Definition Language (IDL). Figure 14.4 involves the following objects:

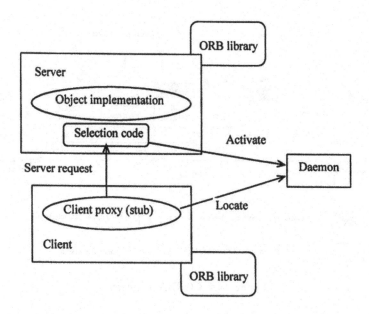

Figure 14.4. CORBA client and server

- IDL compiler generated codes:
  - o Stub code: linked into a CORBA object.
  - o Skeleton code: linked into a CORBA object implementation.
- An ORB agent/daemon process.
- Library code.
- Interfaces among ORB components.

The CORBA architecture is designed to support the role of an object request broker that enables clients to invoke methods in remote objects, where both clients and servers can be implemented in a variety of programming languages. The main components of the CORBA architecture are illustrated in Figure 14.5.

CORBA makes the distinction between static and dynamic invocations. Static invocations are used when the remote interface of the CORBA object is known at compile time, enabling client stubs and server skeletons to be used. If the remote interface is not known at compile time, dynamic invocation must be used. Most programmers prefer to use static invocation because it provides a more natural programming model. We now discuss the components of the architecture.

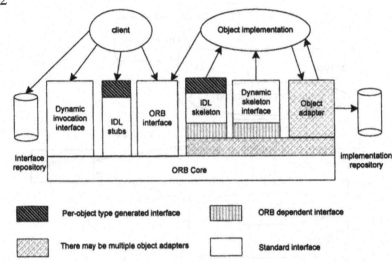

Figure 14.5. CORBA architecture

ORB core. The role of the ORB core is similar to that of the communication module of RMI. In addition, an ORB core provides an interface that includes the following:

- Operations enabling it to be started and stopped;

- Operations to convert between remote object references and strings;

- Operations to provide argument lists for requests using dynamic invocation.

Object adapter. The role of an object adapter is to bridge the gap between CORBA objects with IDL interfaces and the programming language interfaces of the corresponding servant classes. This role also includes that of the remote reference and despatcher modules in RMI. An object adapter has the following tasks:

- It creates remote object references for CORBA objects;

- It dispatches each RMI via a skeleton to the appropriate servant;

- It activates objects.

An object adapter gives each CORBA object a unique name, which forms part of its remote object reference. The same name is used each time an object is activated. The object name may be specified by the application program or generated by the object adapter. Each CORBA object is registered with its object adapter, which may keep a remote object table that maps the names of CORBA objects to their servants.

IDL skeletons. Skeleton classes are generated in the language of the server by an IDL compiler. As before, remote method invocations are dispatched via the appropriate skeleton to a particular servant, and the skeleton unmarshals the arguments in request messages and marshals exceptions and results in reply messages.

IDL stubs. These are in the client language. The class of a proxy (for object-oriented languages) or a set of stub procedures (for procedural languages) is generated from an IDL interface by an IDL compiler for the client langauge. As before, the client stubs/proxies marshal the arguments in invocation requests and unmarshal exceptions and results in replies.

Implementation repository. An implementation repository is responsible for activating registered servers on demand and for locating servers that are currently running. The object adapter name is used to refer to servers when registering and activating them.

An implementation repository stores a mapping from the names of object adapters to the pathnames of files containing object implementations. Object implementations and object adapter names are generally registered with the implementation repository when server programs are installed. When object implementations are activated in servers, the hostname and port number of the server are added to the mapping.

Interface repository. The role of the interface repository is to provide information about registered IDL interfaces to clients and servers that require it. For an interface of a given type it can supply the names of the methods and for each method, the names and types of the arguments and exceptions. Thus, the interface repository adds a facility for relection to CORBA. Suppose that a client program receives a remote reference to a new CORBA object. Also suppose that the client has no proxy for it; then it can ask the interface repository about the methods of the object and the types of parameter they require.

Those applications that use static invocation with client stubs and IDL skeletons do not require an interface repository. Not all ORBs provide an interface repository.

Dynamic invocation interface. In some applications, a client with the appropriate proxy class may need to invoke a method in a remote object. For example, a browser might need to display information about all the CORBA objects available in the various servers in a distributed system. It is not feasible that such a program should have to link in proxies for all of these objects, particularly as new objects may be added to the system as time passes. CORBA does not allow classes for proxies to be downloaded at run time as in Java RMI. The dynamic invocation interface is CORBA's alternative.

It allows clients to make dynamic invocations on remote CORBA objects. It is used when it is not practical to employ proxies. The client can obtain from the interface repository the necessary information about the methods available for a given CORBA object, The client may use this information to construct an invocation with suitable arguments and send it to the server.

Dynamic skeleton interface. This allows a CORBA object to accept invocations on an interface for which it has no skeleton because the type of its interface was not known at compile time. When a dynamic skeleton receives an invocation, it inspects the contents of the request to discover its target object, the method to be invoked and the arguments. It then invokes the target.

14.3.3 Interface Definition Language (IDL)

The CORBA Interface Definition Language, IDL, provides facilities for defining modules, interfaces, types, attributes, and method signatures. IDL has the same lexical rules as C++ but has additional keywords to support distribution, for example, *interface, any, attribute,* etc. It also allows standard C++ pre-processing facilities. The grammar of IDL is a subset of ANSI C++ with additional constructs to support method signatures.

The CORBA IDL is designed to specify the functionalities of objects. Programming language code is generated from the IDL definition to perform the tedious, error prone, and repetitive tasks of establishing network connections, marshalling, locating object implementations, and invoking the right code to perform an operation. The IDL mainly has the following types of definitions:

- *Modules.* The module construct allows interfaces and other IDL type definitions to be grouped in logical units. A module defines a naming scope, which prevents names defined within a module clashing with names defined outside it.

- *Interfaces.* An IDL interface describes the methods that are available in CORBA objects that implement that interface. Clients of a CORBA object may be developed just from the knowledge of its IDL interface. An interface defines a set of operations and attributes and generally depends on a set of types defined with it.

- *Methods.* An IDL method defines a function of an IDL object and can be invoked by clients. The method definition has many constructs indicating what type of data the method returns.

- *Data types.* IDL supports fifteen primitive types, which includes *basic types, structure, array, sequence, exception,* etc. Constants of most of the primitive types and constant strings may be declared, using the const keyword. IDL provides a special type called *Object,* whose values are remote object references. If a parameter or result is of type *Object,* then the corresponding argument may refer to any CORBA object.

- *Attributes.* IDL interfaces can have attributes as well as methods. Attributes are like public class fields in Java. The attributes are private to CORBA objects, but for each attribute declared, a pair of accessor methods is generated automatically by the IDL compiler, one to retrieve the value of the attribute and the other to set it.

- *Inheritance.* IDL can extend the functionality of an existing interface by defining its inheritance. CORBA inheritance is independent of implementation inheritance, as shown in Figure 14.6.

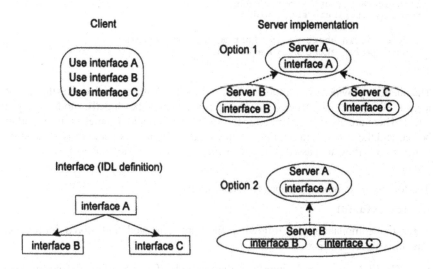

Figure 14.6. Interface inheritance and implementation inheritance

14.3.4 An Example of CORBA for Java

One commonly used CORBA for Java is the Orbix Web developed by IONA Technologies Ltd. The general syntax of CORBA IDL is as follows:

```
module <identifier> {
  <type declarations>;
  <constant declarations>;
  <exception declarations>;
  interface <identifier> [: <inheritance>] {
    <type declarations>;
    <constant declarations>;
    <attribute declarations>;
    <exception declarations>;
    [<operation_type>] <identifier> (<parameters>)
    [raises exception] [<context>];
    ...
    [<operation_type>] <identifier> (<parameters>)
    [raises exception] [<context>];
  }
  interface <identifier> [: inheritance>] {
    ...
  }
}
```

Below is an example of an IDL definition for a grid application:

```
// IDL;
// in file grid.idl

interface Grid {
```

```
readonly attribute short height;
readonly attribute short width;

    void set(in short n, in short m, in long value);
    void get(in short n, in short m);
}
```

The interface provides two attributes, height and width, which define the size of a grid. Since they are labeled *read-only,* they cannot be directly modified by a client. There are also two operations: the *set()* operation allows an element of grid to be set, and the *get()* operation returns an element. Parameters here are labeled as *in,* which means they are passed from the client to the server. Other labels can be *out* or *inout.*

The following command compiles the IDL file:

```
idl grid.idl
```

After the compilation, the following files are generated and stored in a local directory java_output:

- *_GridRef.java.* A Java interface; the methods of this interface define the Java client view of the IDL interface.

- *Grid.java.* A Java class which implements the methods defined in the interface *_GridRef.* This class provides functionality which allows client method invocations to be forwarded to a server.

- *_GridHolder.java.* A Java class which defines a Holder type for class *Grid.* This is required for passing *Grid* objects as *inout* or *out* parameters to and from IDL operations.

- *_GridOperations.java.* A Java interface which maps the attributes and operations of the IDL definition to Java methods. These methods must be implemented by a class in the server.

- *boaimpl_Grid.java.* An abstract Java class which allows server-side developers to implement the Grid interface using one of two techniques available on OrbixWeb; this technique is called the BOAImpl approach to interface implementation.

- *tieGrid.java.* A Java class which allows server-side developers to implement the Grid interface using one of two techniques available on OrbixWeb; this technique is called the TIE approach to interface implementation.

- *dispatcher_Grid.java.* A Java class that is used internally by OrbixWeb to dispatch incoming server requests to implementation objects. Application developers do not require an understanding of this class.

After the implementation of the *_GridOperations.java* program and a client program, the program can be compiled. Then the server should be registered to the registry by using the *putit* command. The client can now access the server from any machine since it knows the machine name, the server name and object names.

14.4 DCOM

Distributed Component Object Model (DCOM) is a viable distributed objects technology to develop distributed computing systems. Distributed COM is nothing more than a wire protocol and a set of services that allow COM components in a distributed environment to intercommunicate. In this section we briefly review this technology.

14.4.1 COM and DCOM

As its name implies, the Component Object Model (COM) is a model that you can utilize to build software components. A component is a package or a module, more often referred to as an executable (EXE) or a dynamic linked library (DLL). Being a model, COM is fully specified in a formal document called "The Component Object Model Specification." The COM specification encompasses several previously successful technologies: object-oriented model, client/server model, and dynamic linking technologies. Object-oriented programming is a successful technology because it supports encapsulation, inheritance, and polymorphism. COM not only accepts and praises these concepts, but it firmly enforces and improves them. The client/server model has been discussed frequently in the previous chapters. It has many benefits, but one notable benefit is systems robustness. In the client/server model, a server can support numerous clients simultaneously. If a single client crashes, it will not bring down the server and all the other clients. Likewise, if the server crashes, it will not bring down its clients, assuming those clients gracefully handle the disconnection. Robustness is the main reason why COM embraces the client/server model. Dynamic linked libraries (DLLs) have been successful, for the most part, because they save space, support upgrades, and allow a runtime selection of functions needed by a client program.

COM supports interoperability within the confines of a single machine, but distributed COM (DCOM) extends COM to support distributed objects. This extension adds support for location transparency, remote activation, connection management, concurrency management, and security. In fact, many presenters and writers speak of DCOM as "COM with a longer wire". As shown in Figure 14.7, the DCOM wire protocol is built on top of Microsoft RPC, Microsoft's implementation of DCE RPC. This upper layer is termed ORPC, since it is a protocol that supports object-oriented remote procedure calls (ORPC).

Simply put, DCOM allows developers to concentrate their efforts on developing the functionality of their applications, without the worries of data marshaling and network protocol management. DCOM provides this support for easy distribution of objects in the global cyberspace. Its accessibility is superb, because it is an integrated part of Windows NT, Windows 95/98/2000, and future Windows platforms. Soon it will be supported on a variety of UNIX platforms; check out Software AG's "EntireX DCOM" product line at *http://www.sagus.com.*

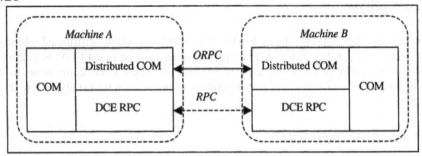

Figure 14.7. Distributed COM is built on top of DCE RPC

14.4.2 DCOM Facilities and Services

DCOM provides many facilities and services. Here we only introduce some of them which represent the main features of DCOM.

14.4.2.1 Location Transparency

When a client invokes a method using DCOM, it thinks that the method is executed locally. But in fact, the method can be anywhere in cyberspace. It could live in the same process as the client, a different process on the same machine, or a process on a machine two hundred miles away. From the client's perspective, there's no difference. This is the idea behind location transparency.

Location transparency depends upon marshaling. To support marshaling, DCOM uses a previous, proven technology known as DCE RPC. DCE RPC supports location transparency in the functional world. DCOM, which is built on top of RPC, supports location transparency in the object-oriented world. Like RPC, DCOM uses an interface to define a set of related functions, which are used for client and server communications. Given an interface, we can use a tool, called the Microsoft Interface Definition Language (MIDL) compiler, to fully generate corresponding marshaling code. This marshaling code is also referred to as proxy/stub code. In DCOM, each interface has an interface proxy and an interface stub. When a remote method invocation is made, possibly because the target object is two hundred miles away, these interface proxies and stubs will come to the rescue.

Location transparency conveys a number of benefits. It permits you to write the code that talks to a target object without worrying about where the object actually exists. The fact that objects can be located anywhere allows for greater flexibility and distribution. Location transparency also allows greater scalability and fault-tolerance.

14.4.2.2 Dynamic and Remote Object Activation

In an RPC environment, a server must be started manually or during computer start up. It must also listen for requests on a specific port. With DCOM, servers don't have to be started manually, because the DCOM infrastructure supports dynamic object activation. In other words, DCOM will dynamically activate servers upon client requests. With DCOM, a server doesn't have to listen for client requests the way legacy servers do in a client/server environment. DCOM handles this transparently. The object worries only about the services it provides, and this is a clear separation of responsibility.

The DCOM Service Control Manager (SCM), which is not the same as the NT SCM, supports remote activation. It lives on every machine that supports DCOM. One of its missions is to locate and activate distributed objects dynamically upon client requests. It works in conjunction with the system registry, since information regarding distributed objects is recorded in the registry. In Windows 2000, this information is maintained by the DCOM catalog, which works with the system registry and the active directory to locate components.

If an object lives in a DLL on the same machine, DCOM will dynamically load the DLL for the client process that uses the object. If an object lives in a separate EXE on the same machine, DCOM requests its local SCM to activate the EXE, so that the client process can use the object. If an object lives in a remote machine, there needs to be some coordination. In this case, the local SCM on the client machine contacts the remote SCM. The remote SCM is responsible for activating the remote EXE or DLL. For a remote EXE, the remote SCM simply spawns it. For a remote DLL, the remote SCM activates a registered surrogate process to dynamically load the DLL.

14.4.2.3 Security

One of the most important attributes of a distributed system is security. DCOM supports *launch, access,* and *call-level* security. Launch security, which is also called activation security, determines who can launch or activate the server component, and thus protects the server machine. With this support, the server component can be launched only by users or groups that are given the rights to do so. Remember that any client anywhere in cyberspace can potentially activate DCOM servers, so it would be disastrous if DCOM lacked support for launch security.

At this point, assume that a client has launch permissions and has successfully launched a remote server. But does the client have access to the component in question? Controlling access to a component, called access controls or access security, is the answer to this question, because it raises authorization to another level. Access controls allow the server component to limit user access to its objects, thereby protecting its objects from offenders.

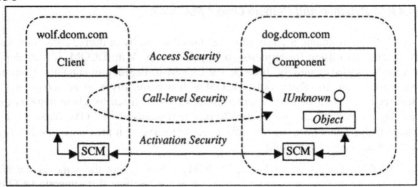

Figure 14.8. DCOM security

Now assume that a client has met both the launch and access security requirements. In other words, you have successfully established a connection and conversation with your remote object. What do you do about sniffers in the wild cyberspace who are tailgating, analyzing, and possibly modifying your packets? Call-level security shown in Figure 14.8 goes a step further to put these offenders to rest. For each method call, you can adjust the degree of data protection by changing the authentication level of the method invocation. There are several authentication levels supported by DCOM, such as data integrity and data privacy.

14.4.2.4 Interfaces

It is best to separate the software interface from its implementation because this allows easier integration among different components. For instance, if we use a service that other people provide, all we want to do is simply use the service via published interfaces. We do not care what they do underneath those interfaces, because we don't care about their implementation, so long as we get the services we need. The same idea applies to DCOM. The DCOM interface can be considered as a contract signed with the world regarding a provided service that will never be changed. Each interface is unique in time and space, because it is assigned an interface identifier (IID), a 128-bit globally unique identifier (GUID). This also means that version support is practically automatic, because each interface contains an identifier that is universally unique.

Interfaces are defined using MIDL, which is based on DCE IDL. MIDL is critical to DCOM because it defines the classes the DCOM library supports, the interfaces these classes support, and the methods offered by these interfaces. Typically, a DCOM object includes a number of well-defined and unalterable interfaces.

In DCOM, all interfaces must derived from a special interface called *IUnknown*. This interface is required to support the fundamentals of a robust and changing component, and it includes three extremely important methods: *QueryInterface, AddRef,* and *Release.* Clients call *QueryInterface* to dynamically discover other interfaces supported by an object, while *AddRef* and *Release* are used for management of an object's life cycle.

14.4.2.5 Binary Interoperability

Binary interoperability is an important aspect of software reuse. In the old days, when you deployed a development library, you had to ship header and library files. The customers had to link your library into their system in order for the system to work. With the advent of component technology, you need to ship only your binary. The customers no longer see header files or need to link with your libraries. Not only does binary interoperability make software integration easier, it allows the development and integration of plug-in components.

In DCOM, binary interoperability is achieved, believe it or not, by the use of interfaces. Each interface has a binary signature, via the use of a vtbl (table of function pointers) and vptr (pointer to a vtbl), as shown in Figure 14.9. To use an object, we must first acquire an interface pointer. The interface pointer points to the vptr, which points to the vtbl. Each instantiated object has a vptr, but there is a single vtbl per class. Once we get to the vtbl, we can find the resulting function. This vptr/vtbl technique is commonly used by C++ compilers to provide support for dynamic binding or polymorphism, and it is used here for binary interoperability.

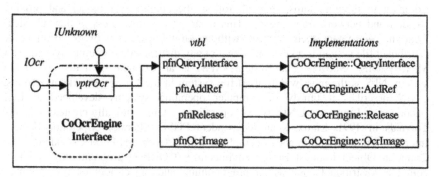

Figure 14.9. DCOM binary specification

The extra level of indirection has a powerful benefit for flexibility in languages. Any language or tool with a facility to support a notion of a pointer/reference can interoperate with DCOM objects.

14.4.3 Applying DCOM

This section lists only the services that are important for a distributed system. The developers' job is to apply and extend DCOM, by adding new interfaces, which are essentially immutable contracts. Make the contracts public, and the whole world can share them. In a sense, these interfaces are immortal. Everyone can communicate with them, like universal languages.

Let us quickly run through a few of the important standard interfaces that Microsoft has provided. Dynamic invocation is supported by the *IDispatch* interface, and event notification is supported by the *IConnectionPoint* family of interfaces. If you look further, there is the *IPersist* family of interfaces, which supports distributed object persistence. There is also the *IMoniker* family of interfaces that supports a smart aliasing, that allow a client to dynamically connect to the object to which the moniker refers. For uniform data transfer, use the *IDataObject* interface. And if you are looking for transaction support, check out Microsoft Transaction Server (MTS).

An interface is just a specification, because there is no implementation attached to it. Any DCOM object can implement these published interfaces to actually provide the corresponding services.

14.5 Summary

In this chapter we investigated several distributed network systems, i.e., distributed file systems, the UNIX/Linux operating system, CORBA, and DCOM systems. Common to these systems, they all follow the client-server model and provide location and network transparency. This means, users, regardless of their physical location, can obtain their services without knowing their network location. A distributed file system is a key component of any distributed computing system. Sun Microsystems' Network File System (NFS) is an example of a distributed file system. NFS is the most widely used file system in local area networks nowadays. UNIX describes a family of computer operating systems developed at Bell Laboratories. Linux is a UNIX type of operating system, originally created by Linus Torvalds in 1991. Linux is an independent POSIX (Portable Operating System Interface) implementation and is compliant with X/Open and POSIX standards. The Common Object Request Broker Architecture (CORBA) programming paradigm combines distributed client-server programming and object-oriented programming methodologies. Distributed Component Object Model (DCOM) is a viable distributed objects technology to develop distributed computing systems. It allows developers to concentrate their efforts on developing the functionality of their applications, without the worries of data marshalling and network protocol management.

Exercises

14.1   What is the purpose of a distributed file system? What services can it provide?   14.1.1

This page intentionally left blank

CHAPTER 15 DISTRIBUTED NETWORK SYSTEMS: CURRENT DEVELOPMENT

In this Chapter we outline the most recent developments in distributed network systems, through exploration of a range of topics that are currently "hot", such as Cluster computing, Computing Grid, Peer-to-peer computing, and Pervasive computing. It is a chapter to broaden readers' knowledge.

15.1 Cluster Computing

Clusters are now an attractive architecture for executing high performance applications and providing data storing and managing services, given their high scalability, availability and low cost to performance ratio. A cluster can be defined as a parallel or distributed system that consists of a collection of interconnected whole computers, that is utilized as a single, unified computing resource.

This rising interest in clusters has led to the formation of an IEEE Computer Society Task Force on Cluster Computing (TFCC1) in early 1999. An objective of the TFCC is to act both as a magnet and a focal point for all cluster computing related activities.

However, cluster programming and use are difficult as clusters suffer from a lack of dedicated operating system providing a Single System Image (SSI). Furthermore, given that cluster are composed of a collection of independent computers used by multiple users, the reliability of clusters are somewhat lacking. The loss of a computer in a cluster or of a single process can cause the failure of a parallel application and a huge computation loss. Hence, fault tolerance functionality is necessary. High availability requirements in clusters vary from general methods for fast application fail-over, to system support of shared data integrity and consistency. Currently, the main methods of preserving data consistency are various logging techniques. This approach can lead a major drawback in large clusters due to the extended fail-over time and the complexity of the recovery protocol, particularly when several nodes or the network fail.

Building cluster services has never been an easy task. One of the most challenging problems is data management. The data store must be scalable, efficient, easy to use and fault tolerant. Distributed replication provides high availability, fault-tolerance and enhanced performance. But these features come at a price: replication adds great complexity to the system development. Most of all, replication jeopardises data consistency. In turn, mechanisms have to be employed to enforce data consistency. Maintaining data consistency is very expensive. Performance and reliability of cluster computing could also be improved by replicating some services, either partially or fully, and distributed across several sites on the cluster.

Replicated services offer fault-tolerance and can improve performance by dispatching service requests to servers near to their users or to a lightly loaded server.

15.1.1 Cluster Operating Systems

Cluster operating systems should provide the following "desireable" features [Buyya 1998]:

- Sharing. The goal of a cluster is to make it possible to share a computing load over several systems without either the users or system administrators needing to know that more than one system is involved

- Manageability: An absolute necessity is remote and intuitive system administration; this is often associated with a Single System Image which can be realized on different levels, ranging from a high-level set of special scripts, down to real state-sharing on the operating system level.

- Stability: The most important characteristics are robustness against crashing processes, failure recovery by dynamic reconfiguration, and usability under heavy load.

- Performance: The performance critical parts of the operating system, such as memory management, process and thread scheduler, file I/O and communication protocols should work as efficiently as possible. The user and programmer should be able to transparently modify the relevant parameters to fine-tune the operating system for his or her specific demands.

- Scalability: If more processing power is needed the user simply "plugs in a new component", and the performance of the system as a whole improves. The scalability of a cluster is mainly influenced by the properties of the contained nodes, which is dominated by the performance characteristics of the interconnect. This includes the support of the operating system to be able to use the potential performance of the interconnect by enabling low-overhead calls to access the interconnect (inter-node scalability).

- Support: Many intelligent and technically superior approaches in computing failed due to the lack of support in its various aspects: which tools, hardware drivers and middleware environments are available. This support depends mainly on the number of users of a certain system, which in the context of clusters is mainly influenced by the hardware costs (because usually dozens of nodes are to be installed). Additionally, supports for interconnect hardware; availability of open interfaces or even open source; support or at least demand by the industry to fund and motivate research and development are important. All this leads to a user community that employs required middleware, environments and tools to, at least, enable cluster applications.

- Heterogeneity: Clusters provide a dynamic and evolving environment in that they can be extended or updated with standard hardware just as the user needs to or can afford. Therefore, a cluster environment does not necessarily consist of homogenous hardware requiring the same operating system; it should run across multiple architectures or at least support a set of standardized APIs to simplify the development of middleware layers enabling heterogeneous use.

- High Availability: If any component in the system, hardware or software fails the user may see degraded performance, but will not lose access to the service

It should be noted that experience shows that these goals may be mutually exclusive. For example, supplying an SSI at the operating system level, while a positive move in terms of manageability, drastically affects scalability. Another example is the availability of the source code in conjunction with the possibility to extend (and thus modify) the operating system on this base. This property has a negative influence on the stability and manageability of the system: over time, many variants of the operating system will develop, and the different extensions may conflict when there is no single supplier.

To provide a single system image – a cluster operating system - on top of a cluster, global management of resourses, such as memory, processor and disk should be performed. A lot of work has already been done in global resource management.

Regarding SSI, at least two variants of it should be distinguished: SSI for system administration or job scheduling purposes and SSI on a system-call level. The first is usually achieved by middleware, running daemons or services on each node delivering the required information to the administration tool or job scheduler. The latter would have to offer features like transparent use of devices located on remote nodes or using distributed storage facilities as one single standard file system. These features require extensions to current single-node operating systems.

An operating-system-level SSI implies detailed state sharing across all nodes of the cluster, and to this point, operating system (OS) researchers and practitioners have been unable to scale this to clusters of significant size (more than a hundred nodes) using commodity interconnects. That does not mean that an OS-level SSI is a bad thing; for the vast majority of clusters, which have less than 32 nodes, an operating-system-level single-system image may be quite workable.

By far the most common solution for cluster operating systems is to run a conventional operating system, with little or no special modification. This operating system is usually a Unix derivative, although NT clusters are becoming more common. The single most popular cluster operating system is Linux. Because it is free, and it is an open source operating system, meaning that one is free to customize the kernel to one's liking.

Sun Microsystems has developed a multi-computer version of Solaris; aptly named Solaris MC [Solaris MC] Solaris MC consists of a small set of kernel extensions and a middleware library. It incorporates some of the research advances from Sun's Spring operating system, including an object-oriented methodology and the use of CORBA IDL in the kernel. Solaris MC provides an SSI to the level of the device, i.e. processes running on one node can access remote devices as if they were local. The SSI also extends to a global file system and a global process space.

Solaris MC includes three key features for controlling and managing the processes running on a cluster:

- It supplies a global view of all the processes and users in the system and allows them to be controlled from a single point. This provides ease of administration and management of the cluster.

- It exports this global view and control of processes through the Solaris Application Binary Interface (ABI) so existing applications can see a global view of the system without modification. For example, we can view everything running on the cluster with the same UNIX command used on a single machine; thus the entire cluster can be managed from a single point, with the same command used in existing systems.

- It harnesses the power of the cluster through features that execute processes in multiple nodes in parallel. Solaris MC provides global control of processes, compatibility with existing software, and ability to use parallelism.

The Puma operating system [Puma], from Sandia National Labs and the University of New Mexico, represents the ideological opposite of Solaris MC. Puma takes a true minimalist approach. That is, there is no sharing between nodes, and there is not even a file system or demand paged virtual memory. This is because Puma runs on the "compute partition" of the Intel Paragon and Tflops/s machines, while a full-featured OS (e.g. Intel's TflopsOS or Linux) runs on the Service and I/O partitions. The compute partition is focused on high-speed computation, and Puma supplies low-latency, high-bandwidth communication through its Portals mechanism.

MOSIX [MOSIX] is a set of kernel extensions for Linux that provides support for seamless process migration. Under MOSIX, a user can launch jobs on their home node, and the system will automatically load balance and migrate the jobs to lightly loaded nodes. MOSIX maintains a single process space, so the user can still track the status of their migrated jobs. MOSIX is a mature system, growing out of the MOS project and having been implemented for seven different operating systems/architectures. MOSIX is free and is distributed under the GNU Public License.

The ChorusOS operating system [ChorusOS] is a highly scalable and reliable embedded operating system that has established itself among top telecom suppliers. The ChorusOS operating system is used in public switches and PBXs, as well as within access networks, cross-connect switches, voice-mail systems, cellular base stations, Webphones and cellular telephones. It is also used in a wide variety of other embedded applications, ranging from printing devices to factory automation. Its main features include:

- Component-based architecture for high configurability – Uses a highly-flexible, component-based architecture that allows different services to be configured into the run-time instance of the operating system

- Exceptional scalability – Component based design allows a very high degree of scalability; based on only the micro core executive, typically requires only about 10 Kilobytes of memory to run

- Multiple OS personalities and APIs – Can be run simultaneously on a common hardware platform using the ChorusOS operating system in such a way that diverse applications can communicate transparently.

- Inter-Process Communication – Allows applications to be distributed across multiple machines; the IPC feature identifies the location of a process (local or remote), and then identifies the shortest path and quickest execution time that can be used to reach it, managing the communication in a way that makes the process location entirely transparent to the application.

Cluster operating systems are similar in many ways to conventional workstation operating systems. How different one chooses to make the operating system depends on one's view of clustering. For some people, each node that runs a cluster operating system must be a full-featured operating system themselves. For others, a small kernal on each node is all it requires, then other common features required by each node will be provided by middleware.

15.1.2 Reliable Server Clusters

A key indicator of today's global business systems is the reliability and uptime [Grimshaw et al. 1999]. This concern is crucial for e-commerce sites and mission-critical business applications. Expensive and powerful servers that are designed as stand-alone systems can be very reliable, but even an hour of downtime per month can be deadly to online-only businesses.

Server clusters are increasingly used in business and academia to combat the problems of reliability since they are relatively inexpensive and easy to build [Buyya 1999], [TBR 1998]. By having multiple network servers working together in a cluster and using redundant components such as more than one power supply and RAID hard drive subsystems, the overall system uptime in theory can approach 100 percent. However, server clusters are only a part of a chain that links business applications together. For example, to access an HTML page of a business web site, a user issues a request that travels from the user's client machine, through a number of routers and firewalls and other network devices to reach the web site. The web site then processes the request and returns the requested HTML page via the same or another chain of routers, firewalls and network devices. The strength of this chain, in terms of reliability and performance, will determine the success or failure of the business, and a chain is only as strong as its weakest link, and the longer the chain, the weaker it is overall.

One way to make such a chain stronger is the use of redundancy (replication) and concurrency (parallelism) techniques. With replication, if one component fails, another replica is ready and able to take its place. If the second component fails, there must be a third one, and so on. With concurrency, multiple requests can be processed simultaneously and the performance can be improved. Redundancy and concurrency also have the potential to shorten the length of the chain since tasks can be allocated to multiple devices in parallel instead of to individual devices in a sequential order.

Another way to make the chain stronger is to increase the reliability of the weakest link of the chain. Nowadays, most web-based applications use the client-server model [Goscinski and Zhou 99]. In such applications, servers are the most likely performance bottleneck and point of failures, and the majority of server failures are software related [Guerraoui and Schiper 1997], [SUN 1997]. Therefore a key issue in building reliable and high-performance applications is to develop software systems for server clusters that are actually able to achieve extremely long uptimes and at the same time, to improve the system performance.

Although building reliable software is of paramount importance in many modern applications, fault-tolerant computing has long been regarded as a luxury in applications mainly due to its complexity and lack of tools to deal with this complexity. To build a reliable and high-performance software system, the developer must not only deal with the complex problems of distributed and parallel processing systems when all the components are well, but also the more complex problems when some of the components fail. The challenge here is to develop tools that enable developers to concentrate on their own application domain by freeing them from the difficulties of dealing with fault-tolerant and high-performance issues.

15.2   Grid Computing

15.2.1 What is Grid Computing?

Increasingly, organisations and academic institutions are using distributed clustering systems to support large-scale, resource intensive applications for scientific and industrial research. These systems are usually geographically isolated, and use a diverse range of clustering platforms to manage the sharing of computer resources on a local scale.

The emerging grid computing paradigm, aims to aggregate these islands of computer resources so they can be used as a single vast computing resource. In a manner analogous to public utilities such as the electric power grid, water and gas services, grid technologies aim to provide dependable, consistent, pervasive and inexpensive on demand access to computer resources [Foster and Kesselman 1998].

Grid computing focuses on large-scale, multi-institutional, resource sharing to deliver high performance. This wide-area sharing of resources can be used to facilitate virtual organisations, which according to [Foster et al. 2001] is the real problem grid computing aims to solve. Grid computing, and virtual organisations, allow multi-disciplinary, multi-institutional collaborations. This requires, co-ordinated, flexible and dynamic resource sharing models to enable a range of collaborative problem-solving and resource brokering strategies.   Therefore, the participants in a virtual organisation can share their resources to accomplish a common goal.

Grid computing can be divided broadly into two categories: computational grids and data grids. Computational grids provide access to pools of distributed processing power, whereas data grids access distributed data resources. Computational grid systems exploit the aggregate computing capacity of heterogeneous computer resources. These may include dedicated computer clusters, super computers, or the idle processor time of a department's workstations. In comparison, data grids focus on the efficient management, distribution and replication of large amounts of data [Stockinger 2001].

This data is typically distributed geographically and as with computational grids can be stored on workstations or dedicated clusters and supercomputers. The information aggregated in a data grid can be stored in distributed database systems or on file servers as a series of flat files. Once the data within a data grid system has been placed appropriately it can be processed computationally.

The difference between cluster and grid can be summarized as following:

- A Cluster requires a "Single System Image (SSI)" while a Grid does not require a single system view (although is could have SSI).

- A Cluster emphasises on performance of parallel processing while a Grid emphasises on resource sharing.

- Geographically a Cluster is located in a central location while a Grid is distributed in many places.

- Normally computers in a cluster are homogenous, while a grid involves heterogeneous computers and other resources.

Basic functions needed for a grid application include resource discovery and brokering, metering and accounting, data sharing, resource management, security, reliability and availability, virtual organizations, monitoring, and policy implementation and enforcement.

At the moment grid technologies are still developing, and open standardised grid architectures have not yet fully materialised. This section outlines the current direction of grid computing, highlighting the implications and short comings of current strategies and examining some of the possible future work [Casey and Zhou 2004].

15.2.2 Background to the Grid

Here we provide an overview of current grid technologies, and examine how they have developed from existing distributed and parallel systems. The applications of grid infrastructures are reviewed, followed by a discussion of virtual organisations and trust. Finally, the different classes of grid application are categorised in terms of their different application requirements, performance metrics, and levels of collaboration.

In part, the evolution and development of the emerging grid computing paradigm can be attributed to the major technology trends of the last 10 years. Over the past decade, distributed and parallel systems composed of cheap commodity computer resources have increasingly been used to support large-scale applications. In many institutions these systems have largely taken over the processing and storage roles super computers once had. Typically, these distributed resources use local-area networks as their communications channel and are geographically isolated from one another. However, these islands of resources can now be linked together using wide-area networks to exploit an enormous aggregate computer capacity. These fast wide-area networks have developed at a national scale in many countries, to provide Internet access for major cities, and high speed communications links between partner organisations [Foster and Kesselman 1998].

Clearly, distributed systems research is a critical area that has had a major influence on the development and evolution of grid computing systems. However, there are many differences in the systems and architectures that have been developed for the tightly coupled distributed systems and those created for the loosely coupled, high latency grid environment. High-performance distributed systems usually run within a local environment where the entire system can be tuned and controlled for maximum reliability and performance. These environments are typically, highly coupled, low latency, and have been designed for a single application domain [Casanova 2002].

In contrast, grid environments provide flexible application service environments that can be re-configured to support multiple application domains. These environments, work at a national or global scale, and cross multiple organisational and administrative boundaries. This allows grid applications to utilise the resources of multiple sites in an on-demand, and flexible manner. Grid systems operate as independent, decentralised, scaleable, dynamic services in which no single location has complete control over the entire grid system. Typically, these systems comprise loosely coupled, heterogeneous, resources that are bound by high latency communication systems. Consequently, these environments have multiple points of failure and require complex administration and security arrangements [Foster and Kesselman 1997].

The individual members of a grid system retain autonomy over their local systems and are able to clearly define which resources are to be shared, who is allowed to share, and the conditions under which sharing occurs. The sharing of a grid's resources is restricted, and the producers and consumers of resources must come to an agreement on the service level for a particular resource [Czajkowski et al. 2002]. This creates problems in controlling the reliability and performance of the grid, as no single location can has complete control over the entire system. Therefore, the resources of a grid system are more likely to be dynamic rather than static as grid resources can become available or unavailable for processing at any time.

According to [Iivonen 2004] an important step in the building of teams is the development of trust. In the context of virtual organisations the development of productive and efficient teams, is a critical issue. However, the development of group synergy, trust and identity follows a different path in virtual organisations, where often, team members hardly know each other and are unlikely to meet face to face [Lacono and Weisband 1997].

Traditionally, trust relationships develop over time as team members learn the advantages and disadvantages of trusting behaviour. Team members learn who to trust and how predictable people are in their trusting behaviour. Finally, the demonstration of trust allows a team or group to form a shared set of beliefs and values that defines the group's collective identity [Suzanne and Suzann 1997].

In contrast, the formation of virtual organisations is often on a temporary basis and can occur dynamically. Therefore, in the situation of a virtual organisation the gradual and incremental development of trust cannot occur. Typically, the goals of teams in temporary collaboration are efficient and speedy completion of project goals. In these circumstances, Meyerson, Weick and Kramer [Meyerson et al. 1996] suggest that group members concentrate on the completion of project tasks in absence of complete trust. Consequently, the aligned goals of group members help propel the temporary groups towards their collective goals. This concept is termed "swift trust" [Meyerson et al. 1996] and overcomes the need for traditional trust building exercises, allowing group members to move ahead quickly as if trust was already in place. The issue of trust is critical to collaborations in virtual environments, and can mean the difference between the success and failure of a project.

Virtual organizations facilitate the coordination of disparate and geographically isolated resources, in a flexible, collaborative and scaleable manner. Through the use of grid technologies virtual organizations facilitate the efficient use of computer resources, so that collaborative efforts do not generate redundant sets of data or perform duplicate processing. The mechanisms that grid infrastructures use to coordinate these resources are discussed in the next section.

Foster and Kesselman summarise the application of grid technologies into a number of categories, including distributed supercomputing, high throughput, on demand, data intensive, and collaboration.

Distributed supercomputing applications require vast amounts of processing time and storage space to solve complex simulation and analysis problems. In comparison, high throughput applications utilise the idle processor time of workstations connected to the grid to schedule loosely coupled or independent tasks across available hosts. On demand grid applications integrate the local resources of a company with those of the grid to meet the short term resource requirements for projects where it is inconvenient or economically unfeasible to use local resources. Data intensive applications concentrate on the creation of information from geographically distributed resources. This process can be demanding in terms of computational and communication performance. Collaborative computing applications facilitate person to person communication between different organisations. This communication supports the sharing of different resources and equipment and allows virtual organisations to be formed [Foster and Kesselman 1998].

15.2.3 Grid Architectures and Infrastructures

Here we first examine the components and services that make up a grid, then in the following sections, we highlight and review a selection of grid systems that are currently being developed. The systems reviewed include Globus, a layered system, which is one of the most widely deployed middleware systems; Legion, an object oriented virtual machine, and Condor, a cycle scavenging and opportunistic scheduling system. Finally, the technologies that comprise data grid systems are examined and reviewed.

15.2.3.1 Grid Architectures

Grid architectures build upon a large base of prior work and integrate a wide range of technologies to facilitate the development and use of virtual organisations and grid applications. These prior works encompass a range of computer technologies such as distributed systems, load balancing, security, fault tolerance, mobile agents, and wide-area networking. The services provided by these systems form the core components of grid architecture and middleware systems and allow grid users and applications to coordinate and use remote resources.

Currently, grid architectures and middleware services are un-standardised and there are many competing grid service models. Two of the most successful system architectures that have been deployed in grid systems are the layered protocol and the virtual machine environment. In the layered protocol architecture, successive system layers build upon the functionality of the lower levels. The layering of the system facilitates grid resource and application independence, as heterogeneous grid components can interact using the interfaces defined by the protocol.

Similarly, virtual machine architectures abstract the heterogeneity of grid resources. However, the abstraction of the virtual machine architecture is at a much higher level and grid components and resources are integrated into a single computing entity which is globally addressable. In comparison, layered systems abstract a grid's application domain and underlying resources to provide a common interface that is independent of the various hardware and software components contained in a grid.

15.2.3.2 Grid Components

Overall, the virtual machine and layered grid architectures support the same basic functionalities, such as resource allocation, process management, cycle scavenging, grid information services, security, communication, replication, data management and access, fault tolerance, as well as quality of service parameters. These system mechanisms are not particular to grid systems and have been modified to address the requirements of grid systems from the parallel and distributed systems research area.

Here we provide a brief introduction to a selection of core grid components highlighting the issues that are particular to grid systems. The remaining grid components and systems are discussed later in further detail in the relevant sections.

- Resource Allocation and Scheduling Systems: Resource allocation and process management systems schedule, match service requirements and migrate grid transactions, across the multiple, distributed, heterogeneous resources of a grid. These systems are complimented with load balancing and grid wide coordinating mechanisms, which are used to maximise the utilisation of a grids' resources. Allocation schemes primarily use two mechanisms to schedule transactions in a distributed environment. These are the state and model based allocation schemes, and these can be pre-emptive, or non-pre-emptive. Typically, grid systems employ decentralised grid resource allocation systems as their centralised counterparts do not scale well to the size and scope of grid environments.

  Pre-emptive systems allow jobs to be migrated to idle systems whilst programs are running, whereas jobs in a non-pre-emptive system remain on the same node. State based allocation systems, query the resources of a distributed environment to assemble an accurate picture of the systems' state. This allows jobs to be re-allocated or migrated to idle systems within a distributed environment. Unfortunately, this process is very expensive as every node in a distributed system or grid has to be queried about its state. In comparison, model based allocation schemes define system models that reflect the way resources are used in distributed systems. This allows the state of a distributed system to be predicted, and is efficient as the state of the system does not have to be retrieved. However, this may not be accurate, and depends on the system model used.

  Cycle scavenging systems utilise the idle processor time of workstations, and use their own allocation schemes and brokering systems to allocate and migrate jobs to idle hosts. Once a host has resumed foreground processing and is no longer idle, jobs are moved and re-allocated to idle systems. The systems that provide by cycle scavenging mechanisms are reviewed in further detail later.

- Grid Information and Directory Service Systems: Grid information and directory service components provide information relating to the state of a grid infrastructure. State information may relate to an individual node or the global state of an entire system and the supporting information services maybe centralised or decentralised. These information components are central to the function of a grid and publish information relating to the structure, system load, system failures, and hardware and software of a node. Grid information and directory service components provide functionality, in the allocation and scheduling of grid transactions.

  In the Globus system, information service components are distributed and report information relating to the status of individual nodes rather than the entire system [Czajkowski et al. 2001].

Similarly, Condor uses decentralised information system and uses a publishing mechanism to announce information relating a hosts' system load, and operating environment to other systems [Raman et al. 1998]. In comparison, Legion uses a combination of global and local information resources, which are both centralised and decentralised. Legion's global information database or collection object stores information relating to the state of resources in a single administrative domain. This collective database can be joined with those of other Legion domains to gain a global view of a Legion system [Chapin et al. 1999].

- Security: Authentication and Encryption: As with other networked systems that utilise public networks, such as the Internet, security in terms of authentication and encryption is an essential component. Grid authentication systems verify the identity credentials of users, grid transactions, grid resources and processes operating within grid environments. Similarly, encryption systems are used to encode and decode the messages of grid transactions to authenticate the messages and protect their contents.

The Globus toolkit provides basic interfaces to support various authentication and encryption systems and does not specify a particular system. Binding mechanisms have been created for plain text messages, the Kerberos authentication system, the X.509 certificate system, and SSL a public key cryptography scheme [Foster et al. 1998]. In comparison, the Legion system defines its security policies at the object level by over riding a class's default methods. These specify what an object is, and what it can do. The policies defined by these methods are then enforced by Legions' Magistrate objects, which can authenticate and specify the type of object that can run in a particular Legion jurisdiction [Lewis and Grimshaw 1995].

- Communication Links. The computer networks and protocols that service grid environments and other wide-area systems form a communications backbone that acts as a conduit for information flowing through a grid environment. Therefore, the choice of communication system, architecture and protocol can have a significant affect on the performance, availability and reliability of a grid environment. Currently, all the major grid systems Globus, Legion, and Condor use standard TCP/IP streams as their basic communication protocol. Grid specific protocols are then layered on top of TCP/IP to deliver grid messages, transactions, and to coordinate and manage grid components.

Typically, grid infrastructures use peer-to-peer network architectures to support the decentralised structure of grid environments. In some cases, vestiges and variations of the client-to-server architectures can be seen. For example, the Condor system utilises a central manager to schedule and allocate resources within the local environment, whilst also exploiting the resources of remote systems by linking multiple off-site central managers using a process known as flocking [Thain et al. 2003].

Grid communities are linked primarily with high speed, wide-area links and are generally on a performance scale similar to Internet 2 based systems. These underlying network links maybe composed of a range of wide-area network technologies such as microwave ATM links, satellite connections, and fibre optic cables. Consequently, the network systems that link grid environments are just as heterogeneous as the computer systems they integrate. Therefore, network latency and bandwidth are highly variable.

Currently, there are many projects underway to create multi Gbps wide area links between the major universities and research centres of various countries and regions around the world. For example, the Internet 2 system being developed in the United States currently links a number of high performance computer centres in various universities and national laboratories at speeds upto 10 Gbps using fibre optic cables. Similar, projects are underway through out the world to link the capital cities of different countries and regions with high speed wide-area communication links.

15.2.4 Layered Grid Architecture: The Globus Architecture

The Globus infrastructure uses a layered service model that is analogous to other layered services such as the OSI network protocol. The components of each layer share common characteristics, and build upon the capabilities and behaviours provided by the lower layers [Foster et al. 2001]. The Globus project defines a set of standard grid protocols that specify how grid resources are managed and coordinated across wide-area networks. The Globus toolkit and middleware services and protocols are used in many grid projects such as GriPhyN [Avery and Foster 2001], Nimrod-G [Buyya et al. 2000], and Condor-G [Frey et al. 2001] to name a few. The Globus toolkit has been developed in collaboration with Argonne National Laboratory, the University of Chicago, the University of Southern California Information Sciences Institute, and the High Performance Computing Laboratory at the Northern Illinois University.

The Globus architecture has five layers: Application, Collective, Resources, Connectivity, and Fabric. The Globus architecture supports the sharing of compute resources as well as data resources [Foster et al. 2001].

The fabric layer provides a transparent interface for high level grid components to coordinate, access, and share grid resources such as storage systems, catalogues, network and computational capacity, as well as scientific equipment and sensors. Fabric layer components can access distributed resources as an aggregate logical entity or as a distributed computer pool. In the case of a distributed resource pool the fabric layer can interact with the resources using their own protocols' and APIs' encapsulating the resource from the higher level components.

The different resources accessible by the fabric layer use implementation, resource specific fabric components to expose their functionality to the higher layer grid components. For example, the fabric components handling computational resources provide interfaces for starting, monitoring and controlling the execution of processes. In comparison, storage resource components provide mechanisms to send and receive files, manage quota systems, file replication schemes and striped file transfers. Therefore, the different functionality of the lower level resources can easily be mapped into the fabric layer transparently for use by higher level components.

The connectivity layer functions as a communications conduit between different fabric layer components, and defines a suite of core communications and authentication protocols for efficient and secure grid access. These protocols build on existing network and security protocols such as TCP/IP and public key infrastructure systems, respectively.

The resource layer builds upon the core transport and security protocols of the connectivity layer, supplementing them with job management and control functions as well as resource inquiry protocols. These resource level protocols provide an interface to individual grid resources, acting as common interface to heterogeneous resources.

This abstraction of a resources interface, allows the higher level collective and application layers to coordinate a grid's resources in a uniform manner, without having to consider the operation and idiosyncrasies of individual grid resources.

The job management and control protocols initiate, control and secure grid resource operations, specifying quality of service parameters as well as payment functions. In comparison, the resource inquiry protocols are used to inspect the state and configuration of a particular resource, and to provide monitoring and accounting functions on sharing operations.

At the resource level, the Globus toolkit defines several protocols to control, manage, and inspect the state of individual grid resources. These protocols are the HTTP based GRAM (Grid Resource Access and Management); GRIP (Grid Resource Information Protocol); GRRP (Grid Resource Registration Protocol); and GridFTP a grid enabled extension of the FTP protocol. The details of these protocols will be later in this section.

In comparison to the resource layer which controls access to individual resources, the collective layer coordinates access to the combined resources of a grid. Therefore, the protocols, services, API's and SDK's of the collective layer provide a broad range of sharing mechanisms that consider the interactions of multiple resources combined within a grid. These mechanisms support multiple sharing behaviours through the abstractions of the resource layers interface. As a result, extra functionality does not need to be added to individual resources to support various modes of sharing.

A number of applications are used to coordinate access to grid resources at the collective layer. These collective services typically extend the protocols of the resource layer so that the resources of an entire grid can be controlled and managed. Typical, applications include directory services, scheduling, monitoring and diagnostics as well as a number of programming interfaces.

The top level application layer provides a consistent interface to a grid's resources, allowing grid and virtual organisation applications to transparently access the distributed resources of a grid infrastructure. Grid applications may access any of the layered components of a grid. However, typically they customise the general services and program interfaces of the collective layer to form a specific application.

15.2.5 Virtual Machine Environment: The Legion Architecture

In contrast, the Legion system architecture specifies a globally addressable, object oriented, virtual machine environment that simplifies the integration and function of grid components. Legion transparently, integrates system components into a single grid architecture, which has a single address space and file system as well as global functions for process management, input-output, inter-process communication, and security [Natrajan et al. 2001]. Similar, distributed, object orientated, virtual machine architectures are used in Harness [Migliardi and Sunderam 1999], SUMA [Hernandez et al 2000], and Globe [Steen et al. 1997].

The Legion architecture provides the user with a single coherent system view, in which objects represent hardware and software components. These objects are active processes, and can communicate with each other through method invocations. Every object in Legion has its own address space, class, name and set of capabilities [Grimshaw et al. 1994].

The Legion system is developed at the University of Virginia and has evolved from their earlier work Mentat [Grimshaw 1993] an object-oriented parallel processing system. Mentat has heavily influenced the development of Legion, and a modified version of mentat with added capability for heterogeneous resources was originally used as a prototype of the Legion architecture [Grimshaw and Wulf 1997].

Extensibility and flexibility are the main philosophy of the Legion system, and this allows developers to either use the pre-defined Legion system classes or to develop their own specialised classes. This is in keeping with the viewpoint that different applications have different requirements and allows developers to make their own choices about system functionality and performance.

The Legion system comprises a runtime library [Ferrari, et al. 1996] as well as a set of core class components [Lewis and Grimshaw 1995] that support the basic system level functions required by a grid architecture. These system classes support a rich set of functionalities such as data access, object management, persistence, as well as inheritance, and object binding functions. Every class in the Legion universe derives from these system classes, inheriting their methods and data structures.

The core classes of the Legion system are the LegionObject from which every class is derived, the LegionClass which provides methods for managing objects, inheritance, and object binding. The LegionVault class handles object persistence and the LegionBindingAgent class binds an object to a particular address [Lewis and Grimshaw 1995].

In Legion class instances can be either active or inert. When in an active state an object has its own address space and thread of execution and can receive messages.

Conversely, inert objects are stored on disk, and are not running. Therefore, they cannot receive or process messages. Legion's object management system transparently activates and deactivates objects on demand at runtime, deactivating unused objects, and re-activating objects that are awaiting processing [Grimshaw et al. 1994].

When deactivating objects, the Legion system supports the persistence of an objects state to disk. Using this process, the state of a deactivated object can be reloaded when an object is re-started. State persistence is optional, and is defined by the class of an object. Stateless objects can be thought of as pure functions [Lewis and Grimshaw 1995].

In a Legion system site control is decentralized through the use jurisdictions and magistrate objects. Jurisdictions are a logical extension of an organizations control, and the resources of a grid system are partitioned into separate domains of control. The sphere of influence a jurisdiction has may overlap with other jurisdictions.

The core functionality of Legion is prescribed using several abstract classes and these are described below [Lewis and Grimshaw 1995]:

- LegionObject: The LegionObject class acts as an abstract base class providing essential access and persistence methods. Every class and object in the Legion system is derived from the LegionObject class. Therefore, each class in the Legion system is an object.

- LegionClass: The LegionClass is derived from the LegionObject class and defines interfaces for several mandatory class functions, such as object creation, deletion, inheritance, and binding information. Every class in the Legion system is derived from the LegionClass.

- LegionHost: The LegionHost class defines an abstract interface to represent a host environment. Subclasses of the LegionHost override the abstract class's methods to suit different environments. LegionHost objects, control resources, create and execute objects and define the policies that control which objects can execute on a particular host.

- LegionVault: Vault objects provide interfaces to persistent storage devices and are able to store and retrieve the state of an object, onto a particular storage device. Vault objects, exist on every host of a Legion system, and they are used in the migration of objects from one node to another. Therefore, when objects and their state are transferred or replicated to new sites, they are initially persisted into a vault object, and then transferred to a remote node. Finally, the inert object is re-activated on the new node.

- LegionMagistrate: Magistrate objects form the basis of Legion's trust management system and are used to control access to the different jurisdictions of a Legion grid system. For each jurisdiction, magistrate objects control which Legion objects are able to access a particular resource, and the operations they can perform on that resource. Therefore, sub classes of the magistrate class can be used to define the access rights, and system policies of an organisation participating in a Legion environment.

- Legion Object Identifiers (LOID): Every object in a Legion system is identified by a unique system wide, Legion Object Identifier. Object identifiers contain three sections, and these are a class identifier, a class specific section and a public key section. The class identifier section is used by LegionClass to define a unique identifier for a new derived class. The class specific section is set to zero for class definitions, and can be used by class instances as a method for ensuring unique system identifiers for each class instance. The public key section is used security and authentication. However, the location of an object is not specified and this is handled by a Legion Binding agent discussed below.

- Legion Binding Agent: In Legion binding agents bind the address of an object to its object identifier (LOID). The LegionBindingAgent class is an abstract class that provides the necessary interface, to query an objects address based upon an object identifier (LOID), and to add and remove object bindings.

In comparison to the static layering of the Globus architecture, Legion defines an extensible layering system that can be re-configured to use extra service layers that support additional functionality. The Legion runtime library uses event handling mechanisms to control the order in which the layers of the protocol stack are called. For example, when an event is announced it is typically handled by the default service, except in cases where the default handler has been overridden (it has a higher priority). In these cases the new handler intercepts the event, performs the required functionality and passes the event onto the original default service. In this way, the service layers of the Legion protocol stack can be reconfigured [Ferrari, et al. 1996]. Legion objects are autonomous, and communicate with each other using non-blocking unordered function calls. The interface of Legion objects is described using an interface description language (IDL), which specifies the methods of a particular object. To support site autonomy, the Legion environment is partitioned into a set of independent jurisdictions. These jurisdictions are controlled and managed by magistrate objects that reflect the policies of a particular jurisdiction.

The main advantage of the Legion system is that every component is defined as an object. This simplifies the development of complex distributed environments, and facilitates software re-use, modularization, and component interoperability. However, the object oriented paradigm can cause problems as legacy software and grid resources have to be wrapped in objects. Therefore, the underlying systems of a node in the Legion environment have to be masked within an object wrapper so as to be integrated into the environment. This adds another layer of complexity to the system.

The Legion system has since been transformed into a commercial product, through a spin off company, Avaki Corporation. The Avaki system is essentially the same as the original Legion environment. However, the configuration and installation of the Legion/Avaki grid system has been improved dramatically to ease the creation of a grid environment using Legion/Avaki software [Grimshaw et al. 2003].

15.2.6 Cycle Scavenging Schemes: The Condor System

Cycle scavenging systems utilize the computational resources of idle desktop workstations. These systems use opportunistic scheduling mechanisms, to allocate and migrate processes and grid transactions to idle systems, without impacting the performance of a system owner's applications.

Condor [Thain et al. 2003] and Entropia [Entropia 2003] are two popular systems that utilise cycle harvesting mechanisms to exploit the idle resources of networked computer systems. These systems essentially use a similar function to allocate, schedule and migrate jobs across the idle resources of workstation class computers. However, there are some differences, Entropia for instance can only utilise the resources of Microsoft Windows 2000 based machines.

Whereas, Condor can make use of both UNIX and Windows based workstations as well as aggregating the computer capacity of dedicated systems such as clusters.

Other systems include SETI@Home, Distributed.net, DAS (Distributed ASCI Supercomputer), GUSTO Popular Power, Mojo Nation, United Devices, and Parabon. In this section the architecture of Condor is examined in detail.

Condor is a batch scheduling system that utilizes cycle scavenging mechanisms to exploit both opportunistic and dedicated compute resources and has been developed at the University of Wisconsin since 1988. Condor facilitates the integration of computer resources through out an organization, allowing the scheduling and allocation of jobs to both dedicated systems such as clusters and idle workstations [Thain et al. 2003].

Dedicated distributed systems including clusters are typically composed of many, cheap commodity computers that are linked using standard Ethernet communication links, and housed in their own controlled environment. These systems make use of dedicated scheduling algorithms, which assume a constant, controlled, error free environment.

However, Miron Levny and the Condor development [Wright 2001] team contend this assumption, and argue that dedicated systems as with other systems cannot be expected to be completely available over the long term due to uncontrollable hardware and software failures as well as maintenance tasks. Therefore, Condor's opportunistic scheduling mechanisms assume that resources will not be available for the complete duration of a job. Consequently, the design of Condor's dedicated allocation system leverages the checkpointing mechanisms exploited by Condor's opportunistic scheduling algorithms.

Condor's job check pointing system, transparently and periodically records the state of jobs being processed in a Condor system. This allows Condor to subsequently resume jobs and continue job execution, from where they left off by reading a processes state from a checkpoint file. Therefore, Condor's check pointing system affords a level of fault tolerance by allowing interrupted jobs to be resumed in the face of failures and random system availability. Consequently, Condor's check pointing system is able to maintain the cumulative time spent executing a job.

Additionally, Condor's check pointing mechanisms also facilitate job migration from one system to another. This allows Condor to re-allocate jobs to idle systems once a system is no longer idle [Wright 2001].

The Condor system architecture has developed incrementally over the years, as new technologies and extra requirements have been integrated into the project. Originally, the Condor system could only be used at a single location using LAN technology. Since then, faster wide are networks have developed so Condor has been extended to integrate the resources of multiple sites using a mechanism known as flocking. Several components comprise the Condor system and these components manage and provide services such as "resource management, job management, matchmaking and so on" [Wright 2001].

Condor pools are controlled using a central manager, which runs two daemon services the Collector and Negotiator respectively.

- Collector: The Collector service, acts a directory and information service component, storing and relating information pertaining to the state of each resource within a Condor resource pool. Periodically the machines that make up a Condor pool send updated information, describing their system state and availability. This information is related using a mechanism known as a ClassAd, which is a simple data structure containing information, describing the various conditions a system resource can be under.

- Negotiator: Once jobs have been submitted to the Condor pool, they're resource requirements are advertised to the central manager's Negotiator daemon, also using the ClassAd mechanism.

The Negotiator service, performs a matchmaking operation, and attempts to find compatible requirements between resource requests, and resource offers. After resource request is satisfied, "both parties are notified and are responsible for acting on that match" [Wright 2001].

15.2.7 Data Grids

The architecture of grid environments can be further broken into two broad application domains, computationally intensive grids and data intensive grids. Computational grids pool, and aggregate the processing capabilities of geographically isolated and administratively independent machines into an integrated grid system. Similarly, data grids focus on the distribution and replication of large amounts of raw data at geographically disparate computing sites. Therefore, despite the differences in application domain, the core low level services of computational grids and data grids are essentially the same. Consequently, there is a significant overlap in the functionality of these systems. Nevertheless, the components of the resource and collective layers in computational grids and data grids necessarily support different functionalities to support the sharing of compute and data resources respectively.

Data grid technologies deal primarily with the efficient management, placement and replication of large amounts of data [Stockinger 2001].

Here we examine these issues in detail, and reviews the data grid tools and mechanisms of the Kangaroo, Legion, Globus and Storage Resource Broker (SRB) projects. The Globus toolkit provides core infrastructure capabilities such as resource management, information services, security, fault tolerance and transport services that are common to grid systems. In comparison, SRB provides basic storage functions such as data and metadata access for distributed, heterogeneous environments such as databases, file systems, and archival storage systems [Baru et al. 1998]. Together, these systems form the basis for a number of developing data grid applications and projects such as GriPhyn [Avery and Foster 2001], PPDG (Particle Physics Data Grid) [PPDG], IPG (Nasa Information Power Grid) [NIPG], NEESgrid (Network for Earthquake Engineering Simulation) as well as many others.

15.2.7.1 Kangaroo

Kangaroo [Thain et al. 2001] is a data management system for grid environments uses an opportunistic process to cache and schedule grid input/output transactions in a similar manner to its parent project Condor the high-throughput computing project. Kangaroo temporarily uses a workstation's storage resources to buffer data resources across chains of workstations. This process works transparently and facilitates the replication of file and object resources across multiple workstation resources. Therefore, Kangaroo can offer high availability and high reliability data access mechanisms to resources, as system failures and errors can be overcome by the access of alternate file and object replicas. Kangaroo processes input and output operations uses a background service, allowing foreground applications to share a workstations processor time concurrently. This promotes a higher aggregate system performance as there are more resources available to handle parallel and striped data transfers.

15.2.7.2 Legion

The Legion grid environment facilitates data grid functionalities [White et al. 2001] such as wide-area replication, and data transport using the Legion File System (LegionFS) and its BasicFileObject class. The BasicFileObject instances provide fundamental read(), write() and seek() method calls that allow file data to be stored within an object. ContextObject instances manage the Legion namespace, and provide a directory system abstraction. The BasicFileObject instances are linked directly to underlying filesystems using ProxyMultiObject instances which aggregate multiple file objects and write and read their contents to and from disk. Files and object instances can be replicated within Legion by classes which map object identifiers (LOIDS) to multiple physical objects.

15.2.7.3 Storage Resource Broker

The Storage Request Broker (SRB) has been developed to provide seamless access to a variety of distributed storage systems using a common interface. The SRB middleware supports get and put functions on remote storage devices, query and update operations in conjunction with the metadata catalogue, as well as transport operations for the sending and retrieval of remote files and information. The heterogeneous resources that SRB links are wrapped in driver programs, which are able to map a resources interface into SRB's uniform interface. Additionally, SRB also provides authentication and encryption mechanisms as required [Baru et al. 1998].

Information written into an SRB is organized using a hierarchical structure, similar in nature to traditional directory structures in local file systems. The structure is logical and defines collections and sub-collections to map the relationships between various files and objects. These files, objects and collections maybe distributed across numerous heterogeneous resources. Collections are defined by grouping various physical storage resources (PSRs) into logical storage resources (LSR's), which can optimize file access using replication. Consequently, the logical structure of a collection has no mapping to the physical location of a resource [Baru et al. 1998].

MCAT a standalone system is the metadata system SRB uses and is able to define hierarchical access control, the physical location of a file, object or data item and its logical name. Currently, the systems schema is hard coded but systems are being developed to create an extensible metadata schema.

In a manner similar to Condor, SRB uses a client-to-server architecture to manage the physical storage resources (PSRs) of local-area network sites. These servers are later combined into a larger federation, whereby individual SRB servers are connected in a fashion akin to Condor's flocking mechanism.

15.2.7.4 Globus Data Grid Tools

Conversely, the Globus data grid system leverages a number of existing data access systems and core grid infrastructure services, such as storage resource services provided by SRB, MCAT and the resource discovery, management and directory service components of the Globus toolkit. Together, these low level components are combined to form the core data access and management components of the Globus data grid. As with the other components of the fabric layer, system components independent of Globus are integrated into the system using a uniform interface. This allows the functionality of various storage and resource systems to be mapped into the Globus system transparently, for use by higher level service components, which manage and coordinate a grid's data access functions.

Globus uses a number of high level components to perform functions such as data management, transport, replication and replica selection. Data management and transport functions, allow remote access and control of data that is distributed through out a grid system. Whereas, the replication systems copy or cache distributed files and objects to local systems to optimise file access time and file availability.

The Globus data transport system gridFTP [Allcock et al. 2002] leverages a number of established technologies such as the long standing FTP (file transfer protocol), the Kerberos authentication system and the Globus GSI (Grid Security Infrastructure) to provide a fast, secure and robust data transfer service. To these systems Globus adds a number of key features such as parallel TCP/IP data streams, striped and partial data transfers, third party control, and fault recovery [Allcock et al. 2002].

Parallel data streams utilize the aggregate bandwidth of multiple TCP/IP streams to improve the overall data transfer performance. Similarly, striped data transfers further enhance the bandwidth available to data transfers by interleaving data transfers across multiple hosts. The partial file transfer function facilitates the transfer of arbitrary sections or regions of files to support file fragmentation schemes. The third party control mechanism allows authenticated applications or users to initiate, monitor and control data transfer operations between source and destination nodes. GridFTP's fault recovery system ensures the reliable transfer of data between nodes, and uses a number of operations to detect and restart failed transfers. These maybe the result of problems such as as transient network communications and server outages.

The Globus replica management system is responsible for creating and deleting file and object replicas at multiple storage sites as well as registering and de-registering replica information within the system replica catalogue. The Globus replica management system acts as file and object caching system and copies objects and data files to local systems for improved access performance. However, Globus does not enforce consistency when accessing replicas and dispenses with complicated locking schemes and atomic transactions as used in some distributed databases. Therefore, for the majority of cases Globus replicas are used in a read only manner. The replica catalogue maps logical filenames to physical storage resources recording site addresses and filenames of replica instances.

The Globus replica selection system is the process that ensures the efficient selection of file replicas distributed throughout a grid system. As with other resource allocation schemes, a matchmaking process is used to select a particular resource. The Globus system borrows the classAd matchmaking system developed by Condor to match resources based upon advertised storage capabilities and storage resource requirements. These storage classAds publish information such as hostname, storage space, bandwidth, latency, reliability, system policies, and volume name. The attribute value pairs of these advertisements are then matched using a decentralized storage brokering system. This system searches for replicas matches based upon capability and requirements, and initializes access to these resources using gridFTP [Vazhkudai et al. 2001].

15.2.8 Research Issues and Challenges for Grids

Grid Computing aims to couple geographically distributed resources and offer transparent, powerful, and inexpensive services irrespective of the physical location of resources or access points [Foster et al. 2002a]. To achieve such a vision, however, it is still a challenge to develop tools and middleware that can seamlessly integrate computing devices, clusters, data storage, and networks; can provide a available and reliable source of computing power; can automatically allocate resources according to user preferences and computational demand; can provide sophisticated analysis, debugging and visualisation services, and can facilitate and enable information and knowledge sharing.

The nature and application of Grid architectures and technologies is currently solidifying as large scale scientific, medical and engineering research programs increasingly adopt grid technologies. This has led to the development of industry and research based standards such as the Open Grid Services Architecture (OGSA) which define the functionality and application of a number of core service components. However, there are still many hurdles to overcome before Grid applications become as pervasive as web applications and the Internet are today. This section examines a number of research issues providing reference to related work as well as outlining some possible solutions.

15.2.8.1 Software Engineering Problems

As with other distributed systems there are a number of significant challenges in regard to the development and analysis of grid applications. Currently, programmers are exposed directly to the raw complexities of grid environments and are faced with systems that require them to coordinate several independent system components. Until application level system libraries, which hide the Grid's underlying complexities become widely available the development of grid applications will be hampered. At the moment several application programming interfaces (API) are being developed to simplify access to a grid's resources. These systems integrate various grid service components into a single coherent interface. Systems which use this approach include MPICH-G2 [Karonis et al. 2003], Cactus [Allen et al. 2001] and the Grid Application Development Software (GrADS) [Berman et al. 2002].

System errors and faults as with other sequential and distributed systems is an inevitable component of an applications life cycle. Typically, programmers employ sophisticated debugging and monitoring toolkits to trace system failures, break on specific conditions and step through erroneous code blocks. This allows programmers to isolate, diagnose and correct system errors. However, in distributed environments such as computational and data grids, applications can use thousands of heterogeneous systems. Therefore, in these environments system maintenance operations such as debugging and process monitoring can become very complicated. Some of the major issues associated with parallel and distributed debugging systems are examined here briefly:

- Difficulty obtaining a global snapshot of a grid system

- Multiple independent program components execute concurrently

- Cannot re-create execution sequences exactly, due to variance in system load

- Large-scale heterogeneous grid systems

- Increased network latency in wide-area environments.

Currently, a number of parallel and distributed process debuggers are available and these are actively being scaled up to work with grid systems. These include p2d2 a portable parallel/distributed debugger [Hood and Jost 2000] which is currently being modified for use with Globus and NetLogger a dynamic grid monitoring and debugging service [Gunter et al. 2003].

Finally, performance evaluation is another application of critical importance to the development of grid environments. System performance is a measurement of the efficiency with which different grid components complete their tasks under different conditions. Unfortunately, at the moment it is nearly impossible to create controllable reproducible test results using current grid environments, due to changing conditions such as network latency, congestion, system load, and various system failures. Therefore, results taken from grid environments can really only provide a rough indication of a particular algorithms efficiency. This has lead to the development of simulation environments such as GridSim [Buyya and Murshed 2002] and Bricks [Takefusa et al. 1999] which use discrete event simulation to model interactions between the components of a grid and record performance results. These systems provide a controlled and reproducible environment in which to generate test results.

15.2.8.2 Load Balancing and Scheduling

As with other distributed systems, request allocation, job scheduling and load balancing is an important issue that has a direct effect on system throughput and job turn around time. Scheduling systems typically analyse or predict a systems state to determine the best node to allocate a job to. Current, grid systems primarily use predictive models which allocate jobs to idle systems based upon an approximation of a system's state. These models are more efficient as the global state of a system does not have to be queried.

At the moment, there is a trend for grid systems to use market and economic based models. These models partition grid resources into a computational economy where resources are traded as if they were physical currency. Users can then specify a budget and job deadline, allowing the scheduling system to allocate computer resources to meet the deadline and budget requirements. Several scheduling systems facilitate computational economies and these include Nimrod-G [Abramson et al. 2002], GRaDS [Berman et al. 2002] and Condor-G [Frey et al. 2001].

Other models allocate resources based upon predicted performance, and allocate jobs to machines based upon how fast a job is predicted to finish on a particular system. Unfortunately, these performance model systems are often greedy and do not consider other jobs entering a system, which can lead to lacklustre performance. Systems which use these models include AppLeS [Berman et al. 2003] and Matchmaker [Raman et al. 1998]. Finally, many job scheduling systems attempt to rebalance system resources dynamically and migrate jobs from busy to idle systems. This technique can improve performance and facilitates improved resource utilisation.

15.2.8.3 Autonomic Computing

Autonomic computing systems combine sensors, reactive computing and data mining techniques to automatically manage, detect and respond to system events. This means autonomic systems will be able to configure, and optimise themselves as well mitigate system failures and malicious attacks and intrusions.

In a manner analogous to immune systems autonomic agents use sensors to monitor system events and components, and to respond and adapt to them [Kephart and Chess 2003]. These concepts include:

- Self-configuration. Automated configuration of components and systems follows high-level policies. Rest of the system adjusts automatically and seamlessly.

- Self-optimization. Components and systems continually seek opportunities to improve their own performance and efficiency.

- Self-healing, System automatically detects, diagnoses, and repairs localized software and hardware problems.

- Self-protection. System automatically defends against malicious attacks or cascading failures. It uses early warning systems to anticipate and prevent system-wide failures.

Therefore, in the future it is envisaged that successful grid systems will to some extent include some form of autonomic functionality. Consequently, grid platforms will eventually have to integrate agent technology, and data mining and machine learning processes.

Autonomic computing is an emerging technology, which provides many exciting opportunities and possibilities in the areas of configuration-management, system optimization, and protection in large-scale grid environments.

15.2.8.4 Replication

File and object replication is an important optimisation strategy used in data grids to copy or cache data on local systems to improve the reliability and performance of data access. Therefore, the schemes data grid applications use to create, place, update and select replicas can have a significant impact on the performance, reliability and scalability of data grid applications.

Replica placement strategies must decide, where, when and by whom replicas are propagated through out a distributed system. Primarily, there are two distinct methods used to propagate replica data. These are the server initiated "push" and client initiated "pull" strategies. Server based push strategies actively enhance performance by replicating data items close to client/server systems, where high demand exists for particular file and object data sets. Therefore, deciding or predicting which files and data sets are likely to be in high demand and determining a feasible threshold for replication is a key issue [Tanenbaum and Steen 2002]

In comparison, client based pull strategies passively store copies of files they have previously requested and downloaded. Therefore, clients manage their own cache system and can access previously requested files and data directly from local file systems. This process can significantly improve performance by reducing latency and bandwidth requirements. A key issue for client based replication systems is the size of the cache and when to update or remove old or stale replicas.

For subscription based publication systems such as the World Wide Web and Grid, file and data sets are often published with minimal changes or update operations [Opyrchal et al. 2000], [Casanova 2002]. Therefore, it can be assumed that the majority of file operations are read functions. Consequently, replication and caching systems that function in these environments can implement weaker cache coherency and consistency controls because there are fewer updates. In these circumstances, prediction based push mechanisms can be used to broadcast replica data to peer groups that are interested in the same or similar topic. As a result performance is improved because data and documents are sent to local systems before they are required. However, for Grid environments the situation may not be so simple because data grid publishing mechanisms may not conform to the assumption that data is usually only published once and rarely modified. Current, virtual organisation and grid systems follow this assumption but there is no reason to expect this trend to continue as data grid applications develop.

Another interesting assumption that can be used to improve performance in routing replica data, is regionalism as discussed in [Opyrchal et al. 2000] a web caching paper. This paper utilises IP multicast to broadcast replica data to geographically neighbouring systems. In this way the under utilised links of edge systems and local area networks can be put to better use to broadcast replica data directly to topologically grouped systems. As with the previous assumption this is only useful if a high level of regionalism exists between the data sets of grid applications. According to Cassanova's work [Casanova 2002] this may not hold true over the long term as multidisciplinary grid applications emerge.

In general, depending on different circumstances and application scenarios, data grid applications should exhibit some form of access pattern in the reading and writing of replica data. Therefore, conclusions can be drawn to give a rough guide to the location, time frame and type of data that needs to be replicated.

Additionally, once the different classes of data grid transaction have been identified, data access models could be developed to approximate the behaviour of file access requests. This could allow replica placement schemes to predict where replicas are required using data access models to minimise costly state inquiry operations.

Unfortunately, the accuracy of such models is not always so good. Therefore, model based placement strategies may generate a large proportion of cache misses.

However, data grid applications are still developing and the way they access file and object replicas is changing. Therefore, accurate conclusions cannot really be drawn about the type of access pattern for every single class of data grid application. As a result, replica placement schemes will have to adapt automatically to work with different usage scenarios. Once these patterns have been established the replication scheme can simply choose an optimal strategy for a particular class of application and system environment.

15.3 Peer-to-Peer (P2P) Computing

15.3.1 What is Peer-to-Peer Computing?

"Peer" is defined in the Webster Dictionary as "one that is of equal standing with another". So Peer-to-peer (P2P) computing can be viewed as the computing between equals. It has been estimated that the Internet connects 10 billions of megaherz CPUs with 10000 terabytes of storage. The problem is that most of these resources is unused.

A P2P system can be unstructured or unstructured [Kent and Tewari 2002]. Unstructured P2P architectures include Napster, Gnutella, Freenet, in which no "logically" deterministic structures to organize the participating peers. Structured P2P architectures include CAN, Chord, Pastry, Tapestry, Tornado and they use a "logically" deterministic structure to manage peers.

When designing P2P applications, it is important to assume that peers are untrusted and are mostly connected and communicate with each other [Senior and Deters 2002]. However, these peers can dynamically join and departure the P2P application and there will be failures in peers or communication links. Peers can also shutdown or terminate at any time. With these assumptions in mind, it makes the development of P2P applications a very challenge task. In particular, the issues must be considered when developing commercial P2P applications include security, scalability, gigh object availability, load distribution, self-configuration, self-healing, performance, and legal implications.

The difference between the client-server model and the P2P computing can be outlined below:

- In the client-server paradigm, the client is basically a dumb device; the server performs the computation, keeps the data and handle the control. This centralized fashion is simple, but it introduces some problems including performance bottlenecks and the single point of failures.

- In the P2P paradigm, each peer in P2P can be a client, a server, or as an intermediate entity where it relays requests and responses for other peers. Also, P2P is fully decentralized.

The P2P simulteneous client-server method creates a situation where servers are not the most important infrastructure for resource sharing. P2P systems support a variety of services without relying on an expensive central server. In particular, P2P systems offer high availability without the significant cost of a highly redundant and thus failure proof, central entity.

P2P technology can be applied to many applications, although most consumer-targeted P2P systems available is primarily focused in file sharing. These systems allow files to be shared and propagated through the Internet quickly without powerful servers to host those files.

15.3.2 Possible Application Areas for P2P Systems

Possible business applications include collaboration, distributed computing, file serving, edge services and intelligent agents.

- Financial Services. One market expected to reap great potential is financial services. Such companies processing extremely number-intensive calculations require a great deal of computing power. Under a P2P model, instead of having to buy high-end computers, the financial firms would be able to use computers they have already got at different offices around the world.

- Military Applications of P2P. Modern, military P2P networks require something where there will be no central server - routing and indexing tasks must be distributed equally across all P2P members.

- Health. P2P computing can give companies the ability to use the collective power and storage of their computing systems to actively share corporate information without the need for a central repository, and without overloading the network.

- Neuroscience. Many problems in computational neuroscience require sophisticated software systems that are beyond the development scope of a single individual or research group. Projects where huge calculation is required or data storage is high, P2P can be used for better performance instead of buying big mainframe Computers.

- Education System. P2P software can be used for distance-learning, research and thesis classes, so that far-flung students can collaborate.

- Corporations or research companies. Corporations or research companies require large amounts of computer capacity for tasks like Genom-Analysis or climate research. the P2P technology offers an enormous cost saving potential especially for less-heeled companies. In fact the retrievable CPU-performance is enormous.

15.3.3 Some Existing P2P Projects

Here we list a number of well known P2P projects from academia and industry.

- IBM Advances P2P Messaging. IBM has launched ICT, IBM Community Tools, P2P widgetry - apparently a dynamic messaging client - that's supposed to let users interact with various communities using instant and broadcast messaging.

- NetBatch. One of the most well-known pure P2P business applications is Intel's NetBatch. Instead of buying a massively powerful super-computer to do complex modelling for semiconductor design, Intel created a technology that allowed its employees to take advantage of the company's existing PCs.

- SETI@Home project. Another example is the SETI@Home project, run by the University of California at Berkeley, which allows amateur searchers of extraterrestrial Intelligence to scour radio telescope data and share findings. Launched in May 1999, the project aimed to hook up the spare computer time of 150,000 users. At present, it has more than 1.6 million users, with more than 500,000 active at any time.

- VXNET. Virtual X:/net Technology (VXNET) is a secure, distributed networking application and a platform for rapid development of P2P applications. VXNET users are able to set up "Persistent Communities", private networks where P2P file sharing and communications with trusted individuals may be enabled over broadband, wireless or dial-up connections. VXNET is free of spyware and advertising, and includes Instant Messaging (IM) and 128-bit file encryption.

- Mnemosyne: P2P steganographic storage. Mnemosyne provides a high level of privacy and plausible deniability by using a large amount of shared distributed storage to hide data. Blocks are dispersed by secure hashing, and loss codes used for resiliency. It takes advantages of the widespread availability and low cost of network bandwidth and disk space.

- ConChord: Cooperative SDSI Certificate Storage and Name Resolution. ConChord, a large scale certificate distribution system built on peer-to-peer distributed hash table. ConChord provides load-balanced storage while eliminating many of the administrative difficulties of traditional, hierarchical server architectures. ConChord is specifically designed to support SDSI, a fully-decentralized public key infrastructure that allows principals to define local names and link their namespaces to delegate trust.

- PeerDB. PeerDB is a P2P distributed data sharing system. It distinguishes itself from existing P2P systems in several ways. First, it is a full-fledge data management system that supports fine-grain content-based searching. Second, it combines the power of mobile agents into P2P systems to perform operations at peers' sites. Third, PeerDB network is self-configurable, i.e., a node can dynamically optimize the set of peers that it can communicate directly with based on some optimization criterion. By keeping peers that provide most information or services in close proximity (i.e., direct communication), the network bandwidth can be better utilized and system performance can be optimized. Fourth, to the end-user, it provides a keyword-based frontend for searching data without knowing the database schema.

15.3.4 P2P File Sharing and its Legal implications

P2P file sharing is a product of the P2P file networking technology. Unlike Client-Server technology, P2P communication involves two systems sharing services or files amongst themselves. This eliminates the need of an intermediate server to channel the data via itself. This makes the data transfer faster if the two clients are geographically close to each other; moreover P2P file sharing allow users to share whatever work they had created with a big user group over the Internet.

The problems come quite expectedly when the technology is commercialised. The legal implications of sharing music files over the Internet by millions of users without any care for copyright infringement laws and similar regulations is a problem need to be addressed.

15.3.4.1 P2P File Sharing Systems

P2P file sharing systems fall under two main categories: hybrid P2P and pure P2P [Kant, Iyer and Tewari, 2002].

In a hybrid P2P system all files are indexed at a central directory server. The central server maintains a 'master list' of all connected computers and the types of files stored on each connected peer. The actual file transfer occurs between the requester and owner nodes. A classic example of this kind of P2P system is Napster.

The pre-lawsuit Napster software had a file sharing capacity that could allow users to look at the index of a music database that was provided by Napster and downloads the preferred music from an online user. Even though the songs were downloaded from the remote Napster's client, the indexed database that provided the search results for the user was located on a centralised server in the Napster Company.

When Napster started actively advertising the ability to download the music from their database of thousands of music files, they got the attention of music copyright protection agencies like the Recording Industry Association of America (RIAA). The problem with Napster's architecture was the presence of a centralised Napster server that had a collection of all the songs provided by their clients. This part of the technology was highlighted in the following law suits saying that Napster used these databases to distribute non-copyrighted music to the general public and that the music companies were suffering heavy losses due to this free propagation of music sharing. This was due to the fact that the Napster server collected all the list of songs available at its clients for downloading. Hence the Napster server served as a central location to store the database that would provide searches with the name of the music files and the user from whom to download.

In a pure P2P system there is no central server or router. The routing structure either is a distributed catalogue which uses indexes as parameters or direct messaging where the message is sent to a peer group until the inquiry is found. All nodes within a pure P2P system are peers, meaning that each peer can operate as a router, client or server depending on the query. A popular example of this type P2P system is Gnutella.

The situation where Napster failed was in involving a server into their file searches. Gnutella managed to get over this problem by allowing the individual clients to search other computers connected to P2P networks to obtain search results. This left Gnutella, out of the picture in file sharing.

The closest thing that Gnutella or for that matter Kazaa comes to a server is the presence of supernodes in the P2P networks. A supernode is a powerful system in the network that allows different users to come together and share online files. This is no way connected to any of the servers of Gnutella and hence avoids any legal implications. The only link the softwares have with the mother company is the regular updating by the producers of the software and to get an up-to-date location of the supernodes. Even the supernode updating option can be turned off by the client providing completely autonomous and provides true P2P file sharing without the involvement of an intermediate server. Staying clear from personally hosting any type of information that may aid in infringing the copyright infringement and other sorts of legal implications has allowed the Gnutella and similar networks to thrive in a legally hostile environment.

Napster and Gnutella are both popular file sharing systems. The main difference between Napster and Gnutella P2P file sharing is that Napster requires a centralised server to manage the database management of the system. Gnutella on the other hand, does not rely on centralised servers, but rather provides direct P2P communication between peers without server intervention.

15.3.4.2 Legal implications for P2P File Sharing

The controversial popularity of file sharing among users of P2P file sharing applications such as Napster and Gnutella has created a complicated web of legal implications.

According to the U.S Copyright Law, practically all shapes of expression that can be of use in any tangible form are protected by copyright law [Lohman, 2003]. This includes such forms as books, artwork, digital works and the like. U.S Copyright Law, states that Copyright protection commences from the instant that the expression (in any median form) is fixed (meaning complete), and carries on for the lifetime of the author, and an additional 70 years.

Throughout this stage, copyright law set asides certain rights entirely to the owner of the work, such as the right to distribute (make available), reproduce (make copies) and publicly display (make freely available) the work and so on. The nature of digital file-sharing technology within a P2P environment unavoidably alludes to copyright law. First, every digital file stored on a user's machine can be a potential risk of copyrighted work. Secondly, the sharing of a file to another results in a reproduction and distribution which turn, infringes copyright law.

15.3.5 Some Challenges for P2P Computing

P2P is still developing and lots of research work is going on for the P2P technology. As suggested earlier in this section there can be many possible other P2P applications. P2P will have a big impact on B2B and B2C, but it will take a long time because there are many issues that need to be worked out to prepare the way for this technology. Application authors must design robust applications that can function in the complex Internet environment, and network designers must build in capabilities to handle new peer-to-peer applications. In the near future P2P will be adopted in most large/distributed companies as a cheaper means of storing and sharing files internally. Though P2P has some issues to be resolved but it also provides lot of advantages which cannot be neglected. Some of the most challenge issues include:

- Standardization: it is going to be a big issue, as it is necessary that all the flavors of P2P would talk to each other.

- Search is slow and sometimes unreliable.

- For enterprise wide P2P networking, further research is required to address security, authentication, authorisation and trust issues..

- Legal implications.

15.4 Pervasive Computing

Pervasive computing has been identified as the future of computing, that is, computing that is seamlessly integrated into every aspect of our day-to-day lives [Saba and Mukheriee 2003]. With the fast development of computing hardware, network technology, distributed computing, and more importantly, mobile computing, the realisation of the vision of pervasive computing is getting more realistic.

Mobile computing has been one of the major driving forces for pervasive computing [Beresford and Stajano 2003]. When mobile devices become "invisible", the idea of pervasive computing becomes reality. However, pervasive computing is more than just mobile computing [Fano and Gershman 2002]. Apart from the invisibility, there are other key issues for pervasive computing, such as integration with the environment, scalability, intelligence, and the impacts to our business operations, social lives and legal systems.

15.4.1 Pervasive Computing Characteristics

Pervasive computing finds its roots in ubiquitous computing [Satyanarayanan, 2001] where it aims to provide availability and invisibility of its application to the user. It can be defined as availability of software applications and information anywhere and anytime. Pervasive computing also means that computers are hidden in numerous so-called information appliances which we use in our day-to-day life [Birnbaum, 1997].

From a more general point of view, pervasive computing applications are often characterised as interaction transparent, context aware, and experience capture and reuse capable [Abowd, 1999[. Interaction transparency means that the human user is not aware that there is a computer embedded in the tool or device that he or she is using. Context awareness means that the application knows, for instance, the current geographical location. An experience capture and reuse capable application can remember when, where, and why something was done and can use that information as input to solve new tasks.

The following points provide further detail for each of the aforementioned characteristics. Though it is stated as the main characteristics of pervasive computing, this list was compiled from characteristics put forward by [Abowd 1999] in presenting software issues for ubiquitous computing..

- Interaction Transparency. An example of interaction transparency is the electronic white-board project called Classroom 2000. An electronic white-board has been designed that looks and feels like a white-board rather than a computer. With ideal transparency of interaction, the writer would just pick up a marker and start writing with no configuration. This transparency contrasts with the actual non-transparency of current interactions with computers. Input-output devices such as mouses, keyboards, and monitors are pure artefacts of computing. So are manipulations such as launching a browser, selecting elements in a Web page, setting up an audio or video encoding mechanism, and entering authentication information.

- Context Awareness. A pervasive computing system that strives to be minimally intrusive has to be context-aware and modify its behaviour based on this information. A user's context can consist of attributes such as physical location, physical condition, emotional state, personal history and daily behavioural patterns to name a few. A context-aware application can sense the environment and interpret the events that occur within it.

  The project Cyberguide [Abowd, 1997] is a pervasive computing application that exploits awareness of the current physical location. It mimics on a PDA the services provided by a human tour guide when visiting a new location. The Cyberguide project was an attempt to replicate the human tour guide through the use of mobile and hand held technology and ubiquitous positioning and communication services such as the Global Positioning System (GPS).

- Automated Capture of Experiences. Capture and storage of past experiences can be used to solve new problems in the future. Experiences are made of events and computers have the ability to record them automatically. Human users only have to recall that information from the computer when it is needed. For example, a context-aware electronic wallet could capture and store locations, times, and descriptions of payments made by a traveller. Back home, the traveller could use the recorded events to generate an expense report.

A general challenge in ubiquitous computing is to provide automated tools to support the capture, integration and access of this multimedia record [Barbeau, 2002]. The purpose is allow people to carry on with their task without having to worry on the details for capturing and recording the session for later use. In Classroom2000 [Abowd, 19999], the system showed the capacity to capture all the events associated with the teaching session, and made it possible for students to come back to it at a later time and see it in detail with all its activities. Every stroke of the pen, movement and web page visited where captured by the system and presented in the same sequence to the user, allowing for the students to concentrate on the material presented rather than manually capturing what the lecturer had to say.

15.4.2 Elite Care: An Application Using Pervasive Computing

Founders Bill Reed and Lydia Lundberg established Elite Care to improve housing and health care for the elderly. Elite Care developed all aspects of the technology, including construction, care giving, and pervasive computing, without venture funding and on a limited budget. Design goals included low-cost integration of technologies, unobtrusiveness, and an elderly friendly software interface.

By building pervasive computing into the environment, Elite Care's Oatfield Estates gave residents as much autonomy and even responsibility for themselves and their environment as possible [Stanford, 2002]. Focus was on creating a personalised environment that avoided the traditional institutional care model used in nursing homes for the elderly.

The system consists of the following components:

- Locator badges. Residents each carry a dual-channel infrared radio frequency locator tag that acts as their apartment key and emits periodic IR pulses to the sensors in each room and in the common areas. The pulses are unique to individual badges and support real-time updating of personal location databases.

  Status bits let residents summon immediate assistance by pressing the proper button and automatically alert the staff when the battery charge gets low. The RF component enables location tracking to about a 90-foot radius when a badge is out of sight of an IR sensor, such as when the person wanders.

  Elopement alarms alert staff if a resident prone to disorientation starts to leave the campus. Motion sensors in the rooms enable energy management or convenience functions such as turning on the lights when people enter a space The locator badge can be worn in a wristwatch form factor for those who might be prone to misplacing their badges.

- Embedded weight sensors. Each apartment bed has a built-in weight sensor. As with locator badges, the pervasive computing infrastructure makes many uses of the signatures obtained from these sensors. For example, a daily weight measurement is taken, but transients during sleep periods can also indicate tossing and turning, which might imply wakefulness, perhaps due to pain or stress caused by illness.

Frequent trips to the bathroom might indicate a urinary tract infection, alerting staff to arrange for a check-up. Doctors receive notification of any sudden weight loss, but because some residents might be sensitive about their weight, they can opt out of this measurement.

- In-apartment computers. Each apartment has a networked computer with a touch screen interface that provides access to a standard suite of applications residents use to communicate with families and friends. Tools include email, word processing, audio for speech recognition, and video conferencing using web cams. The applications suite defaults to large fonts for easier viewing.

  Residents can also communicate with their neighbours and summon staff assistance. Staff can use the consoles in their apartments to monitor the status of residents in their care as well as for personal use. These systems connect to the wired network infrastructure extending across the cluster.

- Personalized databases. The database server for the system is implemented with SQL Server. Elite Care maintains individualized resident databases that enhance care delivery, like documenting vital signs such as weight and blood pressure changes over time and activity logs. The caregivers use this data to call for qualified medical attention when needed. Medicine delivery databases let staff know if the residents are current on their prescription medications.

  Managers use the databases to monitor staff performance in timely delivery of services and communicate with the residents' adult children. Residents also use the personal histories in the databases to foster social relationships with others who have common points of history, such as having attended the same college or high school.

With the advancements made with distributed and mobile computing, the Elite Care facility was able to provide an effective and unobtrusive pervasive computing environment that took into consideration the privacy of the residents. Providing a seamless interaction with the needs of the aged, the application showed how beneficial and useful it can be in making the day to day task of caring for the residents easier for the employees.

15.4.3 The Challenges for Pervasive Computing

As devices and users move from one location to another, applications must adapt themselves to new environments. Applications must be able to discover services offered by distributed components in new environments and dynamically reconfigure themselves to use these new service providers [Barbeau 2002]. This characteristic of pervasiveness, that is to weave into the fabric of everyday life, was referred to by Mark Weiser [Weiser 1991] in his vision for ubiquitous computing.

During that period of Weiser's vision, the technology to implement pervasive computing was not available as it is now. Viable commercial products such as, handheld and wearable computers, wireless LANs and devices to sense and control appliances are readily available in our modern era. This allows us to be better positioned to take full advantage of this vision.

Pervasive computing will be a fertile source of challenging research problems in computer systems for many years to come. Solving these problems will require us to broaden our discourse on some topics, and to revisit long-standing design assumptions in others [Satyanarayanan, 2001]. When describing his vision, Weiser was fully aware that attaining it would require tremendous creativity and effort by many people, sustained over many years.

Current research in pervasive computing focuses on building infrastructures for managing active spaces, connecting new devices, or building useful applications to improve functionality. Security and privacy issues in such environments, however, have not been explored in depth. Indeed, a number of researchers and practitioners have admitted that security and privacy in this new computing paradigm are real problems. The reasons that make pervasive computing environments convenient and powerful also make it vulnerable to new security and privacy threats. In many cases, it is inproper to use traditional security mechanisms to deal with new exposures and vulnerabilities.

15.5 Summary

In this chapter we have presented some of the most recent development in distributed network systems; surveyed some key techniques used in advanced distributed network systems; and investigated how the these techniques can be used in the design and implementation of future distributed network systems. In particular, we studied the topics related to cluster computing, grid computing, peer-to-peer computing, and pervasive computing. After the reading of this chapter, we hope readers will have gained a broad knowledge about cutting edge topics in distributed network systems, particularly those relating to industry and potential development.

Exercises

15.1 What is a cluster and why does it attract attentions from both academia and industry? 15.1

15.2 Why Single System Image (SSI) is so important in Cluster computing? 15.1.1

15.3 Image that you were a CTO of a large company (say, with 100 architects located in three cities designing high rise buildings). Currently your company uses a very powerful parallel computer to run various CAD pakages and architects use normal PCs to run the user interface of these CAD pakages. Outline a few reasons to convince your CEO and the company board that moving to a cluster computing platform would greatly improve your company's compatitivity. 15.1

15.4 How do you differentiate cluster and grid? 15.2.1

15.5 Describe the ways that Grid computing can facilitate the coordination of disparate and geographically isolated resources in a virtual organization. 15.2.2

15.6 Describe the core grid components and their basic functions. 15.2.3

15.7 What are the major challenges of grip computing and why? 15.2.8

15.8 Why P2P applications can be scalable and what are the measures to make a P2P application scale? 15.3.1

15.9 Try to suggest some new "killer" applications for P2P computing. 15.3.2, 15.3.3

15.10 Summarise the current methodologies for service discovery in P2P file sharing environments. Discuss their pros and cons in various situations. Propose new ways / ideas to improve the functionality of service discovery in P2P environments. 15.3.4

15.11 What are the possible legal implications for file sharing in a P2P environment? 15.3.4

15.12 What is the vision of pervasive computing and the major challenges to achieve such a vision? 15.4

15.13 Suggest a number of new "killer" applications for pervasive computing that may greatly impact on our lives. 15.4

15.14 Discuss the possible impact of pervasive computing to entertainment industry. 15.4

15.15 Discuss the possible legal impact of pervasive computing. 15.4

15.16 If pervasive computing becomes a reality, discuss its impact to a university (in particular, the impact to students, staff, and teaching and learning). 15.4

REFERENCES

[Abowd 1997] Abowd, G., Kooper, R., Long, S. and Atkeson, C. Cyberguide: A mobile context-aware tour guide, *In proceedings of wireless networks of the ACM,* vol 3, 1997.

[Abowd 1999] Abowd, G. Software engineering issues for ubiquitous computing. *In Proceedings of the 1999 International Conference on Software Engineering,* pp. 5 – 84, 1999.

[Abramson et al. 2002] D. Abramson, R. Buyya, and J. Giddy, "A Computational Economy for Grid Computing and its Implementation in the Nimrod-G Resource Broker," *Future Generation Computer Systems,* vol. 18, pp. 1061-1074, 2002.

[Adler 2002] M. Adler, Tradeoffs in Probabilistic Packet Marking for IP Traceback. In *Proceedings of 34th ACM Symposium on Theory of Computing (STOC).* 2002.

[Agarwal *et al.* 1998] D. A. Agarwal, L. E. Moser, P. M. Melliar-Smith, and R. K. Budhia, The Totem Multiple-Ring Ordering and Topology Maintenance Protocol, *ACM Transactions on Computer Systems,* pp. 93--132, May 1998.

[Agha 1986] Gul. Agha. *Actors: A Model of Concurrent Computation in Distributed Systems.* Cambridge, MA: The MIT Press, 1986.

[Aiello et al. 2002] W. Aiello, S. M. Bellovin, M. Blaze, R. Canetti, J. Ioannidis, A. D. Keromytis and O. Reingold, Efficient, DoS-Resistant, Secure Key Exchange for Internet Protocols. In *Proceedings of the 9th ACM Conference on Computer and Communication Security, (CCS 2002),* Washington D.C., USA, pp. 48-58. 2002.

[Aljifri 2003] H. Aljifri, IP Traceback: A New Denial-of-Service Deterrent?. *IEEE Security & Privacy 1,* 3, pp. 24-31. 2003.

[Allcock et al. 2002] B. Allcock, J. Bester, J. Bresnahan, A. L. Chervenak, I. Foster, C. Kesselman, S. Meder, V. Nefedova, D. Quesnal, and S. Tuecke, "Data Management and Transfer in High Performance Computational Grid Environments," *Parallel Computing Journal,* vol. 28, pp. 749-771, 2002.

[Allen et al. 2001] G. Allen, T. Dramlitsch, I. Foster, N. Karonis, M. Ripeanu, E Seidel, and B. Toonen, "Supporting Efficient Execution in Heterogeneous Distributed Computing Environments with Cactus and Globus," presented at Super Computer, 2001.

[Amir *et al* 1992] Y. Amir, D. Dolev, S. Kramer, and D. Malki, Membership Algorithms in Broadcast Domains, *Computer Science Technical Report, CS 92-10,* Computer Science Department, The Hebrew University of Jerusalem, Israel, 1992.

[Amir *et al* 1993] O. Amir, Y. Amir, and D Dolev, A Highly Available Application in the Transis Environment, *Computer Science Technical Report, CS 93-10,* Computer Science Department, The Hebrew University of Jerusalem, Israel, 1993.

[Ammann and Knight 1988] P. E. Ammann and J. C. Knight, Data diversity: an approach to software fault tolerance, *IEEE Transactions on Computers,* 37(4): pp. 418–425, 1988.

[Anml 2001] Anml, Advanced Networking Management Lab (ANML) Distributed Denial of Service Attacks (DDoS) Resources, *DDoS History in Brief,* http://www.anml.iu.edu/ddos/history.html.2001.

[Arnold and Gosling 1996] Ken Arnold and James Gosling. *The Java Programming Language.* Addison-Wesley Publishing Company, 1996.

[Ashenfelter 1999] John Paul Ashenfelter, *Database Design For The Web,* Webreview, March 1999, http://www.webreview.com/1999/03_26/developers/_03_26_99_1.shtml.

[Attiya and Welch 1994] Hagit Attiya and Jennifer L. Welch. Sequential consistency versus linearizability. *ACM Transaction on Computer Systems,* 12(2): pp. 91--122, May 1994.

[Aura et al. 2000] T.Aura, P. Nikander and J. Leiwo, DOS-resistant Authentication with Client Puzzles. In *Proceedings of the 8th International Workshop on Security Protocols, LNCS 2133.* 2000.

[Avery and Foster 2001] P. Avery and I. Foster, "The GriPhyN Project: Towards Petascale Virtual-Data Grids," GriPhyN 2001

[Avizienis 1995] A. A. Avizienis, The Methodology of N-Version Programming, *Software Fault Tolerance,* Edited by Michael R. Lyu, Published by John Wiley & Sons Ltd, 1995.

[Baba and Matsuda 2002] T. Baba and S. Matsuda, Tracing Network Attacks to Their Sources. *IEEE Internet Computing 6,* 3, pp. 20-26. 2002.

[Bacon and Hamilton 1987] J. M. Bacon and K. G. Hamilton, Distributed Computing with RPC: The Cambridge Approach, *Technical Report No. 117,* Computer Laboratory, University of Cambridge, October 1987.

[Baentsch et al 1996] M. Baentsch, G. Molter and P. Sturm, Introducing Application-level Replication and Naming into Today's Web, In *5ᵗʰ Int'l WWW Conference http://www5conf. inria. fr/fich_html/papers/P3/Overview. html,* France, May 6-10,1996.

[Baker and Sullivan 1992] M. Baker and M. Sullivan, The recovery box: using fast recovery to provide high availability in the UNIX environment, In *Proc. of Summer USENIX,* pages 31-43, June 1992.

474

[Ballardie 1997] A. Ballardie, Core Based Trees (CBT version 2) Multicast Routing, *IETF Network Working Group RFC 2189,* September 1997.

[Banerjee et al 1998] Sandeepan Banerjee, Vishu Krishnamurthy, etc, Oracle8I-the XML Enabled Data Management System, Oracle Corporation, *Proceedings of the 16th International Conference on Data Engineering,* 1998.

[Barbeau 2002] Barbeau, M. Mobile, Distributed, and Pervasive Computing, In: I. Stojmenovic, *Chapter 27 - Handbook of Wireless Networks and Mobile Computing,* John Wiley and Sons, Inc., (ISBN: 0-471-41902-4), pp. 581-600, February 2002.

[Bargteil et al. 2001] A. Bargteil, D.Bindel, and Y. Chen, Quantifying Network Denial of Service: A Location Service Case Study. *ICICS 2001, LNCS 2229,* Xian, China. 2001.

[Baru et al. 1998] C. Baru, R. Moore, A. Rajasekar, and M. Wan, "The SDSC Storage Resource Broker," presented at CASCON, Toronto, Canada, 1998.

[Basseville and Nikiforov 1993] M. Basseville and I. V. Nikiforov, *Detection of Abrupt Changes: Theory and Application,* Prentice Hall, ISBN 0-13-126780-9. 1993.

[Bayardo et al 1997] R. J. Bayardo, et al, *InfoSleuth: Agent-based semantic integration of information in open and dynamic environment,* http://www.mcc.com/projects/infosleuth. 1997.

[Beresford and Stajano 2003] A. R. Beresford and F. Stajano, "Location Privacy in Pervasive Computing", by in *Pervasive Computing*pp. pp. 46-55, January-March, 2003.

[Bellardo and Savage 2003] J. Bellardo and S. Savage, 802.11 Denial-of-Service Attacks: Real Vulnerabilities and Practical Solutions. In *Proceedings of the USENIX Security Symposium,* Washington D.C., USA. 2003.

[Bellovin 2000] S. M. Bellovin, ICMP Traceback Messages. *Internet Draft,* Network Working Group. 2000.

[Bergsten 1998] H. Bergsten, *Servlet are for Read,* http://webdevelopers journal.com/columns. 1998.

[Berman et al. 2002] F. Berman, A. Chien, K. Cooper, J. Dongarra, I. Foster, D. Gannon, L. Johnson, K. Kennedy, C. Kesselman, J. Mellor-Crummey, D. Reed, L. Torczon, and R. Wolski, "The GrADS Project: Software Support for High-Level Grid Application Development," *International Journal of High-Performance Computing Applications,* vol. 15, 2002.

[Berman et al. 2003] F. Berman, R. Wolski, H. Casanova, W. Cirne, H. Dail, M. Faerman, S. Figueira, J. Hayes, G. Obertelli, J. Schopf, G. Shao, S. Smallen, N. Spring, A. Su, and D. Zagorodnov, "Adaptive Computing on the Grid Using AppLeS," *IEEE Transactions on Parallel and Distributed Systems,* vol. 14, pp. 369-382, 2003.

[Bershad *et al* 1987] B. N. Bershad, D. T. Ching, E. D. Lazowska, E. D. Sanislo, and M. Schwartz, A Remote Procedure Call Facility for Interconnecting Heterogeneous Computer Systems, *IEEE Transactions on Software Engineering,* Vol. SE13, No. 8, pp. 880-894, August 1987.

[Bianchini and Buskens 1991] R. Bianchini, Jr. and R. Buskens. An adaptive distributed system level diagnosis algorithm and its implementation, In *Proc. of 21st International Symposium on Fault-Tolerant Computing (FTCS21),* pp. 222-229, July 1991.

[Biles 1994] Sally A. Biles. ONC+ distributed computing, In *Distributed Computing—Implementation and Management Strategies.* Edited by Raman Khanna, Prentice Hall PTR, 1994.

[Birman 1991] Kenneth P. Birman, Andre Schiper, and Pat Stephenson. Lightweight causal and atomic group multicast. *ACM Transaction on Computer Systems,* August 1991.

[Birman 1993] Kenneth P. Birman, The process group approach to reliable distributed computing, *Communications of the ACM,* 36(12): pp. 37-53, 1993

[Birman 1994] Kenneth Birman, A Response to Cheriton and Skeen's Criticism of Causal and Totally Ordered Communications, *Operating Systems Review,* Vol. 28, No. 1, pp. 22-28, January 1994.

[Birman 1996] Kenneth P. Birman, *Building Secure and Reliable Network Applications.* Manning Publications Co., 1996.

[Birman and Joseph 1987] K. P. Birman, and T. A. Joseph, Reliable Communication in the Presence of Failures, *ACM Transactions on Computer Systems,* Vol. 5, No. 1, pp. 47-76, February 1987.

[Birman and Renesse 1994] Kenneth P. Birman and Robbert van Renesse. *Reliable Distributed Computing with the ISIS Toolkit.* IEEE Computer Society Press, 1994.

[Birman *et al* 1991] Kenneth P. Birman, Andre Schiper, and Pat Stephenson. Lightweight Causal and Atomic Group Multicast. *ACM Transactions on Computer Systems,* August 1991.

[Birrell and Nelson 1984] A. D. Birrell and B. J. Nelson, Implementing Remote Procedure Calls, *ACM Transactions on Computer Systems,* Vol. 2, No. 1, pp. 38-59, February 1984.

[Birnbaum 1997] Birnbaum, J. Pervasive information systems. *Communications of the ACM,* 40(2): pp. 40–41, February 1997.

[Blakeley and Deshpande 2000] José A. Blakeley and Anand Deshpande, Tutorial: Data Access, *Proceedings of the 2000 ACM SIGMOD on Management of Data,* Page 579, 2000.

[Blane 2003] J. V. Blane, *Cybercrime and Cyberterrorism: Current Issues,* Nova Science Publishers, Inc. 2003.

476

[Blazek et al. 2001] R. B.Blazek, H.Kim, B. Rozovskii and A. Tartakovsky, A Novel Approach to Detection of "Denial-Of-Service" Attacks via Adaptive Sequential and Batch-Sequential Change-Point Detection Methods. In *Proceedings of the 2001 IEEE Workshop on Information Assurance and Security*, pp. 220-226. 2001.

[Boasson 1993] M. Boasson. Control Systems Software. *IEEE Transactions on Automatic Control*, vol. 38, nr. 7, pp. 1094-1107, 1993.

[Boasson 1996] Maarten Boasson. Modeling and Simulation in Reactive Systems. *Proc. of the 4th Workshop on Parallel and Distributed Real-time Systems (WPDRTS '96)*, pp. 27-34, IEEE Computer Society Press, 1996.

[Boasson 1998] Maarten Boasson. Software Architecture for Distributed Reactive Systems. *Lecture notes in computer science*, no. 1521(1), Springer-Verlag, 1998.

[Bond 1995] A. Bond, *An Introduction to OSF DCE*, DSTC P/L, 1995.

[Booch 1994] Grady Booch. *Object-Oriented Analysis and Design*. The Benjamin/Cummings Publishing Company, Inc., second edition, 1994.

[Borg et al 1989] Anita Borg, Wolfgang Blau, Wolfgang Graetsch, Ferdinand Herrmann, and Wolfgang Oberle. Fault tolerance under Unix. *ACM Transactions on Computer Systems*, pp. 1-24, February 1989.

[Bouchaib et al 1999] Bouchaib Bounabat, Rahal Romadi, and Salah Labhalla, Designing Multi-Agent Reactive systems: A Specification Method Based on Reactive Decisional Agents, Nakashima et al.(Ed.): *PRIMA'99*, LNAI 1733, pp. 197-210,1999.

[Bouguettaya 2000] Athman Bouguettaya, Supporting Dynamic Interactions among Web-Based Information Sources, *IEEE Transactions on Knowledge and Data Engineering*, Vol. 12, No. 5, September/October 2000.

[Bouguettaya et al 1999] Athman Bouguettaya, et. al., Using Java and CORBA for Implementing Internet Database, *Proceedings of the 15th International Conference on Data Engineering*, 1999.

[Bounabat et al 1999] B. Bounabat, R. Romadi and S. Labhalla. Designing Multi-Agent Reactive Systems: A Specification Method Based on Reactive Decisional Agents. *Lecture notes in computer science*, no. 1733, pp.197-210: Springer-Verlag, 1999.

[Boussinot 1991] F. Boussinot. Reactive C: An extension of C to program reactive systems. *Software - Practice and Experience*, 21(4): pp. 401-428, 1991.

[Brey 1995] B. B. Brey, *The Intel 32-Bit Microprocessors: 80386, 80486 and Pentium*, Prentice-Hall, Inc., 1995.

[Briot et al 1998] Jean-Pierre Briot and et.al. Concurrency and distribution in object-oriented programming. *ACM Computing Surveys*, pp. 291-329, September 1998.

[Brustoloni 2002] J. C. Brustoloni, Protecting Electronic Commerce from Distrituted Denial-of-Services Attacks. *WWW2002,* Honolulu, Hawaii, USA, ACM 1-58113-449-5/02/0005, pp. 553-561. 2002.

[Budhiraja *et al* 1992] N. Budhiraja, K. Marzullo, F. Schneider, and S. Toueg. Optimal primary-backup protocols. In *Proc. of the Sixth International Workshop on Distributed Algorithms,* pp. 362-378, Haifa, Isracl, 1992.

[Budhiraja *et al.* 1993] Navin Budhiraja, Keith Marzullo, Fred B. Schneider, and Sam Toueg. The Primary-Backup Approach, In *Distributed Systems,* Sape Mullender, editor, Addison-Wesley Publishing Company, second edition, 1993.

[Burch and Cheswick 2000] H. Burch and B. Cheswick, Tracing Anonymous Packets to Their Approximate Source. In *Proceedings of the 14th Systems Administration Conference (LISA 2000),* New Orleans, Louisiana, USA. 2000.

[Buretta 1997] Marie Buretta. *Tools and Techniques for Managing Distributed Information.* Wiley Computer Pub., 1997.

[Buss and Jackson 1998] Arnold Buss and Leroy Jackson, Distributed simulation modeling: a comparison of HLA, CORBA, and RMI, *Proceedings of 1998 conference on Winter simulation,* pp. 819 – 826, 1998.

[Bussmann and Demazeau 1994] S. Bussmann and Y. Demazeau. An Agent Model Combining Reactive and Cognitive Capabilities. *Proc. Int'l Conf. on Intel. Robots and Systems (IROS'94),* Munchen, 1994.

[Buyya 1998] Rajkumar Buyya, Editor, *High Performance Cluster Computing, Vol. 1 System and Architecture, Vol. 2 Programming and Applications,* Prentice Hall PTR, Upper Saddle River, 1998.

[Buyya 1999] R. Buyya (ed.), *High Performance Cluster Computing: Architectures and Systems,* Prentice Hall, 1999.

[Buyya et al. 2000] R. Buyya, D. Abramson, and J. Giddy, "An Economy Driven Resource Management Architecture for Global Computational Power Grids," presented at International Conference on Parallel and Distributed Processing Techniques and Applications, 2000.

[Buyya and Murshed 2002] R. Buyya and M. Murshed, "GridSim: A Toolkit for the Modeling and Simulation of Distributed Resource Management and Scheduling for Grid Computing," *The Journal of Concurrency and Computation: Practice and Experience (CCPE),* 2002.

[Cabrera et al. 2001] J. B. D. Cabera, L. Lewis, X. Qin, W.Lee and Ravi, Proactive Detection of Distributed Denial of Service Attacks using MIB Traffic Variables A Feasibility Study. In *Proceedings of International Symposium on Integrated Network Management.* 2001.

[Cabri et al. 2000] Giacomo Cabri, Letizia Leonardi, and Franco Zambonelli, MARS: A Programmable Coordination Architecture for Mobile Agents, IEEE Internet Computing, 1089-780/00, Vol. 4, No. 4: pp. 26-35, July-August 2000.

478

[Carter et al 1991] John B. Carter, John Bennett, and Willy Zwaenepoel, Implementation and Performance of Munin, *Proc. of the 13th ACM Symp. on Operating Systems Principles (SOSP-13)*, 1991.

[Casanova and Dongarra 1997] H. Casanova and J. Dongarra, Network Enabled Solvers for Scientific Computing Using the NetSolve System, *Proceedings of the 3rd IEEE International Conference on Algorithms and Architectures for Parallel Processing*, pp. 17-33. Eds. A. Goscinski, M. Hobbs, and W. Zhou, World Scientific, 1997.

[Casanova 2002] H. Casanova, "Distributed Computing Research Issues in Grid Computing," *ACM SIGAct News*, vol. 33, pp. 50-70, 2002

[Caspi et al 1994] P. Caspi, A. Girault and D. Pilaud. Distributing Reactive Systems. *The ISCA Int'l Conf. on Parallel and Distributed Computing Systems (PDCS'94)*. Las Vegas, USA, 1994.

[Ceri *et al* 1991] S. Ceri, M. A. W. Houtsma, A. M. Keller, and P. Samarat, A classification of update methods for replicated databases, Technical Report STAN-CS-91-1392, Stanford University, *Computer Science Technical Report*, October 1991.

[Ceri *et al* 1995] S. Ceri, M. A. W. Houtsma, A. M. Keller, and P. Samarat. Independent updates and incremental agreement in replicated databases. *Journal of Parallel and Distributed Databases*, 3(3):July, 1995.

[CERT 1996a] CERT. 1996a. *CERT Advisory CA-1996-01 UDP Port Denial-of-Service Attack.* http://www.cert.org/advisories/CA-1996-01.html.

[CERT 1996b] CERT. 1996b. *CERT Advisory CA-1996-21 TCP SYN Flooding and IP Spoofing Attacks.* http://www.cert.org/advisories/CA-1996-21.html.

[CERT 1996c] CERT. 1996c. *CERT Advisory CA-1996-26 Denial-of-Service Attack via ping.* http://www.cert.org/advisories/CA-1996-26.html.

[CERT 1997] CERT. 1997. *CERT Advisory CA-1997-28 IP Denial-of-Service Attacks.* http://www.cert.org/advisories/CA-1997-28.html.

[CERT 1998] CERT. 1998. *CERT Advisory CA-1998-01 Smurf IP Denial-of-Service Attacks.* http://www.cert.org/advisories/CA-1998-01.html.

[CERT 1999a] CERT. 1999a. *CERT Advisory CA-1999-17 Denial-of-Service Tools.* http://www.cert.org/advisories/CA-1999-17.html.

[CERT 1999b] CERT. 1999b. *CERT Incident Note IN-99-07.* http://www.cert.org/incident_notes/IN-99-07.html.

[CERT 2000a] CERT. 2000a. *CERT Advisory CA-2000-01 Denial-of-Service Developments.* http://www.cert.org/advisories/CA-2000-01.html.

[CERT 2000b] CERT. 2000b. *CERT Advisory CA-2000-11 MIT Kerberos Vulnerable to Denial-of-Service Attacks.* http://www.cert.org/advisories/CA-2000-11.html.

[CERT 2000c] CERT. 2000c. *CERT Advisory CA-2000-20 Multiple Denial-of-Service Problems in ISC BIND.* http://www.cert.org/advisories/CA-2000-20.html.

[CERT 2000d] CERT. 2000d. *CERT Advisory CA-2000-21 Denial-of-Service Vulnerabilities in TCP/IP Stacks.* http://www.cert.org/advisories/CA-2000-21.html.

[CERT 2000e] CERT. 2000e. *CERT Incident Note IN-2000-04.* http://www.cert.org/incident_notes/IN-2000-04.html.

[CERT 2000f] CERT. 2000f. *CERT Incident Note IN-2000-05.* http://www.cert.org/incident_notes/IN-2000-05.html.

[CERT 2001a] CERT. 2001a. *CERT Incident Note IN-2001-04.* http://www.cert.org/incident_notes/IN-2001-04.html.

[CERT 2001b] CERT. 2001b. *Denial of Service Attacks.* http://www.cert.org/tech_tips/denial_of_service.html.

[Chakrabarti and Manimaran 2002] A. Chakrabarti and G. Manimaran, Internet Infrastructure Security: A Taxonomy. *IEEE Network,* 16, pp. 13-21. 2002.

[Chang and Maxemchuk 1984] J. M. Chang and N. F. Maxemchuk. Reliable broadcast protocols. *ACM Transactions on Computer Systems,* 2(3), August 1984, pp. 251-273.

[Chang and Scott 1996] J. W. Chang and C. T. Scott, Agent-based Workflow: TRP Support Environment (TSE), *The Fifth Int'l World Wide Web Conference,* Paris, France, http://www5conf.inria.fr/fich_html/papers/P53/Overview.html. May, 1996.

[Chapin et al. 1999] S. J. Chapin, D. Katramatos, J. Karpovich, and A. Grimshaw, "Resource Management in Legion," *Future Generation Computer Systems,* vol. 15, pp. 583-594, 1999.

[Chappell 1994] D. Chappell, The OFS Distributed Computing Environment (DCE), in *Distributed Computing: Implementation and Management Strategies,* Ed. R. Khanna, Prentice- Hall, Inc., 1994.

[Chen and Pu 1992] Shu-Wie Chen and Calton Pu. *A structural classification of integrated replica control mechanisms.* Technical Report (CUCS-006-92), Department of Computer Science, Columbia University, USA, 1992.

[Chen and Zhou 2000a] C. Chen and W. Zhou. Design and Implementation of Reactive Systems for Building Fault-tolerant Applications. *Proc. of the 18th Int'l Conf. on Applied Informatics (AI'2000),* pp. 497-500, ACTA Press, USA, held in Innsbruck, Austria, Feb. 2000.

[Chen and Zhou 2000b] C. Chen and W. Zhou. An Architecture for Resolving Network Partitioning. *Pro. of the ISCA 15th Int'l Conf. for Computers and Their Applications (CATA-2000),* pp. 84-87, New Orleans, USA, March 2000.

[Chen and Zhou 2000c] C. Chen and W. Zhou. Building Distributed Applications Using the Reactive Approach. In *Proc. of the 11th Australasian Conference on Information System (ACIS-2000),* Brisbane, Australia, Dec. 2000.

480

[Chen and Zhou 2000d] Changgui Chen and Wanlei Zhou, Modelling and Simulation of Reactive Systems, *Proceedings of the IEEE 2000 International Conference on Algorithms and Architectures for Parallel Processing (ICA3PP'2000)*, pp. 327-332, World Scientific, held in Hong Kong, December 10-13, 2000.

[Chen *et al.* 2001] Changgui Chen, Wanlei Zhou and Shui Yu, A Reactive Architecture For Web-based Information Systems, *Proceedings of the International Conference on Internet Computing (IC'01)*, pp.1028-1034, CSREA Press, USA, held in Las Vegas, USA, June 2001.

[Cheriton and Skeen 1993] D. Cheriton and D. Skeen, Understanding the Limitations of Totally Order Communications, *Fourteenth ACM Symposium on Operating System Principles, Operating System Review,* Asheville, NC, Vol 27, No 5, 1993.

[Cheriton 1988] D. R. Cheriton, The V Distributed System, *Communications of the ACM,* pp. 314-331, March 1988.

[Cheriton and Zwaenepoel 1985] Cheriton and Zwaenepoel, Distributed Process Groups in the V Distributed System, *ACM Trans on Computer Systems,* Vol 3, No 2: pp. 77-107, 1985.

[Cheung et al. 2000] D. Cheung, S. D. Lee, Thomas Lee, William Song, and C. J. Tan, Distributed and Scalable XML Document Processing Architecture for E-Commerce Systems, *The 2nd International workshop on Advanced Issues of E-Commerce and Web-based Information System (WECWIS 2000),* 2000.

[Chin and Chanson 1991] Roger S. Chin and Samuel T. Chanson. Distributed object-based programming systems. *ACM Computing Surveys,* 23(1): pp. 91-124, March 1991.

[ChorusOS] ChorusOS
http://www.experimentalstuff.com/Technologies/ChorusOS/index.html.

[Ciancarini et al 1996] P. Ciancarini, A. Knoche, R. Tolksdorf, and F. Vitali, PageSpace: An Architecture to Co-ordinate Distributed Applications on the Web, *The Fifth International World Wide Web Conference,* Paris, France, http://www5conf.inria.fr/fich_html/papers/P5/Overview.html. May, 1996.

[CISCO 1999] CISCO. *Characterizing and Tracing Packet Floods Using Cisco Routers.* http://www.cisco.com. 1999.

[CISCO 2003] CISCO. *NetFlow,*
http://www.cisco.com/warp/public/732/Tech/nmp/netflow/. 2003.

[Coulouris *et al* 1994] George Coulouris, Jean Dollimore, and Tim Kindberg. *Distributed Systems -- Concepts and Design.* Addison-Wesley, second edition, 1994.

[Cristian 1991] Flaviu Cristian, Understanding Fault Tolerant Distributed Systems, *Communications of the ACM,* Vol. 34, No. 2, pp. 56-78, Feburary 1991.

481

[Cristian 1996] Flaviu Cristian. Synchronous and asynchronous group communication. *Communications of the ACM*, pp. 88--97, April 1996.

[Cristian *et al* 1996] Flaviu Cristian, Bob Dancey, and Jon Dehn. Fault-tolerance in air traffic control systems. *ACM Transaction on Computer Systems*, Vol. 14, No. 3, pp. 265--286, August 1996.

[Crosby and Wallach 2003] S. A. Crosby and D. S. Wallach, Denial of Service via Algorithmic Complexity Attacks. In *Proceedings of the 12th USENIX Security Symposium*, pp. 29-44. 2003.

[Cruickshank 1998] Alex Cruickshank, Web-based databases, 1998, http://www.zdnet.co.uk/pcmag/labs/1998/04/database/

[Czajkowski et al. 2001] K. Czajkowski, S. Fitzgerald, I. Foster, and C. Kesselman, "Grid Information Services for Distributed Resource Sharing," presented at Proceedings of the Tenth IEEE International Symposium on High-Performance Distributed Computing (HPDC-10), 2001

[Czajkowski et al. 2002] K. Czajkowski, I. Foster, C. Kesselman, V. Sanger, and S. Tuecke, "SNAP: A Protocol for Negociating Service Level Agreements and Coordinating Resource Management in Distributed Systems.," presented at Proceedings of the 8th Workshop on Job scheduling Strategies for Parallel Processing, 2002.

[Davidson 1984] Susan B. Davidson. Optimism and Consistency In Partitioned Distributed Database Systems. *ACM Transactions on Database Systems*, vol 9, No. 3, pp. 456-481, Sept. 1984.

[Davidson 1985] Susan B. Davidson. Consistency in Partitioned Networks. *ACM Computer Surveys* 17(3), pp. 341-370, Sept. 1985.

[Dean et al. 2001] D. Dean, M. Franklin and A. Stubblefield, An Algebraic Approach to IP Traceback. In *Proceedings of Network and Distributed System Security Symposium (NDSS 01)*, 3-12. 2001.

[Deering 1989] S. Deering, Host Extensions for IP multicasting, *IETF Network Working Group RFC* (Request for Comments) 1112, August 1989.

[Deering 1991] S. Deering, ICMP Router Discovery Messages, *RFC 1256*, September 1991.

[Deering and Hinden 1995] S. Deering and R. Hinden, Internet Protocol Version 6 (IPv6) Specification, *RFC1883*, December 1995.

[Dennis 2000] S. Dennis, Mobile Phones Emerge as New Virus Target Kaspersky, *Newsbytes.com*, http://www.newsbytes.com/news/00/153195.html. 2000

[De Paoli *et al.* 1995] D. De Paoli, A. Goscinski, M. Hobbs and G. Wickham, Microkernel and Kernel Server Support for Parallel Execution and Global Scheduling on a Distributed System, *Proceedings of the First International Conference on Algorithms and Architectures for Parallel Processing*, Brisbane, Australia, April 1995.

482

[Dietrich et al. 2000] S. Dietrich, N. Long and D. Dittrich, Analyzing Distributed Denial Of Service Tools: The Shaft Case. In *Proceedings of the 14th Systems Administration Conference (LISA 2000)*, New Orleans, Louisiana, USA, pp. 329-339. 2000.

[Dolev and Malki 1996] Danny Dolev and Dalia Malki, The Transis Approach to High Availability Cluster Communication, *Communications of the ACM*, pp. 64-70, April 1996.

[Dragan 1997] Richard V. Dragan, *Web Database Development Tools*, November 18, PC Magazine, 1997.

[Droms 1993] R. Droms, Dynamic Host Configuration Protocol, *RFC 1541*, November 1993.

[Droms 1997] R. Droms, Dynamic Host Configuration Protocol, *RFC 2131*, March 1997.

[Duan 1996] Nick N. Duan, Distributed Database Access in a Corporate Environment Using Java, 5th *International World Wide Web Conference*, France, May 6-10, 1996, http://www5conf.inria.fr/fich_html/papers/P23/Overview.html,.

[Duffield and Grossglauser 2000] G. N. Duffield and M. Grossglauser, Trajectory sampling for direct traffic observation. *ACM SIGCOMM 2000*, 271-282. 2000.

[Edwards, *et. al* 1997] S. Edwards, et. al. Design of embedded systems: Formal models, validation, and synthesis. *Proceedings of IEEE*, 85(3): pp. 366-390, 1997.

[Entropia 2003] Entropia, "The Entropia Approach to Distributed Computing," Available: http://www.entropia.com/pdf/EntropiaApproachtoDistributedComputing.pdf, 2003.

[Eronen 2000] P. Eronen, Denial of Service in Public Key Protocols. In *Proceedings of the Helsinki University of Technology Seminar on Network Security.* 2000.

[Estan and Varghese 2001] C. Estan and G. Varghese, New directions in traffic measurement and accounting. In *Proceedings of the 2001 ACM SIGCOMM Internet Measurement Workshop*, San Francisco, CA, pp. 75-80. 2001.

[Etkin et al. 2000] D.Etkin, E. Olander and S. Bhattacharya, Selective Denial of Service And Its Impact To Internet Based Information Systems. *International Conference Advances in Infrastructure for Electronic Business, Science, and Education.* 2000.

[Fabre and Prennou 1998] Jean-Charles Fabre and Tanguy Prennou, A Metaobject Architecture for Fault-Tolerant Distributed Systems: The FRIENDS Approach, *IEEE Transactions on Computers*, pp. 78-95, January 1998.

[Fan 2001] C. Fan, *Fault-Tolerant Cluster of Networking Elements*, PhD Thesis, California Institute of Technology, Pasadena, CA, UAS, 2001.

[Fano and Gershman 2002] A. Fano and A. Gershman, "The Future of Business Services in the Age of Ubiquitous Computing", in *Communications of the ACM,* December 2002, pp. 83-87

[Fenner 1997] W. Fenner, Internet Group Management Protocol, v2, *RFC2236,* Nov. 1997.

[Ferguson and Senie 2000] P.Ferguson and D. Senie, RFC 2827 - Network Ingress Filtering: Defeating Denial of Service Attacks which employ IP Source Address Spoofing. *Network Working Group.* 2000.

[Ferrari, et al. 1996] A. J. Ferrari, M. Lewis, C. L. Viles, A. Nguyen-Tuong, and A. S. Grimshaw, "Implementation of the Legion Library," University of Virginia 1996.

[Fidge 1988] Colin Fidge. Timestamps in message passing systems that preserve the partial ordering. In *Proc. of 11th Australian Computer Science Conference,* pp. 56-66, 1988.

[Fischer et al 1985] M. J. Fischer, N. A. Lynch and M. S. Paterson, Impossibility of distributed consensus with one faulty process, *JACM,* vol. 32, no. 2, April 1985, pp. 374-382.

[Foster and Kesselman 1997] I. Foster and C. Kesselman, "Globus: A Metacomputing Infrastructure Toolkit," *The International Journal of Supercomputer Applications and High Performance Computing,* vol. 11, pp. 115-128, 1997.

[Foster and Kesselman 1998] I. Foster and C. Kesselman, *The Grid: Blueprint for a New Computing Infrastructure:* Morgan-Kaufmann, 1998.

[Foster et al. 1998] I. Foster, C. Kesselman, G. Tsudik, and S. Tuecke, "A Security Architecture for Computational Grids," presented at 5th ACM Conference on Computer and Communication Security, 1998.

[Foster et al. 2001] I. Foster, C. Kesselmen, and S. Tuecke, "The Anatomy of the Grid: Enabling Scalable Virtual Organizations," *Supercomputer Applications,* 2001.

[Foster et al. 2002a] I. Foster, C. Kesselman, J. M. Nick, and S. Tuecke, "Grid Services for Distributed System Integration", in *IEEE Computer,* June 2002, pp. 37-46.

[Foster et al. 2002b] Foster, I., Kesselman, C., Nick, J. and Tuecke, S. *The Physiology of the Grid: An Open Grid Services Architecture for Distributed Systems Integration,* Globus Project, 2002. www.globus.org/research/papers/ogsa.pdf

[Foster and Gannon 2003] I. Foster and D. Gannon, *Open Grid Services Architecture Platform,* 2003, http://www.ggf.org/ogsa- wg [Agha 1986] Gul. Agha. *Actors: A Model of Concurrent Computation in Distributed Systems.* Cambridge, MA: The MIT Press, 1986.

[Fithen 2000] K. T. Fithen, *Internet Denial of Service Attacks and the Federal Response.* CERT, http://www.cert.org/congressional_testimony/Fithen_testimony_Feb29.html. 2000.

[Floyd and Jacobson 1993] S. Floyd and V. Jacobson, Random Early Detection Gateways for Congestion Avoidance. *IEEE/ACM Transactions on Networking 1*, 4, 397-413. 1993.

[Floyd 1994] S. Floyd, TCP and Explicit Congestion Notification. *ACM Computer Communication Review 24*, 5, pp. 10-23. 1994.

[Floyd and Fall 1999] S.Floyd and K. Fall, Promoting the Use of End-to-End Congestion Control in the Internet. *IEEE/ACM Transactions on Networking*. 1999.

[Floyd et al. 2001] S. Floyd, M. S. Bellovin and J. Joannidis, Pushback Messages for Controlling Aggregates in the Network. *INTERNET DRAFT*, Internet Engineering Task Force. 2001.

[Francis and Sato 1997] Paul Francis and Shin-Ya Sato, Design of a Database and Cache Management Strategy for a Global Information Infrastructure, *Proceedings of the 3rd International Symposium on Autonomous Decentralized Systems* (ISADS '97).

[Fraternali 1999] Piero Fraternali, Tools and Approaches for Developing Data – Intensive Web Applications: A Survey, ACM Computing Surveys, Vol. 31, No.3, September 1999.

[Frey et al. 2001] J. Frey, T. Tannenbaum, I. Foster, M. Livny, and S. Tuecke, "Condor-G: A Computation Management Agent for Multi-Institutional Grids," presented at 10th International Symposium on High Performance Distributed Computing, 2001.

[Gammage and Casey 1985] N. Gammage and L. Casey, XMS: A Rendezvous-Based Distributed System Software Architecture, *IEEE Software*, Vol. 2, No. 3, May 1985.

[Gammage *et al.* 1987] N. D. Gammage, R. F. Kamel and L. Casey, Remote Rendezvous, *Software Practice and Experience*, Vol. 17, No. 10, October 1987.

[Garber 2000] L. Garber, Denial-of-Service Attacks Rip the Internet. *Computer 33*, 4, pp. 12-17. 2000.

[Garbinato *et al* 1993] Benoit Garbinato, Rachid Guerraoui, and Karim R. Mazouni. Distributed programming in GARF. In *Object-Based Distributed Programming, ECOOP'93 Workshop, LNCS 791*, pp. 225--239. Springer-Verlag, July 1993.

[Garcia-Molina and Spauster 1991] H. Garcia-Molina and A. Spauster. Ordered and reliable multicast communication. *ACM Transactions on Computer Systems*, 9(3), August 1991, pp.242-271.

[Garg and Reddy 2002] A.Garg and N. A. Reddy, Mitigating Denial of Service Attacks Using QoS Regulation. In *Proceedings of International Workshop on Quality of Service*, Miami Beach, USA. 2002.

[Geng and Whinston 2000] X. Geng and A. B. Whinston, Defeating Distributed Denial of Service Attacks. *IEEE IT Professional*, pp. 36-41. 2000.

[Geng et al. 2002] X. Geng, Y. Huang and A. B. Whinston, Defending wireless infrastructure against the challenge of DDoS attacks. *Mobile Networks and Applications 7,* 3, pp. 213-223. 2002.

[Gerrity *et al.* 1991] G. Gerrity, A. Goscinski, J. Indulska, W. Toomey and W. Zhu, Can We Study Design Issues of Distributed Operating Systems in a Generalized Way? RHODOS, *Proc. of the 2nd Symposium on Experiences with Distributed and Multiprocessor Systems (SEDMS II),* Atlanta, March 1999.

[Gil and Ploetto 2001] T. M. Gil and M. Ploetto, MULTOPS: a data-structure for bandwidth attack detection. In *Proceedings of 10th Usenix Security Symposium.* 2001.

[Goscinski 1991] Andrzej Goscinski, *Distributed Operating Systems: The Logical Design,* Addison-Wesley, 1991.

[Goscinski and Zhou 1999] Andrzej Goscinski and Wanlei Zhou, Client-Server Systems, *Encyclopedia of Electrical and Electronics Engineering,* Volume 3, Ed. J. G. Webster, John Wiley & Sons, Inc., New York, pp. 431-451, 1999

[Gosling 1997] James Gosling. A Feel of Java. *IEEE Software,* Vol. 30(6), pp. 53-57, June 1997.

[Gould 1998] Nick Gould, Web/Database Integration with Active Server Pages, *http://nt2.ec.man.ac.uk/aspcourse/material/slides/aspcourse/index.htm*, 1998.

[Gregg et al. 2001] D. M. Gregg, W. J. Blackert, D. V. Heinbuch and D. C. Furnanage, Analyzing Denial of Service Attacks using Theory and Modeling and Simulation. In *Proceedings of the 2001 IEEE Workshop on Information Assurance and Security,* pp. 205-211. 2001.

[Grimshaw 1993] A. S. Grimshaw, "Easy to Use Object-Oriented Parallel Programming with Mentat," *IEEE Computer,* pp. 39-51, 1993.

[Grimshaw et al. 1994] A. S. Grimshaw, W. A. Wulf, J. C. French, A. C. Weaver, and P. F. R. Jr., "Legion: The Next Logical Step Toward a Nationwide Virtual Computer," University of Virginia 1994

[Grimshaw and Wulf 1997] A. Grimshaw and W. Wulf, "The Legion vision of a worldwide virtual computer," *Communications of the ACM,* 1997.

[Grimshaw *et al.* 1999] A. Grimshaw, A. Ferrari, F. Knabe, and M. Humphrey, Wide-Area Computing, Resource Sharing on a Large Scale, pp. 29-37, *IEEE Computer,* May 1999.

[Grimshaw et al. 2003] A. S. Grimshaw, A. Natrajan, M. A. Humphrey, M. J. Lewis, A. Nguyen-Tuong, J. F. Karpovich, M. M. Morgan, and A. J. Ferrari, "From Legion to Avaki: The Persistence of Vision," in *Grid Computing: Making the Global Infrastructure a Reality,* F. Herman, G. C. Fox, and A. J. G. Hey, Eds.: John Wiley & Sons, 2003.

[Guerraoui and Schiper 1997] Rachid Guerraoui and Andre Schiper. Software-based replication for fault tolerance. *IEEE Computer,* pp. 68-74, April 1997.

486

[Guerraoui *et al.* 1995] Rachid Guerraoui, Benoit Garbinato, and Karim R. Mazouni, Lessons from Designing and Implementing GARF, In *Object-Based Distributed Programming, ECOOP'95 Workshop, LNCS 791,* pp. 238-256. Springer-Verlag, July 1995.

[Gunter et al. 2003] D. Gunter, B. L. Tierney, C. E. Tull, and V. Virmani, "On-Demand Grid Application Tuning and Debugging with the NetLogger," presented at 4th International Workshop on Grid Computing (Grid2003), Phoenix, Arizona, 2003.

[Habib et al. 2003] A. Habib, M. Hefeeda, and B. Bhargava, Detecting Service Violations and DoS Attacks. In *Proceedings of Network and Distributed System Security Symposium (NDSS 03),* San Diego, CA, pp. 177-189. 2003.

[Hadzilacos and Toueg 1993] Vassos Hadzilacos and Sam Toueg. Fault-tolerant broadcasts and related problems. In *Distributed Systems,* Sape Mullender, editor, Addison-Wesley Publishing Company, second edition, 1993.

[Hagelin 1988] G. Hagelin, ERICSSON safety system for railway control, In *Software Diversity in Computerized Control Systems,* pp. 11-21, U. Voges, editor, Springer, Wien, New York, 1988.

[Haines et al. 2003] J. Haines, D. K. Ryder, L. Tinnel and S. Taylor, Validation of Sensor Alert Correlators. *IEEE Security & Privacy 1,* 1, pp. 46-56. 2003.

[Halpern and Moses 1990] J. Y. Halpern and Y. Moses. Knowledge and Common Knowledge in a Distributed Environment. *Journal of the ACM,* 37(3): pp. 549-587, 1990.

[Hamilton 1984] K. G. Hamilton, *A Remote Procedure Call System,* Ph.D. Thesis, Technical Report No. 70, Computer Laboratory, University of Cambridge, December 1984.

[Hanks et al 1994] S. Hanks et. al., Generic Routing Encapsulation (GRE), *RFC 1701,* October 1994.

[Hara et al. 2000] Hideki Hara, Shigeru Fujita and Kenji Sugawara, Reusable Software Components based on an Agent Model, *Proceedings of the 7th Int'l Conf. on Parallel and Distributed Systems: Workshops (ICPADS'00 Workshops),* 2000.

[Harel and Pnueli 1985] D. Harel and A. Pnueli. On the development of reactive system. *Logics and Models of Concurrent Systems.* Krzysztof R. Apt. Spring-Verlag, Berlin, Heidelberg, New York, Tokyo. pp. 477-498, 1985.

[Harel and Politi 1998] D. Harel and Michal Politi. *Modeling Reactive Systems with Statecharts: The Statemate Approach.* McGraw-Hill Companies, January 1998.

[Harel and Shtul-Trauring 1990] D. Harel and A. Shtul-Trauring. STATEMATE: A Working Environment for the Development of Complex Reactive Systems. *IEEE Trans. on Software Engineering,* 16(4): pp. 403-414, 1990.

[Harkins and Carrel 1998] D. Harkins and D. Carrel, RFC 2409 - The Internet Key Exchange (IKE). *The Internet Society.* 1998.

[Harold 1997] Elliotte R. Harold. *Java Network Programming.* O'Reilly & Associates, Inc., 1997.

[Hecht and Hecht 1986] H. Hecht and M. Hecht, Fault-Tolerant Software, *Fault-Tolerant Computing: Theory and Techniques,* Vol. 1, Edited by D. K. Pradhan, pp. 658-696, Prentice-Hall, 1986.

[Hecht *et al.* 1989] M. Hecht, J. Agron and S. Hochhauser, A distributed fault tolerant architecture for nuclear reactor control and safety functions, In *Proc. Real-Time System Symposium,* pp. 214-221, Santa Monica, 1989.

[Helal *et al* 1996] A. A. Helal, A. A. Heddaya, and B. B. Bhargrava, *Replication Techniques in Distributed Systems,* Kluwer Academic Publishers, 1996.

[Herbert 1994] Andrew Herbert. Distributing objects. In *Distributed Open Systems,* Frances Brazier and Dag Johansen, editors, IEEE Computer Society Press, 1994.

[Herlihy 1986] Maurice Herlihy. A quorum-consensus replication method for abstract data types. *ACM Transactions on Computer Systems,* 4(1): pp. 32--53, February 1986.

[Hernandez et al 2000] E. Hernandez, Y. Cardinale, C. Figueira, and A. Teruel, "SUMA: A Scientific Metacomputer," presented at US/Venezuela Workshop on High Performance Computing, 2000.

[Hewitt 1977] C. Hewitt. Viewing Control Structure as Patterns of Passing Messages. *Journal of Artificial Intelligence,* 8(3): pp. 323-364, 1977.

[Hightower 1997] Lauren Hightower, Publishing dynamic data on the Internet, *Dr. Dobb's Journal,* v22 n1, p70(3), Jan. 1997.

[Hinden 1991] R. Hinden, Internet Routing Protocol Standardization Criteria, *RFC 1264,* October 1991.

[Hood and Jost 2000] R. Hood and G. Jost, "A Debugger for Computational Grid Applications," presented at 9th Heterogeneous Computing Workshop, Cancun, Mexico, 2000.

[Houle and Weaver 2001] K. J. Houle and G. M. Weaver, *Trends in Denial of Service Attack Technology.* CERT, http://www.cert.org/archive/pdf/DoS_trends.pdf. 2001.

[Householder et al. 2001] A. Householder, A. Manion, L. Pesante, G. M. Weaver and R. Thomas, *Managing the Threat of Denial-of-Service Attacks.* CERT, http://www.cert.org/archive/pdf/Managing_DoS.pdf. 2001.

[Huang and Jalote 1992] Yennum Huang and Pankaj Jalote. Effect of fault tolerance on response time -- analysis of the primary site approach. *IEEE Transactions on Computers,* 41(4): pp. 387--403, April 1992.

[Huang and Kintala 1995] Y. Huang and C. Kintala, Software Fault Tolerance in the Application Layer, *Software Fault Tolerance,* Edited by Michael R. Lyu, John Wiley & Sons Ltd, 1995.

488

[Hussain et al. 2003] A. Hussain, J. Heidemann and C. Papadopoulos, A Framework for Classifying Denial of Service Attacks. In *Proceedings of the ACM SIGCOMM Conference,* Karlsruhe, Germany. 2003.

[Iivonen 2004] M. Iivonen, *Trust in knowledge management and systems in organizations:* Idea Group Publishing, 2004.

[Ioannidis 2000] Yannis Ioannidis, *Database and the Web: an Oxymoron or a Pleonasm,* the 1st HELDINET Seminar, Athens, Hellas, July 2000.

[Ioannidis and Bellovin 2002] J. Ioannidis and S. M. Bellovin, Pushback: Router-Based Defense Against DDoS Attacks. In *Proceedings of Network and Distributed System Security Symposium,* San Diego, USA. 2002.

[IPSEC 2004] IPSEC. http://www.ietf.org/html.charters/ipsec-charter.html. 2004.

[Jajodia 1996] Sushil Jajodia, Database security and privacy, *ACM Computing Surveys,* Vol. 28, No.1, March 1996.

[Jalote 1989] Pankaj Jalote, Fault tolerant processes, *Distributed Computing,* 3: pp. 187-195, 1989.

[Jalote 1994] Pankaj Jalote. *Fault Tolerance in Distributed Systems.* Prentice Hall PTR, Englewood Cliffs, New Jersey, 1994.

[Jaworski 1998] Jamie Jaworski. *Java 1.2 Unleashed.* Sams, 1998.

[Jia 1997] Weijia Jia. Implementation of a reliable multicast protocol. *Software-Practice and Experience,* 27(7): pp. 813-850, 1997.

[Jia et al 1996] W. Jia, J. Kaiser and E. Nett, RMP: Fault-tolerant Group Communication, *IEEE Micro,* 16(15), pp. 59-67, April 1996.

[Jia et al 1999] W Jia, W Zhao, D Xuan and G Xu. An Efficient Fault-Tolerant Multicast Routing Protocol with Core-Based Tree Techniques, *IEEE Transactions on Parallel and Distributed Systems,* 10(10), Oct., 1999, pp.984-999.

[Jia et al 2000] W. Jia, D. Xuan, and W. Zhao, Integrated Routing Algorithms for Anycast Messages, *IEEE Communications Magazine,* 38(1), January, 2000, pp.48-53.

[Jia et al 2001] Weijia Jia, W. Zhou, and Joerg Kaiser, Efficient Algorithms for Mobile Multicast using Anycast Group, *IEE Proceedings–Communications,* Vol. 48, No. 1, February 2001.

[Jin et al. 2003] C. Jin, H. Wang and K. G. Shin, Hop-count Filtering: An Effective Defense Against Spoofed DDoS Traffic. In *Proceedings of the 10th ACM Conference on Computer and Communication Security, (CCS 2003),* Washington D.C., USA, pp. 30-41. 2003.

[Johnson 1989] B. W. Johnson, *Design and Analysis of Fault-Tolerant Digital Systems,* Addison-Wesley Publishing Company, Reading, Massachusetts, 1989.

[Johnson and Deering 1999] D. Johnson and S. Deering, Reserved IPv6 Sunnet Anycast Address, *RFC2526,* March 1999.

[Joyce and Goscinski 1997] P. Joyce and A. Goscinski, Group Communication in RHODOS, *Proceedings of the IEEE Singapore International Conference on Networks SICON'97,* Singapore, 1997.

[Jung et al. 2002] J. Jung, B. Krishnamurthy and M. Rabinovich, Flash Crowds and Denial of Service Attacks: Characterization and Implications for CDNs and Web Sites. In *Proceedings of the International World Wide Web Conference 2002,* pp. 252-262. 2002.

[Kaashoek *et al* 1989] F. Kaashoek, A. Tanenbaum and et al. An efficient reliable broadcast protocol. *ACM Operating Systems Review,* 23(4): pp. 5-20, 1989.

[Kaashoek and Tanenbaum 1991] M. F. Kaashoek and A. S. Tanenbaum, Group communication in the AMOEBA distributed operating system. *Proc. 11th Int'l Conf. on Distributed Systems,* 1991, pp.222-230.

[Kaashoek and Tanenbaum 1994] M. F. Kaashoek, and A. S. Tanenbaum., Efficient Reliable Group Communication for Distributed Systems, *Dept. of Mathematics and Computer Science Technical Report,* Vrije Universiteit, Amsterdam, 1994.

[Kargl et al. 2001] F. Kargl, J. Maier and M. Weber, Protecting Web Servers from Distributed Denial of Service Attacks. In *Proceedings 10th International WWW Conference,* Hong Kong, pp. 514-524, 2001.

[Karnouskos 2001] S. Karnouskos, Dealing with Denial-of-Service Attacks in Agent-enabled Active and Programmable Infrastructures. *25th IEEE International Computer Software and Applications Conference (COMPSAC 2001),* Chicago, Illinois, U.S.A (ISBN 0-7695-1372-7). 2001.

[Karonis et al. 2003] N. Karonis, B. Toonen, and I. Foster, "MPICH-G2: A Grid-Enabled Implementation of the Message Passing Interface," *Journal of Parallel and Distributed Computing,* 2003.

[Kaufman et al. 2002] C. Kaufman, R. Perlman and M. Speciner, *Network Security,* Second Edition, Prentice Hall PTR, Upper Saddle River, New Jersey. 2002.

[Kaufman et al. 2003] C. Kaufman, R. Perlman and B. Sommerfeld, DoS Protection for UDP-Based Protocols. In *Proceedings of the 10th ACM Conference on Computer and Communication Security (CCS 2003),* Washington D.C., USA, 2-7. 2003.

[Kent and Atkinson 1998a] S. Kent and R. Atkinson, 1998a. *RFC 2401 - Security Architecture for the Internet Protocol.* Network Working Group.

[Kent 1998b] S. Kent, 1998b. *RFC 2402 - IP Authentication Header.* The Internet Society.

[Kent 1998c] S. Kent, 1998c. *RFC 2406 - IP Encapsulating Security Payload (ESP).* The Internet Society.

[Kent and Tewari 2002] K. Kent, R. Iyer, and V. Tewari, "A Framework for Classifying Peer-to-Peer Technologies", in Proceedings of the 2nd IEEE/ACM International Symposium on Cluster Computing and Grid (CCGRID'02), 2002.

490

[Kephart and Chess 2003] J. Kephart and D. Chess, "The Vision of Autonomic Computing," *IEEE Computer,* 2003.

[Kerberos 2004] KERBEROS, *Kerberos: The Network Authentication Protocol.* http://web.mit.edu/kerberos/www/. 2004.

[Keromytis et al. 2002] A. D. Keromytis, V. Misra and D. Rubenstein, SOS: Secure Overlay Services. In *Proceedings of Network and Distributed System Security Symposium (NDSS 02).* 2002.

[Kim and Welch 1989] K. H. Kim and H. O. Welch, Distributed execution of recovery blocks: an approach for uniform treatment of hardware and software faults in real-time applications, *IEEE Transactions on Computers,* 38(5): pp. 626-636, 1989.

[Kim and Yoon 1988] K. H. Kim and J. C. Yoon. Approaches to implementation of a repairable distributed recovery block scheme, In *18th International Symposium on Fault-Tolerant Computing,* pp. 50-55, Tokyo, 1988.

[Kohler 2004] E. Kohler, M. Handley and S. Floyd, Datagram Congestion Control Protocol (DCCP). *Internet Draft,* Internet Engineering Task Force. 2004.

[Kong 1990] M. Kong, T. H. Dineen, P. J. Leach, E. A. Martin, N. W. Mishkin, J. N. Pato and G. L. Wyant, *Network Computing System Reference Manual,* Prentice-Hall, Englewoods Cliffs, New Jersey, 1990.

[Kurose and Ross 2002] J. Kurose and K. W. Ross, *Computer Networking: A Top-Down Approach Featuring the Internet,* Second Edition, Addison Wesley. 2002.

[Kutz and Ramakrishnan 1997] Ken Kutz and Sub Ramakrishnan, *Web-based Database Application Technologies - An Overview,* WebdevShare 97, 1997, http://webdev.indiana.edu/webdevShare97/pre-conference.html.

[Kuzmanovic and Knightly 2003] A. Kuzmanovic and E. W. Knightly, Low-Rate TCP-Targeted Denial of Service Attacks. *SIGCOMM03,* Karlsruhe, Germany, pp. 75-86. 2003.

[Lacono and Weisband 1997] C. S. Lacono and S. Weisband, "Developing Trust in Virtual Teams," presented at Proceedings of the 30 th Annual Hawaii International Conference on System Sciences, Hawaii, 1997.

[Ladin *et al* 1992] Rivka Ladin, Barbara Liskov, Liuba Shrira, and Sanjay Ghemawat. Providing high availability using lazy replication. *ACM Transactions on Computer Systems,* 10(4): pp. 361-391, November 1992.

[Lamport 1978] Leslie Lamport, Time, Clocks and the Ordering of Events in a Distributed System, *Communications of the ACM,* Vol. 21, No. 7, pp. 58-65, 1978.

[Lamport *et al.* 1982] Leslie Lamport, Robert Shostak, and Marshall Pease, The Byzantine generals problem, *ACM Transactions on Programming Languages and Systems,* 4(3): pp. 382-401, July 1982.

[Laprie *et al.* 1990] Jean-Claude Laprie et al., Definition and analysis of hardware and software fault-tolerant architectures, *IEEE Computer,* 23(7): pp. 39-51, 1990.

[Lau et al. 2000] F. Lau, S. H. Rubin, M. H. Smith and L. Trajkovic, Distributed Denial of Service Attacks. In *Proceedings of 2000 IEEE International Conference on Systems, Man, and Cybernetics 3*, 2275-2280. 2000.

[LeBlanc 1982] T. J. LeBlanc, *The Design and Performance of High-Level Language Primitives for Distributed Programming,* Ph.D. Thesis, Computer Science Technical Report #492, Computer Science Department, University of Wisconsin-Madison, December 1982.

[Leckie and Ramamohanarao 2002] C. Leckie and K. Ramamohanarao, Learning to Share Distributed Probabilistic Beliefs. In *Proceedings of 19th International Conference on Machine Learning (ICML 2002),* Sydney, Australia. 2002.

[Lee 1992] Lee, L., *The Day the Phones Stopped: How people Get Hurt When Computers Go Wrong,* Donald I. Fine, Inc., New York, 1992.

[Leiwo 1997] J. Leiwo, A Method to Implement a Denial of Service Protection Base. In *Proceedings of Australasian Conference on Information Security and Privacy,* pp. 90-101. 1997.

[Leiwo et al. 2000] J. Leiwo T. Aura and P. Nikander, Towards Network Denial of Service Resistant Protocols. In *Proceedings of 8th International Security Protocols Workshop,* Cambridge, UK, pp. 301-310. 2000.

[Lemon 2002] J. Lemon, Resisting SYN Flood DoS Attacks With A SYN Cache. In *Proceedings of USENIX BSD Conference 2002.* 2002.

[Levy 2003a] E. Levy, 2003a. Crossover: Online Pests Plaguing the Offline World. *IEEE Security & Privacy 1,* 6, pp. 71-73.

[Levy 2003b] E. Levy, 2003b. The Making of a Spam Zombie Army: Dissecting the Sobig Worms. *IEEE Security & Privacy 1,* 4, pp. 58-59.

[Lewandowskl 1998] Scott M. Lewandowskl. Frameworks for component-based client/server computing. *ACM Computing Surveys,* pp. 3-27, March 1998.

[Lewis and Grimshaw 1995] M. Lewis and A. Grimshaw, "The Core Legion Object Model," University of Virginia Agust 1995.

[Li et al. 2002] J. Li, J. Mirkovic, M. Wang, P. Reiher and L. Zhang, SAVE: Source Address Validity Enforcement Protocol. *IEEE INFOCOM 2002.* 2002.

[Li et al. 2003] M. Li, C. Chi, W. Jia, W. Zhou, J. Cao, D. Long, and Q. meng, Decision Analysis of Statistically Detecting Distributed Denial-of-Service Flooding Attacks. *International Journal of Information Technology and Decision Making 2,* 3, pp. 397-405. 2003.

[Liang *et al.* 1990] L. Liang, S.T. Chanson, G.W. Neufeld, Process Groups and Group Communications: Classifications and Requirements, *IEEE Computer,* No. 2, pp. 56-66, February 1990.

[Lin and Morris 1997] D. Lin and R. Morris, Dynamics of Random Early Detection. *ACM SIGCOMM 1997.* 1997.

[Lin and Ye 2000] Lin Lin and Ye Chengqing, The Research for Cache in Web, Department of Computer Science, Zhejiang University, *Journal of Computer Science,* Vol. 27, no. 9, 2000.

[Linthicum 1997] David S. Linthicum, Next-generation middleware, *DBMS,* v10, n10, p69 (6), Sept 1997.

[Linthicum 1997] David Linthicum. *David Linthicum's Guide to Client/Server and Intranet Development.* John Wiley & Sons, Inc, 1997.

[Liskov *et al.* 1981] B. Liskov, C. Schaffer, R. Scheifler and A. Snyder, CLU Reference Manual, *Lecture Notes in Computer Science,* No. 114, Springer-Verlag, 1981.

[Long *et al.* 1992] J. Long, W. K. Fuchs and J. A. Abraham, Compiler assisted static checkpoint insertion, In *Proc. of 22nd International Symposium on Fault--Tolerant Computing (FTCS22),* pp. 58-65, July 1992.

[Low *et al* 1996] G. C. Low, G. Rasmussen, and B. Henderson-Sellers. Incorporation of distributed computing concerns into object-oriented methodologies. *Journal of Object-Oriented Programming,* pp.12-20, June 1996.

[Lowman 2003] Lowman, F. A, "Peer-to-Peer File Sharing and Copyright Law: A Primer for Developers". Media: [Online]. Available: [http://iptps03.cs.berkeley.edu/final-papers/copyright.pdf]. Acessed: [27/08/03].

[Lyu 1995] Michael R. Lyu, *Software Fault Tolerance,* John Wiley & Sons Ltd, 1995.

[Maconachy et al. 2001] W. V. Maconachy, C. D. Schou, D. Ragsdale and D. Welch, A Model for Information Assurance: An Integrated Approach. In *Proceedings of the 2001 IEEE Workshop on Information Assurance and Security,* West Point, NY, USA. 2001.

[Maffeis 1995] Silvano Maffeis, *Run-Time Support for Object-Oriented Distributed Programming.* PhD thesis, Zurich University, February 1995.

[Maffeis 1997] Silvano Maffeis, Piranha: A CORBA Tool For High Availability, *IEEE Computer,* pp. 59-66, April 1997.

[Mahajan et al. 2001] R. Mahajan, S. Floyd and D. Wetherall, Controlling High-Bandwidth Flows at the Congested Router. In *Proceedings of IEEE ICNP 2001,* Riverside, CA. 2001

[Mahajan et al. 2002] R. Mahajan, M. S. Bellovin and S. Floyd, Controlling High Bandwidth Aggregates in the Network. *Computer Communications Review 32,* 3, pp. 62-73. 2002.

[Manber 1996] Udi Manber, Future Directions and Research Problems in the World Wide Web, *Proceedings of the 15th ACMSIGACT-SIGMOD-SIGART Symposium on Principles of Database Systems,* pp. 213 – 215, 1996.

[Mankin et al. 2001] A. Mankin, D. Massey, C. Wu, S. F. Wu and L. Zhang, On Design and Evaluation of Intention-Driven ICMP Traceback. In *Proceedings of Computer Communications and Networks.*

[Mansfield et al. 2000] G. Mansfield, K. Ohta, Y. Takei, N. Kato and Y. Nemoto, Towards trapping wily intruders in the large. *Computer Networks 34,* 4, pp. 659-670. 2000.

[Matsuura 2000a] K. Matsuura, 2000a. Evaluation of DoS Resistance in Relation to Performance Dynamics. *The 2000 Symposium on Cryptography and Information Security (SCIS2000),* Okinawa, Japan.

[Matsuura and Imai 2000b] K. Matsuura and H. Imai, 2000b. Modification of Internet Key Exchange Resistant against Denial-of-Service. *Pre-Proc. of Internet Workshop 2000 (IWS2000),* pp. 176-174.

[Mccumber 1991] J. Mccumber, Information System Security: A Comprehensive Model, In *Proceedings of the 14th National Computer Security Conference,* Baltimore, MD, USA. 1991.

[Meadows 1999] C. Meadows, A Formal Framework and Evaluation Method for Network Denial of Service. In *Proceedings of The 12th Computer Security Foundations Workshop.* 1999.

[Mehra *et al* 1997] Ashish Mehra, Jennifer Rexford and Farnam Jahanian. Design and evaluation of a window-consistent replication service. *IEEE Transactions on Computers,* pp. 986-996, September 1997.

[Melliar-Smith and Moser 1998] P. M. Melliar-Smith and L. E. Moser, Surviving network partitioning, *IEEE Computer,* 31(3): pp. 62-68, March 1998.

[Melliar-Smith et al 1990] P. M. Melliar-Smith, L.E. Moser and V. Agrawala. Broadcast protocol for distributed systems. *IEEE Transactions on Parallel and Distributed Systems,* 1(1), pp. 17-25, Jan. 1990.

[Meyer 1997] Bertrand Meyer. *Object-Oriented Software Construction.* Prentice Hall PTR, second edition, 1997.

[Meyerson et al. 1996] D. Meyerson, K. E. Weick, and R. M. Kramer, "Swift trust and Temporary Groups," in *Trust in Organizations.* Thousand Oaks: Sage Publications, 1996, pp. 166-195, 1996.

[Microsoft 1998] Microsoft, *Distributed Component Object Model Protocol -- DCOM/1.0,* http://www.microsoft.com/com/resources/specs.asp 1998.

[Migliardi and Sunderam 1999] M. Migliardi and V. S. Sunderam, "Heterogeneous Distributed Virtual Machines in the Harness Metacomputing Framework," presented at Heterogeneous Computing Workshop of IPPS/SPDP99, Puerto Rico, 1999.

[Mili 1990] A. Mili, *An Introduction to Program Fault Tolerance,* Prentice-Hall, 1990.

494

[Mirkovic et al. 2002a] J. Mirkovic, J. Martin and P. Reiher, 2002a. A Taxonomy of DDoS Attacks and DDoS Defense Mechanisms. *UC Technical Report.*

[Mirkovic et al. 2002b] J. Mirkovic, G. Prier and P. Reiher, 2002b. Attacking DDoS at the Source. *10th IEEE International Conference on Network Protocols,* Paris, France.

[Mirkovic et al. 2003] J. Mirkovic, G. Prier and P. Reiher, Source-End DDoS Defense. *Second IEEE International Symposium on Network Computing and Applications,* Cambridge, Massachusette. 2003.

[MIT 1994] Massachusetts Institute of Technology, *Documentation and Source Code for the Current Implementation of Kerberos,* 1994.

[Mohiuddin et al. 2002] S. Mohiuddin, S. Hershkop, R. Bhan and S. Stolfo, Defending against a Large Scale Denial of Service Attack. In *Proceedings of the 2002 IEEE Workshop on Information Assurance and Security,* pp. 30-37. 2002.

[Moore et al. 2001] D. Moore, G. Voelker, and S. Savage, Inferring Internet Denial-of-Service Activity. *Proceedings of the 2001 USENIX Security Symposium, Washington D.C.* 2001.

[Moore et al. 2003] D. Moore, V. Paxson, S. Savage, C. Shannon, S. Stanford and N. Weaver, Inside the Slammer Worm. *IEEE Security & Privacy 1,* 4, pp. 33-39. 2003.

[Morein et al. 2003] W. G. Morein, A. Stavrou, D. L. Cook, A. D. Keromytis, V. Misra and D. Rubenstein, Using Graphic Turing Tests to Counter Automated DDoS Attacks Against Web Servers. In *Proceedings of the 10th ACM Conference on Computer and Communication Security, (CCS 2003),* Washington D.C., USA, 8-19. 2003.

[Moser *et al.* 1996] L. E. Moser et al, Totem: A Fault-Tolerant Multicast Group Communication System, *Communications of the ACM,* pp. 54-63, April 1996.

[MOSIX] MOSIX, *http://www.mosix.org.*

[Mullender 1993] Sape Mullender. *Distributed Systems.* Addison-Wesley Publishing Company, second edition, 1993.

[Mutaf 1999] P. Mutaf, Defending against a Denial-of-Service Attack on TCP. In *Proceedings of the 2nd International Workshop on Recent Advances in Intrusion Detection (RAID 99).* 1999.

[Natrajan et al. 2001] A. Natrajan, M. A. Humphrey, and A. S. Grimshaw, "Grids: Harnessing Geographically-Separated Resources in a Multi-Organisational Context," presented at 15th Annual International Symposium on High Performance Computing Systems and Applications, 2001

[Narasimhan 1999] Priya Narasimhan, *Transparent Fault Tolerance for CORBA,* PhD Thesis, University of California, Santa Barbara, USA, December 1999.

[Nelson 1981] B. J. Nelson, *Remote Procedure Call,* Ph.D. Thesis, CMU Report, CMUCS81 119, 1981.

[Neufield *et al.* 1990] G. Neufield, L. Liang, and S.T. Chanson, Process Groups and Group Communications: Classifications and Requirements, *Computer,* Vol. 23, No. 2, pp. 56-67, 1990.

[Neumann 2000] P. G. Neumann, Denial-of-Service Attacks. *Communications of the ACM 43,* 4, 136. 2000.

[Nielsen 1999] Jakob Nielsen, User Interface Directions for the Web, *Communications of the ACM,* January 1999.

[NIPG] "Nasa Information Power Grid," Available: http://www.ipg.nasa.gov

[OMG 1995] Object Management Group (OMG). *The Common Object Request Broker: Architecture and Specification.* OMG, 2.0 edition, July 1995.

[OMG 1998] Object Management Group, *The Common Object Request Broker: Architecture and Specication,* Revision 2.2: February 1998, http://cgi.omg.org/docs/formal/98-07-0l.pdf.

[OMG 2000a] *Fault Tolerant CORBA: Draft Adopted Specification,* OMG TC Document ptc/2000-03-04, OMG, March 30, 2000.

[OMG 2000b] *Fault Tolerant CORBA: Modifications to CORBA Core Specifications,* OMG TC Document ptc/2000-03-05, OMG, March 30, 2000.

[Opyrchal et al. 2000] L. Opyrchal, M. Astley, J. Auerbach, G. Banavar, R. Strom, and D. Sturman, "Exploiting IP Multicast in Content-Based Publish-Subscribe Systems," presented at IFIP/ACM International Conference on Distributed Systems Platforms, 2000.

[Orfali and Harkey 1997] Robert Orfali and Dan Harkey. *Client/Server Programming with Java and CORBA.* John Wiley & Sons, Inc, 1997.

[Orfali *et al* 1996] Robert Orfali, Dan Harkey, and Jeri Edvards. *The Essential Distributed Objects Survival Guide.* John Wiley & Sons, Inc., 1996.

[Orfali *et al* 1999] Robert Orfali, Dan Harkey, and Jeri Edwards. *Client/Server Survival Guide.* John Wiley & Sons, Inc., 1999.

[OSF 1990] OSF, *OSF Distributed Computing Environment Rationale,* Open Software Foundation, 1990.

[OSF 1992] OSF, *The OSF Distributed Computing Environment,* Open Software Foundation, 1992.

[Ott et al. 1999] T. J. Ott, T. Lakshman and L. Wong, SRED: Stabilized RED. *IEEE INFOCOM 1999,* pp. 1346-1355. 1999.

[Papadopoulos et al. 2003] C. Papadopoulos, R. Lindell, J. Mehringer, A. Hussain and R. Govindan, COSSACK: Coordinated Suppression of Simultaneous Attacks. *DARPA Information Survivability Conference and Exposition III,* 2-13. 2003.

[Papastavtou et al 1998] Stavros Papastavtou, George Samaras, and Evaggelia Pitoura, Mobile agents for WWW distributed database access, *Proceedings of the 15th International Conference on Data Engineering,* 1998.

496

[Park and Lee 2000] K. Park and H. Lee, A Proactive Approach to Distributed DoS Attack Prevention Using Route-Based Distributed Filtering. *Tech. Rep. CSD-00-017,* Department of Computer Sciences, Purdue University. 2000.

[Park and Lee 2001a] K. Park and H. Lee, 2001a. On the Effectiveness of Probabilistic Packet Marking for IP Traceback under Denial of Service Attack. *IEEE INFOCOM 2001,* pp. 338-347.

[Park and Lee 2001b] K. Park and H.Lee, 2001b. On the Effectiveness of Route-based Packet Filtering For Distributed DoS Attack Prevention in Power-law Internet. *Proceedings ACM SIGCOMM 2001,* pp. 15-26.

[Park et al. 2000] Yong Woon Park, Jong Hyun Kim and Ki Dong Chung, Frequency–based Selective Caching Strategy in a Continuous Media Server, *Proceedings of the 7th International Conference on Parallel and Distributed Systems (ICPADS'00),* 2000.

[Paris 1992] Jehan-Francois Paris. Using Volatile Witnesses to Extend the Applicability of Availability Copy Protocols. *Proc. 2nd Workshop on the Management of Replicated Data,* pp. 30-33, 1992.

[Partridge et al 1993] C. Partridge, T. Mendez and W. Milliken, Host Anycasting Service, *IETF Network Working Group, RFC 1546,* November 1993.

[Paxson 1999] V. Paxson, Bro: A System for Detecting Network Intruders in Real-Time. *Computer Networks 31,* 23-24, 2435-2463. 1999.

[Paxson 2001] V. Paxson, An analysis of using reflectors for distributed denial-of-service attacks. *ACM SIGCOMM Computer Communication Review 31,* 3, pp. 38-47. 2001.

[Peng 2001] T. Peng, Defending Against Denial of Service Attacks and other High-Bandwidth Traffic Aggregates. *Conversion Report for Ph.D. Candidature,* Department of Electrical and Electronic Engineering, The University of Melbourne. 2001.

[Peng et al. 2002a] T. Peng, C. Leckie and R. Kotagiri, 2002a. Adjusted Probabilistic Packet Marking for IP Traceback. *Networking 2002,* Pisa, Italy.

[Peng et al. 2002b] T. Peng, C. Leckie and R. Kotagiri, 2002b. Defending Against Distributed Denial of Service Attacks Using Selective Pushback. *ICT 2002.*

[Peng et al. 2003a] T. Peng, C. Leckie and R. Kotagiri, 2003a. Detecting Distributed Denial of Service Attacks by Sharing Distributed Beliefs. *8th Australasian Conference on Information Security and Privacy,* Wollongong, Australia.

[Peng et al. 2003b] T. Peng, C. Leckie and R. Kotagiri, 2003b. Protection from Distributed Denial of Service Attack Using History-based IP Filtering. *IEEE International Conference on Communications (ICC 2003),* Anchorage, Alaska, USA.

[Peng et al. 2004] T. Peng, C. Leckie and R. Kotagiri, Detecting Distributed Denial of Service Attacks Using Source IP Address Monitoring. *IEEE Infocom 2004*, Hongkong. 2004.

[Perkins 1994] C. Perkins, Minimal Encapsulation within IP, *RFC 2004*, October 1994.

[Perkins 1996a] C. Perkins, IP Encapsulation within IP, *RFC 2003*, October 1996.

[Perkins 1996b] C. Perkins, IP Mobility Support for IPv4, *RFC 3220*, October 1996.

[Perkins 1998] C. E. Perkins, *Mobile IP: Design Principles and Practices,* Addison Wesley 1998.

[Peterson et al 1989] L. L. Peterson, N. Buchholz and R. Schlichting. Preserving and using context information in interprocess communication. *ACM Transactions on Computer Systems,* 7(3), pp. 217-246. August 1989.

[Petrou et al. 1998] C. Petrou, S. Hadjiefthymiades and D. Martakos, An XML-based, 3-tier Scheme for Integrating Heterogeneous Information Sources to the WWW, *Proceedings of the 10th International Workshop on Database & Expert Systems Applications,* 1998.

[Pfleeger and Pfleeger 2003] C. P. Pfleeger and S. L. Pfleeger, *Security in Computing,* Third Edition, Prentice Hall PTR, Saddle River, New Jersey. PICTON, P. 2000. *Neural Network,* Second Edition, Palgrave, New York. 2003.

[Pollak 1986] M. Pollak, Optimal detection of a change in distribution, *Ann. Statist. 13,* pp. 206-227,1986.

[Porras and Neumann 1997] P. A. Porras and P. G. Neumann, EMERALD: Event Monitoring Enabling Responses to Anomalous Live Disturbances. In *Proceedings of 20th NIST-NCSC National Information Systems Security Conference.* 1997.

[Postel 1980] J. Postel, User Datagram Protocol, STD 6, *RFC 768,* August 1980.

[Pour 1998] Glida Pour 1998, Enterprise JavaBeans, JavaBeans & XML Expanding the Possibilities for Web-based Enterprise Application Development, *Proceedings of the 31st International Conference on Technology of Object-Oriented Language and Systems,* 1998.

[Powell 1994] David Powell, Distributed Fault Tolerance: Lessons from Delta-4, Vol. 14, No. 1, pp. 36-47, February 1994.

[Powell 1996] David Powell. A special section: group communication. *Communications of the ACM,* 39(4), pp. 50-97, April 1996.

[Powell and Verissimo 1991] David Powell and Paulo Verissimo. *Delta-4: A Generic Architecture for Dependable Distributed Computing.* Springer-Verlag, 1991.

[PPDG] "Particle Physics Data Grid (PPDG)," Available: http://www.ppdg.net/

498

[Pradhan 1986] D. K. Pradhan, Fault-Tolerant Multiprocessor and VLSI-Based System Communication Architectures, in *Fault-Tolerant Computing: Theory and Techniques,* Vol. 1, Edited by D. K. Pradhan, pp. 467-576, Prentice-Hall, 1986.

[Prescod 1997] Paul Prescod, XML: the intersection of documents and database on the Internet, *Database web advisor,* v15 n12 p36(4), Dec 1997.

[Puma] Puma, *http://www.cs.sandia.gov/puma.*

[Qie et al. 2002] X. Qie, R. Pang and L. Perterson, Defensive Programming: Using an Annotation Toolkit to Build Dos-Resistant Software. In *Proceedings of the Fifth Symposium on Operating Systems Design and Implementation,* Boston, MA. 2002.

[Quintero 1996] J. A. Davila Quintero. Reactive PASCAL and the Event Calculus, in U. C. Sigmund and M. Thiels-cher, editors, *Proc. of the Workshop at FAPR'96: Reasoning about Actions and Planning in Complex Environments.* Darmstadt, Germany, June 1996.

[Rajagopalan and McKinley 1989] B. Rajagopalan and P. K. McKinley. A token-based protocol for reliable, ordered multicast communication. *Proc. 8th IEEE Symposium on Reliable Distributed Systems,* Seattle, WA, pp. 84-93, Oct., 1989.

[Ramakrishman 2000] Ragbu Ramakrishman, From Browsing to Interacting: DBMS Support for Responsive Websites, *Proceedings of the 2000 ACM SIGMOD on Management of data,* 2000.

[Raman et al. 1998] R. Raman, M. Livny, and M. H. Solomon, "Matchmaking: Distributed Resource Management for High Throughput Computing," presented at Seventh IEEE International Symposium on High Performance Distributed Computing, 1998.

[Randell and Xu 1995] B. Randell and J. Xu, The Evolution of the Recovery Block Concept, in *Software Fault Tolerance,* Edited by Michael R. Lyu, John Wiley & Sons Ltd, 1995.

[Rashid 1986] R. F. Rashid, Experiences with the Accent Network Operating System, Networking in Open Systems, *Lecture Notes in Computer Science,* No. 248, Springer Verlag, pp. 252-269, 1986.

[Raynal 1992] M. Raynal. About logical clocks for distributed systems. *ACM Operating Systems Review,* 26(1): pp. 41-48, 1992.

[Reiter 1996] Michael K. Reiter. Distributing trust with the Rampart toolkit. *Communications of the ACM,* pp. 71--74, April 1996.

[Renesse *et al.* 96] R. van Renesse, K. P. Birman, and S. Maffeis, Horus: A Flexible Group Communication System, *Communications of the ACM,* pp. 76-83, April 1996.

[Rennhackkamp 1997] Martin Rennhackkamp, Implementing Integrated Web to Database, *DBMS,* v10 n5 p95(4), May 1997.

[Reynolds and Postel 1994] J. Reynolds and J. Postel, Assigned Numbers, STD 2, *RFC 1700,* October 1994.

[Ricciulli et al. 1999] L. Ricciulli, P. Lincoln and P. Kakkar, TCP SYN Flooding Defense. *CNDS 1999.* 1999.

[Roiger and Geatz 2003] R. J. Roiger and M. W. Geatz, *Data Mining: A Tutorial-based Primer,* Addison Wesley, Pearson Education Inc. 2003.

[Rosenberg *et al* 1992] Ward Rosenberry, David Kenney, and Gerry Fisher. *Understanding DCE.* O'Reilly & Associates, Inc., second edition, 1992.

[Rozier *et al.* 1988] M. Rozier, V. Abrossimov, F. Armand, I. Boule, M. Gien, M. Gulllemont, F. Herrmann, C. Kaiser., P. Leonard, S. Langlois, and W. Neuhaser, Chorus Distributed Operating System, *Computing Systems,* Vol 1, pp. 279-305, 1988.

[Rubin and Geer 1998] Aviel D. Rubin and Daniel E. Geer, A Survey of Web Security, *Computer,* pp. 34-41, Vol. 31, No. 9, September 1998.

[Saba and Mukheriee 2003] D. Saba and A. Mukheriee, "Pervasive Computing: A Paradigm for the 21st Century", by in *IEEE Computer,* pp. 25-31, March 2003.

[Saltzer *et al.* 1984] J. H. Saltzer, D. P. Reed and D. D. Clark, End-To-End Arguments in System Design, *ACM Transactions on Computer Systems,* Vol. 2, No. 4, 1984.

[Sanchez et al. 2001] L. A. Sanchez, W. C. Millken, A. C. Snoeren, F. Tcjakountio, C. E. Jones, S. T. Kent, c. Partridge and W. T. Strayer, Hardware Support for a Hash-Based IP Traceback. In *Proceedings of the DARPA Information Survivability Conference and Exposition 2001 2,* pp. 146-152. 2001.

[Sandberg *et al.* 1985] R. Sandberg, D. Goldberg, S. Kleiman, D. Walsh and B. Lyon, Design and Implementation of the Sun Network Filesystem, *Proceedings of the Summer USENIX Conference,* pp. 119-130, 1985.

[Sandewall 1996] E. Sandewall, Towards a World-Wide Data Base, *The Fifth International World Wide Web Conference,* Paris, France, http://www5conf.inria.fr/fich_html/papers/P54/Overview.html.May6-10,1996.

[Satyanarayanan 1989] M. Satyanarayanan, Distributed File Systems, in *Distributed Systems, an Advanced Course,* S. Mullender Ed., 2nd Ed, ACM Press/Addison-Wesley, pp. 353-383, 1989.

[Satyanarayanan 2001] Satyanarayanan, M. Pervasive computing: Vision and challenges, *IEEE Personal Communications,* 8(4), pp. 10 – 17, August 2001.

[Savage et al. 1999] S. Savage, N. Cardwell, D. Wetherall and T. Anderson, TCP Congestion Control with a Misbehaving Receiver. *Computer Communication Review 29,* 5, pp. 71-78. 1999.

[Savage et al. 2000] S. Savage, D. Wetherall, A. Karlin and T. Anderson, Practical Network Support for IP Traceback. *ACM SIGCOMM 2000.* 2000.

[Savage et al 2001] S. Savage, D. Wetherall, A. Karlin and T. Anderson, Network Support for IP Traceback. *ACM/IEEE Transactions on Networking 9,* 3, pp. 226-237. 2001.

500

[Schlichting and Schneider 1983] R. D. Schlichting and F. B. Schneider, Fail-stop processors: an approach to designing fault-tolerant computing systems, *ACM Transactions on Computer Systems*, 1(3): pp. 222--38, 1983.

[Schnackenberg et al. 2000] D. Schnackenberg, K. Djahandari and D. Sterne, Infrastructure for Intrusion Detection and Response. In *Proceedings of the DARPA Information Survivability Conference and Exposition 2000*. 2000.

[Schneider 1990] Fred B. Schneider. Implementing fault-tolerant services using the state machine approach: a tutorial. *ACM Computing Surveys*, 22(4): pp. 299-319, December 1990.

[Schoenfeldinger 1995] W. Schoenfeldinger, WWW Meets Linda: Linda for Global WWW-Based Transaction Processing Systems, *World Wide Web Journal, Issue 1: Conference Proceedings, Fourth International World Wide Web Conference*, O'Reilly and Associates, December 1995.

[Schöning and Wäsch 2000] Harald Schöning and Jürgen Wäsch, Tamino - An Internet Database System, *EDBT 2000*, LNCS 1777, pp. 383-387, 2000.

[Schuba et al. 1997] C. L. Schuba, I. V. Krsul, M. G. Kuhn, E. H. Spafford, A. Sundaram and D. Zamboni, Analysis of a Denial of Service Attack on TCP. In *Proceedings of the 1997 IEEE Symposium on Security and Privacy*. 1997.

[Schwartz1995] David G. Schwartz. *Cooperating Heterogeneous Systems*. Kluwer Academic Publishers, Dordrecht, 1995.

[Scott *et al.* 1985] R. K. Scott, J. W. Gault and D. F. McAllister. The consensus recovery block, In *Proc. of Total System Reliability Symposium*, pp. 74-85, 1985.

[SEARCHSECURITY 2003] SEARCHSECURITY. 2003. mail bomb. *searchSecurity.com Definitions*, http://searchsecurity.techtarget.com/sDefinition/0,,sid14_gci212514,00.html.

[Selic et al 1994] Bran Selic, Garth Gullekson and Paul T. Ward. *Real-Time Object-Oriented Modeling*. John Wiley & Sons, Inc., 1994.

[Senior and Deters 2002] M. Senior and R. Deters, "Market Structure in Peer Computaiton Sharing", in Proceedings of the 2nd International Conference on Peer-to-Peer Computing (P2P'02), 2002.

[Shah and Ramakrishnan 1994] A. Shah and G. Ramakrishnan, *FDDI - A High Speed Network*, Prentice-Hall, NJ, 1994. ISBN: 0-13-308388-8.

[Sherriff 2000] L. Sherrif, *Virus launches DDoS for mobile phones*, http://www.theregister.co.uk/content/1/12394.html. 2000.

[Shirley et al 94] John Shirley, Wei Hu, and David Magid. *Guide to Write DCE Applications*. O'Reilly & Associates, Inc., second edition, 1994.

[Shrivastava *et al.* 1991] Santosh K. Shrivastava, Graeme N. Dixon, and Graham D. Parrington, An Overview of the Arjuna Distributed Programming System, *IEEE Software,* pp. 66-73, January 1991.

[Siewiorek 1986] D. P. Siewiorek, Architecture of Fault-Tolerant Computers, in *Fault-Tolerant Computing: Theory and Techniques,* Vol. 1, Edited by D. K. Pradhan, pp. 417-466, Prentice-Hall, 1986.

[Siewiorek and Swarz 1992] D. P. Siewiorek and R. S. Swarz, *Reliable Computer Systems: Design and Evaluation,* 2nd Ed., Digital Press, 1992.

[Sinha 1992] A. Sinha. Client-server computing. *Communications of the ACM,* 35(7):77-98, July 1992.

[Sipe 2000] Steven E. Sipe, XML Gets Down to Business - XML's promise of open-platform data exchange is finally being realized, *PC Magazine,* August 1, 2000.

[Smith et al. 2001] F. D. Smith, F. H. Campos, K. Jeffay and D. Ott, What TCP/IP Protocol Headers Can Tell Us About the Web. In *Proceedings of ACM SIGMETRICS 2001.* 2001.

[Snoeren et al. 2001] A. C. Snoeren, C. Partridge, L. A. Sanchez, C. E. Jones, F. Tchakountio, S. T. Kent and W. T. Strayer, Hash-Based IP Traceback. *ACM SIGCOMM 2001.* 2001.

[Snoeren et al. 2002] A. C. Snoeren, C. Partridge, L. A. Sanchez, C. E. Jones, F. Tchakountio, S. T. Kent and W. T. Strayer, Single-Packet IP Traceback. *IEEE/ACM Transactions on Networking,* pp. 721-734. 2002.

[Snyder 1993] A. Snyder. The essence of objects: concepts and terms. *IEEE Software,* pp. 31-42, January 1993.

[Solaris MC] Solaris MC, *http://www.sunlabs.com/research/solaris-mc.*

[Soloman 1998] J. D. Soloman, *Mobile IP: the Internet Unplugged,* Prentice Hall PTR, 1998.

[Solomon 1996] J. Solomon, Mobile IP Applicability Statement, *RFC 2005,* October 1996.

[sommer and Paxson 2003] R. Sommer and V. Paxson, Enhancing Byte-Level Network Intrusion Detection Signatures with Context. In *Proceedings of the 10th ACM Conference on Computer and Communication Security, (CCS 2003),* Washington D.C., USA, pp. 262-271. 2003.

[Song and Perrig 2001] D. X. Song and A. Perrig, Advanced and Authenticated Marking Schemes for IP Traceback. *IEEE INFOCOM 2001,* pp. 878-886. 2001.

[Spatscheck and Peterson 1999] O. Spatscheck and L. L. Peterson, Defending Against Denial of Service Attacks in Scout. In *Proceedings of the 3rd Symposium on Operating Systems Design and Implementation (OSDI99).* 1999.

502

[Spector 1982] Alfred Z. Spector. Performing remote operations efficiently on a local computer network. *Communications of the ACM,* 25(4): pp. 246-260, April 1982.

[Sportack 1999] M. A. Sportack, *IP Routing Fundamentals,* Cisco Press. 1999.

[Sridharan 1997] Prashant Sridharan. *Advanced Java Networking.* Prentice Hall PTR, 1997.

[Stallings 1993] W. Stallings, *Computer Organisation and Architecture: Principles of Structure and Function,* 3rd Ed., MacMillan Publishing Company, 1993.

[Stallings 1998] W. Stallings, *High-Speed Networks: TCP/IP and ATM Design Principles,* Prentice-Hall, NJ, 1998. ISBN: 0-13-525965-7.

[Stanek 1998] William Robert Stanek, XML: Database and Data Integration Solutions, *http://www.zdnet.com/devhead/stories/articles/0,4413,348844,00.html,* 1998.

[Stanford 2002] Stanford, V. Using Pervasive Computing to Deliver Elder Care, *IEEE Pervasive Computing,* March 2002.

[Steen et al. 1997] M. V. Steen, P. Homburg, and A. S. Tanenbaum, "The Architectural Design of Globe: A Wide-Area Distributed System," Vrije University 1997

[Stern 1991] H. Stern, *Managing NFS and NIS,* O'Reilly Associates, Inc. CA, USA, 1991.

[Sterne et al. 2001] D. Sterne, K, Djahandari, B. Wilson, B. Babson, D. Schnackenberg, H. Holliday and T. Reid, Autonomic Response to Distributed Denial of Service Attacks. In *Proceedings of the 4th International Workshop on Recent Advances in Intrusion Detection (RAID 2001),* pp. 134-149. 2001.

[Stoica et al. 1998] I. Stoica, S. Shenker and H. Zhang, Core-Stateless Fair Queueing: Achieving Approximately Fair Bandwidth Allocations in High Speed Networks. *ACM SIGCOMM 1998.* 1998.

[Stockinger 2001]H. Stockinger, "Distributed Database Management Systems and the Data Grid," presented at 18th IEEE Symposium on Mass Storage Systems and 9th NASA Goddard Conference on Mass Storage Systems and Technologies, San Diego, 2001

[Stone 2000] R. Stone, CenterTrack: An IP Overlay Network for Tracking DoS Floods. *9th Usenix Security Symposium,* pp. 199-212. 2000.

[Strassman 2003] P. Strassman, New Weapons of Information Warfare. *Computerworld,* http://www.computerworld.com/printthis/2003/0,4814,87554,00.html. 2003.

[Sun 1988] Sun Microsystems, Inc. RPC: remote procedure call protocol specification. In *Internet Network Working Group Request for Comments,* no. 1057. Network Information Center, SRI International, version 2 edition, June 1988.

[Sun 1989] Sun Microsystems, *NFS: Network File System Protocol Specification (RFC 1094),* Internet Network Working Group Request for Comments, No. 1094, Network Information Center, SRI International, March 1989.

[Sun 1995] Sun Microsystems, *NFS Version 3 Protocol Specification (RFC 1813),* Internet Network Working Group Request for Comments, No. 1813, Network Information Center, SRI International, June 1995.

[Sun 1997] *Sun Clusters: A White Paper,* Sun Microsystems, Palo Alto, CA, USA, 1997.

[Sun 1999] Sun Microsystems, *Jini Technology Architectural Overview,* January 1999, http://wwws.sun.com/software/jini/whitepapers/architecture.html

[Suzanne and Suzann 1997] I. Suzanne and W. Suzanne, "Developing Trust in Virtual Teams," presented at Proceedings of the Thirtieth Annual Hawaii International Conference on System Sciences, Hawaii, 1997.

[Svobodova 1985] L. Svobodova, Client/Server Model of Distributed Computing, *Informatik Fachberiche 95,* pp. 485-498, Springer-Verlag, 1985.

[SWEST 1993] South West Thames Regional Health Authority, *Report of the Inquiry into the London Ambulance Service,* 1993.

[Systa 1996] K. Systa. *The Disco tool.* Tampere University of Technology, Tamphere, Finland, http://www.cs.tut.fi/laitos/Disco/tool.fm.html. 1996.

[Takefusa et al. 1999] A. Takefusa, S. Matsuoka, H. Nakada, K. Aida, and U. Nagashima, "Overview of a Performance Evaluation System for Global Computing Scheduling Algorithms," presented at 8th IEEE International Symposium on High Performance Distributed Computing (HPDC), Redondo Beach, California, 1999.

[Tanenbaum 1990] A. S. Tanenbaum, Experiences with the AMOEBA Distributed Operating System, *Communications of the ACM,* pp. 46-63, December 1990.

[Tanenbaum 1992] A. S. Tanenbaum, *Modern Operating Systems,* Prentice-Hall, 1992.

[Tanenbaum 1996] A. S. Tanenbaum, *Computer Networks,* 3rd ed., Prentice-Hall, 1996.

[Tanenbaum and van Renessee 1985] A. S. Tanenbaum and R. van Renessee, Distributed Operating Systems, *Computing Surveys,* Vol. 17, No. 4, December 1985.

[Tanenbaum and Steen 2002] A. S. Tanenbaum and M. v. Steen, *Distributed Systems - Principles and Paradigms;* Prentice Hall, 2002.

[TBR 1998] *Cluster Computing: A Review of Cluster Characteristics Across Several Leading Vendors,* Technology Business Research, Inc, Hampton, NH, USA, 1998.

[Templeton and Levitt 2003] S. J. Templeton and K. E. Levitt, Detecting Spoofed Packets. *DARPA Information Survivability Conference and Expoition.* 2003.

504

[Thain et al. 2001] D. Thain, J. Basney, S.-C. Son, and M. Livny, "The Kangaroo approach to data movement on the grid," presented at The Tenth IEEE Symposium on High Performance Distributed Computing, San Francisco, California, 2001.

[Thain et al. 2003] D. Thain, T. Tannenbaum, and M. Livny, "Condor and the Grid," in *Grid Computing: Making the Global Infrastructure a Reality,* F. Berman, A. Hey, and G. Fox, Eds.: John-Wiley & Sons, 2003.

[Thomas et al. 2003] R. Thomas, B. Mark, T. Johnson and J. Croall, NetBouncer: Client-legitimacy-based High-performance DDoS Filtering. *DARPA Information Survivability Conference and Exposition III 1,* pp. 14-25. 2003.

[Thompson et al. 1997] K. Thompson, G. J. Miller and R. wilder, Wide-Area Internet Traffic Patterns and Characteristics. *IEEE Network.* 1997.

[Toy 1987] Wing N. Toy, Fault-Tolerant Computing, *Advances in Computer Science,* Vol. 76, pp. 201-279, Academic Press, Inc., 1987.

[Traverse 1988] P. Traverse, AIRBUS and ATR system architecture and specification, In *Software Diversity in Computerized Control Systems,* pp. 95–104, U. Voges, editor, Springer, Wien, New York, 1988.

[Triantafillou and Taylor 1995] P. Triantafillou and D. J. Taylor, The location-based paradigm for replication: achieving efficiency and availability in distributed systems, *IEEE Transactions on Software Engineering,* 21(1): pp. 1-18, January 1995.

[Tupakula and Varadharajan 2003] U. K. Tupakula and V. Varadharajan, A Practical Method to Counteract Denial of Service Attacks. *Twenty-Fifth Australian Computer Science Conference (ACSC2003),* Adelaide, Australia. 2003.

[Vazhkudai et al. 2001] S. Vazhkudai, S. Tuecke, and I. Foster, "Replica Selection in the Globus Data Grid," presented at International Workshop on Data Models and Databases on Clusters and the Grid (DataGrid 2001), 2001.

[Veizades et al 1997] J. Veizades, C. Perkins and S. Kaplan, Service Location Protocol, *RFC 2165,* June 1997.

[Veríssimo et al 1989] P. Veríssimo, L. Rodrigues and M. Baptista, AMP: A highly parallel atomic multicast protocol, *ACM SIGCOMM Symposium,* 1989, pp.83-93.

[Vogel and Duddy 1997] Andreas Vogel and Keith Duddy. *Java Programming with CORBA.* John Wiley & Sons, Inc, 1997.

[Voorhies et al. 2003] S. Voorhies, H. Lee and A. Klappenecker, A Probabilistic Defense Mechanism Against Distributed Denial of Service Attacks. 2003.

[Waldvogel 2002] M. Waldvogel, GOSSIB vs. IP Traceback Rumors. *18th Annual Computer Security Applications Conference,* San Diego, California, USA, 5-13. 2002.

[Wang 1999] Li Wang. *A Toolkit for Constructing Service Replication Systems,* Ph.D thesis, Deakin University, 1999.

[Wang and Zhou 1997] Li Wang and Wanlei Zhou. An architecture for building reliable object systems. In *Proc. of the 26th International Conference on Technology of Object-Oriented Language and Systems (TOOLS Asia'97),* Beijing, P.R.China, September 1997. IEEE Computer Society Press.

[Wang and Zhou 1998a] Li Wang and Wanlei Zhou. An object-oriented design pattern for distributed replication systems. In *Proc. of the 10th IASTED Int. Conf. on Parallel and Distributed Computing and Systems (PDCS'98),* pp. 89-94, Las Vegas, USA, October 1998.

[Wang and Zhou 1998b] Li Wang and Wanlei Zhou. Primary-backup object replications in Java. In *Proc. of the 27th Int. Conf. on Technology of Object-Oriented Language and Systems (TOOLS Asia'98),* pp. 78-82, Beijing, P.R.China, IEEE Computer Society Press, September 1998.

[Wang and Zhou 1999a] Li Wang and Wanlei Zhou. Automating the construction of service replication systems. In *Proc. of the ISCA 12th Int. Conf. on Parallel and Distributed Computing Systems (PDCS'99),* pp. 333-338, Fort Lauderdale, Florida, USA, August 1999.

[Wang and Zhou 1999b] Li Wang and Wanlei Zhou. A tool for constructing service replication systems. In *Proc. of the 28th Int. Conf. on Technology of Object-Oriented Language and Systems TOOLS (Asia'99),* Nanjing, P.R.China, IEEE Computer Society Press, Sept. 1999.

[Wang, Zhou, and Jia 2001] Li Wang, Wanlei Zhou, and Weijia Jia, The Design and Implementation of an Active Replication Scheme for Distributed Services in a Cluster of Workstations, *The Journal of Systems and Software,* Vol. 58, pp. 199-210, Elsevier Science Publishing Co., Inc., New York, USA, September 2001.

[Wang et al. 2002] H. Wang, D. Zhang and K. G. Shin, Detecting SYN Flooding Attacks. *IEEE INFOCOM 2002.* 2002.

[wang and Schulzrinne 2003] B. Wang and H. Schulzrinne, A Denial-of-Service-Resistant IP Traceback Approach. *3rd New York Metro Area Networking Workshop (NYMAN 2003).* 2003.

[Wang and Reeves 2003] X. Wang and D.S. Reeves, Robust Correlation of Encrypted Attack Traffic Through Stepping Stones by Manipulation of Interpacket Delays. In *Proceedings of the 10th ACM Conference on Computer and Communication Security, (CCS 2003),* Washington D.C., USA, pp. 20-29. 2003.

[Ware 1998] H. W. Ware, *The Cyberposture of the National Information Infrastructure,* RAND, Santa Monica, CA, MR-976-OSTP, http://www.rand.org/publications/MR/MR976/mr976.html. 1998.

[W3C 2001]W3C, *http://www.w3c.org/markup,* 2001.

[Weaver 2002] N. C. Weaver, *Warhol Worms: The Potential for Very Fast Internet Plagues,* http://www.cs.berkeley.edu/~nweaver/warhol.html. 2002.

[Wegner 1996] P. Wegner, Interoperability, *ACM Computing Surveys,* Vol. 28, No. 1, 1996.

[Weihl 1993] Willian E. Weihl. Transaction-processing techniques. *Distributed Systems,* Sape Mullender, editor, Addison-Wesley Publishing Company, second edition, 1993.

[Weiser 1991] Weiser, M. The computer of the 21st century. *Scientific American,* 265(3): pp. 66–75, September 1991.

[Welch 1986] B. B. Welch, The Sprite Remote Procedure Call System, *Report No. UCB/ CSD 86/302,* Computer Science Division (EECS), University of California, 1986.

[Wellings 1996] A. J. Wellings and A. Burns. Programming replicated systems in Ada 95. *The Computer Journal,* 39(5): pp. 361-373, 1996.

[White et al. 2001] B. S. White, M. Walker, M. Humphrey, and A. S. Grimshaw, "LegionFS: A Secure and Scalable File System Supporting Cross-Domain High-Performance Applications," presented at Supercomputing, 2001

[Winslett 1997] Marianne Winslett, *Databases and the World Wide Web,* University of Illinois, http://cdr.cs.uiuc.edu/pubs/de97tutorial/ index.htm, Version of April 15, 1997.

[Witten and Frank 2000] I. H. Witten and E. Frank, *Data Mining: Practical Machine Learning Tools and Techniques with Java Implementations,* Morgan Kaufmann Publishers, San Francisco. 2000.

[Wodaski 1997] Ron Wodaski, Multimedia: From database to the Web, *Data Based Advisor,* v15 n1, p44 (8), Jan 1997.

[Wreden 1997] Nick Wreden, Forging stronger ties: Web-to-database access, *Internet Week,* n680 p53(4), Sept, 1997.

[Wright 2001] D. Wright, "Cheap cycles from the desktop to the dedicated cluster: combining opportunistic and dedicated scheduling with Condor," presented at Proceedings of Linux Clusters: The HPC Revolution, Champaign-Urbana, 2001

[Xiong et al. 2001] Y. Xiong, S. Liu and P. Sun, On the Defense of the Distributed Denial of Service Attacks: An On-Off Feedback Control Approach. *IEEE Transactions on System, Man and Cybernetics-Part A: Systems and Humans 31,* 4, 2001.

[Xuan et al. 2001] D. Xuan, R. Bettati and W. Zhao, A Gateway-based Defense System for Distributed DoS Attacks in High-Speed Networks. *Proceedings of the 2001 IEEE Workshop on Information Assurance and Security,* pp. 212-219. 2001.

[Xu *et al.* 1993] J. Xu, A. Bondavalli and F. DiGiandomenico, *Software fault tolerance: dynamic combination of dependability and efficiency,* Technical Report, 442, University of Newcastle upon Tyne, Computing Science, 1993.

[Yaar et al. 2003] A. Yaar, A. Perrig and D. Song, Pi: A Path Identification Mechanism to Defend against DDoS Attacks. *2003 IEEE Symposium on Security and Privacy.* 2003.

[Yan et al. 2000] J. Yan, S. Early and R. Anderson, The XenoService A Distributed Defeat for Distributed Denial of Service. In *Proceedings of ISW 2000*. 2000.

[Yang et al 1998] Andrew Yang, James Linn and David Quadrato, Developing Integrated Web and Database Applications Using JAVA Applets and JDBC Drivers, *Proceedings of the twenty-ninth SIGCSE technical symposium on Computer science education*, pp. 302 – 306, 1998.

[Yau et al. 2002] D. K. Yau, J.C.S. Lui and F. Liang, Defending Against Distributed Denial-of-service Attacks with Max-min Fair Server-centric Router Throttles. *Proceedings IEEE International Workshop on Quality of Service (IWQoS)*, Miami Beach, FL, USA. 2002.

[Zaniolo et al. 2000] C. Zaniolo et al., XML: Current Development and Future Challenges for the Database Community, *Advances in Database Technology – EDBT*, pp. 3-17, 2000.

[Zaroo 2002] P. Zaroo, A Survey of DDoS attacks and some DDoS defense mechanisms. *A part of course textbook Advanced Information Assurance (CS 626) in Purdue Univerisity*. 2002.

[Zhang et al. 2000] X. Zhang, S. F. Wu, Z. Fu and T. Wu, Malicious Packet Dropping: How It Might Impact the TCP Performance and How We Can Detect It. *2000 International Conference on Network Protocols, Osaka, Japan*, pp. 263-272. 2000.

[Zhang and Xu 2000] W. F. Zhang and B. W. Xu, Research on framework supporting Web search engine, Department of computer science and engineering, Southeast University, Nanjing, *Journal of Computer research and Development*, 2000.

[Zhong and Zhou 1998] Jianting Zhong and Wanlei Zhou, A Web-Based Design for the Mobile Transaction Management of A Distributed Database System, *Proceedings of the TOOLS Asia'98*, pp. 372-280, Beijing, September 1998.

[Zhou 1996] W. Zhou, Supporting Fault-Tolerant and Open Distributed Processing Using RPC, *Computer Communications*, Elsevier Science B. V., The Netherlands. Vol. 19, No. 6-7, pp. 528-538, June 1996.

[Zhou 1999] W. Zhou, Detecting and Tolerating Failures in a Loosely Integrated Heterogeneous Database System, *Computer Communications*, Elsevier Science B. V., The Netherlands, Vol. 22, No. 11, pp. 1056-1067, July 1999.

[Zhou 2000] W. Zhou, IPV6: the Next Generation of Internet and Web-Based Computing, a half-a-day tutorial presented in *PART'00*, Sydney, Australia, November 28-30, 2000, http://www3.cm.deakin.edu.au/~wanlei/part_ipv6.ppt.

[Zhou and Eide 1998] W. Zhou and E. Eide. Java Sensors and Their Applications. *Proceedings of the 21st Australian Computer Science Conference (ACSC 98)*, 345-356, Perth, Australia, 1998.

508

[Zhou and Goscinski 1997] W. Zhou and A. Goscinski, Fault-Tolerant Servers for RHODOS System, *The Journal of Systems and Software,* Elsevier Science Publishing Co., Inc., New York, USA, 37(3), pp. 201-214, June, 1997.

[Zhou and Goscinski 1999] W. Zhou and A. Goscinski, Managing Replicated Remote Procedure Call Transactions, *The Computer Journal,* Oxford Press, UK, Vol. 42, Issue 7, pp. 592-608, December 1999.

[Zhou and Zhang 2000] W. Zhou and H. Zhang, The Design and Implementation of a Model for Database Publishing on the WWW, *Proceedings of the 4th IEEE International Conference on Algorithms and Architectures for Parallel Processing (ICA3PP 2000),* World Scientific Press, pp. 436-446, Hong Kong, Dec., 2000.

[Zuquete 2002] A. Zuquete, Improving The Functionality Of SYN Cookies. In *Proceedings of Communications and Multimedia Security,* Portoroz, Slovenia. 2002.

Index